I0214458

Exposition Of Colossians

Exposition Of Colossians

Jean Daille

Sovereign Grace Publishers, Inc.
P.O. Box 4998
Lafayette, IN 47903

Exposition of Colossians

ISBN 1-58960-135-1

Printed In the United States of America
By Lightning Source, Inc.

THE AUTHOR'S DEDICATION.

[PREFIXED IN THE ORIGINAL TO THE PART CONTAINING CHAP. I.]

TO MONSIEUR,

MONSIEUR DU CANDAL,

LORD OF FONTINAILLE,

COUNSELLOR AND SECRETARY OF THE KING, HOUSE, AND CROWN OF FRANCE.

SIR:—I present you these sermons, conscious that I owe this acknowledgment to the friendship with which you honour me, and still more to the edification and good offices which the church where I preached them has for a long time received from your piety. For besides the noble example which your life gives us, a life full of virtue and honour, always steady and equal in the profession and holy exercises of the truth of the gospel; there has been presented no occasion of doing service to the people of God, either in past or present times, but you have embraced with zeal, and managed with prudence.

So likewise we see that the good and merciful Lord you serve has crowned your obedience with the benedictions of his grace. For in the vicissitudes of the times, and the variety of affairs, he has still rendered you acceptable, both to those within, and even to them without. And, which is the principal thing, he has preserved his covenant in your house, that neither the vanity of the world, nor the scandal of the time, has been able to make any of the breaches there which we see with grief in other families. To establish this precious heritage of piety in your race, his providence has added to it, by alliance, persons excellent in knowledge and in merit, in whose lineage you daily see your own life renew and flourish. It is true, sir, you have also had your trials, as no true believers are exempted from them; but those which God has dispensed to you have been so tempered with his goodness, as I believe you may truly say, that in this, more than in any other event of your life, he has exhibited the wonders of his grace towards you. Such was, some years ago, the bitter, untimely, but blessed and happy, death of your eldest son, who was removed in the flower and vigour of his age. This was, doubtless, a very grievous stroke, which cut down in a moment the sweetest of your hopes, plucking from your embraces a son as worthy of love as he was beloved, and whose merit had already advanced him to the dignity of a senator in the chief of the parliaments of this kingdom. But however painful his death was to you, it was, notwithstanding, accompanied with grace of God, so visible and ravishing, that I fear not to refresh your memory with it, well knowing that it is no less dear and precious to you for the piety and the noble and truly christian constancy which he showed in those last and happy moments of his life, than troublesome and bitter for the mourning and sadness which it left on your whole house. As soon as his disease appeared to be what indeed it was, he looked on death without perturbation; he prepared himself for it with great courage; and his deportment, his visage, and his discourses were full of resolution and contentment. He comforted us all; and, amid the tenderness and pangs of such a separation, maintained his mental vigour to the last. And though he left on earth some of the dearest and sweetest he could here possess or desire, yet he quitted it, not only without regret, but even with joy; so firm was the hope, or to speak more correctly, so clear and assured the sight, which the Lord Jesus gave him of the bliss and delights to which he called him. He remained in this gracious and holy frame even to his last breath, with an unclouded spirit and a calm soul, speaking to us of his approaching happiness, and of the present grace of his Lord, with such efficacy, that it checked your tears, and repressed the expressions of your grief, that how just soever they were, you had, nevertheless, a secret shame to allow them to appear in the presence and on the account of so virtuous a person, as if lamentations would have offended his piety, and dishonoured the victory of his faith. The same

God that loosed him so supernaturally from earth, to raise him up to heaven, granted you to bear the affliction of his departure with a patience worthy your vocation. After so severe a stroke, he has yet sustained you, and conducted you to an honourable old age, which few persons attain. And now, I doubt not, amidst the agitations of the present world, and the infirmities of age, your chief consolation is the assured hope you possess of arriving also one day at the gate of that blessed immortality, into which, contrary to the ordinary course of nature, you have seen this dear son enter before you.

If in the holy exercises of piety, by which you daily prepare yourself for that state, the reading of these sermons may find a place, and afford you consolation, I shall therein have extreme satisfaction; at least I can well assure you, that it is one of my most ardent desires, who pray God to preserve you with all your family, in perfect prosperity; and remain, inviolably,

Sir,

Your most humble and most obedient servant,

DAILLÉ

Paris, April 1, 1648.

THE AUTHOR'S EPISTLE.

[PREFIXED IN THE ORIGINAL TO THE PART CONTAINING CHAP. II.]

TO MONSIEUR,

MONSIEUR BIGOT,

LORD OF LAHONVILLE,

COUNSELLOR OF THE KING IN HIS COUNSELS, INTENDANT, AND CONTROLLER-GENERAL OF THE GABELS OF FRANCE.

SIR:—Among the advantages which the reformation of the church, embraced by our fathers in these latter ages, has afforded us, we must, doubtless, ascribe the pre-eminence to the free use we have of the word of Christ, which he, of his abundant grace, has recovered for us. This divine taper, lighted up from heaven in the house of God to shine unto his people, to express it in the terms of the gospel, remained hid a long time under a bushel, Matt. v. 15; the negligence and fraud of men keeping it in this shameful condition. It is now set anew in its candlestick, where it diffuses in every direction among us its enlivening and saving light; and that too in such abundance, as that we may truly say in this respect, the word of Christ dwelleth in us richly, Col. iii. 16. It reigns alone in our assemblies, where its voice, and no other, is continually heard to resound; the fables and legends of men being altogether banished from them. It is read there in a familiar language, which every one understands; whereas if it be read any where else, it is in a tongue dead, and barbarous, and unknown to the people. It is explained among us with all fidelity, sincerity, and diligence; whereas amidst the darkness of former ages, it was so unworthily treated by preachers, that, to read their sermons, one would think they had designed to make them openly ridiculous. I confess that those persons who abide in the erroneous opinions of their ancestors are somewhat ashamed of their gross and profanely licentious practice; and they have in some measure reformed it. Yet there remain but too many defects among them still, and this one in particular, that they explain in public only some pieces, and, if it may be so said, shreds of Scripture, sometimes taken from one book, sometimes from another, never showing their hearers any complete body. For it cannot be denied that this manner of handling the word of God deprives the faithful of much edification; it being evident that the view and consideration of an entire book gives us a more complete knowledge and greater admiration of it than the view of any isolated part. This fault is so much the less pardonable in our adversaries, as, besides being less profitable, it is also contrary to the custom and authority of those ancient doctors of the first ages of Christianity, whose true sons and legitimate successors these gentlemen boast that they are. For it was usual at that time for pastors to expound in the church whole books of Scripture throughout, by sermons continued upon the chain of the holy text, from the beginning of a volume to the very end, which is clearly proved by the remains of their writings. There are extant still the Sermons of St. John Chrysostom upon Genesis, upon the gospels of St. Matthew and St. John, upon the Acts of the Apostles, and upon all the fourteen Epistles of St. Paul, which were delivered by this great man, part of them in the church of Antioch, and part in the church of Constantinople, the greatest and most populous churches of all the East. And among the Latins, we have the Tractates of St. Augustine upon the whole Book of Psalms, and upon the gospel of St. John, and upon his First Epistle, which were in a similar manner made and delivered in the assemblies of his people. An evident sign that, about the beginning of the fifth century, when these two excellent and famous personages flourished, this custom was in repute among Christians. Whether then the thing be considered in itself, or the suffrages of the ancients be taken, it is manifest that our fathers and ourselves had the best reasons in the world to re-establish this sacred and just usage in the church.

Now, sir, this book which I address to you is a fruit of it.

For having undertaken, in conformity to this order, to expound in our holy assemblies the divine Epistle of the apostle Paul to the Colossians, and being come to the end of it, by the grace of our Lord, because the whole work could not be commodiously contracted into one volume, I have divided it into three parts, of which this is the second. The piety which has long flourished in your house, sir, and the exquisite knowledge that God has given you of his truth, induce me to believe that this book, which wholly treats of his divine mysteries, and nothing else, will not be displeasing to you. It is this that has given me the liberty to put your name upon it; a name which numerous excellent graces, with which God has adorned both your family and your person, render very dear and very honourable in our church. I am sorry that this present is not more worthy of it. But such as it is, I do not despair of its obtaining from the dignity of its subject, and from the favour of your kindness, that acceptance to which it cannot pretend upon any merit of its own. Please you then to receive it as a sincere testimony of the respect I bear your virtue, and of the grateful sense I have of the friendship with which you honour me; as well as an inviolable pledge of the prayers which I present unto God for your prosperity, and of the fervent affection I have to be, as long as I live,

Sir,

Your most humble and most obedient servant,

DAILLÉ.

Paris, April 1, 1648.

THE AUTHOR'S EPISTLE DEDICATORY.

[PREFIXED IN THE ORIGINAL TO THE PART CONTAINING CHAP. III. IV.]

TO MONSIEUR,

MONSIEUR DE RAMBOUILLET,

LORD OF LANCEY, AND OF PLESSIS-FRANC.

SIR:—THESE sermons will not be new to you; so little time having elapsed since you heard them at Charenton, no doubt you will recognize them at first sight. The support they then received in our holy assembly emboldens them now to present themselves in public. Perhaps it had been better to rest contented with that favour which our people showed them, and not publish them again in this form. For beside that the eye is much more delicate than the ear, and the defects of a discourse are far more easily observed on paper, where they remain, than in the air, where they do but pass; there is also a great difference between an auditor, whom devotion obliges to hear you, and a reader, who owes you nothing. The one thinks he should sin against piety if he denied you his attention; the other, that he does you a favour in heeding you, and may examine you without a crime. The judgment of the one is half made for you, whereas that of the other is at its full liberty. These reasons would have withheld me from hazarding the edition of these small books, if the matter had wholly depended upon my opinion. But the desires of my friends and the entreaties of the bookseller interposing, their violence has overcome my modesty. Yet I should have had vigour and firmness enough to defend myself against it, if the question had been simply of myself and my reputation. For as the present age is so polite and well informed, that the most eloquent speakers, and the most accomplished writers, can scarcely satisfy it; I well know that, to please it, graces and perfections are needed which I do not possess. But that also is not the object I seek; my weakness, and the calling wherewith God has honoured me, have abundantly secured me from such a passion. The motives which caused me to yield to the too favourable opinion of my friends, were the welfare of Christian souls, which they laid before me, and the service they believed this book might render them. The success will inform us whether they had reason to promise themselves so much from it. For my part, the thing being uncertain, I held myself obliged to give place to their judgment, and to prefer the profit which they imagine the faithful may receive from my poor labours to any other consideration. And if it be temerity to hope for this result, at least it is not a crime, but a laudable affection, to desire it. Of one thing, sir, I am well assured, that you will not dislike the gift I make you of this third and last part of my work. For, independently of that sweetness of spirit and obliging disposition which every one observes in you, and to say nothing of numerous evidences which I have received of your kindness towards me in particular, I am confirmed in this opinion, by your piety, well known in our church, both by the excellent fruits of your charity in the ordinary course of your life, and by the services you rendered to our flock in the office of an elder, which you executed among us with much edification and honour. Persuading myself, therefore, sir, may it please you, that you will receive this small present with your usual benevolence and readiness, there remains nothing but that I pray God to preserve you, with your worthy and noble family, in health and prosperity, and daily to augment his most precious blessings, both spiritual and temporal, to you and them. I beseech you to continue me the honour of your friendship, and to do me the favour to believe that I am devotedly,

Sir,

Your most humble and most obedient servant,

DAILLÉ.

Paris, April 1, 1648.

EXPOSITION

OF THE

EPISTLE OF PAUL TO THE COLOSSIANS.

SERMON I.

CHAPTER I.

VERSES 1—5.

Paul, an apostle of Jesus Christ by the will of God, and Timotheus our brother, to the saints and faithful brethren in Christ which are at Colosse: Grace be unto you, and peace, from God our Father and the Lord Jesus Christ. We give thanks to God and the Father of our Lord Jesus Christ, praying always for you, since we heard of your faith in Christ Jesus, and of the love which ye have to all the saints, for the hope which is laid up for you in heaven, whereof ye heard before in the word of the truth of the gospel.

THE assertion of the apostle Paul respecting the afflictions of the faithful, that they "work together for good to them that love God," Rom. viii. 28, is verified by constant experience. Besides the excellent fruit which the afflicted themselves receive from them, sooner or later acknowledging with the psalmist, that it was good for them to have been afflicted, Psal. cxix. 71, they are also serviceable to the edification of others. For as roses, the fairest and sweetest of flowers, grow on a rough and thorny stock; so from the afflictions of the believer, rugged and piercing to the flesh, spring examples of their virtue and instances of their piety, the sweetest and most salutary of all productions. See what a rich store of benefits the trials of Job and of David have yielded us! To them we owe that admirable book of the patience of the former, and a great part of the divine hymns of the latter. Had it not been for their afflictions, we should not now enjoy, after so many ages, those inestimable treasures of instruction and consolation. What shall I say of the sufferings of Paul, which spread the gospel all abroad, and converted the world to the knowledge of the true God! His imprisonment at Rome alone, under the government of Nero, has done the church more good than the peace and prosperity of all the rest of the faithful of that age. It gave reputation to the gospel, and made it gloriously enter into the stateliest court in the world. It inspired preachers of the truth with heroic courage. It awakened the curiosity of some, and inflamed the love of others, and filled all that great city with the name and odour of Jesus Christ. Nor was it of use to the Romans only. It imparted its celestial fruit to the remotest regions and generations. For it was in this very confinement that this holy man wrote several of his divine Epistles, which we read with so much edification to this day: as those to Philemon, to Timothy, to the Ephesians; and that directed to the Philippians, the exposition of which we last finished; and the following Epistle to the Colossians, which we have now chosen to explain to you, if God permit. Paul's prison was a common reservoir, whence have issued those living springs which water and gladden the city of God, and will furnish it even to the end of the world with the streams it needs for its refreshment.

Having then already drawn from one of these sweet springs that divine water with which we have endeavoured, according to the ministry committed to us of God, to irrigate the heavenly plants of your faith and love, we now turn, my brethren, to another, a no less vital and plentiful one than the former. Bring ye to it, as the Lord requires, souls thirsting for his grace; and he will give you, as he has promised, living water, which shall quench your drought for ever, and become in each of you a well springing up to eternal life.

The church of the Colossians, to whom this Epistle is addressed, having been happily planted by Epaphras, a faithful minister of Christ, the enemy failed not, by the hands of some seducers, immediately to sow his tares within it. These men would mingle Moses with our Saviour, and together with the gospel of the one retain and observe the ceremonies of the other. To make their error the more pleasing, they painted it over with the colours of philosophy, terms of science, curious speculations, and other similar artifices. Epaphras, seeing the danger to which this profane medley exposed the faith and salvation of his dear Colossians, informs Paul of it, then a prisoner at Rome. The apostle, to draw them from so pernicious an error, takes his pen and writes them this letter; in which he shows them that in Jesus Christ alone is all the fulness of our salvation, in such a manner that we should deeply injure him to seek any part of it out of him, since we possess abundant stores in his gospel wherewith to teach our faith and form our manners, without the addition of either the shadows of Moses or the vanities of philosophy. In the beginning he salutes and congratulates them for the communion which they had with God in his Son. Next he draws them a lively portrait of the Lord Jesus, in which shine forth the dignity of his person, and the inexhaustible abundance of his benefits. Upon that he encounters the seducers, and refutes the unprofitable additions with which they sophisticated the simplicity of the gospel. Afterwards, from dispute he passes to exhortation, conjuring these faithful people to live well and holily, conforming their deportment to a piety, honesty, and virtue worthy their vocation. He concludes with some particular affairs, of which he speaks to them, and with recommendations which he offers to them, both on his own part and on the part of other faithful persons who were with him. But you will better understand the whole by the exposition of each part of the Epistle, if the Lord grant us to complete it. For the present, we propose to consider only the five verses which we have read; the first two of which contain the inscription of the Epistle, and the other three the joy and thanksgivings of Paul to God for the faith and love of these Colossians. These shall be, God willing, the two points on which we will treat in this discourse.

I. The inscription of the Epistle is contained in these words: "Paul, an apostle of Jesus Christ by the will of God, and Timotheus our brother, to the saints and faithful brethren in Christ which are at Colosse: Grace be unto you, and peace, from God our Father and from the Lord Jesus Christ." At this day it is customary to inscribe letters with the name of those to whom they are written, and within them, after the body of the letter, the name of those who write them; formerly this was not the custom; for the writer wrote both the names within, at the head of the letter, with a brief salutation in these words, Such a one to such a one health; as we learn by numerous Greek and Latin epistles, which are left us in the ancient books of the most renowned personages of those two nations. The apostle, who lived in those ages, uses the same form in all his Epistles, as you know, except that instead of wishing health and prosperity to those whom he addresses, he ordinarily wishes them peace, and the grace of God, and of his Son Jesus Christ.

According to this form, the inscription of this Epistle contains, first, the names and qualities of those who write it, and of those to whom it is addressed; and, secondly, the good and happy wish with which they salute them.

The names of those who write it are Paul and Timothy, sufficiently known to all who are in the least degree versed in the New Testament. They are here described by certain qualities severally attributed to them. To Paul, that of "an apostle of Jesus Christ by the will of God." To Timothy simply that of "brother." The word, "apostle" signifies, in the Greek language, one deputed, a person sent by some one. But in the Scripture of the new covenant it is taken particularly for those first and highest ministers of the Lord Jesus, whom he sent with a sovereign and independent authority to preach the gospel and establish his church in the world:—the highest and noblest charge God ever gave to men: and to exercise it, it was necessary, 1. To have seen Jesus Christ alive after his death, that a good and lawful testimony might be given of his resurrection. 2. They must have received their commission immediately from the Lord himself. And, 3. They must have the Holy Spirit in an extraordinary measure, with the gifts of tongues and miracles. Whence it appears how illogical they are that attribute the glory of an apostleship to the bishop of Rome, who possesses none of these qualifications. It is also clear that this dignity is extraordinary, and was not instituted but for the first establishment of the church; the government of which, after its plantation, the apostles put in the hands of an inferior order of ministers, who are indifferently called in Scripture either bishops, that is, overseers and superintendents; or presbyters, that is, elders.

The history of the Acts informs us that to the twelve apostles before ordained our Lord added Paul; having miraculously appeared to him, and sent him with the same power that they had to convert the Gentiles. He assumes therefore this glorious title at the entrance of this Epistle, and declares moreover that he is an apostle "by the will of God;" signifying that it was the express order and mandate of the Lord which honoured him with this ministry, and not the suffrage and authority of men; distinguishing himself by this means from those false teachers and troublers who had not been sent, but by the will of flesh and blood. The declaration of this his quality was here necessary for him, 1. To maintain his honour against the calumnies of seducers, who disparaged and slandered him as much as they could, under pretence that he had not lived, like the other apostles, in the company of Jesus Christ during the days of his flesh; and, 2. To establish the liberty which he took of writing to the Colossians, and of proving to them their duty, as well in faith as in practice, it being evident that the apostles had a right to use this authority over all and each of the christian churches. To his own name he adds that of Timothy, whom he calls "brother," as having one and the same faith, and labouring in one and the same work; whether it were to authorize his doctrine the more, by the consent of this holy man, every word being more firm in the mouth of two or three witnesses than in that of one; or to recommend him to these believers, that if he wrote to them, or ever visited them, they might receive him as a person worthy of the fellowship of the apostles, and whose name deserved to accompany that of Paul.

As for those to whom he directs this Epistle, he describes them next in these words: "To the saints and faithful brethren in Christ which are at Colosse." I pass by, as childish and impertinent, the opinion of those who say that he means the isle and city of Rhodes, and that he calls it Colosse because of that prodigious statue of the sun which the Rhodians had erected at the mouth of their haven, and which the Greeks called the Colossus. What need is there of these frigid and ridiculous notions, since the ancients show that there was formerly in Phrygia, a province of Asia Minor, a city called Colosse, not far from two others, Laodicea and Hierapolis, which the apostle also mentions in this Epistle, and recommends expressly to the Colossians the communicating this letter to the Laodiceans, after they themselves had read it? Afterwards this city of Colosse changed its name, and was called Chone. Here one of the most eminent writers of the latter times of Greece, Nicetas Choniates, received his birth, taking his surname from that place: he boasts in one of his works that the apostle honoured the inhabitants of Chone, his native city, by addressing to them this very Epistle.*

Paul designates the christians at Colosse "saints and faithful brethren." He calls them "saints," a name he usually gives to all true christians, and which really belongs to them, since God, separating them from the rest of men by the effectual working of his word, and by the sacrament of his baptism, cleanses and purifies them from the filth of sin, delivers them from the servitude of the flesh, and consecrates them to his own name and service, to be to him a peculiar people, devoted to good works. Hence the whole body of the faithful is called in the Creed, "The holy church." Mark this well, my brethren, and be assured that you cannot be christians except you be truly saints. Suffer not yourselves to be abused by the deceitfulness of those who promise you this glorious name, provided only you make profession of faith in Christ, and that you live in the communion of their church, however evil and impious you are in other things. The body of the Lord is too vital and precious to have dead and putrid members. I confess that if you have the industry to hide your vices under the false ap-

* In Thesaur. l. 4. ch. 22.

pearances of an outward profession, you will induce men to give you the name of christians, and to reckon you among the members of the church; as it might possibly be, that, among those whom the apostle honours here with the name of saints and faithful, there were some hypocrites. But God, who sees the secrets of our hearts, and upon whose judgment our whole condition depends, will never account you christians, or members of his Son, if you are not truly saints. Paul likewise, and the church, who by a charitable judgment now call you disciples of the Lord, will change their opinion, and rank you with profane men and worldlings, when they discover your hypocrisy.

The title "faithful," which the apostle gives, in the second place, to the Colossians, is also common to all true christians, and is taken from that faith which they give to the gospel of the Lord. The word "brethren," that follows, signifies the holy communion which they had with the apostle, and with all other believers of whatever rank; as persons all begotten of the same Father, that is, God; all born of the same mother, Jerusalem from on high; all partaking of the same divine nature; all nursed in the same spiritual family; all nurtured in the same hopes; all destined to the same inheritance; all consecrated by one and the same discipline. In fine, he adds, "in Christ," because it is of him, and by him, and in him, that we have all this sanctity, faith, and fraternal union, the titles of which he has given to the Colossians.

After having thus described and designated the persons to whom he writes, he wishes them, according to his custom, "grace and peace from God our Father, and from the Lord Jesus Christ." By "grace," he means the favour and good-will of God, with the saving gifts and divine assistance with which he blesses those whom he loves in his Son. By "peace," he signifies that peace of God which is nothing else but the calm tranquillity of a soul that looks to the Lord with confidence, having remission of its sins by Jesus Christ, and is delivered by the effectual operation of his Spirit from the importunate tyranny of the lusts of the flesh. It is probable that, beside this first and chief peace, the apostle intends also peace with men; a sweet and calm state, exempt from their hatred and persecutions; that without offending them, or being troubled by them, they might lead a peaceable life in all godliness and honesty. You also know that in the style of scripture the word peace signifies generally all kinds of welfare and prosperity; in which sense it may, without disadvantage, be interpreted in this place. But he wishes them these benefits "from God our Father, and from our Lord Jesus Christ." "From God," because he is the first and highest spring of all good; "the Father of lights, from whom cometh down every good and every perfect gift." "From Jesus Christ," for he is the channel by which the benefits of God stream down to us; it being evident that without the death and resurrection, and, in a word, without the mediation of Jesus, we could have no part of the graces of God. He calls God "our Father," because he has adopted us freely in his Son, and on account of this relation he communicates his grace and peace to us; whence it is that Jesus Christ has given us authority to call him "Our Father" in the prayer which he has taught us. He calls Jesus Christ "the Lord," because he is our Master, who has all power and authority over us, as well by the right of creation as by that of redemption. Such is the inscription of this Epistle.

II. Let us now come to the second point of our text, in which the apostle congratulates the Colossians for the part they had in Jesus Christ: "We give thanks," he says, "to God, the Father of our Lord Jesus Christ, praying always for you, since we heard of your faith in Christ Jesus, and of the love which ye have to all the saints, for the hope which is reserved for you in heaven, whereof ye heard before in the word of the truth of the gospel." Here is the preface or exordium of the Epistle, which extends as far as the 13th verse; in which the apostle, by the true commendations which he gives the piety of the Colossians, wins their affectionate regard, and declares his cordial affection to them, to prepare them for a right and faithful reception of the instructions which he would hereafter propose to them, as proceeding from a soul desirous of their salvation. He protests therefore to them,

1. In general, that as often as he and Timothy prayed to God for them, they did so with most humble thanksgivings for the happy spiritual state in which they saw him.

2. He mentions more particularly the grounds of this thanksgiving, and proposes three of them. First, the faith of the Colossians. Secondly, their love. And in the last place, the inheritance reserved in heaven for them. Three particulars which comprise all the felicity of man. The part he takes in the happiness of the Colossians teaches us one of the most necessary offices of our love, which is to interest ourselves in the affairs of our brethren; "to mourn with them that mourn, to rejoice with them that rejoice;" and to be as nearly touched with their good and evil as with our own. Far from our practice be the envy and malignity of the men of this world, to whom the prosperity of others gives trouble, and their adversity gladness; who feed themselves with their miseries, and are sad at their mercies. But the apostle also shows us, by this his example, that the joy which we have for the good of our neighbours should be elevated to God, who is its only source, to render him thanks for it. This is the just and reasonable tribute this liberal Lord demands of us for so many

benefits as he communicates daily to our brethren and ourselves. If our meanness and poverty render us incapable of any other acknowledgment, let us at least faithfully acquit ourselves of this one, which is so easy and so just, and say with the prophet, "What shall I render to the Lord for all his benefits toward me? I will take the cup of salvation, and call upon the name of the Lord," Psal. cxvi. 12, 13. Let us study with so much the more care to render this sacred duty to the Lord, by how much more vile and detestable in this instance is the ingratitude of men. Far from blessing him for the benefits which he gives their neighbours, they scarcely thank him for those which they receive of him themselves. They impute them to their own industry or fortune, and, as says the prophet, "sacrifice to their net," Hab. i. 16, for the good successes that attend them; yea, there are some so insensible, that they do not give the glory to godliness itself, but to their own will, and the strength of their free determination. But it is not enough to render thanks to God for our brethren, there must be also prayer for them. For as it is he who gives them all the good things they possess, so there is none but himself that can preserve or augment them: and thus our thanksgivings should be ever followed or accompanied with petitions; as the apostle shows, in saying that he gives thanks to God for the Colossians, praying always for them. The title he gives to God, calling him "the Father of our Lord Jesus Christ," is not put here in vain, but to distinguish and specify the object of our prayers and thanksgivings. The appellation of God under the Old Testament was, "the God of Abraham, of Isaac, and of Jacob," the patriarchs with whom he contracted the old covenant, and to whom he promised the new. Now his name is "the Father of Jesus Christ," by whom he has abolished the old testament, and accomplished the new. Besides, by this Paul reminds us of that on which we can never sufficiently meditate, that it is by the means of this sweet and loving Saviour God has communicated himself to us; and if we have the honour to be his children, it is by Jesus Christ, of whom he is properly the Father, having, not adopted him, as he has us, but begotten him, from all eternity, of his own substance; by reason of which that also which he assumed to himself, in the womb of the virgin, has the same glory; according to what the angel said to the holy virgin, "The Holy Spirit shall come upon thee and the power of the Highest shall overshadow thee; therefore also that holy thing that shall be born of thee shall be called the Son of God," Luke i. 35.

But the apostle proceeds to add what were those blessings of the Colossians for which he and Timothy so assiduously rendered their thanks to God, the Father of our Saviour:

"Having heard of your faith in Jesus Christ," he says, "and of the love which ye have towards all the saints." He had never been among them, as he says hereafter, placing them, according to the opinion of most interpreters, in the number of those "who had not seen his face in the flesh," Col. ii. 1. Therefore he says it was by hearing that he had knowledge of their faith and love. Here is, faithful brethren, the true matter of our rejoicings and thanksgivings for our neighbours; not that God has given them vigorous health, abundance of riches, the favour of the great, the glory of fame, the knowledge of sciences, and other good things of this world; which in truth are but figures, dreams, and shadows, that secure no person either from diseases of the body, or death, or from trouble and disquiet of conscience, or true misery; but because Heaven has revealed Jesus Christ to them, and shed into their souls that "holiness, without which no man shall see the Lord." For these two graces, faith and love, comprise the whole kingdom of God. Faith is the beginning of it, and love the accomplishment. The one clears our understandings, the other sanctifies our affections. The one is the light of the soul, the other is the heat thereof. The one believes, and the other loves. The one begins, and the other finishes, the happiness of our life.

Now faith respects generally the whole doctrine of God revealed in his word, believing it to be undoubtedly true; but yet it fixes particularly on the promise he has made us, to give us eternal life in Jesus Christ his Son. It is this properly that renders faith saving and vivifying. Without this it would not differ at all from the faith of devils, who believe there is a God, and tremble. But this love of God, which it apprehends and embraces, gives it salvation, and enables it to produce in us all that is necessary for entering into the celestial kingdom; according to the assertions of Jesus Christ and his apostles in numerous places of Scripture, that whosoever believeth in the Lord is already passed from death to life; that there is no condemnation to him; and that "being justified by faith we have peace with God." Hence Paul, to describe true faith, adds expressly these words, "faith in Jesus Christ."

He shows us in the like manner the object of love, by saying, "the love which ye have towards all the saints;" that is, as we have intimated before, towards all Christians, all the faithful. I confess that love extends itself to all men in general, there being none to whom we owe not love, and, when required, the services which a true and sincere affection is ever ready to yield; since all men are the work and image of God; since in Adam they all have one common nature with us, and are all called to the participation of faith and of eternity in Jesus Christ by the gospel, which, without distinction or exception, invites all nations and persons to repentance and grace. But still love embraces not all men equally. It has various degrees in its affections, and loves its neighbours more or less, as it perceives more or less in them the marks of the hand of God, and the tokens of his Christ, and of his Spirit. Seeing then that they appear no where more clearly than in the saints, that is, in true believers, it is evident that these make the first and principal part of the object of love; according to what the apostle says elsewhere, "Let us do good to all men, especially to them who are of the household of faith," Gal. vi. 10. Besides that union which we have with them, a much more strict and intimate one than with any others, their necessity also particularly obliges us to do so; the hatred and persecution of the world putting them generally into such a condition that no creatures more need the offices of our love; neither is there any object more worthy of the affection and succour of a good and generous soul, than innocence unjustly hated and oppressed: therefore it is that the apostle observes here by name the love of the Colossians towards all the saints.

He joins these two virtues together, faith and love, because in fact they are inseparable; it being neither possible nor imaginable, whatsoever error may please to say, that man should believe and truly embrace God, as his Saviour in Jesus Christ, without loving him, and his neighbours for his sake; or that he should love him sincerely without believing in him. He puts faith before love, not because it is more excellent, (on the contrary, he elsewhere openly gives the advantage to love, 1 Cor. xiii.,) but because it goes first in the order of things requisite to salvation. It is the blessed root from which love and all other christian virtues spring forth. It is the foundation of the spiritual building, the gate of the kingdom of heaven, the first-fruit of the workmanship of God, and the beginning of the second creation. As in the old creation light was the first thing he created, so in the new, faith is the first thing he produces; which the apostle elsewhere thus divinely expresses: "God, who commanded the light to shine out of darkness, hath shined in our hearts, to give the light of the knowledge of the glory of God in the face of Jesus Christ," 2 Cor. iv. 6.

After the faith and love of the Colossians, the apostle adds, in the third place, the happiness that was kept for them in heaven: "For the hope which is laid up for you in heaven." Some join these words with what he had now said of the faith and love of the Colossians, and understand that these faithful people laboured with alacrity in the exercise of these virtues, for the hope they had of the celestial crown and reward; according to what the apostle says elsewhere of Moses, that "he chose rather to suffer affliction with the people of God, than to enjoy the pleasures of sin for a season; and esteemed the reproach of Christ greater riches than the treasures of Egypt; because," he says, "he had respect unto the recompense of reward," Heb. xi. 25, 26. And he teaches us in general, respecting all those that come to God, that they "must believe that God is, and that he is a rewarder of them that diligently seek him," Heb. xi. 6. And hence it does not follow either that our works merit the glory of heaven, or that our affection is mercenary. If we might not hope for anything but what we merit, our hopes would be very miserable. But knowing that God is faithful and unchangeable, we hope with assurance for the bliss which he, of his mere grace, promises to us; and the less we merit it, the more love we conceive towards God, who gives it to us; and the greater acknowledgment and service ought we to render him for it. And for this gratuitous salary which he promises us, we look not on it as a prey after which we hunt, and without which we should have no love for the Lord: but as an excellent evidence of his infinite goodness, as a testimony of his admirable liberality. That love of God, which is so resplendent in it, is the thing which most pleases and ravishes, and which inflames our faith, our zeal, and our affection for the service of so good and amiable a Lord.

If we were to combine what the apostle says of the love of the Colossians with the hope which they had of the heavenly glory, we should speak in strict conformity to evangelical truth. But it seems to me more simple and more consistent with the context, to refer it to the 3rd verse, where he says that he gives thanks to God for the Colossians, having understood their faith and love, "for the hope," he adds now, "which is laid up in heaven for you." For considering the condition of these believers on the earth, there seemed no great cause to congratulate them for their faith and love; the afflictions which they drew on them rendering them in appearance the most miserable of men. But though the flesh forms this judgment of them, the spirit, that sees, above all visible things, the crown of glory prepared for the faith and love of believers, esteems them as the happiest of all creatures; congratulates them, and renders thanks to God for the inestimable treasure that he has communicated to them. "I know (saith the apostle) that your piety has its trials and exercises in this world. But I cease not gratefully to bless the Lord that he has conferred on you that great favour. I know the bliss that is prepared for you on high, in the sanctuary of God." He takes the word "hope" here, as often elsewhere, for the thing hoped for; that is, the blessed immortality and glory of the world to come. I confess we do not yet possess it, for hope is the expectation of a future good. "We are saved," says the apostle, "by hope: but hope that is seen is not hope: for what a man seeth, why doth he yet hope for?" Rom. viii. 24. But this good, though absent and future, is as certified to us as if we had it already in our hands. This the apostle shows when he adds that this hope is reserved in heaven for you. It is a treasure which God has set apart, having fully prepared it, and keeping it faithfully for us in his own bosom. Hence we are assured of this felicity, for he has deposited it in the hands of Jesus Christ, in whom is hid our life and immortality; so that if we are assured of the safety of those things which a man of probity and honour keeps in trust for us, how much more certain should we be of the life and glory to come, seeing God has put them for us into the keeping of so faithful and powerful a depositary! The place where this rich treasure is kept for us confirms us yet more in the hope and the excellence of it; for, saith the apostle, it is reserved for us in heaven. Fear not, ye faithful. Your bliss is not on earth, where the thief steals, or infidelity and violence spoliate; where time itself ruins all things; where crowns the best secured are subject to thousands of accidents. Yours is on high, in the heavens, in the sanctuary of eternity, elevated above all the capricious and uncertain changes of human affairs; where neither vicissitudes, nor the causes that produce them, have any access. This same place shows you also the excellence and perfection of the bliss you hope for, since all celestial things are great and magnificent. Weakness, poverty and imperfection reside here; heaven is the habitation of glory and felicity.

In fine, the apostle mentions briefly, in the last words of this text, whence the Colossians had derived this sublime hope: "Of which," he says, "ye heard before in the word of the truth of the gospel." This sovereign bliss, which is reserved for us in heaven, is so highly raised above nature, that neither acuteness of sense, nor vivacity of reason, nor even the light of the law, could discover it to us, much less give us the hope of it. That same Jesus Christ who has destroyed death, hath "brought life and immortality to light through the gospel," 2 Tim. i. 10. Before this they were either entirely unperceived or imperfectly known and hoped for. It is therefore precisely from the gospel that we draw both the faith and the hope of them. He calls the gospel "the word of truth," not, as some have said, because it is the word of Jesus Christ, who is the truth and the life, an exposition more refined than solid, but because it is the most excellent of all truths; for those which are learned in the school of nature and of the law, are mean and unprofitable in comparison of those which the gospel discovers to us. We may justly conceive that the apostle designs also secretly to oppose the doctrine of the gospel to those of the seducers, who still recommended shadows and figures, as we shall hear in the following chapter; whereas the gospel presents to us the substance and the truth of things. And it seems to be in this sense that John, after he had said, "The law was given by Moses," adds, in a form of contrast, "but grace and truth came by Jesus Christ," John i. 17, because the law had only dark lineaments and shadows; but, on the contrary the Lord Jesus brought us the lively image, the body, and the truth of celestial things. The apostle reminds the Colossians that they had "heard before this word of truth," as it were to protest to them that he would advance no novelty among them, having no design but to confirm them more and more in the holy doctrine which they had already received by faith, from Epaphras, and other ministers of the Lord. See, beloved brethren, what we had to offer you for the exposition of this text.

It remains that we briefly direct you to the principal subjects of reflection which we should gather from it, for the instruction of our faith, the edification of our love, and the consolation of our souls. As for faith, it is for its security that Paul tells us, at the commencement, that he is "an apostle of Jesus Christ by the will of God," apprizing us by the title which he assumes, that we required not to receive any doctrine into our belief which has not been announced by these great and highest ministers of the Lord. Let us try the spirits, and admit only the word of the apostles. If any one preaches a gospel beyond that which they have preached, let us hold him an Anathema. We have their Scriptures. Let us assuredly believe all that we read in them. Let the doctrine which appears not there be suspected by us; and praised be God that, according to this rule, we have banished from our religion that which error and superstition had thrust into christianity. You know that the God, the Christ, the heaven, the worship and sacraments, which we preach, have been given to us by the apostles of the Lord, established by the will of God, and appear in all their Gospels and Epistles; whereas the mediators whom our adversaries invocate, the high priest which they acknowledge, the traditions which they maintain, the purgatory which they fear, the greatest part of the sacraments which they celebrate, the adoration of the host, the veneration of images, and the voluntary worship which they practise, are not found either in the Old or the New Testament. Let us therefore firmly retain our religion, as instituted by the will of God, and constantly reject what is beyond it, as coming from man, and not from the Lord; from earth, and not from heaven. But it is not enough to make profession of it; we must plant this doctrine in our hearts by a lively belief, in such a manner that we may be able to say with truth, that we have faith in Jesus Christ, and love towards all the saints.

With the apostle, we render thanks to God that of his great mercies he has vouchsafed to communicate to us this treasure of his gospel; and not in vain, since there are among us those who have truly profited by these spiritual riches. But the life of the greater part renders them unworthy of the praise which Paul here gives the Colossians. Is this to have faith in Jesus Christ, to serve him so remissly as we do? to evince so little zeal for his glory? so little respect to his commandments? so little belief of his doctrines? and so little affection for the interests of his kingdom? As for love, I am ashamed to speak of it, so chilled is ours. For if we loved all the faithful, should we leave the lives of some of them, and the reputation of others, without succour? Should we injure them instead of defending them? Should we take away their substance instead of communicating to them our own? Should we vilify their honour instead of preserving it? Would their prosperity offend us? Would their miseries satiate us? Faithful brethren, remember that they are the saints of God, his children, and the brethren of his Christ. Respect those sacred names, and spare those persons who have the honour to be related so nearly to your Lord. He will judge you by the treatment which you give them, and charge to his own account the good and the evil which they shall receive from your hands, recompensing it or punishing it in the very same manner as if you had honoured or violated him in his own person. He will sever you from his communion if you do not carefully improve theirs, and will never avow you for his children if you acknowledge them not for your brethren. And allege not, I beseech you, that you have faith. I know well that this divine light cannot dwell in souls which are cold and destitute of love. But suppose that this were possible, I solemnly tell you that all your pretended faith, though you possessed it in the highest degree, without love, would be but a shadow, an idol, and an illusion; and, as James saith, a corrupt carcass, James ii. 26. Do all you will, have as much faith and knowledge as you please, if you have not love, you are not a christian; you are but a false and deceitful image of one. Love is absolutely necessary to the perfection of a christian. It is the distinctive mark of this holy discipleship; it is the honour and the glory of it; and the apostle, as you see, sets it down here among its essential parts. Faith will cease in heaven, where vision will supersede believing. But love will remain for ever. Possess then a blessing so great and so necessary for you. If you have not hitherto realized it, ask it of God incessantly with prayers and tears, and leave him not before you have obtained it. If you have it, thank him for it, more than for all the goods of the universe; and forget not that in giving you love, he has given you the life, the kingdom, and the crown of heaven. Exercise this precious gift continually; let there be none of your neighbours without feeling it. Do good to all. Communicate what you have received: the light of your knowledge, to the ignorant; the succour of your good offices, to the afflicted; the sweetness of your patience, to enemies; the consolation of your visits, to the sick; the assistance of your alms, to the needy; the example of your innocence, to all with whom you converse. But have a particular care of saints, the members of the Lord Jesus, who serve him here with you, and however poor they are, yet have been redeemed with his blood, and predestinated to his glory, as well as you. Dear brethren, your labour shall not be in vain; your love will bring forth its fruits in their season with a most abundant interest. For terrestrial and perishing good things, which you sow here below, you will one day reap on high those that are celestial and immortal; for a little bread and a little money that you now give to Jesus Christ, you will receive from his liberal hand the delights of paradise, and the treasures of eternity. This is the hope which is reserved for you in heaven. It is not the word of weak and vain men which has promised you this. You have heard, by the gospel, the word of truth, which cannot lie.

And as so magnificent a hope should inflame our love; so should it comfort us in our tribulations, and render us invincible under the cross to which the name of Christ subjects us. Consider a little what the men of the world do and suffer for uncertain hopes, that whirl in the air, float on the sea, and depend on the wind and on fortune. To how many dangers they expose themselves! to what toil and disquietude they condemn themselves! voluntarily passing nights and days in a most laborious servitude for an imaginary good, that has no existence, and perhaps never will have, and which, however successful in their designs, they will not enjoy at most but for a few years! Christian, shall it be said that you have less zeal for heaven than they have for the world? Their hope is doubtful; yours is certain. Theirs depends on the will of men and the inconstancy of the elements; yours is in heaven. Pursue then nobly so high and glorious a design. And since your hope is in heaven, have incessantly your heart, your affections, your thoughts there. Regard no more either flesh or earth; your bliss is not here. Jesus Christ has placed it on high at the right hand of the Father, in the palace of his holiness. Let this excellent hope sweeten all the evil which you suffer here below. If you are not at ease here, if you are despised, if you have no part in the wealth or honours of the world, think that neither is it here that Jesus Christ has promised you the rewards of your piety. That heaven which you see so fixed and immutable keeps them faithfully for you. You will there receive, on a future day, the honour, the glory, and the dignities which you now breathe after; not to possess them during a few miserable months, as worldlings enjoy their boasted riches, but eternally, with perfect and unspeakable satisfaction, in the blessed communion of saints, of angels, and of Jesus Christ, the Lord of both. To whom, with the Father and the Holy Spirit, the only true God, blessed for ever, be honour and glory to ages of ages. Amen.

SERMON II.

VERSES 6—8.

Which is come unto you, as it is in all the world; and bringeth forth fruit, as it doth also in you, since the day ye heard of it, and knew the grace of God in truth: as ye also learned of Epaphras our dear fellow servant, who is for you a faithful minister of Christ; who also declared unto us your love in the Spirit.

DEAR brethren, the gospel of our Lord Jesus Christ is the most excellent and most admirable doctrine that was ever published in the universe. It is the grand mystery of God, the wisdom of angels and of men, the glory of heaven, and the happiness of earth. It is the only seed of immortality, the perfection of our nature, the light of our understandings, and the sanctity of our affections. There is no philosophy, or other doctrine, but this, which is able to deliver us from the slavery of devils, and make us children of the Most High. It is this only that truly purifies us from the filth of sin, and clothes us with a complete righteousness; that plucks us out of the hands of death and hell, and gives us access to the throne of God, there to receive of his bounty life and supreme felicity. All other religions, invented and followed by flesh and blood, are ways of perdition, instructions of error and vanity, that present themselves to wretched men in the thick darkness of their ignorance, as those seducing fires that sometimes mislead travellers in the obscurity of night, conducting them into the deeps of death and eternal malediction. The law itself, though it descended from heaven, is as much beneath the dignity of the gospel as Sinai is beneath heaven, and Moses beneath Jesus Christ. The law affrights consciences, the gospel gives them confidence. The one slays the sinner, the other raises him up again. The one makes grace desirable, the other gives the enjoyment of it. The one presented the shadows and figures of truth, the other gives us the lively image, the very body of it. Whence you may judge, my brethren, how much it concerns us to know so saving and divine a doctrine, that we may embrace and obey it. The repose and happiness of our souls are based on it, which we shall unprofitably seek everywhere else. It is to inflame us with an ardent desire for this holy and blessed knowledge that the apostle Paul so often proposes to us in his Epistles the praises of the gospel; scarcely ever naming it without immediately adding something in its commendation; as the custom is of those that are ardently attached, never to speak of what they love without giving it some eulogy that testifies both its excellence and their estimation of it. Such is the manner of our Paul towards the gospel of his Master. He has his soul so full of the love and admiration of this heavenly doctrine, that he can neither pronounce nor write the name of it, but he accompanies it with praises, as the just and due attentions of its dignity. Of this we have an example in the text which you have now heard. For having said before that the Colossians had heard of the hope which is laid up for us in heaven by the word of truth, that is, the gospel; he thence takes occasion to introduce in this verse something in its commendation, describing to us the diffusion and efficacy of this divine word of life. "The gospel," he writes, "which is come unto you, as it is in all the world; and bringeth forth fruit, as it doth also in you, since the day ye heard of it, and knew the grace of God in truth." In the two verses which follow, he commends Epaphras, who had by his ministry converted the Colossians to the knowledge of the Lord, bearing a strong testimony to his fidelity and goodness, and mingling with it his praises of the Colossians themselves: "As also ye have heard of Epaphras our dear fellow servant, who is for you a faithful minister of Christ; who also hath declared unto us your love in the Spirit." This shall be, if it please the Lord, the subject of this sermon; and to proceed with it in order, we shall consider the two particulars that present themselves in the text of Paul, that is, the praise of the gospel in the former verse, and that of Epaphras in the two next; alluding also to what the apostle intermingles with them in commendation of the Colossians.

I. As to the gospel, he touches on two points. First, its admirable progress, and its great and sudden spread. It "is come unto you, as it is in all the world." And, secondly, its divine efficacy to convert men and change their courses of life: "And bringeth forth fruit, as it doth also in you, since the day ye heard of it, and knew the grace of God in truth."

He says therefore, first, that the gospel had come to the Colossians. Secondly, that it had also come into all the world. About the first there is no difficulty; for as there was a church in the city of Colosse, it is evident that the gospel, by which christian churches are founded and builded, had been preached there. Only we should observe in this event the marvellous goodness of God towards the Colossians; for they were a barbarous and an idolatrous people, very far off from the country and the religion of Israel; a portion of Phrygia, a province infamous for its abominations, whence had issued the mysteries and infernal devotions of Cybele, called by the Gentiles the mother of the gods, the most detestable of all pagan idols, and in whose service were committed the most unclean and shameful horrors. The Colossians, as other inhabitants of Phrygia, were immersed in this vile gulf, when the Lord vouchsafed to visit them, and make the light of his gospel to arise upon them. Whence it appears that the knowledge he gives us of his word is a donation from his mere grace, and not the payment of our vaunted merits. For what had the Colossians, in their deplorable condition, that could invite him to communicate to them this rich treasure? what had they, on the contrary, that might not have diverted him from that design, all of them being saturated with an inveterate love of idols? You see also the apostle says, not that they had come to the gospel, but that the gospel had come to them; to show us that it is God who comes to us, who prevents us by his grace, according to the determinate purpose of his good pleasure. The sick go or send to the physician, and solicit the aid of his skill. Here, perfectly contrary, the supreme Physician of souls seeks the sick. He comes to them in his benignity. He sends them his ministers, and presents to them his remedies, when they dream of nothing less than of their malady, and the cure necessary for them. "The Son of man is come to seek and to save that which was lost," Luke xix. 10. He despatches his servants to Colosse, and other places, to bear thither his salvation to men who were intent on nothing but their own destruction. He causes himself to be "found of them that sought him not;" and says "unto a nation that was not called by his name, Behold me, behold me," Isa. lxv. 1. Let a man search as much as he pleases, he will never be able to find any reason of the dispensation of God in communicating his gospel at certain times, and to certain places, but his mere good pleasure. And that we may the more carefully note this truth, he often directs the light of his word to those who conducted themselves the worst of all men in the state of nature, and hides it from them who seemed less defiled than others. He imparts his gospel to the Colossians, to the Ephesians, to the Corinthians, and others, who were of all people the most abandoned to superstition and vice. He says nothing to the gymnosophists, the brahmins, or to various others, as well barbarians as Greeks, who at the time were esteemed the most innocent of all mankind, and who, in fact, appear from history to have possessed much more justice and integrity than any other people. Why has God taken this course? Because if he had acted in a different manner, if he had called only those in whose religious systems and lives was seen a glimmer of exterior goodness, passing by those whose manners had nothing but what was detestable, we should have believed, without doubt, what some cannot even now forbear to say, that the works of men oblige God to call them, and impart to them his gospel; and that, as they speak in the schools of Rome, if in rigour they are not worthy of this favour, yet they merit it at least in a seemliness of equity and congruity. The Lord therefore very often takes a perfectly opposite course, to make us understand that the persons whom he calls are as devoid of all merit as they are whom he leaves; and that if he vouchsafes to illuminate any with the light of his gospel, he does so of the sole good pleasure of his grace, and not in the least degree for any of their merits. Indeed it is most certain that no man whatever, in his native depravity, can do any good work, the most splendid of their pretended virtues being only a deceitful daub, which by a fair appearance hides deformity and corruption. It was therefore a miracle of the divine goodness that this saving doctrine came to the Colossians, who, by their nature, were so far from it; and the apostle reminds them of it, the more to excite their sincere gratitude to the Author of this great benefit.

But that which he adds is much more strange and incredible, that the gospel was come into all the world. He makes the same assertion in a succeeding verse of this chapter; "The gospel is preached to every creature that is under heaven." And in the 10th chapter of the Epistle to the Romans, he applies to the ministers of the Lord Jesus what the psalmist had sung of the heavens; "Their sound is gone forth through all the earth, and their words unto the ends of the world." And in the 15th chapter of the same Epistle, speaking of himself, he says, "From Jerusalem, and round about it, even to Illyricum, I have fully preached the gospel of Christ;" and after this he sowed the good seed in the isle of Malta, and at Rome. Now if the other twelve apostles, and the seventy disciples, and the evangelists, laboured each according to his measure in proportion with Paul, and that they did so is not to be doubted, it is not astonishing that by that time they should have carried the gospel through the whole world. We read also in the writings of the first Christians, Justin, Clement, Tertullian, and others, that in their time, that is, about one hundred and thirty and one hundred and sixty years after the Lord's death, all places were filled with Christian churches, and that there was no nation among either the Greeks or the barbarians, nay, the very Scythians or Tartars, where Christ Jesus had not his servants. And though these testimonies cannot be rejected without extreme arrogance, there being no probability that either Paul, or the other writers now mentioned, would have asserted such a fact without reason; yet, entirely to disarm incredulity, I will add, that the very same statement is made in the books of heathen authors of that age. For Tacitus, a Roman historian, a violent enemy to Christianity, though dispassionate in other things, and of great esteem among his countrymen, has recorded that in the eleventh year of Nero, that is, eight years after the date of this Epistle of Paul to the Colossians, a severe search having been made, there was found a very great multitude of Christians at Rome.* This is sufficient to justify the statement of the apostle. For as the gospel in the west was able to penetrate quite through the provinces that constituted, as it were, the heart of the Roman empire; it would more easily extend itself to Parthia and the Indies, where Thomas conveyed it; and other eastern parts, where its vestiges remain to this day; and in Egypt and Ethiopia in the south, where, according to ecclesiastical history, Matthew preached it; and towards the north, which occupied the attention of other disciples. This was almost the whole world that was then known by the Greeks and Romans; and, without doubt, in this sense we are to understand the apostle's statement. For as to those extensive countries discovered in the west, about one hundred and fifty years ago, which are commonly called the West Indies, or the New World, it is evident that the ancients had no certain knowledge of them, and it is very probable that they were not peopled at the apostle's time; the memorials which those nations have preserved of their own history reaching back for not more than four or five hundred years at most. We may therefore conclude, that, taking the world, as it is commonly understood, for countries inhabited and known at the time, the gospel had, when the apostle addressed the Colossians, come into all the world.

The apostle mentions this to the Colossians, first, to confirm them the more in the faith of the gospel. I confess that its truth depends not on the success attendant on its promulgation, nor on the number that believe it. Though all the world were to reject it, though heaven and earth were to persecute it, the faith of a Christian should continue firm and unshaken, founded, as it is, on the word of God, and not on the approba-

* Annal. l. 15.

tion of men; as, on the contrary, though the universe maintained error, it would be our duty to reject it, our condemnation to receive it. The command of God is in force for ever, "Thou shalt not follow a multitude to do evil." But though this is true, yet it is a great consolation to a believer to see the extensive diffusion of the truth. And as the admirable power of the Lord is the more impressively manifest in proportion to the greater number of converts it brings to his Christ, so it is evident that this extension of the gospel confirms our faith; furnishing us with an eminent testimony of the power of God, and of the efficacy of his word.

I add, also, that the success here mentioned by the apostle contains a strong argument for the divinity of the gospel, and that in two respects: First, if you consider the thing in itself; it is so great and marvellous that it shows sufficiently that this doctrine is not only true, but even divine and celestial. When Paul wrote this Epistle, it was not full thirty years after Jesus Christ had suffered death in Judea, and yet the gospel, as he says, had already come into all the world. How could it have made so much way in so little time, surmounted so many obstacles, flown into so many places infinitely distant, if it had not been of celestial origin, and was not carried by a divine power? Certainly, as the extension of the light of the sun, that in a short time illumines the whole hemisphere, and by its rapid motion visits all climes of the globe in four and twenty hours, evidently shows us that it is a work of God, and of a nature altogether different from that of earthly and elementary things; so the swift and sudden course of the evangelical doctrine, that filled the world in so little time, penetrated and dissipated its moral darkness, and so speedily made itself visible from one end of the heavens to the other, invincibly proves that it is a divine and not a human production. Look at all the systems of religion that have ever prevailed in the world, and you will not find one of them that was established in this manner, and that in so short a time was equally progressive. The pagan religions existed only in the countries where they were generated; and if sometimes they extended farther, their growth was owing rather to the love of novelty in travellers, who transported them from the place of their birth, than to their own native genius and energy. All the celebrated systems of philosophy among the Grecians lived only in the soil that produced them. And the doctrine which the popes of Rome have established in their communion arrived at the state in which we see it, only by a long succession of ages; gaining something in every period, till it took its present consistence and form, and in which it is maintained, by the terror of inquisitions, the pomp of worldly power, and the favour of the mighty, who find their own interests combined with it. It is only the gospel of the Lord that, from its birth, had the courage and the power to fly every way, penetrating with incredible swiftness all the regions of the habitable world in less than five and twenty years. And here let none allege the seduction of Mohammed, which infected the east, and the south, and a part of the west itself, in a very little time. For there is no similarity between the progress of these doctrines. I pass by other observable differences. I will touch upon only one of the most essential; namely, that Mohammed and his successors were unable to advance their impostures but by the force of arms, and propagated their creed no where except in the countries which they conquered, and among the nations which they subjugated. It was their iron, and not their Koran, that passed through and devasted the world. Was there any thing marvellous or supernatural in their success? or that a troop of robbers, whom their own necessities, or the cowardice and distractions of others, had fitted for enterprises, should, by force or stratagem, capture certain towns? or that, elated with their first successes, and receiving great accessions to their numbers, they still advanced, and, passing out of Arabia, they attacked the extremities of the Roman empire, which at that time were almost defenceless? and that, aided by the disunion and imbecility of their enemies, they found themselves, at the end of three or four score years, in possession of the east and the south? Surely in all this there was nothing superhuman. In earlier times, Alexander the Macedonian was equally victorious in less than fifteen years, as was Sesostris also, and others both before and after him. It is then no miracle that the religion of the Saracens, borne, if I may so say, on the wings of their victorious ensigns, saw much of the world in fifty or sixty years. If we marvel at anything, it is at the success of their arms, not at the exploits of their Koran, which never gained admittance into any place whose gates were not opened for it by fire and sword. On the contrary, the gospel of the Lord Jesus was not sustained and advanced in the world by military force, the favour of arms, the successes of war, or the achievements of any conqueror. It was not promoted either by the charms of eloquence or the subtilties of philosophy; in one word, it had no conceivable human succour. Those who carried it were twelve or thirteen fishermen, with a small number of others of no higher rank in life; without credit, without arms, without courage, without experience; the offscouring and refuse of the world; mere weakness and imbecility; who, far from invading the rights of other men, had renounced all their own; who, instead of smiting and slaying, were scourged and stoned at every turn; and, instead of attacking others, did not resist those who maltreated them; living in very great humility and innocence. With this poor equipage the gospel undertook the conquest of the world, and though it met every where with gates shut and walls garrisoned with all that was terrible to repel it; though the Jews persecuted it, the Gentiles derided it, the great and the little held it in abomination; though magistrates banished it, or put it under the most cruel punishments; though all rent it by outrage and reproaches; yet, unprotected as it was, it made itself room, and, in spite of so many dreadful obstructions, ran from east to west, and from south to north. Constantly despising all earthly aid, it reigned in a hundred and twenty years in every place, before it had one magistrate or captain on its side, and disarming them when it received any; so far was it from making advantage of their arms or authority. We may affirm therefore that this progress of the gospel is a thing altogether peculiar to itself, never occurring at any time in the world, and with which neither Mohammedanism, nor any other religion, has any thing in common. It follows that this is an evidence of the truth and divinity of this holy doctrine, those that are human neither having nor being able to have that admirable power and energy which are here seen.

This will be further evident, if we contemplate this event in another light, inasmuch as it was a manifest accomplishment of the ancient oracles, given by the Lord to his ancient people, and registered in his Scriptures, which foretell, in numerous places, that the Messiah would universally diffuse the knowledge of the true God, which was before confined within the narrow limits of Judea; that the nations should walk in his light, and that the "people walking in darkness should see a great light," Isa. ix. 2; words which the Lord Jesus, in the days of his flesh, had thus interpreted, "This gospel of the kingdom shall be preached in all the world," Matt. xxiv. 14. These predictions, therefore, appearing at that time so punctually, so admirably, and in so short a time fulfilled, who can doubt any more whether the Lord Jesus is the true Christ? and especially since he alone revealed the God of Israel and his service to the world, and declared that his apostles were the servants of this same God, who, having many ages before predicted these things, so mightily in the fulness of time executed them by their ministry?

But besides the confirmation of the faith of the Colossians in general, I conceive that by this eulogy of the gospel, the apostle designed more particularly to fortify them against the new doctrines which some seducers were sowing in their church. For since other churches, founded in divers parts of the world, had heard nothing of these doctrines, it was very evident that they were not any part of the gospel, that is, of what the apostles preached. Whence we may deduce, as we pass on, an invincible proof, both of the truth of the doctrine which we believe, and of the vanity of that which we contest with our adversaries of Rome. For as to what we hold, it is evident that the apostles taught it in all the world, both by word of mouth and by writing, as all the necessary, positive, and affirmative articles of our faith fully appear in the monuments of apostolic preaching; that is, both in the books which they wrote, and in the churches they founded. As for our adversaries, it is no less evident that they can never show that the monarchy or infallibility of their pope, or the adoration of their host, or the service of their images, or their invocation of saints, or purgatory, or the traffic of their indulgences, or any other of the points which we debate with them, was preached in all the world at the time of the holy apostle. Not a single trace of them can be found in any of the books or memorials remaining of that age, or of a long time beyond it; only a man may perceive them, some ages after, growing up, one in one place and another in another, at various times and in different regions; an evident sign that they are not parts of the gospel of Jesus Christ, which was fully preached in all the world in Paul's lifetime, but the inventions and traditions of men that have arrived since.

II. Having mentioned this sudden and admirable diffusion of the gospel, the apostle directs us, in the second place, to its efficacy in the places where it had been preached. It is not only "come into all the world," but, which is more, it "brings forth fruit" there, "as it doth also in you." It bears the same fruits there which it has produced among you. You discern that these fruits of the gospel are nothing but that faith, love, integrity, modesty, temperance, and other spiritual graces, which it produces in the souls of those who hear it and receive it as they ought, and in which the sanctification of men consists. It is this energy of the gospel which the Lord would represent to us in the parable of the seed, to which he compares it, Matt. xiii.; and which, according to the various properties of the places where it fell, brought forth more or less fruit; in some a hundred-fold, in other sixty, and elsewhere but thirty. Never was seen a thing more marvellous. In a few years the gospel transformed the whole earth. It crowned with flowers and fruits plants that were barren and accursed. It filled the deserts, the plains and the most desolate heaths with exquisite and delicious trees. That which the laws of nations, that which the most excellent philosophy had for many ages cultivated in vain, no sooner felt the hand of these evangelical vine-dressers and husbandmen, than, losing the austerity of its primitive juices, it became bland, and was laden with celestial fruits. Piety, sweetness, and philanthropy were seen to flourish where nothing had ever appeared but the horrors of superstition, of atheism, of cruelty, and of all other vices. This is the change which the Lord had foretold in Isaiah, in those figurative words, "I will plant in the wilderness the cedar, the shittah tree, and the myrtle, and the oil tree; I will set in the desert the fir tree, the pine and the box tree together," Isa. xli. 19. And elsewhere, comparing the gospel to rain that waters the earth, and makes it bud and bring forth fruit, he says, "So shall my word be that goeth forth out of my mouth: it shall not return unto me void, but it shall do all my pleasure, and prosper in the things for which I send it," Isa. lv. 10, 11. And this divine fruitfulness of the evangelical doctrine, which miraculously changed the world, is also a most evident argument for its truth, and its heavenly origin; for never has a system of religion or morals been known in our world possessing so animative and universal an efficacy.

But the apostle particularly commends the fruits which it had brought forth among the Colossians: "It bringeth forth in you, since the day that you heard and knew the grace of God in truth." He praises both their teachableness, for this word had produced fruit in them from the first day they heard it; and their constancy, for it still continued to yield fruit. The earth produces not fruit as soon as it receives seed; there must be time to mollify the grain, to make it germinate, to invigorate it, and decorate it with fruits. It is not so in this spiritual husbandry. The gospel, from the very moment that it is rightly received into your heart, will produce fruit. Receive it, then, faithful brethren. Defer not till to-morrow. This day, while you hear the voice of the Lord, "harden not your hearts," Psal. xcv. 7, 8. It is one of the most pernicious artifices of the enemy, to suggest to men that they defer their conversion to the future. Give me, says he, this day, and give God the next. Give me the present and him the future; to me the flower and vigour of thy life, to him the remnant and thine old age. So men find at last, when all has been given to Satan and the world, nothing remains for them to give the Lord, to whom they have left only the future, that is, what was not theirs; disposing of the present, which alone was in their power, to the service of their mortal enemy. Christians, take ye heed of his wiles, and hasten out of his snares. Imitate these faithful Colossians. Receive the word of God so deeply into your hearts, that it may bring forth fruit there from this very day. You cannot be the Lord's too soon. Put not off the design of being happy to another time; consider that time flies, and life escapes, and death comes, while you deliberate. But if we are required at once to bear fruit worthy of the gospel, it follows not that we may soon after cease to do so, as certain trees, which, if they are the first to flourish, are also the first to fade. The plants of the Lord soon begin, but never cease to yield fruit. They bring forth fruit in the hoariness of old age; and are even then "fat and flourishing," as the psalmist sings, Psal. xcii. 14. If you have embraced the gospel with ardour, retain it with invincible constancy. For salvation is prepared for none but those who persevere, who retain the verdure of heavenly principles, in defiance of the scorching heats of summer and the chills of winter; so that no season, however severe and adverse, ever strips them of their spiritual flowers and fruits.

As to what remains, the apostle calls the faith of the gospel "the knowledge of the grace of God," because it is not possible to enjoy this heavenly doctrine, if a man has not received and experienced the mercy which it offers us in Jesus Christ. This grace is the heart and substance of the gospel. Whence it appears, that to thrust into it the doctrine of the satisfactions and the merits of men, is to corrupt it and to change its nature, for these things are wholly incompatible with grace, or such as at least extremely darken and enfeeble it. When he says that they "heard and knew the grace of God in truth," he means, either that they received it truly, in sincerity of heart, without hypocrisy, or that they knew that this grace was delivered to them pure and sincere, without any mixture, either of Pharisaical superstition or philosophical vanity; or, finally, so as it is declared in the gospel, not in error, and in fictions, and lies, as in false religions, nor in shadow and in figure, as in the law of Moses; but nakedly and simply, as it is in itself. Of these three expositions, all good and convenient, the first is commendatory of the Colossians, the second of Epaphras their pastor, and the third is to the praise of the gospel itself.

As to Epaphras, he speaks of him by name in the second part of this text, consisting of the last two verses. And to commend him to the Colossians, and secure to him their hearts and regard, he bears a strong testimony to his fidelity, his sincerity, and his goodness: "As ye also learned of Epaphras our dear fellow servant, who is for you a faithful minister of Christ, who also hath declared unto us your love in the Spirit." This holy apostle knew how very important it is that churches should, for their edification, have a good opinion of their pastors; and with what artifices the enemy usually labours to decry the faithful servants of God, and ruin their reputation among their flocks: on this account he here exalts Epaphras as his piety deserved: and, to remove from the Colossians all suspicion against the purity of his teachings, expressly assures them that the doctrine which they had learned of him was the very same gospel of which he had spoken. And from this great anxiety of the apostle for the reputation of Epaphras, the ministers of the Lord should learn the necessity of insuring the high and cordial esteem of their people; abstaining not from evil only, but also from its appearances, and whatever might cause them to be suspected of it. It is not enough to obtain the approval of our own conscience, we should also be prepared to satisfy the judgment of our neighbours. Innocence is necessary for ourselves, and reputation for others. And since it serves to edify them, we are evidently bound to preserve, not only our own, but also the reputation of our fellow servants, whom God has appointed to the same office. And who does not see that, if we bite and rend one another, the disgraceful conduct of individuals will involve us all in one common infamy and ruin? And you see also that as the reputation of pastors is a public good, tending to the edification of the whole church, each believer owes it a peculiar respect, and that the crime of those who unjustly violate it is a kind of sacrilege. It is robbing the church, stealing from it its means of edification, to calumniate the life and doctrine of them who serve it, or to expose them to ridicule and contempt by your defamations.

But to return to Epaphras; the apostle honours him with two or three very great eulogies. First, he calls him his "dear fellow servant." Admire, I beseech you, the ingenuousness, the kindness, the humility, and modesty of this holy man. His ingenuousness; for whereas there is commonly a jealousy between persons of the same profession, Paul, contrarily, acknowledges and exalts the gifts and piety of this servant of God. His kindness; for he tenderly loves him, and everywhere plainly shows that of all men there were none whom he more tenderly esteemed than the faithful ministers of the gospel. Finally, his humility; in that being raised to the throne of apostolic dignity, the highest in the church, he makes Epaphras, as it were, to sit there with him, owning him for his fellow. Next he styles him a "minister of Christ." It was much to be fellow servant with Paul, but it is much more to be the minister of Christ, the Lord of glory, the Head of the church, the sovereign Monarch of men and angels. Judge with what reason some of our adversaries deride the title that we assume, denominating ourselves ministers of Christ, or of his gospel, since it is the word that the apostle expressly uses here, to denote that holy service to which God has called us. But he calls not Epaphras simply a "minister of Christ," he says moreover that he is a "faithful minister:" the appellation of minister was his in common with many others, the praise of faithfulness with few. It is all that the apostle required in a good steward of the house of God: "Let a man so account of us, as of the ministers of Christ, and stewards of the mysteries of God. Moreover it is required in stewards, that each one be found faithful," 1 Cor. iv. 1, 2. To have this praise the minister of the Lord must, first, seek the glory of his Master, and not his own: and, secondly, he must keep close to his orders; not parsimoniously concealing from his sheep any of the things committed to him for their edification; and without setting before them anything of his own invention beyond, or contrary to, the will of the chief Shepherd. But though all these good qualities greatly recommended Epaphras to the Colossians, yet the apostle adds another, which, no less than the former, obliged them tenderly to love and cherish him, namely, that he employed the Master's talents to their edification: "He is a faithful minister of Christ *for you.*" They ought therefore to love him both for the dignity of his office, and for the profit that thereby came to them. For though we are bound to love and respect all the faithful servants of God in general, yet, doubtless, we owe those particular affection and reverence who specially consecrate their ministry to our edification. In fine, the apostle tells them that this holy servant of God had informed him of the pure and spiritual love they bore him. He "hath declared to us" (that is, both to him and to Timothy) "your love in the Spirit." I conceive that by *love* he means here, not the christian grace which we ordinarily call by this name, (for of the love of the Colossians, in that acceptation of the word, he had already spoken in the 4th verse,) but the affection which these believers had for Paul. And he calls it a "love in Spirit," that is, spiritual; because it was founded on the Spirit, and not on the flesh; upon the interests of heaven, and not on those of earth. And here consider, I beseech you, how prompt and active Epaphras was to cement spiritual friendships. The Colossians had never seen Paul; doubtless it was he who had recounted to them the eminent virtue and piety of this great man, and by this means had enkindled in their souls that holy and spiritual love which they felt for him. And behold, also, how, by his narration of the love that these believers bore to him, he excites in his soul a corresponding affection for them. O holy and blessed tongue, that sowest nothing in the hearts of the faithful but charity and love, how far from thy candour and goodness, are those mouths of hell of these days, that inspire nothing but hatred, and kindle nothing but animosity, envy, and revenge, in the souls of all on whom they breathe; who busy themselves in making dissensions among brethren, in dividing and arming against each other those whom nature or grace has most strictly united!

But it is time to conclude this discourse. That which you have heard may, I think, suffice for your understanding this text. Nothing remains for me, but to conjure you to seek most earnestly to profit by it, and to draw from this subject the holy uses which it contains, whether for correction in the duties of life, or the consolation of your souls. The gospel of Jesus Christ is come unto you; the same gospel which aforetime changed the world, which abolished idolatry and paganism, and made the knowledge and service of the true God everywhere to flourish. The Lord has raised you up Epaphrases, faithful ministers of his word, who have published it to your fathers and to you with exquisite sincerity and truth entirely, as Paul preached it to the nations, without any leaven of superstition or error, acquitting themselves in their stewardship with so much uprightness of conscience, with so much zeal and ardour, that I assure myself, were the great apostle now on earth, he would do them the honour to own them for his dear fellow labourers. You have seen this sacred doctrine repeat the evidences of its divinity by the swiftness of its course, and its mighty efficacy. In a short time it flew through all christendom, and, in spite of the oppositions of hell and earth, raised up everywhere noble and flourishing churches to the Lord. We may say particularly of your church, that the gospel yielded fruit in it from the day that it was heard there. The blood and the sufferings of so many of the faithful, who therewith nobly sealed its truth, their charity, their zeal, their good and holy works, still fresh in our memories, are unexceptionable testimonies of this fact. But I know not whether I may justly add what the apostle says here of his Colossians, that the gospel bringeth forth fruit still in you; for those few fruits which it produces here are choked up with so many thorns and briers, so many sins and vices, that they scarcely deserve to be considered. I mean not that the gospel itself is changed. It has still that immortal energy which God gave it, to germinate, and grow up, and produce the fruits of righteousness and life. It is ever the incorruptible seed of God, his word living and abiding for ever, full of efficacy and vigour. Whence then comes this sterility? Dear brethren, it comes from the bad quality of our ground, and not from the weakness of the heavenly seed. The gospel is not yielding fruit among us, because it falls in stony places, and by the highways, or among thorns; on souls full of worldly lusts or carnal cares; or it is exposed to the feet of evil spirits, who are ever going to and fro in the land; or it is frozen and hardened with the fear of temporal evils. This is, christians, the true cause of our barrenness.

Let us then cleanse our hearts, and, as a prophet says, "break up our fallow grounds," Hos. x. 12; Jer. iv. 3. Let us pluck up the thorns which the world has planted there, avarice, the desire and deceitfulness of riches, ambition, and the love of our flesh, sensuality, and vanity. When you receive the gospel into souls so prepared for it, it will not fail to show its fecundity; it will bring forth its fruit abundantly, in some an hundred for one, in others sixty, in others thirty. Without this it is in vain that we boast us of Jesus Christ and of his word; his word is given to us that it may bring forth fruit. If we continue barren, far from proving beneficial to us, it will aggravate our condemnation, and draw upon us a judgment terrible in proportion to the plenty in which it was communicated to us. Remember that dreadful threatening, verified in the lamentable experience of multitudes, which the apostle denounced to the Hebrews: The earth that bringeth forth thorns and thistles "is rejected, and nigh unto cursing; whose end is to be burned," Heb. vi. 8. "It is a fearful thing to fall into the hands of the living God," who is the most severe to punish the contempt of his word, when he has been the most liberal in imparting it to men. For not continuing to bear fruits worthy of their vocation, these very Colossians, whose faith and love the apostle here commends, and their neighbours, the Laodiceans and the people of Hierapolis, saw, some years afterwards, their cities demolished and buried by a tremendous earthquake. And all those noble churches of Asia, so much celebrated in the Acts and the Apocalypse, are at this day desolate, for not having profited by the gospel; and God has already begun to avenge this contempt of his word in various places in christendom, which the briers and thorns of the old superstition now cover again, instead of the gospel which lately flourished there. God forbid, dear brethren, that we should fall into the like condemnation. To prevent it, let us recover the zeal of our fathers; let us do our first works. Let the gospel again be fruitful in the midst of us, abundantly prolific in love, meekness, honesty, peace, humility, patience, alms, prayer, fasting, sobriety, chastity, and the other fruits of the Spirit; and above all, a spiritual love of Paul and the other apostles who report the gospel to us, that we may respect them and walk in their doctrine, and in concord and love among ourselves. If we make this use of the gospel, God will take pleasure in the midst of us. He will daily visit us, he will cherish us, as his paradise, his heritage, the garden of his delights. He will pour out upon us here below graces of all kinds, blessings in abundance. And after having seen us fruitful on earth, he will one day transplant us into heaven, that we may for ever live and flourish in the courts of his own blessed and eternal habitation. Amen.

SERMON III.

VERSE 9.

For this cause we also, since the day we heard it, do not cease to pray for you, and to desire that ye might be filled with the knowledge of his will in all wisdom and spiritual understanding.

THE love of beauty and excellence is so natural to us, that we cannot discover so much as the earliest germs of them anywhere but with delight; and the secret pleasure they excite within us always makes us wish for their growth and their perfection, unless envy, or some other malignant passion, check the natural emotions of our hearts. Thus, when we see lovely and docile children, there is no soul having any of the sympathies of man that is not delighted, and utters a similar prayer for them to that which Joseph offered for Benjamin, when he was presented to him by his brethren, "God be gracious unto thee, my son," Gen. xliii. 29. From such sentiments flow those benedictions which we cordially pronounce on persons that are employed in beneficial affairs, whether natural or civil; as when, with the psalmist, we see the busy reapers of a luxuriant field in harvest time, and address them, "The blessing of the Lord be upon you; we bless you in the name of the Lord," Psal. cxxix. 8.

But if natural beauty and perfection engage our affections and good wishes to those in whom we perceive them, the gifts of divine grace, which are incomparably more excellent, should much more affect us, and kindle in our hearts more ardent flames of love and of desire for those that possess them. For as high as heaven is above the earth, and as much as eternity is preferable to time, so much advantage have the beauties and perfections of grace above those of nature. If, therefore, we estimate them according to their worth, we cannot see them shine out in any without advancing towards them, and attaching ourselves to them as holy and as happy persons. An eminent example of this motion of christian love, we have in our text; for the apostle Paul here shows us that he was no sooner informed by Epaphras of the faith and love of the Colossians, than his soul was seized with ardent love to them; and being hindered by his absence from giving them other evidences of his affection, he presented incessant and earnest prayers to God for their advancement and perfection in piety; that is, for the continuation and the perpetuity of their felicity.

The sum of his desires for them is contained in three verses, each verse evidently relating to a distinct kind of benefits: for he wishes them, first, in the 9th verse, the benefits that respect a perfect knowledge of the truth; then, in the 10th, those that respect the exercise of sanctity; and, finally, in the 11th, such as concern perseverance in faith, and patience in afflictions. For the present, we will meditate only on the first of these three articles, deferring the two next to another discourse: "And for this cause," saith the apostle, "we also, since the day we heard it, cease not to pray for you, and to desire that ye might be filled with the knowledge of his will in all wisdom and spiritual understanding." For the right understanding of this text, we will consider in it three particulars, by the help of the grace of God, which we implore to produce this effect. First, the motive of the apostle's prayers. Secondly, their form, manner, and quality. And, finally, which is the most important, the subject of them, that is, the blessings which he requested of God for them.

I. The motive that induced the apostle to pray for the Colossians, he expresses in these first words: "And for this cause, since the day we heard it, we cease not to pray for you." For these words sending us back to the former verses, with which they are connected, teach us that the information which the apostle had received from Epaphras, of the faith of the Colossians towards Jesus Christ, and of their love towards the saints, of their heavenly hope, and their other spiritual graces, of which he spake before, that this knowledge, I say, having filled him with love towards them, made him continually pour out prayers before God to complete their salvation. I confess the affection they bore him in particular, and which he mentions in the verse immediately preceding, contributed something to his anxiety to pray for them. But its principal cause was their piety and sanctification, because they had the first-fruits of the Spirit, and the beginnings of the kingdom of heaven. Seeing the foundations of the gospel, and of the building of God, so happily laid and established among them, he beseeches the supreme Master and Architect of this spiritual work by his power to finish it. The same reason made him also present his prayers to God for the Ephesians, as he testifies at the beginning of the Epistle which he wrote them, using almost all the same words that he does here. Having "heard of your faith in the Lord Jesus, and love unto all the saints, I cease not to give thanks for you, making mention of you in my prayers; that the God of our Lord Jesus Christ, the Father of glory, may give unto you the Spirit of wisdom and of revelation," Eph. i. 15—17. Faithful brethren, learn by this example of the apostle to pray to the Lord principally for those in whom you see the work of his Spirit manifest. Rejoice ye for their faith and zeal, and love them for the integrity and purity of their life; but remember that the first and principal office which your love owes them is the continual succour of your prayers. Object not that they are too far advanced to need them. During the course of this life, the progress of a christian is never so great that the prayers of his brethren for him are unnecessary. When he is most advanced, the enemy makes most attempts, and lies most in ambush for him. The nearer he is to the crown, the more need he has of divine assistance. As there are none in the lists whom we favour more with our wishes, acclamations, and applause, than those who come nearest to victory; so in this career of the gospel, we should love those most who run best, and accompany with our vows, prayers, and benedictions those who are nearest to the mark of the heavenly calling. We never utter more wishes for a vessel than when, after a long and dangerous voyage, it arrives near our coast, or we see it ready to come into the haven. When the believer having escaped the shoals and tempests of the world, steers the direct course for heaven, and makes, (if we may so say,) with oars and sails, for the port of salvation, it is then we should redouble our wishes and benedictions for his safety; it is then we should fear more than ever lest some accident mar his progress, and bereave him of the reward of all his pains.

II. But let us now consider, in the second place, the manner and quality of the apostle's prayers: "Since the day that we heard this good news, we cease not to pray for you." First, he did not pray alone. "*We* cease not to pray;" where you see he speaks of more praying with him, comprising in this number Timothy, whom he had expressly named at the beginning of this Epistle, and the other believers who were at Rome with him. Urged by one and the same love, animated with one and the same desire, they all lifted up their hearts and voices to God with the apostle for the spiritual prosperity of the Colossians. As there is nothing on earth more grateful to the Lord than this divine concert of many souls thus mingling their voices and supplications, so there is nothing more effectual to draw down his blessing and obtain his graces in the behalf of our neighbours. "If two of you agree on earth concerning anything that they shall ask," saith our Lord, "it shall be done for them of my Father which is in heaven," Matt. xviii. 19. In addition to the conjunction of believers who prayed unanimously with the apostle for the Colossians, they had also two other qualities which gave them much power; assiduity, and the devotion of heart from which they issued.

He expresses their *assiduity* in prayer, when he says that he "ceased not to pray for them, since the day he heard of" their piety, of their zeal in the gospel. As soon as he was informed of it, he deferred not this duty to another time. He commenced praying for them immediately, and pleading with God for the completion of their faith; so ardently did this holy soul love all who bore the badges of his Lord. But he was not satisfied with praying once or twice for the salvation of these dear disciples of his Master. He went on constantly, and ceased not to solicit the goodness of God for them. For it is not enough that Moses lifted up his hands once or twice for Joshua's victory: for the entire defeat of Amalek, this holy man must continue to hold his hands stretched out towards heaven. Hence Isaiah commands the watchmen of Jerusalem, that is, its pastors, not to hold their peace, nor give the Lord any rest, "till he establish and make Jerusalem a praise in the earth," Isa. lxii. 6, 7. And our sovereign Master expressly teaches us in one of his evangelical parables that we "ought always to pray, and not to faint," Luke xviii. 1. And his apostle enjoins us to "continue in prayer," Col. iv. 2; and elsewhere, to "continue instant in prayer," Rom. xii. 12; and again in another place, to "pray without ceasing." 1 Thess. v. 17. So you see he very carefully practised himself what he commanded others. Think not that this holy man was on his knees from morning to evening, employing himself in nothing but the recital of prayers, as the Messalians or Euchites did, a sect of heretics condemned by the ancient church, who professed to be always in prayer, and under this fair mask concealed a most profound and infamous laziness. The greater part of the monks of the communion of Rome at this day, who retire to cloisters, as to so many refuges of idleness, pass their time in saying litanies and orisons, usually without any attention or devotion, and under pretext of this pretended service to the public unjustly draw the tribute of immense alms, righteously due to the true poor, and not to them, who are willingly so by a vow directly contrary to the command of God. The prayer of a believer interferes not with his other duties. The same Lord who commands him to pray orders him also to labour. He who obliges him to the one does not exempt him from the other. He intends that he acquit himself of them both. Let prayer begin, guide, and end his labour; let his labour seal, follow, and accompany his prayer. Let him pray with his hand upon his work; let him work with heart and eyes lifted up in prayer. Let these two exercises fill up his whole life; parting its days and hours between them, and keeping faithful and indissoluble company to its end. Paul prayed; but his devotion did not hinder him from preaching to them who were present, from writing to the absent, from instructing the teachable, or reprehending transgressors; from confirming them who were within, or drawing those without; from fortifying the faithful, or convincing the adversaries;

and from employing his time in a multitude of good and holy actions. What means he then by saying that he ceased not to pray for the Colossians? He intends to say that he assiduously pursued it, that he offered it as often as time and place permitted, that neither day nor night passed but he did them this charitable office. Not to allege here what Augustine elegantly says, that our desires being prayers, these are continual when our desires are continual.* This example of the apostle teaches pastors in particular, that beside preaching the word, they owe to their flocks the succour of their prayers, offered not only in public, but also in private. For how can they, without crime, forget persons who are so strictly united to them—their crown and their glory, the ground of their joy and the subject of their most precious labour?

But the apostle, besides the assiduity of his prayers for the Colossians, shows us their ardour and devotion, when he says that he prays and *desires* for them. For the first of those words signifies the elevation of the soul to God; when fixing its eyes on the greatness of this supreme Majesty, it adores him, and gives him the glory of perfect goodness, power, and wisdom. This is as the exordium and preface of prayer, to move the Lord, that he give us favourable audience. Then follows that which the apostle calls here the desire; that is, the very request we make to the Lord, beseeching him to give liberally to us, or to our brethren, the benefits we need. From which we observe, by the way, the order we should keep in our prayers, that they may be legitimate and grateful unto God; namely, that at the entrance we present him a heart full of humble and affectionate respect to him, that reveres him as almighty and all-wise, that loves him as infinitely good, and praises and glorifies him as perfectly blessed. The requests which are heedlessly presented to him, without this preparation, are more apt to provoke his wrath than attract his beneficence. After this, we should next make our requests with an ardent desire and filial confidence. Thus the apostle prayed for the Colossians.

III. Let us now come to the third point, and see what was the matter or subject of his prayer: "We cease not," saith he, "to desire of God that ye may be filled with the knowledge of his will in all wisdom and spiritual understanding." It sufficiently appears, by the commendations he gave the Colossians before, that they were already much advanced to the knowledge of God, and of his gospel; therefore he does not simply desire of the Lord that they may be made partakers of this knowledge, but that they may be filled with it. For there are great differences in knowledge; first in regard of its extent,

* Augustine in Psal. xxxvii.

and next in regard of its degrees. For its extent, it comprehends those things which can be known, which being almost infinite, it is evident a man may know some who does not know others. And as for its degrees, the same thing is known more clearly and more distinctly by one, more obscurely and confusedly by another. It is the same in this as in seeing; one sees and discovers more objects than another; and of those who see one and the same object, one beholds it more clearly than another; and whatever is the cause of this diversity, whether the inequality of their eyes, or the difference of their attention, or that of the light which irradiates them, so it is that their seeing is very different; that of the one being imperfect and defective in comparison of the other. The apostle therefore, beseeching the Lord that the Colossians might be filled with knowledge, intends that they might obtain of his goodness a perfection of both kinds: first, that if there were any points of the gospel not yet come to their knowledge, he would grant them grace to observe and comprehend them. And, secondly, that if they did not clearly enough comprehend the things they knew already, he would so shine on them by the light of his Spirit that they might plainly and distinctly perceive them. In these two points the fulness or perfection he wishes them in this place consists; the one, not to be ignorant of any of the necessary particulars of the mystery revealed to us by the gospel of Jesus Christ; the other, to know each of these particulars clearly and distinctly, seeing the truth of them as in a resplendent light. Besides, we must remember that as the state of a believer, during his journey in the world, differs from that which he will enjoy in heaven, where he will live in the bosom of God; so the perfection of his knowledge is of two sorts, the one earthly, and the other heavenly. This is his last and highest perfection; that is but the propensity and beginning of it: the one is the perfection of his infancy, the other of his full age. And though the first may be in a sense truly termed fulness and perfection, yet in comparison with the other it is imperfect. Hence the apostle elsewhere puts these two kinds of knowledge in opposition to each other: "Now we know but in part, and see but darkly in a glass, whereas in the other world we shall see face to face, and know as we have been known," 1 Cor. xiii. And in the same place he compares the knowledge we have here below to the thoughts of a child, and that which we shall have on high to the thoughts and judgment of a perfect man. Then all the arguments of the truth of the gospel shall be so magnificently displayed before our eyes, that a doubt of it shall never be able to enter; and whereas now we see but the images of things, then we shall touch the substance of them; besides which the light of our understandings will be incomparably more clear and perfect than it is here below. But though, considering the thing in itself, only the knowledge of a believer enjoying the vision of his Lord in heaven can be called perfect, yet referring and adjusting it to the state in which we now are, there is also on earth a sort of knowledge which may be called perfect, namely, the highest measure a believer can attain while he is here below. As, though the knowledge of a child is far below the understanding of a man, yet there is a certain form and measure of knowledge proportionate to the capacity of its age, to which, when the child has arrived, we say it is an accomplished child, yea, most accomplished. For every age has its perfection, and every greatness its full height. It is then of this second kind of perfection and fulness that the apostle speaks, when he prays the Lord that the Colossians might be filled with knowledge; that is, not that they might see the Lord face to face, (this is not given but in the other world,) but that they might receive of his goodness all the light necessary for their state on earth, and as great and rich a measure of knowledge as may be necessary for attaining one day the utmost degree in the kingdom of heaven. And remark here, by the way, the holy artifice of the apostle. By praying God that the Colossians might be filled, he secretly intimates to them that they yet wanted something, that he might render them teachable and attentive to the instructions he wished afterwards to give them. For those who think they are perfect, and have the consummation of knowledge, disdain instruction as superfluous and unprofitable. Therefore he seasonably removes this imagination from the Colossians, that they may patiently suffer him to instruct them, and finish in them what was only rough-drawn. To the same end, he adds, that they might be filled with the knowledge of the will of God. For by the will of God he rejects and removes far from this subject all the inventions and doctrines of men, the disputes and subtilties of philosophy, the voluntary devotions and superstitions which had been sowed among the Colossians by false teachers, as things rather contrary than useful to the perfection and happiness of man, and restrains all the knowledge he desires for them to the sole will of God, as its true object and its just measure.

Upon which we have to remark, first, that the word which the apostle uses in the original, and which we have translated knowledge, signifies properly a great and ample knowledge; and these holy authors employ it ordinarily to express that knowledge of God which is given us by the gospel of Jesus Christ. The law of Moses and the doctrine of the prophets teach what is the will of God. But they were not designed to declare it so clearly and so fully as the gospel. Hence Peter compares the light of the prophets to that of a candle shining "in a dark place," and that of the gospel to the brightness of the day, 2 Pet. i. 19. And to this John had respect, when he said that "no man hath seen God at any time; the only begotten Son, which is in the bosom of the Father, he hath declared him," John i. 18; because the knowledge given of him before the manifestation of the Lord Jesus was so weak, that it is scarcely worthy of comparison with that which is given to us. It is therefore properly this evangelical and christian knowledge which the apostle wishes for the Colossians, opposing it to that of the law, the rudiments of which some endeavoured to re-establish among them.

Secondly, we must observe what is the object of this knowledge, the knowledge (saith he) of the will of God. All men naturally desire knowledge. Every kind of real knowledge is beautiful and grateful, and adds some ornament to our understanding. Yet it must be confessed that generally none are capable of giving us the perfection and happiness we desire, and which are necessary for our nature. Such are all mundane sciences, discovered and cultivated by the sages of the world; not only their philosophy about nature, and the motions of the heavens and elements, and about the properties and effects of things animate and inanimate, but also that part of their doctrine which immediately concerns us, and explains what our conduct should be, both in private, and towards those who govern us, or are governed by us, either in the family or in the state. To say nothing of the variety and extreme uncertainty of their opinions, which change every day, and float in infinite doubts, no man, after having passed a whole life in this study, and made the utmost progress, becomes more contented, or happier, or more assured. All the pretended light of their school cannot dissipate from our minds either the horror of death or the fear of the judgment of God. The knowledge of the Lord alone can remove them from us, and by consequence it alone is necessary for us; the rest will not render us either more happy if we have them, or more miserable if we have them not. It is then only this knowledge which the apostle desires for the Colossians.

But we must consider, in the third place, that he wishes them the knowledge, not of the nature, or the majesty, or the other essential perfections of God, but of his will. For as to the essence of this supreme and incomprehensible Lord, as to the immensity of his power, as to the ineffable manner of his understanding, and the wonders of his judgment, it is not necessary for us to know them clearly. It is sufficient for us to adore them, and many have lost themselves in endeavouring to sound them. We must know his will to attain salvation, as the true rule of our duty and his judgment. He has fully declared it to us by the ministry of his heralds, the apostles and prophets, who have published it by word of mouth, and consigned it to us in writing by the holy books which they have left us. We must seek it there, and not in the discourses of vain men. There we shall find it manifested, as far as it is necessary for us to know and do it. It has two principal parts, faith and obedience. For the will of God, as the apostle understands it here, is nothing else but that which God would have us believe and do to be happy. For faith, his will is, says our Lord, that whosoever seeth the Son, and believeth in him, shall have eternal life, and be raised up at the last day, John vi. 40. For practice, "This is the will of God," says the apostle, "even your sanctification," 1 Thess. iv. 3. These are the two principal parts of the will of God, to which all other instructions in Scripture refer. In the knowledge of these things Paul prays God that the Colossians might be perfect and complete.

He adds "in all wisdom and spiritual understanding." We call them wise men in the world who know how to obtain their end, who use means fit for this purpose, and skilfully avoid all that might hinder it; so dexterously conducting their affairs that one of two things follows: either they accomplish that which they desire, or, if disappointed, some accident, and not their fault, has caused such ill success. But because they propose to themselves ends vain, evil, and unprofitable to their happiness, however wise they are esteemed by the world, all their industry is nothing but folly and error. Those then, on the contrary, are wise after the Spirit who constantly hold the right course of piety, guiding themselves in it with such skilfulness that they avoid scandals, and all that might divert them from their mark. And though the world commonly account them extravagant, yet their conduct evinces true wisdom, since, at the end, it will be found that none but they attain to salvation. It is then this skilfulness which the apostle terms here spiritual wisdom; both because it respects the things of the Spirit, which appertain to a celestial and spiritual life, and also because it is a gift of the Spirit of God, coming from on high, from the Father of lights. Neither the sense nor the reason of nature is able to bestow any knowledge of the divine will, which is the matter and subject of wisdom. Wisdom is the use and employment of the knowledge of God. For to be wise after the Spirit it is not enough to know what is the will of God. There must be the use of this knowledge; first, by laying down, as a certain and unalterable maxim, that it is in this will our bliss consists; and consequently, that it must be the limit of our desires. Secondly, by practising what we know of this divine will, aiming at the mark it shows us, and, to attain it, employing the means which it prescribes, watching and labouring continually thereto. For certainly that servant in the parable, who knew his master's will and did it not, was any thing but wise. In the last place, as for the spiritual understanding which the apostle desires for the Colossians, it is real and exquisite prudence, to judge aright of things which are presented to us, and to discern the good from the evil, the true from the false, and the real from the apparent; and this gift, you perceive, is also a fruit of the knowledge of God, and consists only in a strict application of what we know of his will to the doctrines and counsels which the flesh and its ministers set before us to turn us out of the way of salvation. This Eve wanted when she was seduced by the serpent, and the Galatians when they were misled by those impostors. The apostle feared lest the same should befall the Colossians, and, to divert this fatal blow, supplicates the Lord to give them the understanding necessary for happily distinguishing the false colours, the dissimulations and enticements of error, from the simplicity that is in Christ. Therefore he desires of God not only that they might be filled with the knowledge of his will in wisdom and understanding, but in *all* wisdom and understanding; that is to say, very abundantly, in so great and rich a measure, that none of the parts or operations of this divine ability should be deficient in them; after the same manner as when he asks elsewhere, "Have all faith?" to signify so high and elevated a measure of it, that no kind or degree of faith is wanting. Such is, well-beloved brethren, the ardent and affectionate prayer which the apostle continually offered for these Colossians, that they might be filled with the knowledge of the will of God "in all wisdom and spiritual understanding;" that is, in such a manner that this knowledge might form in them an accurate spiritual prudence.

To conclude. It remains that we briefly touch upon the principal lessons which we are to derive from it for the instruction of our faith and the amendment of our practice. First, you see how far the judgment of the apostle is from the doctrine and practice of Rome. The apostle wishes the faithful to know the will of God, that they may be filled with this knowledge. Rome teaches that their faith is better defined by ignorance than by knowledge, and that it is sufficient for them to have I know not what implicit faith, (as they call it,) which, without knowing anything itself, refers us to the faith of another. The apostle desires that believers be endowed with all wisdom and spiritual understanding. Rome fears nothing so much as this, and commands the people, without knowing or understanding anything themselves, to leave this whole study to their clergy; contented with saying they believe what the church believes, not knowing in the meantime what it does believe. Darkness is not more contrary to light, than this pretended faith to wisdom and understanding. Their practice is conformable to their doctrine. For they hide the Scripture from their people, the sacred and authentic evidence of the will of God, the living and teeming source of all wisdom and heavenly understanding; and if in their service they repeat any passages of it, they repeat them in a strange language, that their people may hear and not understand it. Faithful brethren, thank God that he has withdrawn you from this kingdom of darkness; enjoy with gratitude the light he has set up among you. Learn, in the brightness thereof, what is the will of the Lord, the head and the foundation of true wisdom. Esteem this knowledge as the gate of heaven, the entrance of eternity, the seed of the divine nature, and the principle of celestial life. Without it, how will you love God? as no one loves what he knows not. Without it, how will you obey God? since to obey him is only to do his will. Without it, how will you resist the enemy? how will you free yourselves from his wiles? how will you discern his frauds from divine truth? Judge how the apostle estimates it, since it is the first thing he asked of God for these Colossians, whom he so ardently loved. If you will attain the salvation to which he directs them, possess that which he with so much earnestness desires for them. Remember you are the people of the Sun of righteousness, of the eternal Wisdom and Word, the workmanship of his Comforter, who is a Spirit of wisdom and of understanding; and that one of the greatest reproaches God ever gave to his Israel, was his calling them a "foolish people and unwise," Deut. xxxii. 6; Isa. i. 3, who had neither knowledge nor understanding.

And since you see that the apostle asks of God this divine wisdom for the Colossians, address yourselves also to that Father of lights from whom comes down every good gift and every perfect gift. Press him; importune him; quit him not till he has revealed his mysteries to you, till he has enlightened your eyes and your hearts to make you see the wonders of his wisdom. But to prayer add study; read and hear his word carefully; meditate on it here and at home; render it familiar; commune about it with your neighbours, and instruct your children in it. I grant that without the grace of of the Lord this labour is unprofitable, but I maintain that with it it is most efficacious. Paul would preach to Lydia in vain, if God were not to open her heart. But if God set to his hand, it is not without success that Paul labours for it.

And to attract this saving hand of the Lord, join to prayer the offerings of your alms, the perfume of a good and holy life. Make use of what you know. Manage these first-fruits of light which you have received already. Employ the talent that has been given you, and the Master will add to it others and greater. How can you think he will communicate new graces to people who so vilely abuse the first? You know his will, and do that of Satan and of the flesh. He has made you a present of the gospel, and you drag it in the dirt. He has marked you with his seals, and you pollute them with the filth of vice. You shamelessly wear his livery amidst the debauches of the world, and the disciples of heaven are as ardent as the children of this generation after the dissipations of time. God forbid that "wisdom and spiritual understanding" should lodge in hearts so profane. They are jewels too precious to shine anywhere but in heaven, that is, in pure and holy souls. So far will you be from increasing your light, if you change not your conduct, that God will take away the little which remains, and let you return into Egypt to live once more in its miserable darkness. But God keep us from so great an unhappiness, my beloved brethren; and to prevent it let us in good earnest turn to him, renouncing the lusts of the world and the filth of the flesh, living in exemplary purity and righteousness, that the Lord may take pleasure in us, that he may make the knowledge of his will abound in us "in all wisdom and spiritual understanding;" and, after the faith and hope of this life, receive us, in the eternity of the other, to the vision and fruition of his glory. So be it; and unto him, the Father, Son, and Spirit, the true God blessed for ever, be all honour and praise. Amen.

SERMON IV.

VERSES 10, 11.

That ye might walk worthy of the Lord unto all pleasing, being fruitful in every good work, and increasing in the knowledge of God: strengthened with all might, according to his glorious power, unto all patience and long-suffering with joyfulness.

PHILOSOPHERS, pagan as well as christian, commonly divide the sciences into two kinds; the speculative, which aim only at the understanding of their subject, resting there, when they have once acquired it, without going any further; and the practical, which aim at action, and regard things only with respect to the use made of them. Of the first kind is astronomy, whose only design is to comprehend the motions of the heavenly bodies; and the mathematics, which relate to the study of magnitude and number, without any other end than a knowledge of them. Of the second kind is moral science, which teaches us for practical purposes, and shows us the nature of each virtue, that we may practise it, and live according to the rules she gives us. It is disputed in the schools to which of these two kinds of sciences belongs sacred theology; that is, the doctrine of divine things revealed to us in the gospel of our Lord Jesus Christ. For on one hand it teaches us several things of the nature of God and of angels, and of the world to come, and other mysteries, which seem to be merely objects of contemplation, and not of action; on the other hand it gives us divers rules for practice: and this mixture has induced some to think that it is a discipline not simple and uniform, but miscellaneous, and composed of both kinds. Our apostle, in my opinion, clearly decides the question in this place. For having before wished the Colossians a rich and full knowledge of this divine doctrine "in all wisdom and spiritual understanding," he stays not there, but adds, in the text we have read, the end to which it is subservient: "That ye may walk worthy of the Lord unto all pleasing, being fruitful in every good work." Here he states expressly that the end of this knowledge is practice; holy walking and fruitfulness in every good work being evidently practical. Consequently it ought to be placed among the active sciences, since they are characterized by their end, and that which properly gives them the rank they are to hold. I grant that it treats of the essence and attributes of God, but it is with the design to carry us by such means to the love and service of his divine Majesty, that is, unto action; whence it is that in Scripture, knowledge of God is almost always taken for obedience to him, as far as he has revealed himself to us.

But it is of no great importance for us to know the rank of this heavenly discipline among the sciences, provided we hold fast this principle of the apostle, that the end of our instruction in the knowledge of God is a godly life, and not our mental amusement, or the gratification of our curiosity with a vain delight; much less the being able to divert our companions with such high mysteries. We do not call that man an architect who can fluently discourse of buildings, but him who has the art to erect them; and we do not give the name and glory of a captain to one who can eloquently speak of war, but to him who can manage it, and is able to conduct an army skilfully, and can withstand and fight an enemy, and acquit himself in all the functions of a military command; nor can we regard him as a christian who knows the duties of the faithful, and can pertinently explain them, but him who performs them. This science consists in the life, and not in talk; in the heart and in the doings, not in the brain and in the tongue. Let this then be our sole aim in this holy study. Let us learn not simply to know or to speak, but to do, carefully reducing to practice all the precepts of this heavenly doctrine. And that we may duly comprehend this legitimate end of our knowledge, let us meditate on the lesson which the apostle now gives us concerning it. It contains two particulars: First, the nature of the life and practice at which we are to aim. And, secondly, the constancy and patience with which we should persevere in them. These shall be, God willing, the two subjects we will treat of in the present service.

I. The apostle explains the former of these in the 10th verse, "That ye might walk worthy of the Lord unto all pleasing, being fruitful in every good work, and increasing in the knowledge of God." In these words he shows us, first, the end of the knowledge of the gospel in general, which is a walking worthy of the Lord. Next he sets before us the principal parts of this worthy walking. The first respects the object proposed, the pleasing of God in all things. The second, the manner in which it ought to be attempted, by becoming fruitful in every good work. The third, its progress, advancing in the knowledge of God.

Here then, christian, in the first place, is the proper and sole end of that heavenly light which has been communicated to you, that you "walk worthy of the Lord." You do not require to be informed that the Scripture often compares the life of man to a journey, and his designs and occupations to a path, or way. The simple fact is, that having entered the world, at once we leave the moment of our nativity, as a starting place, and incessantly advance towards death, as a common habitation, where, sooner or later, all men meet. Other travellers may, if they please, delay their journey, or retrace their steps; but we cannot do either. Time, infolding us from the first moment of our life, perpetually carries us forward, whether we wake or sleep, whether we consent to it or resist, without permitting us to turn back, or indulge in the shortest repose. We are like him on board a vessel propelled by sea and wind, whose personal motion does not arrest or abate his course. But as the roads and projects of travellers are very different, so there is a great diversity of habits and manners in men's lives. Wicked men follow one way, and good men another. The Pagan steers one course, the Jew another, the Mohammedan another, and the Christian another, each wholly different from the others. This is what the Scripture calls "the way of man;" that is, the fashion and method of life which each man follows. And suitably to this expressive figure, it often makes use of the word *walking*, to signify a regulating and framing of the life after some certain manner, whether good or evil; meaning the tenor of our lives, and our customary deportment. There is nothing more common in the Psalms, and in the Proverbs, than these forms of speech; "to walk in integrity;" or, on the contrary, "to walk in fraud and iniquity:" and in the writings of the New Testament, "to walk in light," or, "in darkness;" "after the Spirit," or, "after the flesh;" with other similar phrases, all signifying a certain manner and condition of life, good or evil, as it is qualified. Agreeably to this scriptural style, the apostle says here, "that ye might walk;" meaning, that you may live, that you may regulate and form your lives.

But how does he wish us to walk? "Worthy of the Lord." It is word for word in the original, worthily of the Lord; or, in a manner worthy of the Lord. The apostle intends that we should lead a life corresponding to our honour, as the children and disciples of Jesus the Lord; his co-heirs, and heirs of his Father. He often uses this manner of speaking, or others very similar to it. As when he exhorts the Philippians to conduct themselves in a way that "becometh the gospel of Christ," Phil. i. 27; and the Ephesians to "walk worthy of the vocation wherewith they were called," Eph. iv. 1; and when he adjures the Thessalonians "to walk worthy of God, who has called them to his kingdom and glory," 1 Thess. ii. 12. The teachers of human merits have drawn from these passages that superb denomination which they commonly give them, calling them "merits of condignity;" pretending that to walk worthy of God, signifies, a meriting of life by their works, in a proper sense, and according to strict justice. But they are evidently deceived. For not to speak of the vanity of this presumption, which Scripture and reason itself strike as with a thousand lightnings, it is plain that to be worthy of anything does not in the least degree mean, in any of these passages, to merit it properly and strictly. For who would interpret in this manner the apostle's words, "walk worthy of God," that is, "lead a life that merits God?" There are persons found, who have so sublime an opinion of themselves, as to imagine that they merit heaven, and the glory of the life to come. No one has yet been seen, that I know of, who vaunted that he merited God. This language would be monstrous, and surpass the pride of devils themselves. It is very presuming to affirm that any man merits even the gifts of God. Common sense permits not any one to think, or say, that he merits God. No more will what the apostle says elsewhere suffer this comment: "Let your conversation be worthy of the gospel;" and, "Walk worthy of the vocation of God." For who ever affirmed that our works merit the gospel, or the vocation of God—a thing which was past, and which we received from the liberality of the Lord, before the performance of any one good work? It is clear that, in all these places, the worthiness of which the apostle speaks is nothing but a certain seemliness, arising from our corresponding with those things of which he says we are worthy. Just as when John the Baptist exhorts the Jews to bring forth fruits worthy of repentance, he means, not that merit repentance, but that answer to it; that are suitable to the sense we have of our own sin, and of the grace of God. In like manner here, an eminently holy and pious life, abounding in good works, is worthy of God, not because it merits him, but because it has some suitableness with his sanctity and glory. It is worthy of the gospel, because it is correspondent to it, and conformable to what it requires of us. It is worthy of the vocation of God, because it is incited to those things to which he calls us, and produces the fruits which he demands of us.

Do you wish then to know, O christian, how you should live? Live worthy of the Lord. Paul has comprised all in these few words. When it was demanded of a prince, who had fallen into the hands of his enemy, how he would be treated, he answered, "As a king," signifying by that one word all the forbearance and generosity he desired should be used towards him. So the apostle, in these two words, embraces the whole model of our behaviour. How shall we live? Lead, says he, a life that is worthy of the Lord. This is enough to let us understand that avarice, cruelty, hatred, envy, or any other of the passions of the world, can have no place in us; but that justice, kindness, and all other pure and celestial affections, should be resplendent in us: that nothing base or abject should be mingled with them; but that all should be great, and generous, and elevated above the dunghills of the flesh. Keep then, believer, this supreme Lord continually before your eyes. Ask your conscience, upon everything presented to you, whether it is worthy of him; and do not anything that may not be so accounted. Flee all that is repugnant to the noble birth of his disciple; all that deviates from the rule which he has given you; all that diverts you from the kingdom to which he conducts you. This Lord is purity and holiness itself; he is entirely separate from sinners; he never had any communion with sin. This Lord is supremely good; he hates no man; he prayed even for them who crucified him, and conferred infinite benefits on them who injured and blasphemed him. This Lord neither possessed nor coveted the honours and grandeurs of the world. All his glory is divine, and his grandeur celestial. His discipline is like his life; he invariably enjoins us nothing but eminent innocence, sanctity, and goodness: and the good things he promises us are spiritual, and not carnal; the inheritance he has purchased for us, and to the possession of which he lead us, is in heaven, and not on the earth. From this it is easy to conceive what is this manner of life worthy of him which the apostle commands us. It is a life resembling his life, in which shine forth the examples of his divine excellencies, and the characteristics of his doctrine, and the badges of his house, and the first-fruits of his glory.

It is a life that treads under foot all the villanies of sin; that disdains what the flesh and the world promise to their slaves; and, beholding with contempt all that the world adores, is ardent only in the pursuit of heaven. It is a sweet, humble, and inoffensive life, obliging all men, and injurious to none; that, without turning to the right hand or the left, glides on, incessantly advancing towards the mark of the celestial calling. It is thus you must live, believer, if you would not depreciate the light you have received of the knowledge of God. It is, I confess, a high design. But then it is not for mean and common things that God has given you his Son and his Spirit. If our infirmity makes us fear, let the power and the might of the Lord imbolden us. And if sometimes any act escapes us that is unworthy of him, as in this flesh wherewith we are clothed too many do escape us, let us combat our own weaknesses, and have recourse to the grace of God, who, pardoning us what is past, will fortify us for the future.

But the apostle, after having enjoined us in general that our life should be worthy of the Lord, treats, in the second place, of the principal duties we have to perform, that such may be our lives. First, he specifies that we should wholly aim to please him; that is, that in all things we should seek to please the Lord, attempting nothing but what will be acceptable to him, that this be the scope of our life. Consequently the first point of a celestial life, a life truly worthy of the Lord, is to take his will for our supreme rule, conforming to it all our thoughts, words, and actions. For this is the apostle's meaning, when he says we must entirely please him; that is, in all things, in all the parts of life; both in what respects the sentiments of our hearts, and in what concerns the words of our mouths, or our external actions. This is as the soul of the service of God. You serve a man, or yourselves, and not the Lord, when you act to please yourselves, or others. The best action, and in itself most holy, loses its worth when the design of pleasing God is wanting. Let us then banish from our life, first, all those things which God has not instituted. For however noble their appearance, we cannot assure ourselves that they please the Lord, if he has not ordained them. Let us not suffer ourselves to be beguiled by the paint and tinsel of human devotion. Since the question is of pleasing God, we must give ourselves to the study and practice of that, which himself has expressly commanded in his word. This, I am most certain, is acceptable to him. But for that which superstition or the pretended wisdom of men has invented, I cannot be assured whether it please the Lord or not. Then next, in the very performance of the things which he has commanded, let us aim still to please him. Let us offer not our sacrifices but to his Deity alone. If our actions are also acceptable to men, so let them: this will not offend us. But in whatever way they judge of us, let us ever aim to please the Lord. Provided that our oblations are grateful to him, let the world judge of them as it pleases. We have what we sought, and it suffices us to have found favour in the eyes of our Master. Let us renounce our own wills, and regard his alone, wishing daily that it might be done by us and by all other creatures, as the Lord Jesus has commanded.

The apostle adds, secondly, the productions of Christian life: "Being fruitful (saith he) in every good work." This necessarily follows from the affection which he has recommended to us. For if we entirely study to please the Lord, we shall certainly addict ourselves to good works, as they only can be acceptable to him. But to denote this production the apostle uses a remarkable term; "being fruitful in every good work." The Scripture often compares believers to trees, because they are planted by the hand of God, having sprung from his celestial and incorruptible seed, that is, his word; and you know how the prophet, in the first Psalm, describes to us a good man, and one fearing God, under the image of a tree planted by a stream of living water, yielding its fruit in its season, and crowned with a green and grateful foliage which never fades. And elsewhere he compares him to a flourishing and fruitful palm tree in the courts of the Lord, Psal. xcii. 12—14. Jesus Christ says in John, chap. xv., that he is the Vine, and we are the branches; and Paul compares the Israel of God, that is, the whole society of his children, to a true olive, into which each of them is grafted to partake of its sap and fatness, Rom. xi. Suitably to these metaphors, with much beauty and propriety, the apostle says, Be fruitful, to express the production of our good works. That immortal sap which has been poured into us from on high by the word and Spirit obliges us to this fecundity; it having been communicated to us only to produce in us the fruits of righteousness and holiness. This the Lord expects from his mystical vineyard, and demands it as the just recompense of his assiduous cultivation. And as we prize trees which do not unprofitably occupy our ground, but yield us an abundance of fruit as well as leaves and bloom; so is it with the heavenly Vineyard-keeper. He seeks for fruit on his spiritual trees. The fig tree that bears none he condemns to the fire. He loves and purges that which bears. Good works are the fruits he requires of us; yea, every sort of good works: "being fruitful in every good work." Nature imparts not to any of its trees the faculty of bearing more than one kind of fruit, because the seed of which they grow is earthly and material. But grace, which originates the Lord's mystical plants of a spiritual and divine seed, makes them capable of bearing infinite fruits of every sort. These the apostle calls good works, commanded by God in his word, useful for the advancement of his glory and the edification of our neighbour. Let no one flatter himself that the fruitless verdure of leaves, the outward profession of christianity, would suffice him to be numbered among the plants of the Lord. He acknowledges no trees but those that bear fruit. This is not all. It is not enough to bear one kind of fruit, there must be a fertility "in every good work." Your alms will not serve you if they are not accompanied with the fruits of integrity and sanctification. In vain will you be adorned with meekness and gentleness, if you have not also chastity and beneficence.

The apostle requires, in the third and last place, that we increase in the knowledge of the Lord. See, faithful brethren, how this holy man every where combines knowledge and action, faith and love. He begs of God that the Colossians might be perfect in wisdom and spiritual understanding; to the end that they may walk in a manner worthy of the Lord, and be "fruitful in every good work." But lest they should imagine that they had no need to acquire any more knowledge, he returns to the topic, and adds, "increasing in the knowledge of God." For as our sanctification is during life imperfect, so there is always a deficiency in our knowledge. We must endeavour equally to attain the one and the other. And as the light of knowledge incites and directs us to the practice of good works, so the exercise of good works cleanses the eyes of our understandings, and increases true wisdom: on the contrary, the neglect of sanctification diminishes this divine perspicacity in us, and gradually brings back the darkness of ignorance. For as the Lord gives new graces to him who faithfully employs his first donations, so he takes away his talent from him that abuses it. They who cast away a good conscience make shipwreck also of faith; and they who hold the truth in unrighteousness are given up to a mind despoiled of all judgment; and God sends them strong delusions who receive not his holy doctrine in love. On the contrary, he reveals his secret to them, and augments their light, who seek his commandments, and are inclined to do his will. Let us hold fast therefore these two precious gifts of the Lord, knowledge and practice, faith and love, and study to increase in both, meditating on the mysteries of God, and learning them that we may obey his will, and obey his will that we may confirm ourselves more and more in the knowledge of his mysteries.

II. Dear brethren, that which the apostle desired for his Colossians is no trivial thing; it is a complete knowledge of the divine will, a life worthy of the Lord, a spiritual fecundity, a "being fruitful in every good work," and a continual advancement in heavenly wisdom. Yet this is not all. For great and excellent as these things are, they suffice not without perseverance to conduct us to salvation, and it is impossible to persevere in them without supernatural strength and courage. Therefore Paul desires, in the last place, that these believers "may be strengthened with all might, according to his glorious power, unto all patience and long-suffering with joyfulness." This succour is necessary for us, as well because of our own infirmities as for the multitude, violence, and obstinacy of our enemies. For as to ourselves, though that Divine Spirit, with which God baptizes us at the beginning of our vocation, invests us with a new vigour, yet there remains much weakness in us while we live on earth, our inward man being yet but in its infancy; a weak age, and quite unable to stand if not sustained. And as for our enemies, they are multitudinous; they watch night and day to destroy us; and arranged in divers bands, under the ensigns of the devil, the world, and the flesh, the chief commanders of this black army, sworn to effect our ruin, they cease not to trouble us, leaving neither wile nor assault, neither malice nor violence, neither threatening nor promise, unemployed against us. If we repulse one of them, he returns with many others, who on all sides attack us, spy where we are weak, and often turn our own weapons against us. If we overthrow avarice, voluptuousness presents itself. If that is defeated also, ambition enters in its place; hatred unites with it; desire of revenge urges us on; wrath provokes us; envy assails us; persecution troubles us; prosperity elates us; the success of our own conflicts gratifies our vanity. Often that which helps us on one hand hurts us on the other; as in a complication of diseases, when the remedies counteract each other, or that which is good for the liver is detrimental to the stomach. Who sees not that to preserve ourselves in so mixed a conflict, and against so many confused and obstinate attacks, (for they last as long as our lives,) we, who are so weak that we are insufficient even for one good thought, require an extraordinary degree of might? But God arms us with the power of his Spirit as with an impenetrable shield, and under this covert we stand secure amid the tempest of blows that falls continually around us. This is that divine power which the apostle desires for the Colossians, when he prays that they might "be strengthened with all might;" that their souls might be confirmed, their hearts hardened as a diamond to resist all assaults; their courage vested with an heroic ardour and constancy, which all the violences of hell and earth may never be able to overcome.

He prays they may be "strengthened with all might;" because, as we have to do with various enemies, and are sick of divers infirmities, we need not one or two kinds of strength only, but strength of every kind. For, as you see in nature, the strength of bodies is different; one resisting one thing, and yielding to another; one having the virtue to repulse the force of one element, but not to guard itself from another: so in a manner is it in the souls of men. One will bravely liberate himself from the temptation of one vice, who is not able to defend himself from another. A man who resists the assaults of the world yields to the charms of its caresses. And as they lose a victory who are overcome, though by only one of innumerable enemies, it is with great reason the apostle prayed that these Colossians might be blessed "with all might," lest the honour of their crown and triumph should be endangered; that is, a perfect strength, which would be proof against all the strokes of the enemy; which might boldly undertake good and holy services, however high and difficult; which might valiantly combat all sin, resolutely despise earthly things, vigorously repel temptations, and nobly suffer afflictions.

He shows us also, as he proceeds, the source of this heavenly might, when, having expressed his desire that the Colossians might be "strengthened with all might," he adds, "according to his glorious power." Whence do these faithful people receive this admirable strength necessary for their salvation? From the "glorious power" of the Lord, says the apostle; that immense and efficacious might of God which nothing can resist. The Holy Spirit is so styled in Luke, chap. xxiv. 49, where the Lord commands his apostles to tarry at Jerusalem until they were "endued with power from on high," that is, the Spirit he had promised them. And Paul, making a request for the Ephesians very similar to that which he here presents to God for the Colossians, distinctly calls that the Spirit of God which in this passage he calls the virtue or power of his glory. God grant, says he, that you may be "strengthened with might by his Spirit in the inner man," Eph. iii. 16. He calls this power of the Spirit of God "glorious," to express its admirable and invincible energy, which magnificently triumphs over all that opposes its operation; which with the weakest means accomplishes the greatest things; which changes, when it pleases, shepherds into legislators and kings, herdsmen into prophets, and persecutors into apostles; which demolishes the proudest fierceness, and preserves invincible the most despicable weakness; which hardens the bodies of its humble warriors as steel, sustains them in the flames, and confounds with their lowness the fury of men, of elements, and of devils. For this is what the sacred writers usually call glory, even an abundance of beauty, of power, and perfection, so rich that it overpowers our senses, and bends beneath it all the vigour of our spirits, reducing them to admiration and astonishment. And Paul not unfrequently uses the word in this sense, as when he says that "Christ was raised up from the dead by the glory of the Father," Rom. vi. 4, that is, by his great and unspeakable power. We learn from this that the virtue which converts us to God, and that which preserves us in his grace, is not a common and ordinary power, but an invincible efficacy which nothing can resist. Seek it not in your own nature, O christian, seek it in God; and, acknowledging your weakness, ask of him the remedy for it. Whenever you resist the enemy, and remain victorious in combat, render all the glory of it to this sovereign Lord, without attributing it, in the least degree, to yourself.

But the apostle shows us, in what follows, what is the use and effect of the succour which the glorious power of the Lord affords us: "Strengthened with all might, unto all patience and long-suffering with joyfulness." These are the two productions of the Spirit of God in a believer, "patience," and "long-suffering," or long-waiting, in which principally our strength consists. These are as the two hands of heaven that sustain us in perils, and keep us from sinking under the weight of those evils with which we often find ourselves surcharged. And though they are of a very similar nature, yet each of them has something peculiar to itself. Patience bears the evil without bending, humbly submitting to its infliction, and firmly standing under this heavy load. The Spirit, which is long-suffering, or long-waiting, (for so the word used here in the original properly signifies,) afterwards assists it, and without murmuring expects deliverance from the evil felt, and the enjoyment of future good. Patience respects the weight of the affliction. The long-suffering, or the long-waiting, of the patient spirit respects its duration. These two excellences are absolutely necessary for a christian; for without them how should he bear either the chastisements of God or the persecutions of the world? How could he be steadfast in the exercise of other graces, to discharge the duties attendant on them, against the impediments that hourly thwart him? Patience, says Tertullian, is the superintendent of all the affairs of God, and without it, it is not possible to execute his commands or to wait for his promises. It defeats all its enemies without toil. Its repose is more efficacious than the movements and deeds of others. It renders those things salutary to us which, of their own nature, are most pernicious. It changes poisons into remedies, and defeats into victories. It rejoices the angels, it confounds devils, it overcomes the world. It subdues the greatest courage, and converts the most obstinate hearts. It is the strength and the triumph of the church, according to the saying of the ancient oracle, "In returning and rest shall ye be saved; in quietness and in confidence shall be your strength," Isa. xxx. 15.

But to show us what this patience is to which the Spirit of God conforms his children, the apostle says that it is "with joyfulness." This is the true character of christian patience. Sometimes the hypocrite suffers, but not without murmuring; and the ancient philosophers made a great show of their patience; but this was only an effect, either of their pride or of their insensibility, which was not in any degree accompanied with the joy which the Holy Ghost pours into the souls of those who suffer for the name of God. Not that they are insensible, or that they receive without pain the evil brought on them. But if the evil they bear makes them sorrowful, this very thing rejoices them, that by the grace of their Lord they have the strength and the courage to bear it, and know that their suffering shall turn to their good, and that from these thorns they shall one day reap the flowers and fruits of a blessed immortality. To which may be added the sweetness which is then shed into the heart by the lively and profound impression of that inestimable Comforter, who, on such occasions, communicates himself to them more freely than ever, and by the ineffable virtue of his balm assuages their most painful wounds. This is what, dear brethren, we had to say to you on this text of the holy apostle.

Let us receive his doctrine with faith, and religiously obey his voice. He shows us what our task is here below; let us acquit ourselves in it with care. God of his grace has raised up among us a great light of knowledge; let us use it for its true purpose, and walk with it in such a manner as is worthy of so holy and merciful a Lord, whose name we bear. Let this great name awaken our senses and affections; let it draw them off from the earth, and elevate them to heaven, where he reigns who has given it to us. Let this name put into our hearts a secret shame to do or think anything that may be unworthy of it. Brethren, remember, whenever the flesh or the world solicits you to evil, that you are christians. Give up the world. It is not to please it that you have been regenerated by the Spirit from on high. The world is so unjust, so capricious, and so mutable, that it is impossible to satisfy it. See in what continual pain and torment they live who attempt it. And though you should effect it, the success would cost you dear. By pleasing the world you would displease your own conscience; to satisfy which is infinitely more important to you than any other thing. It is quite otherwise with God. His will is constant and always the same, without any variation. Nothing is pleasing to him but what is just and reasonable. Your conscience will find in it its entire satisfaction, and will never reproach you for having served so good a Master. Not to allege to you, that the world, after you shall have killed yourself to serve it, will pay you only with ingratitude and contempt, as experience daily shows us; whereas the Lord will magnificently reward the care you shall have taken to do his will; comforting and blessing you in this world, crowning and glorifying you in the next. If you demand what must be done to please him, the apostle shows you in a word, "Be fruitful in every good work." As often as the Lord shall cast his eyes on this vineyard, let him see it always laden with good fruits. Let him never have cause to complain of it, as he formerly did of that of Israel. "I looked," says he, "that it should bring forth grapes, and it brought forth wild grapes," Isa. v. Surely he has had no less care of ours than of theirs. He has planted it, in like manner, with the choicest vines; he has also encompassed it with a lofty and admirable hedge; he has watered it with the rain of his clouds, and made the beams of his Sun of righteousness to shine on it, and may justly say of it, "What could be done more to my vineyard, that I have not done in it?" Let us not be ungrateful to so sweet a Master. Let not our sterility confound his expectation. Let our fruits be answerable to his cares, and our fecundity to his husbandry. Let there be no soul barren and unprofitable among us: let every one be fruitful of what he has, every one improve the dressing and sap the Lord has given us. Let the sinner present him his repentance; the just, his perseverance; the rich, his alms; the poor, his praises; old age, its prudence; youth, its zeal. Let the learned abound in instruction, the strong in modesty, the weak in humility, and all together in love. And as it is the good pleasure of our heavenly Father that here we should have many conflicts, as none can live piously without persecution, let us prepare also for this part of our duty, and, with the apostle, supplicate the Lord that he may strengthen us with all might, according to his glorious power; that he may grant us firm and unmovable patience, to persevere constantly in the holy communion of his Son; so that neither the promises nor the threatenings of the world, neither the lusts nor the fears of flesh, may be ever able to entice us from his service. O God, our task is great, and we are feeble. Our enemies are giants, and we but dwarfs. Therefore, do thou thyself perform within us, merciful Lord, the work which thou commandest us. Perfect thy glorious power in our infirmities. Strengthen our hands, and confirm our hearts, that we may fight vigorously, and achieve great things in thy name; and, after the trials and temptations of this life, may hereafter receive from the sacred and sweet hand of thy Son the glorious crown of immortality, for which we ardently breathe. So be it.

SERMON V.

VERSES 12, 13.

Giving thanks unto the Father, which hath made us meet to be partakers of the inheritance of the saints in light: who hath delivered us from the power of darkness, and hath translated us into the kingdom of his dear Son.

DEAR brethren, the first creation of man is a most illustrious masterpiece of the goodness, power, and wisdom of God, when this great artificer made Adam of the dust, and formed him after his own image, to live and reign on the earth in sovereign felicity; yet it must be confessed that our restoration by Jesus Christ is much more excellent and admirable. For whether you consider the things themselves which have been given us, or have respect to the condition of those to whom they have been communicated, or to what the Lord did for communicating them, you will see that in every way the second of these divine benefits surpasses the first. The first gave us a human nature, the second has communicated to us a divine one. The first made us a living soul, the second makes us a quickening spirit. By the one, we had an earthly and animal being; by the other, we receive a spiritual and heavenly one. The one placed us in the garden of Eden, the other elevates us to the heaven of glory. There we had dominion over animals, and the empire of the earth; here we have the fraternity of angels, and the kingdom of heaven. There we enjoyed a life full of delight, but not stable, and dependent, like that of other living creatures, on the use of meat, and drink, and sleep; here we possess a life full of vigour and strength, which, like that of blessed spirits, is sustained by its own virtue, requiring no other nourishment. The one was subject to change, as the event has declared; the other is truly immortal and immutable, and above the accidents which altered the first. The advantage of the first man was, that he might not have died; the privilege of the second is, that he cannot die. But the difference will appear no less in the disposition of the persons to whom the Lord has communicated these benefits, if you attentively consider it. I confess that the dust which God invested with a human form did not merit a condition so excellent, and received it from the mere liberality of the Creator. But if it was not worthy of such a favour, certainly there was nothing in it which, in the rigour of justice, rendered it incapable of it; whereas we not only have not merited the salvation which God gives us in his Son, but have most abundantly merited that death which is opposite to it. If the matter on which the Lord wrought, in the first creation of man, had no disposition for the form he gave it, so neither had it any repugnance to it; but in our second creation, that is, in our redemption by Jesus Christ, he finds in us souls so far from complying with his operation, that they powerfully resist it. So you see that, to effect the first work, he merely issued his will and word; but, for creating the second, it was necessary that he should shake the heavens, send down his Son to earth, deliver him up to death, and do miracles that astonished men and angels. With this grand and incomprehensible mystery of God the apostle now engages our attention, my brethren, in the text which you have heard. For having finished the exordium, or the preface, of this Epistle; and intending thence to enter on his principal subject, in order to glide the more gently into it, after mentioning to the Colossians the prayers that he offered to God for them, he now adds the thanks which he offered him for their common salvation; and by this means opens his disquisition, touching the sufficiency and inexhaustible abundance of Jesus Christ for the salvation of believers, which renders it unnecessary to make any addition to his gospel. "Giving thanks unto the Father," says he, "who," &c. As this text consists of two verses, so it may be divided into two articles. In the first the apostle gives thanks unto God, who "hath made us meet to be partakers of the inheritance of his saints." In the second is proposed what he has done to make us meet for this happiness; namely, "delivered us from the power of darkness, and translated us into the kingdom of his dear Son." These are the two points we will handle, if it please the Lord, in this discourse; humbly beseeching him to guide us in meditating on this sacred subject, and to touch our hearts so vividly with it, that it may effectually promote our edification and consolation.

I. The benefit of our redemption being very great, and most admirable in all respects, (as we intimated,) it is with great propriety that the apostle begins his discourse concerning it by giving thanks to God. And in his Epistles he scarcely ever speaks of it without extolling it, or admiring the goodness of the Lord. He directs his thanksgiving to the Father, as the first and supreme author of this excellent work. Think not that he denies the Son or the Spirit their part in it, or that he would deprive them of the glory due to them for it. For as these three persons are only one and the same God, the works of the Deity appertain to all three of them. But as they subsist in a certain order, the Father of himself, the Son of the Father, who generated him, the Holy Spirit of the Father and the Son, from whom he proceeds from all eternity; so likewise they act in the same manner. And as the Father is the first in this order of their subsistence and of their operation, Paul addresses his benedictions particularly to him, as the prime and sovereign source of the Deity, whence originally has flowed down to us all the good and grace that we have received in our redemption.

But let us see how the apostle describes this work of our salvation for which he gives the Lord thanks: " He hath made us meet," saith he, " to be partakers of the inheritance of the saints in light." After sin had made a separation between God and us, it was naturally impossible for us to have a part in any of his blessings: the Lord, therefore, designing to save us, took care first of all to remove this obstacle to our communication with him. This he did, satisfying his justice by the expiation of sin through the death of his Son Jesus Christ. By this means that free commerce between his goodness and our poor nature which our sin had interrupted was again opened, so that now there is no obstruction, except on man's own part, to his approaches to God, and participation of his grace through faith and repentance. Bnt this is not what the apostle intends, when he says that the Father has made us meet to have a part in his inheritance. For this grace, by which he has opened a way to the throne of his beneficence through the expiation of sin, generally respects all men; nor is there any one who will not find free access if he present himself with faith and repentance: but the grace of which the apostle here speaks is appropriate to him and the Colossians, and such as resemble them; that is, in a word, it is peculiar to true believers, and not common to all men. It must be observed, therefore, in the second place, that besides this first impediment, which shut the gate of God's house against us, I mean the inexorable severity of his avenging justice; there is another and as difficult to be surmounted as the former, though it is of another kind, and of a different nature. It is the malignancy, the insensibility, and the blindness of our corrupt nature. For as the justice of God would not permit a creature polluted with sin to approach him except its sin were expiated; so his wisdom could not suffer it to touch any of his divine favours, except it repented of having offended him, and believed his promises. But in our fallen state our souls are so depraved by sin, that they are incapable of themselves either to think aright of God, or to put affiance in his goodness; and so this great miracle of the love of God towards us (I mean the expiation of sin by the death of his Son) would remain without any saving effect with respect to us, if, leaving us in our native condition, he simply presented to us in external means, the declarations of his grace. And therefore this kind and compassionate Lord, not satisfied with having opened the gate of his bounty by the cross of Christ, also delivers us from the grave of our impiety, and gives us the will and the strength to come to himself. It is properly this second benefit, peculiar to those who believe, which the apostle intends, when he says that God hath made us capable to partake of his inheritance. The first gift of the Father capacitated his hand to communicate his treasures to us; and the second capacitates us to enjoy them. Without the death of his dear Son he could not give us life; and without his effectual calling we could not receive it from him.

Faithful brethren, mark well this lesson of the apostle, who gives thanks to God that he hath made us meet to partake of his inheritance. He first brings down, by this means, the pride of those who give this glory to free-will, boasting that they have made themselves meet for salvation, either by some kind of predispositions which oblige God at least by the way of decency to give them his grace, or by the proper management of afflictions, as well as the pride of all those in general who pretend that it is in a man's own power to prepare himself for the heavenly inheritance. No, says the apostle, this wholly appertains to God. It is he that "hath made us meet." Of ourselves we cannot so much as think a good thought; so he elsewhere affirms, 2 Cor. iii. 5. I confess that this impotency of man is voluntary, and consequently criminal; it proceeds from the extreme wickedness of his heart, and from no defect in any of those things which are necessary from without for producing this effect. For what besides his own rebelliousness hinders him from believing in God, and embracing with repentance the exhibitions of divine grace which are presented to him, either in the course of nature, or in the law, or by the gospel? Yet so it is, that however voluntary this his wickedness, it is also invincible, and altogether refractory. It is no longer a weakness. It is a formed impotency, which nature is not able to correct. And the Scripture always speaks of it in this sense. "The natural man receiveth not the things of the Spirit of God, because they are spiritually discerned," 1 Cor. ii. 14. And, "The carnal mind is enmity against God: for it is not subject to the law of God, neither indeed can be," Rom. viii. 7. John, speaking of the Jews, says, "They could not believe," John xii. 39. And Jeremiah of their ancestors, "Their ear is uncircumcised, and they cannot hearken," Jer. vi. 10. "Can the Ethiopian change his skin, or the leopard his spots? then may ye also do good, who are accustomed to do evil," Jer. xiii. 23. Such is by nature the miserable state of all men.

Let us learn then, in the second place, to give the Lord alone the whole glory of all that we are in his Son, as in reality it belongs to none but him. He has not only given us this rich inheritance, the purchase of the blood of his Son

Christ, he has even given us the meetness to enter into it, and possess our part of it. Besides his making us the gift, he has also imparted to us the strength to receive it. For it is not with the inheritance of God as with the honours of earthly princes; these often fall into the hands of persons most incapable of enjoying them. That divine honour of the heavenly inheritance is given to none but those that are "meet" for it; that is, who have the circumstances requisite for partaking of it, which are faith and repentance. But the same God who has prepared the heritage for us, gives us also the preparation which is necessary for entering into it; according to what the apostle says elsewhere, "Our" meetness, or "sufficiency, is of God," 2 Cor. iii. 5; and what our Lord himself avers in John, "No man can come unto me, except the Father which hath sent me draw him," John vi. 44. This also is what the apostle intends in the Epistle to the Philippians: "It is God who worketh in you both to will and to do of his good pleasure," Phil. ii. 13. And elsewhere he comprises this whole work of the grace of God in one only word, saying, "He that hath wrought us for the selfsame thing is God," 2 Cor. v. 5. Therefore he calls us, in one place, the workmanship of God, and his creation in Jesus Christ, Eph. ii. 10; and in another, his husbandry and his building, 1 Cor. iii. 9. Consequently it appears that the offer of grace, which is made to all by the gospel, if there be nothing else, gives us not a part in the heavenly inheritance. I grant that it is sufficient in itself, and would produce its effect in man, if the wickedness of his heart had not blinded him. But this deplorable blindness obstructs the effect which these offers of the divine grace should produce. Wherefore God himself makes us capable of them, by that inward operation of his Spirit with which he accompanies the preaching of the gospel in the hearts of his elect, by reason of which they are called the "taught of God," John vi. 45. It is this teaching which renders them meet for entering into the communion of his Son, according to what he says in John, "Whoever hath heard and learned of the Father cometh unto me," John vi. 45. Thus he made Lydia capable of having part in his inheritance, opening her heart to understand the things that were spoken by Paul, as the sacred history informs us, Acts xvi. 14. Doubtless, in the same manner, he also made both Paul and these Colossians, and all the rest of the faithful, capable of the same effect, inwardly enlightening them, and leading captive their hearts into the yoke of the gospel.

In fine, we may again observe how contrary to apostolic doctrine is the presumption of those who boast of meriting salvation. If there is anything in us to which merit can be attributed, without doubt it is our capacity and sufficiency, that we are meet to partake of the kingdom of God. But this very thing is a donation from God, for which we owe him most humble thanks. How then and by what right can we in justice demand wages for it? Would it not be as preposterous as if a patient were to enter action against his physician, and insist on compensation for being cured by his art? or as if a poor man were to demand wages of us for receiving our alms? or a prisoner for having been redeemed with our money? Let a man turn and transform things as much as he pleases, it is clear that grace and merit are incompatible; and that he who is justly obliged to render thanks cannot, without folly, pretend to have merited that very thing for which he renders thanks. Our sufficiency or meetness is a gift of God, or it is not. If it is his gift, why maintain ye that it is meritorious? If it is not, why does the apostle thank our Lord for having made us meet to have part in his inheritance? The word inheritance, which the apostle here employs, evidently confirms the same truth, as an ancient instructor of the church has well observed. Why is it, says he, that the apostle uses the word inheritance? To show us that no man obtains the kingdom of heaven by his own works or performances. But as an inheritance depends upon happiness, and not upon merit, so is it in this matter. None can exhibit a manner of life and conversation so excellent as to be worthy of the kingdom. The whole is derived from the gift of God.*

To proceed, I doubt not but Paul took this term from the Old Testament. There we find that the land of Canaan, destined and given to the children of Israel for an inheritance, according to the promises made to their fathers, was the figure of this blessed, spiritual, and divine life, which God puts us into possession of by the gospel of his Son, beginning it here below by the consolation and sanctification of his Spirit, and designing to complete it on a future day in the highest heavens, by the communication of his immortal glory. For as each Israelite had his portion in the land of Canaan, the same in substance with the rest, but diversely qualified; so each believer has his share in celestial life; but in such a manner, that though all substantially possess the same life, yet it is variously proportioned and attempered to each of them. Again, as none but the children of Abraham had right and title to that ancient inheritance; so there are none but the children of the promise who are born of the word of God, and not of flesh or of blood, that have part in the new. For this cause the apostle entitles it the inheritance of the saints. Depart, ye unbelieving and profane. It is not for you that God has prepared this glorious inheritance. "Be not deceived: neither fornicators, nor idolaters, nor adulter-

* Chrysostom in loc.

ers, nor effeminate, nor thieves, nor covetous persons, nor drunkards, nor revilers, nor extortioners, shall inherit the kingdom of God," 1 Cor. vi. 9, 10. It is designed for saints alone. The portion of the profane and ungodly is elsewhere; during this life, in the world, and in its wretched delights; and when life shall pass away, in the lake of fire and brimstone.

But the apostle having styled that salvation which God communicates to us in his Son "the inheritance of the saints," adds further, "in light." As light is in Scripture the symbol of two things, knowledge and glory, so it may be taken here two ways; either for the knowledge of those divine things which God reveals in his gospel, or for that sovereign joy and felicity which we shall possess on high in the heavens. It is best, in my opinion, to conjoin these two expositions, that so we may comprehend the entire state of the whole inheritance of the saints, who, after they are once united to Jesus Christ, always live in light; first, in that of grace, during their pilgrimage on earth; afterwards, in that of glory, when they shall be elevated to that blessed city, "which hath no need of the sun, nor of the moon, to shine in it; for the glory of God hath lightened it, and the Lamb is the light thereof," Rev. xxi. 23. For this cause all the divine denizens of this heavenly state are called "children of light and of the day," 1 Thess. v. 5; which should shine as lights in the midst of a perverse generation, Phil. ii. 15, and be "the light of the world," Matt. v. 14: as persons born of the light of the Spirit and the word of God, who, being led by the rays of the Sun of righteousness, walk on straight towards the supreme source of lights; where arrived, they shall eternally dwell in that brightness which will transform them into the image of their Lord, from glory to glory, by the power of his omnipotent Spirit.

II. But it is time to come to the other verse, in which the apostle adds what the Father has done to make us thus meet for the inheritance of the saints in light: "He hath delivered us," says he, "from the power of darkness, and translated us into the kingdom of his dear Son." By "darkness" the Scripture ordinarily means ignorance and misery; the two contraries of knowledge and joy, which it expresses by light, as we just now said. For ignorance and error hide the true and proper form of things from our understandings, just as darkness conceals visible objects from our bodily eyes. And because there is nothing more unpleasant to men, nor more terrifying, than the obscurity of darkness; the term is also used to represent horror, trouble, and misery. So "the power of darkness" is nothing else than that tyranny which the devil and sin exercise over their slaves, filling their spirits with deadly errors and brutish ignorance, and their consciences either with terror or insensibility, and drawing them on by little and little under this dismal yoke into the horrors of eternal death, which our Lord often calls outer darkness, where there is weeping and gnashing of teeth. For as knowledge and truth are a light necessary for the attainment of salvation, so error and ignorance infallibly lead to death. Therefore the devil, the sworn enemy of our good, blinds men to the utmost of his ability, spreading before them gross and thick mists, which hide heaven and its blessed brightness from them. This is the sum of his artifices. The well of his abyss ever vomits forth into our air a black vapour, to render our senses useless. By this means he turned, in former ages, the nations of the earth from the service of their Creator, obscuring and smothering by his illusions those sparks of the knowledge of him which they possessed, and plunging them, and holding them down, in such profound ignorance, that these miserable men were not ashamed to adore the work of their own hands, and "change the glory of the incorruptible God into an image made like to corruptible man, and to birds, and four-footed beasts, and creeping things," Rom. i. 23. As for justice and moral deportment, this impostor had so extinguished the lights which Providence had kindled for them in their hearts, and so disordered all their knowledge by his seductions, that the vilest abominations passed among them for matters of indifference. Walking on in such thick darkness, it is no wonder if they were in continual fear; they knew not where they were walking, nor whither they were going, and, after much stumbling and staggering, fell at last over the precipice of eternal perdition. And would to God the prince of error did not in the same manner still abuse the world! Certainly the darkness of ancient paganism was not more gross nor shameful than that which at this very day covers the greater part of the earth.

But as the apostle calls that error wherein the devil keeps men "the power of darkness," and, not simply darkness; this teaches us that that accursed one works effectually in them, doing with their hearts what seemeth him good, and planting all deceit and ignorance in them at his will, so that these wretches cannot defend themselves. The same thing the apostle teaches us in his Epistle to the Ephesians, when he says that this evil "spirit now worketh in the children of disobedience," Eph. ii. 2. Not that he has naturally any just dominion over the souls of men, but their sin brings them under his sceptre; and their hearts being of themselves full of unclean and unjust affections, it follows, through the excess of their corruption, that he never tempts them in vain. And all this domination over them is founded merely on imposture, error, and ignorance; so that it is with great truth and elegance that Paul here calls it "the power of darkness." This is, faithful brethren, the sad and pitiable state in which naturally men lie. Let not the paint and tinsel of their pretended wisdom and justice dazzle your eyes. In the sight of God it is but darkness, and for this reason the Scripture calls them darkness itself. "Ye were sometimes darkness," says the apostle to the Ephesians, chap. v. 8.

Judge by this how horrible is the error of those who dogmatize that liberty is so very natural to men, that they cannot conceive how they could be men without it. Let them philosophize upon this subject as they please, they will never be able to show that a man can be, at the same time, both at liberty and under the power of darkness. He that is under the power of another is not free. Only God can enfranchise men, and take them from this miserable servitude, and bind that strong tyrant who held them captive. To this sovereign Lord the apostle here gives the glory both of his own liberation and of that of the Colossians: "He," says the apostle, "hath delivered us from the power of darkness." But the Greek word,* which he uses in the original, has more emphasis than this, signifying that he delivered us by an exertion of power, drawing us, and, if I may so speak, plucking us by force out of our irons; by which he represents to us, on the one hand, how strong and strait were the bonds of our slavery, and, on the other, how excellent and admirable is the power which God has displayed in bringing us out of this spiritual Egypt. For we daily experience, that though nothing is more sordid and shameful than the tyranny of error, yet we all naturally love it, so horrible is our depravity. The most of them adore their fetters, and leave not the darkness of Egypt and the horrors of Sodom but with regret; and, to draw them out, God must descend from heaven, and take them by the hand, as of old he did to Lot and his children. You know he delivers them from this black power of darkness when he dissipates their error and ignorance, causing his sacred truth to shine into their hearts, in so vivifying and so glorious a manner, that they discern it, maugre all the illusions of Satan and the world. Then the domination which this impostor exercised over them vanishes. They wonder how such mists could hide from them so resplendent a light; and this new flame, or, to speak more correctly, this new sun, discovering to them the true face of things, the false colours wherewith the devil and the flesh endeavour to disguise them, have no more efficacy on them. They then see the naked turpitude and horror of idolatry, of superstition, and of vice; and, on the other side, clearly perceive the verity, the beauty, and the excellence of piety and holiness.

This deliverance is absolutely necessary for a participation in the inheritance of saints, unto which none is received who

---

* Ἐῤῥύσατο.

is not a child of light, and has not renounced the servitude of error and sin. And I confess that to have shaken off the yoke of darkness, and to have issued from its power, is a great thing. But this is not all. If the Lord were to stop there, we, for all this, should have no share in the divine glory of the heavenly Canaan. It is of absolute necessity for admission there, that we bear the marks of the Lamb, and on our going out of darkness enter into his holy light. For this cause the apostle, after he had said that the Father hath "delivered us from the power of darkness," immediately adds, "and translated us into the kingdom of his dear Son." For though, in fact, these two divine benefits are inseparably united, yet they constitute two different graces. It is his goodness, and not anything in them, that has thus combined them. Had not the counsel of his love otherwise ordered, a man might be delivered from the power of darkness, and yet not enter into the kingdom of his Son, but remain in such a liberty as Adam's was before he fell. But now as no man has remission of his sins without becoming a member of Jesus Christ by faith; and as all who have this honour are predestined by the good pleasure of the Father to be conformed to the image of their Head, and consequently to have a part in his kingdom and glory; there must of necessity be an entering into his kingdom, or an eternal abiding under the power of darkness. The apostle, by the kingdom of the Son of God, means that very thing which the evangelists ordinarily call the kingdom of heaven; that is, the church of our Lord Jesus Christ, that blessed city builded by the ministry of the apostles and prophets upon the Son of God, its only eternal and immovable foundation, the state of the Messiah, the new republic of God, his royalty and priesthood. Very pertinently he here calls the inheritance of the saints, the kingdom of the Son of God, because no one but a child of God can have a part in it: this teaches us that we cannot obtain this right except in the kingdom of Jesus Christ; as none but he, the true and proper Son of God, is able to convey divine adoption to us; and it is for a like reason that he styles him the dear or well-beloved Son of God, that we might confidently hope for all the grace and glory which the Father promises us; inasmuch as we have the honour of being related to his well-beloved, him in whom he is well pleased, whom he most peculiarly loves, and as perfectly as he loves himself, his eternal delight and love. Besides, I doubt not but the apostle designed to heighten the grace which the Father has shown us by this fine and impressive contrast between the kingdom of his well-beloved Son, into which he has translated us, and that power of darkness, the dominion of his enemy, from which he has delivered us. God brought us into this blessed kingdom when he gave us the faith of his gospel, the righteousness of his Son, and the consolation of his Spirit, designating us by the badges of his house, and sealing us with his holy baptism. But the word "translated," which the apostle uses, represents also the strength and efficacy of this act by which God has brought us into the communion of his Son. I acknowledge that the operation of this divine grace is sweet and pleasant, for it persuades, it wins the heart, it is accompanied with the extreme joy of him who receives it: still it is potent and effectual: nothing can resist it. There is no rebellion nor hardness of heart but it subdues; it draws men to Jesus Christ, as himself expresses it, John vi. 44; or, as his apostle says here, it translates them into his kingdom.

Thus, beloved brethren, we have delivered to you the exposition of this text. I wish that the same Spirit which of old indited it to the pen of the apostle, would please to engrave it in the lowest depth of our hearts, with the point of a diamond, in characters that could not be effaced, that we might have it day and night before our eyes, that we might carefully peruse it and consult it in all the occurrences of our life. This meditation would suffice to preserve us in a constant and happy exercise of christian piety, and to guard us from all that interrupts our sanctification or our comfort. First, it would inflame us with an ardent love to God, and excite us to a vivid and sincere acknowledgment of his benefits. For what love, what reverence, and what services do we not owe to this sovereign Lord, who has vouchsafed to display on us so much mercy and goodness—who has called us from that eternal death wherein we were sunk with the damned, to the possession of the inheritance of his saints—who has made us meet to enter into the fruition of his light—who, by a miracle of his power and wisdom, has plucked us from the yoke of the devil; has delivered us from the unrighteous and murderous power of darkness; and, to crown all his other favours, has translated us into the blessed kingdom of the Son of his love—who, from brands of hell, that we were, has changed us into living and lightsome stars in his firmament—of dead dogs, has made us the first fruits of his creatures; and from slaves of demons transformed us into angels; and from the accursed state of Satan raised us to the sacred fellowship of his Son, to be henceforth his free-men, his brethren, and his members—O love! O goodness incomprehensible! How have we the heart to still offend a Lord so merciful, so admirable? How is it that his most divine beneficence does not transport our spirits—does not win to his service all our thoughts, and affections, and emotions? Christians, all the acknowledgment he demands of you for his vast goodness is only that you lead holy lives. Refuse him not so just and so reasonable a due. He has made you to partake of the inheritance of the saints; be not so ungrateful as to mix with the profane. Be ye separate from them, and have no communion with the impurity and filth of their sins. Despise not, as Esau, the title you have to so precious an inheritance; let it be dearer to you than all the perishing viands and delights of the earth, none of which are better than that contemptible pottage of lentils for which the profane man bartered his birthright.

This inheritance is in light. Live, then, as children of light. Let your conversation be all radiant with those divine and heavenly excellences which the gospel of our Saviour recommends to you. The darkness is now passed. The Sun of righteousness is at its full height. Let that infamous power of darkness, under which you formerly groaned, have no longer authority over you. Open all your understanding, that you may perceive the glory of the Lord, and suffer no more abuse by the illusions of error. Labour to increase your light, being assiduous at the Scriptures of God, the living spring of all spiritual illumination, the inexhaustible treasure of saving knowledge. But let this light shine also in your deportment; for it is to no purpose that you renounce the darkness of superstition, if you remain in that of sin. "He that hateth his brother," says John, "is in darkness, and walketh in darkness, and knoweth not whither he goeth; for darkness hath blinded his eyes," 1 John ii. 11. Remember, you are no longer in the school of Satan, the prince of darkness; you are in the kingdom of the Son of God. Think and act worthily of so glorious a condition. Let it purify your life of all that is filthy and sordid. Let it elevate your hearts above mortal things, and set them in heaven, the residence of this divine royalty.

But, dear brethren, as this text obliges us to make sanctification a special study; so it opens to us a living source of consolation and joy. For if we knew our blessings, and that wonderful grace which the Father has shown us, who would equal us in felicity? We have a part in the heritage of the saints. The kingdom of the beloved Son of God has been given us. O great and magnificent portion! Let the world boast of and adore its gold, its honours, and its delights, as much as it pleases; we have that better part, which is sufficient to make us eternally happy, though we should be deprived of all other things. Christian, if the world were to bereave you of what you have within its jurisdiction, consider, it cannot take from you the inheritance of the saints. If it denies you its leeks, and onions, and flesh-pots, it cannot debar you from that divine light which shines on you, and which, in spite of all its attempts, will conduct you to your blissful Canaan. If it takes from you its honours, should it drive you even out of its dominions, it will not be able to wrest from you the kingdom of the Son of God, nor the dignity and glory you possess in it. This is not a corruptible kingdom; it is not like those of the earth, that are subject to a thousand and a thousand dishonours, miseries, and mutations. It is an immortal kingdom, firmer than the heavens; so abundant in glory and in goodness, that it changes all those who partake of it into kings and priests. Faithful brethren, let us be contented with so advantageous a portion. Let us enjoy it for the present by a lively and established hope, meekly bearing the inconveniences of this brief journey we are taking to attain it, and patiently except that blessed day, when our heavenly Father, having finished the work of his grace, will elevate us all into his glory, and put on our heads the crowns of life and immortality, which he has promised us in the eternal communion of his well-beloved Son; to whom, with the Father and the Holy Spirit, the true and only God, blessed for ever, be all honour and praise, for ever and ever. Amen.

SERMON VI.

VERSE 14.

In whom we have redemption through his blood, even the forgiveness of sins.

DEAR brethren, as a true and extensive knowledge of that great and glorious Redeemer, whose remembrance we are this day to celebrate, is the only foundation of the religion and salvation of men; so, on the contrary, ignorance of his person, of his offices, and of his benefits, is the source of those errors and abuses which have corrupted religion, and consequently of that unhappiness into which the unbelieving, the profane, the superstitious, and the heretical are ever falling. We may say to all these people, as our Lord formerly did to the woman of Samaria, If ye knew who he is that speaks to you in our gospel, ye would ask of him the refreshment and consolation of your souls; and he would give you living water, springing up to everlasting life, John iv. 10. And as Paul said of the ancient Jews, that if they had known the wisdom of God, "they would not have crucified the Lord of glory;" 1 Cor. ii. 8; so may we say of all the enemies of godliness in general, that if they knew Jesus, the wisdom and word of the Father, they would not injure either his truth, or those that make a profession of it. Jesus truly and fully known, believed, and apprehended, suffices to expel error, doubt, superstition, sin and death from our hearts; and to establish in their room truth, peace, joy, holiness, and salvation. Accordingly, you see that Paul, the instructor of the whole world, the minister of truth, the teacher of life and happiness, protests that to execute this high commission, and to open the eyes of the Gentiles, and bring them from the power of Satan unto God, he determined to know nothing among them but "Jesus Christ and him crucified," 1 Cor. ii. 2. He finds in this rich and inexhaustible subject all that is necessary for him to convert infidels, to confirm believers, to comfort the afflicted, to reclaim them who had been misled, and recover them who had erred. He finds in it wherewith to confute the philosophy of the pagans, wherewith to abase the presumption of the Jews, wherewith to instruct the ignorant, and to convince the learned. It is with the mere science of this Jesus, that he wrests men from idolatry, and liberates them from the slavery of sin. With this also he reforms the abuses and cures the wounds which error has caused in the church. It is his weapon against enemies without, and against the factious within. With this knowledge he builds the house of God; and with this he cleanses and keeps it pure. Whatever enemy appears, he opposes to him nothing whatever but his crucified Jesus. For as in nature no sooner does the sun appear in our horizon, showing his beautiful and luminous visage to the world, but the shades and clouds that filled the air immediately vanish; so in the church, when the Lord Jesus arises in the hearts of men, there diffusing the riches of his saving light, and displaying his beauty, at the same instant error and misconception disappear, unable to sustain the force of this divine brightness; and, as the psalmist sings on another occasion, When he arises his enemies are dispersed, and they that hate him flee before him. He driveth them away as wind driveth the smoke, Psal. lxviii. 1, 2. This then is the only certain means either to preserve or to recover the truth and the purity of heavenly doctrine; that is, to propose Jesus Christ incessantly to believers, and diligently show them all his riches, all his power and his grace. This is the apostle's method. Thus he acts on every occasion, always taking back his scholars to Jesus Christ. So you see in the Epistle to the Hebrews, that he might put aside the shadows of the Jewish law, with which some of that nation endeavoured to darken the gospel, he shows them at the beginning the majesty and divinity of the Lord Jesus, setting him up above men and angels on the throne of a supereminent glory. He does the same in this Epistle, and indeed he combats here a similar error. For after he had saluted the Colossians, and given them some evidences of the affection he bore them, as you have already heard, he now begins to speak to them of Jesus Christ, discovering his divine glory, and the fulness of his goodness to them, that, being satisfied with so rich a treasure, they might not go to beg either the succour of Moses, or the assistance of philosophy, for the saving of their souls. It is precisely at the text which we have read that he begins this excellent discourse. For having before thanked God for the grace that he had shown the Colossians in translating them into the kingdom of his well-beloved Son, he thence takes occasion to speak of him, adding, "In whom we have redemption through his blood, even the forgiveness of sins." This is the great benefit which we have received from God by means of Jesus Christ. Then he describes, in connection with this, the excellency and divinity of his person: "Who is," says he, "the image of the invisible God, the first-born of every creature." But at this time we shall be satisfied with the first topic.

You see, my brethren, that meditation on the subject is very suitable to the service of the holy supper to which we are invited, where the remission of sins, which we have in Jesus Christ, is sealed to us by his sacrament; where the blood, by which he has purchased it, is represented and communicated to us; where Jesus the author of this benefit, is portrayed before our eyes as broken and dead for us, and as feeding us to everlasting life. Let us, then, lift up our hearts with devout earnestness, that having well comprehended the greatness of the grace of God, and the excellency of his Christ, we may present to him souls strongly affected with a sense of his goodness, and may afterwards receive that joy and blessed life which he promises to all them who approach him with such a disposition. To aid you in so necessary a meditation, I will examine, if the Lord pleases, what the apostle teaches us concerning the benefit which we receive of God in his Son; "In whom we have redemption through his blood, even the forgiveness of sins."

In these words he briefly points out the author of "redemption," that is, Jesus Christ; what is its nature, "the forgiveness of sins;" what the means by which Jesus Christ has obtained it for us, "through his blood;" and, lastly, who they are that receive it from God, namely, "we;" that is, believers.

I. He had said before that God hath delivered us from the power of darkness, and translated us into his kingdom. Now he shows us by whom he effected that great work, adding that, we have redemption in Jesus Christ. He is the author of our redemption, our only Deliverer, the Prince of our salvation. The apostle says that it is in him we have redemption; this may be taken two ways, both of them good and suitable: first, as signifying that it is by him we have been delivered. For it is a Hebraism frequent in Scripture to say *in* instead of *by*. And in this sense the apostle declares that it is by Jesus Christ his Son that God has accomplished the work of his good pleasure towards us, having constituted him the Mediator of mankind, who, according to the will of him who sent him, perfectly executed all things that were necessary to put us in possession of salvation. But this word "in" may also be taken in the sense it has in our usual language, as signifying our spiritual communion with the Lord, by reason of which we are said to be in him, and he in us. For though "he is the propitiation for the sins of the whole world," 1 John ii. 2, and the worth of his sacrifice so great that it abundantly suffices to expiate all the crimes of the universe; and although the salvation obtained by him is really offered, and by his will, unto all men; yet none actually enjoy it but those that enter into his communion by faith, and are by that means in him, as that clause of his covenant expressly imports, "God so loved the world that he gave his only begotten Son, that whosoever believeth in him should not perish, but have everlasting life," John iii. 16. Whence it is that John proclaims, "He that hath the Son hath life; he that hath not the Son of God hath not life," 1 John v. 12; which amounts to this, He that is in Jesus Christ hath life, and he that is not in him hath not life; according to what our Lord himself said to his apostles, "Out of me ye can do nothing," John xv. 5. This sense is, as you perceive, grand and lucid, and contains an excellent truth, that to enjoy salvation by Jesus Christ we must be in him. But because the apostle's design is to show us what the Lord has done for our salvation, rather than what he requires of us for our participating it, I prefer the first acceptation of the words, "in whom," that is, by whom, "we have redemption." And this indeed is the most common exposition of the best interpreters, both ancient and modern.

II. Let us next consider what is the divine benefit which we have by Jesus Christ. The original word* used by the apostle particularly signifies a deliverance, effected by some ransom given for bringing him who is delivered out of his miserable condition, and is strictly that which we call redemption. For a man may be delivered many ways: as by being simply taken out of his affliction; as when a master enfranchises his slave, of his good-will setting him at liberty; or when a creditor lets his debtor out of prison, forgiving him the debt; or by exchange, as when one prisoner of war is alienated for another; or by forcible recovery, as when Abraham delivered Lot, by defeating his enemies, and David his people, who had been taken by the Amalekites. The deliverance we have by Jesus Christ is not of this kind. He has procured it by the ransom which he gave for us, and this is the meaning of the

* Ἀπολύτρωσις.

word "redemption" here used by the apostle. But the same term teaches us also that the benefit which we have received from him is not simply the gift of life. It is a deliverance which brings us out of some misery. God gave life and immortality to the angels, but he gave them no deliverance, since they never were in sin or misery; and indeed he promised life to Adam prior to his fall, but not salvation and redemption, because man was then in his integrity without sin and misery. The benefit that we receive from him by Jesus Christ is not simply life and immortality; it is a deliverance, a salvation, a redemption, that not only confers on us some good, but takes us out of sin, and wrests us from misery.

This the apostle explains more particularly, when he adds that this redemption which we have in Jesus Christ is "the remission of sins." True it is that the word "redemption" is of general import, comprising deliverance from any kind of evil; it is also certain that the number of our evils is great, and that Jesus Christ has delivered us not merely from one or two evils, but from all. He has delivered us from the ignorance in which we were by nature overwhelmed. He has delivered us from the bondage of the flesh, the lusts whereof exercised a horrible tyranny in our members. He has delivered us from that death to which we were subjected, and from the curse of the eternal Father which we had deserved. For which cause the apostle elsewhere says that "Jesus Christ is made unto us," not simply "righteousness," but also "wisdom, sanctification, and redemption;" and in a multitude of places, that he has brought us out of darkness, and delivered us from the tyrannous power of sin and death. All this is most certain. But in this place he restrains the redemption which we have in Jesus Christ to the remission of sins, and that, I think, for two reasons:

First, because remission of sin is the first and the principal of his benefits, the basis and foundation of all the rest, which infallibly attracts them, and without which it is impossible to touch any of them. For sin, as you know, is expressly that which separates between God and us. The cause why this most merciful and all-powerful Ruler of the world withholds from us the light of his knowledge and the communication of his goodness, leaving us in the darkness of error and in misery, is not a hatred, or contempt, or disdain of his creatures. It is nothing but our sin, his justice and sovereign equity not permitting him to reward the guilty with his favours. Jesus Christ therefore intervening and procuring for us the remission of our sins, thereby brings us out of our miserable condition, and opens the fountain of celestial good, which before was closed by justice. This obstacle being removed, this sluice, if I may so say, opened, divine goodness recovering its natural course, flows forth upon us, and pours into us light, peace, holiness, and life. It is not then to exclude these other benefits of the redemption which is by Jesus Christ that the apostle defines it "the forgiveness of sins," (for it comprises them all, none having this remission who do not after that receive all other divine graces,) but to show us the due order of all the parts of this redemption, of which remission of sin is the first and principal.

Secondly, the apostle does this because the ransom which the word "redemption" implies was not strictly necessary, except for obtaining the remission of sins. But for this there was no need that Jesus Christ should lay down his life for us. For supposing that a pure and sinless creature should have lain in ignorance and misery, and, if you will, even in death itself, there would have been no necessity that the Son of God should have shed his blood or suffered death to have rescued it. It would have sufficed that he loved it. His good-will would have immediately excited his power to display itself in its behalf, and deliver it out of its distress. There was nothing to hinder this natural operation of his goodness, and so the happiness of such a creature would have been simply a deliverance, and not a redemption. But as we were sinners, it was necessary for our recovery that Jesus Christ should make his soul an offering for sin, and pay the ransom of our liberty. Whence it follows, that, to speak properly and exactly, nothing but the remission of sins should be called redemption, as the apostle here defines it; the other deliverances which we obtain by our Lord being only the fruits and results of the remission of sin.

This then is the grand achievement of the Son of God, the miracle of his goodness and love, that he has procured and obtained for us the forgiveness of our sins. This is our true redemption. Without this redemption we should still be enemies of God; we should have no part either in his grace or in his glory. Be in other respects all that you can desire; possess all the goods of the earth, all perfections of body and mind; be monarch of the whole world; have (if it be possible) the light of angels and the riches of their knowledge: if you possess not the remission of your sins, you are a bondman and a wretch, a slave to devils, and vanity, and death; for true redemption is the remission of sins. But as without it, it is impossible to be otherwise than infinitely wretched, so with it, it is not possible to be otherwise than infinitely happy, The repose of the conscience, the illumination of the understanding, the jewel of sanctification, the graces of the Holy Spirit, life and immortality, inseparably follow it. "Go in peace," said the Lord Jesus to those whose sins he pardoned; as if he had said, Thou hast nothing more to fear, as thy sin is forgiven thee. There is no longer any evil that can hurt thee, or good that can be denied thee, if profitable for thy salvation. Away with that cruel and extravagant doctrine which insists that God remits the fault without remitting the punishment. This is repugnant to common sense and reason; for what is it to remit a sin, but not to punish it, and treat him who has committed it as if he had not been culpable? This is to contradict the apostle, who elsewhere proclaims that "there is now no condemnation to them who are in Jesus Christ," Rom. viii. 1; and here, that the forgiveness of our sins is a redemption. For if God punishes believers, as it is presumed, he does so after having condemned them to suffer; for, being most just, he neither punishes nor absolves any without judgment. And if notwithstanding our forgiveness we escape not burning in the fire of a pretended purgatory, how is our forgiveness a redemption? Is a criminal ransomed by burning him? I grant that believers, after receiving this remission, are not freed from divers afflictions during their temporary abode here below. But I affirm that their sufferings are exercises or chastisements, and not properly punishments of their sin. The Lord sends to them these not in his wrath, but in his grace; not to punish them, but either to amend them or to prove them, and to conform them to the image of his Son, who in the days of his flesh was consecrated by afflictions. Such is this forgiveness of sins, the redemption which we have in Jesus Christ.

III. Let us now see by what means he has obtained it for us. The apostle teaches us that we have it by his blood. We have already said that the word "redemption," here used, shows that our deliverance was effected by the payment of a ransom. This he expressly asserts in another place, saying, "Ye are bought with a price," 1 Cor. vi. 20. Now here he declares what this price is, what this ransom of our deliverance, even the blood of Jesus Christ. Peter insists likewise on the same important topic: "Ye have been redeemed," says he, "not with corruptible things, as silver and gold; but with the precious blood of Christ, as of a lamb without blemish and without spot," 1 Pet. i. 18, 19. And the Lord Jesus distinctly teaches us the same thing, when speaking of the end and design of his mission to the world, he says that he "came not to be ministered unto, but to minister, and to give his life a ransom for many," Matt. xx. 28. In a like manner Paul states that Jesus Christ "gave himself a ransom for all," 1 Tim. ii. 6. And in this sense we must understand what the spirits of the blessed say when they glorify the Lamb for having redeemed them to God by his blood, Rev. v. 9; and Paul in the Acts, that God has purchased the church by his own blood, chap. xx. 28. By these passages, and a multitude of others of similar import, it is evident that the apostle, both in this place and in the first chapter of his Epistle to the Ephesians, where he repeats the words, " through the blood of Christ," means the violent death the Son of God suffered on the cross, with the effusion of his blood, which he shed forth in great abundance through the wounds of his feet, of his hands, and of his side. And it is a thing common in all languages to express life by blood, and the loss of life by a shedding of blood. But the Holy Ghost particularly uses this manner of speaking when there is reference to a sacrifice. For in such cases the blood of the victim is almost always put for the life which it loses when offered. It cannot therefore be thought strange that these divine authors say, " the blood"of Christ, (who is the only Lamb and most perfect oblation, which all the old sacrifices typified,) when they mean the life that he poured out for us on the cross, offering it to the Father as the propitiation for our sins. This now is the great mystery of the gospel, which was not known to men or angels, nor could have been ever thought of or conceived by any but the supreme and infinite wisdom of God, that Jesus Christ, the well-beloved of the Father, the most holy One, should lay down his life for us, be put in our stead, and bear our sins in his own body on the tree, and suffer in his sacred flesh, and in his most holy soul, the pains and sorrows which we had merited, to exempt us from them.

This is precisely what we mean, when we affirm that he satisfied the justice of God for us. And the apostle, in these words, furnishes us wherewith to preserve this glory to our Lord, against two sorts of adversaries: one of them that impudently deny his having satisfied for us at all; the other, of those who grant his satisfaction, but extend this honour to others also, and insist that it pertains likewise to saints, and even to ourselves. As for the first, they deserve not to be accounted christians, since they reject a truth so clearly and so frequently asserted in the gospel, confessed by all the church, and which is also the source of our comfort in life and death, and the only foundation of all our hopes. For if Jesus Christ satisfied not for us, what mean the prophets and apostles who proclaim at the beginning, in the midst, and at the end of all their preaching, that he "died for our sins," "was wounded for our transgressions, and bruised for our iniquities: the chastisement of our peace was upon him; and with his stripes we are healed?" that his soul was made "an offering for sin?" that he is our "propitiation, through faith in his blood?" that he is "the Lamb of God, which taketh away the sin of the world?" that he offered up himself a sacrifice for sin, and sanctified us through this offering, and purged away our sins by himself? 1 Cor. xv. 3; Isa. liii. 5, 10; Rom. iii. 25; John i. 29; Heb. ix. 28;

x. 10; i. 3. I omit, at present, other places, of which the number is infinite; these are sufficient to settle the truth. For, first, as our deliverance is called a redemption, it must needs be that Jesus Christ has purchased it for us, by some ransom which he gave in our behalf. But he gave none at all, unless in dying he expended his life and his blood for us, and in our stead. Again, if it is not thus, why says the apostle, it is by the blood of Christ that we have remission of our sins? If his blood is not a satisfaction for our sins, it is evidently of no use whatever to obtain for us the remission of them. In this case we should have it, not by the blood or death of Christ, which, according to this notion, would have contributed nothing to it, but by the mere goodness of God or of his Son. For to say that the remission of sins is attributed to the blood and death of our Lord, because he by dying sealed the truth of what he preached in his life; this is evidently to mock the world. His miracles also confirmed his doctrine, and yet neither Scripture nor any wise man ever said that we have remission of sins by his miracles, as Paul says here, and in many other places, that we have it by his blood and by his death. Besides, if this reason is valid, as the martyrs suffered to seal the same doctrine, it may be also said that we have redemption and remission of sins by their blood, which we can nowhere read. On the contrary, the apostle vehemently denies that he or any other was crucified for us, but Christ alone, 1 Cor. i. 13.

These reasons destroy also another subterfuge used by these people; namely, that we have salvation by the death of Jesus Christ, because in dying he gave us an example of patience and perfect obedience. For, according to this sentiment, the martyrs, in whose sufferings were the like patterns, should have saved us as well as Christ. We add that patience and obedience constitute part of our sanctification; but the apostle says we have in Jesus Christ, by his blood, the remission of sins, and not simply sanctification. Their third evasion is no better; that Christ has acquired by his death the right of pardoning sins. For either their meaning is that the Lord has rendered sin remissible by the satisfaction he has made for it, or they simply intend that Christ obtained by his death the power of pardoning sins, which he had not before. If they answer, the first, they grant us the very thing that we demand. If the second, they contradict the gospel, which testifies that our Lord often remitted the sins of men prior to his death, and said expressly that he had authority on earth to forgive them. Their last resort (and which nothing but despair of so bad a cause could suggest) is of no more validity; namely, that the remission of our sins is attributed to the death of Christ because it preceded his resurrection, the glory of which enkindles faith and repentance in us, the true causes of that remission. But they cannot produce any one example of so strange a manner of speaking; and to say that the blood of Christ washes away our sins because it was shed prior to his resurrection, the cause of that faith by which we obtain pardon, this is as absurd, if not more so, than if you were to say that by the darkness of the night we are enlightened during the day, because the light of the sun, which then shines on us, was preceded by the darkness of the night. If this were correct, the remission of our sins should be everywhere attributed to the resurrection of Christ Jesus, to his ascension to heaven, and to the miracles of his apostles, and not to his death; but, in perfect opposition to this, it is ever constantly referred to the death, to the blood, and to the cross of the Lord, as to its true cause, and not ever to his resurrection. As to the statement of the apostle, that Christ rose "again for our justification," his meaning is not that our sins obliged him to rise, as they had obliged him to die, according to what he had affirmed, that he "was delivered for our offences," Rom. iv. 25; but, that he might apply to men the fruit of his death in justifying them by the virtue of his blood, he was raised from the grave, and crowned with the highest glory; this being necessary for the production of those divine effects in the world. We say then, that by pouring out his blood and his life on the cross, the Lord truly satisfied the avenging justice of the Father, undergoing for us, and in our room, that death which we deserved; and until this be admitted, there can be no rational ground for asserting, as the apostle does here and in many other places, that we have remission of sins in Jesus Christ by his blood.

But from the same apostolical assertion it is also very evident, that none but our Lord is capable of satisfying for us. For as the forgiveness of sins is our redemption, who sees not that if any one procures it for us he must be our redeemer? a title which, by the unanimous consent of all christians, pertains singly to Jesus Christ. Moreover, by the blood of our Lord this forgiveness has been purchased; so that neither Paul, nor Cephas, nor any other having been crucified for us, it follows that no one of them has either satisfied God for us, or merited the remission of sins. Though their death was precious in the sight of God, said an ancient writer,* yet there were none of them, however innocent, whose suffering could be the propitiation of the world. The just have received crowns, not given them; and from their constancy and steadfastness in the faith have grown up examples of patience, not gifts of righteousness. This glory is due to nothing but the blood of Christ. And as he is the only victim that was offered for our sins, so is it sufficient to expiate them all. Never man found favour

* Leo Mag. Serm. 12, de Passion.

but through this sacrifice. Never did the sword of God spare any, but for the sake of this blood. This Paul teaches us in our text, and this is the last particular which we have to observe upon it. For when he says "we have redemption in Jesus Christ by his blood," he intends not to speak singly of himself and the Colossians, but of all believers that were on the earth, and even of those that had lived from the beginning of the world to that time. There neither was nor ever had been salvation in any other but in him. And as sin and death descended from Adam on all men, so the righteousness and life of all believers come from Jesus Christ. He is "the Lamb that was slain from the foundation of the world," Rev. xiii. 8, and his death intervened "for the redemption of the transgressions that were under the old testament," as well as of those that are committed under the new, Heb. ix. 15. His blood is the remission of the sins both of the one and the other people. That it was to be shed in due time gave it the same efficacy for the generations that preceded his cross, which it had by its actual effusion in those that succeeded. God the Father, appeased by this sacrifice, ever present in his sight, as well before as after its oblation, communicated the fruit and merit of it, that is to say, grace and remission, to all those who believed in him, under the one and the other testament.

Behold, beloved brethren, that which we had to say to you concerning the redemption which we have in Jesus Christ. This the text of the apostle teaches us, and the table of the Lord represents it to us. This is the mystery of the bread which we there break, and of the cup we there bless in remembrance and for the communicating of that sacred body which was broken for us, and of that divine blood which was shed for the remission of our sins. Let us carefully improve a doctrine so necessary, and which is so diligently inculcated on us in the word and in the sacraments of our Lord, applying it for our edification and comfort.

We learn from it, first, the horror of sin; a spot so black that it could not be washed out but by the blood of Jesus Christ. That remission of it might be given us, it was necessary that the Father should deliver up his dear Son to die, and the Son give his blood, the most precious jewel of the universe, a thousand times more worth than heaven and earth, and all the glory of them. From this meditation conceive a just hatred against sin; as it is so abominable in the eyes of this sovereign Lord, on whose communion alone depends all your bliss, shun it, and pluck it out of your consciences and your hearts. As for sins already committed, seek the remission of them in the blood of Christ. Give yourselves no rest till you have found it, till you have obtained grace, till it be confirmed in your souls by the hand and seal of the Holy Ghost. Lay aside the pretended satisfactions and merits of men. Have no recourse but to the righteousness of Jesus Christ, which alone is able to cover our shame and render us acceptable to God. But having once obtained pardon for the time past, return not to sin for the future. When sin shall present itself to you, courageously repel it, opposing to all its temptations this holy and salutary consideration: It is my Master's tormentor, the murderer of the Lord of glory; it is the accursed serpent that separated man from God, that put enmity between heaven and earth, that sowed misery and death in the world, and obliged the Father to deliver up his Son to the sufferings of the cross. God forbid I should take into my bosom so cruel, so deadly an enemy.

But from this same source we may also draw unspeakable consolation against the gnawing guilt of sin, and the troubles of conscience. For, as it is by the blood of the Son of God that we have been redeemed, what cause is there to doubt but that our remisssion is secured? The superstitious have reason to be in continual fear, for man, in whom they put their confidence, is but vanity. The propitiation which I present to you, O believer, is not the blood of a man or of an angel, creatures finite and incapable of sustaining the eternal burnings of the wrath of the Almighty; it is the blood of God's own Son, who also is himself God blessed for ever. It is blood of infinite value, and truly capable of counterpoising and prevailing against the infinite demerit of your crimes. Come, then, sinner, whoever you are; come with assurance. However foul your transgressions, this blood will cleanse them away. However ardent the displeasure of God against you, this blood will quench it. Only bedew your soul with it. Make an aspersion of it on your hearts with a lively faith, and you need no more fear the sword of the executioner of the vengeance of God.

But, believing brethren, having thus assured your conscience by meditation on this divine blood of our Lord, admire ye also his infinite love, which he so clearly shows us and confirms to us. This King of glory has so loved you, that when your sins could not be pardoned without the effusion of his blood, he would die upon a cross rather than see you perish in hell. He poured out his blood to keep in yours, and underwent the curse of God that you might partake of his blessings. Oh great and incomprehensible love! the singular miracle of heaven, ravishing men and angels! what should we fear henceforth, as this great God has so loved us? Who shall condemn us, as he is our Surety? Who shall accuse us, as he is our Advocate? He has given us his own blood; what can he any longer refuse to bestow on us? He has laid down his soul for us; how much more will he grant us all other things that are necessary for our salvation! But as this thought comforts us, so ought it to sanctify us. Of what hells shall not we be worthy, if we love not a Lord who has so ardently loved us—if we obey not his commandments who hath blotted out our sins—if for this precious blood which he has given us we do not render ours to him, and consecrate to his glory a life which he has redeemed by offering his own in sacrifice for our salvation?

And after an example of such admirable goodness, how can we be ill affected to any man? Christians, God has forgiven you a thousand and a thousand most enormous sins; have you the heart to deny your neighbour the pardon of one slight offence? He has given you his blood, you that were his enemies; how can you refuse a small alms to him that is your brother, both by nature and grace? Let the goodness of the Lord Jesus mollify the hardness of your heart; let the virtue of his blood melt your bowels into sweetness, into charity, and into love towards him and towards his members. Dismiss you this very day, at his table, all the bitter passions of your flesh. Put off there pride, hatred, and envy; and there clothe yourselves with his humility and his gentleness. Do him new homage, and bind yourselves by oath to be never any other's but his alone; presenting yourselves with deepest reverence before this throne of his grace. Remember at this time, and ever after, that blood by which he has obtained redemption for you, that is, the forgiveness of your sins. This blood is the peace of heaven and of earth. This blood has brought us out of hell, and opened paradise unto us. It has delivered us from death, and given us life. This blood has blotted out the sentence of our curse that stood registered in the law of God; it has stopped the mouth of our accusers, and pacified our Judge. This blood has effected a renovation of the world. It has quickened the dead, and animated the dust, and changed our mortal flesh into a heavenly and divine nature. Dear brethren, God forbid we should tread under foot a thing so holy, or account such precious blood profane or common. Let us reverence it, and receive it into our hearts with ardent devotion. And may it display its admirable efficacy in them, causing the royal image of God, even holiness and righteousness, to flourish there, to the glory of the Lord and our own consolation and salvation. Amen.

SERMON VII.

VERSE 15.

Who is the image of the invisible God, the first-born of every creature.

DEAR brethren, as the salvation of mankind, the true end of the coming of our Lord Jesus Christ into the world, obliged him to expiate sin, and destroy the dominion of Satan; so the performing of these great works required an infinite dignity and power in his person. For as it was not possible that he should give us eternal life without obliterating our guilt, and satisfying the justice of the Father, and delivering us from the grasp of devils; so it was equally impossible that he could perfect these achievements without an infinite merit and a divine strength; that is, without being God; none but a true God possessing an infinite dignity or an infinite power. As then the streams conduct us to their spring, branches to their stock and root, the house to the foundation that sustains it; so the salvation which is of the Lord Jesus leads us to the deeds by which he obtained it for us, and thence to the dignity that was necessary in his person for executing those acts. Salvation is the fruit of this tree of life. The infinite merit of his cross is as the branch which yielded this noble fruit; and his almighty, most holy, and most divine person is the stock or root that shot forth this beautiful and blessed branch. This order the apostle observes here in the consideration of our Lord Jesus Christ. He sets forth to us, first, his fruit, that is, our salvation or redemption; the end of his whole mediation. Next he represents the means by which he acquired this salvation for us; that is, the effusion of his blood for the remission of our sins. Thence he now ascends to the dignity of his person, which he magnificently describes in the text that you have heard, saying that he " is the image of the invisible God, the first born of every creature;" forasmuch as " by him were all things created." Wonder not, faithful brethren, that Jesus should give us life and eternity; us, I say, poor sinners, who had deserved death and the curse of God. For he purchased remission of our sins by his blood, and by the sweet savour of his sacrifice perfectly appeased the wrath of God, which alone withstood our entering into his heavenly kingdom. Neither account it any more strange that this Jesus, so infirm, clothed with frail flesh, subject to all our sufferings, should be able to offer so great and so precious a sacrifice to God. For however weak and despicable was that form under which he appeared here below, yet he is in reality the true Son of God; his wisdom, his word, and his power; the perfect portrait of his person, his living and essential image, the sovereign Lord and Creator of the universe.

In this description of the dignity and excellency of the Lord Jesus, the apostle compares him, first, with God the Father, saying that he "is the image of the invisible God." In the second place, with the creatures, saying, that he "is the first-born of them;" and adds the reason of it in the two following verses, which is taken from his having made and established them all, as their Creator, their Preserver, their last and highest end. And, finally, he proposes his relation to the church, saying, in the 18th verse, that he is "the Head thereof," the "Beginning," and "the First-born from the dead," having the first place in all things. You see in these three points comprised the sovereign dignity and excellency of the Saviour of the world. But because it would be difficult to explain them all three in a single sermon, the richness and profundity of the matter constrains us to fix, for this time, on the first two, and to defer the remainder to another time. We have then to handle in this discourse the two heads contained in the verse which we have read. One, that Jesus Christ "is the image of the invisible God;" the other, that he is "the first-born of every creature." May the same Lord who, by his grace, will be the subject of our discourse, please to be also our direction and light, inspiring us with conceptions and expressions worthy of him, illuminating our understandings with the knowledge of his high and supereminent majesty, and inflaming our hearts with a fervent love to himself for the glory of his own great name and our salvation.

I. As for the first head, the apostle asserts two things in it: the one is, that Jesus Christ "is the image of God;" the other, that the God whose image Jesus Christ is, is "invisible." For understanding aright how the Lord Jesus is the image of God, we must premise that the word "image" is of great extent, signifying generally anything that represents another; so that things being very variously represented, it happens that there is a great variety and difference of images. Some are perfect, which have in them an entire, an exact, and adequate resemblance of the subjects which they represent; others are imperfect, and express but some particular, nay, that too with some defect, having not properly in them the same features and essence which are in their original. I place in this second rank all artificial images, whether drawn by painters, or engraven or carved by sculptors, or cast by founders, or figured by embroiderers and workers of tapestry; which represent only the colour, the figure, and the lineaments of men, and animals, and plants, and similar subjects, and indeed have nothing of their life and nature. To this same order must be reduced that which Moses writes, that Adam was made after the image of God. It is not to be thought he had such an essence as God has; but this is said because the conditions of his nature had some resemblance to the properties of God; namely, in that he was endowed with intellect and will, and was the master and lord of animals and earthly creatures. In the same manner must we take what Paul says, when, comparing the two sexes of our nature, he terms the man "the image and the glory of God;" but the woman "the glory of the man," 1 Cor. xi. 7. He calls the man "the image of God," because of the advantage and superiority he has over the woman, having no one above himself but God, who is his Head: but man is the head of the woman, because she was created of him and for him, as the apostle teaches.

But besides these kinds of images, which but imperfectly represent their originals, there are others that have a perfect resemblance to them. Thus we call a child the image of his father, a prince the image of his predecessor. For a son has not merely the shadow, or the colour, or the figure of his father, he has his nature, his qualities, and properties, and, if we may so say, the whole fulness of his being, a soul, a body, a life, all of the same several species with those of his father. A prince, in like manner, has not only the shadow or the appearance of the authority and power of his predecessor, but the whole substance and reality. Thus it is that Moses says Adam begat Seth his son "in his own likeness, after his image," Gen. v. 3; by which he suggests that Seth had a nature the same in all things with Adam's. Now the question is, in which of these two senses must we take the word "image," when the apostle says here, and also elsewhere, that Jesus Christ is "the image of God," 2 Cor. iv. 4. The very nature of the subject in question shows us so clearly that we must apprehend it in the second and not in the first sense, that even those who oppose it dare not say that Jesus Christ is an imperfect image of his Father. For where is the christian ear that could tolerate a blasphemy so horrible, and so contrary to all holy Scripture? Surely when the apostle says of our Lord that he is "the image of God," he thereby means quite another thing than when he says elsewhere that man is "the image of God." For, intending here to exalt the Lord Jesus, and to demonstrate that his dignity is so high as to capacitate him to save us, he would ill suit this design if he attributed no more to him than what holds good of any man, whoever he is. But if you do not admit that Jesus Christ is a perfect image of God, the apostle affirms nothing more of him here than he asserts elsewhere of man, when he says he is "the image of God." Beside the apostle's design, the thing he expressly mentions evidently shows us this. For our Lord informs us that he who hath seen him hath seen the Father; and that he who beholdeth him beholdeth him that sent him, John xiv. 9; xii. 45. Where is the portrait of which it may be said, that he who has seen it has seen the subject which it represents? This evidently cannot be found but in such an image as is most perfect, and which fully contains all the nature of its original. Whence it appears that it is in this sense that Jesus Christ is "the image of God." And for our understanding it the better, the apostle has a passage in the Epistle to the Hebrews, which in scope, and terms, and sense very much resembles this béfore us; there he saith that Jesus Christ is the resplendence of the glory of his Father, and the image, or the character, or engraven stamp of his person, Heb. i. 3; terms exceedingly elegant and expressive, and such as clearly decide this case, that the Lord is the image of God in a manner that man is not, and that the same glory which shines in the Father is resplendent also in the Son, and that the same nature which is in the person of the one is likewise in the person of the other. We say therefore, according to the analogy of this doctrine, and the reason of the thing itself, that Jesus Christ is the image of God his Father, but a perfect one, yea, as perfect as an image can possibly be; an image which exhibits to us and represents, not the colour or the shadow, but the truth and substance of the Deity. The Scripture, our only guide in these high mysteries, clearly teaches this. And to aid you in comprehending it, though the Godhead is most simple in itself, exempt from all mixture and composition, yet speaking of it according to the weakness of our understanding, to which God has not disdained to accommodate himself in his word, we will consider three things of him; the nature, the properties, or qualities, (which divines commonly call his attributes,) and his works.

As for his *nature*, it is most perfectly represented in Jesus Christ; for he has really and veritably the same essence and substance with God the Father; as a child, whom we call the image of his father, has the same nature with him, being as truly man as he is. The Scripture teaches us this truth in very many places, where it says that Jesus Christ is God; that he is "the true God;" our "great God and Saviour;" God blessed above all; Jehovah, of old tempted by the Israelites in the desert; he whose glory Isaiah saw in the vision described in the sixth chapter of his prophecies; 1 John v. 20; Tit. ii. 13; Rom. ix. 5; 1 Cor. x. 9; John xii. 41. It lays down the same thing also whenever it presents him to us as a proper object of our adoration; saying that all men ought to honour him "even as they honour the Father," John v. 23; and that the very "angels worship him," Heb. i. 6; it being evident that, according to Scripture, there is nothing but a nature truly divine to whom adoration may be lawfully given.

But the Lord Jesus no less perfectly represents the Father in his *properties* than in his nature. The Father is eternal, so is the Son; and Isaiah calls him upon this account the Father of eternity, Isa. ix. 6. "Before Abraham was I am," John viii. 58. He was from the beginning with God; and before the world was created, even then he was in the bosom of the Father, his love and his delight. The heavens shall perish, but he is permanent. The heavens shall wax old as a garment, and be folded up as a vesture, and be changed; but Jesus is the same, and his years shall not fail, Heb. i. 11, 12. The Father is immutable, without ever receiving any alteration or change, either in his being or in his will. The Son is "the same yesterday, to-day, and for ever," Heb. xiii. 8. The Father is infinite, filling heaven and earth; neither is there anything within or without the world that limits the presence of his being. The Son is in like manner infinite. He is in heaven while he speaks to Nicodemus on earth, John iii. 13. He is here below on earth, in our hearts, and in our assemblies, at the same instant that he is sitting at the right hand of the Father in the highest room of the universe; and though the heavens contain that body and human nature which he assumed, yet they do not enclose his majesty and omnipresent divinity. The Father has a sovereign understanding, knowing all things, present, past, and to come. The Son is wisdom itself. He knows all things; and if on one occasion he says that he knows not the day of judgment, his words are to be understood in respect of his human nature, and not in respect of his divine intelligence. He trieth the reins, and knoweth the heart of man, Rev. ii. 23; a power which the Scripture sets down as the character and specific mark of the knowledge of God, asserting that it is only he who knoweth the hearts of men. The Father knows himself, and no man or angel, to speak properly, ever saw him. The Son so perfectly knows him that he has even declared and revealed him unto men. The Father is almighty, and does whatsoever he will. The Son has all power in heaven and in earth, and there is nothing difficult to him. The Father is supremely good, hating evil and loving rectitude and justice. The Son is the Saint of saints, entirely separate from sinners; goodness itself, justice itself. The Father is merciful and inclined to pity. The Son is the fountain of compassion. The Father maketh his sun to shine on, and his rain to bedew, even the men that blaspheme him. The Son died for his enemies, and prayed for those who crucified him. In short, the Father has not any other essential quality, but the Son likewise has it, and in the same measure with the Father.

I come to his works. Certainly the Son himself informs us that he perfectly represents the Father in this respect; saying, in general, that "what things soever the Father doeth, the same doeth the Son likewise," John v. 19. The Father created the universe. The Son "laid the foundation of the earth, and the heavens are the works of his hands," Heb. i. 10. "All things were made by him, and without him was not anything made that was made," John i. 3. The Father preserves the world by his providence; the Son sustains all things by the word of his power. The Father has set up the princes and magistrates who govern mankind; and there is no power but of him. It is by the Son that "kings reign and princes decree justice," Prov. viii. 15. The Father saved and redeemed the church; the Son is our righteousness, our wisdom, and our redemption. The Father loved us, and delivered up his Son to death for us; the Son gave himself a ransom for our sins. If the Father raised up the Son, the Son also raised again his own temple when the fury of the Jews had beaten it down. If the Father quickens the dead, the Son also quickens them; and the last judgment, the punishing of the wicked in hell, the glory of the faithful in heaven, and all that refers to it, is the work of the one and the other. The Father hath elected us; so likewise hath the Son. "I know," he says, "whom I have chosen," John xiii. 18.

It is the same in all the other operations of the divine nature. If you accurately read the Scriptures, you will not see any of them attributed to the Father which are not likewise attributed to the Son. And as for that right and sovereign authority over all things which accrues to God from these great and high qualities and operations, this glory shines in the person of the Son as it does in the person of the Father. If the Father is Judge of the earth, King of ages, and Monarch of the world, the Son is, in like manner, the Lord of glory, the Commander of the armies of heaven, the Prince of men and angels, the Judge of all flesh. If the name of the Father is great and awful, that of the Son is above every name which is named in this world or in the world to come. If all creatures, both superior, intermedial, and inferior, owe sovereign homage to the Father, and cast down themselves before him, adoring his majesty with the profoundest reverence of which they are capable; so it is clear that before Jesus every knee bows, both of things in heaven, and things on earth, and things under the earth, the Father himself proclaiming when he bringeth him into the world, "Let all the angels of God worship him," Heb. i. 6.

So you see, dear brethren, that the Lord Jesus is truly the image of his Father, as he has, and perfectly displays in himself, the nature, the properties, and the works of the Father; an admirable, a singular, and a truly divine image, which possesses the whole form of its original, without any variation, and faithfully and naturally represents all the features of it in their true and just greatness, measure and nature. I confess that among men there are sons who resemble, in some degree, their fathers; but there are none in whom such resemblance is comparable with that of the Son of God to his eternal Father. If our sons express our nature and manners, it is always with some difference, which a penetrating eye may easily observe; and after all there are none who in their life entirely express the lives of their fathers, with every one of their actions and operations. But the Son of God is a most perfect image both of the nature and the life of his Father, (if we may speak in this manner of these mysteries,) all the works of the one, whether small or great, being also the works of the other.

This sacred truth here taught by the apostle overthrows two heresies, which, though contrary to each other, were at one time equally afflicting to the church of God. I mean, that of the Sabellians, and that of the Arians. The former confounded the Son with the Father, the latter rent them asunder. Those took from the Son his person; these his nature. For the Sabellians dogmatically insisted that the Father and the Son were but one and the self-same person, who according to the various ways and designs of his manifestations assumed sometimes the name of Father, sometimes the name of Son. So that in their account it is the Father who suffered on the cross, and it is the Son who sent him that suffered. Paul demolishes their error, by saying that Jesus Christ is the image of the Father. For no one is the image of himself; and however great and exact the resemblance of the image may be to its original, it has of necessity a subsistence distinct from that of its original. A son has the same nature with the father whose image he is said to be; but nevertheless the person of the father is one, and that of the child another. Since then the apostle declares here and elsewhere, that Jesus Christ is "the image of God," (that is to say, of the Father,) we must either desert his doctrine, or acknowledge that Jesus Christ is another person than the Father. But if you distinguish their persons, it follows not that you must divide their nature, as did the Arians, who made it their position, that the nature of the Father is of one kind, and that of the Son of another; the one uncreated and infinite, the other created and finite. These are two shores which we must equally avoid, steering our course straight between them; shunning on one side the confusion of Sabellius, and on the other the division of Arius. Jesus Christ, saith the apostle, is the image of God his Father. He could not be his image, if he were one and the same person with him. He could not be his perfect image, if he had a nature different from the nature of the Father. How could he represent his eternity, if he had been created in time? how his immensity, if he had a limited essence? how his majesty and glory, if he were but a creature? Let us then hold fast this truth full and entire; and believing that the Son of God is a person distinct from that of the Father, let us acknowledge that his divine nature is the same with that of the Father; that is to say, that he is one only and the same God with him, blessed for ever; as without this the doctrine of the apostle, that Jesus Christ is "the image of God," cannot be fully and firmly established.

But let us now consider how and why he here declares God the Father, whose image Jesus Christ is, to be "invisible." Truly the divine nature is spiritual, as our Lord said to the woman of Samaria, "God is a Spirit," and every spiritual nature is invisible; it being clear that the eye sees no objects but such as are corporeal, such as have some figure and colour, and cast forth from them some kind of species into the air, and into other diaphanous and transparent bodies, through which they gliding with incredible swiftness, come to strike our senses; things which have none of them any place in spiritual and immaterial substances. For this cause Moses, when he would teach the Israelites that there is nothing gross or material in the divine essence, nothing that might be represented by the pencil or the chisel in visible images, expressly remonstrates to them, that on the day the Most High manifested himself, giving them the law upon Mount Sinai, they "heard the voice of words, but saw no similitude," Deut. iv. 12, 15, &c. Whence he infers that they should take good heed to make no graven image, or the likeness of any kind of thing; no image of any form whatever for a religious use, as a representation of God; as the nations then did, and almost all do to this day. This truth is clear and undoubted, nor was it ever contested but by the Anthropomorphites, who attributed to God a human body and members; an extravagance long since condemned and abolished in all Christendom.

But the apostle here styling God invisible, intends not only that neither our eyes nor our other senses can apprehend the form of his nature, but that our very understandings cannot comprehend it, and that it is hidden from all our conceptions. For it is usual in Scripture to put seeing for knowing, and to express the apprehensions and conceptions of the mind by the names of the senses of the body. And on this principle we understand what the apostle says elsewhere, that God, the King of ages, is invisible; and in another place, that he dwelleth in inaccessible light, and that "no man hath seen or can see him," 1 Tim. vi. 16. The angels themselves, however superior their understanding is to ours, cannot comprehend the true form and nature of this supreme and most glorious majesty, because his essence is infinite, and no finite being can comprehend an infinite being. And therefore the seraphim, in Isaiah, standing before God, covered their faces with two of their wings, to testify that they could not bear the splendour of his glory, Isa. vi. 2. I grant that, through his grace, we know something of his nature; and this the Scripture means, when it says of Moses and other believers, that they saw God in proportion to the various degrees of knowledge which he gave them of himself; of which the highest degrees will be those which we shall attain in the kingdom of heaven; and the Holy Ghost, to express this to us, says that we shall see God as he is, that we shall see him face to face, and know him as we are known, 1 John iii. 2; 1 Cor. xiii. 12. But however fair, and clear, and excellent all this knowledge of God which believers and holy angels have in this world or the other, it is not, to speak strictly, a seeing; that is, an apprehension which reaches and conceives the true and proper form of its object; so that this remains still firm, that God, to speak properly, is invisible.

But why does the apostle ascribe this quality to God the Father, particularly in this place? Dear brethren, he does so with great propriety, and thereby shows us how it is that God has manifested himself to us by Jesus Christ his Son. For there is a secret opposition between the word image and invisible. God is invisible, says the apostle, but Jesus Christ is the image of him. This eternal Father has a nature so sublime, and so impenetrable by any of our senses, that without this his image, which shines forth in his Son, neither men nor angels would have known aught of him; he would have remained eternally veiled in that inaccessible light in which he dwells, without being known by any but himself. But now he has vouchsafed to manifest to us that which may be known of him by this eternal and most perfect image of his person, that is to say, by his Son. For first, it is by him he made the world, the theatre of his wonders. And it is by him also he preserves and governs it in so admirable a manner. It is to him likewise that we must refer the revelations of God under the Old Testament. It is the Son, as most of the ancient teachers of the church have very well observed, that appeared to Abraham and the other patriarchs; that led Israel through the wilderness, and inspired their prophets. But the apostle, in this passage, has respect particularly and properly to the manifestation of God in the fulness of time, when his eternal and essential image discovered all his glory to the Jews first, and afterwards to the other nations of the world, rendering it, invisible as it was in itself, visible in that flesh with which he vested himself in the blessed virgin's womb. It was then properly that the Son appeared before our eyes, as he is in reality from all eternity, the image of the invisible God, the brightness of his glory, and the engraven character or express image of his person. For the office of an image is to represent that of which it is the figure. Now it was principally in this last manifestation that the Son made us see all the wonders of his Father, the abysses of his justice and of his mercy, the depths of his wisdom and his infinite power, of which the world knew not before. The creatures of this universe show us only the edges, as it were, and the footsteps, and the stronger lineaments of them; Jesus Christ has unfolded them all to our view in their very nature. The world, and even the law itself, were but imperfect draughts and obscure shadows; Jesus Christ is that living image, in which the majesty, the nature, and the goodness of God appear with all their fulness.

II. But it is time now to come to the second point, in which the apostle, having compared Jesus Christ with God his Father, of whom he is the image, considers him with respect to the creatures, and expresses the relation he has to them, by saying that he "is the first-born of every creature." This passage has variously exercised the heretics. Those of them who deny that the Son of God subsisted at all before he was born of the holy virgin, perceiving that these words place him before all the creatures, to support their error, corrupt the word creature, and insist that in this place it signifies the faithful, who believed the gospel of our Lord. Wretched unbelief; to what extravagancies dost thou lead miserable men! For what delirium can produce anything less substantial and more suspicious than this exposition? First, it renders the apostle's conception frigid and absurd. If you believe these people, the apostle informs the Colossians that Jesus Christ was born before men believed what he preached; is not this a great secret, and highly conducive to the apostle's design? Then again, who gave them the authority which they claim to change the sense of the words of God? Paul says that the Lord "is the first-born of every creature." By what right do they restrain a subject of such vast extent to the faithful alone? The faithful, say they, are created anew of the Lord! Who doubts it? Paul teaches us that they are the "workmanship of God, created in Christ Jesus unto good works," Eph. ii. 20; and elsewhere, that "if any one be in Christ, he is a new creature." But it follows not thence that the word creature, without any adjunct, must be taken merely for the disciples of Jesus Christ and his apostles. The Scripture never uses the term in that sense. As for the eighth chapter of the Epistle to the Romans, where they pretend that the apostle means the faithful alone by all the creatures which "groan and travail in pain together," ver. 22, this is a new dream, no less absurd than the former; it being clear by all the circumstances of the passage, that the creatures there mentioned are not the children of God but of another kind. Paul plainly distinguishes them, saying of those, that they "also shall be delivered from the bondage of corruption into the glorious liberty of the children of God: and that not only they, but we also, (that is, all the faithful,) who have the first fruits of the Spirit, groan within ourselves," ver. 21, 23. All those creatures are no other than the universe, the heavens and the elements, which shall one day be set free from the vanity under which they now groan, and to which they were made subject by sin. That which they allege out of the third of the Revelation, is in no degree more to the purpose; Jesus Christ styles himself there, the beginning or principal of the creature or creation of God, ver. 14. But nothing obliges us to take the creature of God in this place for the faithful alone, any more than in the other. The Lord means all the things which God has created, either in the first or in the second world, he being the principal of the one and of the other, according to what he had said in the same book generally and indefinitely, "I am Alpha and Omega, the first and the last," Rev. i. 8. Besides, though the creature of God should signify the faithful in this place, we are not to infer that the words "every creature" here must be taken for the faithful alone; as when the Scripture calls them men of God, it follows not thence that when we mean the faithful alone we must say all men. The term, "of God," is put there for an adjective epithet, as grammarians speak, according to the use of the holy tongue; the creature of God, that is, a divine and celestial creature; a quality which evidently restrains the sense of the word creature, to which it is annexed, to the most excellent kind of creatures, that is, the faithful. Whereas Paul says here simply, "every creature," without adding, "of God," or "divine" or any other word that might contract the signification of the general term creature to merely one of its species, that is, the faithful. Rejecting therefore the gloss of these critics as impertinent, and contrary both to the scope and style of the apostle, we say that by "every creature" he intends what the Scripture and all the languages of men ordinarily intend by these words, namely, created things, "the heavens and the earth, and all that in them is."

But here rise up the Arians, another kind of heretics, who, insisting upon this interpretation, infer that the Son of God is a creature, as he is called the first-born of them; alleging that the first-born is of the same nature with his brethren; and adding, to fortify their pretension, that in fact, the supreme Wisdom, which is no other than the Son, says in the Proverbs, that God possessed or created it "in the beginning of his ways, before his works of old," Prov. viii. 22; which is nothing else, as they affirm, but what Paul says here, that the Son is the first-born of every creature; and they adjoin also that which is said in the Epistle to the Hebrews, that Jesus Christ is faithful to him who appointed or made him, Heb. iii. 2; that is, as they pretend, to God, who created him. But God forbid that we should rank him with creatures, to whom the Scripture ascribes the glory of having created them all, and to whom it commands us to give that supreme adoration which is due to God alone, and not to any creature. The apostle, in this very place which they abuse, makes a most evident distinction between the Son and other things; for whereas he calls them creatures, he says of the Son that he is, not the *first-created*, (as should have been said, if he were of their order,) but the *first-born;* an evident sign that he received his beginning of the Father by a divine and ineffable generation, and not by creation. As for that which they cite out of the Proverbs, not to urge another exposition of it, the original text imports that God possessed wisdom in the beginning of his ways, (as our Bibles have well rendered it,) and not that he created it, as the Greek interpreters have improperly taken it. And as to what Paul says in the Epistle to the Hebrews, that God made Christ, he means not that he created him, (a notion which would be quite beside his purpose,) but that he ordained and established him High Priest in his church. Even as when Samuel says that God appointed or made Moses and Aaron, 1 Sam. xii. 6, he intends that he established them in the charges which they bore among his people. And in this sense we must understand Peter's language in the Acts, "that God hath made Jesus both Lord and Christ," Acts ii. 36; that is, has ordained him to these great dignities. And so from these passages it strictly follows that the Son of God was called the Anointed, and settled in his office of Mediator, (which we confess,) but not that his divine nature was created (which we utterly deny.) In fine, for these words of Paul, some answer that by saying Jesus Christ "is the first-born of every creature," he means no more than that he was born before all creatures; and perhaps it would be very difficult, that I may not say impossible, to refute this exposition.

Yet there is another which I judge more suitable both to the scope and to the sequel of this text: it is that by the "first-born" is meant the Owner, the Lord, and the Prince of every creature. That which the apostle adds, "for by him were created all things in heaven and in earth," perfectly accords with this sense; it being evident that the creation of things is a true and solid title to that power and lordship which God has over them. Why is the Son of God the Lord of every creature? Because there is not any of them which he did not create; and it is most reasonable that he should dispose of them and govern them at his pleasure, since he gave them all the being or life that they have. And that the word "first-born" may be taken to signify master and lord, is evident both by examples in

Scripture, and by the reason of the thing itself. For the Lord promises in the Psalms to make David the first-born of the kings of the earth, Psal. lxxxix. 27; that is, as every one sees, to make him master and the chief of kings; it being evident that, to speak properly, he was not their elder brother, being neither the brother to other kings, nor more aged than they. Isaiah says also in his prophecy, chap. xiv. 30, "the first-born of the poor," to signify the veriest poor, those that (if I may so say) carry away the prize for poverty, though otherwise they were not born before others, nor of the same family with them. But the passage in Job is more remarkable than any other, where mention is of "the first-born of death," Job xviii. 13. He is meant who has the power and the administration of death, the Angel and Prince of death, and (as the Epistle to the Hebrews speaks) "he that hath the power of death." The reason of this manner of speaking is also perfectly evident. For the eldest born, by the law and custom of most nations, formerly were, and to this day are, the principal of the family, the heads, and in a manner lords, as well of their brethren as of the slaves and goods; hence originated this kind of language, putting eldest or first-born, to signify the head, the lord, and the master. We say, therefore, that it is in this sense we must understand the apostle's words, Christ "is the first-born of every creature," that is, the Master and Lord of them; which no way implies that he himself is a creature; lords not being always of the same extraction and lineage with their subjects, but most frequently of another very different. And as it would be ridiculous reasoning to conclude that he who has the dominion of death is death itself, under the colour that Job terms him, "the first-born of death;" so is it most impertinent arguing to infer that the Lord is a creature, because the apostle says here, that he "is the first-born of every creature." We have a passage exactly parallel with this in the beginning of the Epistle to the Hebrews, where the apostle says that God has appointed his Son "heir of all things, by whom also he made the worlds," chap. i. 2. Here you see, first, that he expresses the Lordship which Jesus Christ has over all the creatures, by a figurative word, styling him the heir of them. For that the word heir was taken by the ancients to mean lord and master, the civilians themselves have observed.* And, secondly, you see further, that the apostle, after the same manner as in the text, founds the dominion which Jesus Christ has over the whole universe upon his being the Creator of it. For this he means when he says that "by him God made the worlds." Be it then concluded that this primogeniture of the Lord Jesus over every creature is nothing

* Instit. l. 2, tit. 19, s. ult.

else but that glorious and sovereign empire which he has over the whole world, and every one of its parts, by the right of creation; being its supreme and absolute Lord, as he that brought all creatures out of nothing, and gave them every degree of that being which they possess.

Thus, dear brethren, we have given you the exposition of this text. Let us profit by it and extract the practical uses that it contains, and the succour it may give us against sin and error.

First, it furnishes us with an answer to those who censure us for having no images among us. Tell them that Jesus Christ, the only most perfect image of God, suffices us. This is an image that we safely honour without fear of offending God, because it is a true one, and shows us to the life, and in reality, all the perfections of the Father; while all other images offered to us are the work of men's hands, inventions of their superstition, and images, not of God, but of their own vain imaginations. Even their visibility discovers their falsity, as God is invisible. For to represent an invisible nature by colours, is much worse than if you should paint anything white with charcoal, or light with darkness. Your images, O adversaries, are dead and insensible, destitute of the advantages which nature has given to the least and lowest animals. Ours is alive and intelligent, the source of life and wisdom. Yours are incapable of seeing or rewarding the service which you do them. Ours knows our hearts, and has infinite goodness and power. For Jesus, the image of God, whom we adore, "is the first-born of every creature," the sovereign Master of the universe. Let us boldly address our most religious services to him. And since it is in him that God manifests himself to us, let us have him ever before our eyes, seeking the true knowledge of God in him alone. There we shall see him as he is.

But let this seeing by no means be idle: he does not set before us this most perfect picture of his perfections, which he has drawn to the life in his Christ, that we may unprofitably gaze on it; but that each of us may imitate him according to his small ability, and express in his soul a draught of that perfect goodness and holiness which shines so gloriously in him, and gradually become an exact and lively image of our Lord. Consider, how he was obedient to the Father, bountiful to men, helpful to the afflicted, compassionate to sinners, mild and kind to enemies. There, christian, is the pattern of your life. Follow these sacred examples. Serve God, like him, patiently bearing all that he lays on you, courageously marching on all occasions wherever he calls you. Love men as he loved them, cheerfully employing all that you are and all you can do for their edification; communicating your goods to the poor, your light to the ignorant, your assistance to the oppressed. Let not their malevolence obstruct your kindness. If they offend you, pardon them, and pray for them; and remember, as the Lord said, that they know not what they do. Let neither their injuries nor their caresses ever turn you from a pious course.

Fear neither the hatred nor the forces of the world. Remember that as this Jesus whom you serve is "the image of God," so he is likewise "the first-born of every creature." He has them all in his hand. He commands the heavens and the elements; he governs men and beasts. All the parts of nature owe him and render him a prompt obedience, and, will they nill they, do nothing against his orders. Having the Master of all things for your Head and Saviour, how is it that you are not ashamed of your timidity? The wind makes us tremble as the leaves of the wood. The least sound affrights us; and instead of glorifying the Lord here in his palace, in peace and joy, while his voice makes the world tremble, we tremble while the world is in repose. Is it this that we promised Jesus Christ? Is this to bear his cross with patience, and resist for his sake even unto blood? Is this that lively and unmovable faith of which we make profession, which should carry us unappalled through waters and through flames? If the providence of the Lord were unknown to us, our weakness would be less inexcusable; but having lived for so long a time by continual miracles of his goodness, why doubt we so readily of a care and fidelity which we have so many a time experienced? You see, on the present conjuncture, what thoughts he has inspired on our behalf into the sacred powers that govern us, and even the supreme among them; what order they have taken for our safety; and what care they declare themselves resolved to take of it for the future, receiving us under the protection of their edicts. Dear brethren, it is an admirable effect of the love with which the Lord regards us. Let us enjoy it with perfect thankfulness both towards him and towards his ministers, the princes of whom he is the first-born in a particular manner. Let us not disturb the work of his grace by our fears and diffidences, but, assured of his infinite goodness and power, let us rely upon the truth of his promises, and rest upon his favourable providence, quietly and comfortably finishing this short journey which we have begun; waiting till this holy and merciful Lord, after having conducted and comforted us in this desert, shall raise us up on high to the mountain of his holiness; where, far from evils, and from dangers, and from fears, we shall glorify him eternally, with the Father and the Holy Spirit, the true and only God, blessed for ever. Amen.

SERMON VIII.

VERSES 16, 17.

For by him were all things created, that are in heaven, and that are in earth, visible and invisible, whether they be thrones, or dominions, or principalities, or powers: all things were created by him, and for him: and he is before all things, and by him all things consist.

AMONG all the reasons which establish our right to the things that we possess, none is more just or more natural than that which arises from the production of them; it being evident that what issues from us should depend upon us, and that it is just every one should dispose of what he has made. Thus among all the nations of the earth children belong to the parents that begat them, and works either of the mind or body are theirs who formed them and set them forth. This right is the first and the most ancient foundation of all human possessions and dominions; the power which men have to give, to sell, or exchange things proceeding from this, that they, or those of whom they received them, gave them, or preserved their existence. For if you go back to the first sources of human laws and institutions, you will find that men assumed not dominion or possession, save of the persons whom they had either naturally begotten, or saved in war, by preserving and giving the life they might have taken from them; and of things which they had either made and composed, as buildings, or at least improved and cultivated, as the ground they cleared and tilled. It is from thence that were formed, by little and little, those good and just establishments of families, of cities, and of states, and of laws necessary for their government, which have maintained mankind to this present time. You see likewise that God our sovereign Lord, to justify the right he has to dispose of us as seemeth him good, and the obligation we have to serve him, ordinarily urges this reason, that he has created us. "It is he that hath made us," saith his prophet, "and not we ourselves; we are his people, and the sheep of his pasture," Psalm c. 3. By the same consideration he silences the refractory and profane, who have the insolence to censure his disposals: "Shall the thing formed say to him that formed it, Why hast thou made me thus? Hath not the potter power over the clay, of the same lump to make one vessel unto honour, and another unto dishonour?" Romans ix. 20, 21.

It is further by the same reason, my brethren, the apostle

proves in this place that Jesus Christ, the Son of God, is the Lord of all things. Having said that he is "the first-born (that is, the Master) of every creature," he now alleges the proof of it, taken from his being the Creator of all things. "For by him," says he, "were all things created, that are in heaven, and that are in earth, visible and invisible, whether they be thrones, or dominions, or principalities, or powers: all things were created by him, and for him: and he is before all things, and by him all things consist." This reason is evident and invincible. For if man, who gives to the things he makes only the form of their being, working in all his operations on borrowed matter, does yet acquire thereby a right of dominion over them, as we said even now, so that he may dispose of them as he will, how much more justly is the Son of God the Master and Lord of all the creatures, as he created them, that is, gave them the whole of their being; not the form only, but the matter also of which they consist; having brought them out of nothing, having entirely made and formed them by the sole might of his power, without any subject for his displaying it upon, existent when he first created them! And this proof clearly determines that which we laid down in the preceding sermon; that is, that when the apostle calls Jesus Christ the "first-born of every creature," he means simply that he is the Master of them, and not (as heretics assert) that he is a creature as they are, and only created before them. For the reason which Paul annexes, taken from his having created them, fully evinces that he is Master of them, but not that he was created himself. Otherwise, it must, from the same premises, be inferred that the Father, who created all things, was also created himself; a blasphemy which the most shameless heretics would abhor. For if the apostle's discourse is good and pertinent, (as all christians confess,) he reasons thus: Whoever has created all things, the same is "the first-born of every creature;" but the Lord Jesus has created all things, he is therefore "the first-born of every creature." You see clearly that this first proposition, Whoever has created all things is "the first-born of every creature," cannot be true except in this sense, that he is the master of every creature; but it is evidently false in the sense that the heretics take of the words "first-born of every creature," that is, created before every other creature; for the Father, who created all things, is eternal and immutable, and was not created. It must, therefore, of necessity be said that the apostle, by "the first-born of every creature," means their Lord and Master. Otherwise his discourse would not be pertinent.

But having in our last discourse sufficiently explained and justified this conclusion of Paul, that the Son of God is "the first-born of every creature," let us consider now the reason he alleges, drawn from hence, viz: that he created all things, and that they are all for him, and all subsist by him; that is to say, he is the Author, the End, and the Conserver of them. It is a truth of infinite importance in the christian religion, both of itself and for its own merit, as also for the great contradictions it has suffered at all times from the enemies of the divinity of Jesus Christ, both ancient and modern, who have applied all their force either to overthrow, or at least to shake it. For this cause we are obliged to examine the present text, where it is so majestically stated, with so much the more care; and that we may omit nothing which is necessary for clearing it, we will consider, in the first place, what the apostle says of the Son of God; that "all things were created by him, and for him;" and that "he is before all things," and that they "all consist by him." In the second place, the division that he makes of all these things which the Lord created; some, they "that are in heaven," others, they "that are in earth;" some, "visible," others, "invisible," as "thrones, dominions, principalities, and powers." These shall be, if the Lord will, the two parts, and, as it were, the two articles, of this discourse. May it please God to guide our meditations by his Spirit on this sublime subject, and to enable us by his grace to aim at his glory and our own edification.

I. In the former of these two articles the apostle says, first, that all things were created by Jesus Christ; secondly, that they were all created for him; in the third place, that he is before all things; and lastly, that they all consist by him. For though these four points nearly resemble each other, and are necessarily combined, yet they are actually distinct, and ought to come severally under consideration; there being none of them but contributes something particular to the glory of our great God and Saviour Jesus Christ.

The first is plain, that all things were created by Jesus Christ. For where is the christian who understands not this, and knows not that to create signifies, in the use of Scripture, to make a thing, either of nothing, or of a matter which had no disposedness to the form that it receives? And as there is no power but the divine that is capable of such an action or operation, this word is never attributed to any but God only. No one but he creates things. For this cause, among the other titles which are given him for marks of his glory, he is styled, The Creator, this title pertaining to him alone. When the apostle then says here, and twice repeats it, that all things were created by the Son, he means that from him they received all the being they have; that it is he who by this noble and divine manner of working, which the Scripture calls creation, brought them from non-being into being, who, by his infinite power, produced the matter of which they consist, prepared it and fitted it as it now is, investing it with those forms and admirable qualities on which all the motions of their nature depend; that is to say, in one word, the Lord Jesus is the Creator of the universe.

It was not possible to express more clearly this truth. And in this sense all christians always received this passage, till those new enemies of the divinity of our Lord appeared, who blasphemously say that he had no actual subsistence in the universe prior to his birth of the holy virgin. Unable to bear so resplendent a light, they have endeavoured to obscure it by the fumes of their frivolous and false glosses, and say therefore that the word create signifies in this place merely to reform and re-establish things, to put them in a better state than they were in, and not to bring them out of nothing, and give them their whole being. They insist that the apostle, by saying all things were created by Jesus, intends not the first creation of the world, when arising out of nothing it received its natural being and form from the Creator; but the renovation of the world, wrought by the preaching of the gospel, and by the word of the apostles, whom the Lord sent to reform the nations, and to put things in an incomparably better and happier state than they were before. Enslaved they were to the empire of sin and Satan, but by the doctrine and power of the Lord Jesus they have now been consecrated to God and sanctified to his glory. To this I answer, that it is true the world was renewed by the gospel; inasmuch as this holy doctrine abolished the ceremonial discipline of Moses, and the false religions of the heathen, and formed in the whole earth a new people serving God in spirit and in truth, being created in righteousness and holiness. I acknowledge also that this renovation is the work of divine power, and could not have been effected by any human or angelic strength, and on this account it may and ought to be called a creation; it being certain that no less virtue was needful to reform the world than to create it. And, finally, I grant too that Jesus, the Son of God, is the true and sole author of this second creation.

But to this I adjoin two things: first, that though this passage might be understood of this reformation of the world, yet it would of necessity infer that Jesus, to whom it is attributed, is the true eternal God. For as this work is no less, nay, as it is greater, than that of creation, it is evident that none but the true God could be the author of it, for creation is proposed to us in Scripture (a point to which we shall have to return) as an argument of true and eternal divinity. And the thing speaks for itself. For as a divine and infinite power is requisite to regenerate men and destroy the servitude of sin and Satan, it must of necessity be acknowledged that Jesus, the author of this great work, has an infinite power, that is to say, is truly

God; no finite subject being capable of an infinite power, and none being infinite but God alone. Thus you see that these heretics toil in vain; their own interpretation (if it were admitted) necessarily establishes the thing which they oppose; namely, that Jesus is very God, infinite and eternal, and subsisting before all ages. But I say, in the second place, that this text cannot be understood of the reparation or second creation of the world: first, because the apostle will soon speak of that in the three verses immediately following; where he sublimely describes it, saying that Jesus Christ "is the Head of the body, the church; the Beginning, the First-born from the dead;" by whom the Father has reconciled all things unto himself, as well celestial as terrestrial, "having made peace through the blood of his cross." Now unless we render Paul guilty of vain babbling and useless repetition, we must confess that as in this second place he speaks of the reparation and renovation of things, so in the former he spake of their first creation. Secondly, this is further evident from his expressly reckoning the angels among the things created by Jesus Christ; yea, he insists on them more than on the rest, (as we shall see hereafter,) saying that "by him were created things in heaven, thrones, dominions, principalities, and powers." But the angels were not renewed nor restored by Jesus Christ, for sin did not ruin their nature, nor make it wax old, nor subject it to vanity. We must therefore conclude that the apostle speaks here not of the reparation of things, but of the first creation of them; it being most certain that the angels are created beings, their nature yet being not eternal and without beginning. I grant, that by the salvation which we have received from Jesus Christ the angels have been reunited to us, and settled again in peace and amity with us, from whom our sin had separated and estranged them; and this is what the apostle means when he says here beneath, that God has reconciled things in heaven and things in earth by the blood of Jesus Christ, ver. 20; and elsewhere, that he has recapitulated or gathered "together in one all things in Christ, both which are in heaven, and which are on earth," Eph. i. 10. But this is not to be called a creating of the angels, nor can any example of such extravagant language be produced, that a creating of persons was employed to signify a reconciling them to those whom they hated, and whose communion they avoided; otherwise, as Jesus Christ reconciled us also to God the Father, incorporating us into his family, so as he is thereby become our Father, and we his children, in the same manner that we are brethren with the angels; it might, to express this, be also said that Jesus Christ created God the Father, which no ear, I say not christian, but that is ever so little rational, could possibly endure. Finally, the context itself of the apostle's words evidently shows that they must be necessarily understood of the first, and not of the second, creation of things. I confess the Holy Ghost sometimes uses the word create to signify the production of the second work of God, that is, the work of his grace in Jesus Christ. But he never does this without some addition and restriction, that evidently limits the word to such a sense; as, for example, when he says in Isaiah that he is about to "create new heavens and a new earth;" and that he is about to create Jerusalem to be a joy, and her people gladness, Isa. lxv. 17, 18; the very form of this language, put in the future tense, as you see, and those new heavens and that Jerusalem, which he says he is about to create, evidently showed that he is not speaking of the first creation of the world. So when the apostle says that God has created them twain (that is, the Jews and the Gentiles) in himself into one new man, Eph. ii. 15; this latter word, "new," admits no doubt that he means here the second operation of God, by which Jews and Gentiles were united into one people; and not of the first, by which they were brought into their natural existence. And likewise, when he says in the same chapter, that "we are created in Jesus Christ unto good works, which God hath before ordained that we should walk in them." The persons of whom he speaks, *us*, that is, believers, distinguished from other men; and the end of this work of God, good works; these sufficiently prove that the creation there meant is the second, and not the first, nor can any reasonable man doubt it. In these places, and others like them, if there are any, the word create is still limited and circumstantiated. When it is used simply and absolutely, it is to be taken only for the first creation, as when Isaiah says that "God created the heavens," Isa. xlii. 5; and John, in the Revelation, that the "Lord created all things," Rev. iv. 11; and in a multitude of similar places; neither can any one be adduced to the contrary. For as to that which the adversaries allege out of the Epistle to the Ephesians, where they insist that the apostle's words, "God created all things by Jesus Christ," Eph. iii. 9, must be expounded of the second, and not the first creation; in this they do not prove, but take for granted, the thing mooted; nothing obliging us to depart in this place, more than in the others, from the common signification of the word.

As then in our text this term create is used simply and indefinitely, without any limitation or restriction, the apostle saying and twice repeating that all things were created by the Son of God, nay, adding, to show more fully the extent of this subject, "both things which are in heaven, and things which are in earth, visible and invisible, thrones, dominions, principalities, and powers," we conclude that the word means, as in other places where it is employed in the same manner, simply and absolutely, that is to say, it must be taken for the first, and not the second creation. If we are at liberty to do otherwise, and to give it anywhere the sense we please, with no other reason than that of our caprice, who sees not but that by such an opening there would no longer be anything fixed or certain left in Scripture? For as these heretics, by this frivolous gloss, would deprive the Lord Jesus of the glory of the first creation; another might, by the same expedient, wrest it from the Father; interpreting those passages of Scripture which affirm that God created the world, not of its first production, by which it issued out of nothing into being, but merely of a reparation, or a renovation of the universe; and in consequence hereof pretend, with some philosophers, that it was assuredly created long before, but not in the condition and the form it afterwards obtained.

But God forbid that christians should ever suffer impiety to have such a power over the word of God. Let us sacredly keep to the truths which the Scriptures teach us, and receive their language with a candid and sincere belief. Let heresy rise in commotion, and be as restless as it will, as the apostle, the mouth of heaven and the trumpet of God, proclaims that all things were created by the Lord Jesus, let us receive this sacred verity; believe it and confess it so much the more, because not only here does Scripture teach us this, but in numerous other places. For, not to repeat what has been already advanced out of the Epistle to the Ephesians, where it is said that the Father "created all things by Jesus Christ," what can be more explicit than the beginning of John, where this divine author, speaking of the Word which was made flesh, and whose glory he and his fellow brethren had seen, and who was in the beginning with God, proclaims, "All things were made by him, and without him was not anything made that was made. And the world was made by him," John i. 3, 10. What more can be uttered or conceived than what we read in the Epistle to the Hebrews, where the apostle, not satisfied with having said at the entrance that the Father made the worlds by his Son, says of the Son a little after, what the prophet sings, "Thou, Lord, in the beginning hast laid the foundation of the earth; and the heavens are the works of thine hands," Heb. i. 10. Certainly this proof is so firm that all the devils of hell will never be able to pluck it from us. And nothing more gross can be imagined than that evasion with which despair has here inspired the heretics: Though, say they, the apostle has alleged these words of the Psalm, yet his intention was not to apply them to Christ, but the following words only, "Thou remainest, and art the same, and thy years shall not fail:" for is not this a plain contradiction of the apostle, who loudly affirms that it is to the Son the Holy Spirit says, "Lord, in the beginning thou hast laid the foundations of the earth?" Besides, if this quotation from the Psalm decides nothing more than that the Son is permanent, and shall not fail, it is inapplicable, and does not at all suffice for the apostle's design. For his aim is to exalt the Son above the angels; but if the passage he brings for this purpose proves only that the Son is immortal and immutable, who sees not that by this procedure he attributes no more to him than what is equally true of the angels, whose nature is likewise incorruptible and immutable?

As then the scope of the apostle is to show that Jesus Christ has excellences which do not belong to the angels; and as, on the contrary, the passage he alleges expresses nothing of that kind, but the creating of the world; it must of necessity be acknowledged that it is the holy apostle's intention to apply particularly to the Lord this first part of the quotation, wherein it is said that he has founded the earth, and that the heavens are the work of his hands. And so you see that the supreme Wisdom, begotten of the Father before all ages, which neither is nor can be any other than the Lord Jesus, protests in the book of Proverbs, chap. viii., that it was with God, its eternal Father, when he created the world, to show us that it was the Governor and Superintendent of that great work. And Moses, in the beginning of Genesis, expresses the same thing, as far as the nature of the time and of the old testament would permit. For he states that God did not create anything but by his word. He represents him as speaking at every part of his work; "God said, Let there be light. God said, Let there be a firmament. God said, Let the waters be divided, and let the dry land appear;" and so in all the rest. Why does so sage a writer make this supreme and unspeakable nature speak thus for the creating of each of his works? Let the Jew weary himself to the utmost, he will never be able to give us such a good and pertinent reason of it as can satisfy our minds. But John calling the Son of God the Word, chap. i. 1, unveils this secret to us, showing us that it is by this his Word that the Father created the world. And Moses, obscurely intimating this, and in a manner accordant with that time, represents God as not creating anything except by speaking. It must then be concluded, against the obstinate fury of heretics, that the Lord Jesus is the Creator of all things.

And this is so evident, that a majority of those very men who deny his eternal divinity have not refused to acknowledge it; and they in particular who, after the name of their old leader, are commonly called Arians, who, while they admit that by him the Father created the universe at the beginning, yet pertinaciously deny that he is eternal God, of the same essence with the Father. In this, as I confess, they show more modesty than the rest, not having the forehead to reject what the Scripture so clearly exhibits; at the same time I must say they discover less common sense and acuteness, admitting a truth incompatible with their own error. For if the Lord Jesus created the universe, as they, in concurrence with the Scripture, confess, it must of necessity be granted that he is very Jehovah, who in time past was worshipped by the Israelites, which, notwithstanding, is the thing that they oppose.

From what we have observed, it follows, first, that the Scripture never ascribes the creating to any one but God. Secondly, that in Isaiah the title of Creator is given to the true God to distinguish him from creatures, as being incommunicable to any other besides him. It is I, says he, who have made the earth, and who have stretched out the heavens, Isa. xlii. 5; xlv. 12; xlviii. 13; li. 13. Finally, the thing speaks for itself. For the power requisite to create the world (that is, to make it of nothing) is so great and so infinite, that the philosophers, with all the light of their reason, could not comprehend it, but were so far from attributing it to any creature, that they denied it unto God himself. Whence we infer that if there is any part of divine glory proper and essential to God, it is most indubitably this. Seeing then it is found in the Lord Jesus, we must necessarily confess that he is in truth the great God, most high, eternal, and blessed for ever above all things. As for the distinction they advance to cover their error, alleging that the Son was but the instrument and minister of the Father in the work of creation, not the first and principal cause, it is vain and frivolous. For this creative power being infinite, it cannot be but in an infinite subject, and in a sovereign and principal agent. It cannot be communicated to an instrument, for every instrument being finite, is consequently incapable of receiving and containing an infinite power; and as it is in the person of the Son, it unavoidably follows that he is not, as they say, the instrumental, but the first and the principal cause in the work of creation. And this John clearly shows in the Revelation, where he says that he is "Alpha and Omega, the first and the last," Rev. i. 11; a thing that cannot be said of an instrumental cause, which has necessarily another and superior agent of a different nature. The apostle also completely refutes this interpretation, when he appropriates that to Jesus Christ which the prophet evidently uttered of the first, the principal, and sovereign cause of the creation; "Thou, Lord, in the beginning hast laid the foundation of the earth; and the heavens are the works of thine hands;" an application which would be evidently false and incongruous if Jesus Christ were only the instrumental cause of the creation. The observation on which they pretend to ground this distinction is equally futile; I mean, that the Scripture says indeed the world was created by the Son, but not that the Son created the world. For, first, Paul says in express terms that the Son "laid the foundation of the earth;" and though he had not said it, who sees not that the one expression is equivalent to the other, and that his words, "all things were created by the Son," are tantamount to his saying that the Son created all things? But if this form of speech proves that the Son is not the first and principal efficient of the creation, the same must be concluded also of the Father, as Paul, speaking of him, says, in like manner, all things are of him, and by him, and for him.

But, secondly, what he says here of Jesus Christ, "all things were created for him," further demonstrates, and most clearly, the same truth. For these words declare that the Son is the last and supreme end of the creation of things, a matter which pertains only to the principal cause, and not to the instrument it uses for the effecting of its work. It is indisputable that the true God is the ultimate end for which all things were created, that the glory of his divine excellencies might be manifested, so that he might be known and worthily served. This cannot be contested. As therefore it is for the Son that all things were created, it must be acknowledged that he is the true eternal God, as it is not possible that a creature should be the end for which all things were created.

Thence the apostle concludes, in the third place, that Jesus Christ "is before all things." For as he created them all, he must necessarily have existed before they existed. And he expressly notices this, that none might suspect him of novelty, as if he had existed only since Moses, under the plea of his having not been manifested till the fulness of time. He is not only before Moses and Abraham, (as he speaks of himself in John, chap. viii.,) but before all things, from the beginning, before there was any thing created, "before the mountains were settled, and before the hills was I brought forth," as says Wisdom, that is, the Son himself, in the book of Proverbs, chap. viii. 25.

But the apostle, after having thus given to the Lord Jesus the glory of creating all things, proceeds, fourthly, to attribute to him their preservation: "All things consist by him." This he elsewhere expresses in other terms, when he says that he "upholdeth all things by the word of his power," Heb. i. 3; that is, he preserves them by his providence, as he created them by his virtue; their being, their life, and their motion, so depending on him, that when "he hides his face they are troubled," and utterly fail, and return to their dust, or their original nothingness, Psal. civ. 29. Here we have additional proof that he is the true God, the eternal One, blessed for ever with the Father; for this preservation of the universe is one of the highest and most incommunicable glories of the Deity.

II. Let us now consider, in the second place, what are those things whose creation and conservation the apostle attributes to the Son of God: "All things were created by him, that are in heaven, and that are in earth, visible and invisible, whether they be thrones, or dominions, or principalities, or powers." He leaves not any creature, of the highest, or lowest, or intermedial rank, without the reach of his assertion; and for the enclosing of them all within it he makes use, first, of a division taken from their elements, I mean the places where their natural abode is, saying, "things in heaven, and things in earth." The Scripture often speaks of them in the same manner. As when we are forbidden, in the decalogue, to make a religious use of any image, or the likeness of anything whatever: "Thou shalt not make to thyself," says the Lord, "any image, of things that are in heaven above, or in the earth beneath, or in the waters under the earth." By "heaven," he means not only the vast region where we see the sun and the other luminaries; but also paradise, the habitation of angels, and of the souls of men made perfect; and this void space, where the fowls fly, and where are formed the showers, and the thunders, and the other meteors. By "earth," he means this whole globe in which we live, with the waters that ebb and flow. As there is then no creature that is not in one of these two places, he evidently comprises them all by saying the "things that are in heaven, and that are in earth." But he adds yet another division no less general, taken from the quality of the things themselves, which all are either visible, as the heavens, the elements, the plants, and the animals; or invisible, as the devils, and the angels, and the souls of men. And that none might imagine the good angels, by reason of the excellency of their admirable nature, were excepted from this number, the apostle makes the most express mention of them, reflecting on the false teachers thereby, who taught the worshipping of angels, as he will hereafter show. To refute this error, he ranks them by name among the things that were created by Jesus Christ, and that depend on him, and were made for him. For there is no doubt but they are the holy angels whom he here calls "thrones, dominions, principalities, and powers;" and he uses these words so often in this sense as Rom. viii. 38; Eph. i. 21, and elsewhere, that I wonder not a little at some expositors who apply them to another subject. It is very probable that this diversity of names expresses a great diversity among the angels. Indeed, there are no creatures of this kind, in the whole universe, which have not amongst them an admirable variety; that sovereign Wisdom which formed them having pleased to set forth the infinite riches of his power and understanding in the diversity of those ranks, qualities, and functions, by which he has distinguished things which are otherwise of a like, yea, of the same nature. To pass by the rest, who can reckon up the differences of states, of conditions, of temperaments and inclinations, which are observed among men? All of them have the same nature, none have the same form nor the same countenance. Doubtless there is something similar to this among the angels, and in their intellectual world there is some semblance of that variety which renders our visible one so beautiful and so marvellous. To express this diversity of their orders, the apostle uses the names of those degrees which are found in the states and polities of the world: there are "thrones," that is, monarchs and kings; "dominions," that is, dignities, which though very high, yet are beneath kings, as dukes and archdukes; then "principalities," as the governors of cities and provinces; and lastly, "powers," such as inferior magistrates are, whom the Latins, in the apostle's time, called by the very name that we read here, and it is yet in use among the people of Italy.* From this, in my opinion, it may be with reason concluded that there is a diversity of charges and ministries among the angels. If you ask me what are their orders, and how many, and what is the difference between them, and whether it consists in the qualities of their nature, or only in the employments God has given them, I am not ashamed freely to confess to you, with Augustine,† that I cannot tell; the Scripture, which alone could inform us, having declared nothing about it. That which the Roman schools chatter on this matter, of nine orders of the celestial hierarchy, is but the fancyings of a man of too much leisure, who amused himself to fashion it, as skilfully as he could, in imitation of some fond Jewish imaginations of like nature; and, to give them the more weight, set them forth under the holy and venerable name of Dionysius the Areopagite. The impotent frothiness of his tumid style, his quirks, and his vanity, and his whole air, being infinitely far from the gravity, modesty, and simplicity of a scholar of the apostles, sufficiently show that he is anything rather than what he affirms of himself; and indeed, long since, some testimonies urged out of his books by heretics have been rejected by the orthodox as apocryphal and uncertain, and such as were not written by St. Denys at all.‡ Laying aside, therefore, beloved brethren, the empty and vain authorities of human opinion, let us be satisfied with what the apostle has told us on this subject, and diligently seek to profit by his divine instructions.

Let us learn from them, first, to adore the Lord Jesus as Creator of the universe, and to acknowledge by this work of his,

---

* Il podesta. † Enchirid. c. 58.

‡ Concil. tom. 3, p. 855. Ep. Joan. Maroniæ Episc. A. C. 532.

his true and eternal divinity. Let no objection or carnal difficulty, let no heretical subtilty, ever pluck up this sacred truth out of our hearts. Let us oppose the apostle's authority against all that men and devils can say or invent to the contrary. And let us constantly admire the goodness and the wisdom of the Father, who gave us such a Saviour as our necessity required. For none was able to recover us but he who first made us, and the hand alone which created us could restore us to that blessed state whence we had fallen by sin. And as God has given us him for Mediator and Prince of our salvation, whom this great frame had for its Creator, let us embrace him with a firm belief. Let us delight in his fulness, and regard none beside him in heaven or in earth. However sublime their nature and their dignity, the angels, after all, are but creatures; not to speak of men, who, beside the infirmity of their being, were all conceived in sin.

But it is not enough to confess that the Lord Jesus is the Creator of all things, and to acknowledge him for our only Saviour and Mediator; this faith must work and bring forth fruit in us; it must spread itself into all parts of our life, must sanctify our affections and actions, arm us against all the temptations of the enemy, comfort us in affliction, and assure us against every fear. For as Jesus created this grand universe, as thrones and dominions are the work of his hands, as it is by his providence that this all subsists in its present state; who sees not with what devotion we should serve so puissant a Monarch? This earth that bears you, this air that you breathe, these heavens that shine on you, these plants and these animals that nourish or refresh you, and these celestial powers which encamp about you; all these things are productions of his power and presents from his bounty. In like manner, your own nature, this body so skilfully composed, and that soul which enlivens it, are works of his providence, which neither were created, nor do now subsist, but by him. Is it not reasonable that you should consecrate to his glory what you hold only from his grace? Remember also what the apostle adds, that as all things were created by him, so they were made for him. Do not frustrate your Creator of his intentions. Live for his glory, as it was for that you were created. For if the heavens, and the elements, and the winds, and the meteors, and the plants, things deaf, and dumb, and inanimate, preach and celebrate the wonders of their Lord, all of them obeying his voice, and faithfully serving his designs; what will our ingratitude be, if, with these senses and this excellent reason he has given us, we alone of all his creatures should cross his counsels and dishonour his name, instead of glorifying it! The glory he requires of us is only that we walk in his commandments; that we abound in good and holy works; that we depart from all evil, and live in such manner as may oblige our neighbours to acknowledge that this Jesus whom we serve is truly a great God. Let us then faithfully acquit ourselves of these duties, and assure ourselves that if we advance his glory, he will provide for our bliss, and guard us from all that opposes it. For as all things, celestial and terrestrial, visible and invisible, were created, and do still subsist, by him, nothing in the whole world should make us afraid. All the armies of heaven, of the elements, and of nature, are in our Master's pay, and neither war nor work, but for his interests and by his order. These very thrones, these principalities, these powers and these dominions, which he has exalted above all his other creatures, do not employ the might and the glory of their nature but for him and for those who fear him. They are ministering spirits, sent forth to serve for their sakes who shall receive the inheritance of salvation. They keep us in all our ways. They defend us in life, they assist us at death, and convey us up into the bosom of our true Abraham. Let us live in confidence under the protection of so good and so great a Lord, that we may one day receive at his hand a most blissful immortality, the great and last donative of his benignity. To him, with the Father and the Holy Spirit, the true God, blessed over all things, be for ever honour, glory, and praise. Amen

---

SERMON IX.

VERSE 18.

And he is the head of the body, the church: who is the beginning, the first-born from the dead; that in all things he might have the pre-eminence.

It is not without just cause, beloved brethren, that, speaking of the union of Jesus Christ and his church, which was represented at the beginning of the world by the marriage of Adam and Eve, the apostle Paul affirms it to be a great secret, Eph. v. 32. For truly there is nothing in this mystery, whatever view you take of it, but what is most grand and worthy of the admiration of men and angels. First, if you regard the thing itself, is it not wonderful, astonishing, and unheard of in the world, that the Creator should unite himself with the creature—the Lord of glory with worms—the King of heaven with dust and ashes—the Saint of saints with sinners? Then again consider the foundation of this union; what can be conceived of more ecstatic than the birth and the death of the Son of God, on which this divine alliance was contracted? this mystical Spouse having had so vehement a passion for the church, that to make her his own he made himself a man like us, and poured out his blood upon a cross! Contemplate the nature of this union; it is so strict and intimate, that it perfectly commingles the parties whom it unites, and makes them only one body, one flesh, and one spirit; combining their persons and their affairs, and in such manner identifying their interests, that Jesus Christ is wholly his church's, and the church wholly her Christ's. The firmness of this union is no less admirable, being such that all the powers of earth, of hell, or of heaven, are not able to dissolve it; and while nature has bound nothing in the whole universe, that time does not in the end separate, innumerable ages will never dissolve, as they roll on, the sacred ties of this eternal union of the church with her Lord, either in this world or that which is to come. Finally, behold its effects; what can be mentioned more glorious and beneficial than the fruits which it produces? It fills our understanding with light; it purifies our affections; it sanctifies our hearts; it keeps the peace of God in them; it changes slaves of devils into children of the Most High; it transforms earth into heaven; and instead of that death and curse which we deserved, it gives us eternity and glory. From this only flow all those divine graces which we enjoy in this world, and all the advantages and felicities we hope for in the other. No wonder therefore that the Scripture employs so many different similitudes to figure out to us so excellent and so rich a subject; no one being by itself sufficiently perfect to represent us all the wonders of it. For this cause it borrows all the unions that nature, or art, or human society affords us, to express this one union: comparing it sometimes to the union of a vine with its branches, or of an olive with the scions that are grafted on its stock; sometimes to that of a foundation with the building which it sustains, or of a cornerstone with the two walls which it binds together; at other times to the conjunction of a prince with his subjects, or of an elder brother with the younger, or of a husband with his wife.

But, my brethren, among all these sacred pictures of our union with the Lord, none are more expressive, or more simple and beautiful, than the two similitudes which the Lord now sets before you; the one in those words of his apostle which we have read to you, and the other on that sacred table whither you are invited to the feast of his Lamb. The first is drawn from the natural union of the head with its members; and the second, from the union of bread and drink with the bodies which they nourish. According to the one, Christ is our Head, and we are his body. According to the other, he is called our bread, our meat, and our drink, and we the creatures whom he feeds and quickens. And though in other respects these two images are very dissimilar, yet in this particular they agree, that they excellently represent to us both our union with the Lord, and the life which is thence derived to us; for it is evident that the head and food give life, though in different manners, to the bodies with which they are united. This has induced me to believe that the meditation of this text will be suitable for the service of the holy supper, for which we are now preparing; since for the main it sets before our eyes, though under a different figure, that same mystery of our union with the Lord which is represented and communicated to us at his holy table. For to accomplish his design, and fully show us the infinite excellence and dignity of Jesus Christ our Saviour, the apostle, after he has told us what he is in regard of the Father, namely, "the image of the invisible God," and what in regard of the works of the first creation, that is, "the first-born," or the Prince and Master, of all the creatures, as having created them all, made and formed them, from the very lowest of them to the highest, considers him, finally, in regard of the new creatures, that is to say, the church; and informs us that he is the Head thereof, and the church is his body; and, for the greater illustration of it, adds, that he is "the beginning, and the first-born from the dead," whence he deduces this conclusion, that so he has "the pre-eminence in all things." These are the three points which we purpose, the grace of God assisting, to treat of in this discourse, for the exposition of this text and your edification. The first, that Jesus Christ is "the head of the body, the church;" the second, that he is "the beginning and the first-born from the dead;" and the third and last, that he has "in all things the pre-eminence."

I. As for the first of these three points, it is not only here that the apostle calls Jesus Christ the "head of the church." He uses the same language in divers other places of his Epistles, as in that addressed to the Ephesians, where he says that the Father hath set his Son above all things, "to be head of the church, which is his body, the fulness of Him that filleth all in all," Eph. i. 22, 23; and again, that "Christ is the head, from whom the whole body fitly joined together and compacted by that which every joint supplieth, according to the effectual working in the measure of every part, maketh increase of the body unto the edifying of itself in love," Eph. iv. 15, 16. And a few verses after our text, we find him repeating that "the church is the body of Christ;" and in the First Epistle to the Corinthians speaking to believers, "ye are," says he, "the body of Christ, and members in particular," 1 Cor. xii. 27. Indeed, it is a figure very common in all languages, to call him the head of a society who guides and governs it, or who, at least, possesses the first place in it; as you see that every one calls a king the head of his estate, and a general the head of the army that he commands, and those the heads of their regiments or companies who conduct them. Hence is derived our common word captain, which signifies nothing else but the head. The master of a household is in like manner termed the head of it, and so in all other societies of whatever nature. But this manner of speaking is exceedingly familiar with the Hebrews, as you may see in very many places of the Old Testament, where everything that has the first place, whether for its authority or for its excellence, or even for its birth, and mere precedency in time, is called the head of other things of the same kind. And the reason of this figure is evident. For the head standing highest of all the parts of the body of man, and having the conduct of it, because it is the seat of the eyes, and other senses, on which depends the directing of our life; the word is very justly used to express, by way of similitude, whatever holds the first place in any society, and consequently has, in this respect, a manifest resemblance to the head, properly so called. It is not therefore strange that this holy apostle makes use of this figure to express the superiority, the dignity, and imperial power which Jesus Christ has over the church, saying that he is its Head. And certainly, if there is a superior in the whole universe, who may and ought to be called head of the society which is under him, Jesus Christ merits it infinitely beyond any other, for in no other do there conspire the same abundant reasons and respects which are necessary to confirm this appellation as in him. For all the qualities, actions, and functions proper to the head of the body of man, which give it its name and dignity, Jesus Christ possesses and exercises much more nobly and magnificently than any general does in reference to his army, or any monarch in reference to his state.

The first and most known service which the head performs for the members, is to direct and guide them in their operations, and govern their motion and their rest by the light of its eyes, and the perceptions of its other senses. Now princes and captains have some shadow of this perfection, in that they observe and reconnoitre those things that concern the communities they govern, watching, and viewing, and scenting afar off whatever respects their interests; their people, in mean time, quietly labouring each of them in his own employment. But Jesus Christ doth these offices to his church much better, and more perfectly. For all the light of this mystical body resides in him. He considers not only its interests in general, but knows all that concerns the least of his members. "He never slumbereth nor sleepeth." His eyes and senses are always open. He sees all the parts of this his state, and discerns the posture and disposition of all, whether its friends or foes, whether nearer hand or further off. He carefully preserves it by his providence, and so prudently governs it, that there is no danger from which he does not deliver it, nor any difficulty but he surmounts it. It is he who conducts his people's wars, overrules their battles, dispenses their truces, and will one day give them an entire and eternal peace.

The second duty which the head performs to the body, is that of infusing into all its members impulse and sensation by means of the animal spirits, which, issuing thence, spread themselves through the whole body, flowing in the nerves as in so many channels which nature has cut out and laid forth for the maintenance of this communication. And I acknowledge that the authority and privileges which a prince distributes into all the parts of his state, causing his subjects, according to what they individually receive, to pursue various occupations; I say, this very strongly resembles the way in which the head governs the body. But it is far inferior to what we find in the conduct of the Lord Jesus towards his church. For he enlivens all its members, from the greatest even to the least; and gives them not power and authority only as princes give their subjects, but the very strength and ability to act, communicating to each of his faithful ones such a measure of his Spirit as is necessary for sensation and motion, and all the other functions of heavenly life, as Paul teaches us in the Epistle to the Ephesians, chap. iv., and more at large in the First to the Corinthians, chap. xii.

Moreover, the head hath this advantage above the rest of the body, that it is more exquisitely constituted and attempered than the other members, according to the rule which nature prudently observes in general, that is, to frame those things best which are designed for the most eminent purposes. Kings and captains deserve also the name of heads in this respect, their dignity being very elevated above their subjects. But their advantage in this particular is nothing in comparison of that which Jesus Christ has above his church; not only by his being incomparably more holy, more wise, and more powerful than any of all the faithful; but especially, in that he is God blessed for ever.

Finally, as you see the head is placed highest in the body of man, this situation being necessary for its commodious exercise of the functions of its government; a thing that kings and princes imitate, dwelling ordinarily in palaces, sitting on thrones, raised above the houses and seats of their subjects: so Jesus Christ has this advantage, but in a far greater degree;

for he sits on high in the heavens, on the throne of God, above the whole church, both militant and triumphant. And if he conversed of old on the earth, that was only for awhile, and by dispensation for the good of his body, which obliged him to do it; even as the head sometimes bows down itself, when the necessity of any of its members requires it. But the proper and natural place of Jesus Christ is that lofty sanctuary of immortality, where he now appears in highest glory; thence governing by his Spirit all the parts of this mystical body, the church, both those which are in heaven, and those which are yet on earth.

Thus, my brethren, you see wherein this dignity of our Lord Jesus consists, and with how much reason Paul expresses it here and elsewhere, by saying that "he is the head of the church." Whence evidently follows what the apostle expressly says, that the church is the body of Christ. For if Jesus Christ is called the Head thereof, for having and exercising towards it all the functions and prerogatives of a natural head towards its members, then certainly the church must also be called his body; as this whole divine society depends on Jesus Christ, and receives of him all the light, all the aptitude, all the sense and motion, that it possesses.

This doctrine of the apostle leads us to the consideration of various things before we pass any further. First, by laying down this proposition, that Jesus Christ is the Head of the church, he opportunely fortifies the Colossians against that error which hereafter we shall find him expressly opposing, the error of those that would subject believers to angels and to Moses, introducing into the church the worshipping of the one, and the pedagogy of the other. For as the Son of God is the head of this sacred society, who sees not that it ought to depend on him alone? that it is to him it owes its obedience and service, and from him it ought to receive its discipline and guidance? But it must also be observed, that the apostle gives this title to Jesus Christ with a design to glorify him, enrolling it among the other praises of his sovereign dignity. Indeed, as the church is the most divine society in the world, as it is a company of kings, of priests, and of prophets, the assembly of the first-fruits of the creatures, and a new world, much more excellent than the old, a world immortal and incorruptible, it is evident that to be its Head is a dignity more sublime than to have been the Creator and Prince of the original universe. Whereby you see, moreover, how unjust (to say no more) is the temerity of those who give this name to another beside Jesus Christ, acknowledging a mortal man for the true head of the universal church. Let them colour this outrage as they please, they will not be able to justify it. This is evidently to despoil Jesus Christ of his royal robe, and to take the diadem from him, which none but he can bear. They allege that the Scripture communicates to others, as well as to Jesus Christ, the names of pastor, of priest, and of teacher, and of light, and various others. It is true; but it never gives that of "head of the church" to any but him. And the difference of these titles is evident, the former signifying charges whereof the faithful exercise some portion and some shadow, whereas that of "head of the church" signifies the supremacy which is incommunicable to any other but the Son of God. As you see that in a state the names of prince, and of governor, and captain, and others of like sort, are not given to the king only, they pertain to others also; but no other may be called the sovereign, or the head of the state, besides him, without incurring the guilt of sacrilege or treason. Yet they endeavour to excuse themselves, and say they make the pope only the ministerial and subordinate head, not an essential and sovereign one. But this is nothing but words arising from their interest, and not founded in the truth of things. There is no prince who would be satisfied with such language, if any one of his subjects, making himself the head and monarch of his state, were to allege in excuse that he had no other intention than to pass for a ministerial head. In the nature of men, whence this similitude is taken, we see no bodies that have two heads of a different rank; and if any such be found at any time, they are accounted monsters, which cannot be said of the church, the most perfect master-piece of all the works of God. In a word, it is not enough to say that the pope is the ministerial head of the church, it must be proved. We plainly read in Scripture that Jesus Christ is "head of the church." Let us believe it, and adore him under that title. But that there is another head in the church, whether visible or invisible, whether ministerial or sovereign, of this we meet with nothing whatever in the writings of the apostles, not to say that we meet there with many things incompatible with such a doctrine. "Faith cometh by hearing, and hearing by the word of God." Permit us then to suspend our believing this other pretended head of the church, as we hear nothing of it in the word of God. But that which the apostle adds, namely, that the church is the body of Christ, demonstrates that none but Christ is the Head of it. For if the pope, for example, were head of it, the universal church would be the pope's body, as it is the Lord's. But where is the christian ear that that doth not tingle at language so strange, so unheard of, and so profane? And so we see, however vehement and inordinate has been the desire of men for this title of "head of the church," no man has ever hitherto called the church his "body;" every one confessing that it is not the body of any one except Jesus Christ. On a similar principle, they should grant that no one is its head but he, for it cannot have any one for its head but him whose body it is.

I request you to observe, in the next place, in opposition to another error of our adversaries, that Christ's being "head of the church" does not at all prove that there is a corporal connection between the church and him, or that the bodies of the faithful are properly and substantially joined to him, as the members of a natural body are joined to their head. Every one admits that this must be understood figuratively and spiritually, and as all men usually take other expressions by which our union with the Lord is represented; as when he is called the foundation of the church, the corner-stone, the vine-stock of believers, and their raiment. No one concludes from these passages, that our bodies must really touch his substance. Why then will they infer it from other places where, to set forth the same mystery, it is said that he is our bread, our meat, and our drink? If he is our head, if he is our raiment, if he governs and clothes us, without touching our bodies with his, why may not he be our bread, and nourish us, without actually entering into our bodily throat and stomach? If the one is spiritually and figuratively understood, why will you force me to understand the other corporally and literally? I say the same on the apostle's express declaration, that the church is the body of Christ. Our adversaries do not deduce from this any transubstantiation; and they confess that to maintain the truth of these words there is no need that either the church should lose its own substance and nature, or be really changed into the substance of the body of Christ. Nevertheless, they pertinaciously insist that where the gospel calls the bread which our Lord took, his body, there a real and literal transubstantiation of the nature of the bread into that of the body of Christ is implied. As if it were not rational and easy to say that the bread, as well as the church, is figuratively and spiritually the body of Christ. If they admit this sense in one of these places, why do they reject it in the other, where the nature of things themselves and the truth of heavenly doctrine no less necessarily require it.

In fine, not to make any longer stay here, Paul clears up to us, in two words, another question which Roman zeal has so horribly perplexed in these latter times, namely, What is the nature and the true definition of the church? The church is, saith he, the body of Christ. These two words overthrow all the philosophizing of our adversaries on this subject, in order to contract or enlarge the communion of the church beyond what is proper. I say contracting, for they permit none to possess this name but those who acknowledge the bishop of Rome; whereas Paul gives it to all who belong to Jesus

Christ, and have his Spirit, for of such there is no one who does not belong to his body, and consequently to his church, wherever he lives, and whoever are his pastors. I say also enlarging it; for these doctors, who are so severe on the one hand, that they give the name of the church only to the Roman communion, are so lax and so very indulgent on the other, that they freely impart it to the most debauched and profane hypocrites, provided they attach themselves to their pope; not requiring, as they affirm,* any interior virtue in them to be members of the true church, but only an exterior profession of the Roman belief and communion. But Paul anathematizes this no less impious than extravagant doctrine, by saying that the church is the body of Christ. For no one can be of his body without being quickened by his Spirit. "He that hath not the Spirit of Christ," says the same apostle elsewhere, "is none of his." Rom. viii. 9. Certainly then it is not that the profane or hypocritical are parts of the church. There is no communion between Christ and Belial. The body and the members of the one cannot be the body and members of the other. Because the church is the body of Christ, it must of necessity be concluded that these people, of whom our adversaries compose their church, which on their own admission have not any piety or internal virtue, and consequently are members of Belial, may very well be, since they will have it so, true members of the Roman, but assuredly not of the christian church; and if the pope owns them for his sheep, we are very certain that the Lord Jesus will never avouch them for his.

II. But it is time to notice, in the second place, the two other titles which the apostle here gives to our Lord Jesus Christ, namely, that he is "the beginning," or the principle, and "the first-born from the dead." Even as when he had said before that Jesus Christ is "the first-born," that is, the Lord "of every creature," he at once assigned this reason for it, that all things were created by him. In like manner now, having said that he is "the head of the church," he establishes this truth on his being the author of the church, he that formed and constituted it; and the Prince of this new generation, he that will give it its true and utmost perfection of being. For the word which we have rendered "the beginning," signifies also the principle, that is to say, the cause and origin of a thing; and "first-born" denotes both him who is born before the rest, and him who is the master or the prince of the rest; he says therefore, first, that the Lord Jesus is "the beginning," or the principle. Certainly this belongs to him on account of the first creation, as he is the author of it, the Word

* Bellarm. 3. de Eccles. milit. c. 2.

and Wisdom which produced the universe; and it may be in this sense that he calls himself, in the Apocalypse, "the beginning of the creation of God," Rev. iii. 14; and elsewhere in the same book, "Alpha and Omega, the beginning and the end," Rev. i. 8; xxi. 6; xxii. 13. But as these words relate to the church and the resurrection, the word "beginning" must be restrained to them, and we are here precisely to understand by it that he is the beginning of this second work of God. Jesus Christ, the eternal Wisdom, may say in respect of this second creation, as of the first, that the Father "possessed him in the beginning of his ways;" and that it is the same wisdom that projected, prepared, and executed all this great design of the renovation of the world.

First, then, it is the Son of God, who, interposing at the beginning in the counsel of the Father, took upon him the expiating of sin, without which it was not possible to found this second universe; and though he actually did it not, till the fulness of time, yet his engaging his word for it being then accepted of the Father, it had as much efficacy as if the thing itself had been immediately executed; which makes the apostle elsewhere say that "Jesus Christ is the same yesterday, today, and for ever." He has always the same efficacy, as well before as after his manifestation. Without this, not a man could have been called into the state of grace. Therefore Paul says, in another place, that God hath chosen us in Christ, Eph. i. 4; considering him as the foundation of our election, because out of him there could not be salvation or happiness for any one of us. He is therefore truly the beginning of this work, as his merit is the foundation of the counsel God has taken to plan and form it; as Peter also observes, when speaking of the redemption wrought by the blood of the Lamb, he says expressly that he "was fore-ordained before the foundation of the world," 1 Pet. i. 20. But beside the merit of his cross, which was ever present in the counsel of God, he is also "the beginning," or the principle, of the church another way, for, by the operation and efficacy of his power he has called to God all believers that ever were. It is he who brought Abraham out of Chaldea; it is he who appeared to the patriarchs, and who led Israel in the desert, and who inspired the prophets. Whence it is that David calls him his Lord, Psal. cx. 1. He builded and kept up that whole ancient church, as well as the latter, by the virtue of his word and Spirit. But he is again the beginning of the church, in the quality of an exemplar and causal pattern; all the faithful of every age having been, as it were, cast into his mould, as the apostle teaches in the eighth chapter of the Epistle to the Romans; "Whom he did foreknow, he also did predestinate to be conformed to the image of his Son." And it is to no purpose to object, that this cannot be said of that time, when he had not yet assumed that human nature, tempted on earth and crowned in heaven, unto which we are conformed. For to this I answer, first, that though that nature was not really yet in being, it is enough that its idea and image were in the mind of God, for the assimilating and conforming his work to it. This suffices to show that he is the beginning and principle of it.

But I adjoin, in the second place, that this work of the church may be considered two ways: either in its beginnings, while being formed; or in its perfection, as finished, when it shall have received all the touches requisite to give it the highest degree of excellence, in which it must abide. I avow that the church, under the first consideration, had its being before the Son of God was made man and raised up to heaven. But if you take it under the second, it is evident that in this respect he is truly the beginning of this divine work; for no one was perfect before him. He is, if I may so say, the first piece fully ended that ever came out of the Father's hand and his own. No one of the rest is absolutely completed. Their bodies are yet under the power of death, the last of our enemies. Christ is the only one that has altogether broken its bonds, and raised up his body from the grave, and clothed it with a glorious immortality. He is the first man of the new world that the universe ever saw, and in him has been shown us the true form of that second nature which we hope for in the time to come, but which no one has, or shall have at the present, save Jesus Christ. This seems to be the strict meaning of the apostle here, when he calls him "the beginning," or principle, because he adds, "the first-born from the dead;" which words, as you see, evidently correspond with this sense. John also gives this title to the Lord: "Grace be unto you, and peace from Jesus Christ, who is the faithful witness, the first-begotten of the dead," Rev. i. 5. And Paul illustrates this expression elsewhere, saying to the same purpose, that Jesus Christ being raised from the dead, was "become the first-fruits of them that sleep." And a little after, In Jesus Christ shall all be made alive; "but every man in his own order: Christ the first-fruits; afterwards, they that are Christ's," 1 Cor. xv. 20, 22, 23. And in the Acts he saith, it was necessary that Christ should be the first to rise from the dead, that he might show light to the people, Acts xxvi. 23. From all these places it sufficiently appears what the apostle signifies when he saith that Jesus Christ is "the beginning, and the first-born from the dead," namely, that he is the first of all mankind who was raised from the state of the dead, and settled in glorious immortality, that he is the first ear of this blessed harvest, that was carried up into the sanctuary, and offered in due season to the eternal Father, until the rest become ripe. This truth is thoroughly evident. For of what other man but the Lord Jesus was it ever heard say that he arose from the dead, and ascended into heaven? I know the Scriptures tell us of some dead who were raised before the resurrection of the Lord, but this does not at all deprive him of the glory which the apostle here gives him. For though I might allege that those persons were raised from the grave, not by their own power and virtue, as Jesus Christ, but by the touching or prayer of Elijah and Elisha, and by God's command, I say that the resurrection which Paul understands is the rising again to glory and immortality. It is a being born again, not to the former life, which is terrene and fading, but to the other, which is celestial and incorruptible. Who seeth not that in this respect there never was any one raised again, except the Lord Jesus alone? For the son of the Shunammite, Lazarus, and others of similar constitution, at their coming forth from the grave, reassumed the same natural and perishing life which they had laid down, a life subject to the same infirmities, and to the same necessity of dying; and, indeed, they died after they had lived again awhile. Their death was rather deferred than abolished. Their bodies corrupted and, in the end, returned to that dust from which they were preserved for some years. But with Jesus Christ it was not so. He, in coming forth from the dead, retook not the life he had quitted, that is, the life of the first Adam, that infirm, natural, and earthly life, a life still subject to death. He left it in the sepulchre, where it must remain, as in eternal oblivion. He put on a new life and nature, such as is spiritual and celestial, as the apostle elsewhere describes it; a life full of strength and glory; not subject either to the use of meat or sleep; not subject to dolour or death; a life appropriate to the second world, and not to the first; a nature peculiar to the future age, not to the present. Accordingly, you see, that being invested therewith, he remained not on the earth; this is the old Adam's element, the habitation of corruption and death; but having only sojourned there forty days, as long as was needful to assure his apostles of the truth of his resurrection, and to show them, in his own person, the first-fruits of the mystical Canaan, he ascended up above the heavens, to the true element of the new man, and the sanctuary of eternity. We conclude, then, that he is truly "the beginning, and the first-born from the dead," since he is the first of all the dead that was born and raised again in incorruption. But these titles signify yet another thing, namely, that it is he who shall raise again all the members of the church in like glory; that he is the Master and the Lord of the dead, for investing them one day in their order with a nature resembling his own, according to what Paul says, that he will fashion our vile body "like unto his own glorious body," Phil. iii. 21. For he would not be "the first-born from the dead," if he did not communicate the privilege and the possession of this second birth to all his brethren, that is to say, to all the faithful.

The apostle adds, in the third place, "that in all things he might have the pre-eminence." Those who are well versed in the reading of these divine books, know the word "that" is often put in them for "so as that," or "in such a manner as;" to signify the event and consequence of an action, rather than the intention or design of the agent: I presume it must be so taken in this place. For the intention of our Lord in being made Head of the church, and the beginning of the new life, was rather to save us and glorify his Father, than to obtain for himself the pre-eminence. Yet true it is that such was the success of his undertaking, that he actually has the pre-eminence in all things. For there are but two sorts of things, one of those which pertain to the first world and its creation, the other of those which are of the second world and of the regeneration. Christ, therefore, being already the Master and Creator of the former, it is evident that, having been also established Head of the church, (which is the state that consists of the latter,) and the beginning, and first-born of the resurrection of the dead, he obtains, by this means, the pre-eminence in all things; that is to say, both in those of the first creation, of which he is the Author, and in those of the second, of which he is the Head. This is the conclusion which the apostle deduces from his whole preceding discourse: there he said that the Lord is "the image of the invisible God, the first-born of every creature," the Creator of the elements and the angels; and moreover the Head of the church, the principle and the first-fruits of the new creation; now he adds, "that in all things he might have the pre-eminence." This, as it appears to me from hence, being clear enough, there is no necessity that we should dwell any longer upon the exposition of this text.

To conclude, it remains that we briefly touch upon the duties to which the doctrine of the apostle obliges us, and the comforts which it affords us. Jesus Christ "is the head of the body, the church." These few words, if we meditate on them as we ought, will teach us all what we owe of obedience to the Lord, of charity to our brethren, and of care and respect to ourselves. As for the Lord, since he has vouchsafed to become our Head, it is evident we ought to honour him with the utmost devotion and submit all the actions of our life to his direction. See with what promptitude the body obeys the head, and with how absolute a submission it follows all its volitions. The body neither stirs nor rests but as the head orders. It depends entirely on its guidance, and never crosses its orders or resists its commands. The head has no sooner conceived a thing, but the spirits immediately present themselves at the place it desires, and each of the members employs all its vigour and strength to execute its will. This is an image of that obedience which the Lord, our mystical head, demands of us; and this is that which the apostle means when he saith that the church is subject to him, Eph. v. 24. In vain therefore they boast themselves to be the church, who act contrary to what the Lord ordains, who are subject to another beside him, and instead of his orders follow the will of a mortal man; owning another head, adoring another oracle, and keeping what he has forbidden. Blessed be his name that he has taught us to disclaim their error, and to hang all our religion upon his sacred lips; believing only that truth which he has revealed to us in his gospel, and engraven in our hearts by his Spirit. But what will it profit us to follow him in our faith, if we resist him in our manners? How can he avouch for his church a body subject to mammon, to pleasure, to ambition, and other idols of the world—a body wholly bended down to the earth, whereas this Divine Head is exalted above the heavens? Dear brethren, let us not deceive ourselves. We cannot be the church of Christ except we are his body, and we cannot be his body except we depend absolutely on him; except we cast out of our members the spirit of the flesh and of the world, and take in his Spirit, to follow its light, and obey its movings. Henceforth then let us so regulate our life that it does not contradict our profession. Let the Lord Jesus be truly our Head; let him be still above us; let him preside in all our designs, let him conduct our steps, let him govern our actions, and inspire all the sentiments we have. Let there appear nothing in our words, in our affections, or our works, but what is his.

But this lesson of the apostle no less recommends to us charity towards our neighbour than submission towards Jesus Christ. For since the church is a body, and even the body of Christ, that is, the fairest and most perfect body in the world, judge ye, what ought to be the union and the love of all the faithful who compose it? Look upon the body of man, from which this resemblance is taken; how great is the zeal of all the parts for the conservation of the whole! how they love it, and conspire for its good! how they act and suffer all things, and each in its rank exposes his life and being for it! Such, ye faithful, ought to be your affection for the church, this divine body of the Lord, whereof you are members. Its peace, its preservation, and its glory, should be the object of your highest and most urgent desires. There is nothing that should not be cheerfully employed in so noble a design. Woe to them that feel not the wounds of this sacred body, that are not affected with its bruises, and look upon the breaches of it unmoved;

who are so far from groaning at them, and endeavouring to repair them, that they inflict more, rending with extreme impiety and inhumanity the most innocent body in the world, and most beloved of God, the body of his Son, which he hath redeemed at the price of his own blood!

But besides the affection we ought to have for the church in general, this similitude teaches us also to love ardently each of the faithful in particular. Paul treats of this expressly in 1 Cor. xii. 25—27: There is no division in the body; the members have a mutual care one for another; and if one of the members suffer anything, all the members suffer with it; or if one of the members be honoured, all the members rejoice together in it. Now ye are the body of Christ, and his members, each one on his part. O God! how great would be our happiness and our glory, if the union and concord of our flock answered this beautiful and glowing picture; if, knit together by a holy and inviolable love, and having but one heart and one soul, as we have but one Head, we amiably conversed together, tenderly resenting the good and evil of each other, and each of us exerting his power to preserve and increase the good of our brethren and to comfort and cure their evils! But, alas! instead of this sweet and grateful spectacle, which would ravish heaven and earth, we behold little among us but quarrels, and coldness, and hatred, and animosities. The welfare of our brethren displeases us, and their adversity does not afflict us. The former raises our envy, and the latter stirs not our compassion. Vanity and self-love make us either disdain or hate all others. There are no bonds which our fierceness does not break, it equally violates both those of nature and those of grace. Is this that great name, the body of Christ, by which we glory to be called? Christ is nothing but sweetness and love. He has laid down his life for his enemies. How are we his, *we* that hate and persecute our brethren? And how are we his body, since we rend one another? Were ever the members of the same body seen at war together, the hand assaulting the foot, and the teeth falling on the hand? If such a thing appear, is it not regarded as the effect of extreme rage, or as a horrible prodigy? Oh! how ordinary is this rage and this prodigy among us, who, being members of the same body, and (which infinitely augments our shame) of the body of Christ, the Saviour of the world, have yet no horror at biting and consuming one another, as if we were a herd of cannibals, and not the flock of the Lord Jesus! I well know that none of us want plausible reasons to palliate our faults, passion itself making us witty in the defence of this bad cause. But let our own conscience be our judge, let it remember it has to do with Jesus Christ and not with men; if it beguile us, it cannot deceive God. Renounce we then unfeignedly all this kind of vices, and cordially loving our brethren, succouring the afflicted, assisting the poor, comforting the sick, and living in concord with all, let us truly be, as we say we are, the body of our Lord Jesus Christ. This peculiarly the bread and the wine of our Lord, the sacred emblems of our mystical union, require of us; they remind us, as the apostle represents it, that we are but one bread and one body, 1 Cor. x.

Finally, this doctrine further shows us with what purity and sanctity we ought to keep our own persons, since all being the body of Christ, we are each one members of him. Against every arrow of temptation that sin shall let fly at us, let us take up this consideration for our succour; say, Shall I take the members of Christ to make them members of Satan? Shall I defile that body in the filth of incontinency, drunkenness, or any other kind of debauch, which the Son of God has cleansed with his blood, which he has united and joined to himself, and of which he is become the Head? Far be it from me to commit so vile a deed. It is thus, my brethren, that we ought to regulate our whole life, that we may be truly the body of Christ. And doubt not, if we be so, this Divine Head will love us and tenderly preserve us. For no one ever yet hated his own flesh. He will feed us, and set us at his own table, and give us the bread and wine of heaven; and after the combats and trials of this life, will clothe us with his own glory and immortality, as being "the first-born from the dead." To him, with the Father and the Holy Spirit, the true God, blessed for ever, be honour and glory to ages of ages. Amen.

SERMON X.

VERSES 19, 20.

For it pleased the Father that in him should all fulness dwell; and, having made peace through the blood of his cross, by him to reconcile all things unto himself; by him, I say, whether they be things in earth, or things in heaven.

As in the frame of nature God has appointed only one great light, namely, the sun, and has united in the body of this admirable luminary all the brightness spread through the universe, that it might enlighten the heavens and the earth, and that from it, as from a common source, all the light and warmth which all things receive might stream forth; so likewise in the kingdom of grace, the same God has given us only one Jesus Christ, the true Sun of righteousness, whom he has filled with all the treasures of wisdom and life, that he might be an exceeding, abundant and inexhaustible fountain of joy and immortality; whence are diffused upon all the parts of the new world, which is created in righteousness and in holiness, all the spiritual perfections and blessings it possesses. This is that heavenly doctrine, dear brethren, which the apostle teaches us in the text you have now heard; where, speaking of the Lord Jesus, he saith, "it pleased the Father that in him should all fulness dwell." He represented to us in the former words the excellency of the person of the Lord Jesus, that he is "the image of God," the Lord and the Creator of all things, visible and invisible; then next his dignity, that he is "the Head of the church, the beginning, and the first-born from the dead;" concluding that he has the pre-eminence in all things. The apostle now produces the reason of it, taken from the decree and will of the eternal Father: "For it pleased the Father that in him should all fulness dwell." And that we might discern the wisdom of the Father in the disposal of this fulness, he sets before us, in the words following, the work, to accomplish which he designed and sent his Son; a work so great and so wonderful, that it is evident without this fulness, which he caused to dwell in him, it was not possible it should be perfected. For by him he purposed to reconcile, and actually did reconcile, all things to himself, those that are in heaven, as well as those that are in earth. And for the more full discovery of the greatness of this divine master-piece, he touches also the means by which it was accomplished, namely, peace, which he made by the blood of his Son's cross. It was not possible to reunite heaven and earth, and reconcile these parts of the universe, that were divided each from other, but by making peace, by extinguishing their hate, and removing the cause of their enmities. Neither was it possible to procure this peace otherwise than by the shedding of divine blood, and the offering up a sacrifice of infinite worth, and by the intervention of a Mediator, who should have in him all the perfections and excellences of the parties who were to be reconciled. The greatness of the work shows us the quality of the means requisite to finish it; and the quality of the means regulates the faculties and nature of the person necessary to perform it. To reconcile earthly and heavenly things in God, there was need to make peace; to make peace, there was need of a blood and a sacrifice of infinite value; to offer such a sacrifice, there was need of a person in whom all fulness dwelt; that is, who had in him fully and perfectly all the graces and excellences of heaven and earth. Certainly, then, it was an order highly reasonable, and most worthy of the divine wisdom of the Father, to make all fulness dwell in his Christ for the reconciling of heaven and earth, by making peace through the blood of his cross. That we may have a fuller view of it, for his glory and our own consolation, we will consider, by his grace, in this sermon, those three points which are distinctly proposed us in the text. First, the good pleasure of the Father, that all fulness should dwell in Christ. Secondly, the work he has wrought by the hand of his Christ thus qualified; namely, the reconciling of all things to himself, both which are in earth and in heaven. And finally, the means by which he has executed this great design, namely, making peace by the blood of the cross of his well-beloved Son.

For a right understanding of the first of these three points, we must inquire, at the entrance, what this "fulness" is which the good pleasure of the Father has made to dwell wholly in Christ, especially seeing that interpreters do not agree about it; some referring it to the divinity of our Lord, others to the graces which were accumulated on him after his manifestation in our flesh. It is certain that the word fulness is variously understood in the Scripture; and, not to speak of other senses, which are beside our purpose, it is sometimes referred to the greatness of things, and signifies their just, their whole and due measure. As when it is said that Saul "fell on the earth" to the fulness of his stature, 1 Sam. xxviii. 20; that is, all along, so as his whole body lay stretched out on the ground: and it is very likely that thus Paul calls the church the "fulness," or the completeness, of Christ, Eph. i. 23; forasmuch as being his body, in it his just and due magnitude consists. Without the church, he would be a Head without a body, that is, without a magnitude and a stature proportionate to his pre-eminent majesty. It seems we might so take the "fulness" mentioned in this text, as signifying all the graces and excellences requisite to the full and entire greatness that becomes the Christ of God; but the word "dwell" which is annexed to it does not comport with it; for it would be a harsh phrase, and without example in any language, to say that a man's stature dwells in him. For the same reason, I exclude another sense, which else would not ill comport with the matter; I mean that which the term fulness has, when it is put for a full and whole measure, and such as wants nothing. We are to observe therefore, beside what has been said, that the word fulness very commonly in Scripture sets forth that which fills anything; as when one prophet styles men, and other creatures of which the earth is full, the fulness of the earth, Psal. xxiv. 1; and another, the fulness of a city, Amos vi. 8, all the people that dwell in it; and again another, the fulness of the sea, the isles, of which the sea is full, with all their inhabitants, Isa. xlii. 10. And, as philosophers speak, because the contents, perfections, and qualities of things fill up their forms and give them all their beauty, as plants and living creatures are the ornament of the earth, people the glory of cities, and isles so many crowns of the sea, it is common by a very elegant figure, to term the graces and perfections of such or such a subject its fulness; for without them it would be empty, and in such a condition as that rude and uncouth mass which Moses describes in the beginning of Genesis, "the earth was without form and void," Gen. i. 2, before the Lord clothed it with the stately ornaments, and filled it with that rich abundance, which we now behold upon it. In this sense, the apostle John gives the name of the fulness of Christ to that total abundance of perfections and divine graces which dwelt in him, his wisdom, his righteousness, his sanctification, and his redemption, when he saith that "of his fulness have all we received," John i. 16. And it is after the same manner that Paul, by "the fulness of the Godhead," means all the qualities or properties of the divine nature; its understanding, its wisdom, its omnipotence, its goodness, and infinite justice, saying, that "in Jesus Christ dwelleth all the fulness of the Godhead bodily," Col. ii. 9. It is therefore in this sense also, as it appears to me, that we must take the word fulness in this text; referring it to the things of which the apostle had just spoken, when he affirmed Jesus Christ to be "the image of the invisible God, the first-born of every creature," by whom all things were created and subsist; "the head of the church, the beginning, and the first-born from the dead," having the pre-eminence in all things. For you perceive these qualities are the perfections and excellences, partly of the divine nature, and partly of the human; the former, namely, his being "the image of God," and the Author and Governor of the creatures, pertaining to the divine; the latter, namely, his being "the head of the church," and "the first born from the dead," to the human: so after these things, when the apostle now adds, "For it pleased the Father that in him should all fulness dwell," it is as much as if he had said it was the Father's will that there should appear in his Christ a rich and a complete abundance of all divine and human perfections; all the beauty, dignity, and excellency that replenish heaven and earth, that adorn the nature of God and of men. Thus the question which interpreters debate, whether this fulness should be referred to the divinity or to the humanity of our Lord, is answered; for this exposition comprises them both; the eternal wisdom and power of the one, with all its attributes; the sanctity and love of the other, with all the graces which were given to it without measure. This is the all-fulness that dwells in Jesus Christ.

And the word *dwell* has here a vast emphasis. For in the style of Scripture, it signifies an abode, not transient, and for a time only, but such as is firm, constant, and durable; so that the apostle saying that all fulness dwells in Christ, thereby shows us that this rich abundance of all divine and human perfections shall eternally be in him; not as the divine glory and majesty was formerly in the tabernacle of Moses, and in the temple of Solomon, where it lodged but for a space; not as the irradiations of the Deity in the souls of the prophets, which they filled but for some hours; finally, not as the graces and perfections which, for some years only, enrich the bodies and spirits of mortal men, of which old age, and a thousand other accidents, and in the end death itself, quickly despoils them, which makes the sacred writers say that the comeliness of flesh and the fashion of this world pass away; that they are like flowers and herbs, in whom beauty tarries but a few days; time, without delay, plucking it from them, and defacing all its lineaments. Our Christ is an eternal temple, which the glory of God fills both continually and for ever. It does not merely lodge there, it dwells there as in its true and incorruptible sanctuary. Never shall that sanctuary lose it. This fulness shall abide eternally in him.

But the apostle saith that "it pleased the Father that in him should all fulness dwell." By the pleasure of the Father, he means, according to the ordinary style of Scripture, the determination and order of the eternal wisdom of God. For Christ did not violently snatch up this glory, nor reassume it of himself. He received it by the will of the Father, who gave him to man, and sent him into the world, pouring into him all the treasures of his graces, that we might draw from his fulness all the good we need for our happiness. But it must be remembered that the apostle considers the Lord Jesus here as Christ and Mediator, and not simply as the Son of God; he considers him in regard of his office, and not in respect to his first and original nature; for if you look upon him this second way, it is clear that, being God eternal with the Father, he received of him his divine essence, with all its fulness, not by any decree of his will, or of his good pleasure, but by a natural communication, that is to say, by an eternal, ineffable, and incomprehensible generation. The creation of the world is a work of the good pleasure of God; the generation of the Son is a natural act of the person of the Father. The first was done in time, the other is before all time. The world, which is the effect of creation, had a commencement of being; the Son, who is the fruit of the generation of the Father, is eternal, without beginning, as well as without end of days. But this Son, who is God by nature, is Christ by the will of the Father; for the name Christ signifies an office, and not strictly an essence or a nature. Originally this office was not attached to the person of the Son. He might have been the Son without being our Mediator, and would have so subsisted if the sin of man had not intervened, or if the justice of God had left us in the misery into which sin had precipitated us. But this good and gracious Lord having had compassion on us, and resolved thereupon to bring us up from those depths of death in which we lay, ordained a Mediator who might effect this great work, and invested him with all the qualities and perfections that were necessary for this end. It is therefore precisely in this respect that the apostle considers Jesus Christ here, when he saith it was the good pleasure of "the Father that in him should all fulness dwell." He thereby means it was the Father's will, that in this sacred person of the Mediator, who was ordained and appointed for our salvation, all perfection, richness, grace, and excellency should meet together, Divinity and humanity, filled with the infinite abundance of all the qualities and properties which pertain to them, should concur. Such being his good pleasure, he chose his Son, God co-eternal and co-essential with himself, who, uniting all the riches of his Deity with the human nature which he assumed, constitutes one only person, in the bosom of which dwells all this fulness that is necessary for his office as Mediator. Whence it appears how vain is the cavil of heretics, who conclude from this passage that the Deity of the Son is not eternal and co-essential with the Father's,* but created and made by the will and good pleasure of the Father. For the apostle does not speak here of the origin of the perfections which are found in Christ, but of their being united and met together in one and the same subject. I acknowledge, it is by the good pleasure of the Father, and by the order of his will, that the Godhead of the Son dwells in the Mediator. But it thence follows that this Godhead of his is an effect of the Father's will. It was, before it filled the Mediator. The same Father who by his will united it to our flesh, for the making up, together with that flesh, the person of Christ, had communicated it to his Son from all eternity by a natural act of his eternal understanding, that is to say, by a divine generation.

Now it is not in vain that the apostle here advances this assertion, that it pleased the Father all fulness should dwell in his Christ. He does it with design to confirm our consciences in the religion of the Lord Jesus only. For these Colossians (as we shall see hereafter) were tampered with by seducers, who mingled the Mosaical ceremonies with the gospel, and the worshipping of angels with the service of the Lord. The apostle, therefore, here seasonably fortifies these believers against this error, and that by two excellent reasons: the first taken from the dwelling of all fulness in Jesus Christ. Poor men, saith he, what seek you for, either in Moses or in angels? we have

* As the whole church believes.

all in Jesus Christ. There is no good, no perfection, nor excellency, either in God or in the creature, but dwells in this sovereign Lord. Having him, we have no need to go to others, since in him we find all. The other reason is taken from the will of God, the supreme rule of religion, the only thing that is sufficient to settle the agitation and natural distrust of our consciences. As for Jesus Christ, saith he, it was the good pleasure of God "that in him should all fulness dwell." The Father has set up him to be the spring of our salvation. But as for Moses and angels, we do not see that ever it was the will of the Father to give them such a dignity. Dear brethren, now that our faith is fought against with similar errors, let us arm it also with the same reasons. If the adversary send us to angels and saints, let us answer him, that the Lord Jesus sufficeth us; that having him we can want nothing, since all fulness dwells in him. I will not inquire for the present what these angels and saints are, whom you recommend to me; whether they have indeed that merit, and that righteousness, and that authority which I need for the expiation of my sin, and for the opening the mansions of God to me. How rich and how abounding soever you represent them to me, I may dispense with their store, since this Christ whom I embrace has all fulness dwelling in him. Let them be all that you please, they will want, however, some part of that infinite plentifulness which overflows in our Christ. And how zealous soever you are for their glory, yet you durst not presume to say that all fulness dwells in them. How great is your imprudence, to go hither and thither groping in pits and cisterns, while you have near you such a living and inexhaustible fountain! Grant that the worshipping of saints is not criminal, (which it evidently is,) it is notwithstanding superfluous, forasmuch as it has nothing in it but we find it surpassed in the fulness of Jesus Christ. But the other consideration which the apostle sets before us here is of no less force, that it was the good pleasure of the Father all fulness should dwell in his Christ. My faith attends on the will of God. This will is its object and its rule. I cannot relish either doctrine or service that does not conform thereto. Tell me how you know it is the good pleasure of God, that this fulness of merit and power, which you ascribe sometimes to saints departed, sometimes to your pope and his ministers, does indeed dwell in them. As for the Lord Jesus, whom I adore, and in whom I seek all my bliss, the Father has proclaimed from heaven, that he is his well-beloved Son; his Scriptures declare, that he has committed all judgment to him, and that all fulness dwells in him. But as for those others, whom you have taken for objects of your devotion, and to whom you have recourse for your salvation, you cannot show me anything that bears a resemblance of these statements. Certainly, then, it must be affirmed that all your devotion in this behalf is but will-worship, founded only on your own passion, and the imagination of your leaders, not upon the good pleasure of the Father. It is strange fire which has issued out of the earth, and was not kindled from heaven; such as cannot, without guilt, either enter into or be used in the sanctuary of God.

II. But I return to the apostle, who, having said that it pleased the Father all fulness should dwell in Christ, adds, in the second place, and "by him to reconcile all things unto himself; by him, I say, whether they be things in earth, or things in heaven." This is the great master-piece of the good pleasure of God; the end for which his will was, that the fulness of all divine and human perfections should be seated in Christ. The particle "and," used by the apostle, signifies this. It does not merely connect the two parts of his discourse, but imports the consecution and dependence of the latter on the former; as if he had said it was the good pleasure of the Father that in Jesus Christ should all fulness dwell, to the end that he might reconcile all things by him. For all this fulness which the Father would that his Christ should have dwelling in him was necessary for his effecting this reconciliation. He needed the power, and the holiness, and the wisdom of the Divinity; and together with it the humility, and the obedience, and the meritorious sufferings of the humanity, that he might finish this design: he could not have been able to reunite heaven and earth with less preparations.

Let us see then what this work is, this reconciling, of which the apostle speaks, of all things terrestrial and celestial in God by Jesus Christ. It is clear by the Scriptures that Jesus Christ has by his death reconciled men to God, has appeased his wrath, and opened to us the throne of his grace, as the apostle teaches us in various places, and particularly in Rom. v. 10, 11, where he saith that we have been "reconciled to God by the death of his Son;" and in 2 Cor. v. 18, that God "hath reconciled us to himself by Jesus Christ." But it seems that this is not precisely that reconciliation which Paul means here; first, because the things in heaven, which he expressly puts among the parties reconciled, have no part therein; the angels that dwell in the heavens, pure and holy as they are, having never fallen into any alienation from God. Secondly, because of that reconciliation the apostle speaks in the words immediately following, in which he saith, "having made peace by the blood of his cross;" so that the former words must of necessity be referred to some other reconciliation, except we render the language of this divine writer culpable of a vain and fruitless repetition. The truth is, they that understand these words of reconciliation with God find themselves much entangled in the matter, and have recourse to divers means for clearing them of this difficulty. Some affirm, that though the angels are holy and blessed, yet they were not exempt from needing the death of Jesus Christ to merit and obtain their confirmation and perseverance in that state; a bold doctrine, and such as it is difficult to find any foundation for in the Scripture. For by this reckoning Jesus Christ should also be the Mediator of angels; a thing that seems to oppose the end and true nature of this office; first, because a Mediator should partake of the nature of the parties whom he reconciles, as you see that Jesus Christ, the Mediator between God and men, is God and man; whereas he took not the nature of angels. Secondly, because every mediator intervenes between parties who are at difference; whereas the angels are, and ever were, at perfect accord with God, holily obeying his will. Lastly, because the blood of Jesus Christ was shed only to wash away sin, and the Scripture everywhere represents the people of God's covenant, his redeemed ones, and those whom he has saved, as justified and cleansed from their filth; for which there was no place in the nature of angels, they being pure and free from all sin. As to that passage in Job, that God putteth "no trust in his servants, and his angels he charged with folly," Job iv. 18, it is evident, and acknowledged by all christians, that this is not said to accuse those blessed spirits, or to suggest that if they were tried by the ordinary and strict justice of God, they would be found guilty, and have need of pardon; but rather to signify either that the authority of God over his creatures is so great and so absolute, that he owes nothing to the angels themselves, how exquisite soever their sanctity, the light of glory wherewith he crowns them being a gift from his own bounty, and not the due reward of their merit; or else that the infinite purity of this supreme Majesty is so splendid and so glorious, that the light of the most holy spirits fades before him, and is found dusky and defective in comparison of his; as the shining of our lights, and of the stars themselves, disappears at the brightness of the sun. Others, not able to approve of this interpretation, (and I think justly,) that the angels were reconciled to God by Jesus Christ, in order to exclude them from this passage, restrain the apostle's words to men only; understanding by the "things that are in heaven," the already hallowed spirits of the faithful, which death had taken out of this world; and by "the things that are on earth," the faithful that yet live here in flesh. But, not to dissemble, this exposition seems both forced and frigid. Forced, because the Scripture, by "things in heaven," ordinarily means the angels, whose element and natural habitation the heavens are; whereas souls separated from their bodies are received in and lodged there by a supernatural grace and dispensation. Frigid, because the sense it attributes to the apostle no way answers the sublimity and dignity of his words. For if his aim were to express nothing but that the faithful are reconciled to God, what need was there to divide them into two ranks, some who are on earth, others who are in heaven? Who doubts but he reconciled these as well as those? But without question he purposed to magnify this work of God by Jesus Christ, and to this end saith that it extends not to men alone, who are reconciled to the Father by the efficacy of the cross of the Lord, but that it exerts an influence in heaven itself, reuniting and reconciling the things that are there.

What shall we say then to these difficulties, and in what sense shall we take the apostle's words, that God hath reconciled all things in himself, both those that are on earth, and those that are in heaven? Dear brethren, we will leave them in their genuine and ordinary sense, and say that these expressions signify the recomposing and reuniting of the creatures, both terrestrial and celestial; not with God, but among themselves, with each other. For as in a state the subjects have a twofold union; one with their prince, on whom they all depend; another among themselves, as members of the same political body, joined together by the bond of mutual concord, amity, and correspondence: in like manner is it with things celestial and terrestrial, the two principal parties of this great state of God, which we call the universe. Besides the union they have with God as their sovereign Monarch, from whose bounty they receive the being and the life they enjoy; they have another alliance and conjunction one with the other, as parts of one corporation, having been formed and qualified for mutual fellowship. It is in this relation, and in this union, that the beauty and perfection of the universe consists, when heaven and earth have amicable intercourse, and conspire to one and the same end, with a holy and reciprocal affection. Sin having broken the first union, and separated man from his Creator, by the same means dissolved the second, loosening us from the creatures. As in a state, when some of the subjects rise against the sovereign, those who remain loyal presently disunite from the rebels, and instead of the intercourse they held before with them, make implacable war upon them, while they continue in their disobedience. Such the event proved in the world. Man had no sooner rebelled against God, but heaven, and all that remained in obedience, separated from man. All nature took up arms against this rebel, and would even then have utterly ruined him, if the counsel of God, who would not destroy us, had not hindered it. And as from one disorder there never fail to spring up many others, this first rupture of man with God and the good creatures brought forth innumerable others, rending mankind itself into several pieces, dividing one from the other by diversity of religions, and the aversions and animosities that attend them. Such was the sad and dismal state of the world, the end of which could be nothing else but ruin and eternal perdition; therefore God, to restore its primitive beauty, yea, to raise it to a perfection higher than that of its first original, reconciled all things by his Christ, both terrestrial and celestial. He took away the wars, hatreds, and aversions that divided them, and reduced them all into that union which they ought to have for his glory and their own good. As to things on earth, you know the enmity of the Jews and the separation of the Gentiles, whom the law, as a partition wall, prohibited from the fellowship of the people of God. Christ laid this enclosure even with the ground, and recalling the Gentiles, associated and reallied them with the Jews, to make them thenceforth one and the same people. He did as much to the distinctions which separated the more polite nations from the barbarous, the Latins from the Greeks, the east from the west, the north from the south. He removed all these marks and differences, and united all nations, sects, and conditions into one only people, into one body, namely, his church. Thus "things on earth" were reconciled. As for "things in heaven," it was the good pleasure of the Father to reconcile them also by his Son. For after sin entered, the angels, the true citizens of heaven, were our foes; whereas they are henceforth our friends and allies, united with us under Jesus Christ, our common Head. Aforetime they were armed against us with a flaming sword; now they fight for us, and encamp about us. They drove us away from the entrance into Paradise; now they bear our souls thither, at their departure from this life. They take part in our interests, are sad at our disasters, and rejoice at our repentance. And to testify how delightful this reconciliation is to them, they saluted the birth of our Lord, who came to make it, with their songs and melodies. For it they glorified God, and blessed and congratulated men. But as the mischief of our sin communicated itself to all parts of the universe, even to those which are without life, putting them all in disorder, and subjecting them to vanity; so I account that this blessed reconciliation must be extended also to them. The will of God was to comprehend them also in it; reuniting the heavens with our earth, and all the elements with us. For heaven, which had nothing but lightnings and thunder for us, and that would rather have reduced us to nothing than receive us into its courts, is now liberal towards us of its comfortable light, and opens to us the most secret sanctuaries of its glory. Life is at agreement with us, immortality is in good understanding with our flesh, the grave is no longer our enemy, the elements shall be serviceable to our welfare, they shall work no more against us. Thus you see how the will of God was to reconcile things on earth and things in heaven by his Son; and reduce all the parts of the universe to good terms each with other. This great work is begun, the foundations of it are laid, the pledges of it are given us. But it will not be perfectly accomplished till the latter day, when the world, freed from the bondage under which it yet groans, shall appear entirely changed; its new heavens, and its new earth, and its new elements, with the angels and saints, and all its other parts, conspiring together in an eternal concord, and an inviolable intercourse, to the glory of their common Creator, who shall then be "all in all," as the apostle declares, 1 Cor. xv. 28. And, in my opinion, he specially means this in this place, when he saith that the Father would reconcile all things in himself, as the original precisely means. For these words signify, not the term, but the end and event of this reconciliation; that is to say, that it shall be made, not with God, (as the greater part of expositors have understood it,) but for the glory of God. For it is plain that heavenly things were not reconciled to God, for they never were opposed to him. But it is no less evident that their reconciliation with us, in the sense we have explained it, will redound to the glory of God, when this whole universe shall return entirely to its true and due union. When therefore the apostle saith, that it is the good pleasure of the Father to reconcile all things in himself, he intends it shall be for himself, that is, for his own glory.

III. It remains now that we speak of the means which God used to bring this great work of the reconciliation of the world to its end. Paul shows this to us, when he adds, having made peace by the blood of the cross of Christ. The war that man had with God, in consequence of his sin, was the true and only cause of the bad understanding which existed between us, the angels, and the other parts of the world. Whence it is clear that, to make the latter cease, it was only necessary to extinguish the former; that is, to reconcile us with the creatures, it required only to recover us to the favour of the Creator. This is the means which the Father in his sovereign wisdom used, and which the apostle means, when he saith that he "made peace;" that is, our peace, having pacified his own justice, and quenched all the fire of his wrath against us. By the sacrifice that Jesus Christ offered on his cross this miraculous change was wrought. This precious blood satisfied the justice of the Father, and the odour of this divine burnt-offering sweetened his Spirit; and, severe and inexorable as he was, rendered him propitious and favourable to us. Instead of fulminating his vengeance, he tenders us the arms of his love; and no man is so wretched but he is ready to receive him, provided he accept the promise of his mercy with a humble faith. Not long since, upon one ot the foregoing texts, we treated of the reality, the worthiness, and necessity of this satisfaction, by which the Lord Jesus made our peace with the Father, through the shedding of his blood on the cross, and his voluntarily suffering there, in our room, the curse which our sins deserved. Therefore we will dispense with speaking more of it at this time; and, to conclude the exercise, will content ourselves with briefly remarking upon each of the three points explained, the principal heads of consolation and edification which they contain.

And here, dear brethren, which shall we most admire—the goodness of the Father, and the will he had to raise us up from our fall, and to reconcile us with the whole creation, whose hatred and aversion we had incurred; or his unspeakable wisdom, in ordering this great word, and in the means he elected and employed to compass it; or the love of the Son, who for our welfare spared not his own blood? Sinner, approach the throne of God with boldness. He is no longer environed with flames and lightning flashes. He is full of grace and clemency. Fear not his indignation or his severity; peace is made. Your rebellions are expiated, your sins are purged. God requires nothing of you but faith and repentance. His justice is satisfied, and doubt not but the satisfaction it hath received is sufficient. He that made it for you is the well-beloved of the Father, the Lord of glory, in whom all fulness dwells. You will find abundantly in him all the good things which are necessary for your felicity; the light of wisdom, to dissipate your darkness, and illuminate your understandings to a perfect knowledge of divine things; a righteousness most complete, and sufficient every way to justify and exempt you from the curse of the law, and to open the entrance of the tribunal of God to you; a most efficacious sanctification, to mortify the lusts of your flesh, and fill you with love, honesty, and purity; and a most plentiful redemption, to deliver you from death, and from all the evils that have connection with it, and put you in eternal possession of immortality. Make your advantage of this divine well of life. Give no ear to them that call you anywhere else. You are happy enough, if you possess the Lord Jesus. He is the only Prince of salvation, the way, the truth, and the life. And as for creatures, whether earthly or heavenly, fear them not. If you are Jesus Christ's, they shall do you no evil. He has reconciled them all to you. He has taken from them all the will and power they had to hurt you. They desire your good, and secretly favour you, owning you for their friends and allies. Heaven looks down on you in peace, and calls you up into its holy place. The angels bless you, and direct all your ways. This earth will hold you no longer than your common

Lord shall judge expedient for his own glory and your salvation.

But if this general peace which you have now with God and the world rejoice you, the means by which it was procured should no less ravish you; even that blood of Christ shed upon the cross, the grand miracle of God, the price of your liberty, the salvation and the glory of the universe. What and how ardent was that love which gave so rich and so admirable a ransom for you! What will he deny you, who has not kept back his own blood from you! who to make you happy, abhorred not a cross, the most infamous of all punishments! who, to raise you up to the most eminent contentment, underwent the extremest dolours; the lowest disgrace, to bring you to the highest glory; the malediction of God, to communicate to you his benediction! Oh, over-happy christians, if you could discern your bliss! Where is the anguish of spirit or the trouble of conscience, or the loss, or the suffering, or the reproach, which the meditation of this love should not console? Who shall condemn us, since the Son of God died to merit our absolution? Who shall accuse us, since his blood and his cross defend us? Who shall take from us the benevolence of the Father, since he has obtained it for us, and preserves it for us? Who shall pluck out of our hands a life he has given us, a salvation that he has so dearly bought?

Dear brethren, these considerations, which open to us so rich a source of consolation, oblige us also to a peculiar sanctification. For how great will be the hardness of our hearts, if these great evidences which God has given us of his love do not affect us! if they kindle not in us an ardent affection towards a God who has so loved us, a sacred and inviolable respect towards a Redeemer who has done so much for us! He has reconciled and reunited all things in him, both terrestrial and celestial. Let us live then henceforth in such a manner as may answer this happy alliance. Let us no more afflict heaven, no more scandalize the earth, by the impurity of our deportment. Let us labour, in conjunction with all the creatures, for the service and to the glory of our common Lord. Let us imitate the purity, the zeal, and the obedience of those celestial spirits, into whose society we are entered by the benefit of this reconciliation. Let us be clothed as they are, with a beautiful and pleasing light. Our lot is, to be one day like them, in immortality; let us be so, for the present, in sanctity. Our peace is made with God. Let us not make war upon him any more. He has pardoned us all the enormity and rage of our rebellion; let us never turn to any of them again. He will be our good Lord and gracious Master. Let us be his faithful subjects and obedient servants. Let the blood of Christ wipe away both our guilt and our filth. Let us fasten our old man to his cross; let the nails that there pierced his flesh pierce also the members of ours. Let the cross that made him die make all our lusts die, and extinguish by little and little in us that earthly, carnal and vicious life which we derive from the first Adam, to regenerate and raise us up again with the Second, to a new, holy and spiritual life, worthy of that blood by which he has purchased it for us, and of that Spirit by whom he has communicated the beginning of it to us, and of that sanctuary of immortality, where he will fully finish it one day to his own glory and our eternal blessedness. Amen.

SERMON XI.

VERSES 21, 22.

And you, that were sometime alienated and enemies in your mind by wicked works, yet now hath he reconciled in the body of his flesh through death, to present you holy and unblamable and unreprovable in his sight.

DEAR brethren, it was long since observed by philosophers, and we still find it by experience, that general things actuate the spirits of men but very little. The cause is, that being naturally bound too closely, every one to his particular interests, they mind only that which affects them, and are not solicitous about a common concern, till by some means they are made painfully sensible that they have a part in it. The ministers of the church therefore should not content themselves with proposing the maxims of heavenly doctrine collectively, and in general terms only, to the souls whose edification is committed to them; but that they may get hold of them, and produce some good effect upon them, they must apply to them in particular each of those divine verities. Paul, whose example should serve as a rule to all the true servants of God, takes this course in several places in his Epistles; and particularly in the text we have now read. For having before represented to the Colossians the reconciliation of things on earth and things in heaven, by means of the peace which was made through the blood of Christ, according to the good pleasure of the Father, he now descends from general things to particular cases; and to excite in the hearts of these faithful persons a more lively feeling of this grace of God, he reminds them by name of the part which they had in it; inasmuch as the efficacy of this grace had been displayed upon them, in drawing them out from perdition, and advancing them to the highest happiness. "And you, that were sometime alienated and enemies in your minds by wicked works, yet now hath he reconciled in the body of his flesh through death, to present you holy and unblamable and unreprovable in his sight." To heighten the excellency of the benefit God had conferred on them, he first sets before their eyes their miserable estate by nature, before the gospel was preached unto them. You were, saith he, formerly alienated from God, "and enemies in your mind by wicked works." Next, he sets forth the favour which God afterward showed them, notwithstanding all their unworthiness. And "yet now," says he, "hath he reconciled you in the body of his flesh through death." Finally, to induce them to pursue a complete sanctification, he represents to them the purpose or end of their reconciliation with God: "to present you holy and unblamable and unreprovable in his sight." These three points we will handle, God willing, in this sermon, distinctly, one after the other. The first and natural estate of the Colossians before grace; their reconciliation with God, made in the body of the flesh of Christ, by his death; and the end of this reconciliation, to be holy and unreprovable before him.

I. Certainly, since the sin of Adam corrupted and infected our nature, there are no men born into the world whose condition of itself is not most wretched. Yet their misery is nowhere so clearly discovered as in the heathen, who are born and live without the covenant of God. For as to those whom he prevents with his grace, by training them up in his church from the beginning of their life, his light and his goodness encompassing them from their nativity, hinder them from discerning so fully the horrid corruption of our nature. Whereas, heathens having no other guide but that nature, its state and strength is to be manifestly seen in them. The Colossians, to whom Paul writes, were of this order, Gentiles by extraction, by religion, and in manners, before Jesus Christ enlightened them. Let us behold in them an image of the condition in which we should be if God had not separated us from the rest of men, and seasonably drawn us out of our original misery. The apostle saith, first, that "sometime," that is, before their conversion, they were "alienated," that is, estranged from God, from his covenant, and from his people, as he explains it more largely elsewhere. Remember, says he to the Ephesians, "that at that time ye were without Christ, being aliens from the commonwealth of Israel, and strangers from the covenants of promise, having no hope, and without God in the world," Eph. ii. 12. They had no communion with the true God; were so far from adoring him, that they not even so much as thought on him, and derided the only nation in the world that knew and served him. This is clear from the books of the ancient heathens which are still extant, as well as from the ignorance and idolatry of the modern.

But the apostle goes further still, and adds, that at that time they were enemies of God; which comprehends two things: first, that they hated God, and warred against him; the second, that God accounted and pursued them as his enemies.

And, first, Paul declares this expressly in the Epistle to the Romans, where, among other characters which he gives the heathen, he mentions that they were "full of envy, murder, debate, deceit, malignity; whisperers, backbiters, haters of God," Rom. i. 29, 30; upon which a question arises, how it is true that the heathen hated God. For either they knew him, or they knew him not. If they knew him not, how did they hate him, since love and hatred are two passions which cannot be exercised but towards objects known, it being as impossible to hate as it is to love that which we know not? And if they knew him, seeing he is the chief good, how is it possible they should hate him, since our will is not capable of hating any known good? To this I answer, first, that when the Scripture says the heathen hated God, it does not mean that God was the proper and formal object of their hatred. For it is certain that in this sense the Deity cannot be hated by them who are ignorant of him, nor can he be otherwise than loved by those who know him. But the Holy Ghost thus speaks, to signify that these wretches act altogether as if they hated God. It is a form of speech familiar enough, to put the cause for the effect, and the antecedent for the consequent. Now these people, in their blindness, defaced the glory of God as much as they could. They battered down the most illustrious marks of his Godhead; they blasphemed his providence, they reviled his nature. They robbed him of the honour of creating and preserving the universe, and gave it to monsters. They despised his will, and reversed all his orders. They passionately loved that which he most abhorred, and abhorred that with which he is best pleased. Are not these the ordinary and natural effects of hatred? It is, therefore, with great propriety that the Scripture, to set forth the impiety and fury of the heathens, says that they hated God, since they treated him in the very same manner as if they had directly hated him. As when the wise man says, that the wicked hate their own soul, or their own life, Prov. xxix. 24; viii. 36, it is not to signify that their will has, properly, any aversion to their own life; on the contrary, they love it too much: but to declare that they conduct themselves just as if they expressly hated it, loving and practising, with extreme vehemency, the things that cause their ruin, and neglecting and abhorring those which would lead them to salvation.

Secondly, though the heathen have some knowledge of God, yet because they suppose him to be quite opposed to that which he really is, they may with propriety be said to hate him. For though it be not possible for us to hate good, so far as it is good; nevertheless it often happens, that error representing things to us as quite contrary to what they are in themselves, we love that which is indeed worthy of hatred, and we hate that which is in truth most worthy to be loved. From such an illusion did the pagans' hatred of God arise. For imagining him a tyrant, full of cruelty and injustice; or an idle king, who has no care of his state; it needs not to be wondered at that, their understanding falsely conceiving him under so monstrous a likeness, their will should be influenced to hate him, rather than to love him. And those among them who had a better opinion of him, nevertheless loved him not; for by an extreme perversion of mind, which placed their supreme happiness in the enjoyment of pleasures and vices, while sensible that God hated them and punished them, they considered him as an enemy to their felicity. Thus the love of vice induced them to hate him. Whence it followed, that God on his side being supremely good and just, condemned their impiety, and resolved to punish it. This is what the Scripture figuratively calls God's hatred; and this is what the apostle means, when he says that the Colossians in their paganism were enemies of God.

But to show us how deeply this enmity was rooted in them, having said that they were enemies, he adds, "in their minds" or understanding. The understanding is the principal and highest faculty of our soul, which moves and guides our wills and affections, and is consequently the governor of our whole life. The apostle says, therefore, that rebellion and enmity against God have taken up their seat in the understanding; seizing, if we may so speak, on this grand citadel of our nature, and from thence continually making war against God. This war, the apostle intends, when he adds, "by wicked works." I should never finish if I were to attempt now to describe all the enormities of the lives of the heathen. Paul gives us an epitome of them in the first chapter of the Epistle to the Romans: he there expatiates upon the principal fruits of their impiety, their injustice, their uncleanness, and their abominations; vice being grown to such a height among them, that they not only committed it, but also favoured it, and took no shame to adore the very persons whom they confessed to have been extremely imbued with it. This dissoluteness and abandonment to wicked works was a clear conviction of their enmity against God, and renders them altogether inexcusable; because however great and universal their corruption, yet they were not ignorant, as the apostle says shortly afterwards, "that they which commit such things are worthy of death," Rom. i. 32.

This doctrine, touching the state of the heathens, deserves great consideration. For it teaches us two things of very great importance: first, the quality of the corruption of our nature by sin; and secondly, its extent. Respecting its quality, you see it is so horrible, that it sets us far from God, and makes us strangers and enemies to him; it is so deep, that it has insinuated itself into all the faculties of our souls, even the understanding itself, the noblest of them all; and finally, it is so contagious, that it infects all our works with its venom, none issuing forth but wicked ones. Hence it appears, first, how false and pernicious is the imagination of those who place this corruption in the lower part of the soul only, in the affections and sensual appetites, and in their resistance of reason; and assert that the understanding has remained in its integrity. Paul plainly declares the contrary, lodging enmity and rebellion against God in the understanding of the heathens; and this truth he testifies in various places: as when he says, that "the natural man receiveth not the things of the Spirit of God; for they are foolishness unto him, neither can he know them," 1 Cor. ii. 14; and that "the carnal mind is enmity against God; for it is not subject to the law of God, neither indeed can be," Rom. viii. 7. And in the Epistle to the Ephesians, that the Gentiles have their "understanding darkened," Eph. iv. 18. We confess, then, that this evil is universal; that it has depraved our whole nature, and left nothing sound or whole in us, from the sole of the foot to the crown of the head. It has extinguished the light of the understanding, and filled it with the thickest darkness. It has made the motions of the will irregular, and dreadfully disordered all the passions and affections. And so palpable is this, that the two masters of pagan philosophy have in some degree perceived it, and as it were, felt it, while they were groping in their darkness. One of them records in writing, that the soul of man is sick of two maladies, ignorance and wickedness; and the other, that there is something in our nature, I know not what, which resists right reason.* On the same ground you may observe again, how vain is the conceit of those who ascribe I know not what merits of congruity, as they call them, to men out of the state of grace. Would you know how the Colossians invited God to gratify them with the light of his gospel? They were, says the apostle, "alienated and enemies in their minds by wicked works." If a subject merits the favour of his sovereign, by

* Plato in Soph. Aristotle, Ethic. l. 1.

turning his back upon him and departing from him; if rebellion and enmity constrain him to be gracious; if wicked works incline the goodness of God to communicate itself to men; then I confess that they who are out of his covenant may merit his grace. But since it is quite the contrary, and everybody well knows that such conduct evidently provokes justice, and enforces punishment; who does not see that man, while he is in the corruption of his nature, merits nothing, either by way of condignity or of congruity, but the curse of God, according to what the apostle says in another place, that "by nature we are children of wrath?" Eph. ii. 3.

Secondly, this text discloses to us the extent of this corruption. For if any sort of men could be found exempted from it, in all probability it would be the Greeks, the most polite and civilized of all people. Nevertheless the apostle involves them here in this universal misery. From this it appears how much some of the most ancient writers of christianity were mistaken, whom the love of learning and secular erudition so charmed, that they hesitated not to say that the Gentiles, by means of their philosophy, might become acceptable to God, and attain salvation.* I admit that they had a very quick understanding, as we discover by their books, in which they have left us admirable specimens of the acuteness of their minds. Neither do I deny that God presented them, both in the nature and government of this vast universe, with very clear and most illustrious arguments of his power, wisdom, goodness, and providence; as Paul says, "He left not himself without witness," Acts xiv. 17; and again, "That which may be known of God is manifested in them," &c., Rom. i. 19, 20. But all this light only shows us the greatness of their corruption. For they, with all the vivacity of their spirits, made no proficiency in the school of providence toward fearing God and serving him, but became vain in their imaginations, and miserably abused the gifts of heaven; so that the only result of this dispensation was, that they were thereby rendered inexcusable. We conclude, then, that all men generally, not one excepted, are by nature such as the apostle here describes the Colossians, alienated, and enemies in their minds by wicked works. There is nothing but the word of the Lord which is able to bring them out of this state by the saving grace of his Spirit with which God accompanies it. And this the apostle represents here to the Colossians, in the second place. For having minded them of their former condition, he adds, "yet now hath he reconciled in the body of his flesh," that is, the flesh of Jesus Christ, through his death.

Their former condition was very miserable. For what can

* Clem. Alexand. Strom. 6.

be imagined more wretched than men far from God and strangers to Him, in whose communion alone all their welfare consists—men, enemies to Him without whose love they can have no true good? Yet, in addition to misery, there was also horror in their case. Misery ordinarily stirs up pity; theirs was worthy of abhorrence and hatred. For what is there in the world that less deserves the compassion of God and men, or is more worthy of the execration of heaven and earth, than a subject who withdraws from his sovereign; who hates him, and wars against him; who insolently violates all his laws, and abandons himself to all the crimes he has forbidden; especially if the sovereign be gracious and beneficent, as the Lord is, the only author of all our being, life, and motion? But, O inestimable and incomprehensible goodness! God, for all this, did not forbear to have pity on the Colossians. He sought them when they were alienated from him; he offered them peace when they made war upon him; he took them for his friends, and chose them for his children, when they showed him the greatest hatred and enmity. Their wicked works deserved his curse, and he bestowed on them his grace. Their rebellion deserved his direful flashes, and he sent them his comfortable light.

II. This contrast the apostle here indicates when he says, "yet now hath he reconciled." A similar contrast he expresses elsewhere, upon the same subject, saying, "God commendeth his love toward us, in that, while we were yet sinners, Christ died for us," Rom. v. 8. To set forth this great grace of God towards these faithful people, he says that God hath reconciled them. Having spoken of their estrangement and of their enmity with God, with great propriety he uses the word reconcile to signify bringing them again into his love and favour. It happens sometimes, in the misunderstandings of men, that aversion and hatred are only on one side, one of the parties seeking the favour of the other. Here, as we have before intimated, the aversion was mutual. For we hated God, and he, because of our sins, hated us. It was necessary, therefore, for our restoration, that both the one and the other of these passions should be remedied; that is, that the wrath of God against us should be appeased, and our hatred and enmity against him extinguished. The word reconcile, of itself, comprehends both; but in the apostle's writings it refers principally to the first, that is, the mitigation and appeasing of the wrath of God; and indeed this is the principal point of our reconciliation. For God being our sovereign Lord, it would not benefit us at all to change our will towards him if his did not operate favourably towards us; as the repentance and tears of a subject are vain, if his prince reject them, and remain still angry with him.

Again, the word *reconcile*, as also most words of the same

form and nature, is taken two ways. For either it signifies simply the action which has the virtue necessary to make reconciliation, or it comprises the effect of it also. It is in the first sense that the apostle used it before, when he said that God hath reconciled all things, celestial and terrestrial, in himself, or for himself, having made peace through the blood of the cross of Christ. For he means simply that God has taken away the causes of hatred and enmity, and opened the way of reconciliation; not that all things are already actually reconciled. It is thus again that we must understand that which he says in another place, "that God was in Christ, reconciling the world unto himself, not imputing their trespasses unto them," 2 Cor. v. 19. But the apostle uses the word *reconcile* in the second sense, when he says that we have obtained reconciliation by Christ; and when he beseeches us to "be reconciled to God;" it being evident that in these places he intends not the right and power only, but the very effect and actual possession of reconciliation. According to this import we must understand the word reconcile in the text. For this reconciliation may be again considered two ways: first, in general, as made by Jesus Christ on the cross; and secondly, in particular, as applied to each of us by faith. In the first consideration it is presented to all men as sufficient for their salvation, according to the doctrine of the apostle, that "the grace of God that bringeth salvation hath appeared to all men," Tit. ii. 11; and that also of John, that Jesus Christ "is the propitiation for our sins: and not for ours only, but also for the sins of the whole world," 1 John ii. 2. Under the second consideration it appertains only to the believer, according to that clause of the covenant which declares that the only begotten Son was given to the world, "that whosoever believeth in him should not perish, but have everlasting life," John iii. 16. Precisely in this sense the apostle here says that God had reconciled the Colossians; he means, not simply that God had not only prepared the way through the cross of his Son for their reconciliation to him by believing, but also that he had effectively reconciled them to himself, and put them in real possession of the benefits that were purchased for us by the merit of Christ; embracing them as his children, pardoning all their sins, and obliviating all his wrath and aversion against them which their offences had enkindled.

But again, the apostle here informs them of the means by which this reconciliation was effected, it being a subject of infinite importance both to the glory of God and their edification. He hath reconciled you, he says, "in the body of his flesh" (that is to say, of the flesh of his Christ) "through death." There is not one of these words that does not possess very great force. First, when he speaks here of the body of our Lord, he intimates to us the mystery of his incarnation.

As if he had said that God so loved us, that he would have his own Son to become man, to reunite and reconcile us to himself. He would have this divine person, whose essence is spiritual and infinite, to assume a visible and finite body. He shows us also by this expression the sacrifice by which the wrath of God was appeased, and our crimes expiated. For it is properly for this that the Son of God had a body, as the apostle teaches us, when, opposing this body of the Lord to sacrifices of living creatures, that were unprofitable and incapable of satisfying the justice of the Father, he introduces him saying, "Sacrifice and offering thou wouldst not, but a body hast thou prepared me;" and further he adds, "by the which will we are sanctified through the offering of the body of Jesus Christ," Heb. x. 5, 10.

But the apostle does not say simply the body of Christ; he adds, "the body of his flesh," that is according to the style of the Hebrews, his fleshy body, his body of flesh. At first it may appear to you that this addition is needless, and to no purpose; but it is far otherwise. For in the language of Scripture every body is not flesh. It gives this name only to a feeble and mortal body. He means therefore that the Lord, to reconcile us, not only assumed a body, which indeed is very marvellous, but that he took a feeble and mortal body, a body sustaining itself by meat and drink, a body like ours, and subject to all their meannesses and infirmities. A consideration, as you perceive, that exceedingly enhances both the excellency of his love towards us, and the value of the means by which he reconciled us; the King of glory, who is the Author and Mediator of this work, having invested himself with poor flesh to compass his design. And this is the reason why the sacred writers so often use this word to signify our Lord's human nature; they say that "God was manifested in the flesh;" that "the Word was made flesh;" that the Son partook of flesh and blood, 1 Tim. iii. 16; John i. 14; Heb. ii. 14. Indeed, this qualification of the body of Christ was necessary for the expiation of our sins, since this could not be effected but by sufferings, of which a fleshy body only is capable. Hence it follows that, in the 6th chapter of John, where he himself speaks of the virtue he has to quicken us, he also uses these very words, "My flesh is meat indeed, and my blood is drink indeed;" and "The bread that I will give is my flesh which I will give for the life of the world," ver. 51, 55. From this I understand this passage as referring to the natural body of Christ, and not to his mystical body, to which some suppose it to refer. I acknowledge that the Lord receives into the union of his mystical body, his church that is, all those who, applying to themselves the promises of his gospel by faith, are effectually reconciled to God. Yet this is not the body to which the apostle here alludes, since the body he speaks of is the body of the flesh of the Lord, which cannot be affirmed of his mystical body. When he says, therefore, that God hath reconciled us in his body, it must be understood as though he had said, by his body. For, as we have often informed you, it is the ordinary practice of Scripture to put *in* for *by*. And hence it appears how extravagant was the imagination of some ancient heretics, who authoritatively affirmed that Jesus Christ had but a vain and false appearance of a body, and not a real, solid, and true body; as was also the error of those who confessed he had a true body, but held it to be celestial, and of quite a different matter and substance from ours. The apostle refutes these foolish fancies by terming the body of our Lord "the body of his flesh."

Having said that we were "reconciled in the body of his flesh," the apostle adds, in the last place, "through death." It was not enough, my christian brethren, that the King of glory, the Prince of life, assumed to himself a body, and even a body of flesh, vile and infirm as yours, to reconcile you to God; it was necessary that he should die. His flesh would have profited you nothing, if it had not suffered that death which you deserved. But of this death of the Lord, of its necessity and efficacy, we have spoken largely, upon the preceding texts. Here we will only make two remarks before we proceed further. The first is, that Christ satisfied the justice of his Father for us, since it is by his death that he reconciled us; for unless this be asserted, it is evident his death will have contributed nothing to our reconciliation; in this respect he would have died in vain. Let it be granted that it was needful that he should die to confirm his doctrine, and to give us an example of patience; though in truth this does not appear to be a sufficient reason why the Son of God should die, still upon this supposition his death will have contributed nothing to our reconciliation with the Father. His own mercy alone, and not any consideration of this death, would have appeased him towards us. And nevertheless, the apostle says expressly, we were reconciled through that death which the Lord suffered in the body of his flesh. Surely then it must be acknowledged that it quenched the wrath of the Father; that is to say, it satisfied his justice for us. The other particular which I would notice here is, that the body of the Lord made propitiation for our sins only as it was mortal flesh that suffered death. Every one confesses that now he dieth no more; yea, that he is invested with a sovereign glory, having for ever put off the infirmity and mortality of the flesh. Certainly then it is vainly and without reason that some imagine that his body is still offered to this day for the reconciling of sinners unto God. It is through death that he hath reconciled us, says Paul; and being now "raised from the dead," he again says, he "dieth no more," Rom. vi. 9.

III. But I come to the third and last particular in our text, in which the apostle asserts that it is "to present us holy and unblamable and unreprovable in his sight" that God hath reconciled us by the death of his Son. It is strictly in the original, to present us, or to make us stand and appear, before him holy, unblamable, and unreprovable, which has given occasion to some of our expositors to refer these words also to our justification before God; as if the apostle meant that he made our peace, and abolished the enmity, that being purified by the virtue of the sacrifice of his Son, and clothed with his righteousness, by faith, we might appear before the tribunal of his grace, without condemnation and without confusion. But there is nothing to induce us to fix on this interpretation; it is much better, in my judgment, to consider it as referring to our sanctification than to our justification. First, because the words themselves agree with it much better; the Scripture, as you know, ordinarily expressing the gift of regeneration by the word holiness; whereas it uses the word justify, or pardon of our sins, and not imputing them unto us, when it would signify the first benefit of God which we obtain by the imputation of the righteousness of Christ. Secondly, because the apostle having already represented it unto us in those words, that God hath reconciled us in the body of the flesh of his Son, through death, which signify that he has received us into favour, pardoning all our sins, as has been explained, it seems needless to repeat the same thing again. And finally, because both Paul and the other sacred writers are accustomed to join those two gifts of God, our justification and sanctification, together, as two inseparable graces, which are never without each other; so that having spoken to us of one, it was not only convenient, but also in some degree necessary, that he should annex the other; just as, elsewhere, having said that "Christ is made unto us righteousness," he immediately adds, "and sanctification," 1 Cor. i. 30; and again, in another place, where having touched the filthiness of the former life of the Corinthians, as here that of the Colossians, he says, "But ye are washed, but ye are sanctified," 1 Cor. vi. 11. Here the apostle not only knits these two graces together, but shows us the order and relation which they have to each other; that the second, namely, "sanctification," is the end of the former, that is, of "justification." He hath reconciled us, says he, through the death of his Son, to present us "holy and unblamable and unreprovable in his sight." The Scripture teaches us the same thing in various other places; as in Luke, where Zacharias says, "That we being delivered out of the hand of our enemies might serve him without fear, in holiness and righteousness before him,"

Luke i. 74, 75. And Peter, in his First Epistle, says, "Who his own self bare our sins in his own body on the tree, that we, being dead to sin, should live unto righteousness," 1 Pet. ii. 24. And Paul tells us that Jesus Christ "died for all, that they which live should not henceforth live unto themselves, but unto him which died for them, and rose again," 2 Cor. v. 15; and again, he says that Christ "gave himself for us, that he might redeem us from all iniquity, and purify unto himself a peculiar people, zealous of good works," Tit. ii. 14; and in another passage similar to that which we are discussing, he says, "Christ also loved the church, and gave himself for it; that he might sanctify and cleanse it with the washing of water by the word, that he might present it to himself a glorious church, not having spot, or wrinkle, or any such thing; but that it should be holy, and without blemish," Eph. v. 25—27.

I insist upon this point, because it is of exceeding great importance. First, you see by it what is the dignity of holiness. For since the end is of necessity always more excellent than the means which are used to compass it, it is clear that sanctification, being the last end of all the things that the Lord employs for our salvation, is the greatest and most excellent of all his graces. And you know that Paul positively declares that charity, which is in substance nothing else than sanctity, is more excellent than either faith or hope; and he proves it, because neither of these virtues shall have any place in heaven, they being but means and helps for conducting us thither; whereas charity, the last and highest perfection of our being, shall eternally remain.

Secondly, from hence it appears how much carnal christians deceive themselves, who pretend to salvation without sanctification. Wretched men, what are you doing! Your pretension is a vain chimera. You pursue an impossibility. For that salvation which you desire is substantially that very holiness which you refuse. Both that faith, and those other qualities which you say you possess, serve only to sanctify men; without this they are unprofitable things. Suppose then that you have them; if they do not change you, if they do not fill your heart with love to God and with charity to your neighbour, in short, if they do not render you holy, they will profit you nothing. So far from giving you immortality, they will aggravate your misery, and sink you deeper into the abyss of death. Never believe that God gave us his own Son, that he clothed him with a body of flesh, that he delivered him up to the death of the cross, that he reconciled us by such precious blood, that he wrought all those grand wonders which ravished heaven and earth, that he might procure for us the privilege of sinning freely; far be it from so wise and so holy a Deity, that he should be thought ever to have entertained such an extravagant and infamous a design. He has shed upon us all the blessings of his grace and love, that he might restore his own image in our nature, that he might abolish sin in it, and transform us into new creatures, pure and holy, so as in some measure to resemble himself and his Son.

I confess that the description which the apostle here gives us of this grace of God in us is high and magnificent, and that it seems to surmount the reach of believers while they are in the present life; for of which of them can it be truly said, while he remains in this world, that he is holy, and unblamable, and unreprovable in the sight of God? But to this I answer, first, that the apostle does not affirm that this great work of the Lord's in us is completed in this life; he shows us only his purpose, and the end of his grace, and how good and glorious that holiness is with which he will clothe us. For if we be truly his, he will not leave us till he has made us such as the apostle's text imports, even holy, without blame, and unreprovable. Secondly, I observe that though the highest degree of sanctification in this life is much beneath that which shall adorn us in the next, and that the former is defective in comparison with the latter; yet it is nevertheless true, and has all its parts, though in an inferior degree. It is sincere and without hypocrisy, and such in substance as is agreeable with the words of the apostle. For true believers, while here below, put off the habits of sin, and put on those of holiness, for which reason they are justly called holy; though at times, through infirmity, they are led to the commission of some acts which are contrary to the christian character. They are washed from those foul and odious spots which before deformed their whole life, and an adversary cannot observe or censure anything in their deportment that is contrary to the profession which they make of the covenant of grace. And with respect to that which the apostle adds, that they are such before God, it is only to signify that their piety is true and real, not feigned nor dissembled; that it is not a mask, which deceives the eyes of men, but a disposition of heart which God discerns within them, as men behold the evidences of it without upon them; in the same sense that Luke said of Zacharias and Elisabeth that they "were both righteous before God." Here, beloved brethren, we close our remarks upon this text.

The severity of the weather obliging us to conclude this discourse, I will only touch in a few words upon the lessons which we should deduce from it for our edification, referring it to your diligence to meditate upon each of them, and above all to reduce them carefully to practice.

Remember, first, the miserable state in which you were before God prevented you by his grace; and reflect, that it is to you also the apostle says, "Ye were sometime alienated and enemies in your mind by wicked works." For our ancestors, before the Sun of righteousness shone on these countries, were in the same, or rather in a worse, condition than the Colossians. Our fathers were Hittites, and our mothers Amorites, living in the darkness of paganism, serving a Hesus, and a Belenus, and a Tautates, and I know not what other vanities, sacrificing men to them, and weltering in the filth of the most infamous vices. Being, by the great benignity of God, drawn out of this gulf, we were again cast into another, in which, under other names, we committed the like crimes; adoring an insensible and inanimate thing, and bending down ourselves before wood and stone, and dumb images, and giving to a mortal man the glorious names which belong only to the Son of God; being corrupted both in our thoughts and in our deeds. These faults were so much worse than the former, by how much less ignorant we previously were of our Master's will.

Admire next the goodness of God, who seeing us in this abyss, though our ingratitude and rebellion merited his heaviest vengeance, yet had pity on us; and visiting us in his infinite mercies, has reconciled us by the body of the flesh of his Son, through his death. He has sent to us Epaphrases, as he did to the Colossians, ministers of his word, who have made the voice of Paul and of the other apostles to resound among us. He has purified us, and washed all our filth in the blood of his Christ. With this he has bedewed our hearts, abolished our enmity, extinguished our hatred, and reunited us unto himself; communicating to us the divine body of his Son, nailed for us to the cross, the source of our salvation, and the treasury of all the good things of heaven. His death has been our life, and his malediction our benediction. Let us acknowledge this great goodness of our God with profound gratitude. Let us give him the glory of all the good that may be in us. If there be any light in our understandings, any peace in our consciences, any pureness in our affections, any rectitude in our conduct, let us bless the kindness of this sovereign Lord, who has vouchsafed to illuminate, to reconcile, and to cleanse us. Without this favourable beaming forth of his grace, we should be yet strangers and enemies, in the bondage and darkness of Egypt, or under the yoke and in the captivity of Chaldea. Let us now make use of the benefits he has conferred upon us. Let us continue united to him, so as that nothing may remove us to a distance from him. Let us love him fervently and serve him diligently, lest we become again his enemies. Let those understandings which were formerly the heads of that wicked war which we made against him, strictly maintain that holy and happy peace which he has vouchsafed to conclude with us. Let us banish thence all thoughts of rebellion. Let us still have before our eyes that sacred flesh with which the King of glory was clothed for us, the blood wherewith he purchased our peace, and the death which he underwent to reconcile us unto God his Father. Let us not profane a blessing which cost him so dear. Let us imitate also his goodness. Let us treat our neighbours as he treated us. If they avoid us, let us seek them; for we also were enemies to God, and warred against him, when he called us to the communion of his grace. Above all, let us remember that the end of all the wonders God has wrought on our behalf is to make us holy, unblamable, and unreprovable in his sight. Let us not oppose so admirable and reasonable a design. Let us not frustrate the intentions of so good and merciful a Lord. Dear brethren, I might here make great complaints of the profaneness of some, of the looseness of others, and of the falterings of us all, who labour after nothing less than that high and accomplished sanctification to which God calls us. But I would much rather end with entreaties than with complaints, and conjure you in the name of the Lord, and by your own salvation, that you would judge yourselves; and that renouncing all the faults of the time past, and all the impieties and lusts of this world, you would live henceforth soberly, righteously, and godly, and keep yourselves holy, unblamable, and unreprovable, to the glory of God, the edification of men, and your own salvation. Amen.

SERMON XII.

VERSE 23.

If ye continue in the faith grounded and settled, and be not moved away from the hope of the gospel, which ye have heard, and which was preached to every creature which is under heaven; whereof I Paul am made a minister.

OUR Lord Jesus Christ, in the gospel according to Matthew, tells us of two sorts of people who hear his doctrine and frequent his school: the one, those who put his words in practice; that is, those who, embracing the gospel with a true and lively faith, render him the obedience he demands of them: the other, they who hear, but put not in practice, what he says to them; that is, those who, giving but little or no belief in his divine truth, take no care to perform what he commands, but content themselves with a vain outside profession, and are not inwardly affected and changed as they ought to be. He compares the former to a wise and prudent man that has built his house upon a rock; and when "the rain descended, and the floods came, and the winds blew, and beat upon that house, it fell not; for it was founded upon a rock." But, on the contrary, he compares the latter to a foolish man that built upon the sand; and, when "the rain descended, and the floods came, and the winds blew, and beat upon that house, it fell; and great was the fall thereof." Dear brethren, this is an excellent parable, and worthy to be deeply engraven on the hearts of true believers; for it shows us, first, that to have part in the Lord's salvation, it is not enough to call him our Master, and make profession of his doctrines. Those who have but this will sooner or later fall, and be infallibly ruined. Secondly, it further teaches us that it is not sufficient to begin, except a man persevere to the end. And lastly, it declares to us, what is the cause both of the perseverance of some, and the revolt and fall of others: those who are founded on the rock stand firm, and resist the scandals with which the devil and the world combat the truth; those who are built only on the sand, are easily borne down, even at the first assaults which are made upon them by the adverse powers. This doctrine Paul represented to the Colossians in the text which we have now read. In the foregoing words, as you have heard, he set before their eyes the wonders of the love of God, which had been gloriously showed upon them by Jesus Christ their Saviour, who had called them to his communion, and of strangers and enemies, as they were, made them friends of his Father, reconciling them in the body of his flesh, through death, to render them holy, unblamable, and unreprovable in his sight. But the apostle knowing there were seducers and deceitful workers among them, who laboured to turn them away from the purity and simplicity of the gospel, in order that they might be preserved from the poison of those men, now informs them that this great salvation of which he had spoken could not be assured to them without perseverance. Qualifying, and in some degree correcting, his simple and absolute assertion, that God had reconciled them to himself, he adds the condition upon which this divine grace was promised to them: "If ye continue in the faith grounded and settled," &c. This lesson, my brethren, is no less necessary for us than it was for the Colossians, since the floods, the winds and storms, which were then raised against the edifice of their faith, in like manner at this day beat upon ours; various deceitful workers, both without and within, endeavouring to overthrow it. Let us, therefore, bring this sacred preservative which the apostle here gives us against their malice; and that we may the better profit by it, let us meditate in order upon the three particulars which his instruction contains. To confirm the Colossians in perseverance, he shows them, First, the necessity and the manner of it; "If ye continue in the faith grounded and settled, and be not moved away from the hope of the gospel, which ye have heard." Secondly, he sets before them an excellent argument of the truth of that gospel which they had heard; namely, "that it was preached to every creature under heaven." And lastly, he alleges a second proof of its verity, taken from his own ministry; "whereof," says he, "I am made a minister." These are the three points which we will handle, if it please God, in this discourse, briefly touching upon each of them, as we shall judge most proper for our edification and consolation.

I. The apostle explains the necessity and manner of this perseverance in these terms; "If ye continue in the faith," &c. Where you perceive he lays it down first, that faith is the means by which we enter into the possession and use of the good things of God, which he promises to us in his Son. The old covenant had also its good things, but the condition which it required of men for obtaining them was quite different to that of the new; for it demanded of them an exact and perfect obedience to the law, and upon any failure of an entire accomplishment of it threatened a curse, leaving the sinner no hope of life; according to that dreadful clause, "This do and thou shalt live;" and, "Cursed be he that confirmeth not all the words of this law to do them." But the gospel differs from the law especially in this, that not only are the good things which it sets before us much greater and more divine than those of the law, but it demands of men for possessing them nothing but faith alone, according to our Saviour's own words, "God so loved the world, that he gave his only begotten Son, that whosoever believeth in him should not perish, but have everlasting life." This the apostle here shows us with much clearness, when, having said that God hath reconciled us to himself in the body of the flesh of his Son, to render us holy and unreprovable, he adds, "If ye continue in the faith." This connection of the two parts of his discourse evidently infers that it is faith which causes us to participate in the reconciliation and peace of God, and in the holiness which the gospel imparts. You know, likewise, that in a multitude of other places the Scripture expressly informs us, that it is by faith we are justified and have peace with God, and that it is by faith our hearts are purified. Faith is the means of our union with God; it is the root of our love, the source of our comfort, and, in a word, the only cause of our felicity. For as a medicine, however excellent and healthful it may be, does no good except to those who take it; so the redemption of our Saviour, and the virtue of his sacrifice, however great and infinite, though able to heal all our sins, and to give us eternal life, and that not to us alone, but to all the men in the world, will communicate none of those benefits to us, except we receive it by faith. It is faith that applies it to us, and sheds abroad its efficacy into all the parts of our nature. But as many deceive themselves in this matter, and take that for true faith which has only the shadow and name of it; the apostle tells us that, to have part in the salvation of Jesus Christ, our faith must be constant and persevering. For as in games and combats for prizes none are crowned but those who hold out to the end; so in the heavenly lists or race, God glorifies them only who run with constancy to the goal. Those that turn aside, or stop in the midst of the course, lose their labour; according to the declaration of our Lord, "He that endureth to the end shall be saved." And the apostle, therefore, in another place, when assuring himself of the crown, among other causes on which he grounded this assurance, says particularly that he had "kept the faith," 2 Tim. iv. 7.

From this it appears that there are two sorts of persons who shall be excluded from the salvation of God, purchased by the merit of Jesus Christ. First, all the rebellious and unbelieving, who have no faith in the promises and declarations of the bounty of God; as our Saviour said, "He that believeth not shall be damned," Mark xvi. 16. "He that believeth not the Son shall not see life; but the wrath of God abideth on him," John iii. 36. Secondly, they who believe, but their faith is only for a time; such as abide not in the faith, but having received it at the beginning, afterwards quit and reject it. Either the scorching heat of persecution dries up and consumes the tender bud, or the overflowing irruption of pleasures or of worldly affairs carries it away. The cares of covetousness or ambition suffocate it; or the deceitfulness of error, and the hand of false teachers, pluck it out of their heart. The apostle therefore requires of the Colossians, in order that they might be partakers of the salvation of God, that they not only have faith, but that they persevere in it. "If," says he, "ye continue in the faith."

But this is not all; he would have them also to be "grounded and settled." I acknowledge that it seldom happens that this vain and feeble faith, which consists only in a bare profession and some slight movings of heart, endures to the end in those who have it. Persecution or temptation generally plucks off their mask, and openly carries them out of the fellowship of the church. Yet it appears not impossible for them to continue in this state even to the last. As a little chaff may abide in the floor, if the wind does not blow; so there is some probability that these persons may, in like manner, remain mingled with true believers even until death, if persecution or offence does not seize upon them. But suppose that this really happens, still they shall not be saved; because the faith which they possess, and in which they will have persisted, is a nullity to which God has promised nothing; it is the shadow and the image, not the substance and reality of faith. It follows, therefore, that as chaff, though it remain in the floor, is not locked up in the granary with the wheat, but is left out or burned, as a useless thing; so likewise these people who have only this vain faith, should they abide in God's floor, that is, in the external communion of the church, unto the end, still they shall not enter into his heavenly garner, that is, his kingdom, but shall be rejected and excluded therefrom, as having no lot or portion with true believers. They will think it sufficient to allege that they have lived in the church of Christ, that they have perhaps even prophesied, and cast out devils, and done wonderful works in his name; but the Lord will openly tell them, "I never knew you: depart from me, ye that work iniquity," Matt. vii. 22, 23. The apostle, therefore, to show that he speaks of perseverance, not in this vain shadow of faith, but in true faith, does not simply say, "if ye continue in the faith," but adds, "grounded and settled."

If the hypocrite or the formalist continue in the profession or in the rudiments of piety, it is not because they are grounded, but because they are not tempted; as a woman that remains chaste only because she has not been solicited to evil. They owe their perseverance to the forbearance of their enemies, and not to their own firmness. This false constancy may deceive a man, who sees only the outside and the event of things, but it cannot deceive God, who knows the inside of them, and who searches the heart, and judges of things by what they are, not by what they appear to be, or by their events. The apostle, therefore, directs that, in order to partake of his salvation, we have true perseverance, and continue in the faith, not simply and in any manner, but being grounded and settled in it. God saves such only. It is but for them that he has prepared his kingdom. The former of these words, here used by the apostle, is taken from buildings, which being fixed deep in the earth upon a rock, are firm and solid, and proof against time and storms; whereas buildings which have no foundation, or are built only on sand, are feeble, and unable to resist the shock. Our Lord made use of this same comparison in the parable which we touched upon at the commencement; and he employs it too in that famous promise which he made to Peter, of building his church in such a manner on the rock, that the gates of hell shall not prevail against it. The other word which the apostle uses has the same meaning, and, properly, signifies in the original a thing in such a state of settlement as that it is difficult to move or shake it; a thing that is fixedly seated and placed, and neither totters nor changes. This is the settlement of true believers, who shall have part in the salvation of God. Their faith, grounded on the eternal Rock, Jesus Christ their Lord, seated and placed upon this immovable basis, abides firm and cannot be shaken. The torrents and the winds assault it in vain; the tempests and the floods may beat upon it, but they cannot overthrow it.

Upon this doctrine of the apostle we shall raise two observations. First, that the faith of those who persevere in the sense he intends differs from the faith of those who revolt, not only in the event, inasmuch as one fails, and the other persists and abides, but also in the nature of the thing itself. For the one is grounded and settled, and the other is not so. Who does not see that there is a great difference between a house which is well founded, and one which is but built upon the sand? Jesus Christ and his apostle expressly declare that such as stand are founded, and that such as fall are not so. Certainly, then, the faith of the former is quite different from that of the latter; and this difference in their results, in that one falls and the other bears up, discloses to us the distinction which is between them, but it does not produce it. It is the effect of it, not the cause; an argument of it, not the original. The same thing also appears from the comparison elsewhere, of the one to wheat, and the other to chaff. The wheat is not wheat merely because it abides in the floor, but, on the contrary, it abides in the floor because it is wheat; and in like manner the chaff does not become chaff because it goes out of the floor, but, on the contrary, it is driven out because it is chaff. This diversity of events proves the weight and firmness of the one, and the inconstancy of the other. Even such is the case with true believers, and such as are merely professors. Persecution and offence make not the difference which is discovered between them, when the former retain the gospel, and the latter quit it: this event only shows that the one were God's wheat, and the others but chaff; according to what John says of apostates, "They went out from us, but they were not of us; for if they had been of us, they would no doubt have continued with us: but they went out, that they might be made manifest that they were not all of us," 1 John ii. 19. The same is further to be evidently seen in the parable of the sower, where the Lord says expressly that those "on the good ground are they, which in an honest and good heart, having heard the word, kept it," Luke viii. 15. Whereas he says of those who revolt, that one heard but understood it not; and another had no root in himself; an evident sign that their disposition was different at first, before the perseverance of the one and the fall of the others. From whence it appears how impertinent is the argument which our adversaries draw from the apostasy of the latter, to prove that the faith of the former may fail; and the contrary. For if the wind carry away the chaff, it does not therefore follow that it shall also bear away the corn; and if the storm beat down a house that is planted on two or three stakes, it is not to be said that it will do as much to a house that is founded on a rock. If the blade that shoots forth and grows up suddenly in the sand, without any root, happens to wither at the first extreme heat that smites it, this does not imply that the same might happen to the corn which is deeply rooted in a good and fertile soil.

The other point which we have to notice is the assurance of true faith, excellently represented here by the apostle in these words, which possess a singular emphasis, "If ye continue in the faith, grounded and settled;" contrary to what is taught in the church of Rome, that faith is in a continual agitation, so that a believer can have no assurance that he is at present in a state of grace, and much less that he shall persevere in it for the future. In conscience, can it be said of these people, as the apostle here says of the Lord's true disciples, that they are "grounded and settled?" How can it be, seeing that they incessantly float in doubt and uncertainty, and are miserably in suspense between the hope of heaven and the fear of hell? I pass by their other error, which is yet more contrary to the apostle's doctrine, namely, that the choicest faith may fail. If this be true, how can it be affirmed that those who have it are "grounded and settled?" Let us then hold fast the truth that is taught us here and in divers other places of Scripture, namely, that faith abides continually; and that, being founded on the merits, death, and intercession of Jesus Christ, it never can fail. The wind causes only the chaff to fly away; it does not prevail upon good grain. It overthrows only the trees that are feeble and ill-grounded; it leaves in their places those which are firm, and have good and deep-grown roots. And as an ancient once said, We must not account them prudent or faithful whom heresy has been suffered to change. None is a christian but he who perseveres to the end.*

But I return to the apostle, who, the more fully to explain this firm and unshaken faith which he requires in us, for obtaining salvation, adds further, "and be not moved away from the hope of the gospel." Thus justly does he join hope to faith; these two virtues being so closely linked together, that they

* Tertul. de Persc.

mutually succour each other, and the one cannot be obtained or lost without the other. For, first, hope is the suit of faith, expecting with assurance the fruition of the things which we believe; so that when the persuasion which we have of them begins to totter, it is impossible but that the hope which was founded on it must come to ruin. Again in the combats which we sustain for the faith, hope is one of our principal supports; while it is firm and vigorous, it repels without difficulty all the strokes of the enemy, opposing to the fear of the evils with which he threatens us, and to the desire of the good he promises us, the incomparable excellency of the glory and felicity for which we look in the other world. He that hopes for heaven cannot be tempted by the paintings and appearances of the earth. For this cause the apostle, in another place, compares hope to an anchor, which, penetrating within the veil, fastened and grounded in heaven, holds our vessel firm and steady, amid the waves and agitations of this tempestuous sea on which we sail below. And it is this, in my opinion, at which the apostle here aims; that believers might be established in the faith, he desires them to have still in their hearts the hope of heavenly bliss and never to suffer this sacred and divine anchor to be taken from them. They are in safety while it holds them fast. But, the better to express it, he calls it peculiarly "the hope of the gospel;" that is, the hope which the gospel has wrought in us, the expectation of those good things which it promises. And so you see he refers hope to the gospel as to its true and genuine object. All the hopes which we conceive from other grounds are vain and failing. There are no hopes but those which embrace the promises of Jesus Christ that are firm and solid, and they are such as never confound those who wait for their fulfilment. The gospel promises us, first, the entire expiation of our sins, and the peace of God in Jesus Christ his Son. They therefore that seek this blessing in the ceremonies and shadows of the law, as the Galatians and false teachers, who would have seduced the Colossians, did; or that seek it in their own merits, and the merits of creatures; all of them, I say, and all that are like them, suffer themselves to be carried away from the hope of the gospel. Then again, the gospel promises us eternal life in heaven by the grace of God in his Son. Those therefore who seek their felicity, either in the earth or in heaven, otherwise than through the Lord Jesus alone, quit this hope. Whereby it appears how very pertinently Paul recommends this hope of the gospel to the Colossians. For in the combat in which they were engaged, it was sufficient to preserve them from all the attempts of impostors. What have I to do (says this hope) with the observations of your disciplines, or the subtilties of your philosophy, since I abundantly have in my gospel all the good things which you vainly promise me?

But as it is common for false teachers to abuse the gospel, and to give that name to the fopperies and vanities which they preach, Paul, to put the Colossians out of all doubt and uncertainty, indicates expressly what this gospel is of which he speaks, that, says he, "which ye have heard," namely of Epaphras, who had preached it among them, and to whom he before gave an excellent testimonial for fidelity and sincerity. I mean, says he, the gospel which you received at the beginning, from the mouth of true servants of God, and not these vain and dangerous doctrines, which evil workers would wish you to receive as the gospel of Christ.

II. But to confirm them the more in the faith, he sets before them in the second place, an excellent encomium of the gospel, which contains a clear proof of its truth, saying that it is "the gospel which was preached to every creature which is under heaven." It is not the doctrine which these false apostles sowed here and there in some out-quarters, whispering and privily advancing among light and unstable spirits. It is the true word of the Son of God, which had been proclaimed through the whole universe by his command, and according to the oracles of his ancient prophets; that word which, going forth from Jerusalem, spread itself every way in a very little time; and, being accompanied with the power of its author, made itself heard and believed in all the provinces of the habitable earth, in spite of the contradictions of hell and the world. His assertion, that the gospel was "preached to every creature which is under heaven," may be expounded two ways, but both of them amount to the same sense.

First, by a figure very common in divine and human speech, the word "creature" may be taken for man, the noblest and most excellent of all the creatures. And our Lord so used the word before upon the same subject, when he commanded his apostles to do what Paul magnifies in this place: "Go ye," said he, "into all the world, and preach the gospel to every creature;" where it is evident that by "every creature" he means men, who alone are capable of hearing and receiving what is preached. In this sense when Paul says that "the gospel was preached to every creature," it is as much as if he had said, to all mankind, and among all sorts of men; agreeably to what he says here shortly afterwards, when speaking of himself, "warning every man, and teaching every man in all wisdom," ver. 28.

Secondly, these words, "to every creature," may, in my opinion, be also taken as signifying in all the world; and the more so, because it is literally in the original, in all the creature, with the article *the*, and not simply "to every creature." Now that Paul sometimes uses this term, "the creature," to signify the world, this great body and collection of all things which

God has created, is manifestly seen in the Epistle to the Romans, where he says, "The earnest expectation of the creature waiteth for the manifestation of the sons of God;" and again, "The creature was made subject to vanity;" and also shortly after, "We know that the whole creation," or all the creature, "groaneth and travaileth in pain together until now," Rom. viii. 19, 20, 22, where it is clear, and confessed by most interpreters, that "the creature" signifies the world; and our Bibles, to make us understand it the better, change the singular number into the plural, rendering it (*les créatures*, and *toutes les créatures*) the creatures, and all the creatures; whereas the original reads simply the creature, and all the creature. Taking it thus therefore in this place, when the apostle saith the gospel "was preached in all the creature which is under heaven," he means in all the world wherein we dwell, wherein God has seated mankind beneath the heavens. I will not stay here now to show you how it might be truly said in Paul's time, that the gospel of our Lord was then preached to all mankind, or in all the habitable world, or how this event is a clear and solid proof of its truth. We have already handled both of these particulars in expounding, if you remember, the 6th verse of this chapter, which affirmed that the gospel was come unto all the world. Upon that text, which signifies nothing else than what the apostle says here, namely, that the gospel has been "preached in all the creature which is under heaven," we showed, first, by good and irrefragable testimonies of ancient writers, both christian and pagan, that the heavenly word had been preached within the apostle's days in all countries then known either to the Greeks or Romans, and received generally with profit; so that taking the word world (according to the style of all languages) not simply and absolutely for all the parts of this terrestrial globe, but only for those which at that time were known to men, and which they understood to be inhabited, it might be said with truth, and without any over-reaching hyperbole, as Paul declares here, that the gospel had been "preached in all the creature which is under heaven," that is, in all the world. And, in the second place, we proved, both by the importance of the thing itself, and by the respect it has to the oracles of the Old Testament, which had predicted it many ages before its event, that this swift, sudden, and admirable progress of the gospel through all the world, in so few years, is a certain and infallible evidence of the truth and divinity of this holy doctrine; obliging, consequently, both the Colossians at that time, and us at the present, to hold fast and persevere in the faith which we have reposed in it, without suffering ourselves ever to be moved away from it, either by the cheating arts of false teachers and their crafty seducements, or by the threatenings and persecutions of the world.

III. These things having before been explained at large, lest the repetition of them should be irksome, I will pass to the third head of our text, in which the apostle sets before the Colossians another character of true christian doctrine, namely, that it is the word, the ministry whereof was committed to him. It is, says he, the gospel, of which "I Paul am made a minister."

He opposes his heavenly call to the temerity of false teachers, who ran without having been sent, and preached not that which heaven commanded them, but that with which earth inspired them; their impulsions and instructions being from flesh and blood, and not from the Lord Jesus. It was otherwise with Paul; all the faithful knew him to have been called from heaven, and suddenly changed by the efficacy of divine power from a wolf into a pastor; made a herald and witness of the gospel immediately by the Lord Jesus; instructed in his miraculous school, and illuminated and consecrated by his Spirit. Who could doubt but that it was from the mouth of this holy man that the mysteries of God should be learned, and that what was contrary to his doctrine ought to be judged false and vain? I confess that his mission was extraordinary and miraculous, and is not to be made a precedent for others; still that which he here says of it affords us two instructions which concern pastors generally. The first is, that they should never intrude themselves into this sacred office, if God call them not, so as that they may say with a good conscience, as Paul does in this place, that they have been made ministers of the gospel. It is true, Jesus Christ now speaks not to men from heaven, as he before did to Paul, to call them unto his work. But this much he does, he makes us perceive his will; first, by the moving of his Spirit within us, which never fails to incite us to his work when God calls us to it; and secondly, by the voice and authority of his church, that is to say, of his faithful people, to the body and community of whom he has given the power to apply the right of his ministry to such as they discern to be meet for it, as the examples of the primitive church, registered in the book of the Acts and elsewhere, show us. And as for ordination, as it is called, which is done by the imposition of the hands of other ministers already established, I confess that this also ought to intervene for the completion and crowning of the call; accordingly you see that it is seriously practised among us. But I add, that it is not so absolutely requisite, but that in case of extreme and invincible necessity, as in places and times when there are no true ministers of Jesus Christ to be found to give it, the call of the church, that is of a body of faithful people, may suffice to a valid instituting of a pastor, supposing the person to have the ability and inclination requisite for such a charge.

The other particular which we have to learn here is, that all pastors, of whatever rank they may be, are ministers, and not masters, of the gospel. It is the title which the apostle here assumes according to the declaration he makes elsewhere, that he has no dominion over the faith of believers, but is a helper of their joy, 2 Cor. i. 24. The duty of a minister is to propose what has been committed to him, what he has received of the Master. If he go beyond it, and will have his own will and his private imaginations to bear sway, he is no longer a minister; he does the act of a master, and consequently sets up a tyranny, since the church neither has nor can have any lawful master but Jesus Christ.

Thus, dear brethren, we have expounded this exhortation of the apostle to the Colossians. Remember, that it is to you also he directs it. Amid the persecutions which Satan casts in the way of your faith, and the temptations he offers to turn you out of it, retain still in your hearts and in your ears this sacred voice which cries aloud from heaven to you, "Continue in the faith grounded and settled, and be not moved away from the hope of the gospel, which ye have heard, and which was preached to every creature which is under heaven; whereof I Paul am made a minister." Oppose the authority of this divine command to the seducements and illusions of the world, to the flatteries and babble of sophisters, to the suggestions and lusts of the flesh. From whatever coast there come counsels contrary to it, whether from within or from without, judge them impious and abominable. And blessed be God, who has hitherto so settled you in the belief of his word, that neither the forcible attempts of open enemies, nor the fraud of false friends, has been able to remove you. But, dear brethren, it is not enough to have stood fast hitherto; there must be a preparation for combats which are still to come. For we have to do with enemies with whom we must look for neither peace nor truce. They will be still setting to work one engine or another; and if repulsed on one side, they will not fail to attack us immediately on another. Let us be therefore as vigilant in our defence. Let us have no less zeal and constancy for our preservation, than they have rage and resolution for our ruin. Let us fortify our faith daily. Arm it with proof armour. Found it on the eternal Rock, and so fasten it that nothing may be able to pluck it out of our hearts. For this purpose let us continually read and meditate that heavenly word from which we have drawn it. Let us fill our souls with this divine wisdom, and render it familiar to us. Let us instruct our youth in it. Let us cause it to abound everywhere among us. Let it be the matter of our mutual entertainments, and the usual subject of our meditations. For, as an ancient once very prudently said, "The reading of the holy Scriptures is an excellent and an assured preservative to keep us from falling into sin; and ignorance of the Scriptures is a huge precipice, a deep gulf of perdition." *

In the design of our perseverance, let us particularly make use of the two means with which Paul here furnisheth us. The one, that the gospel which we have heard has been preached in the whole world; the other, that it is the same which was committed to our apostle. It is in the belief of this gospel that he would have us abide firm. It is to this faith that he promises the peace of God, his favour and his eternity. God, says he, has "reconciled you to himself, that he might present you holy, unblamable, and unreprovable; if ye continue in the faith grounded and settled, and be not moved away from the hope of the gospel." From whence it follows, that if we have this gospel among us, we may certainly assure ourselves that by retaining it we shall obtain the peace and the salvation of God. The only question therefore is, whether the doctrine which we have embraced be truly this gospel or not. If it is, I have no further search to make. I am content to have found that which is sufficient for me, that I may appear before my God without confusion, and receive of him life everlasting. But that the doctrine of which we make profession is the same gospel that Paul preached, the same that he and the other apostles sowed in the world, and which the world, being overcome by the force of its truth, in the end received and adored, is so clear, that I do not think the devil himself, hardened in impudence as he is, can deny it. For do not the God whom we serve, and the Christ whom we adore, and his merit in which we trust, and the worship we give him in spirit and in truth, and the heaven we hope for, and the sacraments we celebrate, and all the other articles of our religion, everywhere appear in the books of Paul, and of the other apostles? Are they not to be seen in all the monuments of these great men, as well in their writings as in the churches which they planted through the earth? Let us therefore, my brethren, abide firm in this faith, since it most assuredly is the gospel which was heretofore preached in all the world, and was committed to Paul's ministration.

And if those of Rome confront us with their devotions and traditions, let us boldly tell them, that if those things were any part of the gospel, they would appear in what the apostles preached, to whom Jesus Christ gave the ministry thereof. Whereas there is not any one of them found in the sacred volumes, which they have left us to be the rule of our faith; neither the adoration of the host, the veneration of images,

---

* Chrys. Hom. 3, de Lazaro.

the invocation of departed saints, nor the other points for which they have excommunicated us. And herein their head evidently shows how apostolical he is, to banish those from his communion whom Paul here expressly declares to be at peace with God, holy and unreprovable before him. For, to have this happiness, he does not oblige us to believe or practise this pretended gospel of Rome. He requires us only to abide firm in the belief of the gospel which he preached to the faithful and left in his Epistles. In them our religion is to be seen, full and whole, but not one article of that which Rome would by all means constrain us to receive. But there is no necessity for us further to dwell upon this matter; the truth of that doctrine which we embrace being so clear, that no man who understands christianity, and owns the divinity of it, can call it into question; and, on the other hand, the absurdity of the doctrine we reject is so palpable, and so rudely beats against the foundations of reason and Scripture that it is very difficult for a man who has had any taste of the gospel ever to yield up his consent to the errors we contest, except God has blinded him by way of punishment for his ingratitude.

The great combat which we have most cause to fear is that of the passions of our flesh. It is these properly that enfeeble faith, that darken its light, that hide the truth from its view, and embellish error. These are the true causes of their change who desert us, and of the offence of many that are infirm amongst us. Experience shows it daily. And accordingly you see our Saviour warned us of it, having said, in one of his parables, Matt. xiii. 21, 22, that it is either the fear of persecution, or the cares of this world, or the deceitfulness of riches, that makes the seed of heaven unfruitful in the hearts of men, and obstructs their perseverance. And Paul somewhere informs us, that they who reject a good conscience make shipwreck also of faith, 2 Tim. i. 19. When a man is once sold over to pleasure, or avarice, or ambition, it is no wonder if, in the sequel, he should loathe the truth and fall into error. The passage from the one to the other is easy. Besides, the slaves of sin not finding the contentment of their passions in the profession of truth, which is generally under the cross, their interest leads them to seek their satisfaction in the world; this gives a violent shake to their minds, and brings them by degrees to relish the side and party of the world, as it is natural to us easily to believe the things we desire. It is for this reason, dear brethren, that we must use every effort and fight in good earnest, if we would continue firm in the faith. Give me a man that, embracing Jesus Christ, has cast off the lusts of the flesh and the world, and I will be security for his perseverance. Take me away the colours wherewith avarice, ambition, and vanity adorn error in the thoughts of the wordly-minded, and I will not fear its seducing any. Cleanse your conscience, and your faith will be out of danger. The devil, without doubt, made use of his best weapons against our Lord; and you know that, having represented to him the hunger and the necessity he was in, he omitted not to spread before his eyes the pomp of the grandeurs and riches of the world. It is a stratagem he still puts in practice, and his ministers do not forget this piece of his device; they fail not to tell those whom they would destroy that they will give them wonders. Faithful brethren, let us fortify ourselves seasonably against this temptation. Let us mortify in ourselves all the lusts of flesh and earth. Let us accustom ourselves to welcome the cross and sufferings of our Lord. Let us not suffer the world to dazzle our eyes, but let us look upon it as a deceitful show, unable to content its own adorers. To the false goods with which it feeds its bond-servants, let us oppose the true ones which the gospel promises. Let the sweet and noble hope of these inflame our souls with an ardent desire of heaven and immortality. Let it sweeten all the bitterness that attends our profession, and make execrable to us all that tends to turn us away from so blessed a design. Courage, christian; yet a little patience, and you will have overcome. Your faith, if you abide firm in it, will open in your heart in the present time a living spring of such joy as is a thousand times sweeter than all the pleasures of worldlings; and it shall be crowned one day with that pre-eminent and immortal glory which the gospel that you have believed promises to all those who constantly persevere in the vocation of the Lord Jesus; to whom, with the Father and the Holy Spirit, the true and only God, blessed for ever, be all honour and praise, to ages of ages. Amen.

SERMON XIII.

VERSE 24.

Who now rejoice in my sufferings for you, and fill up that which is behind of the afflictions of Christ in my flesh for his body's sake, which is the church.

THE gospel of the Lord Jesus possesses many admirable evidences of its divinity, and among them the sufferings of its confessors and martyrs are, in my opinion, not the least illustrious. For if you seriously consider them, you will find that there never was any doctrine in the world that drew more persecutions upon its followers, or that inspired them with so much courage and resolution to endure them, or was, in effect, sealed with so much blood and patience. Other religions, as they sprung from the earth, are welcome there, and the world, that well knows its own nature and spirit, shows them kindness, and receives them gladly. The alliance also which there is between them, being all of them fruits and productions of the flesh, makes them mutually bear with each other. And if a little jealousy at times raise in any of them some aversion for the rest, this passion seldom carries them so far as to an open persecution. But as soon as christianity appeared, they all turned their hatred and their violence against it, as against a religion which was a stranger, and of quite a different origin and extraction from theirs. Who is able to describe the furious excesses of the world against this innocent discipline, and the horrid calamities to which it condemned its professors, banishing them out of all its countries, stripping them of all its honours and possessions, burning them, torturing them, and mercilessly employing its brute creatures and its elements against them! Yet these cruelties did not confound the faithful; they bore them magnanimously, and would rather lose all that was dear to them, even their very blood and life itself, than renounce Jesus Christ. Of all the false religions that were propagated among men in the time of paganism, name one that was consecrated in such a manner. Of all the sects of philosophy which Greece brought forth, and of which the old sages so haughtily boasted, show me one that gave to its disciples the courage to suffer for it, or that was watered with their blood. I will not deny that some persons have suffered, and still are found to suffer, for false religions. But, first, this never happens except when long use, and the superstition of many generations, have authorized their belief; whereas the faithful suffered for christianity at its first springing forth, before the consent of the people or the authority of princes had strengthened it, or any other human considerations made it plausible. Then, again, those sufferings for error are very rare; they are the sufferings of a few persons only, one here and another there, whom vanity or melancholy may push on so far; whereas christians suffered by thousands, of all ages, of each sex, of every rank and condition, so that their resolution can be attributed to no other motive but their religion. Who can doubt that Mahommedanism and paganism would have been immediately extinguished if they had been exposed to the same trials? Whereas christianity was established by them; it flourished in the flames; and the ruder were the shocks that persecution gave it, the deeper root it took. And this character is so essential to this divine doctrine, that in the time of our fathers, when God caused it to come forth again into public light, it did not escape the same treatment that it had anciently experienced, nor did it fail to confirm its truth by the same sufferings, confessions, and martyrdoms which had accompanied its first introduction. To this I further add, that the sufferings for other religions, when any happen, are with constraint and fear, or mixed with pride and obstinate ferocity; whereas in those for the gospel there shine forth humility and modesty, charity and sweetness, celestial consolation and joy. Such, at the erection of christianity, were the sufferings of the apostles and the disciples. For this reason Paul speaks of his sufferings to the Colossians, in pursuance of the design he had to confirm their faith. "Who now rejoice," says he, "in my sufferings for you," &c.

To keep the faith of the Colossians in its purity, and to secure it from the leaven which seducers would mix with it, he presented to them in the preceding text, two strong arguments of the truth of the gospel. One taken from its extension, it having been preached through all the world in a very little time; whereas the new doctrine with which efforts were made to infect them had been heard but here and there, in some by-corners. The other drawn from his own miraculous call, it being a doctrine the ministration of which our Saviour had authentically and magnificently committed to him; whereas he had not ordered any person to preach those traditions with which some would burden them. But because this was a matter of great importance, he employs the rest of this chapter in grounding and clearing it, showing in various ways the truth of his heavenly call. And, first, he confirms it in this verse by the sufferings which he cheerfully and willingly bore to answer that call, secretly opposing his condition to that of the false teachers, who were exempted from the cross by the profession they made of observing the law of Moses. That I, says he, am sent of God, and a true minister of his, these great conflicts which I sustain, and the afflictions which I continually suffer, evidently prove. For instead of fearing them, or being ashamed of them, I rejoice in them; and it highly gratifies me to confirm my preaching with this divine seal, even the cheerful bearing of the cross of Christ, because I am not ignorant how necessary this deportment is in his school, where no one lives without suffering; and how profitable it is for his mystical body, that is, the church, whom he has united to himself, and of whom he has made me a minister. This is the substance of what the apostle here declares concerning his afflictions; and, that we may the better understand it, we will consider, first, the manner in which he bore them. This he expresses in these words; "Who now rejoice in my sufferings for you." Secondly, the reasons of his rejoicing; taken from the nature of those afflictions which were the rest of the sufferings of Christ, which I, says he, "fill up in my flesh." And, finally, the object or the use of them, in that he suffered them for the sake of "Christ's body, which is the church." These three points we will explain, the grace of God assisting us, in this exposition. The apostle's joy in the nature of his sufferings, and the end or utility of them; we will establish and make good the truth of his sentiments, and refute the attempts that error makes to wrest some advantage from his words. The whole shall be elucidated with as much perspicuity and brevity as is possible.

I. Although it is generally true, that all those who will live godly in Christ Jesus suffer persecution; yet this is particularly verified in the ministers of the gospel, who, not content with embracing this profession themselves, undertake to draw and guide others to it. This charge exposes them, more than the rest of the faithful, to the hatred and violence of the world. Paul's history clearly proves this. For he had no sooner received this sacred ministry, than he saw the Jews and the heathen rise against him, as by common agreement, and his whole life from that moment was nothing but a series of afflictions. But the Spirit of him who had called him fortified him in such a manner, that he sustained them all, not only patiently and constantly, but even cheerfully, and there was not one of them of which it might not be said that he rejoiced in suffering it. It is evident, however, that in this place he speaks of one of his afflictions in particular, and not of them all in general. For in saying, "I now rejoice in my sufferings," he intimates his present sufferings, those which he was enduring when he wrote this Epistle, and not others that were past. Every one knows the condition which he was then in; that he lay a prisoner at Rome, bound in a chain for the gospel. It is therefore to this persecution that we must understand him to refer. It is this prison, and this chain, and the inconvenience, pain and ignominy that attended them, with respect to the flesh, which he signifies by his afflictions.

But the question is, how is it that he saith that it is for the Colossians he was afflicted? "Who rejoice," says he, "in my sufferings for you." It does not appear in the history of his persecutions, which we have at large in the book of the Acts, that these faithful people had contributed to them, that they had been either the cause or the occasion of them. To this I answer, that if you carefully consider this sacred history, you will easily be enabled to resolve this difficulty. For it is evident that the hatred of the Jews, his accusers and persecutors, who raised up this long affliction upon him, was principally caused by that commerce which this holy man ordinarily had with the Greeks and other Gentiles; by his imparting the gospel to them, and receiving them into the communion of the people of God without obliging them to observe the law of

Moses. It was this that particularly kindled their hatred against Paul. They suffered James and many other disciples to exercise their ministry among those of the circumcision, as you see in the Acts. But as for Paul, who taught the Gentiles, and freely communicated to them the mysteries of God, him they could not bear; they cry out as soon as they see him, "Men of Israel, help. This is the man that teaches all men everywhere against the people, and the law, and this place." And they add in particular, that he had brought Greeks into the temple, and polluted that holy place; imagining he had caused a disciple of Ephesus, whose name was Trophimus, to enter into it, because they had seen him in the city, Acts xxi. 28, 29. Hereupon the apostle was made prisoner by the captain of the citadel, and from thence sent to Cesarea, and two years afterwards to Rome. So you see that the commerce he had with the Gentiles, and the care he took of their conversion, according to the charge given to him concerning it from on high, was the true cause of all this tedious and terrible tempest being brought upon him. Since therefore the Colossians were of the number of the Gentiles, considering them here under this relation, he had reason to say that it was for them he suffered; it being evident that he incurred the trouble in which he was at that time, for having opened, by his sacred ministry, the heavenly Jerusalem to them and to other Gentiles. And thus he explains himself respecting it in another place, where, speaking of the persecution of which we are now treating, "I Paul," says he, "the prisoner of Jesus Christ for you Gentiles," Eph. iii. 1. He expressly names the consideration under which the Ephesians had a part in his bonds, namely, as they were Gentiles. The truth is, he was not imprisoned either on account of the Ephesians or of the Colossians in particular; but in general, because of the service he did to the Gentiles, converting them, and admitting them to the communion of the people of God. And let none object that he had never preached in person to the Colossians. Some doubt it. But suppose he had not, it is sufficient that those who had converted them, as Epaphras and others, had done it by his order, and after his example, and under his authority; he being the person who had the preaching to the uncircumcision committed to him, and to whom the Lord from heaven had given the charge to go unto the Gentiles, "to open their eyes, and to turn them from darkness to light, and from the power of Satan unto God, that they might receive the remission of their sins, and an inheritance among them which are sanctified by faith," Acts xxvi. 17, 18. Hereafter we shall find him declaring still more plainly to these faithful people, that they, and the rest of the Gentiles, were the occasion of his sufferings. "I would," says he to them, "that ye knew what great conflict I have for you, and for them at

Laodicea, and for as many as have not seen my face in the flesh."

In all this the holy prudence of the apostle appears, who, to win the hearts of these believers, and the better to dispose them to the reception of his instructions, besides the authority of his office, which he sets before them, expressly intimates the affection he bore for them, and the zeal he had for their salvation; and in order to gain them unto God, he hesitated not to endure so long and grievous a persecution; and so far from repenting of it, he still rejoiced in it to that very hour; an evident sign, that if it were to commence again, the consideration of that hard prison would not in the least degree prevent him from exercising his ministry towards them and the other Gentiles in the same manner as he had done before. Thus Paul endured all the afflictions which the gospel and the edification of men entailed upon him. "I endure all things," says he, "for the elect's sake, that they may also obtain the salvation which is in Christ Jesus," 2 Tim. ii. 10. And to them who would have diverted him from the journey he took to Jerusalem, "What mean ye," says he, "to weep and to break mine heart? For I am ready not to be bound only, but also to die at Jerusalem, for the name of the Lord Jesus," Acts xxi. 13. He faithfully makes good what he had promised them. He magnanimously undergoes his bonds. The tumult and fury of an enraged people did not daunt him. The conspiracy of his enemies, the injustice of his judges, and the perils of the sea, did not in the least discourage him. The tediousness of a long imprisonment did not at all change him. Behold how he yet protests that he rejoices in his afflictions! He is as fresh and vigorous as if he were but now entering upon them.

Indeed it is thus that we ought to suffer for Jesus Christ. It is not enough to be patient under suffering, there must be a rejoicing in it. It is not enough to go forth under the cross without murmuring, there must be a marching on with alacrity. He that follows his captain weeping is but a poor soldier; men of valour, on such occasions, go forward with gladness. Paul goes yet further. He would have us to glory in such kind of tribulations, and triumph in them, Rom. v. 3. So did the apostles, who, having been ignominiously scourged by the decree of the council of the Jews, rejoiced (says the sacred history) "that they were counted worthy to suffer shame for the name of Jesus," Acts v. 41. I confess that such joy, in occurrences which would produce shame and sadness in all other men, is strange; it is contrary to the sentiments of nature, and exceeds its strength: yet I affirm that it is just; and although it is above the reach of our reason, it will be found to be a very rational joy.

II. That this may the better appear, let us now consider the two reasons of it, which the apostle here alleges, when he adds, "And fill up that which is behind of the afflictions of Christ in my flesh for his body's sake, which is the church." The word "and," which knits these words with the foregoing, is put here, as in many other places of Scripture, for one of those particles which they call causal. I "rejoice in my sufferings for you, and fill up that which is behind of the afflictions," &c.; that is, forasmuch as I fill up, or because I fill up, that which remains of the afflictions of Christ, as some of the best and most learned interpreters have well observed. The first of these reasons which induced the apostle to receive the sufferings of the gospel with joy is this, that by undergoing them he filled up the rest of the afflictions of Christ in his flesh.

First, it is clear that by "the afflictions of Christ" he does not mean the troubles which the Lord Jesus himself suffered in his own person during the days of his flesh, of which his death on the cross was the last and the chief, the end and crowning of them all. For neither Paul, nor any of the writers of the New Testament, ever uses the term "affliction" to express those sufferings of our Lord. They are always termed either his passion, and sufferings, or his temptations; as in the Epistle to the Hebrews, "Jesus was made a little lower than the angels for the suffering of death." Heb. ii. 9; and in Peter, "The Spirit testified beforehand the sufferings of Christ," 1 Pet. i. 11; and so also in other places.

Secondly, "the afflictions of Christ," of which the apostle speaks in this place, were not finished; there remained still some part of them to be filled up; whereas the Lord's personal sufferings were perfectly completed on the cross, so that in this respect there remained nothing more for him to suffer; according to what he himself testified, when he cried with a loud voice, before he gave up the ghost, "It is finished:" and also according to what the apostle teaches in various places; namely, that Christ "died unto sin once;" that henceforth he "dieth no more," but "liveth unto God," and that he "was once offered to bear the sins of many," Rom. vi. 9, 10; Heb. ix. 28. Those of Rome confess it, and even complain that they should be charged with having other thoughts upon the subject; they acknowledge it would be gross blasphemy to say that the sufferings of the Lord Jesus, by which he expiated our sins on the cross, want anything that should be supplied either by Paul or any other man. What then, are these "afflictions of Christ" which are here spoken of? Dear brethren, they are those which the apostle suffered for the name of the Lord, and in his communion, and by reason of the ministry with which he had honoured him. For it is the practice of these holy men to give this title to all that believers suffer for this holy and glorious cause. "As the sufferings of Christ abound in us," says the apostle, "so our consolation also aboundeth by Christ," 2 Cor. i. 5. Hence you clearly see that by "the sufferings of Christ" are not meant those which the Lord suffered in his own person, but those which the apostle suffered for his sake. As he says to the Philippians, that he desired to be found in Christ, to the end that he might know "the fellowship of his sufferings," Phil. iii. 10; that is, those sufferings by which all his faithful ones are consecrated after his example. The same he elsewhere calls "the afflictions of the gospel," 2 Tim. i. 8; and in another place, "the dying of the Lord Jesus," which he says he bears "about in his body," 2 Cor. iv. 10; just as he here says that he fills up the afflictions of Christ in his flesh. And, in my judgment, it is the same that he means at the end of the Epistle to the Galatians, where he glories in bearing in his body "the marks of the Lord Jesus," Gal. vi. 17, because afflictions are, as it were, the mark that Jesus Christ imprints in the flesh of his servants, the seal and badge of his house. So in the Epistle to the Hebrews, he terms the low and disgraceful condition, the afflictions and inconveniences of the people of God, "the reproach of Christ;" saying that Moses esteemed "the reproach of Christ greater riches than the treasures in Egypt," Heb. xi. 26.

If you now ask me the reason of this mode of speech, it is not difficult to be found. For, first, since it is for the name of the Lord, for his cause, and in his service, that the faithful are afflicted; "suffering," according to Peter's advice, "not as a murderer, or thief, or evil-doer, or as busybodies in other men's matters," but as christians, 1 Pet. iv. 15, 16; all the wounds which they receive upon this account are justly called the sufferings of Christ. Since he is the cause and the true occasion of them, it is reasonable to attribute them to him, and to say that they are his. Secondly, there is so strict a union between the Lord and all his true members, that they with him make up but one body, as the apostle will presently tell us. And by virtue of this conjunction we have part both in his glory and, in some measure, in his very name; as the apostle intimates, when he compares this mystical body to a natural body, and says, "As the body is one, and hath many members, and all the members of that one body, being many, are one body; so also is Christ," 1 Cor. xii. 12. Under the name of "Christ" there Paul comprises not only the person of the Lord Jesus, but with him the whole multitude of his believers. And considering them as united together, he gives the name "Christ" to this whole body, which is composed of the Lord as the Head, and of the faithful as members. Whereby it appears that all that believers suffer, each for his share, makes up part of the afflictions of Christ; as you know we call those injuries ours which we receive in any one of our members, whether the hand or the foot. Paul is the hand of Christ, as one of the members of his body, yea, one of the most excellent. Surely then all that he suffers pertains to Christ. It is his affliction and his hurt. None of the wounds of his servants is alien to him. And you see even among men, it is an offence to a prince to slight his minister, it is an affront to the husband to injure the wife, to attack the servant is to assault the master. Though the connection between these persons is not so close or so intimate as the union of Jesus Christ and his people, yet it is sufficient to denominate these outrages and injuries the prince's, the husband's, or the master's injuries, which are done to the persons who appertain to them under that relationship. Accordingly, you see in civil affairs, that men interest themselves as much in such cases, and take as heinously, or even more so, the outrages done to persons depending on them, and dear to them, as those which are directly aimed at themselves. Thus, in the heavenly state of the church, Jesus Christ owns both the good and the evil that are done to his followers. He says of those who visit, comfort, and feed his poor members, that they visit, and comfort, and feed himself. Of those who refuse them these good offices, he declares that they have denied them to him. And Paul had learned this lesson from his own mouth. For when, in the darkness of his ignorance, actuated by the fury of his zeal without knowledge, he persecuted the disciples, Jesus cried to him from heaven, "Saul, Saul, why persecutest thou me?" Acts ix. 4. It is I whom thou outragest in the person of those faithful people whom thou purposest to bind and imprison. Thou dost not give them a blow that does not reach me. I fail not, though in heaven, to bear a part in all that they suffer on earth. The blood thou drawest from them is mine; and as their persons belong to me, so all their afflictions and torments are mine. The apostle, instructed by this divine oracle, boldly calls the afflictions of Christ all those which he suffered after he had the honour of being his.

But he does not barely say here that he suffers "the afflictions of Christ." He also says that he fills up that which is behind, that which was yet wanting of them. To understand this aright, we must remember what he teaches us elsewhere, namely, "that whom God did foreknow, he also did predestinate to be conformed to the image of his Son, that he might be the first-born among many brethren," Rom. viii. 29; and that one of the principal parts of this conformity is their suffering here below, and their partaking of the cross of Christ, according to the intimation which he constantly gives us in Scripture, that if any one will follow him he must take up his cross, that all who will live godly in Christ Jesus shall suffer persecution, and that we must through much tribulation enter into the kingdom of God. Now as the wisdom and understanding of the Lord is infinite, he has not only ordained this in general, but has defined and decreed in his eternal counsel, both that which the whole body of the church shall bear in the gross, and what each of the faithful, of whom this body is composed, shall suffer in particular, through what trials he shall pass, where his exercises shall begin, and where they shall end. And as his hand and his counsel had before determined all that the Lord Jesus suffered in his own person, Acts iv. 28; for which reason Peter calls him the Lamb that "was foreordained before the foundation of the world," 1 Pet. i. 20; so likewise has he resolved upon, and formed, in the light of his eternal providence, the whole lot of each one of the faithful, all the parts and thrusts of their combat. The case of the head and of the members is alike. Nothing happens to them by mere chance. The procedure and proportion of their whole laborious course is cut out and fashioned before all ages. According to this true and holy doctrine, the apostle doubted not that his task was ordained in the counsel of his God, that the number of his sufferings were determined, and the quality of them regulated. Having then already despatched a great part of them, he means here that which remained for him yet to finish according to the counsel of God. I accomplish, says he, in my present sufferings, "that which is behind," or the remainder, "of the afflictions of Christ." I despatch my task by little and little, and what I now suffer makes up a part of it. It is one draught of the cup which the Lord has ordained for me, a portion of the afflictions which I am to pass through, for his Christ's sake and cause. It is one of the conflicts which I must endure, for the consummation of my whole course.

But it must not be omitted, that the word here used, and which we have rendered "fill up," is in the original very emphatical, and signifies, not simply to "fill up," or to finish, but to fill up in one's turn, in consequence of and in exchange with some other. I consider that there is represented by it a secret opposition between what Jesus Christ had suffered for the apostle, and what the apostle at that time was suffering for Jesus Christ. The Lord, says he, on his part, has completed all the sufferings that were necessary for my redemption; I now, in my turn, fill up all the afflictions that are useful for his glory. He did the work which the Father had given him to do on earth; and I after him, and after his example, do that which he has charged me with. He has suffered for me; I suffer for him. He has purchased my salvation by his cross; I advance his kingdom by my conflicts. His blood has redeemed the church; my imprisonment and my bonds edify it. For you see, my brethren, that the conformity which is between Jesus Christ and each one of his believers, requires that there should be such a resemblance between his sufferings and ours. And this is what the apostle intends by the word here used. To this we must also particularly refer his saying that he "fills up that which is behind of the afflictions of Christ in his flesh." For as the Lord suffered in this infirm and mortal nature which he had put on; and, after he had put off the infirmness of it, and rendered it immortal and impassible, suffered no more; in like manner, it is in this flesh that all the afflictions shall be filled up which we are to suffer by the order and counsel of God. When we shall once have quitted it, there will be no more conflicts and sufferings for us to undergo, than there were for the Lord Jesus after his death upon the cross. It is the same thing which the apostle signifies in the passages quoted before, that he bears the dying of Christ in his body, and his marks in his flesh.

From whence, by the way, it appears how absurd the belief of purgatory is, which makes the faithful to suffer, not in the flesh, but in the spirit; and extends their afflictions and pains beyond the days of their flesh; in which, nevertheless, the apostle teaches us that their sufferings are completed. Thus you see what is the sense of his words, and how much reason he had to rejoice in his sufferings: first, because they were the afflictions of Jesus Christ, the Prince of life, and the author of our salvation. Secondly, because they were dispensed by the order and will of God. Thirdly, because they made up the last part of the apostle's task; being the continuance and remainder of the conflicts which he had to sustain. And lastly, because they contained an illustrious evidence of his gratitude towards the Lord; and rendered him conformable to his holy image, in that, as Jesus had suffered for his salvation, he also suffered in his turn for the glory of his gracious Master.

III. But he adds yet another reason, which likewise sweetened the bitterness of his sufferings, and enabled him to find joy amidst the horror of them; it is that he suffered them for "the sake of the body of the Lord, which is his church." He had already said that he suffered for the Colossians, as we have explained; now he extends the fruit of his afflictions further, saying that they are of use to the whole church. And to show us how much weight this consideration should have to make his sufferings pleasant to him, he gives the church the highest and the most glorious appellation that can be attributed to any creatures, calling it the body of Christ. For what object more illustrious and more precious can we suffer, than for the body of the Son of God, the King of ages, the

Father of eternity? We have already treated of it upon the 18th verse of this chapter, and showed how, and in what sense, the church is the body of Christ, and we will not now repeat it. But his affirming that he fills up these afflictions for the church is true, and appears so in two respects.

First, inasmuch as the church was the occasion, and indeed the cause, of his sufferings. For it was the service he did it, in preaching the gospel, in instructing and comforting it, in grounding and settling it in the faith, which had provoked the Jews against him, and involved him in the afflictions which beset him. As if a prince's servant, zealous for his master's glory, and for the prosperity of his affairs, should through his zeal fall into some disaster, he might say it was for him and his interests that he shed his blood, and lay a prisoner in his enemies' hands.

Secondly, Paul's afflictions were for the church, because he suffered them for the edification and consolation of the church. This was the intention of his patience, and the design of his constancy. It was to the church that all the fruit of these fair and illustrious examples of the apostle's constancy redounded. He himself explains it to be so. "Whether we be afflicted," says he to the Corinthians, "it is for your consolation and salvation, which is effectual in the enduring of the same sufferings which we also suffer," 2 Cor. i. 6. Here you see that the fruit which the faithful reaped from these afflictions consisted in this, that by the virtue of his example they were confirmed in the gospel; were rejoiced, and comforted, and fortified for the same conflicts. And in the Epistle to the Philippians, when treating of the same imprisonment to which he alludes in our text, he says, "I would ye should understand, brethren, that the things which happened unto me have fallen out rather unto the furtherance of the gospel; so that my bonds in Christ are manifest in all the palace, and in all other places; and many of the brethren in the Lord, waxing confident by my bonds, are much more bold to speak the word without fear," Phil. i. 12–14. Behold! how his sufferings were for the church, in that they encouraged the preachers, and enkindled in the hearts of the faithful people the zeal of the house of God; and in those without the church an inquisitiveness about the gospel, for which he was a prisoner. This great man's preaching would never have sparkled as it did, never afforded the world and the church so much edification and consolation, if it had not been accompanied with sufferings sealed with his blood, and confirmed by his wonderful patience amidst the continual persecutions which were raised against him. The conflicts of other servants of God have the same effect. Their blood is the seed of the church. It is from their sufferings that it springs up. It is by them that it grows and gathers strength. It is the patience of these divine warriors that converted the world, that conquered the nations unto Jesus Christ, and planted his cross and his gospel everywhere, even in the most rebellious spirits. Surely, since the church received so much profit from the apostle's afflictions, it is with good reason he here affirms that he fills up that which is behind of them for it. And in this sense we must understand it, when he says to Timothy that he "endures all things for the elect's sake," 2 Tim. ii. 10.

This may suffice for the discussion of our text, which is perspicuous, simple, and obvious. But the error of our adversaries compels us to lengthen this discourse. Not that they deny the exposition which we have given; for how could they do that, without renouncing the doctrine of the gospel and the confession of christians in all ages? But, granting that the apostle's afflictions were for the church in the sense in which we have expounded it, they add, that they were so also in another sense; that is to say, in that by undergoing them he made satisfaction for the sins of other believers, and by this means contributed to the increase and enrichment of the church's treasury of satisfactions, out of which the bishop of Rome, to whom the custody of it is committed, makes largesses from time to time, as he judges meet, for the expiation of the sins of penitents; and hence has arisen the use of indulgences, which is become so common in our days. But, first, what kind of proof is this? To show that the saints have satisfied divine justice for the sins of other believers, they allege that Paul writes, "I fill up the rest of the afflictions of Christ for his church." I answer, his meaning is for edifying and comforting the church. They acknowledge the force of this answer, but add, that the apostle's sufferings serve also for the expiation of the sins of the church, and to fill the exchequer of its pretended satisfactions. Is this fair disputing? Is it not a pronouncing of dogmas after their own fancy? Is not this presupposing their opinion instead of proving it? It is clear that we read nothing in this text either of these satisfactions, of that treasury, or of those indulgences of which they inform us. Certainly, if they will draw these things from hence, it behoves them to show us that they are here, to disclose them to us, to constrain us by the clearness of their proofs to see them. So far, however, from forcing us to this by the weight of their evidence, they do not so much as attempt it, but content themselves with telling us, that though our exposition is good and true, yet theirs also must be added. Since they urge no other proof of it but their own dictate, we may reject it with the same facility with which they offer it. Nevertheless, for your greater edification, I will proceed a little further in the illustration of this text.

First, the apostle's words by no means warrant us in supposing that he is speaking of satisfactions, it being evident that it may be said of all useful things, that they are for those who have the use of them: as, for example, that it is for men the sun shines in the heavens; that it is for them the clouds pour down the rain, and the earth yields its fruits; that it is for the church Paul wrote his Epistles, and preached, and published the gospel; and a thousand other such things, in which no man ever dreamed that there is any satisfaction. And when Paul professes to the Corinthians, that he would most willingly spend and be spent for them, 2 Cor. xii. 15, does he mean for the atonement of their sins? No, says a Jesuit; but he speaks of his great pains in preaching and teaching, which could not have failed of being very useful for the edification of the church, though of no value for the satisfaction of God.* Here, therefore, in the same manner, when the apostle says his afflictions are for the church, it follows clearly that his sufferings were of use to the church, (which I willingly confess,) but not that they were satisfactions for the sins of the church; which is precisely the thing we deny, and which they would prove. But if the words of this text do not support their exposition, the authority of the fathers, which they so highly extol, does not establish it any the more; not one of them ever having been known to infer their doctrine from this text, or to interpret it differently from what we have done.

Lastly, the thing itself as little favours their design; and to demonstrate it to you, we must briefly touch upon all the points of their pretended mystery. It is composed of four propositions, all of which they advance upon their own credit, without founding so much as one of them on Scripture. For, first, they presuppose that when God pardons the sins which are committed after baptism, he remits only the guilt, and the eternal punishment of our trespasses, but not their temporal punishment; this, they consider, he obliges us to expiate, either here or in purgatory. Secondly they add, that various saints, as the apostles, martyrs, and others, have done and suffered much more than they themselves required for the expiation of their own sins; and, as they are provident, thrifty men, lest these superfluous satisfactions (for so they call them) be unprofitably lost, they maintain that they go into the common treasury of the churches, where, being mixed with the superabundant sufferings of Christ, they are preserved for the necessities of the penitent. And, finally, in addition to all this, they give the custody of this treasury to the bishop of Rome alone, who dispenses it as he judges expedient. Here is a chain of imaginations which have no foundation, either in rea-

* Justinian in loc.

son, or in Scripture, or anywhere else, but in their own passion and interest. For, first, who taught them thus to cut in pieces the benefits of God, and to suppose that he remits the guilt without the punishment, as if to remit a sin was anything else than not to punish it—and that he again remits a part of the punishment, namely, that which is eternal, and holds us bound to satisfy for the other? How does this accord with that full and entire grace which he promises to repenting sinners, and with his declaration that he will forget their sins; that he will blot out their iniquities; that he will remember them no more, and that there is no condemnation to them that are in Jesus Christ? Would it not be a mockery, if, after all this, he should exact of men the punishment of their faults to the utmost farthing? And as for the pretended satisfactions of the saints, whence have they drawn them—from what prophets, from what apostles, seeing that, so far from having suffered more than was necessary to expiate their sins, all of them declare that none of them were justified by their doings or their sufferings, that they all needed grace for the expiation of their transgressions, and that all their sufferings were not able to counterpoise the glory wherewith God will crown them? And if we be indebted to them for any part of the expiation of our sins, what will become of the apostle's assertion, that Christ purged our sins by himself, Heb. i. 3; and that he consummated, or made perfect, them that believe, by that one sole oblation which he made on the cross? If Paul, who is in question, did in suffering satisfy for us, why does he protest elsewhere that he was not crucified for us? 1 Cor. i. 13. Surely, according to our adversaries' supposition, he could not in truth deny it. For if his sufferings serve not only for the edification of our lives, but also for the atonement of our sins, as they pretend, there remains no longer any sense in which it may be said that Christ alone suffered for us. These two propositions, that the apostle did suffer, and did not suffer for us, will be irreconcilable; whereas in our doctrine it is easy to harmonize them, by saying, he suffered for us, that is, for our edification; and suffered not for us, that is, not to atone for our sins; this kind of suffering appertaining to the Lord Jesus only.

Besides, if the afflictions of which the apostle here speaks were satisfactory for the church, (as our adversaries will have it,) Paul would not have suffered them with joy; it being evident that pains of this nature necessarily seize those who suffer them with an extreme horror and heaviness, because they are accompanied with the apprehension of the wrath of God against sin, as appears both by the cross of our Lord, which he bore, it is true, with firmness and patience, but without any emotions of joy; and also by the confession of our adversaries themselves, who represent to us that the souls which suffer for their sins, in their imaginary purgatory, are all confounded with horror, and full of excessive sadness.

Lastly, how does this fiction accord with the perpetual voice of the church,* that though the faithful die for their brethren, yet martyrs did not shed one drop of their blood for the remission of their sins; and that none but Christ has done this for us; and that in this he did nothing for our imitation but that for which we should thank him; that he alone took on him our punishment without our sin, to the end that we by him, without merit, might obtain the grace which is not due to us? This foundation being overturned, their pretended treasury, and its distribution, which they invent, fall to the ground. I confess the church has a treasure, or rather a living spring of graces, and of propitiation for its sins, but it is full and whole in Jesus Christ, her eternal High Priest, who was ordained of God, from all time, to be a propitiation, through faith in his blood; and to have possession of these blessings, the sinner needs but to present him a heart full of faith and of repentance, according to the direction of John, "If we confess our sins, he is faithful and just to forgive us our sins, and to cleanse us from all unrighteousness," 1 John i. 9. As for the patience and the sufferings of saints, though they have not the virtue to atone for our sins, yet they are not unprofitable to us. Wherefore the Lord would have them put up and kept, not in the pretended exchequer of the pope, but in the treasury of the Scriptures, out of which every believer has the liberty of receiving them at all times for his use, to the edifying of his life, that he may gather from such fair examples that excellent fruit of piety which they contain, and admire and imitate them to the best of his ability. This is the lesson which we ought to practise upon the sufferings of the apostle in particular, which are represented to us in this text, that we may in reality profit by them, to the glory of God and our own edification.

Let us learn from them, first, not to be ashamed of affliction for the gospel's sake. Paul shows us that it is matter of joy; I "rejoice," says he, "in my sufferings;" and our Lord himself says, "Blessed are ye when men shall revile you, and persecute you, and shall say all manner of evil against you falsely, for my sake. Rejoice and be exceeding glad: for great is your reward in heaven: for so persecuted they the prophets which were before you," Matt. v. 11, 12. Christ was treated thus himself, and his apostles went to heaven the same way. Blush not to bear their marks. If they be ignominious before men, they are glorious before God. Fortify yourselves in this resolution, particularly you to whom God has committed the mini-

* Aug. 34. tract. in Joan. et l. 4. ad Bonif. de Pecc. mer. et remiss.

stry of his word. If the world thwart your preaching, if it threaten you, if it proceed so far as to imprisonments and to banishment, remember that Paul had no better usage, and that it was out of a prison that he wrote this excellent Epistle. As your cause is the same, so let your courage be like his. Conclude, as he did, that these bonds are an honour to you, that these sufferings are the afflictions of Christ. Let this sacred name, and the communion you have with him, sweeten all the bitterness of your troubles.

But, faithful brethren, think not that you shall be exempted from these trials because you are not ministers of the gospel. You also have part in them, each one according to his calling, and the measure of the grace of God. He has no children whom he consecrates not by afflictions. But if you suffer with Jesus Christ, you shall reign with him; if you have part now in his cross, you shall one day have part in his glory. And, to assure you of it, he calls your sufferings his afflictions. He protests that you receive not a blow but what he feels. Doubt not that he takes great notice of the conflicts which he vouchsafes to call his. Think also upon what he has sustained for you, and you will confess it is reasonable that you should suffer something for his glory who has undergone so much for your salvation. He has suffered for you the whole curse of God; will not you bear the reproaches and wrongs of men for him? He has borne and expiated the penalty of your sins on the cross; will you shrink from that which is behind of his afflictions? He has accomplished what was most difficult, that which none but he could discharge, having drunk for us the dreadful cup of God's indignation against our sins. Let us valiantly accomplish the trials which remain for us. It is he himself that dispenses them to us. It is not either the fancy of men, or the rage of devils. God has appointed our task for us. It is from his hand we must receive all the afflictions which we shall suffer.

But besides that we owe this respect and subjection to God, let us learn of the apostle that we owe such examples also to the church. It is not for Jesus Christ alone that we suffer. It is for his body also. As our afflictions advance the glory of the Master, so they likewise serve for the edification of the family. Judge thereby, faithful brethren, what our affection for the church should be. The consideration of it constituted a great part of the apostle's joy. He accounted himself happy, that by his sufferings he could testify the love he bore to this sacred body of his Master. He blessed his chain, how hard soever it was, because it did the church some service. Dear brethren, let us imitate this divine charity. Let us love our Lord's church above all things. Let us make it the chief object of our delight. Let us consecrate to its edification all the actions and sufferings of our lives. Let us embrace all its members with brotherly kindness, and take good heed that we despise no man who has the honour to be incorporated in so august and divine a society. The apostle's example shows us that we owe them even our blood and our life. And we have heard him also at another time professing to the Philippians, that if he should be offered upon the sacrifice and service of their faith, he should joy in it, Phil. ii. 17. And John says expressly, that as Christ "laid down his life for us, so we ought to lay down our lives for the brethren," 1 John iii. 16. If the Lord spare our infirmity, and call us not to such great trials, let us at least testify our love towards the church by all the offices and services of which our condition, and the present occasion, is capable. We owe it our blood. Let us give it, at least, our tears, our alms, our good examples. You that have had the heart to plunge into the vain pastimes of the world while the church was in mourning, that have laughed and sported while she suffered and groaned, repair this disorder. Comfort her with your pious tears, whom you have saddened by your vain pleasures. Break with the world. Have no more commerce but with the children of God. Remember you have the honour to be the body of Jesus Christ. How is it that you have no horror at defiling, in the filth of sin and vanity, those members which are consecrated to the Son of God, washed with his blood, sanctified by his word, and baptized with his Spirit?

The church, besides this purity of life which its edification requires of you at all times, particularly at the present, demands of you the succour of your alms for the refreshment of its poor members. Their number and their necessities increase daily. Let your charity be augmented after the same proportion. Let it relieve the indigence of some, let it allay the passions of others, let it extinguish enmities and hatred among us all. Let it seek not only to those whom you have wronged, but even to them that have offended you without cause, that henceforth you may truly be the body of the Lord, his church, holy and unblamable, "having neither spot, nor wrinkle, nor any such thing;" patient and generous in affliction, humble and modest in prosperity, crowned with good works and the fruits of righteousness, to the glory of our great Saviour, the edification of men, and your own salvation. Amen.

SERMON XIV.

VERSES 25—27.

Whereof I am made a minister, according to the dispensation of God which is given to me for you, to fulfil the word of God: even the mystery which hath been hid from ages and from generations, but now is made manifest to his saints: to whom God would make known what is the riches of the glory of this mystery among the Gentiles; which is Christ in you, the hope of glory.

THE church of our Lord Jesus Christ is the fairest and most glorious state that ever existed in the world; a state formed in the counsel of God before the creation of the heavens, founded on the cross of his Son in the fulness of time; governed by the Father of eternity, and enlivened by his Spirit; it is the most precious of his jewels, the last end of his works, and the only design of all his wondrous performances. It is a state not mortal and corruptible, as those of the earth, but firm and everlasting, situate above the sun and moon, and sees all other things roll under its feet, in continual change, without being subject to their vanity. It is the only society against which neither the gates of hell, nor the revolutions of time, shall prevail. It is the house of the living God, the temple of his holiness, the pillar of his truth, the dwelling-place of his grace and glory. One of the prophets therefore long ago contemplating it in spirit, cried out in transport and ecstasy, "Glorious things are spoken of thee, O city of God," Psal. lxxxvii. 3. But among its other glories, this is in my opinion none of the least, that God employs the hands, the sweat, and the blood of his apostles for its erection. It is for the church that he made and formed these great men, and poured into their souls all the riches of heaven. And as they had received them for the service of the church, so they laid them out in it faithfully and cheerfully, insomuch that they counted it a great honour to suffer on its account, and they blessed the reproaches which they received for its edification. We lately heard Paul, the most excellent of these divine men, protesting that he rejoiced in his sufferings and afflictions for the church; and now, in the text which we have read, he goes on to say that he is the minister of the church. What an admirable and happy community must that have been whose minister and servitor was Paul, the greatest of men, one of the master-pieces of heaven, and the wonder of earth! But by these words he not only justifies the joy he had in suffering for the church, as minister of it; he also grounds upon them his liberty to make remonstrances to the Colossians, and to enforce his doctrine against the errors which seducers were sowing among them. For this cause, he enlarges on this subject, and magnifies his ministry. First, he represents to them the foundation of it, namely, the call of God; and the object of it, or those towards whom he ought to exercise it; and the end of it, in verse 25, in these words; "Whereof" (that is, of the church) "I am made a minister, according to the dispensation of God which is given to me for you, to fulfil the word of God." After this, in the following verse, he extols the subject of this ministry, namely, the word of God; saying that it is "the mystery which had been hid from ages and from generations, but now is made manifest to the saints." Lastly, he adds the efficacy of this divine mystery towards the Gentiles; and declares wherein it consists, namely, in Jesus Christ our Lord. He is the whole matter and substance of this great mystery. "To whom God would make known what is the riches of the glory of this mystery among the Gentiles; which is Christ in you, the hope of glory." These are the three points which we purpose to handle in this discourse, if the Lord permit. First, the ministry of Paul. Secondly, the mystery of the gospel. And thirdly, the riches of its glory towards the Gentiles. The subject is great, the time short, and our abilities small; may it please God to supply our defects by the abundance of his Spirit, and powerfully strengthen and multiply the words of our mouth in your hearts; so that, notwithstanding their scantiness and poverty, they may administer food for your souls, even as the seven loaves and a few little fishes, by virtue of his blessing, formerly sufficed to satiate a great multitude.

I. As for the first of these three points; the apostle, speaking of the church, says, "Whereof I am made a minister, according to the dispensation of God which is given to me for you, to fulfil the word of God." Upon which we have four things to consider. First, the quality of the apostle's office, which he terms the ministry of the church. Secondly, the title to this office, founded on the dispensation which God had given him. Thirdly, the object of the execution of this office, which he expresses by saying, "for you;" that is, for you Gentiles, as we shall show you presently. And in the fourth place, the function and the proximate end of this office, which he declares in these words, "to fulfil the word of God."

Observe then, brethren, first, how this holy apostle, to describe the office to which God had called him, says he had been made, not the master, or the prince, or the judge, or the monarch, or the high priest, but the minister of the church. By which you see, on the one hand, how very far from the mind of this holy man were the doctrine and practice of those who qualify themselves with those vain and haughty titles, which are not to be found among the names of the apostles and pastors in the Scriptures, and who are not ashamed openly to say and to write, that bishops are judges, masters, and princes of their flocks: that he of Rome, in particular, is the monarch of the church, its king and its sovereign Lord on earth, whose feet it ought to kiss, the lowest homage a vassal can do to his master; that he has power to impose laws on the church, which shall bind the conscience, so as that it can have no faith or salvation out of his obedience; that he has, though indirectly, even power and dominion over the temporalities of the church, not excepting the sceptres and crowns of the sovereign powers of the earth. Judge by this if it is not a mockery of the world for such persons to represent themselves as the true heirs and successors of Paul and Peter. Paul calls himself a minister of the church. These men say they are the lords and monarchs of it. Paul protests that he has no "dominion over our faith," 2 Cor. i. 24. These men pretend that they have an absolute empire, insomuch that every man is bound, under pain of damnation, to believe all that they command, and for no other reason than because they command it. Peter styles himself a presbyter, that is an elder, with the presbyters or elders, 1 Pet. v. 1—3. These men say they are their sovereigns and kings. Peter orders the pastors to feed the flock of Christ, not as having lordship over his heritage; these men attribute to themselves a direct and a supreme dominion over them. In short, Jesus Christ, both Paul's and Peter's Master, says expressly to his ministers, "Ye know that the princes of the Gentiles exercise dominion over them, and they that are great exercise authority upon them; but it shall not be so among you," Matt. xx. 25. And yet these men exercise, both upon people and pastors, indeed upon the whole church, a mastership and dominion much more absolute, rough, and rigorous than any monarch ever exercised over his subjects, and such a dominion too as wants neither the pomp of dignity, the splendour of riches, of arms, and guards, nor any other of the ordinary and visible marks and badges of a worldly royalty. But you have to observe here also, on the other hand, how false and unjust is the derision which our adversaries make of the name of minister, which pastors among us assume; imputing, in a manner, their modesty to them as a crime, and almost accusing them of their want of arrogance.

I know well that the word here rendered "minister" is often used in the language of Scripture, and of the church, to signify the ministry of those who have the care of the poor, and of the funds of the church, and we have retained it in this sense in our vulgar tongues; in which they that are put into such charges are called in French *diacres*, in English, deacons, as you know; which is precisely the Greek word here used by the apostle. But however, since Paul has not hesitated to use this name for expressing his office, calling himself a minister of the church, ver. 23, and in other places, a minister of the gospel, a "minister of the New Testament," 2 Cor. iii. 6, a "minister of God," chap. vi. 4, and minister of Christ, it appears to me that no one can blame us, who are so far beneath him, for having followed the example of his humility; and that to censure us for calling our pastors ministers, is evidently to revile this great apostle, who has so often used this name in this sense, and even to signify the highest dignities in the church, such as his apostleship; for it is evident that he means this, when he says in our text that he was made a minister of the church.

He adds, secondly, "according to the dispensation which is given to me." Hereby he shows, first, that it was not man, but God, the supreme Master and Lord of the whole universe, who called and consecrated him to the ministry of the gospel. You all know the history of it, which is told us at length in the book of Acts. It is full of so many wonders, that the vocation of this holy man ought to be counted very singular; many circumstances meeting in it which do not occur in the call of any other apostle. Jesus Christ had called the rest during the days of his flesh; he called Paul after his resurrection, and subsequently to his having taken his seat at the right hand of the Father. He conversed with the rest on earth; to this person he spake from heaven. The others were invited by our Saviour, and won by degrees; him he overcame and subdued at once by an extraordinary exercise of his divine power, seizing him suddenly by the miraculous force of his right hand. If the rest, before their call, had no affection for the Lord, at least they had no hatred or aversion against him. Paul burned with a furious zeal against Jesus Christ, and all his disciples, and made war upon him, and had his weapon in hand when he was plucked by celestial power out of the bonds of iniquity, and in a moment changed from a persecutor to a minister of the church. But in addition to the Author of his call, he here discloses to us the nature of his ministry, by saying that this dispensation of God was given to him. I am not ignorant that the dispensation of God may be taken for the conduct and wise disposal of the providence of God, who governs all things, and particularly the things of the church, by his eternal counsel. And if the apostle had said simply that he had been made a minister according to or by the dispensation of God, it might have been so understood; but he adds expressly that this dispensation of God was given to him, and this necessarily obliges us to understand it, not of the Lord's conduct, which was not given to him, but of the divine office of a steward in his church, to which Paul was called, and which was committed to him. That this was the quality and condition of his apostleship he teaches us expressly in another place: "Let a man so account of us as of the ministers of Christ, and stewards of the mysteries of God," 1 Cor. iv. 1. Whence it clearly follows, since the apostle was a steward, or a dispenser, that his office was a stewardship, or a dispensation, as he calls it here. And from this it appears again how false is the opinion of those who attribute a lordly and absolute authority and a despotic power to ministers of the church over the Lord's flocks. For the steward, or dispenser, has power not to do anything of his own head, and after his own fancy, but only to dispense what the master has given him and precisely in such a manner as he has described to him. If he take upon himself to do more, he exceeds the bounds of his commission; and all that he does or says beyond them is void and of no force, nor does it oblige any one of the household to obey it.

But the apostle describes, thirdly, the object of his ministry; that is, who they are towards whom he ought to exercise it. "This dispensation of God," he says, "is given to me for you." These Colossians, to whom he wrote, being Gentiles by birth and extraction, he considers them here in that quality; and his meaning is, that it was for them, and others like them, that is to say, for the Gentiles, that he had been called to this sacred ministry. It is true, an apostleship was a universal charge, which extended generally to all men, of every nation or condition, having the whole earth for its precinct, according to that clause of the commission which the Lord gave his apostles when he sent them forth, "Go, and teach all nations," Matt. xxviii. 19. And that the ministry of Paul was of the same character evidently appears, both from his procedure and his writings; for he often preached the gospel to the Jews, as you may see in various places in the Acts; and directed to them particularly that excellent Epistle to the Hebrews which remains in the church to this day. But though the extent of his charge was such originally and properly, nevertheless, that he might exercise it more extensively and with greater success, God appointed him to preach peculiarly to the Gentiles, and commissioned him to labour particularly for them, as he expressly informed him when he directed to him his call from heaven: "I send thee," said he, "to the Gentiles, to open their eyes, and to turn them from darkness to light," Acts xxvi. 17, 18. And afterwards, in pursuit of this heavenly mandate, Peter and Paul by a voluntary arrangement divided mankind into two parts; Peter, with the other apostles, taking the circumcision of the Jews, and Paul the uncircumcision, that is, the Gentiles, as he himself informs us in another place. This, however, must be understood of the ordinary exercise of their commissions; Peter not being prohibited from preaching to and converting the Gentiles, nor Paul from labouring among the Jews, if any favourable opportunity should occur in the course of their ministry, Gal. ii. Here we have a general view of the necessity of appropriating a determinate flock to each pastor, and of the vanity and exorbitancy of the pretension of him who calls himself the universal pastor and bishop of all Christendom. For if the apostles themselves, who had the power to exercise this charge, yet considered it so difficult, that for its proper performance they voluntarily divided the district of their commission between them, each of them taking a portion of it only; how can we believe that a man, who is infinitely inferior in gifts to these great ministers of God, should be able alone to govern the whole church of Christ? But the apostle very pertinently declares this to the Colossians, to keep them fast in the purity of the faith. For since he had been sent of God to illuminate and teach the Gentiles, it is evident that they, being Gentiles, owed him a particular respect, and that they were to believe nothing which was not conformable to his instructions, considering him as the minister of their faith, whom God had particularly set over them. From whence it follows that they neither could nor ought to embrace that novel doctrine which certain seducers offered to them, seeing it was neither preached nor approved of by Paul. And since we ourselves are by extraction Gentiles, this consideration, my brethren, should induce us also to reverence this holy man. He is our apostle, and the minister whom God has given to us for an interpreter of his will, and a conductor of our souls to salvation. Let us respect him among all the ministers of Christ. Let us hear him diligently. Let us peruse his divine instructions night and day. Let us abide fixedly hanging on his sacred lips, and hear nothing contrary to his doctrine. Whatever others may be, there never was any but he who received from heaven the particular commission to instruct us.

Lastly, he shows us the nature of his work, and the end of his office. "The dispensation of God which is given to me for you," says he, "to fulfil the word of God." Some there are who understand by this "word of God," of which the gospel speaks, the ancient oracles, which foretold the conversion of the Gentiles to the knowledge of the true God in the days of the Messiah; as, for instance, in Isaiah, where we read that Christ should be given "for a light to the Gentiles," chap. xlii. 6; xlix. 6; and in Zechariah, "Many nations shall be joined to the Lord in that day, and shall be my people," chap. ii. 11;

and in Micah, "Many nations shall come and say, Come, and let us go up to the mountain of the Lord, and to the house of the God of Jacob; and he will teach us of his ways, and we will walk in his paths," chap. iv. 2; and other similar passages, which are to be found in great number in the books of the prophets. As if the apostle meant, that he was appointed the minister of the Gentiles, for the accomplishment of these predictions. Now certainly it cannot be denied that the thing in itself is true, it being evident that his preaching was one of the most excellent means which the Lord used for effecting that which he had promised in those oracles, namely, the conversion of the nations. Nevertheless, to put this sense upon the apostle's words, is, in my opinion, to do them violence. For, first, the word of God, according to the apostle's style, signifies the gospel, which is so called on account of its excellency; it being, without controversy, the most excellent of all the words of the Lord; and these terms are always constantly so understood when he uses them simply and absolutely, as in this place; and I do not think that so much as one passage can be produced in which he uses them otherwise. And if this were not so, it is impossible to understand them in any other way here, as the apostle, to explain what is this word of God, for the fulfilling of which he was sent, immediately adds, "the mystery which hath been hid from ages and from generations, but now is made manifest to his saints;" which is, as you perceive, an illustrious description of the gospel. And as for this phrase, "to fulfil the word of God," which seems chiefly to have settled the authors of this exposition, considering it harsh that it should signify preaching of the gospel, it should be considered that the apostle uses it elsewhere in this very sense, when he says that "from Jerusalem, and round about unto Illyricum, I have fully preached the gospel of Christ," Rom. xv. 19; where he uses the same term as he here does, and clearly calls that "the gospel of Christ," which he here terms "the word of God." What does he mean then by these words? Truly, to fulfil the gospel is to preach it with such efficacy, that it may find reception in the hearts of men; it is to justify the virtue of it by the effect. And, therefore, our French Bibles have judiciously rendered the word, in the place now quoted, by "making to abound." The true and natural perfection of the gospel is, that it is "the power of God unto salvation to every one that believeth, to the Jew first, and also to the Greek." I acknowledge that it is so every way in itself; but this its virtue does not appear, nor display itself, until it be planted by preaching in the hearts of men, and take root and fructify there. Till then, its perfection remains hid and wrapped up in itself. It is with the gospel as with seed, which shows not what it is, but when, having been received into the bosom of the earth, it produces an herb or a plant; or as a sword in the sheath, which does not discover its strength, and the goodness of its temper, but when it is drawn and used. This is what the apostle means, when he says that God gave him the dispensation of the Gentiles, to fulfil or accomplish his word; that is, to spread his gospel, and by his preaching display the virtues and perfections of it; which, indeed, clearly appeared when this heavenly word, which, till that time, had, in a manner, operated upon the Jews alone, in a short space of time converted a great multitude of Gentiles. And the apostle elsewhere uses a similar word, in almost the same manner, when he says that the power of God is completed in infirmity; that is to say, not that it therein acquires its perfection, but that it shows and displays it. Such is the end of the apostle's ministry. He was called to it to fulfil or complete the word of God, to spread the gospel, to preach it for the conversion of men, and for the glory of its author.

By this you see, first, in what the charge of true ministers of the Lord principally consists. It is not in commanding their flocks, or in appearing above them, much less in extravagant exhibitions before the world; but in publishing heavenly truth with a holy order, even to the giving of themselves no rest till it be settled in the souls of their hearers, till it reign there, and show its divine perfections in the change of their conversations. And, secondly, that the gospel is the whole subject of their preaching, so that they have no liberty to mingle with it either their own inventions, or the traditions of men, however fair and plausible they may appear; that they keep themselves faithfully within these bounds, remembering the end of their commission, that the dispensation of God is given to them to fulfil the word, not of men, but of God.

Let us now consider that which the apostle adds concerning this word of God; (that is, the gospel;) "It is," says he, "the mystery which hath been hid from ages and from generations, but now is made manifest to his saints." All this serves to exalt the glory of the gospel. He saith, first, that it is a mystery, that is, a secret; and he often gives it the same name in other places, because it is a doctrine not exposed to the sense and reason of men, but it is secret and hid in God, 1 Tim. iv. 16; such a doctrine as eye saw not, nor ear heard, neither did it enter into the heart of man. Read the books of the sages of the world, and you will see that by the subtlety of their spirits they discovered, and we may say read, various truths in the creatures which the Creator had engraven on them; but you will not find there those of the gospel. They were hid in the deep abyss of his eternal wisdom and counsel, which no created eye can penetrate, nor can we discern anything that is therein until he himself produce it, and set it before our sight. It appears from this, how much they are mistaken, who con tend that evangelical truth may be discovered in the contem plation of nature. I acknowledge that the gospel does not contradict nature, indeed I affirm that it perfects and crowns it; so that when it is once revealed to us, we observe many things in nature which admirably correspond with it, and which could not be clearly seen without this new light. But it is the Son of God alone who brought it out of the bosom of the Father, and published it. By the same consideration you may also judge with what reverence we ought to receive the gospel, since it is a mystery, the secret, not of an earthly king, but of the sovereign Monarch of men and angels.

II. Let us consider this mystery of the gospel. The apostle says that this secret "had been hid from ages and from generations;" that is, from the creation of the world until the revealing of our Lord and Saviour; none of the former times, none of the generations of men that lived in them, having had the happiness to know it. There are many truths in the law which might be termed secrets, or mysteries; as, for instance, those things which it teaches concerning the creation of the world, and the manner of that creation; concerning the judgment of God against sin, and the calling of Israel: but these truths became public long ago, having been made known by the ministers of God to former generations. The gospel alone has this glorious advantage, that it continued hid until the appearance of the Son of God. Paul affirms it here; he repeats it in the Epistle to the Ephesians in almost the same terms, chap. iii. 5, and also in that to the Romans chap. xvi. 25, where he says that the revelation of this mystery had been "kept secret since the world began." But he adds, in fine, that this great secret now is made manifest; that is to say, in the fulness of time, in the latter days, when the Son of God appeared. By the saints of God he means, first, the apostles, to whom the Lord Jesus discovered the whole truth of his gospel by the light of his Spirit, in a very peculiar and extraordinary manner. And, secondly, the rest of the faithful, whom he caused to see the same mysteries by their preaching, accompanied with the effectual operation and light of the same Spirit. Both of them are called saints, because God had separated them by his call from the rest of men. By which you see that there are none but the saints of God who truly know his mysteries, the revelation which is necessary for the knowledge of them most assuredly purifying and sanctifying the heart of man.

But I perceive that some difficulties arise here in your minds against this doctrine of the apostle, which must be resolved for your satisfaction before we pass on further. First, you may ask me in general how it is true that this mystery was hid from the former ages, seeing the gospel is eternal. And then how this accords with so many prophecies of the Old Testament, in which it seems to be so clearly represented; and with the words of our Lord, when he said of Abraham, that he saw his day; and, likewise with the express information of the Scriptures, that the ancient believers were all saved by faith, which seems to have been impossible without the knowledge of the gospel. To the first question I answer, that it is true the gospel was foretold, and, as the apostle says elsewhere, was promised and prefigured, under the Old Testament; but it was not manifested. It was, at that time, in being, but it lay hid in the bosom of the Father, and only wrapped up in the oracles, by which he promised it, and in the types, by which he prefigured it; so that it is nevertheless eternal, inasmuch as, in these latter times it was not made and created of nothing, but only brought out of the obscurities and envelopments, with which, until then, it had remained covered. And as for the prophecies, it is true that they are clear, since the Sun of righteousness has arisen in the horizon of the church, and there shed abroad his light, by the aid of which we easily read what the finger of God has written in them; but before this, while the darkness of the night covered all things, it was impossible for the best sight thoroughly to penetrate into the true meaning of them. As when it is broad day we read distinctly and without difficulty the writing which, during the dimness of the night, appears to be nothing but a few confused strokes and letters. Would you know the difference between these two dispensations? Turn to that chapter of Isaiah, in which we read, "He is brought as a lamb to the slaughter," Isa. liii. 7, and what follows. There is not a child among us that does not instantly understand it of Christ, and his dying for us, in profound humility and love. Yet the Ethiopian, who, without doubt, was very forward in the school of the former people, confesses that he understands nothing of it, and cannot tell whether the prophet says this of himself or of some other man, Acts viii. 34. First, the accomplishment of things, which is the commentary upon prophecies, and the light of figures, has made the ancient oracles and types clear to us, which necessarily remained obscure and inexplicable until that event. Secondly, the law further augmented this obscurity; it being then spread over these mysteries as a thick veil, through which men, however sharp-sighted, were unable to penetrate. Whereas now, the righteousness of God having been revealed to us without the law, (as the apostle says,) and this troublesome veil having been rent, and removed by Jesus Christ, we clearly behold the light of Moses's face, which was indeed of old, but could not be seen so long as it abode covered with the veil of the law. And when it is said that Abraham saw the day of the Lord, and rejoiced in it, we are to understand that he knew and believed that Christ should come and save the world, and exalt the people of God to a pre-eminent glory, which was sufficient for his joy; but this does not imply that he distinctly knew either what the person of Christ would be, or in what manner he would acquire salvation for us, with all the circumstances of these things, which neither men nor even angels knew, but by the manifestation of Jesus Christ in the flesh, and by the consequences thereof. The apostle expressly testifies that it was then, and not before, that the manifold wisdom of God was made known to the angels, whom, according to his ordinary style, he calls "principalities and powers," Eph. iii. 10. The knowledge which the rest of the faithful had of Christ was like that which Abraham had. They believed in his coming, and their redemption, and the restoration of all things by his means; and they desired him, and waited affectionately for him, embracing his promises afar off. But they did not distinctly comprehend the mystery, as we do at this day. Yet this did not hinder their justification by the merit of his death, their salvation by his cross, their being fed with his manna, and their being made to drink of his source, it being clear that there is no other salvation in the world but that which he procured. Nor do the various degrees of faith, by which the redeemed draw from his fulness, vary at all in the essence and substance of his grace; because God requires no other faith of his people than such as is proportioned to the measure of the revelation which he has given them, such revelation being more or less clear as the times were nearer to, or more remote from, the glorious light of his Son. Thus the truth which the apostle teaches us here abides firm, and is beyond all contradiction, namely, that the mystery of God, that is to say, the gospel, was hid from ages and from generations, and was not manifested till now to the saints of God; "to whom," says he, "God would make known what is the riches of the glory of this mystery among the Gentiles, which is Christ in you, the hope of glory."

III. This is the third head of our discourse, the glory and the riches of this mystery. He sets the will of God at the entrance, as a strong bar against our curiosity, to stay and restrain it from intruding into a search of the causes of this admirable dispensation of the mystery of the gospel. Curiosity would busy itself principally about two points, namely, the time and the persons to whom this manifestation has been made. Respecting the first point, it demands why God should suffer so many ages to flow forth, and so many generations to pass away, without discovering the secret of the gospel to them, having reserved the revelation of it to these latter ages only. Let us say, with the apostle, "God would" so do; and let us be contented with his will, assuring ourselves that it is just and reasonable, though we know not his motives. He has reserved the seasons of things for his own disposal. Besides, at whatever time he might have revealed this mystery, man would still have demanded why it was not done sooner or later. Now he complains that God delayed it so long. If God had discovered it at the beginning, he would complain of his having made so much haste. He now objects the interest of the first ages which were deprived of this blessed light. He would have objected the interest of these last generations, that they were too far removed from this sunshine to profit by it. Unbelief never wants pretences. It finds a reply against all the Lord's procedure; and, not desiring that it should be just, easily invents appearances to believe that it is not so. Let us suffer him to be wiser than ourselves; and instead of arguing about his arrangements, let us receive them with respect, and profit by them. Let it satisfy us, that by his grace we find ourselves within the compass of that blessed time in which he has manifested his secret, and let us thankfully make use of the advantage which he has been pleased to give our age above those that have preceded.

But if you ask me why God did not sooner communicate his gospel to the church, I will also ask you why he does not give to men and other living creatures the perfection of their kind at the instant of their nativity; why he lets them lose so much time in the weakness of infancy, which might be better employed in more noble actions, if they had their vigour and maturity at the beginning of their days. Tell me again why he makes not the plants to grow up, to blossom, and to bear fruit in a moment, and why he forms families and states so slowly among mankind. God does nothing suddenly, that we may learn the maturity of his counsels from the gravity of his motions. He has formed the church in the same manner. He has purposed that she should begin to pronounce before she spake distinctly, and that she should pass through childhood before coming to full age. He designed that she should learn her rudiments before she heard the highest lessons of his wisdom, and have at one time, Moses for her schoolmaster, and at the other Jesus Christ for her Teacher, as the apostle shows us in the Epistle to the Galatians, chap. iii. and iv. Since the gospel is the highest of her lessons, it was justly reserved for her ripest age. But if you press me still, and ask me why God ordained such a difference between the ages of the church, I will answer you as before, with Paul, that thus he *would* do. You cannot break over this bound without unsettling the whole nature of his proceedings, and bringing the justice of them into question; it being evident that it was neither more difficult, nor apparently less reasonable, for God to give animals and vegetables their strength and perfection in the first moments of their life, than to give to the church the knowledge of his mysteries in the first centuries of her existence.

The other point, in this dispensation of God, which offends our curiosity, is respecting the persons to whom he has manifested his mystery, and whom he has sanctified by this divine light. Why to these has he done this, rather than to those? Why to poor Galileans, rather than to the scribes and priests of Israel? The apostle cuts the knots of all these questions with only one word, saying that he would make it known to them. It is the reason which the Lord himself assigned for this diversity, when having given thanks to the Father, because he had hid these things from the wise and prudent, and had revealed them unto babes, he adds, "Even so, Father; for so it seemed good in thy sight," Matt. xi. 26. And the apostle treating in another place expressly of this matter, concludes, that God "hath mercy on whom he will have mercy, and whom he will he hardeneth," Rom. ix. 18. At this will we must stop, and not go on vainly seeking for reasons in the persons themselves for the favour which God has showed to them; it being evident that we shall never find in them any which can give us satisfaction. And to this also must we reduce all the diversities which may be observed in the dispensation of the gospel; such as God's making it to abound in one country, and among one people, while another is deprived of it; causing it to shine upon one generation after having denied it to another; and his communicating it here more liberally, and there more sparingly. All this depends merely on his good pleasure; nor can the things themselves afford sufficient reason for it.

But I return to the apostle, who says that by the revelation of his gospel "God would make known what is the riches of the glory of this mystery among the Gentiles." They who are acquainted with this holy man's writings, know that he often uses the word riches to signify abundance: as, for instance, when he exclaims, "O the depth of the riches both of the wisdom and the knowledge of God!" Rom. xi. 33; and when he speaks in another place of the riches of the grace of the Lord, Eph. i. 7; and demands of the impenitent if he "despises the riches of the goodness, and forbearance, and long-suffering of God," Rom. ii. 4. In this sense we must here understand the expression of "riches of glory;" that is to say, a great abundance of glory, or (which amounts to the same thing) a very great and most abundant glory. Whereby you see the zeal of this holy man for the praise of the gospel; insomuch that he cannot satisfy himself upon this subject, but heaps up the most magnificent terms he can think of to represent its excellency. He calls it a mystery, and a mystery of God; and a mystery hidden during all the ages which rolled on from the foundation of the world, and which was at length discovered from heaven in the last time to the saints of God. This is saying much; and there is no other doctrine, either human or divine, of which so much can be said. But it is not enough for Paul. He adds that it is a glorious mystery; and contents not himself with this, but ascribes to it, not glory simply, but riches, and an abundance of glory. And it is not here alone that he so speaks. He treats of it everywhere else in the same manner; as when he says that unto him this grace was given, to "preach among the Gentiles the unsearchable riches of Christ; and to make all men see what is the fellowship of the mystery, which from the beginning of the world hath been hid in God," Eph. iii. 8, 9; and when he calls it the glorious "ministration of the Spirit," and the mirror wherein the face of the Lord is openly beheld, 2 Cor. iii. 8, 18. And indeed he had good reason for so speaking; for it is particularly in the gospel that God has made all the beams of his glory to shine forth. There he manifests and communicates to men all the wonders of his power, of his wisdom, justice, and merciful goodness, in their greatest altitude, and in their richest abundance, which are as the substance and essence of this glory. The gospel is his treasury, in which he presents to us his most divine and glorious benefits; his grace, his peace, his Spirit, his holiness, his consolation, his life, and his immortality.

But the apostle does not speak here of the riches of the glory of the gospel in general, and towards all: he adds particularly, "among the Gentiles." Surely there is no sort of men, whether Jews or Greeks, in whom the gospel does not show forth riches of glory, if they receive it. Yet we must acknowledge that its glory never broke forth with so much splendour as when it was preached to the Gentiles. First, that exceeding great and inexhaustible abundance of goodness and grace, with which the gospel is filled, poured forth itself, and (if I may so speak) overflowed all bounds in saving the Gentiles, the most hopeless of all men, when it raised them from the grave, or rather the abyss of misery, in which they had lain, not for four days, as Lazarus in his sepulchre, but for four thousand years. For this reason, the holy apostle, comparing the grace of God in his Son, which was shown to the Jew, with that showed to the Gentile, at his calling of each, declares that the former received it by promise, and the latter simply and altogether of mercy, Rom. xv. 8, 9. Then, again, how admirable was the virtue of the gospel, which effected that in a few days which the law had not been able to do in so many ages! The ministers of the law compassed sea and land, and after all found it very hard to make one proselyte; and with all their diligence during the two thousand years in which they toiled, they had not reduced so much as one nation to the service of God, though they employed, when they were able, even sword and power for that purpose. But the gospel, quite naked, and without any weapons but its cross, converted many nations from paganism, and brought them unto God. They were men who worshipped stocks and stones, who were sunk in brutish ignorance, and were addicted to the most infamous vices; there was a mixture in them of the stupidity of beasts and the wickedness of devils. Certainly, to make even one of these a christian; to bring him out of this infernal pit, and place him in the church; to make him, who was a slave of Satan, a child of God; was, as Chrysostom writing on this passage justly says, no less a miracle, than if some one should suddenly change an unclean and deformed dog into a man, and raise him from the dunghill whereon he lay to sit upon a royal throne. It was truly therefore a great and an ineffable richness and abundance of glory, for the gospel to transform so speedily, not a small number, but hundreds and thousands of pagans, into so many believers. And in this the apostle secretly strikes at the false teachers, who would mix such a noble and glorious mystery with their feeble traditions, as if it had not in itself strength and virtue enough to subsist without the succour of their inventions.

Finally, he intimates in two words the ground of all this richness of glory which the gospel possesses, "which is," says he, "Christ in you;" that is to say, that Christ whom they possessed, and who dwelt in them by faith. And he adds that he is "the hope of glory;" in the same manner as in another place he calls Christ "our hope," 1 Tim. i. 1; that is, he of whom we hope for highest glory, and in whom we infallibly find all the blessedness that we can either desire or expect. It is not without design that he informs them that Jesus Christ is all the fulness of the mystery of the gospel; by this he lays a foundation for that which he more clearly tells them hereafter, namely, that it is in vain that the seducers attempt to mingle with it the ceremonies of Moses and the service of angels. All this great mystery begins and ends in Jesus Christ, since it is no other thing, as he defines it elsewhere, than "God manifested in the flesh, justified in the Spirit, seen of angels, preached unto the Gentiles, believed on in the world, and received up into glory," 1 Tim. iii. 16; that is, Jesus Christ our Lord, born, put to death, raised again, glorified, and set forth in the gospel for us. Such is the mystery of which the holy apostle here speaks.

Judge now, beloved brethren, what grace God has conferred on us in communicating to us so rich and so admirable a secret. Many kings and prophets have desired to see and to hear it, but have not had that happiness. Heaven and earth, for four thousand years, sighed after the blessing we possess; but only the last ages obtained it. The Jews saw the wonders of God but obscurely, and through veils and shadows. The Gentiles did not see them at all, being covered with a dismal night, living without God and without hope. This divine mystery appearing at once in the end of time, as a great light which suddenly shines forth from heaven, dissipated the shadows of the one, and dispelled the darkness of the other, changing in a moment by its virtue the whole face of the universe. It has particularly shown the riches of its glory among us, having brought our fathers out of the horrors of paganism, which once covered the whole of this land. Let us embrace, therefore, with all the affections of our souls, this great and inestimable favour of the Lord. Let us keep it pure and uncorrupted, without mixing with it anything that is foreign. It is not only sufficient for our happiness, it is even rich and abundant in glory. They who would burden it with ceremonies and services, whether of Moses's teaching or man's inventing, as false teachers formerly did, and our adversaries do at this day, understand not rightly the inexhaustible riches with which it overflows. They obscure the resplendency of its heavenly glory by their additions; they again hide and cover it with the veil which Jesus Christ has rent asunder. Let us say to those who propose them to us, We are content with the mystery which God has vouchsafed to manifest unto his saints. It was sufficient for their bliss. It will well suffice for ours. We do not desire any other riches than those with which it abounds, or any other glory than that with which it shines. It is enough that this Jesus Christ who fills it is in us, the hope of true glory. There is no need to associate with him either Moses, or angels, or saints.

But, my brethren, it is not enough to secure this mystery from the errors of superstition, there must be a putting far away the filth of vice, and of carnal and earthly passions, in order that it may be preserved pure among us, and receive that glory which is its due. God has not lighted up this great Sun among you that you should continue to live in sin, and do those works in such a blessed light which are done in darkness. Far be it from him. He has made known to you the mysteries hidden in old time, that your holy life might be new. As your knowledge is greater than that of other ages, let your holiness surpass theirs. The dimness of their light in some degree excuses their faults; faults committed in the mistakes of childhood, and in the obscurity of shadows. With what pretext can you palliate yours; you, to whom God has communicated all his counsel? How will you defend that ardent and unruly passion which you have for the earth ; you, whom by the gospel he has made to see all the beauties of heaven ? How will you justify the love and the adherence which one has to the pleasures of the flesh, another to the riches and honours of the world ; you, to whom he has shown the riches and the glory of eternity in his Son Jesus Christ ? Surely to sin in such light is not infirmity, nor simply wickedness. It is impudence, and execrable insolence. Take heed then, beloved brethren, that this great grace which God has shown you does not prove your condemnation. If you desire it should be saving to you, purify and cleanse yourselves from all filthiness and pollution. For the mysteries of God are only for saints. Renounce the customs of the world as well as its belief. Walk in the ways of heaven, in honesty and purity, worthy of the vocation with which God has honoured you. Let his mystery show forth the wonders of its glory among you, powerfully changing your whole life into its brightness, and transforming you into the image of that Jesus Christ who has vouchsafed to dwell in you, and to take your hearts for his temple; that, after you have wisely used his talents here below, and happily laboured in his vineyard, he may at length crown you in the heavens with that sovereign and eternal glory which he has promised us, and which we hope for from his grace. Amen.

SERMON XV.

VERSES 28, 29.

Whom we preach, warning every man, and teaching every man in all wisdom; that we may present every man perfect in Christ Jesus: whereunto I also labour, striving according to his working, which worketh in me mightily.

DEAR brethren, there is a great difference between the law and the gospel, both with regard to their own nature, and to the manner of their dispensation. For, to omit other things, the gospel is a mystery; that is, a truth so hid in God, that if he had not vouchsafed to discover it to men himself by a supernatural revelation, no creature, either earthly or heavenly, would ever have been able to bring it forth from the bottomless depth of God's wisdom, or to acquire of it any solid and distinct knowledge by the contemplation of the things of the world. But the law is a truth suitable to the sentiments of nature, and so open to the view of angels and men, that if sin had not dulled and corrupted the strength of our understanding, we should have easily comprehended it of ourselves, without any extraordinary manifestation from heaven. Accordingly, you see, however blind and wretched men are, yet they fail not to discern the things of the law, and the rectitude and justice of most of its requirements. But if you consider the dispensation of these two doctrines, you will find that the law was given by Moses to the Jewish nation only, whereas the gospel of our Lord and Saviour was preached indifferently to every people on earth, there having been no part of mankind to whom the benefit of this new light was not presented by the apostles and their scholars. Paul informed us of it in the preceding text, where he affirmed, first, that the gospel is a mystery, hidden during all the ages and generations which had passed, but now manifested to the saints of God; and secondly, that the Lord has made known the glorious riches of this mystery among the Gentiles, that is to say, among other people of the world besides the Jews; this he further confirms in our text by the extent of his preaching, declaring that he proclaimed this divine word to all men. For having intimated before the subject of this great mystery of the gospel, and declared that it consists wholly in Christ Jesus, who is the author and the substance of this celestial doctrine, he adds, " Whom we preach, warning every man, and teaching every man in all wisdom; that we may present every man perfect in Christ Jesus." And because his labours and sufferings were one of the most glorious marks of the truth, and of the divine authority of his apostleship, he makes mention of them also in the following verse: " Whereunto I also labour, striving according to his working, which worketh in me mightily." His design is to justify what he had before told the Colossians, namely, that he was a minister of the church, set up to fulfil the word of God among the Gentiles, that he might establish the Colossians in the doctrine which he preached, and secure them from the seductions of false apostles, who endeavoured to corrupt it by mixing with it those errors which they were actively employed in propagating, and contended, that besides faith in Jesus Christ, there was a necessity for observing the ceremonies of the law of Moses, and of practising various superstitions, such as the worshipping of angels, which they recommended and greatly extolled, as Paul shows us in the following chapter. It was to set up his own ministry above that of these evil workers that he before urged his heavenly call. It is for this purpose that he again so highly exalts the gospel; and with the same design he here sets forth the exercise of his apostleship, which consists in two things: the first, in preaching, which he describes in ver. 28; the other, in the labour and conflict which accompanied his preaching, declared in the verse following. These are the two points of which we will treat, by the will of God, in the present discourse, the preaching and the combats of Paul; commenting upon each of them, as we shall judge expedient, for your edification and consolation, which is the only aim of all the labour of this great apostle, and the true end both of our word and of your faith.

I. In the first place we will notice the preaching of the apostle; and respecting this we shall have four things to consider: First, the subject of it, namely, Jesus Christ, "whom," says he, "we preach." Secondly, the manner of it, which he expresses in these words, "warning and teaching every man." Thirdly, the object to which his preaching was directed, namely, every man; "warning every man," says he, "and teaching every man." And in the fourth and last place, the end and aim of it, namely, the perfecting of those to whom it was directed; "that we may present every man perfect in Christ Jesus."

First, when he says that he preaches Jesus Christ, his meaning is not simply that he speaks of Jesus Christ to those whom he instructed. There never was a heretic who did not make some mention of him, and who, to colour his false doctrines, did not mingle with them something of the mystery of Jesus Christ; even Mahomet himself, the most desperate of all impostors that ever seduced men from the gospel, speaks of him with honour, and acknowledges in general the truth of the call and the doctrine of Jesus. But the apostle declares that he preaches Jesus Christ alone, that he is the only subject of his preaching, and the substance of his teachings; according to the profession he expressly makes elsewhere, that he determined to know nothing among them, "save Jesus Christ, and him crucified," 1 Cor. ii. 2. His Epistles in which he has left us a lively and true picture of his preaching, sufficiently justify this remark. For those who have read his divine writings see that they are filled from the beginning to the end, with Jesus Christ alone. This adorable name shines forth in them everywhere, and there is no discourse or chapter on which it is not engraven. There are scarcely two periods found together in which it does not appear. If he is to teach, he proposes no other secrets than those of either the nature, offices, actions, passions, or promises of Jesus Christ. If he must combat error, he wields no other weapons than the cross of Jesus Christ. If he aims to clear the obscurities either of nature or of the law, Jesus Christ alone is the light which he uses to dissipate all kinds of shadows and clouds. From him he draws consolation for souls cast down, either by the sense of their sins, or by the heaviness of affliction. In him he finds all his motives and arguments for our sanctification. Jesus Christ alone furnishes him with all that is necessary to pacify our consciences, to make glad our hearts, to raise our hopes, to confirm our faith, to inflame our charity, to enkindle our zeal, to establish our constancy, to encourage our patience, to purify our affections, to loosen us from the earth, and lift us up to heaven. Jesus Christ is all his logic and all his rhetoric. He is the source of his arguments, the magazine of his arms, the great motive of his persuasions, the soul of all his discourses. In the writings of this holy teacher, you nowhere meet with either pope, or mass, or devotions to saints and angels, or purgatory, or auricular confessions, or even one of those pretended mysteries which fill up the modern theology. He was fully content with Jesus Christ. He believed it enough to preach him, and that he needed no more, either to discharge his own duty, or to advance our edification. And not without good reason; for what is there, I do not only say, that is necessary and useful, but that is in any way good, or great, or excellent, which is not in Jesus Christ? If other things which are recommended in religion were as true as they are false, and as innocent as they are pernicious, yet it is evident that in comparison with Christ Jesus they are miserably poor and trivial. In him alone is found such true solidity as is able to content the soul; in him alone is wisdom, righteousness, sanctification, and redemption; all the fulness of the Godhead, all the treasures of wisdom and knowledge, as Paul tells us hereafter. In this Lord alone is grace, truth, and life. There is no "salvation in any other; for there is none other name under heaven given among men, whereby we must be saved," Acts iv. 12. And yet, alas! though this is a truth so clear in itself, and so authentically confirmed by the preaching of our great apostle, yet there are people who, notwithstanding that they profess to believe it, seek that elsewhere which is to be found alone in Jesus Christ; and who, though this living and overflowing spring of grace is opened to all believers by the loving-kindness of the Father, dip in the poor cisterns of the creature for the water of salvation. They acknowledge that the merits of Jesus Christ are infinite, his righteousness absolutely perfect, his grace inexhaustible, his power pre-eminent; still they are not content with it, but add their satisfactions to his, the prayers of angels and saints to his intercession, and mingle the sufferings of men with the blood of the Son of God. But if the lusts of the world, or the false blaze of error, or the corrupt inclinations of the flesh, induce them to approve or to tolerate so dangerous a mixture, let us, for our part, dear brethren, whom God has delivered from such prepossessions, adore the fulness of Jesus Christ. Let us content ourselves with his richness, and never seek any true good anywhere else than in him. Let us bless God that from the pulpits erected among us we hear no name sounded forth but his. Since Paul preaches none but him, he alone should occupy the tongues of preachers, and the faith of their hearers.

Secondly, the apostle having declared the subject of his preaching, goes on to express the manner of it. We preach Christ, says he, "warning and teaching in all wisdom." These are the two parts of the office of a good preacher; namely, admonition and instruction. The first comprises all the remonstrances that are made to sinners, whether to reprehend their faults, to excite their diligence, to comfort their sorrows, or to remind them of any other part of their duty. The second contains all the lessons of heavenly doctrine, the exposition of each article of the mystery of godliness. Admonition reforms manners, teaching informs faith. The one moves the will and the affections, the other instructs the understanding. The apostle asserts, in another place, that he carefully joined these two offices together, not contenting himself with teaching and testifying of the faith in Jesus Christ, but incessantly warning every one with tears, Acts xx. 21, 31. And you see him uniting these two duties throughout his Epistles, where he not only expounds the mysteries of faith, but constantly applies those instructions to the conduct of those whom he instructs; reproving, chiding, comforting, and encouraging them as they had need. And as he thus acted himself, so he gave orders for the like procedure to others, whom God had called to the holy ministry. "Preach the word," says he, to Timothy; "be instant in season, out of season; reprove, rebuke, exhort with all long-suffering and doctrine," 2 Tim. iv. 2. And in other places he directs that every pastor be not only "apt to teach," but also "able, by sound doctrine, to exhort and convince the gainsayers," 1 Tim. iii. 2; 2 Tim. ii. 24; Tit. i. 9. Indeed these two offices are necessary for the edification of the faithful, which is the design of the ministry. It is not enough to propose to them generally the secrets of the gospel; general things do not much affect us. They must be applied particularly; and the word of God, which is the instrument of our profession, is proper for these two operations, as Paul expressly declares, when he says that "all Scripture is profitable for doctrine, for reproof, for correction, for instruction in righteousness: that the man of God (that is, his servant, or his minister) may be perfect, and thoroughly furnished unto all good works," 2 Tim. iii. 16, 17. Such, then, whom the Lord has honoured with this sacred ministry should labour to discharge these two duties; and remember that he calls them, not simply to teach, but also to admonish. For this is not the desk of a professor of mathematics or physic, who has no other business than to explain the secrets of those sciences to those that hear them. The pulpit has been prepared in the church for conducting men to salvation; not merely to make them understand, but to give them everlasting life, to illuminate their minds, to form their lives unto holiness, to pluck them out of the snares of Satan, and cause them to walk in the ways of God. Faithful brethren, since you know that such is the nature of our charge, you should not think it strange or unkind that we execute it in this manner among you. There are some who have a tender ear; they willingly hear information and doctrine, but cannot bear remonstrances. A discourse about the mysteries of religion is pleasing to them, but one about their vices and their duty is burdensome. And this tenderness is a very bad sign, as it shows that their religion is not sound. As a physician judges that there is something amiss, some sinew hurt, or some collection of unnatural humours, in those parts of the body which he cannot touch without putting the patient to pain. If you would have our ministrations to be entirely pleasing to you, reform your manners, that nothing may remain in your life but what is healthy and vigorous. Remonstrances annoy those only who have a diseased soul. But they should consider, that if they are troublesome to them they are necessary; and if the duties of our office oblige us to make them, their eternal interests much more oblige them to suffer them. It is a salt somewhat sharp, but wholesome; a potion bitter, but conducive to health.

But the apostle's addition, that he teaches "in all wisdom," must not be forgotten. There is no occasion for me to inform you that he speaks of heavenly wisdom, of that truth which is necessary to be known for obtaining salvation. It is evident, therefore, when he says he teaches in all this wisdom, he signifies that he declares all the mysteries of it to those whom he instructs, that he hides no part of it from them which it concerns them to know, for their arrival at the inheritance of Jesus Christ. It is the very thing which he speaks more clearly, and in express words, to the bishops or pastors of the church at Ephesus, when he says, "I kept back nothing that was profitable unto you, but have showed you, and have taught you publicly, and from house to house, testifying both to the Jews, and also to the Greeks, repentance toward God, and faith toward our Lord Jesus Christ;" and shortly after he says, "I have not shunned to declare unto you all the counsel of God." Acts xx. 20, 21, 27. From which it appears that the traditions, which are pretended to have been not publicly and generally taught to all the faithful, but delivered in secret by the apostles to some only, are not at all necessary to men's salvation. He who has learned what the apostle taught all men knows enough, since he taught in all wisdom, except men will say that he still wants some knowledge who has learned all wisdom. But it has always been one of the artifices of curiosity to pretend that men of God did not publish all, and that they committed a part of their instructions only to the ears of some that were more perfect than the vulgar, to the end that, under this pretext, it may make its own disquisitions and inventions pass for articles of divine doctrine. I know well that this is a mere imagination, as weak as it is bold, and such as has no other foundation than the invention of those by whom it is advanced. But it is not my business to make any further inquiry into its vanity; for whatever it is, since Paul has taught every man in all wisdom, my simplicity is henceforth my safety. The ignorance of your pretended secrets cannot be prejudicial to me, since all the wisdom of the gospel is comprised in the apostle's public and common teachings. From the same consideration, you may also perceive how extravagant are the visions of those who would cause it to be believed, that the doctrine of the church is polished and perfected from age to age, the succeeding having added to the light of those that went before; and that we should not wonder if the ancients either knew not some of the articles of modern divinity, or even spake contrary to them, inasmuch, say they, as the church not having yet at that time declared them, the belief of them was not necessary. By this account, the faith must have been imperfect in the apostle's time. Yet Paul says here that what he preached to all men was "all wisdom;" and he adds immediately, that by it he rendered "every man perfect in Christ Jesus." Whatever may be said on the subject, it is clear that it is enough to know the things which are sufficient to save us. If that which the apostles preached sufficed for the salvation of the first believers, we have nothing to do with that which men have since added. For we seek but our salvation; and it is foolishness to imagine that what was sufficient to save believers in those days is not sufficient to save them now; as if God had changed his design, and the revelation of his Son, and as if the apostle's preaching were not the seal and the perfection of all his dispensations. The articles which have been declared in the latter ages either formed a part of the wisdom preached by the apostles, or they did not. If they did form a part of it, they were no less necessary for the first ages than for the latter. If they did not, they are now as little necessary as ever. And it avails nothing to plead the authority of the church; for whatever authority may be ascribed to the company which is so called, it has not enough to make that necessary which in reality is not so; to shut up what God has opened, to contract that which he has dilated, or to bind that which he has loosed. If God will save us, without belief of the mass or of purgatory, the church would do well to renounce them; would she not? God will judge us by his own will and word, and not by the fantastical conceits or imaginations of men.

But I return to the apostle, who shows us, in the third place, what is the object of his preaching; "Warning every man, and teaching every man." It is very probable that the false teachers who would seduce the Colossians, to colour that observation of the law which they recommended, alleged that the apostles themselves left the Jews the use of circumcision, and the practice of legal abstinences; and that if Paul acted otherwise, it was towards some only. I consider that it is properly to this we must refer and oppose his repeating here three times, "warning every man, and teaching every man, that he might present every man perfect in Christ." He thus repeats this word, to show that his preaching was the same and uniform throughout, that he declared to all men but one Jesus Christ, and that he preached him indifferently both to Jews and Gentiles, Greeks and barbarians; God having given for them all but one and the same gospel, as he has set up but one sun in the universe to shine on all mankind. I declare, says he, the same Christ unto all, as Saviour and Redeemer of the world. There is no man to whom I preach any other thing. By which he gives a secret blow to the doctrine of these seducers, which was particular, and not preached either by the holy apostle, or by any of his fellows. It is probable also that he aimed to show here in his way the extent of his charge, which enclosed all men on earth within its compass; there being no one to whom he had not authority to preach the gospel, and whom he was not commissioned to admonish and teach; according as he says, in his Epistle to the Romans, "I am a debtor both to the Greeks, and to the barbarians; both to the wise, and to the unwise," Rom. i. 14. This he repeats, in order to establish the power which he presently afterwards uses to admonish the Colossians, and to condemn the seducers. For he shows thereby that there is no person, however learned he may otherwise be, who is not his scholar for this heavenly wisdom, and ought in this respect to be subject to his instructions, and to learn of him the mysteries of the gospel. As if he had said that God has raised him to the doctoral chair of the universe, and made him his public and universal herald, who should be listened to by every man in the world. From whence it follows, that these pretended masters of the Colossians, who would intrude to teach them after their mode, thwarted the institution of God; and that before they commenced the instruction of others, they should first have learned of the apostle the true mysteries of the wisdom of God. I acknowledge that there is not one of the ministers of God who has now this great extent of authority that the apostle here with truth ascribes to himself. Nevertheless, each of them ought to do in his district what the apostle did in his, to admonish and to teach every man, whoever he may be, in all wisdom, to have but one and the same gospel for all; not a pleasing doctrine, or, as it is commonly called, a velvet gospel, for the rich, and another quite different for the poor; but to treat them all without respect of persons, not concealing anything from the one which has been discovered to the others. Each one ought to teach the small as well as the great, to admonish the great as well as the small; to edify them all in common, without despising the littleness of the one, or fearing the greatness of the other.

But let us see, in the last place, what is the end of this preaching Jesus Christ. "Whom we preach," says the apostle, "warning every man, and teaching every man in all wisdom, that we may present every man perfect in Jesus Christ." This was the apostle's aim, this was the design of his labours, even to present all those who heard him holy and unreprovable unto Jesus Christ; to put them into such a condition by his preaching, as that they might appear before the throne of grace without confusion. He expresses it elsewhere in other terms; namely, when he says to the Corinthians in particular, "I have espoused you to one husband, that I may present you as a chaste virgin to Christ," 2 Cor. xi. 2. Here he uses precisely the same word as that in our text. You know that there are two sorts of perfection; one of a believer's minority, the other of his full age; according as the apostle distinguishes our times in the First Epistle to the Corinthians, chap. xiii. 11. The one, that which we have here below, during the course of our pilgrimage. The other, that which we shall have in heaven, our true country. This latter is a perfection every way complete; such as comprehends all the degrees of knowledge, holiness, and glory which our nature is capable of possessing. The former is a perfection begun, having all the parts of sanctification and consolation which are necessary in our present frailty, but not yet brought to its completion, or to its highest degrees. The one is simply and absolutely called perfection; the other is so named with respect to, and in comparison with, either the state in which we and other unregenerated men were, and still are, or the condition of our age. The apostle means the first when he confesses that he is not already perfect; he speaks of the second when he says, "Let us therefore, as many as be perfect, be thus minded," Phil. iii. 12, 15. And both are the end of the preaching of the gospel. For the design of Paul, and of all true ministers of the Lord, is by this means to guide the faithful to eternal salvation; that is, to the last and highest degree of these two kinds of perfection. And so the nearer effect of their preaching, and which immediately follows it, is the believer's perfection on earth; the farther and more remote effect of it, which necessarily and infallibly results from the first, is his perfection in heaven. Moreover, this first perfection, to which preaching immediately tends, consists chiefly of two parts, knowledge and sanctification, faith and charity; and though there be many defects in both, yet if you compare them with the vision and glory of heaven, they are, even at present, perfect in some degree, inasmuch as the true believer wants not any of the knowledge and habits which are necessary to salvation. And it is to this the apostle reduces it, when he restrains the perfection he speaks of to Jesus Christ; "that we may present," says he, "every man perfect in Jesus Christ." It is to his abundance that we owe our perfection, inasmuch as he gives us all that we have of it by his Spirit, and supplies that which we want of it by the riches of his merit. The apostle considers the believer's perfection here in its whole extent; that is, with regard both to faith and holiness. He particularly intends the first; for it seems to me evident that he has an eye to the error of the seducers, who added the observation of the Mosaical law, the worshipping of angels, and such other traditions, to the instructions of the gospel, as if the faith of christians was imperfect without them. Paul, to overthrow these pernicious doctrines, seasonably establishes this fact, that the preaching of the gospel is enough to render every man perfect who receives it with faith, and that there is no need either of Moses or of angels, of the ceremonies of the one, or of the services of the other; that Jesus Christ, in whom we are, is abundantly sufficient, without the assistance of any other. But though this is the apostle's direct aim, yet in that perfection of which he speaks, together with fulness of faith, he comprises pureness of manners and of worship, which inseparably depend on it, and without which that faith cannot possibly be perfect.

Such is the sense of these words of Paul, from which we may learn two things before we proceed further. The first is the perfection and sufficiency of the doctrine preached by the apostles. For since the end to which it tended was to make the hearer of it perfect, it is evident that it had in it all that was necessary to convey this perfection; there being no probability that God would have put a means into the hands of his servants which was not sufficient to reach the end; such a fault being incompatible with his infinite wisdom and power. But it is evident that the apostles' preaching could not have made the faith of their hearers perfect, if they had omitted in preaching any of those particulars, the belief of which is necessary to salvation. It must be concluded, therefore, that not one of them was omitted. Consequently, it is clear by the same argument, that all the traditions which men advance at this day are unprofitable. For what service can they do us, since we may be "perfect in Jesus Christ" without them? It cannot be said that they were a part of the things which the apostles preached. First, the very men who defend them dare not affirm it of most of them, it being notorious that they rose up by degrees very long after the apostles' times. Secondly because Paul himself describes to us the matter of his preaching; "We preach Christ," says he; confining it wholly, as you see, to the mystery of our Saviour, with which these traditions have no more connection than those of the seducers, who sought to mingle divers ceremonies, and the worshipping of angels, with the gospel of Jesus Christ, which traditions he afterwards refutes. And lastly, because the apostle elsewhere gives to Scripture the same sufficiency which he here ascribes to his preaching, saying that "all Scripture is given by inspiration of God, and is profitable for doctrine, &c., that the man of God may be perfect," 2 Tim. iii. 16, 17. But it is clear that these pretended traditions are not to be found at all in Scripture. Surely then it is also manifest that they are unnecessary to make our faith perfect.

But, on the same grounds, it is apparent again, how contrary to Paul the doctrine of Rome is. For he says that the design of his preaching was to make every "man perfect in Jesus Christ;" Rome, on the contrary, allows this perfection only to clerks, in the first place, and next to monks; not reckoning that the people (whom, by an odious name which the apostle Paul never gives but to pagans or the profane, they call seculars, and men of the world, in opposition to men of the church) can or should seek to arrive at perfection. And the presumption of monks is grown so high, that there are no longer any but persons hooded and clothed in their manner who are called religious men, or religious women; as if every man who is a true christian were not also truly religious. And again, they call their condition only the state of perfection, as if all the rest of the faithful were but abortives and imperfect productions. And though this vanity is beyond measure injurious to all other christians, yet their partisans suffer it, and the majority of them seem well pleased with it; imagining, under this pretence, that there are none but monks who are obliged to be perfect, and that, as for themselves, who are in the world, it is not their part to aspire so high; and, in effect, the greater number so freely dispense with this necessity, that truly there is reason to call them seculars indeed. But the holy apostle here overthrows in two words the arrogance of the one, and the security of the other. As to the former, he tells us he preached the gospel that he might render his hearers perfect; he clearly shows us, that for our guidance to perfection we have no need of the rules either of Francis, or Dominic, or Bruno, or Loyola, or the many other pretended regulars, who, as it were, outvying each other, daily set forth some new doctrine before the world. The Lord Jesus has provided long since for our perfection, giving us a most complete and very easy rule to attain it, after which it is an extreme rashness to attempt the establishment of another. Follow that rule, christian, embrace it, and proceed constantly in the way of holiness which it has prescribed you, and be assured that by so doing you shall not fail of arriving at perfection, though you wear not Francis's frock and hood, or Loyola's little band. But the apostle here no less condemns the security of those who are called seculars, than the vanity of such as style themselves religious. For he says expressly and universally that his design is to "present every man perfect in Christ Jesus." He will have no other disciples. He owns none for his scholars but such as aim at perfection, such as resolve to obtain it, and labour after it daily. If you remain secular, and in a state of imperfection, his preaching has not wrought its effects in you; and as you have no part in that perfection to which he would lead you in this life, no more shall you have part in that to which he desires to conduct you in the life that is to come. There is but one sort of christians, even those who, having believed the gospel, mortify the deeds of the body, and crucify their flesh with its affections, and who, forgetting the things which are behind, advance some steps daily towards the mark and prize of their calling; such christians has Paul, whose language respecting it you are now hearing, prevailed to present, by the efficacy of his preaching, perfect in Christ Jesus. It is a mistake, it is a folly, to fancy that any others are christians. These double or middling christians, who would at once be both christians and worldlings, disciples of heaven and of earth, have no more place in the reality of nature than in the Scriptures of God. If you would have a place among the perfect ones of the life to come, be betimes among the perfect of this life. There is no ascending to the one of these perfections but by the other. If you will be one day in the number of full-grown men of Jesus Christ, be now in the number of his children. Walk in faith and in love during this pilgrimage, if you would aspire to the vision and glory of the heavenly country.

II. But it is now time, my brethren, having spoken of his preaching, to say something to you, in the second place, of the apostle's labour and conflicts. "Whereunto I also labour, striving according to his working, which worketh in me mightily."

Surely there is no christian that does not meet in the way to heaven with many thorns, which the flesh, the world, and the devil sow there; for these cannot suffer any one to undertake so glorious a design without crossing him to the utmost of their power. Yet, among all the faithful, there are none that have more labours and conflicts to undergo than the ministers of the gospel. This high office, besides being very painful itself, draws the hatred and persecutions of the enemy more especially upon them; and again, among all those whom God has honoured with this divine employment, it must be acknowledged that the apostles are the men who had most difficulties to surmount and afflictions to wade through. All our strivings for the truth are but children's play, in comparison with the combats which these great warriors had to sustain. For who does not know that in every work of importance the beginning is always much more difficult than the progress and prosecution? The apostles broke up the ground in which we labour; they opened and levelled the race in which we run; they with infinite pain laid the foundations of the house which we build. The business at that time was to overthrow paganism, to demolish Judaism, to fill up great deeps and to level mountains; whereas we enter upon a work already settled and fixed. They went through a country where there was neither way nor path, nor anything favourable to them; whereas we go in the track which they have made. To all this we must add the great extent of their charge, which enclosed the whole universe, and obliged them to take care of all the nations of the world; whereas we labour each of us in a small parcel of this great and vast heritage of the Son of God. What shall I say of the persecutions which Satan raised up and brought upon them in all quarters, animating all the powers of the world against them, and subtlely engaging them in this war, some by a zeal for the religion of their fathers, others by reasons of state; some by a jealousy for reputation, others by their passion for pleasures and vices? To overcome so many difficulties, and to advance, as they did, a work whose success was, in appearance, as impossible as if they had undertaken to displace the bounds of the world, and to change mountains into seas, it was evidently necessary that these holy men should toil in an extraordinary manner, and strive with a far greater vigour than that possessed by any of the rest of the faithful. But though they all applied themselves to such service with an indefatigable and courageous earnestness, and with an admirable constancy of mind, yet Paul particularly signalized himself among those blessed patriarchs of the new people and Israel of God; for with respect to labour, which he mentions, first, none of them preached Christ with more fervour, none of them pressed men to yield themselves to him with more vehemency, none began with more alacrity, nor went on with more assiduity. Never was tongue more active, nor pen more divine, nor mind more vigilant, than his. He alone traversed as many countries as all the rest together. He visited all nations, sowing the gospel everywhere, watering it night and day with incredible pains, by his speech, by his tears, and by his cares. He had no sooner achieved one conquest than he enterprised another; and the end of one labour was to him but the beginning of another. Never did ambition or avarice, though the most restless of our passions, cause men of the world half the anxiety sustained by the apostle in bringing mankind to the perfection which the Lord Jesus promised. And as the inclination which the sun has to communicate his comfortable beams to all creatures keeps him in perpetual motion, without permitting him to have one moment's rest; so Paul's love for souls, and his ardent desire to shed abroad, in every direction, the light, life, and blessedness with which his Master had stored him, pressing him both day and night, caused him to pursue his course without ceasing, and to circulate continually about mankind, presenting his treasures sometimes to one country, and sometimes to another, passing all the days he lived in this glorious activity. Neither did he at all exaggerate when he said to the Corinthians, being compelled to it by the false assertions of his calumniators, that he had laboured more abundantly than any of the rest, 1 Cor. xv. 10. That part of his history which Luke has given to us in the Acts justifies the truth of his words, and the fourteen divine Epistles which he has left us, and which make up part of his admirable labours, as clearly show us how the case really stood.

His strivings or conflicts were not less than his ministerial labours. For by them he means the perils and sufferings which the discharge of his apostleship, and the preaching of the gospel, caused him every hour to experience, and which he frequently compares to the combats which were at that time solemnized in Greece; because those who engaged in them had various pains and inconveniences to suffer, as he shows at large in the 9th chapter of the first Epistle to the Corinthians, ver. 25—27. He had more enemies to sustain than any of the rest; there were Jews and pagans without, seducers and false brethren within. It makes us tremble only to read the persecutions and obstructions which he received from these quarters. He himself has drawn up a little catalogue of them, in which he represents to us through what depths of afflictions he had passed, and was still daily passing; being pursued, out of measure, both by his own countrymen, and also by the Gentiles. He was beaten, imprisoned, scourged, stoned; he was in shipwrecks on the sea, in dangers and deaths upon the land. He was sometimes at the mercy of robbers in deserts, and at others beset round in cities, both with weapons of enemies, and the ambushments of false friends. He was reduced to nakedness, to cold, to hunger, and thirst. It is this hard and terrible chain of labours and sufferings to which he here alludes, when he says, " Whereunto I also labour, striving."

But, oh the deep humility of this holy man! he immediately gives the glory of these marvellous exploits to the grace and assistance of the Lord Jesus alone. I labour and strive, says he, "according to his working, which worketh in me mightily." He exercises the same modesty, elsewhere, when, having said that he had "laboured more abundantly than they all," he presently corrects himself, and adds, "yet not I, but the grace of God which was with me." It is the invincible force of this grace of the Lord Jesus which he calls here "his working;" and he says that it works in him "mightily," or with power, to signify the admirable effects which it produced in him; first, in that it raised up in him the light of knowledge, the love of holiness, charity towards the Lord's flock, and such prudence and wisdom as were necessary for the instruction and government of souls. Secondly, in that it endued him with a more than human courage, with an immovable constancy and firmness, both that he might sustain the burden of such great and continual labour, and patiently and cheerfully bear the persecutions and temptations which were still let loose against him; the Lord overruling these things, which tended to frustrate his purposes, for his glory and the advancement of his work, as he promised him, that his strength should be made perfect in his weakness. Thirdly, in accompanying the apostle's preaching with divers miracles, which ravished men, and gave authority to his words, as he expressly testifies in another place: "I will not dare to speak of any of those things which Christ hath not wrought by me, to make the Gentiles obedient, by word and deed, through mighty signs and wonders," Rom. xv. 18, 19. Lastly, this divine efficacy of our Saviour also magnificently appeared in the success with which he crowned the labours of Paul; opening the hearts of those who heard him, and causing his voice to enter into them, notwithstanding all the impediments of nature, with such a miraculous blessing, that he made his gospel to abound from Jerusalem, and round about even to Illyricum, subduing nations, and converting them gloriously to the service of his Master. It is this that he here represents to the Colossians, when he says, "I labour, striving according to his working, which worketh in me mightily." And it excellently conduces to his design, which is to show the truth of the gospel he preached, which shone forth clearly in those many miracles, they being as seals by which the Lord confirmed it.

This great example especially concerns those whom God has called to the sacred ministry of his house; and it shows them, on one hand, how painful their office is; that it is a work, (as the apostle says when addressing Timothy,) a work, I say, rather than a dignity; a labour, and not a recreation; for the proper discharge of which they must toil and strive, watch in all things, endure afflictions, and do the work of evangelists, 1 Tim. iii. 1; 2 Tim. iv. 5. And it teaches them, on the other hand, that they must not be discouraged by those great difficulties, but trust in the grace of Christ, and expect from the sole efficacy of his assistance that light, that strength, that patience and constancy, which is requisite for finishing so laborious a course, since it is he alone who renders us meet for these things; strengthening us in weakness, comforting us in trouble, encouraging us in difficulties, sustaining us under assaults, and so conducting us, that though we are nothing of ourselves, yet in him we can do all things, who makes us able ministers of the new testament, 2 Cor. iii. 5.

But though Paul's example particularly respects pastors, yet it appertains also to all true christians in general, since there is not one of them who is not the Lord's servant, who has not the management of some of his talents, and who is not called to labour and combat. Let us meditate, then, all of us in common, both upon the preaching and labour of this great apostle, and jointly make our improvement of them. He still at this day declares to us the same Christ, whom he before preached to all the nations of the world. Though the organs that sound it to you be incomparably weaker than his were, yet it is his word that you hear, the same word and the same Christ which in time past converted the universe. The same Paul whose voice had then so much efficacy, speaks yet to you daily. He addresses to you the same doctrine, he sets before you the same wisdom, he admonishes and teaches every man among you. Do not abuse so great a blessing, do not frustrate the true and just effects of this holy man's labour. The end of his preaching is, that you all may be perfect. This is the mark to which he calls you all in general. Say not to me that he speaks to some only. I warn, says he, and teach every man, that I may render every man perfect in Jesus Christ. Object not the employments which you have in the world, nor the duties to which your family and your affairs confine you. If they be incompatible with that perfection which the apostle requires of you, you must renounce them. It is an extreme folly to excuse oneself from being happy. This ought to be the first and last of our cares; and if we cannot attain it but by quitting honours, by losing riches, by retrenching our delights, yea, as our Lord says, by plucking out our own eye, or cutting off our foot or our hand; it is better to forego all this, than keep it, to be cast, at our departure hence, into the torment of eternal fire. But these are vain and mere frivolous pretences to palliate our negligence. If we have truly received Jesus Christ into our hearts, neither a wife, nor children, nor a family, nor an estate, nor the honest and lawful employments of the world, will hinder you from being perfect. The fear of God, honest deportment, plain dealing and justice, charity and beneficence, and, in a word, the holiness in which our perfection consists, is not incompatible with any of these things. For I ask you, Is it your business or your calling which obliges you to offend God and injure men—to pollute your body with the filth of infamous pleasures—to defraud or to rob your neighbour—to drown your whole life in luxury, in debauches, and in slothfulness? No, no, christian, excuse not yourselves by such pretences. The affairs of your family and of your trade are altogether innocent of your faults. They rather invite you to honesty and innocency than solicit you to vice. It is nothing but the rage of your ungoverned passions that causes this disorder. It is nothing but your ambition, your covetousness, your pride, your effeminateness and delicacy, which turns you away from christian perfection. To obtain it there is no need that you should retire into a desert or a cloister, nor that your habits or your food should be different from those of the people among whom you live; there needs for this nothing but a retirement from vice, and a sincere renunciation of the practice of it, plucking its lusts from your heart, changing your life, and not your dwelling, your conduct, and not your clothes. And this it is, my beloved brethren, in which we must labour and strive. The design to which I call you is great and painful, and no less difficult than the conquest of the world, the business of Paul's apostleship. For there is no duty more severe than that of renouncing our passions, or more difficult than that of overcoming ourselves. It is much more easy to wear a cowl, or a hair-cloth, and to blacken the body with blows, yea, to kill oneself, than to put off the desires of the flesh. Labour then earnestly and assiduously, since you have undertaken so difficult a task. Employ all your time in it; let no day pass without engaging in it; watching and praying, mortifying all the members of your old man, with a true penitence; reading the word of God, and meditating upon it; embracing his promises, exercising yourselves in the study and practice of those good and holy works which he has recommended to us. The design is great, and you are weak. But the Lord Jesus, in whom you have believed, is almighty, and all-merciful. He still has the same power which before converted the world by the hand of Paul. If you labour in his work with such zeal as his apostle did, he will also communicate his graces unto you. He will display his virtue upon you. He will work powerfully in you. He will bruise Satan under your feet, and crucify your flesh by the efficacy of his own. He will vivify your spirit by the light of his. He will cause you to triumph over your enemies. He will comfort you in the afflictions which you shall suffer for so good a cause. He will guide you in all your ways. And after the labour and the combat, will crown you on high in the heavens with that glory and immortality, with which all the pains of the present life are not worthy to be compared. So be it; and unto him, as also to the Father, and to the Holy Spirit, the only true God, blessed for ever, be honour and glory, to ages of ages. Amen.

SERMON XVI.

CHAPTER II.

VERSES 1, 2.

For I would that ye knew what great conflict I have for you, and for them at Laodicea, and for as many as have not seen my face in the flesh; that their hearts might be comforted, being knit together in love, and unto all riches of the full assurance of understanding, to the acknowledgment of the mystery of God, and of the Father, and of Christ.

DEAR brethren, as gardeners and husbandmen are not satisfied with sowing good seed in the ground which they have prepared, but also take care to eradicate the weeds which might choke or injure the good plants; so in the spiritual husbandry of Jesus Christ, it is not enough that the ministers of his gospel cast his divine word, the good and saving seed of our regeneration, into the souls of men; they must also exert themselves to weed and cleanse this spiritual soil committed to their cultivation; extirpating those bad and pernicious weeds of error and false doctrine, which, springing up of themselves, or being privily sown by an enemy's hand, would mar all this divine tillage. Hence the apostle Paul, having in the 1st chapter of this Epistle very effectually established the truth, as you have heard, proceeds now in this 2nd chapter, the beginning of which we have read, to refute and reject the errors which certain false workers, ministers of Satan, were artfully endeavouring to introduce; that this people, as a field or a garden of God's, being cleared of all worthless and noxious seed, the precious grain of the gospel, which the apostle had sown there, might take root and spring up, and grow at large, covering and crowning it all over with the flowers and fruits of incorruption, which are sincere piety and true sanctity, no strange plant being mingled with it. These seducers, as we have often intimated, taught, that besides faith in Jesus Christ, of which they made profession, there was also a necessity for observing the Mosaic law, and of worshipping of angels, and of practising certain kinds of superstitious discipline and mortifications of their own invention. And to render all this the more acceptable, they mingled with it some of the subtilties and vain speculations of secular philosophy. This is the weed which the apostle, the church's holy husbandman, now roots up out of his Lord's field; fortifying the Colossians against the craft of such men; and divinely showing them how full and sufficient was the doctrine of his gospel; how unprofitable, and even plainly dangerous, were the additions made by these seducers. This you will hear in the course of the chapter. The two verses which we have read, and the three or four following, are as the entrance or gate of this controversy. In these the apostle is preparing the hearts of the Colossians to receive his instructions, by placing before them the evidences of his ardent desire for their salvation. In the 1st verse, he declares his great anxieties for them and for their neighbours: "I would that ye knew what great conflict I have for you," &c. Then he adds, in the following verse, the design or the cause of this conflict: "That their hearts might be comforted," &c. These two points we purpose to handle in the present discourse, by the assistance of the grace of Christ: Paul's care and conflict for the Colossians and the Laodiceans; then his design, or the end for which he underwent all this trouble for them.

I. In reference to the first of these two points, you may remember that the apostle affirmed, in the end of the preceding chapter, that, to discharge the ministry which God had committed to him, he laboured and fought according to the energy that wrought powerfully in him. Now he descends from generalities to a particular instance; and having spoken definitely of the labour he endured for the edification of all, he tells the Colossians of the great anxiety he felt for them in particular; adding, "For I would that ye knew what great conflict I have for you, and for those of Laodicea." It is not without cause, says he, that I profess to strive and labour for the edification of the faithful. For, not to allege other proofs of it to you, God knows, and I also desire you to know, that I sustain a great conflict for you and your neighbours. Laodicea, which he speaks of, was the metropolis of Phrygia, and nigh to Colosse, which was situated in the same province. The vicinity of these two cities was the cause of a particular intercourse between the churches which God had formed in them; and hence the apostle afterwards salutes the Laodiceans by name, and orders the Colossians to impart this Epistle to them. John also, in the Apocalypse, makes mention of the church of Laodicea; and it is one of the seven churches of Asia to which the Lord Jesus commanded him to write in his name. And by the epistle which he thereupon wrote, and which is registered in the Apocalypse, it appears that there were much laxity, and coldness, and many defects in that flock. Whether such corruption had obtained permission there as early as Paul's own time; or whether, as I judge more probable, it slipped in afterwards, through the carelessness of the faithful and the craft of foes; it is very probable that Laodicea was troubled at this time with the same evils that the Colossians were, and that these seducers who endeavoured to infect the one applied themselves also to the other. Therefore the apostle would have this Epistle, as a preservative against the venom of these false teachers, to be communicated to those of Laodicea; a proof that, since they had need of the same remedies, they were threatened with the same maladies.

But to the Colossians and the Laodiceans, whom he here expressly names, he adds indefinitely all those who have not seen his face in the flesh. His name was so very celebrated among Christians, that there could hardly be one of them who had not heard of him, and who did not know him by report, and consequently had seen him in heart and in spirit. But he speaks of those only who had not seen him present in the flesh, whether by these words he means all the faithful in general, of every cast and country, who had never enjoyed his presence, (for we know that the care of this eminent apostle extended to them all,) or whether he speaks of the faithful in Phrygia or in Asia only, which, in my opinion, is more likely. For as it was impossible that Paul and the other apostles should personally visit every place, they often sent evangelists as their assistants and coadjutors, to travel in various parts for the conversion of souls. And so, though the apostle had traversed the greatest part of Asia Minor, and honoured many of its principal cities with his presence and preaching, and especially the province of Phrygia, (as we gather from the book of the Acts, chap. xvi. 6; xviii. 23,) yet it is probable that there were still many cities to which he had not been able to go in person. Expositors, both ancient and modern, for the most part, conclude from these words of Paul that he had not yet visited the city of Colosse nor the city of Laodicea when he wrote this Epistle; and they suppose that he had converted those people, and founded churches among them, by the ministry of Epaphras. Nor can it be denied but that the words give us some apparent ground so to conceive. For saying that he "had a great conflict" for the Colossians and the Laodiceans, and for all those who had not seen his face in the flesh, he seems to enrol the Colossians and the Laodiceans among those who had never seen him. Nevertheless there are ancient authors,* and than whom none are more eminent for profound learning, as well as for acuteness and solid judgment, who think otherwise, and hold that Paul had been both at Colosse and at Laodicea; thinking it improbable that he should have twice gone through Phrygia, as Luke expressly states, and not have seen those two cities, the princi-

* Theodoret, in his Preface to this Epistle and on the place itself.

pal ones of that country. And for these words, "and all those which have not seen my face in the flesh," they conceive them to be added, not to rank the Colossians and the Laodiceans with such as had not seen the apostle, but, on the contrary, to distinguish and separate them from others who had not; as if Paul had said that he had a great conflict, not only for them, but even for those who had never seen his face in the flesh. But after all, this difference is of no great importance; and as we have no other means for deciding the point, we forbear to insist on it, leaving every one at liberty to take either way of the two, neither of them damaging the truth of faith or holiness of life. And thus we have seen who they were for whom the apostle sustained the great conflict of which he here speaks.

Consider we now the conflict itself. By this he means, I doubt not, first and principally, that care, and solicitude, and thoughtfulness which the consideration of these churches drew upon him. For though their faith and constancy afforded him much satisfaction, and encouraged his hope, yet when he cast his eyes upon the great temptations that surrounded them, the hatred and persecutions of the world, the seducements and artifices of false teachers, and when he reflected on the weakness of human nature, he could not but fear lest so many things, and those of so much force, should draw them off from piety. Love is not without apprehension, no, not in the greatest safety; how much less in the midst of so many dangers! The apostle elsewhere assures us that the affection which he bore to the faithful was so great, that he sympathized in all their miseries, and felt as if he had suffered them himself. The care which I have of all the churches, says he, keeps me besieged from day to day. "Who is weak and I am not weak? who is offended, and I burn not?" 2 Cor. xi. 29. And in the 3rd verse of the same chapter he represents to us the great anxiety he felt for the Corinthians in particular: "I fear lest by any means, as the serpent beguiled Eve through subtlety, so your minds should be corrupted from the simplicity which is in Christ." Just the same he apprehended for the Colossians and Laodiceans, and other christians in Asia, that is, lest the frauds and artifices of seducers should confound their faith, and spoliate among them, as they had done in the church of the Galatians, as appears by the Epistle which he wrote them on the occasion.

Yet these just fears which oppressed the mind of the apostle were not his whole conflict. For under this word he comprises also all that he did to divert the danger which he apprehended. First he was perpetually in prayer for the safety of these dear churches; and as Moses in olden time upon the mountain ceased not to lift up his hands to the Almighty for the victory of Israel, engaged at that time in battle with Amalek; so this great apostle, from that high station where Jesus Christ had set him in his church, continually presented his supplications and sighs to heaven for the good success of the conflicts in which his Master's troops were engaged. He writes, "We pray always for you," 2 Thess. i. 11. "I always make request for you all in all my prayers," Phil. i. 4. "We cease not to pray for you, and to desire that you may be filled with the knowledge of his will in all wisdom and spiritual understanding," Col. i. 9. To prayer he added action; courageously attacking error on all occasions; refuting seducers, and exposing the vanity of their doctrine and the malignity of their design, not only by word of mouth, but also by writing, as we see by those divine Epistles of his which remain with us, and which abound in evidences of his great earnestness against these false apostles. And as he courageously assails the enemy, so he smartly appeals to the faithful; reproving them, admonishing and encouraging them to necessary firmness and constancy. He proceeded with so much magnanimity, that he spared not Peter himself, who, having fallen through weakness and pliancy into certain things which seemed to favour error, Paul boldly engages him, and with much freedom shows him his fault, as elsewhere he has narrated, Gal. ii. In short, he omitted none of the duties of a valiant and vigilant captain, either against the foe, or towards his friends and fellow soldiers, as we may see in his writings. But his combat did not terminate here. He often came to blows, cheerfully suffering for this cause all the persecutions which the rage of the Jews and the malice of seducers could contrive and form against him. And, indeed, the very chain with which he was loaded, and the prison he was in when he wrote this Epistle, made a part of this combat of his; it being clear, by the history of the Acts, that nothing had more inflamed the hatred of the Jews against him, who cast him into this affliction, than the zeal which he showed everywhere against the corruptions of those persons who wished to retain the ceremonies of the Jewish law; and hence it is that he told the Colossians, chap. i. 24, he suffered for them; because in effect, it was for maintaining their liberty, and the liberty of other Gentiles converted to the gospel, and for the keeping of their faith pure from all corruptive leaven, that he fell into this wearisome suffering. Such was Paul's conflict for these faithful people.

Dear brethren, admire the zeal and the love of this holy man. He was in the prison of Nero; he stood, as we may say, upon the scaffold, and had his head on the block, being indicted for a matter which concerned his life. And even in this state his heart is in pain for the churches of Colosse and Laodicea, and for those besides which had never seen him. *Their* danger troubled him more than *his own.* Neither prison nor death was able to extinguish or diminish his affection, or to make him lay aside the least of his cares; having so great a combat against his own person upon his hands, he leaves it, and on so pressing an occasion labours and fights for others. Certainly nothing can be imagined more elevated or more ardent than this love. We may truly affirm of it what is said in the song of Solomon, his "love is strong as death," and his "jealousy is cruel as the grave: the coals thereof are coals of fire, a most vehement flame. Many waters cannot quench it. neither can floods drown it."

But observe again the prudence and suitable procedure of this holy man, in representing these things to these faithful people for so good an end. Having to treat with them on important matters, and to decry errors which seduction had painted over with the deceitful colours of philosophy and eloquence, that he might dispose their hearts to give him due audience, and gain his remonstrances a necessary credit and authority, he sets before them at the entrance the cares that he had for their salvation, the conflicts he sustained for them, and all the effects of that sacred amity he had towards them. As a captain, who, to keep his soldiers firm in their duty, represents to them his watchings, and his labours, and his cares for their preservation; and, in sum, all the marks of his affection to them; or rather as a tender mother, who, to withdraw her dear children from giving ear to seducers, shows them her fears, her solicitudes, and her alarms, the yearning of her bowels, and all that she does or suffers for them. Such is the apostle's holy artifice in the present business: and it is grounded on a maxim which we all understand, namely, that we believe those who love us, and are concerned for our welfare, much more than those who are indifferent to us. He declares to them his pains that they may take in good part his remonstrances, and discovers to them his strong affection that they may receive his counsels. His aim is not to gain renown, or to enhance his esteem among them, (such a childish vanity had no place in the soul of this great man,) but merely to render his instructions the more effectual to the Colossians.

And the conflicts which for this end he mentions to them should serve in like manner for examples to us. Let ministers of the gospel learn by them, what love they owe their flocks, to what cares and conflicts their office obliges them. Let nothing in the world be dearer or more precious to them than the salvation of the souls committed to their charge; let them take part in their joys and in their griefs; let them feelingly resent their wounds, apprehend their dangers, labour incessantly for their edification. To it let them consecrate the thoughts of their mind, and the words of their mouth, and the work of their pen, and the actions of their life; yea, their blood and life itself, if there be need, saying with clear conscience, as the apostle in another place does, "As for me, I will very gladly spend and be spent for your souls," 2 Cor. xii. 15; and "joy to be offered upon the sacrifice and service of your faith," Phil. ii. 17. Let this care and these thoughts fill their hearts day and night; let them be assured that there is no business, no incident, no peril that exempts them from this duty; no, not death itself, in the very gates of which they ought to mind still their flock, and contend for them by their prayers and their devout wishes. Such is the faithful love and care we owe you.

We confess that without this watching and striving for your salvation we cannot avoid the censure and chastisements of the supreme Pastor. Judge if it be not reasonable that you should affectionately regard those whom the love of your salvation engages to so many cares and labours, and if it be not just that you receive their instructions with reverence, and hearken to the product of their studies with attention; that you comply with their zeal for your edification, and attribute much importance to their counsels, and bear with their fidelity, and impute to their affection the severity of their remonstrances when grief and fear draw from them complaints and cries against your behaviour; that you console them in their anxious cares for you by your gratitude, and above all by your progress in the studious pursuit of piety. This is the only fruit which they crave of all their cares and their conflicts; they would account them most advantageously recompensed if you do but profit by them; if they perceive by the purity of your manners, and the sanctity of your lives, that they have not laboured in vain. But do not imagine, I pray, that their solicitude discharges you of all care. On the contrary, it shows you with what earnestness and assiduity you should labour for your own salvation. For if they must heed your affairs with so much diligence, what zeal should you put forth about them yourselves! Their exertion may awaken and animate you, but it cannot save you except you strive yourselves. Their conflict will win you no crown, if you take no part in it after their example. Every one will live by his own faith; no person be crowned for the zeal of his pastor or his brother. If your pastors watch, if they stand on their guard, if they labour and fight, blessed be God, they shall receive their reward. But their labouring will not excuse your loitering, nor will their heedfulness justify your neglects. "Every man shall bear his own burden." Others may give you the example of their piety, but they will not be able to communicate to you its recompenses.

Let us then employ ourselves, both pastors and flocks, about our salvation with fear and trembling. Let us all combat with Paul, if we would be crowned with him. Let us imitate his love, if we desire to partake in his glory. Let us extend our love and our solicitudes as he did, not only to the faithful whom we know, but even to those whom we never saw. I confess that it is bodily sight and presence which enkindles and maintains carnal amities. The eyes of the flesh are the authors and the preservers of them. But in christian friendship it is otherwise; it is the Spirit that unites them. It is his eye and his light that originate and perpetuate them. For since it is properly Jesus Christ and his gospel that love regards, it is evident that it ought to embrace all those who bear the marks of them, whether they be absent or present. The distance of time and place do not hinder this sacred commerce. The apostle strives even for those who had never seen him. Let us also love all true christians, and expand our affections to those whom many seas and many mountains sever from us. Let us strive for them by prayer, and do them (however far off from us) all the services of which our love is capable; labouring with holy tenderness for the salvation and edification of each other.

II. Having considered Paul's conflict, let us now examine the end and design of it. Whence is it, holy apostle, that thou art so very solicitous for, and holdest these Colossians and Laodiceans, and even those who never saw thee, so near thy heart? Why does this carefulness follow thee to the very prison, and enter there to aggravate and imbitter thy personal sufferings? Why labourest thou so for them? To the end, that their hearts may be comforted, they being joined "together in love, and unto all riches of the full assurance of understanding, to the acknowledgment of the mystery of God, and of the Father, and of Christ." Thus the apostle answers our demand. I am in pain, he says, for their consolation and their faith. I fight to secure to them this treasure, and to prevent the enemy's snatching out of their hands so precious and so necessary a possession. By saying that he fights for them, that they may keep these graces, he shows that they were in danger of losing them, if their enemies, that is, the seducers and false apostles, should accomplish their design, and persuade them to receive the errors which they taught. Indeed, their doctrine of man's justification by ceremonies and observances, whether legal or human, is incompatible with the truth of the gospel, disturbs the comfort of believers, breaks the bond of love, deranges and confounds the mystery of Jesus Christ; bereaves him of his glory, and of his plenteous grace; representing him as poor and scanty, and as needing the succour, either of Moses, or of philosophy and the superstition of men, to give us salvation. The apostle names three things which he wishes for these believers, and which he would keep for them by his cares and conflicts: consolation of heart, union in love, and the riches of a full certainty of understanding, or, as he expresses the same thing in other terms, a knowledge "of the mystery of God, and of the Father, and of Christ."

The first of these, *comfort of heart*, is the happiness of believers on earth. For it is that calm and tranquillity which their souls enjoy amidst the tempests of this life, when they sweetly repose themselves on their Master's word, and are assured of his salvation, notwithstanding the menaces and persecutions of the enemy, and their failures and imperfections. All heresy and error in religion necessarily disturb this consolation, because they shake the truth and certainty of the evangelical doctrine on which it is founded. But the error which the apostle sets himself to oppose struck particularly at this part of our salvation; depriving the conscience of that peace which faith in Jesus Christ produces; and casting it into a miserable agitation, by making justification to depend on I know not what observances, that are either vain and unprofitable, or even impious and pernicious. This it is that everywhere animates Paul to fight with vigour. The faithful could not receive this error without losing their true consolation, that is, their only heart's good. And this should make us jealous for the purity of the gospel, and solicitous to keep it free from all admixture of error. Let us not hearken to those who tell us, that if what they have added to the gospel displeases us, yet we cannot deny that they retain Jesus Christ, and the foundation of our salvation in him. This is a most obvious delusion. I confess that Jesus Christ gives salvation and consolation; but he gives it to them who embrace him as he presents himself to us on his cross and in his gospel simply, without adulteration and composition. If you will have either vice or superstition with him, he will avail you nothing, save to augment your condemnation: as food, however good and wholesome, will no less than kill you, if it be mingled with poison. We must either receive Jesus Christ alone, or renounce his salvation. There is no possibility of conjoining him with the world, or with superstition. And this verity, that our hearts cannot have true and solid comfort but in Jesus Christ alone, is so evident, that the erroneous themselves, when closely pressed, are constrained to acknowledge it. After sufficient dispute about the merit of their works, and large boast of the worth of their satisfactions, and of the value of their pontifical indulgences, and of the intercession of their saints, they confess that by reason of the uncertainty of our own righteousness, the safest course is, to put all our confidence solely in the mercy of God.* In other cases, which

* Bellarmin. of Justif. l. 5. c. 7.

concern our amusement only, I think a man may sometimes without blame choose the longest and most hazardous way. In the case of our salvation, it is doubtless an excess of folly not to take the safest. As by your own confession, my doctrine, or rather the doctrine of the gospel, is the safer, suffer me to return to it, and to pity your imprudence, who amuse the world with that which yourself confess has less safety and more hazard.

But I return to the apostle, who having said that he desires for these faithful people, "that their hearts might be comforted;" adds, secondly, his prayer for their *union in love*, "being knit together in love." Their seducers troubled their union, and casting in a new doctrine among them as a matter of contention, ruined as far as it was possible their fraternal concord; drawing them into diversity of opinions, from whence arises contrariety of affections. To prevent this disorder, and preserve union in charity among them, the apostle had so great a conflict. For as the sea is peaceable and united during a calm, but when the winds begin to rage it rises in waves that violently dash against each other; so false teachers, which are as the winds, the hurricanes of hell, no sooner beat upon a church than they disturb its peace, and put all its members into commotion; disuniting them, deranging them, and making them miserably clash with each other, to their common ruin, and the joy of their enemy. But Paul teaches us that the mutual conjunction of believers in love is necessary for the consolation of their hearts; "that their hearts may be comforted, they being knit together in love." Indeed, what joy and what comfort can a pious person have in the trouble of division? Jesus Christ, the only source of our joy, does not communicate himself to any but such as have genuine love, who abide conjoined in his body by the bands of one and the same faith and love.

Finally, the third benefit which the apostle desires to preserve among the Colossians and their neighbours, is *the abounding of a full assurance of understanding:* "being knit together in love, and unto all riches of the full assurance of understanding, to the acknowledgment of God, and of the Father, and of Christ." This order well deserves our attention. For these three things which he has here associated are of such a nature, that the first depends upon the second, and the second upon the third; consolation upon union in love, and union in love upon knowledge. This last is as the first upon which love is erected, and love as the second, which sustains the third, that is, consolation. Of these three jewels, one cannot be had without the others. And as the consolation of the Lord cannot be enjoyed without the sweetnesses of love, so love cannot be had without the illuminations of knowledge. But the apostle does not simply name that knowledge which he desires in the faithful; he describes it in an orderly way, according to his usual manner, and intimates as he proceeds the principal qualities which it ought to have. These he briefly comprises in the following words, "all riches of the full assurance of understanding;" that is, to express the Hebraism in the idiom of our own language, all abundance of understanding, with full assurance and satisfaction.

He would have, then, first, that the knowledge of a christian be "understanding;" that is, that he should perceive and see in the clearness of celestial light those verities which God has revealed to us: not that we are bound to comprehend them all, and penetrate the nature of them to the utmost depth; that, as they are in general divine and supernatural, would be impossible; but that we ought to know them as far as they are revealed, because otherwise we should every moment be liable to delusion, and might take the vain traditions of men for things taught of God. Here we see how far that blinded faith, so satisfactory to our adversaries, is from the knowledge of a believer. This faith, if interrogated about evangelical truth, refers us to the church for an answer, being ignorant all the while of what it believes, and consequently has not a spark of understanding. Black is not more contrary to white, nor darkness to light, than this phantasm of faith, shall I say, or of ignorance, to the knowledge which the apostle here requires. He would have the faithful to be intelligent; these people understand nothing, nay, boast of their ignorance, imagining that it is not without merit. It is therefore the faith, not of a christian, away with such a thought; nor of the collier, as they call it; no, nor of the man endued with reason; but the faith of a brute, which has no understanding, as the psalmist sings.

Secondly, the apostle wishes us to possess not merely "understanding," but "riches," yea, "all riches of understanding;" that is, a great and perfect abundance of knowledge, that we may be rich in this kind of wealth, that we may be ignorant of none of the mysteries of divine truth; that we know not only its elements or its first principles, but also all the practical inferences resulting from it which are necessary to regulate our lives, and to guard us from the snares of Satan around us. If we do not, how shall we discern the voice of the chief Shepherd from the voice of a stranger, to flee from the one and follow the other? Here you see again how contrary to the doctrine of this holy man are the preaching and practice of those, the Romanists, who license their people to be ignorant, and censure them who, not contented with the first and plainest lessons of christianity, study the depths of this saving wisdom, outrageously decrying this laudable desire, as if it were the way to heresy and hell.

Thirdly, Paul would have this intelligence of a believer not only to abound, but also to advance to an entire certainty and "assurance," a word which he often employs to express a full and an assured persuasion of those things which we believe to be sure and indubitable. For though matters of faith are not laid open to the senses or the reason of men, yet the truth of them is so evident, so beautiful, and so well defined, that as soon as those clouds of passion and prejudice which hide it from the eyes of our understanding are dissipated by the hand of the Holy Spirit, it beams forth and shines into our hearts with exceeding brightness, and makes itself to be believed and embraced for what it is indeed. Thus must it be known with certainty, and not with doubting, that, as the apostle says in his Epistle to the Ephesians, " we henceforth be no more children, tossed to and fro, and carried about with every wind of doctrine, by the sleight of men, and cunning craftiness, whereby they lie in wait to deceive," Eph. iv. 14. Whereby you see how false is the opinion of Rome which makes the belief of christianity to depend upon the authority and testimony of her prelates. I pass by the extreme weakness and vanity of this pretended foundation ; this has been proved by a thousand experiments. Whatever it be in other respects, this is manifest, that since they fasten the people's knowledge there, they are bound to confess that their faith ought to change as the doctrines of their prelates change. It follows that their faith is not certain nor assured ; not such a knowledge as the apostle requires in us, whose property is such, that though Paul himself, or angels from heaven, should come and preach the contrary, it would continue, even under such a supposal, still firm and unmoved ; and would rather anathematize apostles and angels from heaven, than let go that divine verity which it has believed and known ; so strong is the sense that it has of its excellency.

The apostle, having thus described the nature of true faith, or a christian's understanding, lastly, confines it within the bounds of its true subject, when he adds, "the knowledge of the mystery of God, and of the Father, and of Christ." This restriction is necessary, because seducers boast of their traditions too, as if they were a piece of wisdom worthy of our faith, and without doubt the false teachers whom the apostle opposes acted in this manner. To arm us against their vanity, he declares expressly that the understanding which he requires of us is a knowledge not of what philosophers talk in their schools about the nature of the world, nor of what seducers produce from their vain imaginations, but only of the gospel of our Lord Jesus Christ, without which there is nothing but error and folly. He calls it a secret, or a mystery, because it was a verity hidden with God, and, as we have already said, incomprehensible to our minds. He says, that it is "the mystery of God our Father," both because he is the Author of it, who graciously has revealed it to us, and because therein he has manifested himself, discovering to us in the gospel all that we need to know of his nature and will for the attainment of salvation. He adds, finally, "and of Christ," for the same reasons; for it is the Lord Jesus who brought this holy doctrine from the bosom of the Father, and set it in our view by the ministry of his servants; and it is he also who is the principal subject of it, as our only Mediator, without whose teaching and merit it is impossible to have any part in true happiness. Of this mystery of Christ Jesus the apostle desired that the Colossians might have a full, firm, and distinct knowledge, in order to abide knit together by charity, and by this means enjoy true and solid consolation. This is the treasure which he is afraid lest they should lose. To preserve it to them he submits to so much pain and engages in so many conflicts.

Dear brethren, his desire teaches us our duty. Since we aspire to the same happiness the Colossians before us possessed, since we serve the same Master and live under the same discipline, let us labour to get and keep for ever the same good things which the apostle wisheth them. God of his great mercy liberally offers them to us, and the fault will be ours if we do not partake of them. As for the knowledge of his mystery, he presents us the treasury of it in his holy Scriptures. This source of light is not shut up and inaccessible to you, as it is to a great part of the world, and even to many who call themselves christians; but open and manifest. Draw out of it the wisdom of heaven, reading, studying, and searching those divine books night and day. We do not envy you this sweet and happy communication, as the pastors of our adversaries envy their flocks; we wish, as of old Moses did, that all God's people were prophets. It is a science that admits all ages, all sexes, and all conditions of men; the Author of this holy doctrine having so attempered it, that it is adapted to the capacity of every sort of persons. There are in it deeps to exercise and humble the greatest minds; there are facilities to instruct and content the least. It is an abyss where elephants may swim, and a shallow where lambs may wade. But as all are capable of this science, so there is no person for whom it is unnecessary. It is the key of the kingdom of heaven, the spring of piety, the root of sanctity, the seed of true life. Study it carefully. Hearken to its teaching here, meditate on it at home with deep intent, beseeching God with prayers and tears to open your hearts and write his doctrine in them. Be not satisfied with having learned some points of it. Take no rest till you know all its wonders; till you have attained not simply understanding, but, as the apostle speaks, "all riches of understanding."

Urge not to me that vain and cold excuse, which is in the mouths of many, that you are not ministers, and therefore do not need extensive knowledge. These Colossians were no more ministers than you, and yet you see what the apostle desires for them; and afterwards he will enjoin that the word of Christ dwell plenteously in them in all wisdom. Why, are you less exposed to temptations because you are not ministers? Are the devil and the world less ardent or less obstinate in assailing you? We are all engaged in the same war, and have all need of the same arms. Ought captains and officers only to be armed? Is it not necessary for private soldiers? The knowledge of the mysteries of the gospel is the armour of all christians, and the Scripture is the public magazine whence both of them should fetch it. But that it may do you service in time of need, this knowledge must be also deeply radicated in your hearts. You must have it with a "full assurance," as the apostle speaks. It should not lightly float in your head, to be plucked away by an enemy, on the first occasion; it must be engraven on your heart with a pen of iron, and the point of a diamond; that is, you should be so firmly persuaded of it, that nothing may be able to efface it or enfeeble your belief of it. I know well every one boasts that he is so. But there is a great difference between words and things. Show it me by your lives, and I will credit it. If you be fully persuaded of the truth of the gospel, how is it that you have not the love which it most absolutely demands? How do you hate men whom it commands you to love, and love the vices which it enjoins you to hate? Let us lay aside words, and possess in deed that "full assurance of understanding" which the apostle wishes for us. This is the true way for us to continue "knit together in love;" to conflict with and overcome our enemies; to edify and preserve our friends; to attract those that are without, to retain those that are within; to enjoy consolation in all the trials of this world, and in the end to obtain the salvation and the glory of the next, through the grace of our Lord and Saviour Jesus Christ; to whom, with the Father and the Holy Spirit, the true and only God, be all honour, praise, and glory to ages of ages. Amen.

SERMON XVII.

VERSE 3.

In whom are hid all the treasures of wisdom and knowledge.

IGNORANCE of the natures and qualities of the Lord Jesus is the source of all the errors and heresies which have exercised the christian church from its beginning down to this day. And as Paul said of the rulers of the Jews, that if they had known the true wisdom, they would never have crucified the Lord of glory, 1 Cor. ii. 7, 8; so may we say of the authors of all the false and pernicious doctrines which men have wished to introduce into religion, that if they had duly known Jesus Christ, they would never have troubled the church. I pass by the scourges of the first ages, the impiety of the Arians and the Dokites, the extravagancies of the Nestorians and the Eutychians, together with their innumerable branches; they all evidently sprung from ignorance of the true being of our Lord Jesus Christ, and strike directly at him, attacking either his divine or his human nature, some attributing to him a created and imperfect divinity, and others an imaginary and chimerical humanity; while others impugned his person by dividing or confounding the two natures which are united in it. From the same source have come those abuses and disorders in the following ages, which gradually raising themselves from weak and obscure beginnings, have at last obtained a superiority, and suffocated the genuine simplicity and purity of the gospel. Hence proceeded that invocation of saints which is at this day practised throughout all the Romish communion. Hence issued that second sacrifice which they call the sacrifice of the altar, and wherein the heart of religion is made to consist. If men had rightly known the excellence of our Lord's mediation, and the extensive efficacy of his cross, they would never have addressed themselves to any other intercessor, never have had recourse to any other oblation. From this ignorance also, as from a common spring of error, have flowed in among people the dogmas of the satisfactions and merits of condignity, and congruity, and indulgences, and the rules and oddly various discipline of monks, and in sum, all superstitions. If people had well known who Jesus Christ is, they would have been assuredly content with his satisfaction, and infinite merit, with that eternal indulgence which he has obtained for all who believe, and with the perfection of his gospel. Hence again has arisen the setting up of another head in the militant church, to be there as the vicar and coadjutor of Jesus Christ. If this Jesus whom the Father has given and placed over all things for a Head to the church, if the fulness of his power, and wisdom, and infinite love, had been well known, never had this second monarchy been erected in his kingdom. In a few words, we may say to these, and to all others who err in religion, as once our Lord himself said to the Samaritan, John iv. 10, If you knew the gift of God, and who this Jesus is that speaks to you in his Scriptures, you would seek all your salvation in him alone, and demand of none but him any of the things that are necessary for the refreshment and consolation of your souls. Judge, faithful brethren, how much it concerns us to know him well, and, to have him ever before our eyes. The knowledge of Christ is an adequate security from error. With what solicitude the apostle exhibits him to us! With what affection he displays to us all the wonders of this great and divine subject! He has before described him to the Colossians in a sublime manner, and, to attach their hearts entirely to him, shown them that in him is found all fulness. But with this he is not satisfied. He now proceeds to inform them in the text, that in him "are hid all the treasures of wisdom and knowledge." In these few words there is a vast extent of meaning and truth; we will therefore employ the whole of this exercise in explaining them, if God permit; observing in order all that shall seem necessary for the elucidation of the text, and the instruction and edification of your souls.

I know well that the relative word here translated "whom" means *which* as well as whom; and may be referred either to Jesus Christ, or to the mystery of God, mentioned in the preceding verse. If referred to the latter, then we understand the apostle to say that in this mystery are hidden all the treasures of wisdom; and I admit that the words so construed express a great truth, for most certainly our Lord's gospel, here called his "mystery," is an inexhaustible treasury of all saving wisdom and knowledge. But we are not obliged to admit this interpretation; and in my mind it is more pertinent, and apposite to the scope of the apostle, to refer this word to the name of Christ, which immediately preceded, and that the apostle's meaning is, that these treasures are hidden in Jesus Christ. But you perceive that these two senses differ very immaterially from each other. For a right conception of the text, we must first refute the exposition which some have given, and then assert its true meaning. Some think Paul would say that Jesus Christ knows all things, and is so rich and so abundant in knowledge, that he is ignorant of nothing. This is to mistake the apostle's intention. But that which they add is yet worse. For from this bad interpretation they deduce a false and dangerous doctrine; concluding from our

Saviour's possessing all the treasures of knowledge, that the infinite wisdom of his divinity was actually transfused into his human nature; and consequently all the other properties also of the divine nature, as its omnipotence, its infinity, and its omnipresence: since there is the same reason for all these attributes of God, which are so inseparable that none can have one of them without possessing the rest. Behold, I beseech you, how prolific is error, and how truly it was said by one of the ancient sages of the world, that one falsity or absurdity being admitted, many others necessarily follow. That which has led, or, to speak more accurately, which has drawn, these authors into this long series of errors, is no more than their false opinion about the sacrament of the eucharist. They incommodiously and unreasonably suppose that the flesh of Jesus Christ is present in the bread; and this absurdity gradually prepared them for others still worse. For, disrelishing the doctrine of transubstantiation, which the Romanists employ to uphold this real presence of our Lord's body, and deservedly rejecting it, as full of absurdities and contradictions, but still determined to retain their own false preconception, they have endeavoured to maintain it by the aid of another error, scarcely inferior to it, namely, that of ubiquity, affirming that the body of Jesus Christ is everywhere present, and consequently in the eucharistical signs. To defend a thing so strange, and so contrary to sense, to reason, and to Scripture, they have advanced the notion that the flesh of Christ, through its personal union with the divinity, has really received all its properties. I mean that, in assuming flesh, the Son of God has rendered it omnipotent, immense, and infinite; a doctrine which has induced them to corrupt divers passages of the word of God, that they might form out of them some prop for their error. This is not the place for a full refutation of their doctrine, nor for an adequate expression of our sorrow, that persons, who in other particulars rejoice in the light of truth, should in this instance continue in darkness. Would to God that we could bury in eternal oblivion a fault which has caused so much scandal in Christendom! I shall very briefly treat the subject of the text in hand, and their abuse of it in favour of their opinion.

I say, then, that, in reasoning on this topic, they commit two observable faults: the one, that they do not correctly state the apostle's meaning; and the other, that their inference is not deducible from the premises. And to begin with the latter of these, they infer that which is not deducible from their premises; for although there is an infinity of science and knowledge in Jesus Christ, it no more follows that his human soul understands and knows all the things that God knows, than because there is an eternal divinity in Jesus Christ, it follows that his flesh is an eternal divinity; or from his having created the world, that his flesh created it. This (if indeed we may compare human things with divine) is as inadmissible as it would be, that the body of man is immortal and intelligent, because he possesses within him an immortal intellect. For as in man there are two substances, the soul and the body, which, though united in the same subject, yet severally conserve their own properties; the soul its spirituality and invisibility, and the body its visibility and palpability; the one a capacity to understand and to will, the other, not: so there are two natures in Jesus Christ, which, though personally united, are not commingled or confounded. Each of them retains its essential and original qualities, and in such a manner that the divine nature continues eternal, infinite, omnipotent, and omniscient; and the human created in time, bounded in place, and endowed with a limited strength, power, and knowledge. When we say of man in general that he possesses understanding and sense, that he has a visible or invisible essence, that he is mortal or immortal, we assign each of these attributes only to that part of his nature to which it corresponds, and do not confusedly apply them to both; so, if the apostle had said (as I grant he truly might) that there is in Jesus Christ an infinity of power or knowledge, that infinity should be referred to his divinity, and not to his humanity. For Jesus Christ being very God, blessed for ever with the Father, who, in this respect, can question whether he is omnipotent and omniscient? But it is not thence inferrible that he is so likewise in regard of his human nature. And for any to deduce it from that attribution is as impertinent reasoning, as if, because there is in Jesus Christ a flesh conceived and born of the blessed virgin, and which was infirm and crucified, you would infer that his divinity was also born of the holy virgin, and was fastened to the cross.

But though it were granted them, that "all the treasures of wisdom and knowledge" are hid in the human soul of Jesus Christ, still they could not legitimately infer from such an admission that the knowledge of his soul is infinite, and the same with that of God. We confess that this blessed soul, having had the honour to be personally united to the eternal Son of God, has in consequence been adorned with all the effulgence of knowledge and wisdom of which its nature is capable; so that it may be said in this respect that all these treasures are hidden in it, and that its knowledge far surpasses the knowledge of men and angels, both for its extent, and for its perspicuity and certainty. But as the nature of the subject in which it properly resides is finite, itself is also necessarily finite; whereas the knowledge of the Father and of his eternal Word is infinite, even as their nature is infinite. And it is to no purpose to reply, that according to this statement the human nature of Jesus Christ will have no advantage above the saints, of whom it may be said in this sense that "all the treasures of wisdom" are hidden in them, since God, who dwells in them, has an infinite knowledge and wisdom. For this consequence is evidently false. First, by reason of the extreme difference between the graces communicated to the saints, and the gifts of light and knowledge infused into the soul of our Saviour. Secondly, by reason of the infinite difference between their persons; for though God dwells in the saints by his grace, yet no one of the saints is God; whereas the eternal Word so dwells in the humanity of Jesus Christ, that the same one who is man is also truly God; these two natures being so strictly united, that they are only one and the same person. From this reason, it may be rightly said, that if the word of the Father is almighty and eternal, as most assuredly it is, omnipotence, and eternity, and infinity are in Jesus Christ; for he is truly the Word of the Father: but it cannot, however, be inferred from this, that Peter (for example) or Paul possessed infinite power or wisdom, because God dwelt in them: God dwelt not personally in them, so that each of them was God, but only by the grace of his Spirit.

I add, in the second place, that all this reasoning is foreign to the scope of the apostle, whose object they have misapprehended. For his intention here is not to speak of what Jesus Christ knows. What would this conduce to the end that he had proposed to himself, namely, our confirmation in the gospel, and the fortifying us against those traditions and speculations which false teachers would add to it, that we might reject them and content ourselves with this Jesus Christ, whom the Father presents to us in his word? Who sees not that the knowledge of all things, which our Lord has in himself, is altogether extraneous to this purpose? For the thing in question is what we must know to serve God aright, and be saved in the sequel. But Jesus Christ does not reveal to us in the gospel all that he knows either as God or as man. And so from his knowing all things, it follows not that it is enough for us to embrace his gospel. For (will the false teachers say) though he know all for his own part, yet he has not discovered in the gospel which his apostles preach unto us all that is necessary for us to believe or to practise.

What then, you will inquire, is the true sense of these words? Dear brethren, it is not hard to discern, if you afford ever so little attention to the thing. The apostle considers the Lord Jesus here, not simply and absolutely, but as he is set forth and revealed to us in his gospel, as far as he is the subject of the apostle's preaching and the object of our faith. In this respect he says that "all the treasures of wisdom and knowledge" are hid in him; meaning that this Christ, who is present with us in the gospel, is an object so rich and so divine, that he contains all the matter of wisdom in him; that all the verities composing it are fully and abundantly found in him; so that, to acquire wisdom, there is no need of studying anything but Christ. If we do but know him, we shall be ignorant of nothing. If I should say that the treasures of wisdom or natural science are hid in the world, my meaning would be, not that the world knows verities which appertain to this science, but that it contains them; that it is a theatre where they are exposed to our view; and that by the study of it we may learn them. Or were I to say that man is the treasury of all the knowledge of living creatures, I should not intend that man knows them, but that he exhibits it, being as an exact model and pattern of all that the nature of living creatures comprehends; so that by careful studying and meditating on him, we may learn all that can be known of them. In this very manner, by saying that in Christ "are hid all the treasures of wisdom and knowledge," the apostle shows us what is the knowledge, not that Christ has in himself, but which he is able to give to us; not what he knows, but what he makes us to know; he being as it were, an abyss of wonders, in which are found all the riches of that heavenly truth in the knowledge of which true wisdom consists. From whence the inference he aims to make upon it clearly flows, namely, that we ought to shut our ears against every other doctrine, however plausible and probable. For as Jesus Christ is the magazine and the treasury of all wisdom, in whom is found all that we ought to know not only for necessity, but even unto plenitude, who sees not that it is extreme folly for men to turn themselves another way, or trouble their heads about the study of any other object? And so this wisdom and this knowledge of which the apostle speaks is meant, not the cognizance which the Lord has, either as God or as man; but that knowledge of divine things which is requisite for us, if we would attain to salvation, and in the possession of which consists the true perfection of our nature. And when he says that the treasures of this wisdom are hid in him, his meaning is not that these divine things are known to our Lord, (such a conception would be frigid and impertinent,) but that they are all displayed and set forth in him; that they dwell in him, that they are found there; that they are enclosed and to be seen in him, through the veil of the infirmity of his cross, which in a manner overspreads and hides them. This is, in my judgment, the true and genuine sense of the apostle's expression.

Let us now examine each of its terms, all of them admirable, elegant, and rich, and afterwards consider the truth of them. First, he calls the wisdom and knowledge which are in Jesus Christ "treasures," to intimate both their excellence and abundance; the word treasure importing both these. You know, we properly call such a collection a treasure as contains things not worthless, as dust or chaff; but precious and exquisite, as gold and silver, and precious stones, and jewels. The term signifies *abundance* also. For you will not say that that man has a treasure who has but two or three pieces of gold or silver, or a diamond, or four or five emeralds. To have a treasure is to have a considerable mass of rare and precious things. And by this the truths which Jesus Christ exhibits, and of which he affords us the knowledge, are distinguished from those elsewhere. Many and various kinds of knowledge are discoverable by other means, but they are comparatively of no value. They do not make a treasure. This worthy title appertains only to rare and precious things. But the truths which Jesus Christ teaches those who study him are so many pearls of inestimable price; they are divine jewels, such as neither the barbarous sea-coasts, nor the mines of the New World yield; such as neither the heavens, nor the earth, nor any of the store-houses of nature, can furnish. But abundance also is in the matter before us as well as worth. I admit that some of these precious truths are hid in the world, and in man himself, and that we may extract them from those sources by attention and meditation; as appears by the knowledge which some heathens acquired who read no other book. I grant too that the ancient tabernacle of Moses afforded a far more ample store. But what is all this, in comparison of that abundance of wisdom and knowledge presented to us by Jesus Christ? Most certainly, in him, and in him only, can this divine treasure be found. And, for the fuller discovery of the immeasurable abundance of his exhaustless riches to us, the apostle contents not himself with calling it a treasure. He says "treasures," in the plural; so great and vast is the opulence of this divine subject. Yea, he says not simply "treasures," but "all the treasures," to show us that there is nothing grand, or exquisite, or precious but what is found in him.

Now in the progress of his discourse Paul subjoins what those treasures are which are in Christ; "the treasures of wisdom and knowledge." Away, ye covetous, who never hear the mention of treasures but ye fancy those of the world; which (to say the truth) are but piles of dross and masses of earth, only varied a little in form and colour from the other parts of this vile and low element. The jewel of which the treasury of Jesus Christ is full is of an infinitely more precious nature than the metals you adore; it is, saith the apostle, "wisdom and knowledge." The term "wisdom" is honourable among men;

and though ignorant of the thing, yet they respect the name; confessing that it is strictly apposite only to such kinds of knowledge as are at once sublime and useful, divine and salutiferous. Surely, to adhere to this their own definition of it, it is clear that no one of all the sciences which they have learned in the world by the strength of their own spirit deserves to be called wisdom. For either they are low, and of things of small elevation, as the skill of their trades, which have no employment but on the earth; or at least they are vain and unprofitable, as that which they tell us of the heavens and their motions, of nature and its mutations, of numbers and figures, and the measuring of bodies. For what service do they derive from that science of which they so contemptuously boast? Are they in any degree the happier for it, or aught the more assured by it? They themselves vilify it, and confess that all of it yields those that excel most in it but a very slender profit. Will you call useless industry by the name of wisdom, and count him a judicious man who busies himself to no purpose? On the contrary, is it not characteristic of a fool to be amused in things of nought, and to toil for that which affords no benefit, as children that pursue their own shadows and chase butterflies? What then is that wisdom which is truly worthy of so illustrious a name? Dear brethren, it is evidently the knowledge of truths necessary to our salvation, those truths that can make us happy, and preserve peace and consolation in our souls, and conduct us through the accidents of this life to the possession of that supreme felicity which is naturally the desire of all men. It is this kind of knowledge that the apostle means. It is this which by way of excellence, he calls "wisdom," as alone deserving the name, while all other kinds of knowledge lie far beneath it. The word "knowledge," which he adds, I think we need not sever from wisdom, as if they were necessarily two different things. I know that critics have distinguished them; some affirming that wisdom is the knowledge of God and of divine things, and knowledge the philosophy of man and of human affairs; while others maintain that wisdom relates to things to be believed, and knowledge to things to be done. But, to speak candidly, I much doubt whether the apostle ever thought of these petty subtilties; for the word "knowledge" in the original generally signifies all knowledge, and we have no reason to restrain its application to moral or terrestrial things. I judge it therefore more accordant with the simplicity of these divine authors to take the words "wisdom and knowledge" in nearly the same sense, and to say that the latter was added only to enlarge and enrich one and the same conception; as if the apostle had said that there is neither wisdom nor knowledge, nor any true and saving knowledge, but it is in our Lord Jesus Christ.

In fine, it must be observed that he says these treasures are "hid" in Christ. This is a very apt prosecution of his metaphor. For treasures are not exposed to the view of all. They are locked up in cabinets, or concealed in remote places, or buried under ground, to secure them from the eyes and hands of men. As this is usually done, the apostle has very elegantly used this word in the matter before him, and the more so, as something analogous may be observed in the dispensation of Jesus Christ. God has not indeed any such design as avaricious men have, nor has he, fearing lest people should see and seize his treasure, actually hid it from them, to prevent their sharing it. Far be it from us to entertain a thought so injurious to the goodness and liberality of this sovereign Lord, who sent his Son into the world for no other end than to save the world, and delights in nothing more than in seeing us search into his treasuries, and enrich ourselves with his good things, and who has also clearly and magnificently displayed in his Christ all his heavenly wealth, calling him the Sun of righteousness, that is, the most visible and most remarkable object in the universe. He has sent his servants in all directions to discover him to mankind, and from the tops of the highest places to call all men to a participation of this treasure of light. Now both his brightness and their voice have spread abroad so gloriously, that it may be justly said, Light has been in the world, but the world perceived it not, John i. Wherefore the apostle says, that "if our gospel be hid, it is hid to them that are lost," and whose understandings the god of this world hath blinded, (that is, the unbelieving,) that the light of the gospel of the glory of Christ might not shine unto them, 2 Cor. iv. 3, 4. Here you see he attributes all the fault of worldly men in not discerning the excellency of this treasure to their own blindness, caused by the darkenings and malice of Satan, and not to the obscurity or concealment of the treasure itself; to which he gives a quite contrary name, calling it light, yea, a glorious light, that is to say, great and sparkling. Why then does he say that the treasures of wisdom are hid in him—for it seems he should say, on the contrary, that they are manifested in him, that they shine out and appear clearly in him? I answer, that both his statements are true, but in different respects. For if you consider the thing in itself, the treasures of wisdom are manifested to us in Jesus Christ; and he who is purified by divine grace sees them in him, and acknowledges them as soon as he sees him as the gospel represents him. But if you have respect to the eyes and perceptions of men, obscured and corrupted by sin as they naturally are, I confess, it is hard for them to discern in Jesus Christ those riches of wisdom and knowledge which the Father has deposited in him, and that this proceeds in part from that veil of meanness and infirmity which is as it were thrown over him. This led Paul to say that Christ crucified, whom he preached, was to the Jews a stumbling-block, and to the Greeks foolishness, though to the faithful who were called he was the power and the wisdom of God. Therefore, it being necessary for our salvation that he should be born, and live in poverty on the earth, and at length suffer the death of the cross, which surpassed all other deaths for cruelty and ignominy, the Father who sent him in this form, clothed with this mean and mournful mantle, that affrights men, has both manifested and hid his treasures in him. He has manifested them in him, as it is in him and by him that he exhibits to us whatever is necessary to be known for the attainment of salvation; he has hidden them in him, as he has covered this treasure with such a veil, as by its poor and contemptible appearance deters men, and makes them say, as Isaiah prophesied, "He hath no form nor comeliness; and when we shall see him, there is no beauty that we should desire him," Isa. liii. 2. But they who have their eyes purified by light from on high, discern under this appearing simplicity and humility all celestial riches in their stateliest and most glorious form. This is the apostle's meaning when he says that these treasures are hid in Christ. He informs us that we must not stop at that infirmity and vacuity which at first sight appears in him, and disgusts vain and earthly minds, but must look within, and contemplate the great wonders which God has there manifested for our complete instruction and consolation.

Hitherto we have examined the words of this text. It remains that we now consider the truth in it. This we shall do in a very summary way. For the prosecution of this rich subject in its whole extent is above the ability of man or angel to be worthily performed, so great is its height and depth. But we will briefly touch its chief heads. Man's true wisdom in his present state is to know his misery, with the means to escape it; and his felicity, with the way that he must take to attain it. As for our misery, nature indeed has given us some perception of it, for there is scarcely a man in the world who sees not some depravation and irregularity in himself, and whose conscience does not reproach him with his faults, and threaten him with the judgment of supreme justice. The law has taught us much more of it, representing God to us as armed with inexorable severity against sinners, and fulminating his curse upon them. But beside that these kinds of knowledge are weak, and are easily smothered in security, there is this sorrow with them, that, having showed us our misery, they do not inform us of the remedy; so, that if they be necessary to draw us out of that folly wherein the most are plunged, (who confidently sleep amid the tempest, and presume they are well, while they have a mortal imposthume in their brain or in their heart,) yet it cannot be said that they are sufficient to make us wise, seeing that for the just possession of this title a man must know not only his malady, but also the means to cure it. But even the knowledge of this would not be sufficient; for we desire not only deliverance from evil, but also the fruition of good, yea, the chief good. But neither the light of nature, nor even the light of the law, reveals to us what this supreme felicity is, which, without distinctly knowing it, we earnestly desire; so far are they from showing us the way to it. But those verities which are necessary to render us wise are found clearly and in all their plenitude in Jesus Christ, as he is proposed to us in the gospel. As to our misery, he declares it exactly to us, not by dubious, inarticulate sounds, as nature does, nor by circuitions and essays, as the law did; but by the fullest and most impressive way of information that the world ever heard, even crying aloud to us from that cross to which our sins had nailed him: Behold, ye sons of men, how horrid are your crimes, since it was necessary for the washing them away that I should come down from heaven and shed my blood. Behold how great and irreparable was your fall, since there was none in heaven or earth that could raise you up again but myself. As much as the life of the Son of God is more precious than the life of all mankind, so much clearer is the proof which his death gives us of the horror of sin, than that which we might take from the death of all that ever sinned, though we should see them stricken down together, and punished by the avenging justice of God. But if this great Saviour makes us so feelingly perceive the wretchedness of our misery, his design is only to make us the more ardently desire and embrace the remedy which he offers us, fully prepared from that same cross to which he was fastened for us.

I grant that the forbearance and kindness of God in his conduct to men, sinful as they were, might give them some gleam of hope, and that his promises under the former covenant had much confirmed it. But the sword of his justice dreadfully flaming in the hand of the law perplexed them not a little, and they found it extremely difficult to reconcile his inflexible righteousness with the mercy that was necessary for them. Jesus Christ has removed all these difficulties, and exhibits to us in his cross the solution of all our doubts. Fear nothing, sinner, says he, I have compensated the justice of God, and satisfied his law. Boldly trust his promises, and approach his throne with full assurance. This blood, which has opened the entrance for your admission, is not the blood of a beast, nor an earthly ransom; it is the blood of God, a ransom of infinite value, more than sufficient to take away your sins, however infinite may be their demerit. But you will say, This is not all

I need for my consolation. I acknowledge that Christ sufficiently assures me of the pardon of my sins. What security does he give me against the numerous foes who are always attendant on my path, the world, the evil angels, and flesh and blood? But, christian, does not the same cross which has merited your pardon give you also clear and undoubted evidence of your safety during the whole course of your life? For since you know that God has delivered up his only Son to death for you, how can you fear that he will withhold from you any of the cares of his providence?

But this is not all. Christ Jesus, who shows us these excellent and sacred truths in his death, engraven, as it were, in capital letters on his cross, holds up before our eyes others of no less importance in his resurrection. Believers, neither the pardon of your sin, nor the assistance of God during your life, would be sufficient for you; for after all, death will swallow you up as well as unbelievers. See then further in your Jesus the truth that is necessary to complete your consolation. By committing his spirit, at the point of death, into the Father's hands, he teaches you that God will receive your souls when you depart out of the world; and by rising again on the third day following, he assures you that your bodies shall one day be raised out of the dust; and by ascending to heaven, he assures you that there you shall be transported, both in soul and body, to live and reign there with him in eternal glory. As for the way which you must take to arrive at this high happiness, his whole life and his death have clearly marked it out to you, and he still shows it you from that lofty throne whereon he is set. Tread in my steps, he says, if you would be exalted to my glory. Follow the example of my innocence and of my love, if you desire to partake of the honours of my kingdom. I have borne injuries with calmness and patience; I have constantly obeyed my Father even unto my death on the cross, and you see the honour wherewith he hath crowned me. Imitate my obedience, and you shall receive my recompense.

This is the lesson which the Lord Jesus gives us, showing us incomparably more clearly than the frame or government of the world, or the Mosaical dispensation, ever did, both the justice of God, that we may dread him, and the power and wisdom of God, that we may reverence him, and his mercy, that we may love and serve him with all the strength of our souls; serve him, I say, not with the sacrifices of ancient Judaism, nor with the feeble and childish devotions of superstition, but with a pure and holy heart, with works worthy of him, with an ardent zeal, a sincere love, a constant integrity and honesty, a profound patience and humility, an immovable hope and confidence: these are the verities which constitute true wisdom; all of them, as you see, high and sublime, but in like degree useful and saving. Here is no inquiry about the nature of elements, of animals, of plants, or of meteors: nor of the motions of the sun, or of the moon, or of the other planets; but of the being, and the counsels, and the conduct of that great and most high God, who made and formed all those things, and in comparison of whom heaven and earth are but an atom of dust. The research is not about numbers and figures, which can neither diminish your miseries, nor make your souls happy; but of your peace with God, of your consolation in this life, and of your glory and immortality in the next. It is this which Jesus Christ teaches us, that divine crucified person who died and rose again for us. It is this he shows us, represented in high and splendid colours through all the pieces of his mystery. Whatever nature and the law might discover of the edges and first lineaments of this celestial wisdom, it is he alone who has exhibited to us the whole body, and showed us its entire frame and structure. We conclude, then, as the apostle saith, that it is verily in him that "all the treasures of wisdom and knowledge" are hidden.

Let us embrace this conclusion with firm belief; and let us bless God, first, that he has vouchsafed to give his Christ to mankind, and particularly that he has communicated him to us, mercifully presenting him in his word and in his sacraments. Next, let us implore him to open our eyes more and more, that we may discern these rich and precious "treasures of wisdom and knowledge" which he has hid in him. Let not the vileness of his cross, nor the veil of his infirmity, nor the simplicity of his gospel, and these sacraments wherein he is offered to us, offend us. This very thing, if we consider it as we ought, makes up one principal part of the wonder; and that we may rightly know and value this treasure, let us cleanse our minds from the clay and mire of the world, let us purify our understandings, and rid them of the sentiments and opinions of the world, which, being fastened to its own dung, prize nothing but the lustre of its false honours, and the vanity of its perishing riches, and the delight of its unseemly pleasures. Let us once set free our souls from these sordid and servile passions, and acknowledge, as experience will completely justify us in doing, that it is an extreme error and folly to seek our happiness in such wretched things. Let us lift up our eyes unto wisdom, and desire the possession and embrace the study of it. It is the jewel and ornament of our nature. In this consists our whole dignity. Without this men scarcely differ from beasts; nay, in some sort are in a worse condition, as sinking beneath themselves, and falling into the utmost misery. But let us be solicitous that we take not a shadow for substance, and a phantasm for true wisdom. Be not deceived. This wisdom is only in Christ Jesus. All that pretended wisdom which obtains the acclamation and applause of the multitude, whether in the courts or in the schools of the world, is but masked folly, a disguised extravagance, and a painted error, which neglects all that is essential to our welfare, and amuses us with things which have no bearing on our real happiness, the true end of wisdom. Let us seek it therefore in Jesus Christ alone. In him you will find the true substance of it.

They who possess treasures often visit them, and have their hearts always where they are. In like manner meditate night and day on this divine Saviour, "in whom are hid the treasures of wisdom and knowledge." Consider him, pry into him, and diligently sound him. He is an abyss of good things. Let your hand be ever there, and draw thence by faith, study, and meditation, all that is necessary for you. Let your whole life be taken up in the continual handling of these divine jewels, in admiring the beauty and using the brightness of them. Let it be all the passion of your souls, the matter of your joys, and the consolation of your troubles. If you have not those false good things which the world so much glories in, remember that you have the treasures of heaven, the portion of angels, the wisdom and knowledge of happiness. Take heed that none bereave you of so rich a possession. Shut your ear against the prattle and plausible discoursings of seducers. Preserve this treasure courageously against their attempts; nor be content to have it only, communicate it to your neighbours; lay forth the wonders of it before their eyes, adorning all the parts of your life with it. Let the innocence, and holiness, and sweetness, and humility of the Lord Jesus shine out in it. Let these be your pearls, and your jewels, and your ornaments before men, which may constrain them to acknowledge that Jesus Christ dwells in the midst of you, and to say, "Of a truth this nation is a wise and understanding people." Above all, instruct your children in this knowledge. Leave them this wisdom for an inheritance. Such a portion is enough to make them happy; whereas without this they cannot possibly be other than fools and wretches, though you should leave them all the wealth of the east and west.

Finally, as the apostle assures us that "all the treasures of wisdom" are in Jesus Christ, let us be satisfied with him alone, and contemn the vanity of those who, under any kind of pretence, would circulate for wisdom doctrines that are foreign, and without the sphere of Christ. Let us not so much as give them the hearing. It is warrant enough for us to reject them, that they form no part of the treasure of Jesus Christ. I stand not to inquire whether they are true or false, useful or hurtful. It suffices me that, whatever they be otherwise, they are not in Christ. Nothing is to be received in religion but what comes out of this treasury. God who has given it us in his abundant mercy, and who calls us to partake also of it the next Lord's day, grant us to preserve it pure and entire, to possess it with joy and respect in this world, and reap the full fruit of it in that which is to come. So be it.

SERMON XVIII.

VERSES 4, 5.

And this I say, lest any man should beguile you with enticing words. For though I be absent in the flesh, yet am I with you in the spirit, joying and beholding your order, and the steadfastness of your faith in Christ.

As men naturally love and desire only those things which have an appearance of good, so they believe only those which have a semblance of truth; and they withdraw their affection from the former as soon as they clearly discover their worthlessness, and their credence from the latter the instant they perceive that they are untrue. Hence being prepossessed upon some general and confused knowledge, with conceit that the enjoyment or belief of a thing would be advantageous to them, they wish it may prove good and true; evidently presupposing that otherwise their very nature could not permit them to love it or believe it. This is observable even in children, who are the sincerest and most natural map of the motions of our nature. For when their nurses tell them anything, they ask if it be true; and if the tale please them, they are troubled when they perceive that it is no more than a tale, and wish it were true, that they might believe it. So deeply imprinted in the mind of all reasonable creatures is this sacred and inviolable principle of their nature, that nothing is believed but what is thought to be true. This advantage which truth naturally has over falsehood compels its very enemies to counterfeit its mark and wear its livery. For they are aware that their errors and falsehoods can find no entrance among men, except they assume the appearance of truth. Even as coiners, that they may put off their copper and lead, give it the colour and resemblance of gold and silver, and counterfeit the image and stamp of a lawful prince; or as they who would travel through an enemy's country, privily disguise themselves with the enemy's badges; so seducers, well knowing that the understanding of man is the proper and lawful kingdom of truth, where nothing passes but under its sanction and mark, paint and disguise the fictions which they propagate, and give them, as finely as they can, the countenance and colour of truth, that by means of this false resemblance they may pass current among men, who would reject them immediately if they saw them in their own natural likeness. There have ever been a great multitude of these cheats in the world, persons who, urged forward by ambition, or some other particular interest, strive to bring their fancies and dreams into reputation. But as the christian religion comprises the best and most important truths in the world; so there never was any system which impostors and the erroneous have more laboured to corrupt, by decrying some of its true doctrines on one hand, and by intermingling falsehoods on the other. And as all the artifice of such unhappy wits tends only to confound truth and falsehood; so ought we to employ the utmost of our industry that we may effectually sever them, and so discern them as never to take the one for the other.

This discerning, dear brethren, is one of the most important duties of our life. It is loss to take copper for gold, and bad money for good; and it is, moreover, ignorance, ever shameful, sometimes not a little hurtful, to receive an error for truth in philosophy and in civil life. But yet the loss and shame that accrue from all this kind of cheats reach no further than the present time; whereas the consequences of those impostures which we suffer in religion extend even to eternity. For this cause the holy apostle often warns the faithful, to whom he writes, to beware of them, and most cautiously to try all things, that they may not be inveigled by seducers, nor receive their traditions for truths, desiring every sincere and real christian to have his senses exercised and habituated to discern between good and evil, Rom. xvi. 17; 1 Thess. v. 21; Eph. iv. 14; Heb. v. 14. You may have observed in the text that this is the happiness which he wishes and would procure to the Colossians, of not being drawn in by the fair speeches of those seducers that courted them. He had before largely represented to them the abundance and excellency of the benefits of their Lord and Saviour; and he protested again in the verse immediately prior to our text, as you may remember, in our last sermon on this subject, that "in Jesus Christ are hid all the treasures of wisdom and knowledge." Now he shows them his design in his immediate recurrence to a theme of which he seemed to have sufficiently treated in the preceding texts. Now "this I say, that none may deceive you with words of persuasion." And to show that he did not vainly or rashly undertake this task, he apprizes them in the following verse of the knowledge that he had of their state, it being as really before his eyes as if he had been at Colosse. "For," says he, "though I am absent in the flesh, yet in spirit I am with you, joying and beholding your order, and the steadfastness of your faith in Christ."

Thus we have two points to handle, that we may give you a full and entire understanding of this text.

First, the apostle's study that these christians might not be seduced. And,

Secondly, the cognizance he took of their present state, though in body he was far distant from them.

If God permit, we shall briefly consider these two things, pointing out what we judge useful for your edification and consolation in them.

1. The first of these points the apostle expresses in these words, "And this I say, lest any man should beguile you with enticing words." On which words we have two things to examine: the danger in which the Colossians were, and the usefulness of the apostle's statement to preserve them from incurring it. The danger was great, and the evil which it threatened grievous and mortal, even the being deceived and seduced by the enticing words which false teachers used in this wretched design. There never was any servant of Christ who was not beset by such a temptation. As soon as Satan sees the truth of the gospel anywhere appear, immediately he raises up impostors to corrupt it, and to alienate those who embrace it from its purity and simplicity. But especially at the beginning of christianity, when it was first preached aud founded by the holy apostles, there arose a multitude of seducers, who did their utmost to deprave and mar this divine seed of salvation; and the devil made similar attempts in our fathers' days, when, perceiving the gospel to revive, eager instantly to obstruct this holy work, he speedily brought into the field a world of spirits, some audacious and extravagant, others subtle and selfish, which endeavoured to scandalize or to seduce the simple; those, by the prodigies of their fond imaginations; these, by the plausible appearances of their false accommodations. But they who troubled the church in the apostle's time addressed themselves, among others, to the Colossians in particular, as we see by what is here intimated, and by what is more fully stated in the course of this chapter. He does not name them; but his saying, "lest any man should beguile you," is a sufficient evidence that there were some craftsmen of this quality about them who laboured to insnare them. At these he aims his weapons, and against the force of their seducements he arms the Colossians. He shows the end to which they tended, the deceiving of the faithful; and the means they used to effect it, namely, "enticing words."

The term he employs to express the first of these signifies not simply to deceive, but to deceive by false and insnaring ratiocination. For these bad men, knowing well that others are not induced to embrace or avoid anything without some reason, our nature demanding that in all our actions and motives the understanding should precede the will, they begin there to effect our ruin; and to entangle our minds in their errors, they propose us reasons, false indeed, but appearing otherwise; such as have the colour and countenance, but not the essential form and substance, of a good and solid argument. This the word paralogism, here used by the apostle, properly signifies. It is a sophism, a false and spurious arguing which, by its vain appearance and fallacious blaze, leads men to error; as those fatuous fires, which, rising sometimes in the dark of night, conduct those who follow them into precipices. Satan, the father of all sophisters, took this course first, having miserably seduced our first parents by the illusion of a false discourse, the vanity of which experience clearly demonstrated; for, that he might corrupt their will, he attacked their understandings in the first place, and beguiled them that he might destroy them, persuading that the forbidden fruit would make them like God. All whom he has in succeeding ages employed in this work have followed the same method. No heretic ever appeared, either under the Old or the New Testament, who did not paint over his impostures with some specious reasons. Only this difference may be observed among such men, that some act maliciously, and in defiance of their own consciences; others, through ignorance. The former sort are genuine children of the devil, and the most execrable of all men. Conscious that they are fighting against the truth, and defending error by most futile reasons, they undauntedly labour in this unhappy design, either for acquiring glory to themselves, or for creating trouble to teachers of truth, to whom they are hostile. Those of the other sort, who do it through ignorance, have, I confess, less guilt and wickedness, but they are no less dangerous; for really believing the errors which they advance, they are the more ardent and strenuous in persuading others to embrace them, as imagining that they serve them when they indeed destroy them, and that they edify when in truth they ruin them. Such were those Jews of whom Paul bears witness, that they had a zeal of God, but not according to knowledge, Rom. x. 2. They believed the error which they recommended, and were caught in those snares in which they sought to entangle others. And in this rank we must place the most of those of the Roman communion, who labour much to draw us into their mistakes; not only those of the people, but also many of their monks and of their doctors, who labour to deceive others because they have been themselves deceived, having run into that erroneous persuasion into which they would induce us, and confirmed themselves from time to time in it, by those sophisms and false reasonings which they offer us, and which they have either learned of their instructors or invented themselves. We must equally take heed of both these sorts of workers. For however different the motive of their acting may be, the effect of it is ever the same, even seduction and perdition. And as poison fails not to kill the man who takes it, though it have been ignorantly given him by a person that knew it not to be poison, who perchance partoók of it himself, thinking it a remedy; so error, from whatever hand it come, has still a bad effect; and the opinion they have of it who present it to us does not change the venom of it, nor impede its corrupting our souls, and extinguishing divine life in us if we receive it.

But the apostle also points out the means which false teachers use for the establishment of their errors: That none, says he, may deceive you "with enticing words." These he calls, Rom. xvi. 18, in the same case, "good words and fair speeches," and declares that schismatics, and such as make divisions contrary to the doctrine we have learned, seduce "the hearts of the simple by good words and fair speeches." These he names again elsewhere the "enticing words of man's wisdom," 1 Cor. ii. 4. Under these terms he comprehends all the advantages and attractives of discourse, all that it has in it which is apt to touch and win hearts; as either probable reasons, with which it is furnished, or beauty of terms and expressions, or artificial disposition and graceful pronunciation. Every one knows how potent are these charms of eloquence. They sometimes dazzle the best eyes, and deceive the firmest minds. Eloquence makes things, as it were by a kind of enchantment, appear quite opposite to what they really are, and gives them colours and qualities that are not their own; it makes honey pass for wormwood, and wormwood for honey; black for white, and white for black. It can subvert a cause, however good, or establish it, however bad. There is no ardour which it cannot allay, no belief which it cannot agitate, no resolution which it cannot break. It has often procured condemnation of the innocent, while the guilty have been acquitted with applause. It is by its sleights that truth, however invincible it may be, has sometimes seemed to be vanquished. To its adroitness and stratagems the friends of error and falsehood owe the greatest part of their mendacious triumphs. For feeling their own great weakness, they commonly have recourse to this kind of sorcery, that they may carry by its illusions what they could never win by genuine and legitimate strength. It is this that maintains sophisters, and wranglers, and mountebanks, and seducers. With the sophistry and loquacity which it lends them, they audaciously stand up and oppose the clearest truths, and recommend the grossest errors. But among all the busy people who use it, none more perniciously employ it than heretics and corrupters of religion. This false rhetoric is their principal instrument for seducing men. Accordingly, it is evident that they have always taken it up, and scarcely ever assailed the truth with any other kind of weapon. And it must be confessed that they handle these instruments with wonderful dexterity. Never was cause, in matter of religion, more sordid, or shameful, or feeble, than that of the pagans; yet they who pleaded it against the ancient christians knew so well how to disguise it with the colours of their false reasons, and the gloss of their fine words, that they made it pass for plausible among the multitude, and rendered christianity ridiculous to them, however holy and luminous was its truth. Those heretics which arose from among christians had no less ability and art to recommend their impostures, borrowing, for this purpose, from the philosophers and orators of the world, the subtilties of their logic, and all the colours of their rhetoric. There are still extant some pieces of both in the books of antiquity; as the discourses of Celsus in Origen: of Cæcilius in Minutius; of Porphyrius and Symmachus, for paganism; various writings of Tertullian, for Montanism; of Faustus, for the Manichees; and of Julian, for the Pelagians, in Augustine. It is wonderful with what dexterity and with what grace and eloquence they manage such bad and infamous subjects; nor can I read them without lamenting that so many excellent and highly approvable things should be miserably profaned in the service of error; indeed one cannot but groan to see the marble, and gold, and azure, and precious stones employed in adorning the temple of an idol.

I wish you particularly to notice this, my brethren, that you may not be confounded if the Romanists at this day are able speciously to defend a very bad cause, nor be much moved at the ostentation they make of it, who are not ashamed to boast of the eloquence and subtlety of their teachers, as if this were one of the marks of truth. I freely consent to the praises they give them, and acknowledge that enticing words (as the apostle here calls them) abound on their side; but I dare affirm, notwithstanding, and am confident that every intelligent and dispassionate person will agree with me, that, however subtle and eloquent their masters are, and whatever pains they have taken for the better colouring and burnishing their doctrine, their works are not more neat, nor more polite, nor more specious and fair, than the words of those pagans and heretics whom I have just named; yea, to speak without prejudice, I believe they are far inferior to them. Let them forbear therefore to urge for a mark of truth an advantage which is common to them with pagans and heretics, an advantage which the most infamous causes employ, which the worst ordinarily seek after more earnestly than the best; so much more cunning being used in their defence, by how much less strength they have in themselves.

I have no wish to decry eloquence and acuteness, or prejudice you against them, as if they were never engaged except in the service of error; I willingly acknowledge they are excellent graces of God, and that he gives them to men properly for the defence of truth, and surely they have not always had the misfortune to contend for falsehood. They have often done good service to the gospel, and employed their might for its glory, both heretofore against the pagans and the old heretics; and in our times against those of Rome, as appears by the writings both of the fathers and of our own learned men; many of whom are in this respect quite equal to their adversaries, besides their having the principal advantage, that is, the truth on their side. Paul himself, who here condemns words of persuasion when they recommend error, does not reject them when they are employed in the service of truth. And though he was not very conversant with the art of secular eloquence, consequently he says of himself, that for speech he was as one of the vulgar, yet his discourses want no strength nor grace; that rich heavenly knowledge which abounded in his heart giving its tincture to the words of his mouth. That great personage indeed felt how it was, who, hearing him speak, was pressed with the force of his discourse, and said aloud, "Almost thou persuadest me to be a christian," Acts xxvi. 28. All my aim is, that since error oftentimes abuses eloquence, and acuteness is used against the truth, as evil men use other gifts of God to evil ends, we should not estimate the value of any cause by this advantage, nor hastily embrace that party that defends itself with the best and most persuasive words, nor reject that which has least of these ornaments in view. As innocence is not always the best clothed, so truth frequently is not the most richly decked. And though of itself it is always more probable, more likely, and more easily maintainable than falsehood, as one of the ancient sages well observed;* yet sometimes it happens through the sleight of seducers, by the false light in which they set it, and the colours with which they shadow it, that it looks worse in the eyes of the ignorant than a lie. Let us take heed, then, of their surprising us, and so well fortify our minds against their illusions, that we may never reject the truth, however deformed and dis-

* Arist. Rhetor. l. 1. c. 6.

gusting it may appear according to their representations of it; nor receive a delusion, however specious and plausible they may render it. Remember, that that Babylon, the mother of error, who is portrayed before us in the Apocalypse, chap. xvii. 4, presents its abominations unto men in a golden cup; that is, she gives her poisons in a pleasing vessel, and shuts up and hides the hideousness of her impostures under very fair and specious words. Thus those seducers formerly acted who solicited the Colossians; their errors were attended with persuasive or enticing words for the purpose of beguiling them. This is the danger from which Paul would here preserve them.

Let us now consider the means which he puts into their hands that they may safely guard themselves from it. This I say unto you, "lest any man should beguile you with enticing words." Here it is evident that what he saith is able, if duly improved, to keep us from falling into seductive error, and to frustrate all the charms of its fine and attractive words. What then does he say? What is that holy and efficacious speech which can dissipate the illusions and enchantments of error? Dear brethren, you heard it in the exposition of the preceding text, where this holy man told us that all the treasures of wisdom and knowledge are hid in Jesus Christ; such is the apostle's meaning. This is that celestial oracle to which he attributes this great virtue. This is the remedy which he gives us against all the poisons and all the charms of seduction. None of the weapons or the wiles of error can bear up before this sacred word. It alone is sufficient, if we use it as we ought, to confound and annihilate all the fictitious wonders of the eloquence and subtlety of false teachers, as in ancient time the rod of Moses swallowed up all the rods of the Egyptian magicians. For whoever holds fast this principle in his heart, that all true wisdom and knowledge are in Jesus Christ, will receive nothing out of Christ. Being satisfied with this treasure, he will despise all other things, however specious and plausible. Seduction will do little by displaying its arts and gilding and painting over its inventions with the fair colours either of ratiocination or of eloquence. It will get no ground upon such a one, since, after all, the thing it so carefully polishes is not in Jesus Christ, out of whom he will know nothing. He will not so much as hear the babbling of error, so far will he be from being affected with it. He will shut his ear against its fine words, so far is he from being seduced by them. Or if he please to cast his eye upon the works of its subtlety and its eloquence, he will look upon them as spiders' webs, or as jugglers' feats, which amuse us and beguile our senses, but make no impression on our hearts. We well know they deceive us, though we cannot tell how. So the faithful man will hold that for a deceit and illusion which leads him out of Jesus Christ, though he does not see wherein the sophism of the error consists, nor is able easily to untie its knots.

This, dear brethren, is the sure and infallible means to exclude and to expel all error from among us. Seducement wins only upon those who betray this gate, and yield that there may be something of good and saving importance out of Jesus Christ and his Scriptures. When once it has this ground given, it never wants paint and pretences to colour its delusions, and to render even those plausible and likely which are otherwise most gross and extravagant. Thus those traditions and ceremonies which have still the vogue among our adversaries were, by degrees, obtruded upon christians;—the invocation of angels and of departed saints; the sacrifice of the altar, and the veneration of relics and of images; the visible head, and the hierarchy, and the infallibility of the church; satisfactions, and the merit of works; prayers and services in a language not understood; the adoration of the host; communion in one kind only; purgatory, suffrages for the dead, and many other such things. Thousands of colours are found to paint them out, and recommend either the belief or the practice of them to poor people. There are huge books made about them, full of wit and eloquence, that drive the matter so far, as to make these things pass for the principal and most useful part of christian devotion. But this short saying of Paul's is enough to ruin all their labours, and to secure us from all their snares: "In Jesus Christ are hid all the treasures of wisdom and knowledge." It is sufficient for me to have him, since, having him, I have all that appertains to true wisdom. However well disputed, and however eloquently pleaded, are all your traditions, I am not concerned in them, seeing I have the treasure of all science in Christ Jesus. And it is not here alone that the apostle gives us this lesson for freeing ourselves from the entanglements and snares of error; when instructing the Hebrews, and exhorting them not to be carried to and fro with divers and strange doctrines, he lays before them, at the entrance, this divine principle, that "Jesus Christ is the same yesterday, and to-day, and for ever," Heb. xiii. 8.

II. But it is now time to come to the second part of our text, in which the apostle declares to the Colossians, the cognizance he took of the state of their church. "For though I be absent in flesh, yet am I with you in the spirit, rejoicing and beholding your order, and the steadfastness of your faith in Christ." This is the reason why he counsels them to take heed of the wiles of seducers, and so carefully puts into their hands the means to preserve themselves. For some might have thought it strange, that being so far from them, and in all probability ignorant of their condition, he should give them such a caution. He prevents this surmise, and answers, that though he was at Rome, yet he attended to what was doing at Colosse; the affection which he bore them obliging him to interest himself in all their affairs. Wonder not (says he) that I address you in this manner, and send you, from so great a distance, preservatives against seduction; for though many seas and hills sever my body from you, yet my spirit is with you, taking part in all that befalls you, rejoicing in the prosperous estate of your piety, but at the same time fearing the attempts of those enemies which I see around you, ready to sow the tares of schism and error upon the least opening they find for it.

Some refer his saying that he was in spirit with the Colossians to an extraordinary and miraculous operation of the Holy Ghost, who, replenishing his soul with light, enabled him to see occurrences at the greatest distance as clearly as if he had been present, after the same manner that God had showed Elisha what his servant Gehazi did with Naaman; a passage which accordingly the prophet expresses almost in the same manner: "Went not mine heart with thee," says he to Gehazi, "when the man turned again from his chariot to meet thee?" 2 Kings v. 26. I confess indeed that God could easily have made known to Paul, while Nero's prisoner at Rome, all that passed in the church of Colosse, with as much, yea, more certainty, than he could have learned by personal observation; and have also revealed to him the whole state of other churches more distant from Italy; as he gave to Ezekiel, while living in captivity at Babylon, the power to see the most secret actions of the Jews, in the city and the temple of Jerusalem. But it is dangerous to argue from what God can do to what he does, and under colour of some slight probabilities to resolve upon things which his word does not at all affirm; and as we may not multiply miracles without necessity, I think it best and safest not to suppose that the apostle was in this very extraordinary manner present with the Colossians, but to interpret his words simply as others do, of a presence in respect of care and affection. For nothing is more common in all languages, than to say that our minds are in those places, and with those persons, who engage our thoughts and affection. This gave rise to the common observation, that the soul is where it loves, because to that spot it generally directs its affections, its wishes, and its reflections. And in this sense we receive what the apostle says to the Corinthians, that though absent in body, he was present with them in spirit, 1 Cor. v. 3. All he means is, that his bonds did not confine his spirit, and detain it a prisoner at Rome; nor, for a single hour, contravene his concern for them, and having his affections and thoughts continually among them.

He represented to himself their estate as vividly as if they had stood before him; and derived from this lively conception the same emotions of joy, satisfaction, and fear, that the sight of them would have produced within him. So that there need be no wonder if, having them so deeply engraven on his heart, and ever present to the eyes of his mind, he became pained for them, and at such distance prescribed them necessary precautions and preservatives against the pleasant but pernicious poisons of error.

Observe, I beseech you, this holy man's prudent and apt procedure. To justify the care which he took of them, he does not urge the danger they were in, their weakness, or the bad inclinations which some of them had; this discourse would have been offensive, as showing a distrust of their piety; but, on the contrary, he here tells them of the prosperity of their spiritual estate, the beauty of their order, and the constancy of their faith: "Joying and beholding your order, and the steadfastness of your faith." Do not imagine, says he, that I have an ill opinion of your piety because I so earnestly advise you to stand fast; I am very well satisfied concerning it, and find you in so good a posture, that I have much consolation at it; this matter being so pleasing to me, that it fills my heart with joy, notwithstanding the sad state that I am in. But from the same root whence springs my joy, my ardent desire to see you go on from good to better also arises, and with it the solicitude and care I take to exhort it, because it would be an extreme regret and displeasure to see error waste or wound so fair and flourishing a church ever so little. See how by praising them he obliges them to regard his cautions, and by the very consideration of their having so well begun, more and more engages them to holy perseverance to the end. Thus he also treated the Philippians: "My brethren," said he to them, "dearly beloved and longed for, my joy and crown, so stand fast in the Lord, my dearly beloved," Phil. iv. 1.

You perceive, without my indication, that when he says, "joying and beholding your order," the meaning is, rejoicing to see, or because I see, your order. For in Scripture language, and even in common speech, the particle *and* is often used in this sense, and signifies because, or, forasmuch as. He praises and extols two things in these faithful persons, in which the happiness and the perfection of a church consist, namely, order, and a firm and constant faith. By the order of these Colossians, he means the good disposition of all the parts of their church, the vigilancy of the pastors, the submission and obedience of the flock, their joint regard of discipline; each keeping themselves within the bounds of their vocation, and both together living in concord and good intelligence, honestly, and without scandal. For that order comprehends also purity and holiness of life the apostle evidently shows in another place, where, to signify those that lead a scandalous life, he says that they walk disorderly, 2 Thess. iii. 6. He praises also the firmness of their faith in Jesus Christ, signifying thereby both that full persuasion they had of the truth and divinity of his gospel, and their constancy to hold it fast, notwithstanding the assaults and temptations of the enemy. This faith, dear brethren, and this order of the Colossians, were the matter of the apostle's joy, and the cause both of the desire he had to see them persevere still in so good a course, and of the advice he gave them, not to suffer themselves to be beguiled by the enticing words of seducers, and likewise of adding that preservative, of meditating incessantly upon the treasures of wisdom which are in Jesus for saving themselves from this destructive danger.

It is now our business to make a good improvement of so excellent a lesson. We are as much environed, or more so, than the Colossians formerly were, with people who endeavour to deceive us with enticing words, who daily make all kind of attempts upon our faith, and do not forget the sophisms of subtilty, or the charms of eloquence, presenting error to us disguised with divers specious colours. To secure our minds from their illusions, let us tell them, as the apostle teaches us, that all the treasures of wisdom are hid in that Jesus Christ whom we have embraced; that he is sufficient to make us wise to salvation; and that we need to know none but him to obtain happiness. If with fair and artful words they represent to us the necessity of an expiatory sacrifice, for recommending that of their own altars; or the utility of satisfactions to make us receive theirs; or the horror of sin, which has no entrance into the kingdom of God, to persuade us about their purgatory; or the need we have of an intercessor, to induce us to have recourse to a mediation of angels, and of departed saints; or of a head, to set up their pope: let us answer them, that we have all this most fully in Jesus Christ; that his cross is our sacrifice, his sufferings our satisfaction, his blood our purgation; that while we possess him, we shall need neither an intercessor to open the throne of the grace of God to us, and render both our persons and our prayers acceptable to him, nor a head to govern and preserve us. Let us account all that would turn us aside from him, or place any part of his treasure anywhere else than in him, to be a seduction and an illusion.

As good physicians not only preserve from poisons, but also draw profit from them, by making them remedies; so let us not content ourselves with keeping the venom of seducements from hurting us; let us treat them in such a way as that they may serve us. Let their ardour in the cause of error inflame our zeal for the truth. Let their pains-taking and industry sharpen our diligence and care. Let us employ that acuteness and eloquence to the defence of the gospel which they profane in the service of an imposture. Let us have no less affection for the cause of God than they have for the matters of flesh and blood. And instead of the extravagance of some who love ignorance and rudeness, because error abuses knowledge and eloquence, let us, on the contrary, thence take occasion to labour in adorning and embellishing truth, that even in this respect falsehood may have no advantage above it.

But if the examples of enemies should be of use to us, much more ought the examples of brethren, which wholly and solely tend to our edification. Let us profit by that of the Colossians, whose faith and order the apostle praises, that we might imitate them. Let us put our church into such a state as may give joy to the Lord, to his angels and to his ministers. My brethren, I admit that your faith and order may, in some degree, be commended without flattery, as by the grace of Christ you persevere in his fear, and assiduously rank yourselves under his ensigns, no temptation having been able hitherto to make you desert these holy assemblies. But you are not ignorant that, together with this well doing, there are many failures among us, that many things occur in our congregations little comporting with the dignity of the house of God; and that the hardness of some stiffens itself against discipline, the only bond of order; and if our faith is steadfast against error, it is far too yielding to sin. Dear brethren, I had rather leave the examination of it to your own consciences, than here publish our sin and shame, and will content myself with telling you that the apostle banishes out of heaven the immoral as well as the idolatrous, 1 Cor. vi. 9, 10. God, who has granted us to persevere in the profession of his truth, be pleased powerfully to correct, by the efficacy of his gospel, the defects with which his gentleness has hitherto borne; and sanctify us so efficaciously, that after we have glorified him on earth by our good order and conversation, and the fruits of a firm and immovable faith, we may hereafter receive, in heaven, from his merciful hand, the reward and crown of blissful immortality, in his Son Jesus Christ, who, in the unity of the Father, and of the Holy Ghost, liveth and reigneth, the only God, blessed for ever. Amen.

SERMON XIX.

VERSES 6, 7.

As ye have therefore received Christ Jesus the Lord, so walk ye in him: rooted and built up in him, and stablished in the faith, as ye have been taught, abounding therein with thanksgiving.

As man naturally loves novelty and variety, the best and most wholesome things become disgusting to him, when he is compelled, for a long time, to continue the use of them. What food was there ever in the world better, more savoury, more nourishing, and more miraculous, than the manna wherewith God fed the Israelites in the wilderness, pouring it down daily from heaven upon them by the ministry of angels; whence it is called the bread of heaven, and angel's food? Nevertheless, this wretched people were soon discontented with it, disdaining that precious gift of God, and foolishly regretting the fruits and fish of Egypt. "Our soul," said they, "is dried away: there is nothing at all, besides this manna, before our eyes," Numb. xi. 6. Dear brethren, this history is a fit emblem of what has befallen men in reference to Jesus Christ and his gospel, the true bread of heaven, sent down from God into the wilderness of this world for the eternal nutriment of mankind; of which that ancient manna, as you know, was the figure, as he himself teaches us in the 6th of John. For our nature is not less fastidious, nor has it an appetite less extravagant, with respect to the doctrines necessary to feed our souls, than it has with respect to the meat that is ordained for the refreshment of our bodies. The truth of the Lord Jesus is embraced at the first with desire and appetite, every one admiring the excellency of this heavenly food, which infinitely exceeds the productions of the earth. But though it be altogether holy and salutiferous, yet because it is simple and uniform, the vanity of man in desiring change, and variety causes him immediately to loathe it, and induces him to search for novelties to season it, and render it more grateful.

The apostles had scarcely sown this sacred doctrine in the church, when evil workers, as in the camp of Israel, quickly rose up, who, to remedy men's disdain, and accommodate this celestial truth to their palate, must needs add to it divers inventions and novelties of their own. And Paul foretold that others would arise as bad or worse than they: "After their own lusts," says he, "shall they heap to themselves teachers, having itching ears; and they shall turn away their ears from the truth, and shall be turned unto fables," 2 Tim. iv. 3, 4. O prophecy too true! how punctually hast thou been fulfilled! This foolish itch of the ear has caused thousands of fancies and novelties to be gradually entertained among christians, which have so borne down, and, as it were, overwhelmed the gospel, that it is hardly to be discerned any longer. The doctrine of Rome is but a heap of traditions, errors, and superstitions, partly copied from Judaism, and some from paganism itself, and partly issuing from the private speculations of some particular persons. In the days of our fathers, the gospel, having been brought out of the dark caverns of ignorance into the light of men, was received in a similar manner with ardour and admiration. But that loathing of the best and most wholesome things, which is fatal to us, quickly overtook it, and stirred up, as it also still does, divers spirits, who, for a remedy, strive to corrupt this pure doctrine, and dress up its simplicity with their own inventions to make it please the world. To cure us of this fastidiousness, the apostle at this time addresses to us the exhortation you have heard; the same which he formerly made to the Galatians for the same purpose, forbidding them novelties and strange doctrines, and enjoining them to stand fast in Jesus Christ, who had been preached to them, without admitting or desiring anything beyond his gospel. Therefore, says he, "as ye have received Christ Jesus the Lord, so walk ye in him," &c.

To give you a full and entire exposition of these words, we have two things to consider:

First, the apostle's exhortation to the Colossians to cleave to the Lord Jesus; this is the sense and intention of the first verse.

Secondly, the manner in which he would have them cleave to the Lord, namely, by the confirmation and abounding of their faith in his gospel "with thanksgiving." Of these two particulars we purpose to treat in this exercise, by the assistance of Christ, for your edification and consolation.

I. You may remember, that in the preceding text the apostle commended the faithful people of Colosse, and rejoiced at the good order he witnessed in their church, and at the firmness of their faith in Jesus Christ. But it is not sufficient to begin well, we must continue in well-doing, inasmuch as salvation is promised only to those who shall persevere unto the end; with good reason, and very pertinently, therefore, he now adds to the praise he gave them an exhortation to continue and abide firm in that good and happy state wherein they were; and the more so, as there were about them certain busy and unquiet spirits, who with their inventions and subtilties, endeavoured to vitiate the sincerity of their belief, as you have already heard, and shall again more particularly hear, at the conclusion of this chapter. "As ye have therefore," saith he, "received Christ Jesus the Lord, so walk ye in him." Jesus Christ is the subject in which he would have them abide. For he is "the way, the truth, and the life;" neither is there salvation in any other. But because these false teachers, the better to propagate their vain traditions, were wont to colour them with our Saviour's name, knowing well that every faithful person would soon hiss at them if they spake openly of departing from Jesus Christ, or of living at a distance from him, the apostle anticipates this danger, and expressly shows the Colossians how he intends they should abide firm in Jesus Christ, saying, "As ye have received Christ Jesus the Lord, so walk ye in him." And to this also that which he adds in the following verse has relation, "as ye have been taught." By this he clearly signifies that the doctrine which had been delivered to them, either by himself (if it be true that he preached the gospel to them, and founded their church as some think) or by Epaphras, as most are of opinion; he signifies, I say, that this doctrine which had been preached to them, and believed by them, was so holy and divine, and sufficient to salvation, that it was their duty constantly to adhere thereto, and to admit nothing beyond what they had heard under any pretext whatever. "This is the way," as Isaiah says, "walk ye in it, when ye turn to the right hand, and when ye turn to the left," chap. xxx. 21.

But by these words the apostle not only points out to them and explains that doctrine which they ought to hold, but he enforces it upon them, as affecting their reputation; for since they had received it, they could not again part with it without convicting themselves either of imprudence or of instability. For he that quits the faith he once embraced, thereby evidently shows either imprudence in having taken a false or imperfect doctrine for good, or instability in quitting and altering a doctrine good and sufficient when he received it. If your belief be good, why do you change it? If it be otherwise, why did you entertain it? It follows, of necessity, either that there was error and precipitation in the one, or that there is weakness and fickleness in the other. So you see that a regard to their own reputation obliged these christians to that constancy to which the apostle enjoins them. Besides, though it be a heinous sin not to receive the Lord Jesus when he presents himself to us in his gospel, yet it is much more enormous to cast him out after having received him; as it is a far greater outrage to thrust a man from your house when you have admitted him, than to shut your doors against him at the first. The one is a simple offence, the other is an affront. In like manner, it is a much more injurious treatment to desert

Christ Jesus after having followed him, than never to have listened to or followed him at all.

And observe here, I pray, the efficacy of sound doctrine; it is such as that in receiving it we receive Jesus Christ himself. For this highest Lord takes up his abode in all such as embrace his gospel. And we may apply to this purpose what he said to his apostles on a similar occasion, "He that receiveth you receiveth me;" whoso gives credit to their preaching shall have their Master to be with him; he shall entertain not men or angels, but the King of men and angels, the eternal Son of God, the Prince of life, and Father of eternity. He that receives the doctrine of an Aristotle, or a Plato, or of a father, or a pope, and, in short, of any man whatever, does not thereupon receive the author of the doctrine himself; because no man has either the ability or the means to communicate himself to those that credit his instructions. But Jesus Christ, being God blessed for ever, of a nature, a wisdom, and a power infinite, he accompanies his own gospel, and communicates himself to those who receive it; he dwells in their hearts by faith; he there sheds abroad the light and influence of his Spirit, and brings thither with him peace, and life, and joy.

Now to close this part of the subject, take heed that you do not stretch Paul's words beyond his intention, as if his meaning were, that generally every one should adhere to that which he has been taught, and never part with what he has once received, whatever may be the things which he has believed, and whoever the persons were that delivered them. God forbid that an imagination so absurd and pernicious, and so very far from the apostle's mind, should ever enter into your heart. In this case, those who have been in an error would do well not to renounce it; and it would not be lawful for those who have taken poison, to take a remedy. Neither should considerations of honour and generosity be urged in this case; perseverance in an error, once known, is not constancy, but obstinacy. It is a part of true generosity to confess a fault, and to forsake it; and it is clearly a feebleness of spirit not to renounce that which is false or corrupt, upon the pretence that you had the misfortune once to embrace it. I confess it had been better to have rejected it at first; but settling in it after conviction is a doubling of your fault and infelicity. And as for honour, it is a pitiful extravagance to place it in things opposed to duty and virtue. If error be honourable, I will admit that he who confirms himself in it is a man of honour. But since, on the contrary, it is most evidently true, as all will confess, that error is a shameful thing, and blame-worthy, who does not see that true honour obliges us to quit it, and not obstinately to persist in it? and that to persevere in error or in sin, under the pretext of honour, is to attempt, as the gospel says, to gather figs from thorns, and grapes from a bramble bush? Luke vi. 44. It is as if a man would attempt to whiten himself with ink, and cleanse himself with mud. In a word, it is seeking honour in shame, and glory in ignominy. But I pass by those who, by such observations, clearly discover either that they have not well pondered what they say, or (which would be still worse) that they hold truth and error, piety and impiety, virtue and vice, to be indifferent things; since according to their doctrine, pagans and heretics are blamable when they forsake the latter to follow the former, which cannot be affirmed without maintaining, at least, that both are indifferent; inasmuch as common sense dictates to all men that it is a prudent action, worthy of praise and not of blame, to quit the worse for the better, and to leave a bad way that we may take a good one.

I now come to those of Rome, who also abuse the apostle's exhortation to the faithful here, and elsewhere, to abide in that which they have received, and which has been taught them, without giving ear to novelties. This, say they, is what you have done, you that walk no longer in the way you were taught among us, who have deserted and abjured the mass, and the service of our saints, and the veneration of our images, and the belief of our purgatory, and many other such things which your ancestors received, and all which, or the greater part of them, have been constantly and openly preached among us from age to age, and from father to son, for a thousand years and more, as you cannot deny. Dear brethren, to this I answer, that this exhortation of the holy apostle is so far from favouring their cause, that, on the contrary, it overthrows it, and establishes ours. For, as we have said, he does not positively declare that every one should adhere to the doctrine he has received of his teachers. God forbid, since by so doing he would have obliged the pagan to remain eternally in his idolatry handed down to him by his ancestors, and the heretic in the error infused into him by his masters, and the Mussulman in the faith of his Mahomet, and the Jew in the tradition of his fathers. He, on the contrary, exhorts the Gentiles to come out of the ways wherein God had permitted them and their ancestors to walk for the time past. He who urges the Galatians to forsake the by-path into which their doctors had misled them, that they might again commence the race they once ran; he who would have Timothy, and all true ministers, labour to draw men out of the snares of the devil, whatever hand it was that entangled them in it, 2 Tim. ii. 25, 26; here speaks to faithful people who had received and kept pure and sincere till then the gospel of Jesus Christ, without any mixture of error or superstition. These are they whom he recommends to stand fast in what they had learned. And if our adversaries resemble them, I confess that they have reason to abide in the doctrine of their fathers, and we have done wrong to recede from it.

The apostle speaks not in general of all kinds of doctrine, but particularly, and by name, of that which the Colossians then believed; to which he expressly gives these two characteristics to distinguish it from all others. First, that it wholly referred to Jesus Christ. Secondly, that it had been delivered to them, either by himself, or at least by some one of his faithful disciples. "As ye have received Christ Jesus the Lord, so walk ye in him," even "as ye have been taught." If such be the doctrine of Rome, if it neither publish nor exhibit anything but Jesus Christ the Lord, if it were delivered by Paul, if it came from his hand, if it be derived from this source, I will candidly confess that we are faulty in having quitted it. But since, on the contrary, it is as evident and as clear as the light of the sun, that what we have quitted and abjured is not that Lord Jesus Christ whom Paul and his fellow labourers and scholars preached, but a leaven contrary to him, which has been superadded by men, and which was not taught by the first ministers of the truth; who does not see that we have in this not disobeyed, but obeyed the apostle's exhortation? that we have done what he commands, and not what he forbids? For in what part of Paul's or the other apostles' discourses can they ever point out to us the mass, purgatory, the worshipping of saints, and, in short, any of those other articles which they retain, and which we have relinquished? Every one sees how all these things vary from the Lord Jesus Christ, and make void his cross and his kingdom, causing men to seek the expiation and purging of their sins by other means than by his sacrifice, and attributing to creatures the honour of invocation, and of presiding over the whole church, which belongs to him alone.

But the other description which Paul gives of the doctrine which ought to be held fast still less accords with their traditions, namely, its having been received from the apostles; it being manifest that not one word of what they so erroneously affirm is to be found in the writings of those holy men, which are the public and authentic records of what they preached; and that those traditions of Rome grew up in after-ages, some at one time, and some at another, issuing, by slow degrees, from the hands of men according as error gathered strength, as they who read the volumes of antiquity without prejudice and prepossession well know. Let our adversaries therefore desist from those odious accusations. They must either show that those doctrines of theirs which we have relinquished are apostolical, or confess that we had reason to relinquish them; this very command of Paul's, which they are not ashamed to produce against us, necessarily obliging us to adhere to that Lord Jesus Christ alone whom he preached, and on whom the Colossians believed, according to his preaching.

It must not here be argued that the doctrine which we contest with our opponents has been their belief for a thousand years or more. Time is no prescription against any truth, and least of all against the truth of Christ and his apostles. That which he pronounced continues in force for ever. "Though we, or an angel from heaven, preach any other gospel unto you than that which we have preached, let him be accursed," Gal. i. 8, 9. I inquire not of what date your opinions are; it is sufficient for me to anathematize those which were not preached as gospel by the apostle. Time cannot have conferred on them the advantage of being true, which they did not possess at their origin. What is not now true or apostolical will never be so. You are not the only men among whom error has grown old; that gross one of idolatry lived among the pagans nearly two thousand years; and their Rome also pleaded her hoary hairs in defence of her doctrines, as does yours at this day, and said, as Rome now says again, that it is an undertaking ill-timed to correct old age, and that to charge it with error is to affront it. A thousand years and more have transpired since the delusions of Mahomet have been entertained, still this does not render them in the slightest degree better. You yourselves observe errors in the same antiquity whose authority you so loudly applaud, and you cannot deny but that those which you condemn in the communions of the Grecians, of the Armenians, of the Jacobites, and of the Coptics, are very ancient. It is an extremely bad defence, when men are convicted of error, to say that they have been a long time of that opinion. However ancient your doctrine may be, it is young in comparison with that of Paul's, as it sprang into existence after his days. Neither its pretended antiquity, nor any other consideration, can secure it from his fulmination. Since he would have us to keep to that which he preached, without receiving anything beside, however stale and mouldy with age may be your traditions, they all ought to perish under pain of an anathema, seeing they are without the compass of Paul's preaching. We are at this day in the same situation in which the Colossians formerly were. They stood bound by this exhortation to reject the worshipping of angels, the distinction of meats, justification by the law, and everything that any way tended to add to the Lord Jesus Christ, whom they had received from the hand of Paul, and who had been taught them by him. Let us then also freely reject the same things; let us keep constantly to that Jesus Christ whom we have received of him, who filled up all his sermons, and still fills up all his Epistles. Let us content ourselves with that primitive and truly ancient doctrine, and boldly despise all the novelties that the world has presumed subsequently to add thereto. Let us walk in this Lord Jesus as the apostle gives us direction. Let him be our only way, the rule of our faith and of our conduct.

You know that this term is ordinarily used in Scripture to signify the ordering and conduct of our life. The various disciplines and persuasions which men follow are compared to ways which lead to different ends. The way of sinners, and the way of the righteous, are spoken of as signifying the apprehensions and maxims by which their lives are governed. Therefore the term walk is used to signify the leading and ordering of the life. And as our Lord and Saviour says he is the way, so his apostle enjoins us to walk in him; that is, to lead our lives, both with regard to knowledge and persuasions of mind, and also with respect to affections, and actions according to his holy gospel, without any forsaking of it, to take another course; judging all that varies from it to be folly, how plausible soever it may appear. And as a wise and prudent traveller never leaves his road, but proceeds constantly therein until he comes to his journey's end, however smiling the meadows may appear, however green and fresh may be the cooling shades, and however wide and beautiful may be the paths which invite his attention; so are we ordered to keep continually to the doctrine of our Lord and Saviour, and not to relinquish it, or receive any other, whatever nature, or colour, or appearance it may assume, assured that whatever is without the dimensions of this model of truth cannot but be dangerous, and must eventually, if we follow it, lead us to perdition.

II. I pass by the observation which some make, namely, that the apostle's command to walk in Christ intimates that we should constantly advance and press forward in our christian course; for though this conception be true as to substance, it being the duty of each true believer to go forward, and not pass a day without improvement in piety; yet it seems to me to be beyond the meaning of the apostle's words, the scope of which is simply to urge us to perseverance in the gospel of Jesus Christ. Besides, what he adds in the following verse sufficiently recommends to us this duty, where he shows after what manner we are to abide in Jesus Christ: "Rooted," says he, "and built up in him, and established in the faith as ye have been taught, abounding therein with thanksgiving."

In these words he prescribes three things; firmness of faith, the abounding therein, and the giving of thanks. He expresses the first two ways: first, metaphorically, "rooted and built up in Jesus Christ;" and next properly, and without figure, "established," or confirmed, "in faith." For this confirmation in faith is the same thing that is intended by the words, "rooted and built up in Jesus Christ." The first of these metaphors is taken from trees, which stand firm, and easily resist the violence of winds, when they have put forth good and deep roots into the earth, which serve for so many stays and bands to hold them fast; whereas the plants which have but little or no root are easily plucked up, the least gust of wind, or the hand of a child, being sufficient to overthrow them. The faithful are often in Scripture compared unto trees. You all know the parable of the fig tree in the gospel, and that of the palm tree in the Psalms: "The righteous shall flourish like the palm tree: he shall grow like a cedar in Lebanon," Psal. xcii. 12. And there is not one in the church who is not acquainted with that excellent tree, a description of which the psalmist gives us, Psal. i. 3, as an image of the true believer, planted by the rivers of waters, which bringeth forth its fruit in its season, and the leaves whereof do not wither. It follows, therefore, that the ministers who labour in the culture of these mystical plants are compared to gardeners, and vine-dressers, and husbandmen; such was he in the gospel parable, who prayed the owners to supersede the sentence pronounced upon one of his fig trees, Luke xiii. 8. And Paul also describes his own labours, and those of Apollos, for the edification of the faithful, in terms derived from the same subject. saying that he planted, and Apollos watered, 1 Cor. iii. 6, 7. In consequence of these figurative expressions, which are familiar in Scripture, you see that it is with much beauty and propriety that the apostle, to recommend firmness of faith in Jesus Christ, here says that they should be rooted in him. He repeats the same elsewhere, when he prays God to strengthen the Ephesians by his Spirit, that "being rooted and grounded in love, they might be able to comprehend with all saints what is the breadth, and length, and depth, and height; and to know the love of Christ," Eph. iii. 17—19. For since the faithful man is compared to a tree, it is proper to attribute to him both the production (that is, fruit) and the parts of a tree, the principal of which is the root. We say, then, that a tree is well rooted, when its root is spread abroad, and thrust deep into the ground, where it is planted in and fastened to it so many ways that it stands upright and firm, nor can be plucked up without extreme difficulty.

Who then is the believer rooted in Christ? Even the man whose whole soul embraces the Lord Jesus; all whose thoughts and affections are stretched forth and fastened to this divine crucified Saviour, who has neither love, nor desire, nor confidence towards any other object than him. It is he who, having rightly understood the excellency and the fulness of this rich subject, seeks all his felicity in it, and, withdrawing the desires, the cares and affections of his heart from earth, (which are, as it were, the strings and roots of our nature, by which it is fastened to the things of time,) thrusts them forth towards Jesus Christ, unites with and binds them about him, and rests on him alone, and draws the nutriment of his life from none other: as you know trees by their root receive all that juice which gives them life, vegetation, and fruitfulness. Not to produce any other example, such a one was Paul; so fastened was he unto, and so incorporated with, his Lord, that he lived in him alone; this divine ground wherein he was planted affording him all the joy, all the contentment, and all the life he possessed. There is no need to fear that those who adhere to Jesus Christ in such a manner, who are so really and deeply rooted in him, can ever be plucked up by any effort, be it ever so violent. In vain do the winds shake them; in vain do the tempests beat upon them; persecutions will not be able to make them bend; nor fraud, nor eloquence, nor the subtlety of sophisters, remove them. Novelties and curiosities do not tempt them, because that sweet sap which they continually draw from Christ, as from a rich soil, contents them, and purges them of that foolish and childish itching humour which opens the ears of the weak and unstable to these unprofitable things.

But if you be not thus rooted in Christ, there will be no great difficulty in plucking you from the station you are in. If it is not this heavenly efficacy of our Lord which induces you to profess christianity, but birth, or breeding, or the discourse or authority of men, or the name of liberty, or any other such cause, I am much afraid you will not long abide therein. If your heart be in the world, if it still spread its affections, as its roots, among perishing things, if it still admire the pleasures of the flesh, the fumes of ambition, and the vanity of riches, your perseverance is really very dubious. The tree that has no root has no hold. The first gust that falls upon it bears it down. And would to God experience had less justified this truth in our eyes. But this is the very cause of all that change in those who have deserted us. If you examine their lives, you will find that they were not well rooted in Christ Jesus. Wonder not that they were overthrown. But let us profit by their unhappiness, and obey the apostle's injunction; and that we may abide firm for ever in the communion of our divine Lord, apart from which there is nothing but misery and perdition, let us be rooted in him with a lively and profound faith and love. Let us love and relish him only, and inseparably cleave, with all the powers of our souls, to him alone, as dead and risen again for us, drawing all our righteousness from his cross, and all our hope and glory from his heavenly state and immortality.

I come to the other metaphor here used by the apostle to

set forth the confirmation of our faith in Jesus Christ; "rooted," says he, "and built up in him." The former metaphor was taken from trees, the present one is drawn from buildings. This is no less famous in Scripture than the other, for the faithful are there often compared to houses, and particularly to temples. The church also, that is, the society consisting of them collectively, is represented to us under the same image. Consequently, the labours of the servants of the Lord are also called edifying; a word so frequently used in this sense, that there is no occasion for us to stay to explain it. And as in material edifices it is the foundation that sustains the whole of the building, so the Scripture gives that name to our Lord and Saviour, upon whom this spiritual structure entirely depends. "Other foundation," says the apostle, "can no man lay than that is laid, which is Jesus Christ," 1 Cor. iii. 11. And this the prophets foretold, when they said respecting him, that God would lay in Zion "a precious corner-stone, a sure foundation," Isa. xxviii. 16; and that the stone which the builders refused should "become the head stone of the corner," Psal. cxviii. 22. The apostle, therefore, desiring to secure his dear Colossians against the danger of falling, continuing this figure so common in Scripture, commands them to be built up in Jesus Christ. And the same expression he uses in another place, where he says that we are "built upon the foundation of the apostles and prophets, Jesus Christ himself being the chief corner-stone; in whom all the building fitly framed together groweth unto an holy temple in the Lord," Eph. ii. 20, 21.

What is it, then, to be built up in Jesus Christ? Dear brethren, we say a house is built on a rock, when a rock is the foundation that entirely bears and sustains it. A soul is built up in Jesus Christ when it wholly relies upon him, so that its faith, its hope, its love, and the other parts of its mystical structure, are all set upon him, and firmly united to him: it believes the gospel, because it is the word of Christ; it is assured of the remission of sins, because they were expiated by Christ; it expects the kingdom of heaven, because he purchased it; it loves neighbours, because they are his workmanship; it meekly bears affliction, because it is a part of his cross; in short, it lays and settles upon him alone the designs, the thoughts, the enjoyments, and the expectations, wherein consist both its present life and that which is to come. One so built up in Jesus Christ is like that wise man commended by our Saviour, who built his house on a rock, so that no violence was able to effect its fall, Matt. vii. 24, 25. For what indeed can overthrow a soul seated on this Rock of ages, which is firm and immovable for ever? Where is the temptation or the persecution that can beat it down? That which is built upon this foundation is not subject to natural accidents. It is a celestial and an eternal edifice. But the misery of men, and the true cause of their weakness and ruin, is that they build either wholly, or for the greater part elsewhere. The world is the ground whereon they set and raise up the designs of their lives; and this ground being nothing but loose and feeble sand, the first force that assaults them brings them down, and their fall (says our Saviour) is great.

Again, the apostle expresses, in proper terms, what he had represented under these two metaphors, and adds, "established in the faith." For it is properly by faith that we are rooted in Jesus Christ, and by this also we are founded upon and built up in him; all these phrases signifying only the spiritual union and connection which we have with the Lord, the sole tie of which is faith. Let us labour therefore continually to confirm our faith, if we would resist the enemy. Let us meditate on the truth of the gospel, study all its mysteries, and taste the excellency of it. Let us carefully hear and read that word in which God has revealed it to us, and by which faith has its being, as the apostle tells us; "Faith cometh by hearing, and hearing by the word of God," Rom. x. 17. From this you may judge how contrary to the apostle's injunction is the command of the church of Rome, who will not grant that the faithful should read the Scriptures. How shall they be confirmed in faith if they have no commerce with this sacred word, the only parent and nurse of faith? And how can they, without it, obey the command which the apostle gives them, in the second place, even that they abound in faith? It is not enough that we be established in it, that we have a little for necessity, he would have us furnished with it even to plenty, possessed of a great and rich measure of it, and would have this sacred light to go on still increasing and augmenting, as he says elsewhere, from faith to faith. Some are of opinion that this word must be referred, not singly to the thing, but also to the sentiment that we have of it. As if, when the apostle speaks of abounding in faith, his meaning were that we should account ourselves to have abundantly, in the faith of Jesus Christ alone, all the saving knowledge we can desire, without needing the addition of anything in any other way. This exposition is elegant and ingenious, and very pertinent to the apostle's design. But as it is followed by few, and the former is more simple, I will not insist upon it.

The apostle adds, in the third and last place, giving of thanks; "abounding in faith," he says, "with thanksgiving." His meaning is, that we should gratefully admire the excellency and abundance of the benefits which are communicated to us by the gospel; and remember the spring from whence they flow, namely, the sole grace of God, who, taking us out of the darkness of error and ignorance wherein we were plunged, has caused us to enter into the kingdom of light by the power of his word and Spirit, that we may continually render to him our grateful acknowledgments of it. And this duty is not only most reasonable in itself, it is also necessary to insure the faith of the gospel unto us; for as God augments his gifts to the thankful, so he takes them away from the unthankful, withdrawing his light from their souls, and giving them up to themselves, as you know he threatens the ungrateful churches to remove his candlestick from them. And the apostle informs us in another place, that to those who receive not the love of the truth he sends strong delusion, so that they believe a lie, which is the most dreadful punishment with which he avenges himself on the iniquity of men.

Dear brethren, that we fall not into so awful a judgment, let us possess this treasure of knowledge which God has given us in his Son with all the gratitude it demands, humbly blessing him that he has vouchsafed to impart even to us, who were so unworthy of it, a blessing so precious, and of such saving importance. Let this be all our love, and all our glory. Let others boast of their might and their skill, of their riches and their greatness; as for us, we will glory only in the knowledge of God, and of his holy gospel, the sole supreme happiness of man. Let us be jealous of this holy doctrine, keeping it pure and sincere, and carefully taking heed of the leaven of superstition and of error. Let us be content with our Lord Jesus Christ, the Prince of life, and with that fulness of grace which we have received, and the holy apostles preached. Mix nothing foreign with it; to add to it is to accuse it of imperfection and insufficiency. Instead of losing time in the inventions of error, and in the laborious but childish exercises of superstition, let us employ the whole of ours in good and holy works, walking in Jesus Christ, rooting and building up ourselves more and more in him; establishing ourselves and abounding in faith; and testifying and proving the truth of it by a pure piety towards God, and an ardent love towards our neighbour; by the fervency of our prayers, the liberality of our alms, the humility of our deportment, the modesty of our persons, the honesty, justice, and integrity of all our words and actions, to the glory of the Lord Jesus, whom we serve and own for our Master, to the edification of men, and our own salvation. Amen.

SERMON XX.

VERSE 8.

Beware lest any man spoil you through philosophy and vain deceit, after the tradition of men, after the rudiments of the world, and not after Christ.

OUR Lord Jesus Christ, comparing the society of his faithful people, in the 10th chapter of John, to a flock of sheep, informs us that there are thieves who lurk about this mystical fold, and come only to steal, to kill, and to destroy; and also that there are wolves which take away and scatter the sheep. You are not ignorant, dear brethren, that under the names of these spiritual thieves and wolves he represents to us evil spirits, and the false teachers whom they instigate, who both, though by different means, earnestly promote the same design, namely, the seducing and alienating the faithful from the communion of Jesus Christ, their only Pastor, gaining possession of, and appropriating them to themselves, as the thief who takes that which is another's, and makes it his own. Whence ensues their death and destruction. For as the wolf kills the sheep which he has seized, so these ministers of Satan destroy those whom they draw away from the flock of Christ, out of whose communion there is nothing but death and perdition. But these wretched workers employ, as I said, various means to compass their cruel and murderous design. Some they take away by open force, compelling them to leave the bosom of the church by the violence of persecutions, or drawing them into the world by the pleasures of the flesh, and thus causing them to renounce even the very name of Jesus Christ the Prince of life. Against others they make use of fraud, drawing them gradually away from Jesus Christ, under fair and plausible pretences, so as that in the end they have nothing of his left to them but a name, and a vain, unprofitable profession, remaining indeed under the power and in the possession of his enemy. It is against these mystical thieves and robbers that the apostle awakens the Colossians in the text which we have read, exhorting them to take heed of them. He besought them, in the preceding verse, to establish, to build up, to root themselves more and more in the communion of the Lord Jesus, acknowledging with humble gratitude the excellency of his gift. Now, to insure this treasure to them, he advises them to watch against the fraud and ambushments of their enemies, who sought to surprise them, and, by the artifice of their subtilties and fair discourses, to pluck Jesus Christ out of their hearts, and render themselves masters of them, and of their life. "Beware," says he, "lest any man spoil," or make a prey of "you," &c.

It is the duty of a good pastor, such a one as was the apostle, not only to feed the mystical sheep, which the chief Shepherd has committed to his care, by giving them the pure and wholesome doctrine of the gospel, the only pasture of souls, but also to preserve them, with all his power, from the paws of wolves and the hands of robbers; warning them of the danger, and dexterously delivering them out of it, by the saving tone of his voice. And as this is the duty of pastors, so, dear brethren, it is your duty to watch for your own safety; to open your eyes and senses, that you may discern a stranger from a domestic, a thief from the shepherd, the hand of a robber from that of a friend. "Beware," says the apostle to you. He would not that the faithful should be silly sheep, that suffer themselves to be led away by the first comer, and indifferently embrace all that is offered to them. His will is that we should have our senses exercised and habituated in discerning between truth and falsehood; and be able to prove all things, that we may hold fast that which is good, and not suffer ourselves to be led away, either by the dignity of a robe, or the blaze of wit, or some fair appearances of deportment, seeing that the angels of Satan sometimes clothe themselves with light. The Holy Spirit commends the prudence of the Bereans, who examined Paul's preaching, comparing what he had spoken to them with the Scriptures, that they might assuredly know the state of the matter, Acts xvii. 11. The salvation of our souls is too precious for us to trust it with any other than God. Hence it appears how dangerous is that security of implicit faith, as they call it, which, without any scruple, receives all that its teachers deliver; and is so far from examining it, that it vouchsafes not so much as to understand it; believing it true without knowing it, provided only that the mouth which publishes it has been opened by the pope's hand. If the question were only of a title, those of whom the apostle here warns the Colossians to take heed were teachers; and he contests not with them about their dignity in any part of this Epistle; he deals with them only about their doctrine. Accordingly, the case is concerning doctrine, whether we ought to believe it or not; and whatever may be the hand which delivers it to us, if it be false, it will assuredly destroy us; as poison does not fail to kill, though he who prescribes it has taken his degrees with all the requisite formalities. Paul, too, in another place, with one word overthrows all the prepossessions that might be entertained for any preachers, however eminent their personal quality, when he exclaims, "Though we, or an angel from heaven, preach any other gospel unto you, than that which we have preached unto you, let him be accursed," Gal. i. 8. Be all that you will, you cannot be more than Paul or an angel of heaven. Since their doctrine ought to be examined by the gospel, in order that it may be received or rejected, as it shall be found conformable with or contrary to it, it will be doing you no wrong if yours be put to the same test.

But consider, I pray you, with what emphasis the apostle recommends to us the importance of this duty. "Beware," says he, "lest any man spoil you." He could not with more propriety, or greater elegancy, express the danger of those who stand not on their guard, than by this expression, which properly signifies to carry away the booty which a man has taken. It is not without reason, says he, that I warn you to use all your abilities in vigilantly defending yourselves against error, for no small matter depends upon it. It is as much as your souls, yourselves, and the noblest part of your being, your understandings, your affections, your hearts, are worth. The wolves and the thieves, against whom men watch with so much care, aim only at their sheep or their purse. Those of whom I warn you aim at your persons. An enemy, against whom cities and states set guards, threatens only their goods, or at most their lives. He, against whom I require you to watch, seeks your souls, and the share they have in eternity. You are the workmanship and the jewel of the Lord of glory; you will be a prey to Satan and his ministers, if you fall into their snares. They will not be content with merely taking you; they will bring you into bondage; and the redeemed of Jesus Christ, whose liberty he has bought at the price of his divine blood, will become slaves of men, and, which is worse, of devils. Good God! how piercing was the eye of that heavenly Spirit which guided the pen of this apostle! How clearly did he discern the nature and qualities of everything of which he speaks! Observe how error triumphs over those whom it infects; see the trophies it sets up of their spoils, the fetters with which it burdens those whom it seduces, the yoke which it puts upon their necks, and the captivity into which it brings them, and you will confess that the effects of its false and damnable conquests could not possibly be more truly and more naturally represented to us than by saying, as Paul does here, that it spoils or makes a prey of christians, and carries them away as booty. For error is ever insolent. The preachers of the truth serve those whom they teach, and only style themselves their ministers, as the apostle before did: whereas the teachers of falsehood usurp dominion over those whom they have corrupted, and boast that they are their judges, their masters, and their lords. Paul observed long since, respecting the seducers of the Corinthians, that they enslaved them, devoured them, exalted themselves over them, and smote them on the face, 2 Cor. xi. 20; that is, put all kind of indignities upon them. And the false teachers among the Galatians, he says, gloried in the flesh of their miserable disciples, Gal. vi. 13. They are blind who do not at this day observe the same conduct in those men who reign over all the multitude whom they have deceived, and who rear up lofty trophies of every poor soul of whom they have made a prey. Dear brethren, if you love the liberty which the Lord Jesus has purchased for you, if you abhor the servitude of men, if you desire the fruit of the one, which is immortality, and detest perdition, the inevitable consequence of the other; in the name of God, take heed that no man make a prey of you. The doctrine of truth is enclosed within the Lord's sheepfold. Abide there, if you would be in safety. If you stray from it ever so little, you will fall into the hands of wolves and robbers. Hearken not unto their babble. Be not taken with their countenance. Let anything among them that promises fair be suspected by you, since they seek only to withdraw you from the simplicity of the gospel.

Now, the apostle here points at three things, of which he particularly advises us to take heed, namely, the vain deceit of philosophy, the traditions of men, and the rudiments of the world; because these were the three sources from which those false apostles, who were then attempting to deceive the Colossians, drew all the heads of their doctrine, and the means which they used to colour it, in order to give it that vain lustre which was needful for beguiling the simple and unlearned. For, as we shall see more particularly at the conclusion of this chapter, they enjoined the worshipping of angels, ver. 18; a doctrine which, in all likelihood, they had raked up out of the sinks of the Platonic philosophers, who related various things of these higher spirits, and of their interposition and mediation between God and us, for purifying us, and rendering us capable of supreme happiness, as we see even at this day in those remains of their writings which we possess. Again, they introduced different voluntary devotions, which did not spare the flesh, and which seemed full of humility, ver. 23, but were indeed only traditions of men, without any foundation in the word of God. Finally, it is also evident that they pressed the observation of days, and the distinction of meats, according to the ordinances of the Mosaic law, which are likewise styled elements of the world. Now though these three points particularly respect the false teachers at Colosse, yet they are common to nearly all those whoever took upon themselves to alter and sophisticate the gospel, the greater part of their impostures having issued from one of these three sources. We will consider them therefore briefly and distinctly, by the will of God, and after them the character or mark which Paul gives to them, namely, that these things are not after Christ.

I. Among these things, of which we are to beware, he gives the first place to philosophy. Its name is very honourable, signifying the love and pursuit of wisdom. But the corruptions of those men who gave their profession this name among the Grecians disgraced so worthy a term, and made it the name of a tool of error and imposture, rather than of an instrument of science and truth. For the common sort of those who styled themselves philosophers amused themselves altogether in vain speculations, in a trade of subtilty and syllogizing, and in endless disputes, which yielded no true profit to men. They thought that they had attained the end of their profession when they had acquired a faculty of speaking on all subjects with some colour and probability, so as to dazzle the eyes of the ignorant, and win the admiration of the half-witted. This vanity rendered them odious first among the pagans themselves, who commonly considered them as extravagant persons, and they were not much better esteemed by the greater part of the superior sort. And as no class of persons more fiercely opposed the gospel of our Saviour, the first christians also conceived a very ill opinion of them, which increased when it appeared that heretics ordinarily derived from the magazines of these men the arms which they used to offend the faith of the church, and to defend their own inventions. This induced one of the most ancient christian writers* to call them the patriarchs of heretics, and to say that all heresies are maintained by their rules, animated with their spirit, and lodged in their thickets and bushments, as in their strong hold. He calls them animals of glory; and all christian antiquity treats them very roughly, as we learn from that portion of the books of that time which is extant, wherein the commerce of philosophy is accounted so dangerous, that it has been charged upon some as a great crime to have but looked into the books of Aristotle, and to have learned his logic. On the other side, we meet also with fathers who have highly esteemed philosophy, and it cannot be denied but that even they who censure it often use it with great success, and to good purpose.

It is not my design to open this question, or to produce here all that may be said either for philosophy or against it. The holy apostle does not render it necessary, as he here blames not its substance, but the ill use which false teachers made of it, employing it either to the invention or the defence of their errors: this he evidently shows; for having commanded us to take heed that none spoil us through philosophy, he immediately adds, "and vain deceit;" by these words limiting what he had generally uttered, and giving us to understand that he rejected the use of philosophy only when it was made to serve

* Tertullian.

error and imposture. We must, therefore, in this, as in all other subjects, carefully distinguish the thing itself from its abuses, and the substance from what is accessory to it, and the truth from that error which is added to it by the wickedness or weakness of men. For there is nothing in the world, however good and laudable in its nature, which our vices do not pollute in using it. Intemperance has defamed wine, meats, and spices; luxury, gold, silver, precious stones, silk, and perfumes—all of them creatures of God, very good, and very excellent. Cruelty, murder, and parricide have defiled iron, a most necessary instrument of our life; and fire, without which we cannot live, has often served the rage and the injustice of tyrants. What is there more admirable than beauty among the ornaments of the body, and eloquence among the ornaments of the mind? Yet they frequently become, through the corruption of men, the means of debauchery and seduction. Even the Scriptures themselves, the most salutiferous effect of the goodness of God, are sometimes profaned by error and vice; ignorance and levity wresting them to men's own ruin, and wretchedly turning that to destruction which was given only for our salvation. It is not meant, that upon this pretence we should discontinue the use of any of the works of God, who, being infinitely wise, has made nothing that is not useful. If this were intended, it would not be lawful to make use of anything, since there is nothing which vice and ignorance does not abuse. I say the same of philosophy; if its authors among the pagans, if heretics among christians have made it serve the interest of error, it does not follow that it must be totally rejected; nor should we do as the man did, who rooted up his vines, because, having taken too much of their fruit, he was overcharged with it; or as he who would have his rose bushes burned, because he had been sometimes pricked in gathering their flowers. All that we should conclude from these things is, that this plant must be discreetly handled; the fruit enjoyed, but with moderation; the flowers gathered, but with heed taken of the thorns. This is all that the apostle forbids in the text, even deceit, and not instruction; that which is vain, and not that which is solid; error and sophistry, not science and reasoning. Philosophy itself washes its hands of its disciples' faults. It disavows their errors, and renounces all that they have brought forth without its direction by false arguments, however great their reputation may be. It is so far from defending them, that itself affords us weapons with which to combat them, and offers us its lights to discover the weakness of their false discourses. For it has observed and taught the rules of legitimate reasoning with such admirable skill, that there is no falsehood to be met with, of which it does not afford us a conviction. So if there be error in the discourses of men of this profession, (and without doubt, there is no small measure,) it is certain that in this unhappy production they have swerved from their own rule, it being impossible that a falsehood should ever be duly and rightly concluded from truth.

It follows, therefore, that no error or doctrine contrary to truth is, properly speaking, philosophy, it is an abuse of it. It may be an imagination and an extravagance of the philosopher, not a part or a true fruit of philosophy. And, when the apostle says here that heretics spoil men by philosophy; that is, as he adds, by a vain deception; he takes the word philosophy, as it is commonly received, for the accustomed and ordinary discourses of philosophers, and not for true philosophy, and that which is properly so called. As long as the philosopher carefully keeps within his own bounds, he instructs, and does not deceive. The bounds which philosophy has set itself are the things that may be known by the light of natural reason. While it keeps this road it travels securely; and I confess that what it teaches in this manner would, so far from clashing with the gospel, do it good service. For who does not see that its discoveries of the nature of plants, of living creatures, of metals and meteors, of the transmutation of elements, the motions of the heavens, of times and seasons, of the concatenation of inferior causes with the superior, and the conclusion it raises from this contemplation of there being above the universe an invisible, eternal, most wise, and almighty God, upon whom it all depends, are laudable, and excellent, and nothing in effect but a report of the handiwork of God, and a demonstration of his divinity? If the philosopher had stopped there, and had deduced nothing from these discoveries but this clear consequence, that the supreme Being, whose footsteps and whose glory he had perceived in his works, ought to be supremely adored, served, sought, and loved; never would the apostle have ordered us to be afraid of philosophy, for he himself makes use of it when he speaks to the Gentiles, as you may see in his oration to the Lycaonians and the Athenians, in the Acts, chap. xiv. and xvii. He also evidently confirms it in his Epistle to the Romans, when he says "that which may be known of God is manifest in them;" and that "the invisible things of him from the creation of the world are clearly seen, being understood of the things that are made, even his eternal power and Godhead," chap. i. 19, 20, they being considered in his works. But the misery is, that the philosophers being carried away by that vanity and curiosity which was natural to them, broke those bounds, and would needs define things which are beyond that compass, and of which reason, in the state we now are, sees not one jot. And here they necessarily fell into error and extravagancies; as persons born blind would do, should they pretend to discourse to us of colours. Such are the fancies of Plato and his scholars concerning the state of the souls of men departed from their bodies, and the purifications he devised to convey us near to the supreme Good; concerning the interposition of demons, as he calls them, or of angels, as the Scripture terms them, to present our supplications to God, and the service which he ordained for them in consequence of this good office, and a thousand other such things. Such also was the mistake of Aristotle, who, not contented with the knowledge of the present establishment of the world, would know what it was in the beginning, respecting which he had no light at all, concluding, because in the present state of things, of nothing nothing is made, that, therefore, it was never otherwise, and therefore, affirming for a certainty that the world is eternal. As if we must needs judge of the beginning of a thing by those laws under which it lives after its settlement, and limit the power of a free agent to the measure of the effect wrought; that is, as if, because God, in this frame of the world, makes nothing without matter, it therefore followed, that absolutely he could not make anything in any other way; which is as impertinent a reasoning as if you should infer, that because a painter has completed a picture with three or four colours only, it were impossible for him to draw or represent a subject with any other.

In this particular, philosophy has offended by excess, undertaking more than it could compass. It often errs likewise by defect, as when it rejects the revelation of God, resolved to admit nothing that is above its own sense and reason; as if a man who had never seen any other light than that of our fires and candles should contend that there was no other in the world. Pride made the greater part of the old philosophers fall into this impiety. It seemed to them to tarnish their glory to acknowledge that there was another school more intelligent than theirs, and that it was an injury to tell them that God had discovered secrets to others which he had hid from them. It was this vanity that spurred them on so violently against the gospel of our Lord and Saviour at the beginning. If philosophy modestly keeps its rank, if it be content with its bounds, and does not thrust away nor injure divine revelation, if it acknowledge it as its mistress, and be subject to it as Agar was to Sarah, we bid it welcome; it may be received and may abide with us. But if it usurp, if it will needs be mistress and command in a family where it has only the quality of a bond-woman, let it depart, and be treated according to the words of Sarah to Abraham: "Drive out the bond-woman and her son." God has vouchsafed to reveal to us by his prophets, and in the last times by his own Son, all the articles of religion. Philosophy ought to adore them with us. It has nothing to enjoin us in the matter. From the mouth of God, not from the mouth of philosophy, do we receive religion. As often, therefore, as teachers of error shall use the authority or artifice of philosophers to render their inventions plausible or probable in our eyes, let us boldly despise all their subtilty. Let not the names of Aristotle and Plato make us afraid; let not their petty subtilties dazzle our sight. We may hear them when the question is only of men and of nature. When God and his service are concerned, we ought to give ear to none but God and the Son of his love, respecting whom he has proclaimed from heaven to us, "This is my beloved Son, hear him." It is this the apostle intends, when he says here, "Let no man spoil you through philosophy."

But, provided the doctrine of our Lord and Saviour remain sound and entire, without diminution, without augmentation or mixture, we are not prohibited the service of philosophy, but may employ its physics and its ethics to confirm and illustrate, as far as they can, the truths of the gospel; its logic to defend them against the sophisms and sleights of gainsayers; and, in short, to adorn and embellish them, we may use anything of worth that philosophy affords; as the Israelites heretofore adorned the sanctuary of God with the gold, and silver, and jewels of Egypt. You may perceive therefore how, in the religious disputes which we have with those of Rome, they for their part evidently abuse philosophy. We duly employ it, but they abuse it. For in addition to their making Aristotle to reign in their divinity school, regarding his edicts, and cherishing much jealousy of his reputation, as if he were a pillar of religion, they found articles of their faith upon the authority of the sages of the world; as when they prove their purgatory by the testimony of Plato, the veneration of images by the custom of nations, and free-will by philosophy, and various other things of a similar nature, which, not being found in the Scriptures of God, they seek them in the writings of men. As for us, it is evident that we have no positive article in our faith but what is in the gospel. Only when our adversaries urge their transubstantiation upon us, having shown that God has nowhere revealed it to us in his word, but even clearly contradicted it, we call in philosophy itself to our succour to prove its absurdity. We produce its testimony in a case which is clearly of its cognizance, namely, the nature of a human body, the place it takes up, the quantity to which it is extended, the quality of substantial mutations, of which kind they pretend this is, whether a body made and formed sixteen hundred years ago may still be every day substantially produced.

II. But it is high time to come to the two other sources of

the deceits of false teachers. The second is the tradition of men, as the apostle calls it. "Beware lest any man spoil you through philosophy and vain deceit, after the tradition of men." The Scripture commonly gives the name of traditions to those instructions which we receive from others. And it frequently uses the word deliver (from which, in the Latin tongue, that of tradition is derived) for to instruct or teach. "I received of the Lord," says the apostle, "that which I also delivered unto you;" that is, taught. It therefore calls those doctrines traditions of men which have men only for their authors, which come from men, and not from God. I confess that errors derived from that philosophy of which he speaks in our text, may also bear the same name, since they flowed from the spirit of man, and had no other source than his imagination; yet the apostle distinguishes the one from the others, as I conceive, for two reasons: First, inasmuch as those derived from philosophy had some colour of abstruse wisdom, having sprung from speculations, in show sublime and excellent, though in reality vain and frivolous; whereas the doctrines which he here calls traditions had no foundation at all but the authority of those that set them up, and the usage of those that practised them; they being otherwise far from all philosophical reasons, not only true and solid, but also probable. Secondly, because the former had some successive continuance among the people of God, having been delivered by the Pharisees, and other zealots of Judaism, from father to son, in a series of no small length; whereas that which he calls the deceit of philosophy was not delivered in that manner, but lately invented by these new teachers, and taken from the fancies of some philosophers.

From this it appears that no productions or institutions of a human spirit are receivable in evangelical religion; whether they are those which are supported by some pretended reasons, or those that are founded upon use and antiquity. They are all of them nothing but folly and vanity in the sight of God, whatever may be the colour with which they are painted. And though men boast of their utility, they are extremely hurtful, as they pester consciences, and busy them about things which God has not ordained, and turn them aside from his pure service to things which do not profit. Accordingly, you see that our Lord Jesus Christ rejects, and roughly thrusts away, all the traditions of the Pharisees, however much esteemed they were for their antiquity and pretended use; reproaching them that by holding fast those traditions of men they let loose the commandments of God, and applying to them those words of the Lord in Isaiah, "In vain do they worship me, teaching for doctrines the commandments of men," Mark vii. 7; Isa. xxix. 13. Indeed it is an insufferable presumption, that man should attempt to prescribe the form of God's service, especially after the declaration which he himself has vouchsafed to make of his holy will; nor is there one who would endure that his servant should treat him in that manner, and instead of obeying his orders, and causing others to despatch them, begin philosophizing in his house, and giving his family a new rule to observe, as if he were wiser than his master. I know well the authors of these traditions, and those that follow them, are not without fine reasons to palliate their temerity. But it is evident that they do the very same in effect; neither is it to be doubted that a servant who should be culpable of such vanity would likewise plead his motives and designs to any that would give him audience. But common sense dictates to the meanest capacities that such undertaking spirits do not deserve even to be heard, especially where God is concerned, in comparison with whom they, with all their sufficiency, are but poor worms of the earth. Let us hold firm, therefore, this foundation of the apostle, that the traditions of men ought to have no place in religion. It does not concern me to inform myself of their antiquity, whether they be the traditions of men ancient or modern. It is sufficient that I know that they are traditions of men. Having the apostle's caution, we should not be moved with any reason, or splendour, or antiquity with which they may come clothed. If you would have me receive them, show me that they are prescriptions of God, institutions of his Christ, doctrines of his Scriptures. Without this, however specious you may cause them to appear to me, I shall ever believe it is but to make a prey of me; and your diligence shall have no other effect than to make me suspect them the more.

III. But the apostle adds a third source from which the seducers drew both their doctrine, and the means to colour it, namely, that which he calls "the rudiments" or elements "of the world." I pass by the opinion of those who refer these words to the elements of nature, water, air, earth, and fire; as if the apostle here taxed these false teachers with reducing the service of them, which was then in full vogue among the heathen; these wretched idolaters having anciently deified all the parts of the universe. There is not a word in Paul's writings, either here or elsewhere, that leads us to such a conclusion; and it is not very likely that the persons at whom he here aims should authorize so brutal a kind of idolatry; persons who covered themselves with the name of Jesus Christ, and made profession, at least outwardly, of retaining his gospel. It is clear that the apostle, in other places, means, by the elements of the world, not these primogenial and more simple substances, out of which all natural generations are framed; but the ceremonies and carnal services of the Mosaic law, under which the ancient people lived, until the revelation of the Messiah. "When we were children," (and you know he calls all that time in which it was under the dispensation of Moses the childhood of the church,) we "were in bondage under the elements of the world;" and a little after, in contempt, he styles them "weak and beggarly elements," whereunto the Galatians desired "again to be in bondage," Gal. iv. 3, 9. Now it is evident the error of the Galatians was, that they would still be subject to the ceremonial law. In the 20th verse of this chapter he uses a similar expression: "If ye be dead with Christ from the rudiments of the world, why, as though living in the world, are ye subject to ordinances?" There is then no doubt that in this place he signifies by these words, "the rudiments of the world," the observations and devotions of the ceremonial law. And, indeed, we shall see hereafter that these seducers whom he combats in this chapter would hold fast that law, either in whole or in part, subjecting the faithful to circumcision, and various regulations about meats and days.

Paul calls them "the rudiments of the world," because they were the first and the lowest lessons which the church received during the time of its childhood; they were as its alphabet. For the word "rudiments," or elements, is often taken for the first lessons, in which they are taught to know their letters. These letters are also called elements, because, in speech, words are made up of them, even as natural bodies are formed of those first and more simple substances which we properly call elements. And he calls the Jewish church "the world," because its state and its worship were carnal and terrestrial, and in a manner worldly, in comparison with that of the new Israel, whom the Lord formed to worship God in spirit and in truth. Consequently he calls all the knowledge of the Jewish rabbis "the wisdom of this world," and those rabbis themselves "the princes of this world," 1 Cor. ii. 6, 8. However hoary-headed and venerable therefore were these rudiments of the world, the apostle would not that the faithful should suffer themselves to be insnared under that pretence by those seducers who advanced their observance. Thus you see what were those three colours with which these men painted their doctrine: the vain speculations of philosophy; the antiquity of tradition; and the authority of the Mosaic ceremonies.

IV. The apostle adds, "and not after Christ." By these very few words, as with one blow, he beats down all the speciousness of these strange doctrines. Let men decorate them (says he) as much as they will; let them colour them with the subtilties of philosophy; let the practice of them be authorized by tradition; let them be recommended under the name of Moses, and by the respect we owe to the rudiments of the former world; still it is our duty to reject them, not only as unprofitable, but as even dangerous, since they are "not after Christ." He says that they are not so, first, because the Lord Jesus has told us nothing of them in his gospel; it therefore appears that we have good ground to reject from our belief all that is not found in the Scriptures of the New Testament. Secondly, because the doctrine of Jesus Christ is wholly spiritual and celestial; whereas those traditions and legal observances were gross and carnal. And lastly, because they not only possess no correspondence with the nature of the gospel, but they also turn men aside from the Lord Jesus, causing them to seek a part of their salvation in some other source than in him, in whom it is so entirely seated, that not the least drop of it is to be had in any other. And whatever show those who follow these traditions make of being resolved to retain Jesus Christ, experience enables us to see that they but very slightly cleave to him; busying themselves wholly in the performance of their own devotions, and placing the greatest part of their confidence in them; and this they do because these observances are more grateful to them, both on account of their novelty, and of their being voluntary, and indeed of less difficulty, it being much more easy to the flesh to perform some external and corporeal observances, than to embrace Jesus Christ with a lively faith, dying to the world, and living to him alone.

Such are the particulars which we desired to notice upon this caution of the apostle. Remember, dear brethren, it is also addressed to you, since you have adversaries who solicit your belief in the same manner as those who at first combated the faith of the Colossians. They propose to you the same errors, and paint and gild them over in the same manner, with the vain colours of philosophy, with the plausible name of tradition, and with the authority of Moses. They are either doctrines drawn from the speculations of philosophers, as the invocation of angels and of departed saints, the veneration of images, the state of souls in purgatory, and other similar doctrines; or human traditions, as prayer for the dead, quadragesimal observances, the hierarchy, the primacy of the bishop of Rome, monkery, celibacy, and others, all erected by men, without any foundation in the word of God. Or, lastly, they are elements of the world, ceremonial observances, originally instituted by Moses, but abolished by Jesus Christ, as the distinction of meats, festivals, unctions, consecrations, sacrifices, and residence in certain places. Of all that we reject in our doctrine, there is not a particular but refers to one of these three heads.

Remember, therefore, when you are assailed with these errors, that the apostle still to this day calls to you aloud from heaven, "Beware lest any man spoil you through philosophy and vain deceit, after the tradition of men, after the rudiments of the world, and not after Christ." Under these fair appearances there is hidden a pernicious design. Men would take you away from Jesus Christ, and make you a prey to, and the vassals of, men. Oppose to all their artifices this one saying of the apostle's, that whatever may be the things which are enjoined, they are "not after Christ;" they are not found in that Testament wherein he has declared his whole will; they have no conformity with the nature of his gospel, but turn away the minds of men from that sovereign Lord, in whom alone is our wisdom and our righteousness, our sanctification and redemption.

But, faithful brethren, as the apostle's lesson should defend you from error, so should it preserve you from vice. Let that Jesus whom he so assiduously preaches to you, be the rule of your conduct as well as the object of your faith. Love none but him, as you believe in none but him. Renounce the customs and vices of the world as well as its religion. Let the leaven of philosophy have no more place in your actions than in your belief. Receive the customs of men into your communion no more than the traditions of men. If you be above the rudiments of the world, be also above its infancy, and its low and childish passions and affections; they were sometimes pardonable in that childhood, but are inexcusable in persons whom Jesus Christ has advanced to perfect men, and such as by his illumination he has brought to a fulness and maturity of age. Let your souls henceforth have thoughts and affections noble and heavenly, and worthy of those high instructions which Jesus Christ has given you. Let your whole life have relation to him, passing by the world and its elements, this present generation, and its lusts and idols, with which the Lord Jesus does not participate. He has crucified all those things for us, and displayed before our eyes a new world, brought forth out of the bosom of eternity; a world incorruptible, and radiant with such glory as can neither fade nor be sullied. Hither, faithful brethren, you should elevate your desires. This is true christian discipline, to die with Jesus to this old world, having no more sentiment or passion for its perishing benefits, and to live again with the same Jesus in that new world into which he is entered for us; to breathe after nothing but its glory, to think of nothing but its purity, to rejoice in nothing but its peace, and the hope of its eternal pleasures; to forget for ever that which is past, and to press with all our might towards the mark and prize of our high calling; justifying the truth of our religion by the holiness of our conversation, so as that there may no more appear among us either ambition, or hatred, or avarice, or any of those loathsome defilements which disfigure the lives of worldlings. May the Lord Jesus, who has given us this excellent divine doctrine, who has founded it by his death, and established it by his resurrection; who also has in these latter times purged it afresh of the vanities of philosophy, of the traditions of men, and of the elements of the world; be pleased to confirm us in it for ever by his good Spirit, and to make it so efficacious for the sanctification of our life, that after we have finished this earthly pilgrimage, and quitted this vale of tears, we may receive from his merciful hand the crown of immortality, which he has promised and prepared for all his true followers. Amen.

SERMON XXI.

VERSE 9.

For in him dwelleth all the fulness of the Godhead bodily.

As the christian religion consists in principles and practices incomparably more sublime and salutiferous than any which the world ever learned in the schools of nature and of the law, so it was delivered and instituted by an author infinitely more excellent than any of those who erected other systems among men. I will not, however, draw a comparison between Christ and the authors of those various religions which prevailed in the time of paganism; who, though they were in esteem among nations, and obtained a high reputation for wisdom and virtue, yet have the taint of extreme ignorance and vanity; as their own institutions will sufficiently show to any one who will take the pains to examine them in the light of reason. It would be injurious to the Lord Jesus, the Founder and Prince of christianity, to compare him with such people. But even Moses himself, the great teacher of the Hebrews, and the prophets, who commented on, explained, and confirmed his law, are all infinitely beneath the dignity of this new Lawgiver. They were, I grant, ministers of God, the mouth and organs of his Majesty, the interpreters of his will, and heralds of his truth; being endued, as was suitable to such high offices, with an excellent sanctity, a rare and extraordinary wisdom, and a heavenly power, which evinced itself in them by miraculous effects. But after all they were men, and never pretended to rank above that feeble nature which was common to them and to us, nor did they receive any of those honours which belong to the divine; whereas the Lord Jesus, who is God blessed for ever as well as man, was so far from refusing divine honours, that he has expressly required them at our hands, and commanded us to adore him with the Father, and to acknowledge him his eternal Son.

This same difference the apostle observes between the Lord Jesus and those other ministers which God made use of in the former ages: "God," says he, "who at sundry times, and in divers manners, spake in time past unto the fathers by the prophets, hath in these last days spoken unto us by his Son," Heb. i. 1. Moses and the rest were prophets of God, Jesus is his Son. The others were his ministers, Jesus is his Heir. The others were faithful as servants, Jesus as Son is over the whole house, Heb. iii. 5, 6. In the others there shone forth some marks of the commerce which they had with God; that sovereign Majesty imprinting on their faces, as upon that of Moses in particular, some sparklings of his glory. But Jesus is his very light, the brightness of his glory, and the express image of his person. Dear brethren, it highly concerns us to know rightly this great dignity of our Lord and Saviour; not only for rendering to his person the worship which is due to him, and of which we must not fail without offending the Father, as he himself has told us, "He that honoureth not the Son, honoureth not the Father which hath sent him," John v. 23; but also for our embracing with so much greater zeal the religion which he has delivered to us, without ever admitting the persuasion that either men on earth, or even angels from heaven, can add anything to the light, the goodness, and the perfection of the gospel, which is derived from so great and so perfect an author. For this cause Paul here holds forth to the Colossians the divinity of our Lord Jesus Christ.

In the preceding verses he exhorted them to constant perseverance in the belief of his gospel, confirming themselves in it more and more, and taking heed that they gave no ear to philosophy, and the vain traditions of seducers, who endeavoured to corrupt sound doctrine by mixing with it divers inventions, as if it were not perfect enough of itself to guide us to salvation. The apostle, to deprive error of this pretext, and to show the faithful not only the sufficiency, but even the abounding of the gospel, represents to them the sovereign perfection and divinity of its author. "For in him," says he, "dwelleth all the fulness of the Godhead bodily." As if he had said, Since you have Jesus Christ, there is no need of recourse to others. In him, as in a living and inexhaustible spring, is all good necessary to your happiness; a divine authority to found your faith, an infinite wisdom to direct you in all truth, an incomprehensible goodness and power to give you grace and glory, a quickening Spirit to sanctify and comfort you. All other things, when compared with him, are but poverty and weakness. See how the apostle fortifies the faithful in the doctrine of the Lord, and in a few words overthrows all that the presumption of flesh and blood would dare to set up beside or against his perfect truth.

For a right understanding of his words, we must consider them particularly. For though the number of them is small, their weight is great; they are rich and magnificent in sense, and contain within their narrow compass one of the noblest and fullest descriptions of Jesus Christ that is found in Scripture. Let us see then, first, what all this fulness of the Godhead is of which the apostle speaks. And then, in the second place, how it dwells in Jesus Christ, namely, "bodily." The Lord be pleased to conduct us by the light of his own Spirit in so high a meditation, that "of his fulness we may receive grace for grace;" and draw from it that which may fill our souls with that life and salvation which overflows in him, and can be nowhere found but in him.

I. As to the subject itself of which Paul speaks, and in which he says that "all the fulness of the Godhead dwelleth," none can doubt that it is our Lord Jesus Christ. For having said, at the end of the verse immediately preceding, that the traditions of men and the rudiments of the world are not after Christ, he now adds, "For in him dwelleth all the fulness of the Godhead." It is therefore clear that the Lord Jesus Christ is the person of whom he speaks, and to whom he attributes all this fulness. That man must have been ignorant indeed who did not know who this Jesus was of whom the apostle speaks. All knew him, at least confusedly, and in gross; they knew that he was a man born of Mary in Judea; who having lived some years among the Jews, had been at length crucified by the sentence of Pontius Pilate; and who, being risen from the grave to a new life, had sent forth his apostles to preach his gospel, and afterwards ascended up into heaven. And though all did not believe that he was risen again and glorified, yet all well knew that this was said of him; so that all who heard Jesus Christ named immediately conceived in their minds the idea of this person, born and dying in Judea, at such times and at such places, having a retinue of disciples during his life and after his death. This then is the subject of whom Paul speaks, even Jesus Christ considered under this form of a man, in which he manifested himself to the world, and in which he was conceived and figured in the minds of those who heard him named. In this man, whose appearance was like that of other men, who was born and bred on earth, sustained during his life with our common food, subject to our infirmities, who passed through the varieties of our ages, suffered our griefs, felt our inconveniences, and experienced the pains of death, yea, of the most cruel death that was ever suffered; in this man, I say, whose body was nailed to a cross, and deprived of its soul, and buried in a sepulchre; in this man, under so mean and contemptible a form, "dwelleth (says the apostle) all the fulness of the Godhead."

It is ordinary in the Hebrew language, to signify by the fulness of anything that which the thing contains; as by the fulness of the earth, Psal. xxiv. 1, are understood men and other living creatures which fill it; and by the fulness of the sea, the isles which the sea contains. After this mode of expression the qualities and perfections of any particular nature may be called its fulness, because they are the things which fill it, and with them it is, as it were, furnished and adorned, as the movables and ornaments of a room or a house are its fulness. Therefore if I should say that in Adam, as he was at first created, was found all the fulness of manhood, every one would easily perceive that my meaning would be, that the perfections of human nature, the faculties, and properties, and beauties of which it is full, and without which it cannot sustain the dignity of that name, were all in Adam,—an immortal soul, a vigorous understanding, a free-will, a body of excellent beauty, acute senses, and all the other faculties which have any place among the perfections of the nature of man. So when we hear the apostle saying that the "fulness of the Godhead" is in Jesus Christ; let us understand that by this he means those perfections and qualities which fill up the divine nature, in which this great and sovereign being consists, and which theologians commonly call the attributes of God. You know what the word Godhead signifies, even the nature and essence of God. "The fulness of the Godhead" then is that rich and incomprehensible abundance of perfections, of which the supreme and adorable nature is full; namely, his life, his power, his wisdom, his justice, his goodness, his immensity, his eternity, his holiness, and all the other properties, which it has in an ineffable manner; and which our understandings, according to their mean capacity, conceive in it; as the form of the Deity, that is necessary for its having that name; a nature that wants it being incapable of being called God otherwise than falsely and improperly. I grant that some resemblances, or rather some touches and lineaments, of these perfections of the Godhead appear in the noblest of the creatures; as in the angels for instance, who are immortal, and endowed with superior holiness, virtue, and power. But the fulness of them is not in any creature at all; neither can it be found that ever the Scripture speaks in this manner of angels, and says that the "fulness of the Godhead" is in them. Besides, these blessed spirits, and other creatures, however excellent you may imagine them to be, participate in these divine perfections only in a very little measure; whereas the Lord Jesus has them wholly. And to make this evident to us, the apostle thought it not enough to say that the "fulness of the Godhead" is in him; but expressly declared that "all" this fulness dwelleth in him; that we might be assured that there is not any perfection, or excellency, or attribute in the divine nature that is not found in him.

Thus, in these two or three words, he has comprised all that the Scriptures teach us in various places of the richness of the perfections of our Lord and Saviour. For instance, it tells us that he is full of grace and truth; that he is the wisdom and the power of the Father; that he has the words of life; that he is the way, the truth, and the life; that in him are hid the treasures of wisdom and knowledge; that he has that might and strength which sustains all things now, and which created them at first; that he is the everlasting Father, and has immortality and incorruption; and has an infinite understanding, whereby he tries the reins and discerns all the thoughts of the hearts of men; that he has a pre-eminent glory, to which all creatures ought to do homage, yea, the angels themselves, who indeed adore him; the empire and dominion over all the world; the right and authority to judge all men, and a multitude of such things as these. Truly Paul has comprised it all in one word, saying here that "all the fulness of the Godhead" is in Jesus Christ; it being evident that if he wanted any of these names, rights, and attributes, he could not have "all the fulness of the Godhead," which is here ascribed to him.

II. But let us now see in what manner he possesses these things: the apostle expresses it very briefly, saying that all this fulness of the Godhead dwelleth in him "bodily." First, the term "dwelleth" is significant, importing that all this copious abundance of perfections does not reside in Jesus Christ for a time only, appearing for a short period and then withdrawing again, so making a transient stay in him for a few moments and no more; but that it abides in him constantly, and for ever; for so the word *dwell* in Scripture signifies. The word and the glory of God appeared in Moses and the prophets, when, being moved by the power of his Spirit, they uttered and acted divine things; but it dwelt not in them. It only rested on them a few hours, in order that by those marks of God's providence, and of his communion with them, his servants might be rendered acceptable and their authority be confirmed. Whereas the whole "fulness of the Godhead" was, and is, and ever shall be in Christ Jesus. Therefore the apostle speaks expressly in the present tense, and says "dwelleth" in him, not that it had dwelt in him, that no one might imagine that at any time it retreated.

But however great and admirable is the signification of the word "dwelleth," yet the Scripture frequently makes use of it to express the continual solicitude which divine Providence has for the faithful; as when it is said in many places that God dwelleth in the midst of his people; and when the Lord himself says, with reference to his ark, whereon he sometime manifested himself to his ancient people, "I will dwell among the children of Israel, and will be their God," Exod. xxix. 45. And when again, speaking of Zion, he says, "This is my rest for ever: here will I dwell, because I have desired it," Ps. cxxxii. 14. The apostle therefore, to distinguish and sever the dwelling of the Godhead in Jesus Christ from the now mentioned and all other kinds of its dwelling other where, adds that the fulness thereof dwelleth in him "bodily." He opposes body to a shadow or an image; as when he says in this chapter, concerning the ceremonies of the law, that they were "shadows of things to come; but the body is of Christ," ver. 17. "The body," that is, the truth and thing itself. The shadow is but a slight and imperfect representation of it. I think therefore that it is in this sense the apostle says here that the fulness of the Godhead dwelleth bodily in Christ; that is to say, really and truly; in substance, and not in shadow; in truth and not in figure. The Godhead dwelt in time past in the ark of the covenant, but in shadow only. For it was not the supreme Majesty itself that was present there; but a symbol only, and some token of his glory; whereas it is the body itself (if I may so speak) of the divinity, and not its shadow, that resides in Jesus Christ; all the perfections thereof being in him really, and in their whole truth.

By this is excellently represented to us that admirable and ineffable union of the divinity with the flesh of our Saviour which the church ordinarily calls personal; so close a union, that this flesh, and the Word which assumed it, make but one and the same person; the human nature of Jesus Christ subsisting only in the person of the Son. For if it were otherwise, it could not be said that the fulness of the Godhead dwells bodily in Christ. He would not have the body of it, any more than the creatures have, to whom it communicates itself. He would have only some lineaments and shadows of it, and not the very thing itself. For example, God dwelt heretofore in his ark, inasmuch as he manifested his presence in it. But because the things which he placed and exhibited there were not his very nature, or the selfsame perfections with which it is filled; but some simple effects of his power, whereby the images of some of his perfections were in a manner delineated; it is evident that it cannot be truly said that the fulness of his Godhead dwelt there bodily. Thus also he manifested himself to Moses in the burning bush; and afterwards to the apostles in cloven tongues as of fire; and before that, the Holy Ghost appeared in the form of a dove. But besides that these manifestations being but transient, it cannot be said that God dwelt in the bush, or in the places where those other symbols appeared. In addition to this, it is evident that the flame at the bush was not at all the divine nature, or any one of its perfections; and that neither the dove nor the fiery tongues were any more the proper essence of the Holy Ghost, or any one of his real and divine perfections; all these things being but forms created by God, and consequently his productions and works, in which he represented to his servants, as in a portrait or rough sketch, some slight resemblance of what he is indeed. Supposing however that it might with propriety be said (which it cannot be) of the places where these things appeared, that the fulness of the Godhead dwelt in them, still it would be false to say that it dwelt in them bodily; it being clear that the things on account of which it would be said to have dwelt there were not the body and the truth of his nature, but its shadow and symbol only. I say the same of prophets, and of saints, and of angels themselves, to whom God most intimately communicates himself. For the things, in consequence of which the Scripture says that he dwells in them, are holiness, joy, and knowledge, which he works and preserves in them. Now every one sees that neither the knowledge, nor the piety, nor the charity, nor the joy, nor the constant and uninterrupted felicity of the saints, are the very nature of God, or the body itself (if I may so speak) of his immense and incomprehensible perfections, in which the fulness of his Godhead consists: these things are only effects and works of God, engravings and impressions of his hand, marks of his operation; so that however high may be their excellency, and however exact the image of God in these saints, yet it cannot be said that the fulness of the Godhead dwells in them bodily, since it is clear from what has been said that it dwells in them by shadows only, by the illustrious and glorious traces which his operation has left in them, and not in substance. We conclude then from the apostle's express assertion here, that all the fulness of the Godhead dwelleth bodily in Christ; that the divinity is in him after a totally different manner than either in the symbols, by which it is represented, or the creatures, on which he sheds his grace and glory; that it so dwells in Jesus Christ, as that he has in him not some delineations and models by which it is portrayed, not those qualities and dispositions alone which it works by the presence of its grace in the most holy of its creatures; but its very self: that he has the body and verity of it, that is, (as the church expresses this mystery in one word,) that the Godhead is personally united with his flesh; it being not otherwise possible that the fulness of the Godhead should dwell in him bodily.

Now that such is this divine union of the eternal Word with the flesh of Jesus Christ, appears, first, from the fact that neitheir the apostle nor any other of the sacred writers, ever said of saints or angels that which we here read of our Lord; namely, that all the fulness of the Godhead dwelleth in him bodily; an evident sign that this is a glory which appertains to none but him alone. Secondly, from the qualities, the actions, and the attributes of the divinity being communicated to the Man who was born of the blessed virgin; and reciprocally the sufferings, the qualities, and the actions of the flesh, which was born of Mary, being attributed to the eternal Son of God; as when the Scripture says that God has redeemed the church with his own blood; that the Lord of glory was crucified; that Jesus Christ is before Abraham was; that he founded the earth at the beginning, and the heavens are the work of his hands; and other similar expressions. Dear brethren, such is the sense of these divine words of the apostle. Admire the force and the richness of the Scripture, which has in so few words blasted and beaten down all the inventions and dogmatizings of error against the truth, respecting the two natures of our Lord and Saviour, and of the union of them in his person.

First, these words overthrow the impiety of those who bereave Jesus Christ of his divinity, and reduce him to the degree and condition either of a mere man, or of a person raised indeed above man, yet made and created at the beginning, as well as other celestial and terrestrial creatures. How can such blasphemy subsist before this sacred oracle, which proclaims not simply that the divinity, but that the Godhead, and not this simply either, but that the fulness of the Godhead, yea, in addition to this, that all the fulness of the Godhead, dwelleth in him bodily? If he be but a man, no part of this fulness of the Godhead dwells in him; neither its power, nor its wisdom, neither its goodness nor its justice, neither its glory nor its eternity. For none of these divine qualities dwell in one who is but a man. We must affirm that he has in him verily those perfections that fill up the Godhead, (that is, the divine nature,) or deny that all the fulness of the Godhead dwelleth in him. But if you grant me (as deny it you cannot, without giving the the apostle the lie) that all the fulness of the Godhead dwells in him, you must of necessity confess also that he is God; no one (if he be not God) being capable of receiving, holding, and possessing in himself the fulness of God. For this fulness being infinite, there is none but God that can contain it, since there is none but he alone who is infinite. Now it dwells all in our Lord Jesus Christ; it must therefore of necessity be confessed that he is God of a nature infinite.

The frigid and frivolous evasions of those impious men are therefore refuted, who, taking away from Jesus Christ the reality and true glory of divinity, leave him only the name, and make a titular God of him; a God (as they affirm) created and raised up some time since, who has but the title of God, not the nature; the office, not the essence. Who can sufficiently detest the audaciousness of these deceivers, who, by this impiety, overthrow all the ground-work of the Scripture, which reveals nothing more clearly or more expressly than the oneness of the true God; who is likewise so jealous of his glory, as that he forbids us, upon pain of death, to give his name, or his worship, or his attributes to any creature, whatever may be his quality? If Jesus Christ be not the true eternal God, Creator of the heavens and the earth, how will you, miserable men, avoid this condemnation, you that give him the name and the adoration of the true God? But Paul lays all their subtilty in the dust, by formally saying that "all the fulness of the Godhead dwelleth in him bodily." The fulness of the Godhead is not an empty name, or a titular dignity. It is that which fills it; it is that glory, that light, that nature, that truth, and that perfection, with which the Godhead is full. It is this therefore that dwells in Jesus Christ, the substance of a true and real divinity, not a hollow and a vain shadow; it is the essence and not the title of Deity.

But as the apostle by these words condemns the impiety of those who bereave our Lord and Saviour of the glory of his divinity, so he likewise confounds the extravagance of others, who deprive him of his human nature, foolishly affirming that he had but a false appearance in the flesh. For here are two subjects clearly presented to us; one that dwells (that is, the fulness of the Godhead); another, in which this fulness dwells, namely, Jesus Christ; the one is the temple, the other is the God that resides in that temple; the one our Saviour's human nature, the other the eternal Son of the Father; two real and veritable subjects, by the wonderful union of which this sacred and adorable sanctuary of God is composed. To take away the truth, either of his Godhead, with the former, or of his flesh with the latter, is to destroy the fabric. Again, these words of the apostle in the same manner overthrow the error of those who have corrupted the union of these two natures in Jesus Christ; on one hand by dividing them, as did the Nestorians; and on the other by confounding them, as did the Eutychians. For if we sever Jesus Christ into two persons, the fulness of the Godhead will not dwell bodily in his flesh. This man will have but gifts of the divinity, which are, as it were, some resemblance and lineaments of it; he will not have the truth and the very body of it. Neither must it be replied, that the temple in which God resides is a substance different from his person; for the body is the residence of the soul; yet soul and body have but one and the same subsistence, and constitute but one and the same person. So that the dwelling of the Son in his human nature, as in his temple, does not prevent his human nature from subsisting with him in one and the same person. Yet though we must not divide these two natures of our Lord, it does not follow that we must mix and confound them, as they do who define the union of them by the human nature being made equal with the divine, and maintain that it is infinite, and immense, and endowed really in itself with all the properties of the divine nature. The apostle says, indeed, that the fulness of the Godhead dwells in Christ, but he does not say that his flesh was really changed into the Godhead. The body, by being personally united to the soul, does not thereby become soul. It preserves its own nature, and derives only this advantage from that intimate connection which knits it with the soul, that they subsist together, and make up but one and the same person. Just so, the flesh of our Lord, by the Word's dwelling in it, becomes with it one selfsame person, being truly the body, and the soul, and, in one word, the nature of the Son of God; yet it still keeps its original being and essential properties. The Lord is a true Divinity, dwelling in a true flesh, and true flesh dwelt in by a true Divinity. There is a Divinity and a humanity truly distinct one from the other, and each of them retaining its own being and proper qualifications; but there is one only and the same person, who takes his name sometimes from the one, and sometimes from the other, and sometimes jointly from them both. For we call him the Son of Mary and the seed of David, by reason of his flesh; the everlasting God, and the Word of the Father, and the Lord of glory, on account of his Divinity; Immanuel, (that is to say, God with us,) and God manifested in flesh, by reason of these two natures together.

I confess that this is a mystery that surpasses our comprehension, and a wonder that has no parallel. But we must not measure the truths of religion by the rule of our understandings, especially when the question relates to God, whose nature reason itself confesses to be infinite and incomprehensible. It is sufficient that the word of the Lord informs us that it is so; and though our reason cannot discern the manner of this union, yet it being once illuminated by divine revelation, it acknowledges a kind of necessity for it. For presupposing what the Scripture reveals and reason approves, of the desert of sin, the infinite punishment that is due to it, and the inflexible constancy of divine justice, which cannot let sin pass unpunished, it evidently follows that man could not have been reconciled to God unless his justice were satisfied, nor his justice have been satisfied without a sacrifice of infinite worth and merit.

So it being the office of Christ to reconcile men unto God, it is clear that for effecting this great design he must offer to the Father a sacrifice of infinite value, and consequently be God; since nothing can proceed from a finite subject but what is also finite, and none is infinite but God alone. It was necessary, therefore, for our redemption, that all the fulness of the Godhead should dwell bodily in our Mediator; not to speak of other advantages which this admirable union of our nature with the divine, in the person of Jesus Christ, affords us—as the assurance it gives us of the infinite love of God, and of our salvation; the title it procures us to the merits of our Saviour, whom it has made our Brother, and consequently rendered us capable of being his co-heirs; the consolation of Him whom we serve which it sheds into our hearts, he having an infinite power and wisdom to defend us in our conflicts, to strengthen us in our weakness, to preserve us against all the assaults of hell and the world, and to redeem us from death, the last of our enemies; it being evident, that if we had but a mere man for a saviour, however holy and excellent he might be, there would remain to us still very great and just causes of diffidence and fear.

Therefore, blessed for ever be the Father of our Lord; blessed be his love, and that great mercy which induced him to send us so excellent and admirable a Mediator, who has all the fulness of the Godhead dwelling in him bodily. Let us receive him with faith, adore him with devotion, and serve him with zeal. Neither let his flesh be an offence to us. It is very flesh I grant, but the flesh of an eternal God; who, under this pavilion of his visible abasement of himself, which the world so insolently despised, has lodged all the glory of heaven, and all the fulness of the Divinity. Nor let his majesty, and this fulness of the Godhead, which dwells in him, affright us. He is a great God I confess, but a God manifested in flesh, dwelling in our nature, humbling himself to our condition, and partaking of our flesh and our blood, that he might bring us to himself. Let us embrace with reverence that most sacred religion which he has brought us from heaven. And, indeed, if the world has followed and held fast, and still in various places follows and holds fast, with so much earnestness, religions invented and erected by vain men, who were full of ignorance and error, what respect do we not owe to our religion, which has been given to us by the hand and mouth of a person in whom dwelleth all the fulness of the Godhead! Moses was but God's servant, and you see what respect the ancient people bore him, and with what severity all disobediences and rebellions against his ordinances were punished; and how that poor nation still at this day in vain adores the sepulchre and relics of the law, which died and was abrogated long ago.

What penalties, then, must we expect, if we despise the doctrine of the Son, who is eternally blest with the Father—this "great salvation," as the apostle calls it, "which began to be spoken by the Lord!" Heb. ii. 3. All other religions are perished, or will in time perish. Even that of Moses waxed old, and in the end was abolished. But the institutions of Christ shall remain for ever all-holy and all-perfect, immutable and unalterable; nor do they need any reformation, or addition or amplification. After the Lord, we do not look for any other new teacher to come into the world. Moses promised the people of God another prophet after his death. Jesus Christ, the Prophet so promised, will have no successor. He does not promise us any; but only assures us of various seducers who would usurp his name, and counterfeit his voice, and put on sheep's clothing, to seduce his disciples. We ought, therefore, to shun all those who pretend to add anything whatever to his sacred doctrine.

Besides, the qualification, our Lord and Saviour, is sufficient to induce us to content ourselves with him, and to give ear to no other. "For in him," says the apostle, "dwelleth all the fulness of the Godhead bodily." Seeing he has fulness, the man can want nothing who possesses him; according to what John saith, "He that hath the Son hath life," 1 John v. 12; that is, eternal salvation, which is all that we desire. This short sentence of the apostle is enough to secure us against the artifices of all seducers. If they set before us the delicacies and subtilties of philosophy, colouring their fond imaginations with a vain semblance of wisdom, let us arm ourselves with this consideration, that we have in Christ Jesus all the true wisdom that is, since in him dwelleth all the fulness of the Godhead. If any man offer to us ancient traditions, let us remember that the authors of them were but men; who, however great and holy, were all liable to error: whereas the gospel which we embrace is his doctrine in whom all the fulness of the Godhead dwelleth bodily, and consequently it is pure and divine truth. As for those ancients, and bishops, and pontiffs, whose names and authority are urged upon us by our adversaries, I know not who they were; or, to speak more correctly, I know well that they were men subject to failing; so that neither you nor I can have any firm and certain assurance that their assertions are true. But as for this Jesus, with whose gospel I am content, we all know that he was the Son of God, in whom wisdom and truth dwell bodily, with all the fulness of the Deity. Moses himself must be silent when the Lord Jesus appears, as the stars withdraw their light when the sun sheds abroad his resplendent beams. The law of Moses is no longer worthy of regard when the gospel of Jesus is risen.

In conclusion: this sentence of the apostle overturns not only all the traditions of men in general, but even each of them singly and in particular. For example, we are pressed to serve and invocate angels and departed saints. I will not for the present allege that God, whose voice is the rule of my faith, has given no command about it. I will not say that religious worship does not belong to any creature. I will not inquire whether saints hear in heaven the prayers which are directed to them on the earth; nor whether, being finite and created, they behold the motions of our hearts: I will only demand of our adversaries why they would have us to serve and invocate saints. To the end (say they) that we may gain their favour and their intercession with the Father. But, poor men, have we not in Jesus Christ all the grace and favour that we need? And if we had nothing else to urge, would it not be great imprudence for us to have recourse to others, since we have him near to us in whom dwelleth all the fulness of the Deity? They extol the merits and satisfactions of the saints, and the indulgences of their popes. I enter not upon a strict examination of these things; nor do I make inquiry for the present, whether or not they are in reality merits, and satisfactions, and indulgences. If they really are what those men affirm them to be, yet it is clear that they are useless to us; since we find in Jesus Christ, who is sufficient for us, all the fulness of the Godhead, dwelling in him even bodily. If you have need of mercy, of grace, of consolation, of righteousness, of merit, of assistance, of life, none of these good things are wanting in him, in whom dwelleth all the fulness of the Deity. And I am well assured that you will find no portion of them anywhere else, either in heaven or in earth. But though some drop of them might be met with elsewhere; yet it is certain (and you yourselves will not deny it) that these blessings are not to be obtained, either in saints or in angels, so undoubtedly, or so abundantly, as in Jesus Christ. Why, then, while I have so rich a treasure in my hands, would you wish me to go begging elsewhere? It is sufficient for me to be saved. Since the fulness of things necessary for my salvation dwells in Jesus Christ, I will content myself with having recourse to him alone, with fixing my trust and my love on him, and with addressing my services and supplications to him; nor will I be so imprudent as to lose, or, at least, hazard my time and my devotions, in directing them to others, while I am sure that I may successfully offer them to him.

Dear brethren, let us hold to this Lord alone. Let us not divide our adorations between him and any other. Let him alone have our whole hearts, and all our desires, since he alone has all that fulness which is necessary to make us happy. He is the true Fountain of living water; let us not draw from any other source: we have no need of cisterns; this divine Rock, that follows the camp of his own Israel, can abundantly satisfy all his people. He wants nothing who has fulness. Only let us bring him souls hungering after his benefits, and thirsting for his righteousness; hearts longing for the pleasures of his sanctuary, and panting after him as the hart after the brooks of water. Let us serve him constantly, and keep faithfully the holy doctrines which he has given us in a continual exercise of piety and charity. This is all that he demands for the love he has borne us, for the favours he has bestowed upon us, and for the glory which he promises us. Let us not deny him, I beseech you, so just a return. Let us do what he requires of us, and he will liberally give what we ask of him. He will, through his great goodness, communicate this divine fulness to us which dwells in himself; that being justified by his merit, guided by his light, upheld by his power, enriched by his treasures, quickened by his Spirit, and fed with his abundance, we may, after the petty conflicts and slight trials of this life, have part in his crowns, and in his glory, to be made eternally happy in him. Amen.

SERMON XXII.

VERSES 10, 11.

And ye are complete in him, which is the head of all principality and power: in whom also ye are circumcised with the circumcision made without hands, in putting off the body of the sins of the flesh by the circumcision of Christ.

DEAR brethren, it was with great propriety that our Lord and Saviour, when he would magnify the love of God towards mankind, said that "he so loved the world, that he gave his only begotten Son, that whosoever believeth in him should not perish, but have everlasting life," John iii. 16; for this gift of Christ which he has presented to us is without contradiction the greatest and most admirable evidence of his love that he could have given us. I confess that this mighty fabric which he freely bestowed on us at the first creation, this world, roofed with those stately heavens which environ us, enlightened by those brilliant luminaries which revolve incessantly about us, and filled with an infinite variety of good things, was an excellent sign of wonderful beneficence and love; and that the psalmist had reason to cry out, as if ravished with the consideration, " What is man, that thou art mindful of him, and the son of man, that thou visitest him? For thou hast made him a little lower than the angels, and hast crowned him with glory and honour. Thou madest him to have dominion over the works of thy hands; thou hast put all things under his feet," Psal. viii. 4—6. Yet it must be acknowledged that all this liberality of God towards us, which, considered in itself is so great and ravishing, is but a small matter in comparison with the ineffable and incomprehensible love which he has exhibited in giving us his Christ; whether you compare the gifts themselves one with the other, or consider the fruit which each of them produces. For, first, the world is a kind of a magazine of the riches of nature; Jesus Christ is the treasury of all the perfections of the Godhead. In the one, God has set forth and put together only the works of his hands, which are effects, and as it were shadows, of his greatness: in the other, he has poured out all the abundance of his own nature; and as the apostle told us in the preceding verse, " in Christ dwelleth all the fulness of the Godhead bodily;" whereas in the world dwells only the fulness of the creature. As much then as the operator is greater than his work, and the Creator than the creature; so much more excellent and admirable is the gift which God has made us of his Son in the economy of grace, than that of the world in the administration of nature. Again, the difference of the fruit which we gather from each of these gifts of God is suitable to this disproportion which we observe between the things themselves. For, first, the enjoyment of the world could only continue life to man, who before possessed it; it could not restore it to any that had lost it: whereas Jesus Christ gives life to the dead, and perpetuates it to the living. Again, that life which the due use of the world could sustain was terrestrial, carnal, and liable to perish; whereas the life which we have from Jesus Christ is celestial, spiritual, and immutable.

The holy apostle, having represented in a few words the infinite greatness of Christ in himself, as having all the fulness of the Godhead dwelling in him bodily, goes on to unfold the admirable abundance of fruit which we draw from him; the whole, as we have often told you, being designed to confute the ingratitude and vanity of certain seducers, who, not content with that inexhaustible source of blessings which God has opened for us in his Son, would needs join with it philosophical inventions and legal ceremonies. The apostle prosecutes this intention down to the 15th verse; and beginning it at the text which you have heard, tells the faithful Colossians, first, that they are made complete in Jesus Christ, " who is the head of all principality and power." Afterwards, entering upon a particular deduction of this completeness which we have in

Christ, he adds, in the following verse, that we are circumcised in him "with the circumcision made without hands, in putting off the body of the sins of the flesh by the circumcision of Christ." Then, in conclusion, he sets forth other graces and benefits which we derive from the fulness of our Lord. But we, for the present, will content ourselves with the two verses we have read. And for giving you a full exposition of them, to your edification and consolation, we will consider, by the favourable assistance of God, the two points which offer themselves to our notice. First, in general, the completeness which the apostle says we have in Jesus Christ. Secondly, in particular, the circumcision made without hands, which, he adds, we have in him.

I. Let us notice the completeness which we have in Jesus Christ. The perfections and riches of anything are of no advantage to us if they are not communicated. A spring, however fair and fresh, does us no service if it is sealed up; and a garden-plot walled in rather pains then pleases our desires; neither does an inaccessible treasure lessen our need. The tree of life, and the other wonders of the Paradise of Eden, enriched that delightful place, but afforded our first parents no refreshment, when entrance into it was prohibited. For this reason the apostle considers it not enough to have told us that all the fulness of the Deity dwells bodily in Jesus Christ. Perhaps the false teachers themselves did not contest this abundance in him, but, confessing that he had all in himself, only denied that he would communicate it entirely to us; he having it only for the perfection of his own person, and not for our happiness. To banish this false conceit from our hearts, the apostle adds, that we are made "complete in him;" that is to say, his fulness is communicative: the Father has poured forth into him those precious gifts and graces with which he is filled, that each of us might draw out as much as we need. He is the true tree of life, laden with fruit, that we might gather; set open before our eyes and to our hands, not shut up (as the other was after the fall) in a place inaccessible. He has received, to give unto us. He is rich, to enrich us. He is full, to replenish us. His abundance is our bliss, and his treasures the relief of our necessity. The Father gave him to the world, and in him life and immortality.

Neither suppose that he will impart only some of his benefits; as he has an all-fulness of them in himself, so he communicates them *all* to us. He leaves no part of our nature empty. He fills up all with his graces. We derive from him all that is necessary to complete us. This is that which the apostle signifies by these words; and they may be taken two ways; either as importing that we are filled, or (as our Bibles have rendered it) that we are made "complete in

Jesus Christ:" but both amount to the same sense, the difference being only in the manner of signification, and not in the thing signified. For each of these expressions denotes that we receive of Jesus Christ our Lord all things requisite to the perfection and happiness of our persons, which things, namely, the grace of God, righteousness, wisdom, consolation, and sanctification, reside most abundantly in him. If you read that we have been filled in Jesus Christ, it will be a similitude taken from empty vessels, which are filled with extraneous substances. For our nature being of itself empty, and destitute of the glory of God, and of its necessary perfections, our Lord Jesus Christ fills it from his own abundance, and furnishes it with all perfective graces. He clothes it with his righteousness, that it may appear with freedom before the throne of the Father. He illuminates it by his Spirit unto saving knowledge. He comforts it with his peace, and decks it with holiness and love, and in his treasury on high keeps for it that blessed life and immortality with which he will enrich it at the day of resurrection.

This sense, as you perceive, has a very clear coherence with the expression of the apostle, "In him dwelleth all the fulness of the Godhead bodily;" and is exactly parallel to that of John in his gospel, that "of his fulness have all we received, and grace for grace," John i. 16. As in nature the sun has not only in itself a fulness of that resplendent light which renders it so beautiful and admirable, but also diffuses it abroad from itself, and replenishes with it all the luminous bodies which circulate around it, as the moon, the planets, and this earth whereon we dwell; all which have no other brightness than that which this great luminary sheds upon them: so in grace (if we may compare the mysteries thereof with natural things) Jesus Christ, the true Sun of righteousness, has not only in himself all the fulness of the Deity dwelling there bodily, but he also communicates his fulness to all the souls of men that look to him, and move and live in his communion. He fills them with his abundance, and clothes them with his light, changing them into his image, and of dim and dark lumps, as they were originally in themselves, making them so many stars and luminous bodies.

Now if you take the apostle's words in another sense, as importing that we have been made complete in Jesus Christ, they will still be very pertinent. For we, being destitute of all perfections meet for our nature, it will exceedingly well express the grace of Christ to say that we have been made "complete in him," as signifying that it is he who has filled up our breaches, and repaired in us what the first Adam had ruined, by giving us all that we needed. Besides this, I observe that this term will also very aptly answer to that title which the apostle gave a little before to the ceremonies of the Mosaic law, where he called them "the rudiments of the world;" that is, the beginnings, the first and plainest lessons of piety; and such as consequently were unable to bring to perfection, as he says expressly in another place, Heb. vii. 19; Gal. iv.; for which reason he styles the time of the law the infancy of the church, that, is the age of its imperfection. Opposing therefore Jesus Christ to the law in this respect, he now says that we are "complete in him," and that with great propriety, as he has the body, whereas the law had but the shadow; he has fulness, whereas the law had but some small parcel of the requisites of our salvation. For the same reason he calls the ceremonies of it weak, and poor or "beggarly elements," Gal. iv. 9. As for the law, says he, it only began with us, and drew some slight and dark lineament upon us of that true form which God purposed to imprint; whereas Jesus Christ has finished us. In him it is we have that perfection, that entire body, that truth and fulness, of which the law had but the beginning, the shadow, and figure.

By this the holy apostle gives those seducers, with whom he is combating, a fatal blow, discovering the foolishness of their design in endeavouring still to enforce the ceremonies of the law upon those who were made complete in Jesus Christ; an attempt no less ridiculous than if one should put a man to his A B C again, who had received the last tincture of highest erudition in the university; pretending that he could not be thoroughly intelligent and accomplished, except he still daily study the rudiments and plainest lessons of children. But that which follows in the apostle's words, namely, that Jesus Christ "is the head of all principality and power," is added to prevent another error of those deceivers, who, as we shall hereafter hear, taught the worshipping and serving of angels; pretending that it was necessary that we should address ourselves to them, as to spirits capable of interceding with God for us, and of obtaining by their interposition with his Supreme Majesty those graces and perfections which we need. Paul shows, in these few words, the vanity of this false doctrine. For since the Lord Jesus is the Head of angels, who does not see that we have most abundantly in him everything which these people could expect from them—and that possessing Jesus Christ, as we do by faith in his gospel, we have no need to repair to angels, who depend upon him, and have nothing but what is found much more richly in their Head? As if a man who possesses the son of a prince, should, nevertheless, make use of the favour and interpositions of his servants with him. Members have neither motion, nor sensation, nor life, which is not found much more abundantly in their head.

Subjects and servants possess nothing which the prince cannot far better and more easily communicate to us than they. Since Jesus Christ is the Head and Prince of angels, it is clear that, having him, we can want nothing which the angels can give to us. Upon the same ground the impiety of the error of these seducers also appears. For since the angels are subject to Jesus Christ, it is evident, by the light of Scripture, that no one can render to them that religious worship which these people ascribe to them without becoming guilty of idolatry, the greatest and most flagrant outrage which man can perpetrate against his Creator. For no christian can be ignorant that God throughout his whole word forbids us to serve any creature, however high and excellent he may be esteemed; religious worship being a homage which belongs to the divine nature, and cannot be performed to any other without sacrilege.

I presume you all are aware that by these principalities and powers of which the apostle speaks he signifies angels, as we explained in the preceding chapter, ver. 16. He says that Jesus Christ is their Head, that is, their Lord. And this quality belongs to him, not only as he is the eternal Son of the Father, of the same essence and power with him; who, having created them at the beginning, and continuing to preserve them by his goodness and might, is by every kind of right their true Master and natural Lord; but also as he is the Christ and Mediator. For since he, in this relation, and under this quality, has been constituted the Lord of all things, superior, inferior, and intermediate; having, in consequence of his humiliation, received such a name as is above every name, and unto which every knee bows, both of those that are in heaven, and that are on earth, and that are under the earth, Phil. ii. 9, 10; it is evident that in this sense he has dominion and empire over angels as well as others. And this also Peter expressly teaches us, saying that angels, and authorities, and powers have been made subject to him, 1 Pet. iii. 22. For this cause these spirits are often called the angels of Christ, as in Matthew, "The Son of man shall send his angels," chap. xiii. 41; xxiv. 31; and in the Apocalypse, where John says that Jesus Christ sent by his angel the things that were revealed to him, chap. i. 1; and in the same book, "I Jesus have sent mine angel," chap. xxii. 16. Only we must observe, that the Lord Jesus is not called the Head of the angels in the same manner and sense as he is styled the Head of his church. The former title signifies only the empire and lordship which he has over the angels; the second signifies also the union which he has with his true believers, who are saved and redeemed by the merit of his death, and are animated and quickened by the Spirit of his resurrection. For he indeed commands the angels, as their true and legitimate Master; but he has not assumed their nature, nor washed them from their sins; these holy and blessed beings having never committed any: nor has he, by his merit, obtained for them that life and bliss which they enjoy; these being benefits pertaining to none but men. Accordingly, we do not find that the angels are called his body or his members. These titles are peculiar to his believers, agreeably with what the apostle says to the Ephesians, namely, that Christ is the Saviour of his body, chap. v. 23; and every one knows that he is not the Saviour of angels, since they, having not fallen from their original purity and felicity, have had no need of being saved.

II. We now come to the second point of our text, which the apostle lays before us in these words: "In whom also ye are circumcised," &c. He begins here to notice particularly, and in detail, that of which he had before spoken generally, namely, our having been made complete in Jesus Christ; specifying, in order, the perfections for which those false teachers fruitlessly sought in vain observances; and showing that they are to be found plentifully in Jesus Christ, so that there is no need to have recourse to any besides, or to add anything to his gospel for their requirement. Among all those observances which these seducers sought to force into religion, there was none which they more strenuously pressed than circumcision, which, as you know, was one of the sacraments of the old covenant, in which, by cutting off the foreskin, was prefigured and exhibited to the Israelites, not only the purification of their nature by the abolition of their sins and excision of their vices, but also their entrance into the communion of God. In effect, this ceremony was of infinite importance. For it was the seal of all the old covenant; the person who received it being thereby consecrated and initiated to the discipline of Moses, and solemnly obliged to observe his laws; as the apostle represents to the Galatians, when he says, "I testify again to every man that is circumcised, that he is a debtor to do the whole law," chap. v. 3. For this reason he commences with it in this place, well knowing of what consequence was this error, which annihilated the cross of Christ, and overthrew the whole mystery of his grace. Let none object, says he, against this completeness which you have in Jesus Christ, that having not been circumcised, you want the first and principal piece of sanctification. This part of your perfection is no more wanting than others; and if you carefully consider what Jesus Christ has given you through his gospel, you will find that though the knife of Moses has not touched you, yet you have a circumcision through the goodness of our Lord; yea, one that is not only equally excellent with the other, but even much more perfect. Whence you see to how little purpose these men endeavour to make you subject to this ancient incision of the law; it being altogether superfluous to those who have passed through the hands of Jesus Christ. The apostle sets this consideration before the Philippians, in his dispute against the same seducers: "We," says he, "are the circumcision, which worship God in the spirit, and rejoice in Christ Jesus, and have no confidence in the flesh," chap. iii. 3. But here he explains, in what follows, this admirable circumcision which we have received in Jesus Christ; and says, first, that is not made with hands: he next states in what it consists, namely, in putting off the body of sins: and lastly, he terms it the circumcision of Christ.

He says, then, first, that this circumcision which we have in our Lord and Saviour is not made with hands; by which he affirms that it is not formally and precisely that circumcision which Moses gave the Jews, the hand of man effecting that in their flesh; whereas this is made by the operation, not of man, but of God; with the instrument, not of Moses, but of Christ; that is, by his word accompanied by his Spirit, which is "sharper than any two-edged sword," Heb. iv. 12. In which respect alone it has a great advantage over the circumcision of the Jews, it being evident that the works of God are incomparably more excellent than the works of men. And as the apostle, when telling us, in another place, 2 Cor. v. 1, that the building which we look for, after the dissolution of this earthly tabernacle, is not made with hands, by that very reason demonstrates the excellency of it, even that it is a work not of human art or nature, but of the wisdom and power of God; in the same manner he here represents the worth and value of our circumcision in Jesus Christ, by saying that it is "made without hands."

Secondly, the thing itself no less demonstrates its superiority than the quality of the operation by which we receive it. For this "circumcision made without hands," which we have in Jesus Christ, is, as the apostle here defines it, the "putting off the body of the sins of the flesh." You know what he and the other holy writers signify by the flesh; they mean not only this infirm and mortal body, but also our defiled and corrupted nature, which we all bring into the world; comprehending not only the body and the senses, but also the soul, all which are tainted and infected with the pollutions of sin, and in a manner transformed into flesh by the carnal qualities and habits with which they are invested; the understanding being wholly dull and sensual, the will earthly and brutish, and the affections rebellious against the law of Heaven, and all of them cleaving to the flesh. This nature of man thus framed is that which Paul, both here and in other places, calls flesh. The sins of this flesh are the habits of those various vices which cover and envelope it on all sides; not only those which properly relate to the body, and the gratification of its irregular appetites, such as gluttony, drunkenness, and luxury; but also all others which militate against the law of God, and overthrow that order of righteousness and holiness which he has appointed for all the faculties, motions, and sentiments of our nature, as we are taught by the apostle in many places, and particularly in the Epistle to the Galatians, chap. v. 19, 20, where he places among the works of the flesh, not only adultery, fornication, and drunkenness, but also idolatry, heresy, enmity, clamours, envyings, wrath, murders, and other such sins.

The mass of all these vices is that which he here calls "the body of the sins of the flesh;" and he uses this mode of speech again in another place, Rom. vi. 6, when he says that "our old man is crucified with Christ, that the body of sin might be destroyed." And it must be confessed that this figure is exceedingly elegant and appropriate; for as the body comprehends in itself its several members, which have each of them their particular function and exercise; so this mass of corruption which we bear about in our nature is composed of many different vices, which have each of them their peculiar motion and operation. Ambition tends one way, avarice and intemperance another. Envy defiles us in one manner, cruelty in another; and each of these pests has its own sentiment and ends. Their motions are sometimes even contrary, and thwart one another, as unclean spirits which do not agree; but all these evils nevertheless come from one and the same source, and live in one and the same mass; as all the members make up but one and the same body. Hence the apostle sometimes, speaking of sins under this idea, calls them our members, or the members of our flesh; as when he commands us to mortify our "members which are upon the earth; fornication, uncleanness, inordinate affection," and other such vices, Col. iii. 5. Moreover, as this body, in which we live, covers us all around; so that mass of vices, with which our nature is infected, encompasses and infolds us on all sides, there being no part or faculty in us but what is, as it were, invested and besieged with it. Such is the corruption which we derive from the first Adam, for which reason the apostle sometimes also calls it the old man. He says, therefore, that the circumcision which we have in Jesus Christ is the putting off this body of the sins of the flesh; when the true believer, by the virtue of the word and Spirit of the Lord Jesus, cuts off all the vices of the flesh, which are its members, and strips himself of this old habit of sin and death, with which the first Adam clothed us. This is what, in another place, he calls a putting off the old man as to the former conversation, " which is corrupt according to the deceitful lusts," Eph. iv. 22. And in this present Epistle, chap. iii. 8, a putting off "anger, wrath, malice, blasphemy," and other such sins; and again, in another place, a crucifying of "the flesh, with its affections and lusts," Gal. v. 24. All this amounts to the same sense, and signifies the mortifying of the flesh, and the cutting off its vices, that there may be an abstinence from all the sins which they are accustomed to produce in the lives of men of the world.

The apostle adds, in conclusion, that this is the circumcision of Christ. First, because our Lord and Saviour has expressly instituted it in his gospel, commanding us to be born again, to deny ourselves, to change our deportment, to put on a simplicity and humility like that of little children, and to break all the ties which fasten us to the flesh and the world, if we will follow him and have part in his kingdom. This is the first and most important instruction contained in the Scriptures. Secondly, it is the circumcision of Christ, because it is he alone who is the author of it, and effects it in us; neither is there anything besides his gospel which can unclothe man of this body of the sins of the flesh; for it is impossible that a soul on whom the doctrine of Jesus Christ has been imprinted by the power of the Holy Ghost should fail to renounce the world and the flesh. Philosophy was so far from curing this malady, that it did not so much as exactly understand it. The law discovered it indeed, and made man to feel the tyrannous strength of this rebellious body of the flesh, which naturally clothed and surrounded him. But it was unable to subdue and mortify it, as the apostle teaches us at large in the 7th chapter of the Epistle to the Romans. There is none but Jesus Christ who, by the efficacy of his heavenly truths, and the divine example of his holiness, implanted in our hearts by the hand of his Spirit, can circumcise us in this manner, unloosing these wretched bonds, stripping us of them by degrees, and weakening and extinguishing the life of the flesh in us.

Compare now this circumcision of our Saviour with that of Moses, and you will, without difficulty, perceive that it infinitely surpasses it in dignity and excellency. That of Moses wounded the body; this of Christ enlivens the soul. The one pared away a little skin; the other mortifies the whole body of the flesh. The one was in itself but a typical ceremony; the other is a mystical truth. The one wounded the flesh; the other heals and ennobles the heart. Without the one, a man could have no part in the communion of the carnal Jews; and by the other we enter into the alliance of the spiritual Jews, whose praise is of God and not of men. Whereby you may judge how extravagant was the conception of those seducers whom the apostle here opposes, who, notwithstanding that excellent and divine circumcision which christians have received in their Saviour's school, would yet bring them under that of Moses, which was poor and weak, and in so many respects defective, as if christians could not, upon a far better ground than the Jews, glory that they truly are the circumcision of God.

Now for a right comprehension of the force of the apostle's reasoning, it must be remembered that circumcision, as well as the other ceremonies of the Mosaic law, was a figure which represented the abscission of the vices and lusts of the flesh, as the prophets themselves clearly show, when they promise the ancient people that God will circumcise their heart, and the heart of their seed, that they may love him and live, Deut. xxx. 6; and when they command them to circumcise themselves unto the Lord, and to take away the foreskin of their hearts, Jer. iv. 4; an evident sign that this external action referred to the internal mortification and sanctification of the soul. Since then the figure is unprofitable when the truth is attained, and models are serviceable only until the things themselves be formed and perfected, the use of them when this is done being no longer necessary; you plainly perceive that, from the apostle's assertion here, that in Jesus Christ we have this putting off, or cutting off, the sins of the flesh, (that is, the truth, of which circumcision was the figure and model,) it evidently follows that it is no longer necessary for us, and that wilfully to retain it still is to accuse Jesus Christ of having not fulfilled in his discipline the thing represented by this ancient type. It is true, that even in the time of the old testament the faithful had some part of the sanctification signified by their circumcision; but what they had was weak and small in measure, because the true causes on which it depends, being all comprised in the mysteries of the new testament, were then but foretold and promised, not fully and clearly revealed, as they are now by their accomplishment. It was therefore meet that during the whole of that time they should be exercised in the observance of these typical rites, and held in and kept under the discipline of Moses until the fulness of time, according to the apostle's doctrine in the Epistle to the Galatians. Now that Jesus Christ has openly exhibited the very body of truth, and fully brought to light all the causes and motives of true sanctification, these exercises, so suitable to the infancy of the church, are no longer seasonable; and they who still adhere to them are no less ridiculous than he who would still keep up the supports of an arch or the models of a building after the fabric is finished and brought to its perfection, or retain under the scourge of a schoolmaster, and in the restraints of childhood, a man grown up and come to years of maturity.

Thus we have finished the exposition of this text. It remains for us, in conclusion, to extract those instructions and consolations which an attentive consideration of it will afford.

First, Since the apostle assures us that we are complete in Christ, you see how vain are the pretensions of those men who set forth certain rules of perfection, as they call them, which are not to be found in the gospel. Let us content ourselves with our Lord's fulness, and seek our perfection in him alone; and instead of amusing ourselves with the inventions of men, embrace and practise the doctrines of Christ, advancing daily towards the utmost degree of perfection; for we must not flatter ourselves with an imagination that a man can be united to Christ while he leads a vicious and corrupt life. Paul here protests plainly to us, that all those who are in him are made complete. It therefore necessarily follows, that those who are not complete are not in his communion, and consequently should not promise themselves any share in his salvation; it being prepared for those only who are in him. If this doctrine trouble us, let us impute it to our vices and our irresolution; and taking once this truth to heart, endeavour with all our might to obtain that perfection which is in Jesus Christ, accounting that without it we cannot possess either his grace in this world, or his glory in the world to come. I well know that, to speak absolutely, no one is perfect; and that if we compare our condition on earth with that in heaven, all our perfections are but weaknesses. Yet it is true that Jesus Christ, even in this life, in some sense, completes his faithful people, and this perfection which he gives them is not a vain name or an imagination; it is something substantial, a real truth; it is a piety and love sincere and free, and without hypocrisy; and though it may sometimes vary, it nevertheless produces true fruits and works quite different from those of worldlings and hypocrites, according to what our Lord said, "Except your righteousness shall exceed the righteousness of the scribes and Pharisees, ye shall in no case enter into the kingdom of heaven." Tell me not that you are yet on earth, and that perfection is not to be found but in heaven; and that to live as an angel one should be without a body. It is not the perfection of heaven which we demand of you. The Lord will not reject you for not having had in this life the transcendent brightness of the next. But though a child is not expected to conduct his life with as much prudence and reason as a man of years, it does not follow that he has a license to live without rule, and in the intemperance and disorders of slaves. Every age has its bounds, and its measures, and its perfection. Our childhood here below must not be without discipline, under the pretence that it is not come to full growth. Christians, I complain not that there are defects in your knowledge and practice which have no place in heaven; but that there are in you vices which ought to have no place on earth. I blame you not that there is a great difference between you and angels; but that there is none between you and worldly men. I require not what is above the strength of your age, but what is worthy of your profession, and does not at all exceed your light. I beseech you only to labour as much for Jesus Christ as the children of this generation do for the interests of their lusts. This does not exceed the capacity of our nature, since you see what the servants of sin do; and it is necessarily your duty, except you imagine that we owe less to Jesus Christ than worldlings do to their foolish and vain passions.

The first piece of that completeness which we have in him is this divine circumcision, which is not made with hands but by the efficacy of his Spirit. Without it we can have neither place in the communion of his people, nor right to his inheritance. It is a circumcision of which we may truly say, that every soul who does not receive it shall be cut off from his people. The apostle shows us in what it consists, namely, "in putting off the body of the sins of the flesh." Jesus Christ has put into our hands the sword which is necessary to cut away this wretched flesh, namely, his sacred word, in which he discovers the hideousness of sin, the infernal venom of vice, and the vanity and iniquity of all the lusts of the flesh. He has showed us the perdition into which they fall who serve it, and has put it to death on his cross, and buried it in his sepulchre. He has spread before our eyes the wonders of God's love, and the eternity of the kingdom appointed for faithful servants. He has given us rules and examples of this part of our sanctification in his gospel and in his life, and offers us the lights and consolations of his Spirit to lead us in this work. Let us then grasp this divine sword of his gospel; let us thrust it resolutely into our hearts, and cut out thence all the impurity of our vices; let us rid ourselves of them, and cast them behind us. Let us exterminate all the productions of the flesh as execrable things, and leave not one of them in ourselves. Having subdued avarice, let us combat ambition. Let us pluck out luxury and all its passions from our inward parts. Let us root up hatred, and wrath, and cruelty, and spare the life of none of these monsters. Let us not rest until we have cleansed our hearts of all this cursed brood. For it is not enough to cut off some of them. One enemy alone abiding in our bosom is able to destroy us. "The body of the sins of the flesh" must be put off, says the apostle, and not one or two of its sins only. I confess the labour is hard, but is necessary, and that at all times, (for it is the task of our whole life,) in an especial manner at present, now that the death of our Lord and Saviour, and his resurrection, and his holy supper, call us to extraordinary efforts of piety and holiness. And if the labour be great, the felicity and the glory that follow it are infinite. Let us employ ourselves in it, my beloved brethren, with ardour and generosity, putting off the body of all our sins, that having truly crucified our old man with the Lord Jesus, we may also rise again with him, to be enlivened by his celestial food, and have part for ever, after the short trials of this life, in his blessed immortality. Amen.

SERMON XXIII.

VERSE 12.

Buried with him in baptism, wherein also ye are risen with him through the faith of the operation of God who hath raised him from the dead.

DEAR brethren, it is very true that the solemnity of this great day, which has been consecrated by all christians to the resurrection of the Lord Jesus, and sanctified by the mysteries of his table, at which we have communicated, requires of us more than ordinary devotion and meditation; yet there was no need for me to seek a subject suitable for the present exercise in any other place than the regular series of texts which I have undertaken to expound to you; the words which I have read, and which immediately succeed those you heard last Lord's day, excellently suiting each of those duties to which this day is particularly dedicated; inasmuch as they treat of our Lord's resurrection, and of the fruits which thereby redound to us: of baptism, in which they are communicated to us, and which ordinance, for this reason, was formerly solemnly administered in the ancient church on the night before Easter; and of that faith by which we become possessed of this divine resurrection. Lastly, they speak of the interest which we have in his burial, the consequence of his precious death, the blessed commemoration of which we have celebrated this morning. These are subjects which are, as is plain to all, eminently adapted for the devotion of this day. This, then, shall be, by the will of God, the subject of this discourse. Dear brethren, afford it a vigorous and a deep attention, elevating your thoughts to Jesus Christ, the Prince of our salvation, and Author of our immortality, while we shall endeavour to represent to you what his apostle here teaches about our communion in his burial and resurrection.

You may remember, that to confound the impiety of certain

seducers, who would urge upon christians the necessity of being circumcised according to the law of Moses, this holy man alleged, in the preceding text, that we have in Jesus Christ that substance and truth of which the Judaical circumcision was but the shadow and model, having in him put off the body of the sins of the flesh; so that having received, through the grace of Jesus, this mystical and divine circumcision, the other carnal and typical one is altogether useless, and cannot be desired or practised by christians, without wronging their Saviour. He still prosecutes that same intention; and to show how rich that sanctifying grace is which we have in Jesus Christ, he adds, that besides our being circumcised by the virtue of his word, and divested of the body of the sins of the flesh, we have moreover been buried with him in baptism; and further, that we are therein risen again with him, "through the faith of the operation of God, who hath raised him from the dead."

For a right understanding of these words, we will consider, first, the communion which we have both in the burial and resurrection of our Lord Jesus Christ. And, secondly, the twofold means by which this communion is given to us, namely, baptism, and the faith of the operation of God, who has raised our Lord from the dead.

I. We are to notice the communion which we have both in the burial and resurrection of Christ. The apostle expresses this point in these words, "Buried with him in baptism, wherein also ye are risen with him." As for our burial with the Lord, you know that, having suffered on the cross that painful and accursed death which we had merited, his sacred body was loosened from the mournful tree, and being wrapped up in a sheet, was by Joseph of Arimathea laid in a new sepulchre, where it remained in this sad state, (the last of our infirmities,) without motion, without respiration, and without life, until the beginning of the third day, when he gloriously rose again. The transcendent wisdom of the Father, which ordained all the parts of this great work, thus fitly ordered it for the purpose of justifying the truth of his Son's death, by his continuance in the grave. For if he had resumed his life immediately after he laid it down, and had descended from the cross alive, I confess such a miracle might have astonished and transported the minds of the spectators, and demonstrated that this divine crucified person was more than man; but, on the other hand, it would have rendered his death suspicious, and without doubt would have led men to imagine that it had been but a feigned and false appearance, and not a real separation of his soul from his body, which opinion would evidently have shaken and overthrown our salvation, it being entirely founded on the death of the Lord Jesus. Therefore as it so highly concerns us to believe the fact of his death, God has so assured and certified the truth of it, that we have not even the shadow of a reason to call it in question. It was his will, therefore, that the Lord Jesus, after having commended his spirit into his hands, should be laid in the sepulchre, and continue there three days; there remaining after this no more reason to doubt that he was truly dead, since he was so long a time in the state of the dead. Moreover, our consolation required that he should enter into our sepulchres, to take away for us the horrors of them, and to assure us, by his example, that they have not force sufficient to detain our bodies for ever, or to hinder them from rising again. It is for these and other similar reasons that Jesus Christ went down into the grave, death's last entrenchment.

The apostle says then that true believers have been buried with him. How so, you will say, seeing that they, being living persons, were never laid in the grave; and surely not in our Lord's, which was situate on Mount Calvary, nigh to Jerusalem, places very far distant from our abode? Dear brethren, there is no man so ignorant but that he must plainly see that these words are not to be taken according to the letter, but figuratively; and that they signify not a natural, but a mystical sepulchre. And in such a sense it may be said two ways that we have been buried in Christ, or with him. First, with regard to our justification; that is, the remission of our sins. And, secondly, with regard to our sanctification, and the mortifying of the old man. Concerning the first, it is evident that Jesus Christ was buried for us, as he was neither crucified nor put to death but for us only. Burial is nothing else but a consequence of death. It is the sad and dismal state to which it reduces men ever since they became guilty; that is to say, it makes up a part of the punishment of sin; for it is indeed a hideous and mournful spectacle to see so noble and excellent a creature, in whom the image of God shines forth, and who had been formed for immortal glory, to be brought down to the grave, under the power of worms and putrefaction. Jesus Christ, therefore, having undergone this ignominious infirmity for us, and for our salvation, that he might leave none of our penalties unpaid, it is evident that, when he was buried, we were buried in him, and with him, since it was properly for us that he descended into the sepulchre. He bore us upon the cross; he bore us in the grave. We all were in him, forasmuch as he, in all this work, acted but for us. We did and suffered these things, since we are the cause of his doing and suffering them. We were buried in him, inasmuch as by his burial he has discharged this part of our punishment, and so changed the nature of our graves, that instead of being prisons, and places of execution, they are now so many beds and dormitories, in which our bodies repose until the resurrection. Thus his burial has freed ours from the curse, which is naturally upon it; and this benefit makes up a part of that justification which he has merited for us, comprehending an exemption from all the penalties which are due to our sins.

But it is not in this sense that the apostle says we have been buried with Jesus Christ; for he speaks here of the first part of our sanctification, which is nothing else but the mortifying of the body of sin or old man in us, and its burial, that is, its destruction. It is therefore properly in this respect Paul says that we have been buried with Jesus Christ, even inasmuch as by the virtue of his death and burial our old man has been destroyed, and suffered a death and burial analogous to that of Jesus Christ's. For as his flesh, after it was deprived of life, was laid in a grave; in like manner the old man of true believers, having been slain, is interred and reduced to nothing. And as the Lord Jesus left in the sepulchre his funeral linen clothes, together with all the infirmity and mortality he possessed, and came forth vested with a nature and a life fully refined from all that weakness of the first Adam which appeared in him during the days of his flesh; even so believers put off for ever that body of sin with which their first parent had first enwrapped them, and leave it in their mystical sepulchre, to be resumed no more, but that they may henceforth lead a life free and exempt from all its filthiness and turpitude. Lastly, as the burial of our Saviour was properly but a progression and continuation of his death; so likewise that of our old man is but a prosecution of his destruction; it is the state this puts him in, and under it he abides for ever, without rising any more. Paul elsewhere clearly shows us that it is thus we must understand his words, when he says, in the 6th to the Romans, ver. 4, 5, that "we are buried with him by baptism into death; that like as Christ was raised up from the dead by the glory of the Father, even so we also should walk in newness of life;" and immediately after he says, that "if we have been planted together in the likeness of his death, we shall be also in the likeness of his resurrection." To which must be also added, that it is in him, and with him, we have been buried in this manner, because in his death and burial the principles and causes of ours were contained. His death has destroyed our old man, and his burial has interred him; it being evident, that if our Lord had not suffered both for our salvation, sin would still live and reign in us; for it is the love of God, and his peace, and the hope of glory, the true effect of our Saviour's death and burial, that gives the death's wound to our old man, and that abolishes and buries his whole life.

See then how we are buried with him; not that our bodies really enter into the sepulchre in Joseph of Arimathea's garden, where his abode three days; (away with so childish a conception!) but the virtue of his death and holy sepulchre produces in us an image and a copy of his burial, destroying and burying our old man by his efficacy, and bringing on him a mystical death and burial conformable to his own real and mystical one. That which the apostle now adds, that we are also risen again together with him, must also be understood in the same manner. As our death and burial with him is mystical and spiritual, so is likewise our resurrection; these words signifying nothing else than that he, by the virtue of his resurrection, works and produces one in us which bears a resemblance and an analogy with his own. And this resurrection of the faithful, in consequence and by the efficacy of that of Jesus Christ, is their being renewed unto a holy, spiritual, and evangelical life. For even as the Lord, having put off on the cross, and left in the grave, that earthly, infirm, and natural life which he had led here below, during the days of his flesh, put on a new one, that was glorious, spiritual, and immortal, rising from the grave a heavenly man, and living to eternity by the sole strength of a quickening Spirit: so likewise all his true members, having quitted their old man, as destroyed and abolished by the virtue of his death, put on the new, which is formed in righteousness and holiness; and instead of that vile and wretched life which they led before in the guilt and pollution of sin, they take up another wholly new, which is quickened by the Spirit from on high, upheld by his power, and which shines all over with the glorious lights of his holiness, love, and purity.

But besides this conformity between the new nature, which we receive in Jesus Christ, and that which he put on at his coming forth from the grave, we are said to rise again with him, because it is the virtue of his resurrection which produces all this change in us. His resurrection is the cause of ours; without it we should still lie dead, and in bondage to sin. This will appear if you consider it with ever so little attention; for that which forms the new man in us, and gives us the courage to renounce the world, that we may live pure and holy, is, as every one knows, the persuasion of the love of God, and of the remission of our sins, and the hope of a blissful and glorious immortality. Now it is the resurrection of Jesus Christ which gives us all this assurance, putting into our hands a convincing proof of the satisfaction of divine justice, by the deliverance of our Surety; and of our immortality, by his having taken possession there for himself and us; so that our souls being assured of the transcendent goodness of God, and of their own happiness, ardently embrace his instruction, and endeavour to lead a new life. Besides, that faith which purifies our hearts, and by which, as we shall hear presently, we are risen again in Jesus Christ, could not take place in us, if he were not risen from the dead, since it is by that he was "declared to be the Son of God with power, according to the spirit of holiness," Rom, i. 4. Therefore Peter says it is by the resurrection of Jesus Christ from the dead that God "has begotten us again unto a lively hope," 1 Pet. i. 3. And Paul, for this very reason, protests, that if Christ were not risen, our faith would be vain, and we should be still in our sins, 1 Cor. xv. 17. It must then be concluded that in rising again he raised us up also by the same means, inasmuch as by rising he gave being and clearness to the principles and causes of our mystical resurrection. Opening his own tomb, he by that means opened ours. He broke in pieces the doors and bars of our sepulchres by quitting his own; and raising himself from the dust, he drew us up out of the earth, and brought us forth from the abode of death; that glorious life also with which he then vested himself has inspired into us all the spiritual life, motions, and sentiments which we possess.

O holy and blessed communion! O divine and incorruptible fruits of the sepulchre of Jesus Christ! The death of the first man killed us, but the death of the Second makes us alive. The sepulchre of the one is our prison, that of the other is our liberty. In the former appear horror and malediction, the signs of our guilt and of the just wrath of God; but from the latter peace and life germinate, and glory and immortality shoot forth. The grave of Adam extinguished, and shut up for ever in a state of inanition, all the beauty, strength, and life of our nature. The sepulchre of Jesus Christ has destroyed nothing but our sin; it has shut up and kept in only our old man, that is, the loathsomeness and misery of our lives; and instead of this abominable body of sin and death, of which it has divested us, it has, as it were, teemed with and brought forth a celestial and immortal nature, which it puts on us together with our Saviour. And thus you see what are the fruits of our communion with Jesus Christ, namely, the destruction of our old man and the creation of the new, signified by the apostle in these words, we are buried and risen again with him.

II. Let us now consider the twofold means, here intimated by the apostle, by which God makes us partakers of them. The first is baptism: "Buried," says he, "with Christ in baptism, wherein also ye are risen with him;" for so I take these words, rendering "wherein," not in whom; and referring this term, not to Jesus Christ, but to baptism; as if it had been said, in which baptism ye are also risen again together with the Lord; this construction being more natural and more convenient than the other, as they who understand the original language in which the apostle wrote will easily perceive, if they take the pains to consider this text; though, in reality, it makes no difference which of these two ways it is taken, both amounting to the same sense, whether you say that we are risen again in baptism, or in Jesus Christ.

In truth, all the means of which God makes use in religion have no other tendency than to communicate Jesus Christ to us, as dead, buried, and risen again for us, to the destruction of our old man and the vivification of the new. Nor do they ever fail to produce these two effects in any of those who receive them as they ought. Therefore the holy apostles frequently ascribe them to the word of the gospel, which is the first and principal means which God employs to save us, in consequence of which it is called his power to salvation, Rom. i. 16. As for the destruction of the old man, the Epistle to the Hebrews attributes to the word the virtue which operates and effects it in us, saying that it is "quick and powerful, sharper than any two-edged sword, piercing even to the dividing asunder of the soul and spirit, and of the joints and marrow," Heb. iv. 12; and Paul elsewhere calls it a "weapon mighty to the pulling down of strong holds, casting down imaginations, and every high thing that exalteth itself against the knowledge of God, and bringing into captivity every thought to the obedience of Christ," 2 Cor. x. 4, 5. And as to the life of the new man, you know Peter teaches us that the gospel which is preached to us is the seed of this life, telling us that it is thereby we are born again, 1 Pet. i. 23, 25. That holy supper, of which we have participated this morning, has also the same effects. For since it communicates to us the body of Jesus Christ, dead and buried, and risen again for us, we need not doubt that it gives us also the virtue which it possesses, and which is inseparably adherent to it, for the putting to death the old Adam, and making the new to live in us, by its bedewing our consciences with his blood, and feeding our souls with his flesh.

But although these two effects are common to all the means which God has instituted and makes use of in religion, yet the apostle speaks here only of baptism, first, because it is the first seal which we receive of our Saviour, and the proper sacrament of our regeneration, which contains the initials and beginning of our spiritual life in the house of God; consequently, when treating of the same subject in his Epistle to the Romans, chap. vi. 3, 4, he makes mention of baptism in the same manner: "Know ye not," says he, "that so many of us as were baptized into Jesus Christ were baptized into his death? Therefore, we are buried with him by baptism." Secondly, he so speaks that he might with more clearness confute the error which he here combats, even by opposing to the circumcision which the seducers pressed that baptism which we have received in Jesus Christ, by which has been fully communicated to us all that these people pretended to draw from the use of circumcision. Their folly was, therefore, so much the more insupportable, as they not only retained a shadow, of which Jesus Christ has given us the true body, but also would not allow one of the old sacraments of Moses to give place to one of those which Jesus instituted. If the question be of the substance and very effect of circumcision, we have that truth and fulness in Jesus Christ, of which it had only some part shadowed out by its figure. If the subject be the sacrament itself, the Lord has given us one highly excelling, namely, baptism. So that, whichever way it is taken, there is no reason whatever that any man should desire still to retain circumcision.

But to proceed: it is not only in this place that the apostle attributes so great an effect to baptism; he speaks thus of it constantly: as, for example, when he says that Christ sanctifieth the church, "cleansing it with the washing of water by the word," Eph. v. 26; "and that, as many as have been baptized into Christ, have put on Christ," Gal. iii. 27; and again, that "by one Spirit we all are baptized into one body," 1 Cor. xii. 13. For the sacraments of Christ are not vain and hollow pictures, in which the benefits of his death and resurrection are nakedly portrayed, as in a piece of art, which gives us merely an unprofitable view of what it represents. They are effectual means, which he accompanies with his virtue, and fills with his grace; effectively accomplishing those things in us by his heavenly power which are set before us in the sacrament, when we receive it as we ought. He inwardly nourishes, by the virtue of his flesh and blood, the soul of him who duly takes his bread and his cup. He washes and regenerates that man within who is rightly consecrated by baptism. And if the infirmity of infancy prevents the effect from appearing at the instant in children baptized, yet his virtue does not fail to accompany his institution, to preserve itself in them, and to bring forth its fruits upon them in their season, when their nature is capable of the operations of understanding and will. In the primitive church, this double effect of baptism was more clearly represented in the external performance of the sacrament than it is at this day. For the greater part of those who were baptized, being persons of age, who came over to christianity from Judaism, or paganism, they were unclothed, and then plunged into the water, from whence they immediately came forth, and so were baptized in the name of the Father, and of the Son, and of the Holy Ghost; by which they testified that they put off the body of sin, the habit of the first Adam, and buried it in the saving waters of Jesus Christ, as in its mystical grave, and came forth thence risen up to a new life; for a symbol of which they took up a white habit, and wore it a whole week. Now, though the water with which we baptize does not carry so express a figure of this mystical sepulchre and resurrection as that of the ancients, since this ceremony cannot be practised towards infants without very great inconvenience, and even danger to their lives, in so tender an age, and especially in such cold countries as ours; nevertheless, the virtue of holy baptism is still the same; that Jesus, whom in it we put on, communicating to us, by the virtue of his Spirit, the mystical image of his burial and resurrection; that is, as we have showed, the annihilation of the old man, and creation of the new. [See note on page 333.]

If we meet with any baptized persons, as there are but too many, in whom the old man is so far from being buried, that he lives and reigns with absolute power, and the new man has neither life nor action at all, it must not be imputed to Jesus Christ, who always accompanies his sacraments with his saving virtue; but to the person's own unbelief, who wretchedly repels the operation of the grace of Christ, and deprives it of all the effect which it would have assuredly produced in them, if their unworthiness had not frustrated its efficacy towards them. For I acknowledge that neither baptism nor the word works in any but such as receive them with faith. And in this, as in all other things, the admirable wisdom of our Lord appears. For the subject being man, a reasonable creature, he deals with him in a way proper and suitable to his nature. The means he uses for his salvation do not operate in him as drugs and simples, by a physical action, which produce their effect, whatever may be the disposition of the man who takes them. But the operation of the word and sacraments depends upon the preparation of their hearts to whom they are administered. They work when they are received with faith; they produce nothing when they are received with unbelief. And thus it is fit that the understanding, which is the guide and ruler of all our moral actions, should be first persuaded of the truth of God, and then our wills and affections should take impression, and be changed by the efficacy of his power.

This very thing the apostle here shows us with much clearness, by saying, in addition to baptism, that we are buried and raised again with Christ by faith; an evident token that the sacrament mortifies sin in us, and raises us up unto holiness, according to the faith in us with which it meets. It left Simon Magus in the bonds of iniquity and in the gall of bitterness, because it found in him no faith at all, but a heart hardened in unbelief, and full of hypocrisy. But as for Lydia, and all those who have a true faith, it assuredly mortifies sin in them, and causes the new man to live in them unto righteousness and holiness. For it is impossible that the person who is firmly persuaded of the truth of the gospel can live in sin, the venom and horror of which this divine doctrine so clearly reveals;

on the contrary, he will embrace that holiness whose beauty and blessedness it so magnificently sets before us; man naturally flying from what he believes to be pernicious and destructive; and adhering, with the same necessity, to that which he judges healthful and advantageous.

But the apostle, who everywhere exalts the grace of God, and casts down the pride of man, lest any one should imagine that this faith, upon which all our felicity depends, is a production of our own will, by the way informs us that it is a gift of our Lord, calling it "the faith of the operation" or of the efficacy "of God," that is to say, which the efficacy of his hand produces in us. By this he refutes the error of those who contend that God, for the producing of faith in us, merely sets before us, either outwardly by his word, or inwardly by his Spirit, the object of truth, leaving it to the liberty of our will to believe or to reject it. Upon this supposition, faith would not be the faith of the operation of God; since, according to this doctrine, he would exert upon us none at all. But the apostle styles it "the faith of the operation of God." We must conclude, therefore, that in giving us faith he operates in us, powerfully forming our hearts, and opening them by the might of his Spirit, that they may receive his truth; yea, that he imprints and engraves it on them himself by a most efficacious action. The term energy (for such is the original, and it is that which we have rendered operation) deserves great consideration, properly signifying, in the style of the book of God, a powerful operation, which surely accomplishes its design, and infallibly produces its intention; such as the action by which God created the world; an evident sign that the operation by which he produces faith in us is so strong, that it bears down all contradiction; so that none of those upon whom he vouchsafes to confer it can resist it, or hinder their understanding from believing.

The apostle adds, that God has raised Jesus Christ from the dead, either to determine the object of our faith, which is principally Jesus raised from the dead by the glory of the Father; or (which I think to be more pertinent) to compare our mystical resurrection with that of Jesus Christ. For seeing it is God who, by his efficacious operation, gives us that faith by which we rise again in Christ; and seeing it is he again who has raised our Lord from the dead; it is evident that both these works have the self-same principle, namely, the almighty power of God. Christians, judge with what power he works in his faithful people, since he exerts the same power to give them faith as that by which he raised his own Son from the dead, as the apostle informs us yet more clearly in another place, where he prays that "we may know what is the exceeding greatness of his power to us-ward, who believe, according to the working of his mighty power, which he wrought in Christ, when he raised him from the dead," Eph. i. 19, 20. Neither let his saying that the Father raised him disquiet you, as if this contradicted our Lord's assertion in another place, that he himself raised up the temple of his body when the Jews had destroyed it, John ii. 19. It is true that he raised up himself; but since his power is the power of the Father, they being one only and the same God, it is evident that it may be truly said that the Father raised him up; the work of one being the work of the other, as our Saviour declares in John, that "what things soever the Father doeth, these also doeth the Son likewise," chap. v. 19. Consequently the Scriptures attribute the creation of the world indifferently to both the Father and the Son.

Dear brethren, this is what the holy apostle, the great minister of God, tells us in this text. Oh, how happy should we be, if we had these divine instructions written in our hearts, and engraven in capital letters upon all the parts of our lives! if our actions justified what our words profess, that we are buried and risen again with Jesus Christ by baptism, and by the faith of the operation of God, who raised him from the dead! But, alas! it must be confessed, to our shame, there appears in the lives of most of us no print of the burial, and least of all of the resurrection, of Jesus. The flesh lives, and exercises as horrible a tyranny in them as it does in the lives of the men of the world. It has all its sentiments and all its motions at liberty. The new man, that breathes nothing but heaven, and loves nothing but holiness, has no place in them; it is so far from reigning there that it is banished thence, and acts no more than a dead body fast shut up in the grave. Yet if nothing depended on the matter but our shame, impudence would bear it out; but the worst is, our salvation and our eternal damnation depend upon it; for Jesus Christ saves none but his members, such as are made conformable to his image, and have been buried and raised again with him. Let us awake, therefore, from this mortal lethargy, which has benumbed our senses to this day. Let us labour day and night in prayer, with sighs and tears, and not cease until we feel the old man die, and the new live in our hearts. As for the former, both nature and experience sufficiently show us the extravagance of its desires, and the vanity of all its motions. Tell me, I beseech you, what profit the flesh receives from all the trouble which it takes itself, or which it gives to others? What benefit has it from the turmoiling of its avarice, or the burning of its ambition, or the shamefulness of its pleasures, or the sweetness of its revenges? It torments itself, it wearies itself, it embraces wind and smoke, and then perishes, oftentimes shortening its own duration by the violence of its agitations. It has but a little body (which daily weakens) to lodge, and feed, and clothe for some years; yet it travails and disquiets itself as much as if it had a million to maintain for the space of many ages. Was there ever a greater folly? Certainly, should a man of composed mind behold our busy employments in the earth, with the motives and designs of those numerous motions and troubles in which we consume ourselves, I have little doubt that he would take nearly every man for frantic or foolish, and cry out, not simply with the wise man, "Vanity of vanities, all is vanity;" but yet louder, and in a tone more tragical, O madness! O frenzy! all the world is but a company of senseless men!

But merely seeing the vanity of the flesh is not sufficient for a due conception of its horror. Christian, enter into the sepulchre of your Saviour, and you will there perceive that, besides vanity, the life of the old man is completely full of venom and wretchedness. This sacred body which you see lying in that tomb, in so pitiful a state, was pierced with nails, potioned with gall, crowned with thorns, covered with the reproaches of men and the curse of God, separated from its soul, and brought down to the dust, to divert from you the punishments justly prepared for the disorders of your flesh. Think what hells it deserved, since it was necessary that the Lord of glory should suffer such strange usage to redeem it from them. Having once discerned, by such sensible evidences, the vanity and malignity of the old man, and the perdition into which he leads his vassals, how can you have the heart to let him live within you? Beloved brethren, away with him from the world, crucify him! He is unworthy to live. Pierce him through with the thorns and nails of your Jesus. Give him his gall to drink. Put him to death with him, and bury him in his sepulchre, to come forth no more. Let his avarice, and ambitions, and all his concupiscenses remain eternally extinct in the dust of that salvific grave, that there may henceforth no more appear any of his track in your whole course. And instead of that infernal vigour with which he heretofore influenced and disturbed your whole life, put on that new man, whom Jesus has on this day caused to come forth out of his sepulchre. Drink in his Spirit, fill your veins with his blood, and your arteries with his fire. Receive his sentiments, and deck yourselves with his light. Lead henceforth a life worthy of his resurrection, and of his baptism, and of that immortal food which you have taken at his table. Let your actions aim at nothing but heaven. It is there your treasure is. Christian, what do you yet seek on earth? Your Lord is no longer here. This day saw him arise to take his seat on high, at the right hand of God, and to carry up your hearts with him, giving them all his motions, that where he is ye may be also. And if his will is that you shall tarry yet a while on earth, spend the whole time in the same manner that he spent his forty days after his resurrection, in a continual meditation on heavenly things, in the company of apostles, in the entertainment of saints, in the exercise of an ardent love, in the preparatives of your ascension to his kingdom; wholly managing this short space to his glory and to the instruction and edification of men. This is what we owe, dear brethren, to the burial and resurrection of our Lord. There is no occasion to run to Palestine, nor to go up Mount Calvary, to enter into his sepulchre. You are entered into it, and buried with him, if you by the faith of his gospel mortify and destroy sin, according to the intention of your baptism. Nor is it any more necessary, in order to have part in his resurrection, to go and kiss the last print of his feet upon Mount Olivet. You are risen again with him, if you are affected with the glory which he brought out of his tomb, and persuaded of the truth of the discoveries which he made of blessed immortality, and live according to the form of his gospel, in purity and holiness.

May God, who raiseth the dead by his glorious power, be pleased to reveal the same might upon our hearts, and form such a lively faith in them, as may be the true workmanship of his hand, and the faith of his efficacy, that we may thereby be buried and raised up with Christ; and after these first-fruits of his holiness, be hereafter transformed into a perfect resemblance of his glory, that we may eternally possess that great and blessed heavenly kingdom with him, which he has purchased for us by the merit of his death, and insured to us by the virtue of his resurrection. So be it.

[Note referred to p. 329.—The Presbyterian Board are not to be regarded as fully endorsing the views of the author on the efficacy of Baptism, or as adopting all his expressions.—ED. PRES. BD.]

SERMON XXIV.

VERSE 13.

And you, being dead in your sins and the uncircumcision of your flesh, hath he quickened together with him, having forgiven you all trespasses.

DEAR brethren, philosophers commonly, and very properly, say that contraries illustrate each other; for nothing enables us better to understand the excellence of liberty than the consideration of the miseries of bondage; and there is nothing which shows us the nature and advantages of virtue more than the deformity and wretchedness of its opposite vices.

The beauty and usefulness of light is perceived by the hideousness of black obscurity, and the sweetness of health by the inconveniences of sickness. For this reason the ministers of God, to teach us the true worth of his benefits, frequently represent to us the misery of that state out of which he delivered us. The prophets of the Old Testament likewise continually put the Israelites in mind of their once sad and pitiful state in Egypt under the tyranny of Pharaoh. They would have them keep it in their eye, that they might thereby duly relish the redemption of God, and the sweetness of that liberty which he had given to them. Under the New Testament the apostles are no less intent to represent, at every turn, the extreme hideousness of our original condition, that we may acknowledge so much the more grace which God has showed us in his Son, by translating us out of the kingdom of darkness into his marvellous light. Thus Paul, in the text which we have read, that the Colossians might be brought more fully to comprehend the inestimable excellency of the benefit they had received from God in Jesus Christ, when they were raised again with him in baptism by the faith of his operation, as he expressed in the foregoing verse, now lays before them the misery in which they were before ingulfed: "And you, being dead in your sins and the uncircumcision of your flesh," &c.

Now this discourse also hits the mark at which he principally aimed in the whole dispute; which is, as you have often heard, to refute the pernicious error of those who considered the observance of circumcision, and other ceremonies of Moses, necessary for christians. Surely all the profit which they could pretend would be reaped from them was either the remission of our sins, or the sanctification of our lives. But the apostle here shows us, in a few words, that we have both these graces in Jesus Christ. The first, since God has freely forgiven us all our offences in him. The second, since being dead, as we were in ourselves, he has made us alive with him; which renders it evident that the ceremonies of the law are henceforth wholly useless to us. There is no need of the knife of Moses any longer. God, by the sole gospel of his Christ, dying and risen again for us, the true sword of heaven, infinitely sharper than any of the metals of nature, has cut off all the corruption of our flesh. He has done even much more; for by the power alone of the same Christ he has rescued us from death, and animated us, and given us new life. And as for the sins of which we were guilty, he has pardoned them all. His pure grace in Jesus Christ has effectually fulfilled whatever was promised or prefigured by the law of Moses. You have experienced it, says the apostle to the faithful at Colosse; you have seen and felt the efficacy of Jesus Christ in yourselves. Remember what you were, when you believed on him, and consider what you are since you passed through his hands. Ye were dead, and ye are alive: ye were covered with crimes, and are fully absolved from them. Do not so affront your Deliverer, as to think that, having wrought such great miracles by his own power alone, he needs the elements of the law to finish his work in you; and that he cannot complete, without Moses, what he so magnificently began and advanced without him. This, my brethren, is the apostle's express design, in these words.

We, who through the grace of God are not troubled with the error of these false teachers, which died and was buried long ago, will consider this text more generally, and view it in its whole extent, for our edification and consolation, without insisting precisely upon that particular use for which it was first written to the Colossians; and that nothing in it may escape us, we will examine, if God permit, the two heads which are proposed in it, distinctly one after the other.

The first is, the state we were in before the vocation of God in his Son; ye were "dead," says the apostle, "in your sins and the uncircumcision of your flesh."

The second is, the grace that God has showed us in Jesus Christ; he hath "quickened you," says he, "together with him, having forgiven you all trespasses."

Here is, in substance, the map of our whole redemption. The first part represents to us our misery by nature. And the second, our happiness under grace. That is, the achievement of the first and of the Second Adam; the death into which the one had sunk us, and the life unto which the other has raised us.

I. There are none so ignorant as not to know what life and death are. As life is the sweetest and dearest of all our good things; so death is the greatest and the last of all our evils. Accordingly, you see how prudently nature has given to animals such an instinct, as to use all the strength and skill they possess to preserve themselves alive, and to prevent them from dying. Every other evil takes from us but some part of our comforts. Death bereaves us of them all. Bondage deprives us of liberty, banishment of our country, sickness afflicts our bodies, shame or infamy our souls, pain troubles our senses, poverty embarrasses our life. But there is no calamity so great as not to leave us the use or enjoyment of some good, or at least of ourselves. Death extinguishing our life, and by this means sapping and overthrowing the very foundation of our enjoyments, at the same time despoils us of all other good things together. Wherefore the holy apostle, and the other sacred writers, that they might represent the hideousness and misery of the condition of men who are without the grace of God, do not call it simply a bondage, a banishment, a sickness, a disgrace, a blindness, a poverty, a calamity, a nakedness; they term it a death, to signify that it is the utmost of all the evils which can befall our nature; that it is a privation not of some good things only, but generally of all; so that nothing remains either in the spirit, or in the senses, or in the body of these miserable creatures, which deserves to be called good. It is the term Isaiah makes use of to express the state of people while they had no part in the covenant of God: "They that dwell in the land of the shadow of death, upon them hath the light shined," Isa. ix. 2. And the Lord Jesus puts us all in the same condition before he has called us. "The hour is coming, and now is, when the dead shall hear the voice of the Son of God, and they that hear shall live," John v. 25. And without doubt it is to these kinds of dead that he commanded one of his disciples to leave the care of burying their dead, Matt. viii. 22. And you know what the apostle says of that widow who passes her time in the pleasures of sin, that she "is dead while she liveth," 1 Tim. v. 6. And our Saviour tells that person who led a wicked life, under a false reputation of piety, "Thou hast a name that thou livest, and art dead," Rev. iii. 1. Paul, following the style of the Holy Ghost, calls them dead who, abiding in the ignorance which is natural to all men, neither know God nor his will: "Ye were dead," (says he to the Ephesians, speaking of the time they spent in the darkness of paganism,) "ye were dead in trespasses and sins," Eph. ii. 1. And a little after, putting himself in the same number, though he was a Jew, he says, When we were dead in sins, God "quickened us together with Christ," ver. 5; which are precisely the same terms as those which he here applies to the Colossians, whose original condition was in effect the same with that of the Ephesians, they being both by birth pagans.

I well know that the men of the world, and generally those who have no part in the grace of God, have life, sense, and motion; they desire, and fear, and hope, and exercise, in general, all the actions in which life is ordinarily made to consist. Yea, I confess that, to measure things by appearances, and by the outside only, there are none but they who seem to live, filling the world with the noise of their actions and motions, while the majority of the faithful groan in some corner, or pass their days obscurely in the silence of retirement, unsought and unobserved; so that it may be said of them, in this respect, as the apostle says in another, that "God hath chosen things which are not to bring to nought things that are," 1 Cor. i. 28; the flesh no more accounting the faithful to be anything than if they neither lived nor existed at all, but considering none but men of the world when they would reckon up the things that live, and which indeed are. But Paul himself clearly shows us that he speaks not here of the privation of this kind of life, inasmuch as he says not simply that we were dead, but that we were dead in sins and in the uncircumcision of our flesh. We must know, therefore, that there are two kinds of life: the one carnal and natural, which consists in the exercise of natural actions and faculties, such as are common to us, partly with sensitive creatures, as drinking, eating, sleeping, and the like; and partly with evil spirits, as sinning, offending God, and our neighbour. The other sort of life is spiritual and divine, having for its principle the image of God and his grace, and for its actions the exercise of piety towards God, and of love towards our neighbour; such a life as Adam's would have been if he had persevered in the innocence in which he was created, and such as is the life of the holy angels now in heaven. To these two kinds of life answer two kinds of death: the one natural, which is the separation of the soul from the body, and an abolition of the actions, and motions, and sensations, which the union of these two parts of our being produces in us; the other spiritual, which is nothing else than a privation of the image of God, and of those good and holy faculties, habits, and actions with which it is accompanied. It is this second kind of death which the apostle here intends, when he says that we were dead in sins and in the uncircumcision of our flesh. For the Holy Ghost, the true judge and estimator of things, counts all those for dead which have not the life of God, however full of life they may be with respect to the earth and the flesh: and that truly for a just cause; for if we consider the thing in the light of true reason, we shall find that what men call life in them is unworthy of that name; it being, properly speaking, mere death. For living is right acting, and the exercise of the faculties suitable to one's nature, with that satisfaction and pleasure of which he is capable; so that the true life of man (for of such we speak) is nothing else but a continual exercise of good, and holy, and just actions, suitable to his true nature, and worthy of that immortal soul which was given him at the beginning, with such high contentment as must needs accompany them. Now it is evident that those who are in the flesh do nothing like this. Instead of those excellent and noble actions for which they were created, they perform none but base and bad ones. Instead of meditating on God their Creator, and on heavenly and divine things, they dream of nothing but the flesh and the earth, unworthily weltering in these bogs with all the sense and understanding they have. Instead of loving God above all, of adoring and serving him with all the strength of their soul, their whole will is set on creatures and vanity. And their appetites, instead of being subject to right reason, drag it into corruption and unrighteousness. Surely this universal disorder in actions and motions is not, properly speaking, the life of a man; it is a depravation from it, and an overthrow of it, which deserves the name of death rather than that of life. As when a clock is damaged, and all its works are put into disorder, there is no longer the going of a clock; though it still has the parts, it no longer performs its office; it has only the name of a clock, it is not one in reality. So is it with man; he has still the broken remains and ruins of his primitive nature; but the pieces being confused, the wheels pressed together, and all the motions disordered, he has no longer the true life thereof, but only a false and deceptive image of it. Again, acting in this horrible confusion, is it impossible that he can have that pure and calm contentment without which his life is not life. He must of necessity be always in doubt, in distrust, in fear, and disquietude, and must at last fall under those just executions which this disorder deserves; that is, into that eternal death which is the wages of sin. And though he does not yet suffer this final misery while he is on earth, yet because it is infallibly his portion, and will, ere long, assuredly befall him, we are to count him even at present a dead man, and to look upon him as on a malefactor who is on the point of being condemned and executed. For though he, in the mean time, lives and breathes, yet we hesitate not to say that such a one is a lost man, because his punishment is certain. Thus you see it is very justly that the apostle reckons all those to be dead who are without the grace of God, inasmuch as they perform none of the actions of true life, and that eternal death is unavoidable while they remain in this state.

But the apostle's words signify still something more. For to be dead is not simply to cease from exercising the actions of life, it is a loss of the principles of life, and an incapacity for performing the actions thereof. You do not call him a dead man who is simply without action, and does not exercise sensation or motion; (for they who are asleep, or in a swoon, are in that condition, yet they are not dead;) but him who cannot any longer act, or feel, or move, and with action has lost the faculty or power of it. Surely, then, since the apostle says that carnal men are dead, he means not only that they are without the operations, and motions, and sentiments of true life, but that they also lie destitute of the faculty and power to perform them. He expressly teaches us this in another place. For as to their understanding, which is the foremost and ruling guide of all actions properly human, he does not simply say that it comprehends not the things of God, but also that it cannot discern them: "The natural man receiveth not the things of the Spirit of God, for they are foolishness unto him; neither can he know them, because they are spiritually discerned," 1 Cor. ii. 14. And as for the affections, which are another principle of human actions, he affirms likewise, in his Epistle to the Romans, that "the carnal mind," or the affection of the flesh, "is enmity against God," that "it is not subject to the law of God, neither indeed can be," Rom. viii. 7. Our Saviour also says of such as are in this miserable state, that they cannot believe, John v. 44; and one of his prophets had said long before, that the ear of that people was uncircumcised, and that they could not hearken; and, in general, that they could no more do any good than the Ethiopian could change his skin, or the leopard his spots, Jer. vi. 10; xiii. 23.

But the apostle here further shows us the quality and the cause of this death under which we lay before the Lord called us; ye were "dead," says he, "in your sins and the uncircumcision of your flesh." I acknowledge that this word is sometimes taken in the Scripture for the external condition of the Gentiles; and circumcision, on the contrary, for the state of the Jews: it follows, therefore, that the former of those terms is used to signify the Gentiles, and the latter the Jews; as when the apostle says elsewhere that the preaching of the gospel to the uncircumcision was committed unto him, and the circumcision unto Peter; that is, he received the charge of publishing the gospel to the Gentiles, and Peter to the Jews. I confess also, that these Colossians to whom he writes were by birth Gentiles; so that it may be said of them, that they were dead in that miserable heathen-like state in which they formerly were. Yet I do not think that this is intended by the apostle in this place. For in that case it would have been sufficient to say simply, when ye were "dead in uncircumcision," *i. e.* in paganism, and there would have been no occasion to add, as he does, "in the uncircumcision of your flesh." Besides, it appears evident that he makes here a secret opposition between that uncircumcision of which he speaks, and that circumcision which the Colossians had received from the hand of Jesus Christ, of which he spake immediately before, saying that in Jesus Christ they had been "circumcised with a circumcision made without hands, by putting off the body of the sins of the flesh." Therefore, as by circumcision in that passage a spiritual and mystical cutting off was signified, so in the text the apostle takes the word "uncircumcision" mystically, and not literally, for the internal corruption of our nature, and (as he expressed it before) for the body of the sins of the flesh, not simply for the external condition and mark of paganism. Ye were "dead in the uncircumcision of your flesh;" that is, in the corruption of your flesh; precisely in the same sense that Moses meant, when he commanded the Israelites to circumcise the foreskin of their heart, that is, to cut off the vices and corruptions of their hearts. This mystical uncircumcision of the flesh is nothing else than the depravity of our nature; the sins and perverse habits and qualities which have seized on all its faculties; the blindness, error, and folly of the understanding; the disorder of the will, and its adherence to vanity and earthly things; the rebellion of the appetites and lusts, all tainted with gall and bitterest poison. This is properly the principle of that death with which we all were struck before the vocation of God. This is the cursed root from which it springs in us. In the stirrings and motions of this hateful source, which boils incessantly in us, and which casts up filth continually, does this spiritual death consist.

I confess, in this respect, there is a difference between the condition of the dead, commonly so called, and the condition of these spiritually dead, of whom the apostle speaks. For the former, as they do no good, so neither do they commit any evil. Their faculties are equally disabled for the one as for the other. Whereas these spiritually dead men have lost sense and motion only in reference to that which is good. They have both these faculties in sufficient exercise, but it is only with reference to evil. They understand, they love, they desire, but not that which is good; their thoughts and affections being full of error, extravagance, and malignity. As for true good, they neither comprehend, nor discern, nor love it, any more than if they had neither understanding nor will at all. Consequently, while the deadness, the insensibility, and immobility of other dead are an innocent misery, deserving our pity and not our hatred, those of these men, on the contrary, are an evil infinitely culpable, and merit not compassion, but abhorrence and execration from every reasonable creature: inasmuch as their inability to love God does not proceed from their being destitute of natural faculties of understanding and loving, but from a strong and obstinate rebellion of those faculties, and from that invincible passion which carries them to evil; as our Saviour shows us, when he says to the Jews, "How can ye believe, which seek honour one of another, and seek not the honour which cometh from God only?" John v. 44. An evident sign that the impotency of these wretched people to believe came from nothing but their impiety, their stiff and inflexible aversion to the glory of God, and that ardent and invincible affection which they had for vanity and their own glory.

See then, beloved brethren, what is the condition of all men before the Lord effectually calls them to the grace of his Son. Where now are they who pretend that they have the power of a free determination, and a will equally capable of good and evil—who contend that they can either convert themselves to God, (as said the Pelagians of old,) or at least prepare themselves for conversion, and dispose themselves for grace, as the greater part of the doctors of Rome, and with them some others also, maintain at this day? The apostle blasts all this pride in one word, when he says that we were dead in our sins, and in the uncircumcision of our flesh. If a dead man is able to make himself alive, or to prepare himself for the reception of life, by any action that proceeds from him, I will confess that the error of these men is not incompatible with the doctrine of Paul. But since common sense assures us that the dead are deprived, not of the actions alone, but also of the power of life, and that there is nothing but a supernatural action of God which is able to restore them to the society of the living, so that they can contribute nothing thereto themselves, we must needs either charge a falsehood upon the apostle, who says that before grace we are dead in our sins; or confess, in consequence of his doctrine, that men neither have nor can have, of themselves, any action or disposition unto spiritual life; and that the power of the hand of God, working supernaturally in them by his grace, is the only strength that raises them out of this miserable state. If their will be free, it is free to evil only, which it embraces and follows most freely, that is, most voluntarily, and without any constraint, taking all its delight therein. If their understanding act, it is for error, which it conceives and most obstinately embraces. But as for the life of God, they have no more liberty or light for it than if they had neither will nor understanding at all; according to that which our Saviour has taught us, saying, "No man can come to me, except the Father which hath sent me draw him;" and again, "If the Son make you free, ye shall be free indeed," John vi. 44; viii. 36. Without this, a man can have neither life nor liberty.

II. The apostle clearly shows it, when, having represented the death in which we were, he adds, in the second part of our text, that God hath quickened us together with Christ, having forgiven us all trespasses. For there is no doubt that we must refer this action to God, of whom he just before was saying that he "raised Jesus Christ from the dead." It is therefore the same God who raised up the chief Shepherd from the dead who also quickens his faithful flock, bringing them out of that spiritual and eternal death into which they were naturally sunk, and giving them a celestial and immortal life. As there is none but he who could inspire and quicken that dust of which he at first formed us; so there is none but he who can expel out of our flesh that death which has seized upon it, and restore that life which sin has extinguished in us. Each of these vivifications is the work of his hand alone; though, to say the truth, it is needful for him to put forth more might in the accomplishment of the second than he did in effecting the first. For if that handful of earth of which he created Adam had no disposition at all to that form and life which he put in it, yet it had at least no repugnancy thereto; whereas he not only now finds in us no disposition to a heavenly life, but he meets also with resistance and contrariety; a spirit of rebellion animating the whole mass of our flesh, which he must necessarily cast out, in order to infuse celestial life. Now as that death in which we lay comprehends two things—namely, first, the corruption of a nature destitute of all just and rational apprehensions and motions; and, secondly, the guilt of sin, and an obligation to eternal punishment; in like manner that life to which God calls us by his grace consists in two particulars: first, a restoration of his image in us, by the infusion of principles and faculties of true life; and, secondly, the remission of our sins. The apostle here briefly speaks of them both: of the first, in saying that God has quickened us together with Christ; of the second, in adding that he has forgiven all our trespasses.

God has quickened us, first, in that, delivering us from the death we were under, he has put into us, by the grace of his Spirit, the principles of a heavenly life, and formed in us new hearts; hearts illuminated with a new light, namely, the good knowledge of his truth, and of the mysteries of his will. Then, in the second place, by the virtue of this divine flame, he enkindles in our souls the love of his most excellent Majesty, charity towards our neighbour, affection for just and honest things, zeal for his glory, abhorrence and hatred of sin, and, in a word, sanctification, and all the virtues which it comprehends, and which are the sproutings and productions of that second celestial and happy life which in his great mercy he confers upon us. From this new nature, as from a blessed root, issue good and holy actions, prayer, worshipping of God, frequent meditation, and reading of his word, ecstasies of love to him, exertions for his glory, sufferings for his name, relieving, instructing, and assisting our neighbour, and many others, which are, as it were, the flowers and fruits; in the production of which that life which God has given us in his Son properly consists. It is the same thing which the apostle, in his Epistle to the Ephesians, comprises in a few words, saying that "we are the workmanship of God, created in Christ Jesus unto good works, which God hath before ordained that we should walk in them," chap. ii. 10; and again, in another place, that our new man (that is, the second nature, which he forms in us when he quickens us by his grace) "is created after God in righteousness and holiness," chap. iv. 24. The Holy Spirit, being rich and magnificent in his expressions, explains this admirable and blessed operation of the grace of God in us by various terms, taken from different resemblances, but all amounting to the same sense. To set it forth, he says not only, as here, that God has quickened us, but also that he has created us, Eph. ii. 10; and in another place, that he "hath begotten us again," 1 Pet. i. 3. The same is meant when he says that God "will take away the stony heart out of our flesh, and will give us a heart of flesh," Ezek. xxxvi. 26, in which he will write his laws, Jer. xxxi. 33; that he renews us, and forms us into new creatures, or new men, Eph. iv. 23, 24; that he grafts us by his power into the true olive, Rom. xi. 24; that he translates us out of the kingdom of darkness into his marvellous light, Col. i. 13; that it is he who gives increase, the ministers of the word being nothing, 1 Cor. iii. 6; that he opens our hearts, Acts xvi. 14, and works in us effectually "both to will and to do of his good pleasure," Phil. ii. 13; and other similar phrases, which are found in various parts of the Scriptures.

But the apostle adds here, that God has thus quickened us together with Christ; showing us, by these words, the cause and the manner of our vivification; namely, that it was effected in Jesus Christ, and with him and by him. For as that death which we before bore in ourselves came from Adam, the stock and origin of our carnal being, who by destroying himself destroyed us also with him; and, corrupting his own nature, corrupted ours likewise; as it is in him and from him that we inherit this misery: so, on the contrary, that life which we have now received from God comes in the same manner from Jesus Christ, the stock and root of the new nature; who, raising up himself to life, raised us up also; according to what the apostle saith elsewhere, that "as in Adam all die, even so in Jesus Christ shall all be made alive," 1 Cor. xv. 22. But his assertion, that God has quickened us together with Christ, particularly refers to his resurrection; as if God, in restoring him to that glorious life, which he received at his issuing from the sepulchre, had at the same time given us also part therein. And he speaks in this manner, principally, for two reasons: first, because it was then that Jesus Christ brought to light that blessed life of which we have been made partakers; and from him, as from its source, has it been communicated to us; so that the day of his resurrection was the day of our new birth. For if he had not been made alive, no more should we ever have been. Not but that the Father had all the might and power which were necessary to give us life again. But his justice could not have suffered him to give life to any of the sons of men, if their Surety and Mediator had abode under death. The second reason is, that he being our Head, and we his members; he our Pattern, and we copies drawn (if I may so speak) from his original; when God raised him, he re-enlivened us also by the same means, since by this action he bound himself to vivify us likewise; it being evident that without this we should not have that conformity with our Head to which he predestinated us; not to mention, for the present, the efficacy this resurrection has to form in us faith, and hope, and love of glorious immortality, which are the principles of that new life that God puts into us by his Spirit, as we intimated in the exposition of the preceding verse.

It remains now for us to consider the other part of this blessed life which God gives us in his Son, namely, "the remission of our sins." Paul sets it before us, when he says that God has forgiven us all trespasses. For the Spirit of sanctification, which is as the soul of that new life which he creates in our hearts, indeed turns away our affections from vice, and obstructs our commission of unjust, ungodly, and impure actions, in which we wallowed before; yet this respects only the present and the future; and if there were no more, the guilt of sins committed in time past, during our spiritual deadness, would nevertheless remain in its strength; it being clear, that though the act of sin be past, the guilt with which it defiles him who commits it does not depart so soon. It subsists still, both in the conscience of the sinner, if he have any, and in the registers of the justice of the supreme Judge of the world, binding over the sinner to punishment. From which it follows, that supposing a man to be perfectly cured of vicious habits and inclinations, yet he would nevertheless be guilty, in consequence of his former sins, and upon that account liable to the curse; with which, and the terrors that precede it, true life is so incompatible, that it is not to be supposed that a man in such a state could ever resolve to serve God freely and sincerely. Therefore God, that he may thoroughly quicken us, does not only deliver us from the tyranny of vice, and of the flesh, by that princely Spirit which he pours into our inward parts; but also pardons all the sins of which we are guilty: and it certainly appears, if we accurately observe the moments of his action in us, that it is there he begins, first remitting our former offences, to the end that the sense of this his goodness may cause us to love him, and incline us to obey him, and conform ourselves with all our might unto his holy will.

The apostle attributes to this remission two remarkable qualities: one, that God forgives "all our trespasses;" that is, does not impute to us any of our sins, either in whole or in part; but treats us as if we had committed none at all. Another is, that he does it freely, and of mere grace, for so the original properly signifies. The Scripture tells us not of any other kind of pardon. For as to that which our adversaries assert, namely, that the fault is remitted, but the punishment exacted, either in whole or in part, or is bought out with the payment of our own satisfaction, or the satisfaction of others, it is a fiction of their own schools, of which the Holy Ghost says nothing anywhere; but, on the contrary, he represents that remission which God gives the faithful, either at the beginning or in the progress of their regeneration, as an entire pardon, and purely gratuitous. As for that satisfaction by which our Lord and Saviour obtained it for us, it is so far from any way diminishing, that it infinitely exalts the bounty of God towards us, inasmuch as it shows that he so loved us, that in order to pardon our sins with the consent of his justice, he gave his only Son to shed his precious blood for the satisfaction thereof. Thus we have expounded this text of the apostle.

Dear brethren, let us hold fast what it has taught us of the condition in which all men naturally are before God calls them to his grace. Let not their outward appearance, nor the pleasures of their flesh, nor the splendour of their pretended virtues, either civil or moral, deceive you. All this is but a false image of life, covering a carcass loathsome and abominable before God. Account them to be dead; and if they walk, consider it not to be a true principle of life, but sin, the poison of life, which animates them, and incites them to action. The issue will one day clear it to us all; when the just judgment of God, having stripped them of that fallacious disguise which now hides the deformity of their nature, shall show it before heaven and earth, and make us plainly see that they were but sepulchres, whited without, and full of filth and infection within; and consequently cast them into that wretched and eternal death, which is prepared for them with the devil and his angels.

Let us bless God, who has delivered us from this perdition by his great mercy, and hate sin, and the corruption of the flesh, which had involved us in it. Let us consider them as pests and poisons which destroy our life, and reckon that we have lived only during that time which has been exempted from their service. You deceive yourself, worldling, who count the days of your unclean pleasures, or your vain honours, the best part of your life. To speak plainly, it was the time of your being dead, and not of your being alive. After so many years as you have roamed up and down the earth, you have not yet lived a moment. You have all along been in a state of death; and they who write upon your tombs, that you lived so many years, and died such a day, grossly err. You did not live when you offended God and your neighbour, or lost your time in the filth of your infamous delights. And on the day that you shall quit the earth, you will not cease to live (for, properly speaking, you never lived); but from one kind of death you will pass into another, from the death of sin to a death of torment. Christians, if you love life, and hate horror at death, renounce sin and mortify your flesh. You cannot live, except it die. Put in exercise that noble life which the Lord has given you in his Son. Act according to the principles which he has put into you by his Spirit, and exhibit continually in good and holy works the graces with which he has vested you. Faithfully love and serve him. Let your minds meditate on nothing beside him, your hearts desire none but him, your tongues speak only of him. Let the contemplation of the wonders of his love, and the hopes of his glory, be the whole food of your souls. Respect those men in whom you see his image shine; love and serve them for his sake, looking upon their lives, their estates, their honour, their bodies, and souls, as sacred and inviolable things. Endeavour to enrich them by communicating your prosperity to them: offend no man; do good to all: let your charity and your innocence be conspicuous in the sight of God and man.

Faithful brethren, this is that life, truly worthy to be called life, which God rewards for the present with a joy and contentment of conscience, a thousand times more sweet and savoury than any of the vain delights of the world, and which he will crown one day with that glorious immortality which he has promised. It is for this that he has vouchsafed to forgive us freely all our trespasses, all those heinous crimes which had merited hell-fire, and is still ready to pardon all the sins which we have since committed. This his great and admirable loving-kindness tends only to withdraw us from sin, and to constrain us to love and revere so good a God. It is for the same design that he has raised up his Son from the dead, and quickened us with him, giving us faith, hope, and charity, the principles of a new life, even that henceforth renouncing sin and the flesh, and turning our hearts towards heaven, where our treasure and our glory are, we might live soberly, righteously, and godly in the present world, looking for that blessed hope and the glorious appearing of the great God, and our Saviour Jesus Christ. Amen.

SERMON XXV.

VERSE 14.

Blotting out the handwriting of ordinances that was against us, which was contrary to us, and took it out of the way, nailing it to his cross.

DEAR brethren, that remission of sins which God gives to all those who believe in his gospel is, in truth, of itself a great and inestimable grace; for who does not see that it was an effect of the transcendent goodness in God to be willing to pardon such persons as had grievously offended him; and to consent to their happiness who had provoked him, by their wickedness and ingratitude, to make them eternally miserable? But the manner in which he has pardoned us, and the price which our grace cost him, infinitely heightens the wonder of this benefit; for he has not forgiven our sins by a single act of his will, as a creditor remits a debt to his debtor, because to such a man, having absolute power to dispose of his estate in favour of whom he pleases, it is sufficient, for the performance of such a kindness, that he will do it. With God it was not so, in the remission of our sins. His justice, and the majesty of his laws, were concerned in the favour which he would show us, and formed an opposition against it, withholding and staying the motion of his clemency towards us; so that while his own holiness permitted him not to despise the voice of reason, and the rights of justice, for the sake of any one whatever, the will he had to pardon us was not sufficient alone to bring it into effect. And here it was that his love to us showed itself to be wonderful and truly divine; for seeing that sin could not be forgiven us, without satisfying that justice which we had violated; and, on the other hand, that this inexorable justice could not be satisfied but by the cross of his only Son; this good and merciful Lord so desired our bliss, that, to take away the legal impediments which justice laid against it, he resolved to deliver up his Son to that cruel and shameful death; as our Saviour himself has declared in the gospel, saying that "God so loved the world, that he gave his only begotten Son, that whosoever believeth in him should not perish but have everlasting life," John iii. 16. Here, then, is properly the highest pitch of this wonder, which justly ravishes men and angels, that the pardon which God has given us was bought at the price of the death of his well beloved Son. And, in truth, our consciences could not have been assured of his grace without this; nature having planted in our hearts so quick a sense of the right that God has against sins, that we could not put an entire confidence in his mercy until we knew that his justice was recompensed and satisfied. Therefore the holy apostle, having represented to the faithful at Colosse, in the preceding verse, the great favour which God had showed them in forgiving their trespasses, now adds the foundation of this remission, and the means by which it had been obtained. He has forgiven you, having blotted out "the handwriting of ordinances that was against us, which was contrary to us, and took it out of the way, nailing it to his cross." By this consideration he gives them to see the greatness of this blessing, and assures their consciences against all the doubts which the rigour of the law might raise in them, and particularly against the contendings of those false teachers who would make them believe that the grace of Jesus Christ was not sufficient for their salvation except they submitted to the ceremonies of Moses. This shall be, by the will of God, the subject of this exercise; and to give you a full understanding of this text, we will consider two things.

First, what this "handwriting" or obligation is of which he speaks, that lay in ordinances, and "was contrary to us." And,

Secondly, how God blotted it out, took it out of the way, and nailed it to the cross of his Son.

I. Let us consider this "handwriting" or obligation. It is the ordinary practice of Scripture to liken sin to a debt; whence comes that phrase which is so common in the language of God and of the church, of remitting or acquitting sin for pardoning it. Our Saviour used it in the prayer which he gave us, where the petition for the pardon of our sins is couched in these words in the gospel of Matthew, "Forgive us our debts, as we forgive our debtors," chap. vi. 12; that is to say, (as Luke has interpreted it, chap. xi. 4,) "Forgive us our sins: for we also forgive every one that is indebted to us," or that has offended us. This form of speech was so ordinary among the Chaldees and Syrians, that they put the word debtor for sinner, or a guilty person, as appears by the ancient Chaldee paraphrase upon the Psalms, which says, "Blessed is the man that standeth not in the way of debtors," instead of saying "sinners," as the Hebrew text of the first Psalm imports. And our Lord used the same word in this sense, when, upon mention being made of certain Galileans, whose blood Pilate had cruelly mingled with their sacrifices, he says, "Suppose ye that these Galileans were sinners above all the Galileans?" Luke xiii. 2. Thus also we must take it in that tradition of the scribes and Pharisees, reported by Matthew, he that hath sworn by the gift which is upon the altar is a debtor; that is, he sins, or is culpable. The reason of this metaphor is founded upon the resemblance of the things themselves, debt and sin having some conformity. For as the one obliges the debtor to payment, the other obliges the sinner to punishment. And as a debt gives the creditor a certain power over his debtor; in like manner sin consigns over the offender to God, or to the magistrate. For he has a just power to punish the sinner, as a creditor has to make his debtor pay; though, as we said not long since, there is some difference between the powers of the one, and those of the other; public justice being concerned in the punishment of an offender, whereas, in a debtor's making payment it is not so; consequently, debts may remain unpaid, if the private person, to whom they are due, is pleased to remit them; whereas justice does not leave a sin unpunished, though the offended party forgive the offender. And this difference is seen in human affairs, where you know that, for the exemption of a criminal from punishment, it is not enough that he satisfy his adversary; the prince also, who is guardian of the law, and the conservator of public justice, must give him an abolition of his crime. But setting aside this difference, there is, in other respects, such an analogy between a debt and sin, that the name of the one is justly applied to signify the other. This similitude is the cause of Paul's here giving the name of a "handwriting" to the law or testament of Moses.

The word which he makes use of in the original signifies generally any acknowledgment written, or at least signed with our hand, by which we confess ourselves to owe a man a certain sum, and bind ourselves to pay him it at such time, and in such manner, as we have agreed upon. Such are those which are commonly called bills and schedules. But because of all contracts of this kind, an obligation that passes before notaries with certain solemn forms is the most juridical, the French Bible has made use of that name in particular. An obligation then in civil matters is a creditor's title, and an evidence of the power which he has over his debtor, to convince him of his debt, and compel him to make payment, if he refuse. It is an authentic testimony of his owing such a sum; it condemns him to pay, and makes his body and goods liable in this behalf to his creditor. From which it appears that this handwriting of which the apostle speaks in the text is the instrument of our condemnation, and an authentic declaration and demonstration of our sin, which gives valid testimony that we are guilty, and subjects us by this means to the avenging justice of God, giving him a clear and undisputable right to prosecute and punish us. All agree that the word handwriting must be so taken in this passage. But respecting the proper and precise meaning of the apostle by this expression, there is found some difference among expositors; some conceiving it to be one particular, and others another. I will not stay to report their several opinions, it being no way necessary for your edification. I will content myself with representing to you that sense which I consider the most true, and which has likewise been followed by various eminent servants of God. I say, then, that this handwriting of which the apostle speaks means nothing else than the old law, given in time past to the Israelites by the ministry of Moses, and of them accepted at Mount Sinai. This appears, first, from Paul's saying that this handwriting was one of ordinances. For every one knows that this properly belongs to the law of Moses, which consisted in a great many moral, ceremonial, and political ordinances. The Jews, who are very exact and scrupulous in such matters, reckon them up to six hundred; and their most learned authors divide them into fourteen classes or ranks.* The whole body of these ordinances is precisely the law of Moses; so it is evident that it is to this law the apostle alludes, since he says that it is "the handwriting of ordinances." He thus explains it himself, in a passage which has great alliance with the text before us; where, speaking of the reuniting of the Gentiles with the Jews into one only people by our Lord Jesus Christ, he says that he "abolished in his flesh the enmity, even the law of commandments contained in ordinances," Eph. ii. 15; where it is evident that he signifies the law of Moses, both by those express words, "the law of commandments," and also by the nature of the thing itself; it being certain that this enmity of the Jews and Gentiles (that is, the thing which separated them before our Saviour's dispensation) was nothing else but the Mosaic law, which the one of them had, and the other had not. The same appears again clearly, from that conclusion which the apostle draws from this doctrine, in the 16th and the following verses of this chapter. For from his position here, namely, that the handwriting of ordinances has been effaced or blotted out; he concludes that none ought to condemn us in eating, or in drinking, or in distinguishing a festival, or a new moon, or Sabbaths; and again, that it is impertinent for any to burden us with ordinances such as these, "Touch not, taste not, handle not," ver. 21. Now every one perceives that these ordinances make up a part of the law of Moses. Certainly, then, it is that law which he here means; for otherwise it would not follow, from the blotting out of our handwriting, that we are no longer subject to such things.

But the truth of this interpretation will be fully perceived by an exposition of the apostle's own words themselves; there being no other subject but the Mosaic law with which all the

---

* R. Moses ben Majm.

circumstances and qualities he here attributes to it properly agree. First, he terms it "handwriting against us." Secondly, he says that it was one "of ordinances." In the third place, he adds, that it "was contrary to us." And in the fourth place, he says that it has been blotted out, taken away, and nailed to the cross. These are things which cannot, all of them together, be verified of any other subject. First, the law of Moses was a handwriting or an obligation against such as lived under its dispensation; that is, as we have explained it, an evidence and infallible argument of their sin, and of the just power that God had to condemn them to punishment. For the law of Moses proclaiming aloud that all such as failed to observe any one of its ordinances are accursed, it is manifest that all those who accepted it for the terms of their covenant with God, by that act passed condemnatory sentence on themselves, and submitted to the curse; both the conscience of each one in particular, and the common experience of all in general, showing that there was not a man who punctually observed all things written in the law. And as he who signs an obligation in favour of his creditor condemns himself to make payment; and if he fail therein, makes his goods, and sometimes his very person, liable to him; in the same manner, they who received the law, and signed it (if I may so say) after they had heard and understood it; these, I say, condemned themselves to the curse of God, and put their persons, and all their goods into the hands of divine justice, since it is clear that none of them ever fully satisfied all the clauses which that contract contained. Therefore, as a bond given by a debtor to his creditor in acknowledgment of what he owes him is an obligation, which makes it clearly appear that he is responsible to him, and deprives him of all excuse, and leaves him no defence to the contrary; so the law of Moses is an authentic obligation, which demonstrates, and invincibly proves, that the sinner is guilty, and liable to the avenging justice of God, without having any means left him to defend himself from that punishment which it ordains for all such as violate its commands. As for the ceremonies, I grant, they promised, in appearance, some satisfaction of the justice of God, and some expiation of sin, inasmuch as they prefigured the mysteries of Christ who was to come. But, in themselves, they, in effect, contained no such thing. On the contrary, they were so many obligations upon a sinner, openly testifying that he stood obnoxious to the justice of God. For the aspersions and purifications which were made by washing, or pouring water upon men, evidently showed that those who received them were defiled and unclean. And circumcision was a public confession of the impurity of our nature, which declared that it needed to be cut or retrenched. And they who offered beasts to be slain for sacrifices, by that very act acknowledged that they had deserved death. Those who observed the fasts, and other mortifications of the law, protested that they were unworthy to use the creatures of God. And thus it was in the rest of their ceremonies. All their devotions of this nature were either emblems of the punishment they deserved, or a declaration of their guilt, and so many proofs and convictions of their sin. For to imagine that these carnal ceremonies truly expiated their offences was not possible, both on account of the absurdity and extravagance of the thing itself; and also of the frequent and express declarations of God to the contrary made by the mouth of his prophets.

So you see clearly that the whole of the law of Moses was no other than an obligation against us, an instrument of our condemnation, an evidence of our sin, and a justification of our punishment. Wherefore, the apostle elsewhere in the same sense, and for the same reason, calls it "the ministration of death," and "of condemnation," 2 Cor. iii. 7, 9; because, in effect, it properly served only to form, and prosecute, and finish the sinner's arraignment; as affording full demonstration both of his guilt, and of the penalty due to him; giving in evidence concerning his crimes, and making known the justice of God in judging and punishing him. And to this must be referred that which he says in other places, namely, that "by the law" was given "the knowledge of sin," Rom. iii. 20; and that "it was added because of transgressions," Gal. iii. 19; and again, that without the law he "had not known sin," Rom. vii. 7.

As for what the apostle adds here, in the second place, that this handwriting of which he speaks consists in ordinances, we have touched upon it already, and referred it to that large multitude of commandments in which it consists. For I do not see that anything obliges us to restrain this clause to the ordinances of the ceremonial law, as some do. It comprehends generally everything that the law ordains. And it appears to me that the apostle's scope and aim requires that it should be so understood; for he urges God's having abolished that handwriting of ordinances, to prove what he had been saying respecting his having forgiven our trespasses. Why? and how so? Because, says he, he has cancelled, by the cross of his Son, "the handwriting that was against us." It certainly appears that this reason will be beside the purpose, if the obligation that was made void were not that of the whole law; as the offences which have been forgiven us, in consequence of the abolition of this obligation, are generally all sins committed against any part of the law whatever, and not transgressions of the ceremonial ordinances only. And as to the apostle, in the following verses, arguing from this doctrine against the ceremonies only, who does not know that it is ordinary to reason from the whole unto one of the parts? As when in the Epistle to the Galatians, having laid it down in general, that the law of Moses cannot at all justify us; he thence infers against the seducers, that, by consequence, neither circumcision nor the other ceremonies can have this virtue; just as in this place, having settled this principle, that the Mosaic law was abolished by the cross of our Saviour, he afterwards justly concludes that we are no longer obliged to its ancient ceremonies.

But the apostle says, in the third place, that this handwriting or obligation of which he speaks "was contrary to us." This, as you see, also well agrees with the law. Of itself, I confess, it is good, and holy, and profitable, and salutary unto man, as it is that which would lead him unto life; but it is become contrary to us through sin, of which we all are guilty. For it serves to convict us of it; as an obligation, which being produced in judgment, stops the mouth of an unfaithful debtor. It is as it were our adversary, that impleads us, and lays open our crimes, and brings upon us that condemnation to which we have submitted in accepting and signing it. And as for its ceremonies, they not only bore witness against the sin of those who observed them, as we have said; but they were also contrary to us in another sense, even as they put a new yoke upon us, which, through their vast multitude and diversity, was heavy and insupportable. Yet it must be observed that this does not appear to be properly the meaning of the apostle here; the word he makes use of in the original* signifying that this obligation was not simply contrary to us, but contrary in some measure. I think, then, that by this word he prevents an objection which might be urged. For though the law is an obligation against us, perhaps some one may say it is nevertheless useful, since it shows us our sin and misery; and by that means forces us to have recourse to the mercy of God, that we may seek our salvation in his grace alone; which was in effect the true end for which God gave it to the Israelites. The apostle granting this as a truth, affirms that this obligation was, notwithstanding, in some measure contrary to us. For, first, by telling us only of obeying, or being punished, and thundering out on all sides that dreadful voice, "Cursed is every one that continueth not in all things written in the law to do them;" it darkened the clearness of the grace of God, and perplexed poor sinners, filling them with terror, and hindering them from fully discerning the clemency and mercy of the Lord. Then again it aggravated their pains by its ceremonies; the true scope of which was at that time very difficult rightly to comprehend. And lastly, it shut the gate of the house of God against the Gentiles, of whose number the Colossians were,

* ὑπεναντίον.

separating them from his people, and consequently from his grace and pardon, which he gives to none but those who are in his covenant. If therefore it is not absolutely contrary to us, yet it cannot be denied that it was so in some degree.

Finally, the apostle says that this obligation which was against us has been blotted out, and entirely abolished, and fastened to the cross; which also agrees very properly with the law of Moses, which Paul everywhere tells us was disannulled and abrogated by the death of the Lord Jesus, to make room for the gospel, according to the oracles of the prophets, that God would make a new covenant with his people.

II. Here then is the second head of our discourse, how God has abolished this obligation which was against us by the cross of his Son. He tells us two things concerning it: the one, that this obligation is made void; the other, that it was made so by the cross of Christ. He expresses the former in his usual manner, with great elegance; using three most significant terms, all of them taken from the nature of civil promises and obligations, in pursuance of the similitude with which he began. First, he says that this handwriting has been blotted out, or effaced. For so it is usual with men, when they have a debt discharged, to efface the name of their debtor, which was upon their books, and the sum which he owed them. The apostle says that God has done the same with reference to us; that he has effaced this handwriting, or obligation of our mystical debt, which was written in his law, and signed in our particular consciences. And this term has the greater elegance in this place, because there intervened, for our acquittal, something similar to that which men are accustomed to do. For they strike out their debtor's promises with some liquid, as ink, or the like, which they draw over the lines of their writings. So was our obligation made void by the effusion of a liquid, namely, the blood of Jesus Christ, which was poured forth, as it were, from the cross upon that dismal book of the law, to efface all the clauses of our condemnation in it. For as to the writing of men, ink is enough to blot it out; but there was nothing, save the blood of the Son of God, that was able to efface this doleful writing of the law, in which the sentence of our death was contained. Now it appears that it would be sufficient to satisfy a debtor to tell him that his obligation is effaced. Yet the apostle does not content himself with this; he adds, that ours has been taken out of the way, or abolished. You know that men, who are exact and punctual, not only efface their debtors' writings, but tear them and reduce them to pieces, that no sign of their debt may remain. God has done so towards us. He has not only effaced the obligation he had against us; he would not have so much as the erasures of it to appear. He has disannulled it, and abolished it, and rent it with the nails of the cross of his Son. He has, says the apostle, "nailed it to his cross." It is impossible to say anything better or more elegant. The same nails and the same thorns which pierced the body of our Lord upon that fatal tree, on which he died for us, by the same means tore and cut in pieces the obligation which was against us, that evidence of our debt and instrument of our death; that is to say, the cross of Jesus Christ has disarmed the law, and divested it of that killing force which it had naturally against us, and reduced it to such a state, that we being under the covert of his cross, it can no more harm us than if all the letters of it were effaced, and its papers rent in sunder. This divine crucified person has, by dying himself, slain the law; and that which sometimes happens in the combats of men has taken place here; both the combatants, even Christ and the law, remained dead upon the place. The law slew our Lord, who sustained this combat for us, to the end that he might take and bear the terrible blows, the thunderings and lightnings of our principal enemy, But he has also bereaved the law of life, and left it in the same state as that to which it had reduced him; though, indeed, with vast difference in the issue. For our Lord raised himself up from that death which he received and suffered for us, rising again gloriously alive the third day; whereas the law shall never resume the life or the strength of which he has deprived it. It shall remain for ever in that death he has given it. This is what the apostle teaches us very clearly, when he says that "Christ hath redeemed us from the curse of the law, being made a curse for us," Gal. iii. 13. His wounds have been our cure, his death our life, and his curse our bliss. The blood which issued from his sacred body blotted out the sentence of our condemnation; and the blows which pierced him broke in pieces the instrument of our ruin.

Now this great and admirable effect which Paul attributes to the cross of Christ furnishes us with a clear proof of his satisfaction. For if his death were nothing but an example of patience and humility, to what purpose, says this holy apostle, was the obligation which was against us abolished and fastened to his cross? Who sees not that, according to this opinion, the cross of our Lord would have done the law no harm at all—that his blood would have been so far from making void our obligation, that it would not so much as have made the least erasure in it? What does his death contribute to my deliverance from that curse under which this fatal writing puts me, if he died only to give me a noble pattern of constancy, and not to discharge my debts? The saints have verily suffered for our example, and their deaths are patterns of our patience. Yet it cannot be found that the prophets or apostles ever said that by virtue of their deaths the obligation which was against us has been made void, or that the evils which they suffered have redeemed us from the curse of the law. And besides the blasphemy of it, it would render a man evidently ridiculous to use such language respecting them, or to say of them, as the Scriptures speak of our Lord alone, that they have borne our griefs, and carried our sorrows, and been wounded for our transgressions, and bruised for our iniquities; and that the chastisement of our peace was upon them, and by their stripes we are healed. We conclude, therefore, that he verily died in our stead, and satisfied on his cross the justice of the Father for us. For this being presupposed, as the Scripture teaches, there is no longer any difficulty; and it is clear that his cross struck out and abolished the obligation which was kept in the cabinet of God against us, and which alone had the right and power to destroy us. As when a surety pays the sum which the man for whom he is security owes, he makes void the obligation which had been given to the creditor respecting it, and by virtue of which he was to have been imprisoned, of all the force it had to injure him. He effaces it, cancels it, and makes it void. He renders useless all the preparatives of justice against his friend. He puts the adversary, and all his advocates, to silence. He stops the mouth of the judge, which was even open to decree against him. He stays the officers of justice, and secures his liberty from their outrages. This is just the thing which our Lord and Saviour has done for us. But what, do I say he has done thus for us? He has done for us infinitely more than all this. Death and the curse were due to us as the wages of our sins. The sentence of it was written in the obligation of the law, which we ourselves had signed, and by which we had submitted to this penalty. The Judge was ready, and execution could not be avoided. The Lord Jesus, moved with compassion and sent by the goodness of the Father, puts himself in our room as Surety and Mediator for us. He pays what we owed. He suffers on the cross the punishment we deserved. His cross, therefore, has struck out that formidable obligation which was against us. He has abolished and made it of no effect. He has broken all the forces it was preparing against us. He has pacified our Judge, confounded our accusers, stayed the officers and ministers of justice, and saved our persons from the fetters and torments which were prepared for us.

But here again it appears how vain is the error of those who pretend that God only half pardons our sins; that, having remitted the fault, he exacts of us part of the punishment, and makes us suffer it, either in this life or after death, in a certain partition of hell which they call purgatory. How could they more rudely clash with the apostle's doctrine? He says that

God has blotted out, cancelled, and abolished the obligation which was against us. These men affirm, that he still makes us pay some part of our debt. Surely then our obligation is not yet torn. It is a thing unheard of in the course of justice, to bring an action against that debtor whose obligation you have effaced. If it be torn, if it be made void and of no effect, you have no longer any right to bring him before the judge, much less to get him condemned to pay it. If God, who does nothing unjust, should make us pay any part of the penalties of our sins which he has forgiven us, the obligation, by virtue of which he condemns us, is still in its full force. But the apostle protests that it has been effaced, and remains blotted, and nailed to the cross of Christ for ever. The obligation which was against us imported all the punishments, both temporal and eternal, to which we are obnoxious. It is made void and annihilated. We therefore no longer owe any of them. Fear not, christian, you have to do with a faithful Creditor. Having remitted your debt, yea, cancelled the evidence of it, and torn the obligation, he has no intention at all, after this, to demand of you any part of it. I confess that the payment which Jesus Christ has made is of no use to those who remain in unbelief; and though he has, in point of right, nullified the obligation which was against us; yet their ingratitude and infidelity operate against their reception of this benefit from his kindness; even as the unthankfulness and obduracy of that servant, of whom we are told in that parable in the gospel, deprived him of the favour which his master had showed him, in forgiving the ten talents which he owed. For God has affixed this reasonable condition to the covenant of grace which he has made with mankind, that the payment of our debts, made by our Surety, should not be allowed to any but to those who believe; so that they who obstinately abide in unbelief have no share in that immunity, or in those other benefits which this great Mediator has obtained for us. But as to the man who believes, and by a true faith applies to himself the death, and blood, and merit of the Lord Jesus, there is no more any condemnation to him, as the apostle says in his Epistle to the Romans, chap. viii. 1; nor, by consequence, any punishment; the obligation, by virtue of which alone he could be condemned at the tribunal of God, having been blotted out, abolished, and nailed to the cross of his Saviour.

Thus you see, beloved brethren, what that grace of God is which the apostle has here made known, and by what means we may become partakers in it. Sinners, you that groan under the heavy load of your crimes, who feel your misery, and perceive the cords of that damnation in which the law entangles you, come to the cross of Christ, and you shall find rest to your souls. Your consciences accuse you, and compel you to subscribe your own condemnation, acknowledging the justice thereof. But however just it may be, the cross of Jesus frees you from it, inasmuch as it has fully satisfied for you. Beware of the error both of the ancient and the modern Pharisees, who pretend ability to pay what they owe, and even more than they owe; and to justify themselves by their works, that is, by the law. The law is the instrument of our condemnation, and the ministration of our death; and a man who would be justified by the law, commits no less an extravagance than he who, to prove that he owes nothing, should produce in judgment the bills and bonds he has given to his creditors. Confess your debts. Divest yourselves of all confidence in your own righteousness. Declare that of yourselves you are bound over to eternal malediction; that you have deserved it; and present yourselves naked before God, who justifies the ungodly, and he will clothe you with the righteousness of his Son.

And you, faithful brethren, who are already entered into this blessed covenant, live in peace, and quietly wait for the fruit of your faith, according to the promises of God. Let not the thunderings and lightnings of the law make you afraid. Let not that death with which it so severely menaces the sons of men in the least terrify you. Let not the world or the devil, the executioners of its justice, astonish you. Jesus Christ has brought to nought all their strength by effacing the obligation that was against us. Satan, thou cruel enemy of our repose, object not to us our sins. We confess they are greater, and yet more grievous, than thou canst express. Lay not before us that clause of our old covenant which places all who have sinned under the curse. We confess we have merited this curse. But know, Satan, if we have deserved death, Jesus Christ has suffered it for us; and if we have committed sins worthy of thine hell, the blood of the Son of God has blotted them out. His cross has made void that old piece about which thou makest such a clamour; that rough obligation with which thou incessantly threatenest us. How hast thou the insolence to accuse those whom God justifies, and to condemn those for whom the Son of God died and rose again? It is thus, dear brethren, that we must repel the temptations of the enemy, and, notwithstanding his assaults, possess in peace the loving-kindness of God, adoring his bounty, and ardently employing ourselves to his glory. For this is the scope and the end of his grace. He has acquitted us of all our debts, and made void the obligation which was upon them; that we, being ravished with a goodness so divine, might love him with all our strength, and all our soul, according to that true maxim, acknowledged by Simon in the gospel, He to whom much is forgiven ought to love much, Luke vii. 43. He has delivered us, by his Son, " out of the hand of our enemies, that we might serve him without fear, in holiness and righteousness before him, all the days of our life," Luke i. 74, 75. And, indeed, how can we have the heart either not to love at all, or to love but coldly, a God who is so good to us—who, seeing us overwhelmed in debt, has freely forgiven us all—has made void the obligation; and, for the blotting it out, and making it void, has spent the blood of his only begotten Son; and, for the rending it in pieces, suffered his divine body to be all rent with strokes? After a goodness so ravishing, must not that man be worse than a devil who loves not this Father, who has given us his Son; and this Son, who has by his death obtained our salvation? Oh, how much reason had the apostle to count him execrable who loves not this great Saviour! "If any man," says he, "love not the Lord Jesus Christ, let him be Anathema Maranatha," 1 Cor. xvi. 22. God forbid that there should be so wretched and odious a person in the midst of us. Yet, if there be such, surely he believes not of our Saviour that which he makes profession to believe; for it is not possible to believe him without loving him.

Let us love him then, and faithfully serve him, setting his name and honour above all the interests of the world and our flesh. Let us obey his holy instruction, and conform all that life to his will which we hold only by his grace. Let us imitate that divine pattern he has left us, diligently walking in humility, and patience, and charity, of which he has given us such great and admirable examples. Let us have compassion and tenderness for our brethren, resembling those which he has had for us. He has pardoned all our sins, and acquitted us of all our debts. He has shed his blood to blot out the obligation which was against us. He died on a cross, that he might thereunto nail up and for ever abolish all the instruments of our condemnation. Having experienced so great a goodness towards ourselves, how can we dare to have so little towards others—to be obdurate to them, and implacable, when they have offended us—cruel and inexorable, when they owe us anything? He has forgiven us talents, and we exact of them even farthings. He has pardoned us thousands of crimes; we retain against them the slightest offences. What shall we answer when he shall one day say to us, Behold, "I have forgiven thee all this great debt because thou desiredst me; shouldest not thou also have had compassion on thy fellow servant, even as I had pity on thee?" Without doubt, my brethren, we should. It is a duty too just and too reasonable for us to fail in. If yet our flesh oppose, let us pray the Lord to subdue it to his will by the power of his Spirit;

granting us to do what he commands, that after we have had part here below in his grace, and in his sanctification, we may hereafter participate on high in his eternal glory. So be it.

SERMON XXVI.

VERSE 15.

And having spoiled principalities and powers, he made a show of them openly, triumphing over them in it.

DEAR brethren, the cross of our Lord Christ, which, at the first preaching of the gospel, was a scandal to the Jews and the scorn of Gentiles, is in truth the greatest mystery of the wisdom of God, and matter of highest admiration to angels and men. In it the Supreme Majesty has mixed together, with incomprehensible art, and reconciled most contrary and most incompatible things, death and life, ignominy and glory, condemnation and absolution, defeat and victory. The devil having put it into the heart of Judas to betray Jesus, and pushed on the princes of the Jews to take him and deliver him to Pilate, who condemned him, and caused him to die a cruel death upon a cross; this determined enemy of our salvation seemed to have gained the victory, inasmuch as by his artifices he had brought the Prince of life to so shameful an execution. But it happened quite otherwise. The blow which he gave our Lord struck himself, and our Saviour, by suffering death, overthrew for ever all the power of the devil; as Samson, the hero of Israel, who, when he died, pulled down and involved in the same ruins some thousands of his enemies. This cross, on which Jesus hung, was, to say the truth, the instrument of his glory rather than of his ignominy; and the trophy of his victory, rather than the gibbet of his execution. He suffered death on it, I grant, but a death that lasted no longer than three days, and gained him immortality; whereas he there defeated and ruined the devil and all our enemies without recovery. It is this the apostle represents to us in the text, where, in connection with that which he had said before, namely, that the Lord "blotted out the handwriting which was contrary to us, and took it out of the way, nailing it to his cross;" he now adds, "having spoiled principalities and powers, he made a show of them openly, triumphing over them in it." Good God! what a change is this! He tells us of the death of Christ, the most painful, the most shameful, and most execrable punishment in the world, as of a triumph, and does not hesitate to compare that fatal tree on which he suffered to a triumphal chariot. He puts in chains those who put him to death, and causes them to go not for authors or spectators of his sufferings, but for part of the pomp of his victory.

This is the sight, my brethren, to which the apostle invites us, the triumph, not of a Cæsar, or some other of the world's great captains, but of the Son of God, the Father of eternity. In it you shall see this King of glory riding in a chariot bathed in his divine and victorious blood; and, as the prophet Isaiah formerly represented him, chap. lxiii. 1, 3, with princes and people under foot, while he marched over them with his garments dyed red. In it you shall see, not soldiers and commanders in chains, but demons, the princes of this world, bound and fettered fast for ever. You shall see, not arrows broken, and cuirasses battered, and arms cut in pieces, but sin abolished and death destroyed. You shall see the spoils, not of an army or a country, but of the lords of the world, and of the governors of the darkness of this age. Lastly you shall behold in it, not the image of some petty fortress taken by assault or by surrender, or of some river forced, or some province subdued; but hell finally beaten, heaven gained, and an eternal world brought under the power of our victorious Lord. Let us apply ourselves to the fruition of this magnificent spectacle, and afford it all the sense and attention that we have. To this end we will consider, first, what these principalities and powers are which Jesus Christ has spoiled; and then see, in the second place, how he made a show of them, and triumphed over them on the cross. These are the two heads of which we will treat, if the Lord please, in this discourse.

I. The apostle ordinarily makes use of the words principalities, powers, dominions, thrones, and virtues, to signify the angels; as, for instance, in the 1st chapter of this Epistle ver. 16, in the 8th of the Epistle to the Romans, ver. 38, and in the 1st of that which he wrote to the Ephesians, ver. 21. He gives those spiritual beings these names, both because of the strength and power with which they are endowed, which far surpasses the virtue of material and elementary things, and also on account of the various orders into which God has distinguished them, according to the difference of their ministrations; placing some of the angels, as it were, chiefs, in a superiority to others. And though the sin of devils has corrupted the perfections of their nature, yet it appears, by different passages of Scripture, that it has not quite destroyed this order among them; Satan being represented to us as the head of this black band, and as having other evil angels under him; so that they may, in this respect, be still termed principalities and powers. Nevertheless there is another reason which the apostle had his eye principally upon in giving them these names, as he himself intimates in the 6th chapter to the Ephesians, ver. 12, "We wrestle not against flesh and blood, but against principalities, against powers, against the rulers of the darkness of this world, against spiritual wickedness in high places." Here you plainly see he calls them principalities and powers on account of that dominion which they exercise in this world, under its present state of subjection to sin and vanity. Not that such a superiority of right belongs to them; for, having rebelled against their Creator, they have lost all true and lawful dignity. But the sin of man having enslaved him to those evil spirits, has also made these elements subject to them, of which he was the true and natural Lord. And God has permitted it so to be for the execution of his justice against sin. For since man shook off the yoke of God, having wretchedly preferred the pernicious counsel of his enemy to the just commandment of his Master, it is but just that he should be subject to him to whom he betrayed his own liberty. Such, then, is the order, or rather the confusion, of the world, since the fall, namely, that the devil exercises an insupportable tyranny in it, governing it at his pleasure, as if he were its lord. For, first, he works upon all the ungodly with wonderful force, swaying their souls unto brutal passions, setting on fire their lusts, and by that thick smoke which he raises from their hearts blinding their minds, and depriving them of all the light that is necessary for distinguishing truth and falsehood, good and evil, as the apostle elsewhere informs us, saying that this unclean spirit works effectually "in the children of disobedience," Eph. ii. 2; and in another place he tells us that he has the wicked in his snares, and makes them do his will, 2 Tim. ii. 26. Not that he compels them to evil by coercive force, and however much they dislike it; but their nature being corrupted as it is, he never tempts them without effect, their souls voluntarily surrendering themselves to his pernicious persuasions. Moreover, he disposes of material things, turning and changing them at his pleasure, raising tempests in the air, seditions and wars among men, putting in commotion all that murderous violence which makes havoc of mankind, and presiding over all the instruments of the creatures' damage and death; on account of which the apostle, in the Epistle to the Hebrews, chap. ii. 14, calls Satan "him that had the power of death." And although he executes none of his bad purposes without the permission of God, as the Scripture clearly shows us in the history of Job, where you see he touches neither the goods, nor the children, nor the person of that holy man, until leave has been obtained of this Supreme

Majesty; yet because he works commonly in the world, the greater part of which is depraved and rebellious against God, he seems master of it, and he himself glories in it; as when he said to our Saviour, in his temptation, after he had showed him all the kingdoms of the earth, "All this power will I give thee, and the glory of them: for that is delivered unto me, and to whomsoever I will I give it," Luke iv. 6. And indeed for these reasons our Saviour styles the devil "the prince of this world;" as when he says, "Now shall the prince of this world be cast out," John xii. 31; and, "The prince of this world cometh, and hath nothing in me," John xiv. 30; and Paul calls him, in the same sense, "the god of this world," 2 Cor. iv. 4.

Represent unto yourselves the world as it was under the darkness of its old heathenism, when God left all nations to walk in their own ways. In it the devil absolutely domineered; and all those poor multitudes he held under his tyranny. He had put out the eyes of their minds, and in this blindness made them commit all kinds of vileness and abominations. He inspired into them hatred of the true God and of his service; and so effectually beguiled them by his fallacious illusions, that he caused them to adore himself under the forms of various idols. These same spirits are they whom the apostle intends here by those principalities and powers. For though the Scripture particularly marks out one of them, whom it calls Satan, as the head of this abominable monarchy; yet it ranges under him a vast multitude of spirits, who all travelling upon the same design, and employing in it all the might and industry they have, bear a part in his accursed empire. And there is great probability, too, that they are divided into certain bands, each of which is drawn up under their particular chiefs, and all of them depending upon Satan as their general. For which reason the apostle calls them, in the plural number, "principalities and powers." These are the enemies whom the Lord Jesus has overcome and utterly defeated on the cross, as he himself declared the evening before his passion, saying that the prince of this world was then judged; that is, was about to be condemned. And Paul elsewhere says that Jesus has by his death destroyed "him that had the power of death, that is, the devil," Heb. ii. 14.

II. Let us now see how our Saviour has spoiled these principalities and powers, and openly made a show of them, triumphing over them on the cross. First, it is evident that all this language of the apostle is figurative, and taken from that which great captains who had been victorious over their enemies were formerly accustomed to do. For after they had spoiled them, not only of their arms, habits, jewels, and baggage, but also of their estates and all their glory; they led them away prisoners, and made a show of them to their countrymen on the day of their triumph. This name the Romans gave to the pomp of that entry which the captains and generals of a victorious army made into their city. For when any of them had won a battle, taken towns, conquered countries, or performed any great and notable exploit of war, one of the principal and most prized honours decreed him for a reward of his valour was a triumph, which was performed with incredible pomp and ceremony. The conqueror was mounted on a stately chariot, magnificently clothed and crowned. His whole army marched before and after him in military order, every troop under its ensigns and colours. The heads and principal of the enemies followed his chariot, bound, and in chains. There were carried along all the gold and silver, and other treasures, he had won from the enemy. The towns he had taken, the rivers he had passed, the provinces he had subdued, the battles he had fought, were represented in picture, and exposed to the view of the people, who with great festivity and rejoicing accompanied in throng, or beheld him from the windows of their houses, and filled the air with their acclamations and applauses. He entered Rome in this equipage, and passing through the fairest streets of the city, ascended the Capitol, the chief of their temples, where he offered sacrifices, after he had thus displayed the fruits of his victories before the eyes of all the world, and received all kinds of benedictions and praises from his fellow citizens. This is properly that which was called a triumph. The apostle therefore borrowing his terms from this custom, which was well known at that time, and familiar to every one, applies them to our Lord and Saviour, because of that resemblance which we find between the pomp of his mystical victory, and this triumph of secular rulers and captains. He tells us that he has spoiled these hostile principalities and powers; that he has openly made a show of them; and that he has triumphed on the cross; expressions all of them manifestly taken, as you see, from that glorious pomp of the Roman triumphs which we have now described; and which in substance signify nothing else than that Jesus, dying on the cross, has fully vanquished and defeated the devil with all his power in the view of heaven and earth.

In prosecution hereof, we are to refute the false expositions which some give of this passage, and after that render you an account of the true. Some of the most famous interpreters of the church of Rome* understand it of the deliverance of the fathers, whom our Saviour, as those men say, took out of that limbus in which their spirits were, and led them to heaven with him. He "spoiled principalities and

* Thomas, Loranus, Cajetan.

powers," that is, the devils, from whom he took away what they kept in hell; inasmuch, say they, as he caused Adam, Noah, Abraham, Isaac, and Jacob, with the rest of the faithful who died under the Old Testament, to come forth from their limbus, which is one of the partitions of the infernal regions. Then, they say, he led them, carrying them up to heaven, and giving them entrance into Jerusalem on high, from which they had been until then excluded. And he made them triumph in himself (for so the same authors read the apostle's words); that is, he made them to participate in his triumph, in that they had the honour to accompany him and to enter into heaven with him. But scarcely anything can be uttered more false, more forced, and more impertinent, than this whole interpretation. First, that which it supposes of the abode of the spirits of the old believers in a subterraneous and infernal limbus is uncertain and fabulous, being founded only upon the tradition of men, and not on any authority of the word of God. As for that which they commonly quote to prove it, namely, the saying of Jacob, that he would go down into hell unto his son Joseph, Gen. xxxvii. 35, they who are versed in Scripture well know that the word *inferi*, or hell, in that place in particular, and almost everywhere else in the book of God, signifies the grave. Consequently the same patriarch says elsewhere to his sons, that if any evil befel Benjamin, they would bring down his grey hairs with sorrow *ad inferos*, to hell, as many read it; where it is clear that by the same word he means the grave, into which the dead go down with their hair; and not limbus, into which only souls descended, who surely have no hair. And as to what they produce respecting the pretended soul of Samuel, called up from hell by the charms of the sorceress, where is the christian who does not feel indignant at such power being imputed to the ministers of devils over the spirits of prophets? God forbid that we should credit so gross an absurdity. That which the enchantress saw came from hell I confess; but it was not in truth the soul of Samuel, which was at rest with God in Abraham's bosom. It was nothing but a vain shadow and a phantom of that prophet, called by his name because it resembled him, as the greater part of the ancient fathers affirmed, and as some of the most famous authors, even of the Roman communion,* at this day maintain. They again abuse what the psalmist sings respecting the Messiah, "Thou hast ascended on high: thou hast taken" or led "a multitude of captives," as it is rendered, Psal. lxviii. 18. These captives they will have to be the spirits of the fathers. But it is manifest to all who have the least knowledge of the holy tongue, that the phrase there used

* Leo Allatius in Eustath. Antioch.

by the prophet signifies to take or to make prisoners, not to free them; and to lead, not into liberty, but into captivity; so that if this passage be meant of the fathers, we must say, not that the Lord brought them out of prison, (as is supposed,) but that he put them in; a thing that would be infinitely absurd and ridiculous. "The spirits in prison," of whom Peter speaks, 1 Pet. iii. 20, cannot upon any better ground be taken for the souls of the faithful detained in limbus, since those spirits it is said were sometime rebellious, or disobedient, in the time of Noah, and perished in their sin; which cannot be said of the patriarchs and the faithful. In fine, the apostle's saying that the way into the holy places was not manifested while the first tabernacle was standing, signifies indeed that the High Priest of the church, our Lord Jesus Christ, did not carry nor introduce our nature into heaven in soul and body, nor discover and make manifest the way to our mansion of immortality, until the veil of the first tabernacle was rent, which is very true. But it does not follow from this that the spirits of the faithful, consecrated before our Saviour's coming, did not experience the fruit of his death, and much less that they were detained in hell. But this tradition not only has no foundation in Scripture, it also plainly contradicts it. For our Lord promised the good thief that the very day he was crucified he should be with him in paradise, Luke xxiii. 43; whereas, according to our adversaries' supposition, he could not have entered it till the forty-third day after. And the parable of that bad rich man plainly shows us that at that time, as the souls of impenitent sinners were cast into the torments of hell-fire, so the spirits of the faithful were carried up into the repose and felicity of paradise. For that bosom of Abraham in which Lazarus rested, Luke xvi. 22, 25, 26, was not a pit without water, as the pretended limbus is counted to have been, but a place of refreshment and consolation; not situate in the vicinity of hell, but severed from it by a great gulf set between them. And in truth, since the faithful even then drank of the mystical Rock as well as we, were sprinkled with his blood and partook of his sufferings; why should any one imagine that our Saviour's sacrifice had less virtue to introduce them into heaven after their death, than it had to justify, and sanctify, and comfort them in the days of their life? As they bore a part with us in the same faith and conflicts on the earth, so they had a share of our repose and joy in heaven; neither is there any reason for our being admitted, if you will needs have them excluded. Accordingly, it is certain that those ancient christian writers, who excluded from heaven the souls of the faithful who died under the Old Testament dispensation, denied also reception there to the souls of christians; as they did not assent that either the one or the other were admitted till after the resurrection: so that our adversaries, rejecting (as they have reason to do) the one half of this error, and confessing that christian souls sufficiently purged are received into heaven, it is nothing but pure obstinacy in them to retain the other half, and to pretend that the condition of the faithful departed under the Old Testameut was different to that of those who died under the New. Let it be then concluded, that all this pretended deliverance of souls brought out of limbus is but the fiction of a human spirit, not only having no foundation in Scripture or reason, but even contrary to both.

But I add, in the second place, that if it were as certain as it is dubious, and as true as it is false, yet it would not be possible to refer the passage before us to such a doctrine. First, the spirits of departed saints are not at all in the power of Satan, but in the hands of God, to whom they committed them at their death; so that though Jesus Christ had brought them out of limbus, yet it could not be said that he had therein spoiled the devils, since to spoil them is to take from them that of which they were possessed; and it is clear, that if the souls of the faithful had been in this imaginary limbus, yet they would not have been in the devil's possession. Secondly, the original word here used, which signifies to lead about for a show, is always taken in an ill sense, for a shameful and ignominious show, such as that of malefactors, when they are led through the city and publicly executed, that the sight of their shame and punishment may keep men to their duty. Now if our Lord had delivered the souls of the faithful out of such a limbus, it could not be said that he had made a show of them in this sense; it being evident that in this case they would have accompanied his triumph by way of honour, and that it would not have been any ignominy, but a glory for them to have followed his victorious chariot. Moreover, the apostle's words are so placed in the original, that the spoiling, and making a show of, and triumphing over, of which he speaks, necessarily respect the same persons; that is, those whom he spoiled are those of whom he made show, and over whom he triumphed. Now he spoiled not the spirits of the fathers; he, on the contrary, enriched them: surely then it is not they of whom he made a show; neither can the action which the verb imports be referred to them, without depraving the whole of the apostle's context. This is all spoken of one and the same subject, namely, those powers and principalities; that is, the devils, as we have demonstrated, and as all agree. They are the devils whom Jesus spoiled. It is the same of whom he publicly made a show, and over whom he triumphed.

As for the Latin interpreter's* saying the Lord triumphed

* Zanchy.

over them in himself, I acknowledge that various Greek copies read the text in that manner, and some of our writers have so expounded it; conceiving that our Saviour, upon his crucifixion, brought the devils whom he had overcome out of their hell, and showed them to the angels and the spirits made perfect, bound and chained, as a glorious token of the victory he had achieved over them; and they add, that his triumph also continued until his ascension into heaven. But as the Scripture tells us nothing of this, I think it is dangerous to assert it; it being better and more safe to keep to that which God has revealed in his word, than to take the liberty of following our own imaginations, however plausible they may appear. And the reason which seems to have influenced those men to advance this conjecture is exceedingly slender: for they have been induced to do so merely because they considered it absurd to say that Jesus Christ triumphed over his enemies on the cross; seeing that, to speak properly, he overcame them on the cross, but triumphed only at his resurrection and ascension. But, first, if there were some inconvenience in this, yet nothing would induce us to assert what they propose. It would be sufficient, in order to avoid this inconvenience, to say that our Saviour triumphed over his enemies in himself, or by himself; that is, according to the ordinary style of Scripture, by his own strength and virtue, he being raised from the dead and gloriously lifted up to heaven by the potency of his own arm. But, I say, in the second place, that there is no absurdity at all in attributing these things to the very death of our Lord, understanding them, as we ought, spiritually and mystically. And, without doubt, it is much more fluent and clear to refer the last words of this verse to the cross of our Saviour, of which the apostle had spoken immediately before, (he fastened the obligation to the cross, having spoiled principalities and powers, over whom he triumphed on it, that is, on the cross,) than to take it of our Lord himself, and say that he triumphed over his enemies in himself, which is frigid, harsh, and obscure.

We say then, with the greater part of the modern, and with the more learned and illustrious of the ancient expositors, that it is on the cross our Saviour spoiled principalities and powers, and that it was there also he publicly made a show of them, and triumphed over them. I confess, if we look upon him as suffering on that execrable tree, amid the scoffs and sarcasms of the Jews, in the lowest state of his humiliation, flesh will find in him something less than victories and triumphs. But you know, likewise, that this mystery must not be judged of by the senses of the flesh. It is faith alone that is able to discover and to contemplate the wonders which are in it. Now if you open the eyes of faith, you will easily perceive that Jesus has spoiled all hostile powers on the cross, and that it is with this weapon properly that he surmounted those strong and potent tyrants, and took from them all the instruments of their violence, and made a prey of all their riches. For, to say the truth, that harsh and cruel dominion which the devil exercises in the world is not founded upon anything but sin. If this pest had not infected us, all the forces of hell, though they were a thousand times greater than what they are, could not have hurt us. It is upon our sin that this fierce tyrant has built all his power, and it is upon our ruins that he has raised his grandeur. For, first, if we were not culpable by reason of the sins we have committed, the justice of God would never have suffered this executioner of his judgments to trouble and prosecute us as he has done. It would not permit him so much as to open his mouth against us to accuse us. But sin having provoked the wrath of God, and his law prohibiting access unto his throne, and pronouncing a curse upon us, it is evident that justice delivered up our persons to the evil angels, and gave them power to execute its judgment upon us. Again, besides these evils, which are termed penal, and which could not terminate at last but in an eternal death, the devil annoyed men in another way, even by urging them on to vice by his temptations, and causing them to commit a multitude of sins, some by means of avarice, and others by the furies of ambition; casting some into the excesses of luxury, others into the disorders of drunkenness and gluttony. But it is sin also that gives him this power over men; that concupiscence which reigns in them, and which the Scripture calls the old man, because it is the inheritance, and succession, and image of the first Adam. It is by this, as by a handle, that the devil seizes on them, and drags them into such sins as he pleases. Were it not for this, he would have no hold upon them; and each of them, if he were exempted from it, might say as our Lord did, "The prince of this world cometh, and hath nothing in me." Now Jesus Christ has abolished by his cross both the guilt and the vices of men: the guilt, in that he bore the punishment thereof, and satisfied divine justice for them, and extinguished all the flames of the law, and opened the throne of grace to every impenitent sinner; their vices, in that he crucified and destroyed our old man on the cross, and mortified all its lusts, and discovered its impostures. Surely then it is by his cross that he divested the devils of the dominion which they exercised over mankind, having sapped and demolished all the foundations thereof by his admirable sufferings.

That which the apostle adds, in the second place, namely, that he openly made a show of those hostile powers, excellently well agrees with his cross. For this show signifies nothing else than an extreme confusion and ignominy, as we have already intimated; and who is there that knows not that the evil angels never received a greater than that with which the cross of our Lord and Saviour covered them? They thought to have overcome him, and found themselves overcome; instead of ruining his dominion, as they imagined, they saw their own utterly overthrown. And this was publicly done, in the view of heaven and earth; our Saviour having been crucified in the greatest city of the East, in broad day, and at the solemnity of the most sacred festival of the Jews. The angels looked on it from on high, and never beheld anything with more attention and astonishment. Jews and Gentiles were spectators of it; and nature itself, however mute and insensible, sufficiently showed that it took part in it, shutting (if we may so say) its eye, through horror at seeing its Creator suffer. But fear not, poor creatures, the shame and confusion will wholly remain to our enemies. Our Sun will soon come out of this eclipse, and his suffering is the salvation, not the ruin or damage, of the universe.

Finally, the apostle's further assertion, that our Lord triumphed over these hostile powers on the cross, is also easily verified. For, as an ancient * said, There were two crucified persons on that cross, the one Jesus Christ, who was nailed to it visibly, voluntarily, and for a short time only; the other, the devil, invisibly fastened to the same cross, and to his great regret, and for ever; inasmuch as this cross of our Saviour has destroyed his life and power, having given him that deadly blow from which he will never recover. Faith sees upon the cross, above, the Son of God combating and conquering for us; and it sees, beneath, all the bad angels put in chains, vanquished, and in vain raging under his feet.

Yet do I ingenuously confess, that, to speak properly, the resurrection and ascension of our Lord have more analogy with a triumph than his death, which rather resembles a conflict. But it is a very common mode of expression to attribute the name of an effect to the cause which produced it. It is, in my opinion, principally in this sense that our Saviour triumphed over his enemies on the cross, because the death he there suffered was the true and only cause of his triumphs. It was the tree of this cross that bore the palms and laurels with which he has been crowned. It is there that all the causes and foundations of all his glory are found. It is this cross that opened his sepulchre, and brought him out from thence, and raised him up in immortality. It is this also that a little after opened heaven to him, and seated him on the right hand of the Most High. It is this that loosed the

* Origen.

tongues of his apostles, and changed the world in a short time; that defeated paganism, that is, the greatest part of Satan's empire; that threw down idols, and drew all people to the service of that divine crucified person whom it bore. It is this likewise that will pluck us hereafter out of the hands of death, and lift us up into the sanctuary of eternity. Lastly, it is this that has founded that glorious throne on which Jesus shall sit, and both his subjects and his enemies shall see him truly triumphing; the one with eternal joy, the other with a confusion that shall never end. Since the cross of our Lord and Saviour is the cause of so many triumphs, who does not see that it is not only with truth, but also with much elegance, that the apostle here says he triumphed on it over his enemies?

Let us, dear brethren, adore the mystery of it, and look upon it, notwithstanding the sad appearances of its infirmity, as the only cause of the glory of our Head, and of the liberty of his people. If the Jew stumble at it, and the Greek deride it, it is an effect of their ignorance and infidelity. For our part, let us who know its virtue say with the apostle, "God forbid that we should glory, save in the cross of our Lord Jesus Christ," Gal. vi. 14. It has taken us out of the cruel bonds of the devils, and placed us in the liberty of the sons of God. It has spoiled our old tyrants, and broken their iron yoke, and overthrown those infernal principalities and powers. Let us not fear them. After the blow which they have received from the cross of Christ, they are but back-broken serpents, that only hiss and crawl along the dust. I grant that they yet stir, and wind about us, and do not cease to threaten us; but they can no longer hurt us, if we keep fast to the cross of our Saviour, by which the world is crucified unto us, and we unto the world. They are our enemies, they are no more our masters. We are to wrestle with them; we are under their yoke no longer. And if God sometimes permit them to strike us in our goods, or in our bodies, and in what we have on earth; yet he preserves our persons, and does not suffer them to take from us anything that his Son has purchased in heaven for us. And he so governs these combats that they ever turn unto our glory and their confusion, as that of Job's formerly did. God permits them to attack us that we may overcome them; or, to speak more correctly, that the cross of Jesus may stand up once more victorious in each of us, and bruise Satan under our feet, Rom. xvi. 20, as it has already bruised him under his. Let us, with good courage, follow the victory of our Head, and stoutly march on in his steps. Let us pur sue the vanquished enemy, and not quit him till we, in this holy war, bear away the laurel, and the honour of a triumph. Take heed that he rally not his dissipated forces, and do us some injury; for henceforth there is nothing but our negligence that can give him the advantage. Our victory is as sure as it can be, if we have courage sufficient not to destroy ourselves. For what can he do to us if we watch, if we pray, if we keep upon our guard, and under the ensign of the cross of our Lord? Will he accuse us? God justifies us, and his Son defends and intercedes for us. Will he batter us with the curse of the law? The cross of Christ has annulled it. Will he stir up against us the hate and persecutions of the world? In these things we are more than conquerors through him that loved us; who can so turn and change them in favour of us, as that they shall all work together for our good. Will he take hold of us, on the other side, by the baits of sin, and pleasures and benefits of the present world? Our Saviour's cross has extinguished and mortified the desire of them in our hearts; showing us that all this beauteous figure of the world is but a vanity, that passes away, and ends in eternal misery. Will he menace us with death? He may; but the cross of Jesus has disarmed it of all its stings, and so altered its whole nature, that whereas it was of itself the wages of sin, and an effect of our Judge's wrath, and the beginning of hell, it is now a token to us of the grace of God, the end of our conflicts, and the entry of our paradise. Let us, therefore, my beloved brethren, live in repose, and take possession, with humble thankfulness, of the good things which the Lord Jesus has obtained for us by the merit of his cross; serving and religiously adoring him; consecrating all our life to his glory, as he gave his for our salvation: and assuring ourselves amidst all the storms of this generation, that "neither death, nor life, nor angels, nor principalities, nor powers, nor things present, nor things to come, nor height, nor depth, nor any other creature, shall be able to separate us from the love of God, which is in Christ Jesus our Lord." So be it.

SERMON XXVII.

VERSES 16, 17.

Let no man therefore judge you in meat, or in drink, or in respect of an holy-day, or of the new moon, or of the sabbath days: which are a shadow of things to come; but the body is of Christ.

DEAR brethren, our Lord Jesus Christ beautifully shows us the difference of that evangelical service which he has instituted in his church from the legal service which existed in Israel under the Old Testament; when speaking of it to the Samaritan, he says, "Woman, believe me, the hour cometh, when ye shall neither in this mountain, nor yet at Jerusalem, worship the Father. But the true worshippers shall worship the Father in spirit and in truth," John iv. 21, 23. Under the law the service of God was confined to certain places, as the temple at Jerusalem, and the land of Canaan; to certain times, as sabbaths, new moons, and those great feasts of the passover, pentecost, and tabernacles; to certain corporeal things, as beasts, and other kinds, which were offered upon a material altar, with various ceremonies; and to certain sorts of meat, it being not permitted at that time to eat of any other than that which was pronounced clean. But now the Lord Jesus has abrogated this adhering to places, to times, and to the elements of this world, as a low and childish exercise, and appointed for his people a service altogether spiritual and divine, proportioned to that admirable light of knowledge which he has shed into the hearts of the faithful; a service that wholly consists in love to God, charity and beneficence towards our neighbour, and in honesty and purity with respect to ourselves. This is the true service of the Deity, worthy of man who presents it, and of God who receives it; since man is a reasonable creature, and God a Spirit infinitely good and holy; according to what our Saviour adds, that "the Father seeketh such to worship him;" and that, being a Spirit, "they that worship him must worship him in spirit and in truth." But though this kind of service is so just and rational in itself, and though the Lord Jesus has so clearly instituted it by his divine authority; yet on the other hand, the inclination of our nature is so violent towards gross and earthly things, that even among those who make profession of acknowledging Jesus Christ for the Son of God, a multitude is found who cannot let go these bodily exercises, in which a part of divine service heretofore consisted. The apostle testifies in several places that there were such in his time, 1 Tim. iv. 3; and he informs us in others that there would also be such in after-ages; and the event has precisely answered his prediction; an evident sign that it was the spirit of truth, that is, the Spirit of God, which illuminated his understanding, and caused him to see in those days things hidden in futurity, far beyond the reach of the natural sight of men. It is against these people that he labours in this chapter, to fortify against their attacks, not only the Colossians, to whom he writes, but also the faithful in all ages. He laid firm and immovable foundations of truth in his foregoing discourse; showing us, according to his usual custom, with great strength, and glorious evidence, that we have all those advantages plentifully in Jesus Christ, for which error would introduce its inventions and carnal observances; that in him we have all fulness necessary to complete us; that his resurrection and his Spirit divest us of all the vices of the flesh; and that his cross gives us full remission of our sins; since it has both made void the obligation concerning all the punishments we owed to divine justice, and triumphed over all those powers that were capable of accusing or tormenting us. Whence it clearly follows, that it is useless for any to urge the necessity of legal and material observances, seeing that we most perfectly have, in the death and resurrection of our Lord, all that sanctification and justification, for the advancement of which it is pretended that these things are needful. This is, dear brethren, the direct conclusion that the apostle now deduces from that excellent and divine doctrine which he before established. Therefore, says he, "let no man judge you in meat, or in drink, or in respect of an holy-day, or of the new moon, or of the sabbath days: which are a shadow of things to come; but the body is of Christ." He first forbids them to suffer themselves to be put in subjection to these legal things; and next, he affords them a reason for it, taken from their nature, inasmuch as these things were but shadows; of which Jesus Christ has exhibited and given to us the true body. These shall be, by the will of God, the two points which we will handle in this discourse; commenting on each of them, as we shall judge most conducive to your edification.

I. Those seducers whom the apostle opposes in this place had drawn the devotions which they would add to the gospel, partly from the Mosaic law, partly from heathen philosophy, and partly from their own imagination; wherefore in one of the preceding verses he advised the Colossians to beware lest any man spoil them "through philosophy and vain deceit, after the tradition of men, and the rudiments of the world." They had borrowed from Moses circumcision, and the distinction of meats and days; they had begged from the schools of philosophy the worshipping of angels, and the vain discourses with which they coloured over this abuse; and they had invented of themselves certain austerities and pretended mortifications, which they held to be highly advantageous in religion. See, I beseech you, what a heap of strange things the spirit of superstition, even at that time, thrust into Christianity; be not amazed therefore, if men, in so many ages as have rolled away since those days, pursuing the same design, according to the passion of their flesh, have by degrees quite filled up religion with similar services and observations; and, as it were, defiled and polluted that pure and clear fountain of our Saviour's discipline with the dregs and sediment of their inventions. For if flesh had the impudence to promote such abuses during the lives and under the eyes of the apostles, how much more would it have the boldness to enterprise, and the facility to execute it, during the night of so many ages, which were not only destitute of the light of those great tapers, but also overspread with the darkness of grossest ignorance!

Let us see how Paul condemns the traditions of those of his age, to the end that we may preserve ourselves from those of our own, by the example and authority of his doctrine. He spake before of circumcision, to which they would have had christians still submit. He now condemns their other abuses; and first, the distinction they made of days and of meats; and next, in the verses following, their doctrine touching angels, and the worship they gave them; and last of all, their discipline and mortifications, from the 20th verse to the end of the chapter. We will consider, by the grace of God, the two other parts of his dispute, each of them in its place. As for the former, the apostle here censures two sorts of distinctions, or observances, which these men held in religion; the one of meats, the other of days. And as to the latter, he notices particularly, and by name, some of the days which they observed, namely, "holy-days" or festivals, "new moons, and sabbaths." But about the other he expresses himself in general only, saying simply, "Let no man judge you in meat, or in drink," without declaring particularly the kind of meat or drink which they prohibited or permitted; so that as the apostle does not particularly inform us of it, and as we have no light respecting it from any other source, it is not easy for us to know precisely what the meats were, the distinction of which these people set up. For, first, the law of Moses, from which they had taken some part of their discipline, forbade a great number of meats, and contained several very scrupulous regulations about eating, as you may see in the eleventh chapter of Leviticus, and in other places. Among the beasts of the field, it permitted the Jews to take none for meat but such as chew the cud, and divide the hoof; and among fishes, none but such as have fins and scales; and by this rule it banished from their tables hares, rabbits, leverets, the hog, the lamprey, the tortoise, and many other things; not to speak of several sorts of birds which were interdicted them. It was an abomination for them so much as to touch any of these things. And for drink, though there was no general rule given, yet they had various particular observances which refer to it; as, for instance, they were not to drink any liquor drawn out of a vessel that had no close cover, Numb. xix. 15; and the more devout abstained from wine and strong drink, either for ever, or for a time only, according to the law of the Nazarites. And that they might not fall unintentionally into the transgressing of some of these rules, they never ate with pagans, or of any meat which they had dressed, for fear there might have been some lard in it, or other mixture of things prohibited; or that their meat and drink had been offered to idols, as with the pagans was customary; a thing which they greatly had in abomination. For this cause Daniel and his fellows would not taste of the meat or of the wine of the king of Babylon's table, Dan. i. 8; desiring rather to eat nothing but pulse, and drink nothing but water, than incur the danger of being defiled. And to this we must refer that eating herbs, Rom. xiv. 2, which the apostle reports of those weak ones, who still retained the Mosaic distinction of meats. The meaning is, that living among pagans, and fearing lest the victuals they sold in their shambles and shops were defiled one way or other, they abstained from them, and confined themselves to herbs, in which they feared no such thing. The Judaical rules about eating and drinking being such, it is hard to say whether the seducers retained them all in general, or observed only part of them. There is great probability that they adhered to them in some manner, either in whole or in part. Yet, drawing a part of their observances (as they did) from the sinks of secular philosophy, it is probable that, beside what they had taken out of Judaism for this purpose, they mingled with it some observances of the philosophers also, who likewise had their abstinences, as we understand by the books of the ancients. And that of the Pythagoreans is sufficiently known, who fed on herbs and fruits only, forbidding the use of all animated things. It is very likely that those false apostles, upon whom Paul here has his eye, had some such discipline, considering that which he adds afterwards of the nature and ends of their abstinences. Thus much we may say concerning their laws about eating and drinking.

As for the days which they observed, all those which the apostle names in the text were taken out of Judaism. For that the new moons, by which the Hebrews began all the months of their year, (as do most of the people of the East to this day,) were solemnly observed among the Jews, appears both from various places in the books of Moses, where he ordains that a trumpet should be sounded at the beginning of the month, and that certain peculiar sacrifices should be offered to God, Numb. x. 10; xxviii. 11; and also from that Psalm where the prophet commands to sound the trumpet on the new moon, upon the solemn feast-day, Psal. lxxxi. 3; and again, from Isaiah, where God, rejecting the vain services which hypocrites presented to him, without any true faith or devotion, says, "The new moons and sabbaths, the calling of assemblies, I cannot away with; it is iniquity, even the solemn meeting. Your new moons and your appointed feasts my soul hateth; they are a trouble unto me; I am weary to bear them," Isa. i. 13, 14. As concerning the sabbath, that is, the seventh day of every week, which we call Saturday, no one is ignorant with what devotion it was observed and kept holy by the Jews, according to the ordinance of God, repeated in various parts of the books of Moses, and even registered among the ten articles of the decalogue. Again, by the festivals which Paul mentions, he means those high days which besides the sabbaths and new moons which occurred in the ordinary succession of weeks and months, were solemnized at certain seasons of the year; as the passover, on the fourteenth day of the first month, remarkable for the immolation of the lamb, and for the unleavened bread, which lasted seven days; pentecost, which was kept fifty days after the passover; and the feast of tabernacles, which was celebrated the fifteenth day of the seventh month, and lasted seven days, during which time the people resided under tents and booths, Numb. xxviii. So, you see, the apostle here points at all the three kinds of Jewish feasts; those of the year, which he calls simply festivals, namely, the passover, pentecost, and the tabernacles; those of months, which were the new moons; and finally, those of the weeks, which were the sabbaths.

Now whereas the French has translated it, "in the distinction of a festival day," it is word for word in the original, "in part of a festival day," which some take to signify, in respect of festivals, or upon the account of festivals; in the same sense that Peter seems to use the word, when he says, "If any man suffer as a christian, let him not be ashamed; but let him glorify God on this behalf," 1 Pet. iv. 16; that is, in this respect, and as to this matter. And thus the apostle in this place would say, Let no man condemn you in regard of festivals or for festivals; that is, in the matter of the observation of certain days. But the word here used being the root of the other, which in Greek signifies to distinguish, to sever, to divide, as in French *partir* and *partager* come from the word part, or party, that interpreter has not succeeded ill in rendering it, "the distinction." For they who keep holy certain days, and make them festivals, distinguish them from others and set them apart, to observe and celebrate them differently to ordinary days. In substance, the apostle's intention is clear; namely, that he forbids every man, whoever he may be, to condemn christians for using certain meats, and observing certain days. Let no man judge you, says he, in eating, or in drinking, or in distinguishing of a festival day, or of a new moon, or of sabbaths. This word "judge" aptly suits the apostle's sense. For these seducers would make their ordinances, about the distinction of meats and days, to pass for necessary laws, which they meant to impose on the faithful, and by these judge them; praising and approving such as abstained from the meat they forbade them, and observed the days they had marked out to them; and condemning, as guilty of a sin, those who failed to do the one or the other. And the apostle, shortly afterwards, ridiculing their pretended laws, shows us the form of them. Why, says he, are ye subject to ordinances, namely, "Touch not, taste not, handle not?" And this should be particularly noticed; for those who, through a certain feebleness of mind, at that time still scrupled to violate these Mosaic distinctions, but, however, without condemning those who acted otherwise, or obliging them to such observances as necessary things; those the apostle would have to be treated with patience and sweetness; and he sharply reproves those who gave them any offence. But though he has this condescension for the weak, yet he is altogether rigid and inexorable against these pretended teachers; who, acting the legislators, would put christians under their yoke; and, not content with that support which would have been given to their infirmity, pretended to make others subject to it, and fiercely condemned those who observed not their traditions. It is to them that he says, "Let no man judge you." And if, notwithstanding his prohibition, these men have the presumption to proceed, and condemn christians for such things, it is evident that in this case he would have us despise all their judgments, their fulminations, and their anathemas; holding them worthy of condemnation, since they dare to make laws in the house of God; according to the instruction which he gives to the Galatians upon the same subject: If any man preach any other gospel unto you, than that ye have received, let him be accursed, Gal. i. 9. It is thus that the apostle guards and fortifies the liberty of christians, with reference to meats and days, against the attempts of all who would intrude to make laws in the church about such things as were in their own nature indifferent.

II. But as these false teachers clothed themselves with the authority of Moses, the apostle, in order to prevent this pretext from dazzling the eyes of the simple, shows, (even granting that such distinctions formerly prevailed in Judaism by the ordinance of God,) from the quality of their nature, that the usage of them is ceased now under christianity. This is the signification of those words, which he adds in the second part of the text: "Which are a shadow of things to come; but the body is of Christ." It is evident that he means the distinction of meats, the feasts, the new moons, and the sabbaths, of which he had been speaking; and, in general, all other similar things: and he says that they are "shadows of things to come;" not to signify that they still subsist of right, (on the contrary, he affirms that they have been abolished,) but simply to declare to us what their nature is, and for what end they were instituted of God and practised, during their time, by his people. He says, then, that they are shadows of things to come, of which the body is in Christ. A shadow is the representation of a body, but an obscure and imperfect one, and such as shows us merely some of its lineaments, and not the lively colour and true form of its members. Consequently, this word is taken in the Greek language, in which the apostle wrote, for that which we call a rough draught, which is a dark and imperfect painting, executed only with lines, and not with the lustre and diversity of colours, opposed to that which they call painting to the life. And Paul himself elsewhere makes this opposition, when he says that the law had "a shadow of good things to come, and not the very image of things," Heb. x. 1; and again, in another place, he styles the law "the example and shadow of heavenly things," Heb. viii. 5. But here, as you see, he takes the word shadow properly, and not figuratively for a rough draught; opposing it to the body itself which it represents, and not to another kind of more express and lively representation. What then is this body, of which the legal observances were shadows? It is, says the apostle, things to come; a body which is of Christ, or in Christ. The things he means were already come, and accomplished, for the most part, at the time he wrote; forasmuch as Christ, in whom they are, having been manifested, has fulfilled all the mysteries of salvation. But the apostle considering them as in the time when the shadows continued under the law, calls them things to come, because at that time they were indeed not come, Christ, who was to exhibit them, being not then revealed. At that time they were future, now they are present. These things, my brethren, are the offices and the benefits of our Lord Jesus, and all the parts of that heavenly discipline which he has brought into the world. The apostle therefore, saying that legal observances were shadows of them, means, first, that they prefigured them, and referred to them; and, secondly, that that representation of them which they afforded was dusky, obscure, and imperfect; that it was not a clear, distinct, and lively portrait of them, but only as it were a rough, naked, and simple delineation; such as a shadow is with respect to the body which projects it. This was one of the principal offices of the Mosaic law, even to prefigure Christ that was to come. For God having purposed in his infinite wisdom, for just and great reasons, not to send Christ into the world until the last ages, and, as the Scripture speaks, the fulness of time, judged it meet to give, in the mean time, the figure, model, or design of this great masterpiece of work in the law of Moses. First, for the employment of his people, during this time of their minority, in those low and puerile exercises, which suited with the weakness of their age, until the revelation of Christ; as the apostle excellently teaches us in his Epistle to the Galatians, chap. iii. 24. Secondly, he proceeded in this manner for the justification of his gospel, when it should be once come. For the shadows and delineations of it which we see in the law clearly show us that it is the workmanship and design of God; and the admirable resemblance between these ancient figures, long since drawn by his own hand in the tabernacle of Moses, and the bodies of the things, which have been revealed in Jesus Christ, irrefragably prove that he who heretofore took the care to make those draughts is author of the realities which they represented, and that the body descends from the same heaven which at first made the shadows of it to be seen. I pass by for this time the lamb, and the sacrifices, and the aspersions, and expiations, and all the Levitical priesthood; a true delineation of our grand victim offered for the salvation of the world, and of that eternal righteousness which his blood has procured for us, and other similar things, which cannot but with extreme difficulty be maintained, nor made to agree with the ways of the ordinary wisdom of God, except by acknowledging and receiving as true what the apostle here teaches us, and which is evident enough of itself, namely, that all this was heretofore ordained to prefigure Christ.

I will only speak a few words of the distinction of meats and days. The apostle opens the mystery of it elsewhere. For as to observance of meats, giving us direction in the Epistle to the Corinthians to keep the feast of our passover, "not with the old leaven of malice and wickedness, but with the unleavened bread of sincerity and truth," 1 Cor. v. 8; does he not clearly show us that abstinence from leavened bread, observed by the first people, was a picture of the innocence and holiness of the second—and that, by consequence, it is to the same that we must refer the distinction of other legal meats—the beasts which were forbidden them representing by the characters of their natural qualities those moral imperfections, that is, those vices and corrupt affections, from which our lives ought to be exempt? As, for example, abstinence from swine's flesh, which was an abomination to them, signified that the people of the Messiah should have no commerce with that uncleanness and filth of deportment in which men of the world, fitly represented by the genius of this animal, wallow. And when the same apostle tells us that we should keep our feast in truth and sincerity, and, in another place, that there remaineth unto us a sabbath, or a rest, Heb. iv. 9; does he not show us again that the old feasts of Israel were shadows of ours, even of that feast which the Messiah has procured and appointed for the faithful, and which consists in two things: the one, that they abstain from the works of sin and of the flesh, the common works of men; and the other, that they celebrate a rest in God with eternal joy? Now that the body of these shadows is in Jesus Christ, it is evident. For innocence, sanctity, abstinence from sin, joy, and immortality dwell in him fully. There it is, and nowhere else, that the truth, the example and pattern, the doctrine, and all the cause of them, are to be found, together with an Almighty Spirit of light, which alone is capable of producing these divine things in every one of us. Whereby you see it is so far from being consequent, upon these distinctions having been heretofore ordained of God, that we ought now fully to observe them, that, on the contrary, it is to be concluded we may insist no longer on them. For since they were appointed in the quality of shadows, until Christ should be revealed; who does not see that now, when Christ has been fully manifested, it would be mere folly in us to adhere to them still? even as, if seeing and having in hand the very body of a thing, we should occupy ourselves in following after and embracing the shadow of it?

Precisely such was the extravagance of these false teachers who are here noted by Paul; and such also is the error of all those who, upon similar pretences, impose laws upon christians concerning the use of, or abstinence from, such things as are in their nature indifferent. And it is in this matter, for one, that our adversaries of Rome are infinitely to blame; who, notwithstanding the reason of the things themselves, and the clear doctrine of this great apostle, both in this place and in many others, have made and constituted no less a number of laws, about the distinction of days and meats, than were among the Jews themselves. They have marked more than half of the days of the year, some with black, and others with white. I call those marked black which they have devoted to the sadness of fasts and abstinences, as all the Fridays and Saturdays of the year, the Ember weeks, the Rogation-days, the Advent, the Eves, and Lent. Those marked with white are such as they consecrate to joy, as that great throng of holy-days which they disperse through all the four seasons. Jesus Christ, the Father of eternity, has made his disciples free from the laws of time, raising them up above the heavens, which make and measure it. But these men put them in subjection to days and months, and reduce them under the yoke of the Jews, and make their piety to depend upon the almanac. If they do not observe all the days of the year; if they fast not one day; if they eat not on another; if on one they do not perform penance; if they make not mirth on another; though upon the former they should have cause to rejoice in God, and upon the latter to afflict themselves for their sins or their sufferings, they commit a heinous sin, though they did it without contempt or scandal. Was there ever a discipline less reasonable, or more contrary to the doctrine of Paul, who would not have christians condemned for the distinction of a festival day, of a new moon, or of the sabbaths; who reprehends the Galatians for their observing "days, and months, and times, and years," Gal. iv. 10; and counts it for a weakness in faith to esteem "one day above another?" Rom. xiv. 5.

Neither may it be replied here, that we also discriminate Sundays, and Easter, and Christmas, and Pentecost. We observe them for order's sake, not for religion; for the polity of the church, and not upon scruples of devotion.* For what a confusion there would be, if we had no days appointed for the assembling of the faithful! It is for our mutual edification, and not for the worth and value of the days themselves, that we observe them; and, as St. Hierom said, not that the day on which we assemble is more holy or more glorious than another, but because on whatever day we assemble, it is a consolation to us to behold ourselves all jointly employed in holy exercises. Generally, all days to us are equal; as uniform parts of the same time, which flow on by the order of one and the same Lord, and are all employable to his glory: but the necessity and infirmity of this poor life constrain us to divide and part them out for various uses. If it be thus, O adversaries, that you discriminate days, I shall confess I have done wrong to accuse you of acting contrary to the doctrine of Paul. But who knows not that it is a devotion for days, and not the profit of men, that makes you observe them? You believe that you do God's service in this very thing, that you feast one day, and fast another. You give it to the dignity of the day, and not to the necessity of order, or to your edification; neither do you esteem days alike. Those which you observe you set up very high above others, not only on account of the command of the church, but because they have the honour to represent and signify some mysterious thing. Accordingly, you hold that, besides the use which festivals may be of for your instruction, and your having time for works of piety, your very solemnization of them is a religious act, such as makes up a part of divine service, and is, as you say, meritorious in the sight of God; which is exactly the opinion and the practice of those whom the apostle in this place opposes. For they condemned christians, not for absence from the assembly of the church on the day appointed, or for having profaned such hours in the world as were destined to the service of God, or for having scandalized their neighbour by this kind of fault; but only and precisely, as you do, for not having celebrated a festival day.

What shall I say of the other point, namely, the use of, and abstinence from, meats? The apostle says, "Let no man judge you in meat." In conscience, dare you affirm that you judge none of the faithful in this respect? What mean then those

* It is much to be regretted, that the author should have been so influenced by the prevailing opinions of the times, as not to distinguish the Sabbath above other festivals, as a divine institution of perpetual obligation.—Ed. Pres. Bd.

rigorous laws of yours against those who eat any flesh—those laws of yours which deprive christians of this liberty for more than one third of the year, and condemn that man who, during all this time, shall taste one morsel of beef or mutton, to penalties as heavy as if he had committed a deadly sin? You are come so far, that you look not upon those who violate these fine laws as sinners; you abhor them as profane persons and atheists, and count them not for christians. Is this a grave and holy discipline, worthy of Paul and Jesus Christ, to make the service of God to consist in meat; neither the abstinence nor use of which (as reason shows every one, and as our Saviour and his apostle teach, Matt. xv.; 1 Cor. viii. 8; Rom. xiv. 17) pollutes or sanctifies, or produces loss or gain—it being a thing purely indifferent in itself, good or evil only as it hurts or helps the interest of temperance and charity? But we shall have shortly a fitter occasion to speak to you at large upon this subject.

For the present, beloved brethren, make your profit, I beseech you, of Paul's instruction. Use the liberty which the Lord Jesus has obtained for you, as his apostle declares. It is not reasonable that men should take away what God has given you, and bought with the precious blood of his Son. Only see that you take not this liberty for an occasion to live after the flesh, Gal. v. 13. Lay by shadows, since you are no longer children; but embrace the body which is in Jesus Christ. His kingdom is neither meat nor drink; and no one will he condemn for having eaten any of the things which he has created for the faithful to use with thanksgiving. If he formerly prohibited some of them, it was to delineate and portray by this fleshly abstinence that body which is mystical and spiritual, into which he has shaped you by his cross. Your abstinence, christian, is to renounce the meat that perisheth, to loathe the passions and productions of vice, on which the world feeds. It nourishes itself with the works of sin. Avarice, and ambition, and injustice, and luxury, and the filth of wantonness, and the infamous sweets of revenge, are the aliments after which it runs, and without which it cannot live. This is, O ye faithful, that flesh the use of which is forbidden you. This is the Lent which Jesus Christ and his apostles have in truth enjoined, a Lent to be observed, not forty days only, but all the year long; even that we abhor what is evil; that we eschew vice, as poison; that our lives be pure, and innocent, and clean from all the filthiness of the flesh. This is in truth that abstinence which makes a christian, and without which no man can have place among the members of Christ: "For they that are Christ's have crucified the flesh with the affections and lusts," Gal. v. 24. "The world is crucified" to them, chap. vi. 14. Its provisions, its pleasures, its allurements, are had in execration of them. Whoever properly fasts this Lent shall have part in the resurrection of Christ Jesus. Not a man shall attain thereto in any other way. Prosecute it in good earnest, christian souls, and powerfully mortify in yourselves all the lusts of this accursed flesh, which perishes itself, and will cause all those likewise to perish who desire its delights, and cannot wean themselves from its deadly dainties. See what Jesus Christ has done and suffered for its destruction. See the excellency of that other divine food on which he would have you live. Your true food is to fulfil the will of his Father. This is the food of the Prince of glory, and of all his angels; food that is holy and immortal; which will leave in your souls a divine relish and contentment, much better than all the feasts on earth; and after the consolations with which it will solidly strengthen your consciences in this life, it will eternally repast you in the heavens with the delights of blissful immortality.

Brethren, this is the body, of which the abstinence of the Jews was the shadow and delineation only. As for their festivals, they were also figures: verily, not of those in Rome (which, to say the truth, are mere shadows and weak representations themselves, no less than these of the Jews; only they are instituted by men, whereas the Jewish were ordained of God); they were, I say, figures of the resting and spiritual contentment of the faithful. Our festival (as one of the ancients formerly answered a pagan, who reproached christians for their having none*) is to do our duty; to worship God, and offer him the bloodless sacrifices of our holy supplications; to rest from our own works, and entirely sequester ourselves to the work of God; to exterminate from among us that really servile and mechanical labour of vicious actions, and spend our lives in the truly noble and divine exercise of sanctification. Our passover is to eat the flesh of the Lamb, to make use of his blood, to pass out of Egypt unto Canaan, out of the world unto God, and from earth to heaven; leaving the things that are behind, and advancing daily towards the mark and prize of our calling. Our pentecost is to converse with Christ in heavenly places, to think and meditate on him, and to receive from his hand the divine fire of his Spirit, that we may speak of his wonderful works. Our feast of tabernacles is to live as strangers in the world, without cleaving to it, still aspiring unto Jerusalem which is above, the mother and the city of the faithful. Our new moons are the praise we continually sound forth unto God, not with silver trumpets, but with heart and understanding. Finally, our sabbath is to do not our own will, but the will of God; repressing and restraining the motions and sentiments of our nature, that space may be left for Christ to

---

* Origen against Celsus, l. 8, p. 404.

work in us, so that it may not be we that live, but Christ who liveth in us.

This is, christians, that true body which was formerly represented by the Jewish shadows. These are your festivals, your solemnities, and your devotions. Keep them holy, and celebrate them religiously. It is the great Prince of your salvation who has instituted and consecrated them. He recommends them to you everywhere in his gospel; and has indissolubly bound you to them by that death, the remembrance of which we are to celebrate next Lord's day. If you acquit yourselves worthily herein, be assured that after that stay which for a time you make here below, he will raise you up to heaven, there to celebrate with him and his angels that last mystical feast of the great day, which, rising at the point of our resurrection, shall not go down for ever but shine eternally, and render us happy in the fruition of that life and immortal glory which was prepared for us before the foundation of the world. So be it.

SERMON XXVIII.

VERSE 18.

Let no man beguile you of your reward in a voluntary humility and worshipping of angels, intruding into those things which he hath not seen, vainly puffed up by his fleshly mind.

DEAR brethren, it is a thing exceedingly strange, and which shows the extreme corruption of our nature more sensibly than any other, that men should have so vehement and invincible a passion for the service of creatures. God, the sovereign Lord both of them and of the universe, manifested himself clearly to them, causing the illustrious and glorious marks of his goodness, and wisdom, and infinite power to shine forth every where, above and beneath, upon and about them; yea, bringing them home even to their hearts; and giving them a feeling of him, by the innumerable benefits which he pours out continually upon all parts of their lives. In short, he showed himself, and drew near, and represented himself in so lively a manner to their understanding and perceptions, that they could not (if I may presume so to speak) be ignorant of him if they would. Besides all this, he vouchsafed to reveal himself to them at the beginning in a particular manner; speaking familiarly to Adam and Noah, and others of the primitive patriarchs, who were the sources of the first and second world. You are aware, however, that notwithstanding all these lights, the rage of that passion which men had for idolatry was so violent, that it made them forget all those holy and admirable displays of the Deity; and induced them, instead of their great and abundantly good and omnipotent Creator, blessed for ever, to serve the creature; and their frenzy rose to such a height, that besides the luminaries of heaven, and the invisible powers which govern them; besides kings, and sages, and persons whom worth or authority had raised above others; they were not ashamed to adore things of the lowest order in nature, such as beasts, plants, and elements; and to complete their extravagance, they added to all the rest images and figures, things absolutely insensible and unprofitable; changing, as the apostle says, "the glory of the uncorruptible God into an image made like to corruptible man, and to birds, and four-footed beasts, and creeping things," Rom. i. 23.

This brutish error having overwhelmed all mankind, the Lord was so gracious that he drew Abraham out of it, as a brand out of a universal conflagration; and afterwards, manifesting himself more clearly unto his posterity by the ministry of Moses and giving them his law, he raised up amidst this people a public testimony of his truth, against the general misdemeanour of the world, fulminating thousands of maledictions against all such as served creatures. But the love of idolatry was so strong, that it broke this bar of heaven, and violated this divine declaration; which proved to be so far from reducing the nations to their duty, that it could not keep the very Israelites in theirs; but they, as we learn by their history, often gave up themselves to worship the creature. At last, after so many significations of his mind, God sent his only begotten, the Sun of righteousness and truth, into the world, who opened to us the manner and the reasons and causes of the worship of God, and fully discovered that of which the Gentiles were ignorant on account of their stupidity, and the Jews but imperfectly knew in their minority. Now who would think that so shameful and gross an error as the worship of creatures should have the shamelessness to show itself in so noble and so glorious a light? Yet you know this wretched passion found the means to gratify itself; bringing in, by degrees, under various vain but plausible pretences, the worship of angels and men among christians. But, however, it is not strange that a corruption should gain such ground in the latter ages, when it was favoured by a universal ignorance, by a decay of truth, and by the depravity of men; such a thing frequently happens in their discipline and constitutions; generally, as they go on they grow worse. That which surpasses all astonishment is, that in the time and under the eyes of the holy apostles of our Lord and Saviour, there should be men found of so impudent a spirit as to promote so vile an error in the profession of christianity. We should scarcely be able to believe it, if Paul did not give us that testimony respecting it which we have just read to you. And God permitted it, as well to exercise and prove the primitive church as to confirm ours; this occasion having here drawn from the apostle's pen a clear and magnificent condemnation of this abuse. He has rejected already, in the context, those observances which the false teachers, whom he opposes, had taken from the Mosaic law; now he refutes those which they had borrowed from the philosophers of the world. For, as we shall show presently, that worshipping of angels which these men would have introduced among christians was a fruit and an invention of heathen philosophy. Paul strikes down this vain impiety in a few words. "Let no man beguile you of your reward in a voluntary humility and worshipping of angels, intruding into those things which he hath not seen, vainly puffed up by his fleshly mind."

Dear brethren, here is a remarkable sentence pronounced, which overthrows, in express words, all the worship that the superstition of men, whether ancient or modern, attributes unto creatures; it being clear that there is not one of them whom we can lawfully serve in religion, since the apostle forbids us to serve the angels themselves, who are, without contradiction, of all creatures the most excellent. You know the interest we have in this affair; those of Rome anathematizing us, because, being content to adore and serve God our Creator and Redeemer only, we refuse to render unto angels and departed saints that religious worship, and those divine honours, which they decree and prefer daily to them, to the great prejudice of the glory of God and the irreparable offence of men. Let us therefore exactly consider this oracle of the holy apostle; and that we may leave nothing in it behind us, we must see, first, what the doctrine of those seducers is which he condemns. He expresses it in these words, "Let no man beguile you of your reward in a voluntary humility and worshipping of angels." And then we are to examine, in the second place, the marks which he gives these false teachers; these are contained in the following words, "intruding into those things which he hath not seen, vainly puffed up by his fleshly mind, and not holding the Head." But we will satisfy ourselves, for the present, with the former of these parts, remitting the second to another opportunity, on account of the cavils and inventions which our adversaries make use of to corrupt this passage, and which we must refute as briefly as we can.

I. The word that Paul uses at the commencement, and

which we have translated "beguile," is difficult, and seldom found in the authors of the Greek tongue. St. Hierom, one of the most learned of the ancients, says it was peculiar to the country of Cilicia;* of which Paul was a native, he being born at Tarsus, the capital city of that province. However this may be, the derivation of the word is clear, and sufficiently expresses what is nearly its signification. For those who understand the Greek know that this term comes from another, which signifies the reward that was given to those who won the victory in those games, or combats for prizes at which certain judges and moderators at that time presided, who had the superintendence of the whole business, regulating and bounding the race, assigning the ground, and receiving the champions into it, judging of their courses and combats, proclaiming that man victorious to whom they yielded the advantage, and solemnly putting a crown upon his head. Consequently, they were called by a name that signifies, Givers of the reward; and the term, which signifies what they did on such occasions, is generally used to express governing, regulating, ruling, and having the superintendence of a matter. It is expressly from this term that that which the apostle uses here is formed; except that it seems to signify governing and ordering, not simply, but to the prejudice and damage of the person concerned. Therefore some have thought that Paul, comparing here the faithful to racers, or combatants, as he very often does, exhorts them not to let the prize, or reward of the victory, be taken from them by the artifice of seducers, who made it their business to turn them out of the true and lawful lists of their race, which are no other than believing and obeying the doctrine of the gospel; and to cause them to enter into another career, namely, that of their own inventions and services; in the same sense that he said to the Galatians, who were injured by a similar impostor, "Ye did run well; who did hinder you that ye should not obey the truth?" chap. v. 7. If this exposition were as well adapted to the apostle's phrase as it is to his sense, it would be excellent; showing us how this serving of angels here forbidden is an error of no small importance, since it causes those who turn aside unto, or employ themselves in it, to lose the prize of their heavenly calling.

The Latin interpreter, canonized by those of Rome, having respect to the effect of such false doctrine, namely, the driving of the faithful out of the right way, translates it simply, Let no man seduce you. There is no occasion to introduce the interpretations of others. But I affirm that there can be hardly found an expression more proper, more suitable, and

* Ep. ad Alg. 9, 10.

agreeing better with either the term or the scope of the apostle, than that of the French Bible, Let no man master it over you; which naturally expresses the magisterial authority which these seducers assumed to themselves; enjoining and commanding their fancies to the faithful, as if they had been installed superintendents of their religion and their lives; and giving them to understand that, without practising what they prescribed, it was not possible to obtain the prize of their high calling. By this the apostle gives them a blow, and renders them ridiculous, as men who, having, in truth, no lawful authority, would, nevertheless, cause it be believed that they had; and spake and commanded with as much confidence as if it belonged to them to distribute the crown of heaven at the last day, or that they had it already in their hands to impart to whom it should seem to them good. But that which Paul adds exposes their folly still more; Let no man master it over you, at his pleasure, or at his will; which may be referred either to their office or to their doctrine, or, as I think, to them both. To their office; meaning that they are voluntary superintendents, and that their own will alone, not the voice of God or men, elevated them to this pretended mastership; well nigh as the Roman orator calls a certain man a voluntary senator, who thrust himself into the rank of the senators, but had no right to be there, having been elected only by himself. But this respects also their doctrine, and signifies that the worshipping of angels, which they commanded, was founded merely on their own good pleasure, and not upon any precept of God; that their will alone was the reason and ground of it, not the will of the Lord; that it was nothing but an imagination of their own head, and a fruit either of their folly or their malice. Whence we may observe, by the way, that those who teach in the church ought to set forth nothing but what is founded on the word of God. "To the law and to the testimony: if they speak not according to this word, it is because there is no light in them," Isa. viii. 20. This rule is enough to cashier all the doctrines of Rome which we contest with her. For if you examine their worshipping of saints and angels, their sacrifice of the mass, their papal monarchy, and other similar opinions, you will find that they have no foundation but their will; and when they are pressed, they go so far themselves, and boldly assert that they are judges of all things, judges of the faith of men, and of the Scriptures of God; and that a declaration of their popes ought to suffice for the reason of anything, into which also their whole religion and belief is finally resolved. So that if ever there was a generation of whom it might be said that they mastered it over the faithful, at their pleasure, without doubt it is they, who call themselves their judges, their lords, and their monarchs; who make their will to pass with them for the supreme law of the church; who obtrude upon them an endless multitude of traditions and services, upon the sole credit of their good pleasure; and undertake to distribute to them the rewards of their piety after their death, merely according to their fancy; exalting some to be saints, others to be beatified; ordaining for some the service of *hyperdulia*, for others of simple *dulia* (as they call it); commissioning some to be over one country or city, or over one sort of diseases or affairs, and others over another; (as kings distribute, according to their good pleasure, the honours, charges, and dignities of their state;) while they cannot produce, for one particle of all this, any command or foundation from the word of God.

But let us come to our apostle, who declares, in that which follows, what the discipline was which these voluntary masters of the faithful pretended to impose upon them: "Let no man," says he, "master it over you by a voluntary humility and worshipping of angels." In these words he shows us what it is to which they would oblige christians, namely, the worship of angels; and what was the pretext upon which they promoted this new service, namely, a humility of spirit: as for the former, the word used in the original signifies not in general all kind of service, but particularly that of religion; whence the Latin interpreter renders it, "the religion of angels." This religious service comprehends in it those pieces of worship and those ceremonies which are performed to the Deity, and the actions by which homage is done to him in that character, as adoration, invocation, thanksgiving, trust, and such others. The meaning of these men, therefore, was, that besides that supreme worship which christians render to God the Father, Son, and Holy Spirit, they should serve angels also, as their mediators and intercessors with God, and that under this character they should address prayers, and thanksgivings, and other duties of religion to them. This was their error. The pretext which they used to authorize this service was a humility of spirit; alleging that we are too unworthy to present ourselves directly to God, and address ourselves to so sublime a Majesty, and also that Jesus Christ, being the Son of God, and God with him blessed for ever, it would be presumption in us to present ourselves immediately to him; whereupon they concluded that we must have recourse to angels, who are middle natures between God and us, to the end that they, receiving our prayers, may present them to our common Sovereign, and interceding with him on our behalf, may obtain access for us to his otherwise inaccessible throne. Such were the false and plausible pretences with which these people painted over their tradition.

Upon which you may observe, first, in general, that the alleging of some specious and plausible reasons is not sufficient to authorize a worship or an observance in religion. All that is proposed to us on this subject must be founded on the word of God, who alone has the wisdom and authority necessary for settling the doctrines of religion. For if we once license the mind of man to rely upon its own imaginations, there is no error nor extravagance upon which it will not put some colour. Surely the discourse of these seducers is not destitute of show; for men have found so much of that in it, that both heathens, and the heretics which have troubled Christianity, and indeed those of Rome, have all of them used it to colour their superstitions. Yet you see the apostle, without dwelling at all upon this vain lustre, without deigning even so much as to examine it, rejects and absolutely condemns that service for the promotion of which it was designed; only because such service was not ordained of God, but founded solely on the will of men. Let this example make us wise to abhor and refuse, without delay, whatever men would introduce into religion without the order and the word of God. Let us not for a moment regard those gaudy reasons with which they endeavour to paint over their inventions. Let us not so much as hearken to them. It is a sufficient warrant for the rejection of their services that they are not ordained in the word of God. From this alone it follows that they assuredly are vain and unprofitable; neither is there any pretext, however specious, that can or ought to authorize in religion a thing that God has not appointed.

Again, you see here, in particular, that that humility of spirit with which our adversaries at this day colour over the services they perform to angels and saints, is but an old paint which ancient heretics used for bad purposes, and the apostle long ago expressly rejects; so that it is not only a vanity, but an impudence, for them to avail themselves of a thing so condemned. Let them cease to allege that we are too poor to present ourselves directly to God; let them forbear to lay before us the courts of earthly kings, where men make use of the mediation of officers before they speak to the princes themselves, to infer therefrom that we must make use of the intercession of saints and angels in a similar manner, that they may lead us to God, and present to him our persons and requests. Paul has blasted all this artifice; and they should be ashamed to use a pretext which the first heretics took up to cover their errors, and which this great apostle has manifestly taken from them. In truth, all this pretended humility of spirit, with which these people mask themselves, is but a cover of real presumption, which, disdaining to be subject to the commands of God, would serve him after its own fancy, and not as he has appointed. It is like the humility of Ahaz, who haughtily refused the grace which the goodness of the Lord offered to him, upon pretence that he would not tempt him, Isa. vii. 11, 12. God, in his great mercy, gives us his Son Jesus to be our Mediator; he humbles himself, and is made man, that he might be more accessible unto us. He proclaims in a thousand places that he is the "the way, the truth, and the life;" and that "no man cometh to the Father, but by him," John xiv. 6; that it is he by "whom we have boldness and access with confidence by the faith of him," Eph. iii. 12. He calls us unto himself: "Come unto me, and I will give you rest," Matt. xi. 28. And his ministers not only permit us to go to him, they command and press us to do so. Let us go, say they, with boldness to "the throne of grace, that we may obtain mercy, and find grace to help in time of need," Heb. iv. 16. Instead of obeying these holy and divine calls of God and his ministers, you say, No, I will not do it. I am not so presumptuous as to go either to God or to his Son. I must beg the intercession of angels and saints, to present me before that Supreme Light. Can this be anything but exalting yourself above God? Is it not a presuming that you know better than he what belongs to your duty and his service? Is it not a hiding under the fine words of a feigned humility, plain rebellion and disobedience to his holy Majesty? which is in effect the highest pride of which a creature can be guilty, since it is really a pretending that you are wiser than he, and that the way which he prescribes you is neither so good nor so reasonable as that which you have chosen. But let us forbear further argument. For where the apostle speaks, there is no need for us to discourse. His authority relies not on the succour of our reasons. Here, you see, it is express against our adversaries' corrupt usage. He formally condemns the thing which they do. For they approve and daily practise this service of angels which Paul forbids, and ground it upon that same humility of spirit which he has condemned and destroyed; and thus become doubly culpable, inasmuch as they not only rebuild, if I may so say, this Jericho of superstition which he has demolished, but also employ in its erection the very stones which he has blasted from heaven. What can error say against so clear a determination? By what charms can it avert this flash of lightning from falling on its head? Dear brethren, it is too much in love with its own inventions to give glory to God; and will rather renounce his word, than quit its superstitious imaginations. In the present matter, seeing itself pressed, it has recourse to subtlety; and though it both maintains and practises the worship of angels, and cannot deny that the apostle condemns those who teach and practise it, yet it pretends with an incredible boldness that it is not this which the apostle condemns. It has turned itself various ways to effect this illusion; all which, to say the truth, have more hardiness than art in them. And, to begin at this one, the most famous of its last advocates, being, as I think, ill satisfied in his conscience with the subtlety of his fellows, has thought of a new gloss, unheard of till now in all the schools of christianity, both ancient and modern; born of his own conceit alone, a very fruitful breeder of such productions, and begotten by mere despair of his bad cause. This man then affirms,* that Paul means by this expression, not (as all the fathers and all the moderns have believed) the worshipping of angels, but, as he all alone will have it, the law of Moses. First, the novelty of this gloss, and the very consideration that for the space of near sixteen hundred years not so much as one single man has been found who was aware of it, sufficiently shows that it is the heat of disputation, and not the truth of the thing, which suggested it to its author: and the maxims of his church he evidently renounces too, which forbids the Scriptures to be interpreted by any but the fathers; whereas he, laying by their exposition brings in one here that is not only undiscernible in any one of them, but also directly contrary to that of the most renowned of their number,† who understand these words of the apostle of the worship rendered to angels by those seducers whom Paul in this place opposes. But I say, moreover, that it is for a good reason that no man ever thought upon it, since in very deed it is not maintainable; nor can it be made at all to agree either with the apostle's words, or with his scope and design.

Not with his *words*, for they must be interpreted according to the style of the authors of that tongue in which he writes. Now there are but two or three places in Scripture where the word used by the apostle occurs construed as it is in this place. One is in James: "If any man among you seems to be religious, and bridleth not his tongue, but deceiveth his own heart, that man's religion," or service, "is vain," James i. 26. Another is in the book of the Acts, where Paul says, that, from the beginning, he lived a Pharisee, after the straitest sect of his religion, chap. xxvi. 5. The word is found again so construed in the book of Wisdom, held for canonical by our adversaries, and which, though it is not so indeed, yet is written in the same language and style as those of the books of the New Testament. This author makes use of the word in the same manner. The abominable service, says he, or religion of idols, "is the beginning, the cause, and the end of evil," chap. xiv. 27. In all these places the religion or the service of any one signifies either the service he does to some other, as in the two former passages, or the service that is done to him by others, as in the latter of them. Here there-

* Du Perron, in his Repl. to K. James, p. 909.

† Chrysost. Theodoret. Œcumen. Theophylact.

fore, except you think the apostle swerved from the style in which he wrote, the service or religion of angels must of necessity signify one of those two things; either the service which the angels perform to God, or the service which men perform to them. The first of these two senses cannot take place, by the confession of our adversaries themselves, and of every sober person. They must then necessarily admit the second, and confess with us, and with all the ancients, that by the service of angels Paul intends, not the Jewish religion, or the law of Moses, but the religious service which these seducers rendered to angels under pretext of humility.

Moreover, in what prophet, in what apostle, in what rational author, either ancient or even modern, have these men ever found this novel and extravagant manner of speaking, the service of angels, that is to say, the Jewish religion? It is called the law of God, because God instituted it; the law of Moses, because Moses was the mediator and minister of it; the religion or service of the Jews, because that people made profession of it; the elements or rudiments of the world, because it contained but the alphabet, and the first and lowest lessons of piety, and was generally affixed to the corporeal things of this world. But that it was ever called the religion or service of angels we read not. And as for that, which those people allege out of the Epistle to the Galatians, chap. iii. 19, namely, that the law "was ordained by angels in the hand of a mediator;" and its being called, in the Epistle to the Hebrews, chap. ii. 2, "the word spoken by angels;" this I say does not at all justify their pretension. For in these two places the apostle declares only the service which the angels did to God, when he gave the decalogue upon Sinai, where these heavenly ministers accompanied him, and ordered all the pomp of his admirable manifestation; forming the lightnings and the thunders with which the mountain resounded, elevating in the air the smoke and darkness which covered it, shaking its foundations, and making the whole of it to tremble, and distinguishing the thunders into those articulate words which the mouth of God itself pronounced. So far did the operation of angels extend, and no further. For as to the rest, it was God that spake in his own person; "I am," said he at the beginning, "the Lord thy God;" and that gave and uttered all the other precepts which the Israelites heard; so that the law or the religion which he then established might well be termed the religion or the service of God. But it would be an evident injury of his Majesty to call it the religion or the service of angels, since it was given neither in their persons nor by their mediation. Besides, if it were otherwise in this particular, yet it is clear that this title would be proper to the decalogue only, and would not reach that part of the law which is called ceremonial, in the establishment of which the angels did not at all intervene, God having delivered it immediately to Moses, and Moses to the Israelites; and yet it would be this precisely which Paul would be understood to mean here, if his purpose were to speak of the Mosaical law, as our adversaries believe. Since then this name, the religion of angels, can no way belong to it, it must of necessity be asserted, that it is not the law of Moses that the apostle means in these words.

But his *design*, and the thread of his discourse, is no less opposite to this gloss than his words. For first, having already refuted what the seducers took from the law of Moses, in the verse immediately preceding, in these words, "Let no man judge you in meat, or in drink, or in respect of an holyday, or of the new moon, or of the sabbath days: which are a shadow of things to come; but the body is of Christ;" having, I say, so magnificently deposited this, for what reason, or to what purpose, should he repeat the same again? How should the apostle be capable of such vain babbling? Let us say, then, that the error he rejects here is different from that which he condemned just before. That which he condemned before is the observation of the Jewish law or religion; certainly then this is not the thing meant in this place. Besides, that which he adds can no way refer to it: "Let no man," says he, "beguile you of your reward by a voluntary humility and worshipping of angels, intruding into those things which he hath not seen:" where the apostle evidently shows that the service of angels enjoined by the seducers was founded upon hidden things, and such as they could have no knowledge of, either by their own reason or by Scripture; whereas the Jewish ceremonies are so clearly and so distinctly explained in the books of Moses, that every man may see them there. Lastly, the apostle shows us, at the beginning of this discourse, that these seducers had drawn some of their observances from philosophy, which could not have been the case, if by the service of angels you understand the Jewish religion, which, as all know, was delivered by Moses, and not by the philosophers. For our adversaries to understand the discourses of the Jews by the vain deceit of philosophy,* is absurd and ridiculous in the highest degree; it being evident that the Jewish doctors are sometimes called sages, and their science wisdom; as when Paul asks, "Where is the wise? Hath not God made foolish the wisdom of this world?" 1 Cor. i. 20. But never are they called philosophers, or their doctrine philosophy; these names being everywhere constantly referred to the learned men of Greece, and of the heathen, and to their doctrine.

* Du Perron, p. 910.

Let it be then concluded, that the apostle means here, by the religion or service of the angels, not the religion delivered to the Jews by Moses; but the worship, and invocation, and service which these seducers taught men to address to angels, under a pretext of humility; they having borrowed this abuse from the Greek philosophers, in whose books it is still found to this day; Plato, one of the chief of them, writing expressly, that service must be done to the demons, (for so they called the angels,) as holding a middle place between the gods and men, and serving us for interpreters to the divine nature; and all his school has ever thus held and practised, as appears by the works of the latest of his disciples. And this abuse was common among all the heathen. They founded it, too, just as did the seducers here censured by the apostle, and as our adversaries do, upon pretended humility of spirit, as we understand by an ancient commentary upon the Epistle to the Romans, published under the name of St. Ambrose.* The author, speaking of the heathen of his time, says. "They are accustomed to make a miserable excuse, saying that by means of them (that is, of the petty deities they served) they might go to God, as men come to a prince, by means of his counsellors of state and his masters of requests. But, says he a little after, men go to a king by means of his officers, because, after all, a king is a man who knows not whom he may trust with his estate, whereas God is ignorant of nothing, and knows the disposition, and action, and capacity of all men; so that to obtain his favour we want not the suffrages of an interposer; there needs but a devout soul. Such a one he will surely hear, wheresoever he speaks to him.

It is from the sinks of this philosophy of the world that the seducers, here opposed by the apostle, had drawn their pretended humility, and their worshipping of angels.

And our adversaries, well perceiving that generally it cannot be denied that such was the doctrine here condemned by the apostle, advance another of their fancies, telling us that in his time there was a certain sect which some call the Judaic sect, and others give it other names, consisting of people who neither served God nor Jesus Christ, but angels, under the quality of chiefs, and supreme patrons, and protectors of their religion; that it is at these Paul here aims, and not at them, who, it is true, serve angels, but who also serve God the Father, and his Son Jesus Christ. First, all this sect is an idol, which never had subsistence anywhere except in their fond conceit; neither could it indeed be anywhere else. For if they were Jews, who can believe that they served not God, whose service the whole Judaical law and religion expressly com-

*Ambrose, p. 1807. c. 4, 5.

manded throughout, in the beginning, in the middle, and at the end? Again, if they were christians, how served they not Jesus Christ? And if they were either Jews or christians, how did they own no other chief of their religion than the angels? All this is nothing but a mere fiction of our adversaries, who endeavour to put a changeling upon us, and to set up this chimera, that it may receive the blow which the apostle aims at them. It is not lawful for us to forge sects at our pleasure; there must be proof of them produced from good and creditable witnesses, if we would wish to be believed. But so far are they from having any warrant for this fine story in antiquity, that, on the contrary, the ancient interpreters of the apostle, such as Theodoret, Photius, and Theophylact, overthrow it; affirming that those whom Paul aims at alleged that God is great and incomprehensible, and that it is a thing unworthy of the majesty of the Son to conduct such mean creatures as men unto him: whereupon they added that application must be made to angels, to obtain access by their means, and to gain the favour and good-will of God. How is it that they did not serve God, since it was for access to him, and to become acceptable with him, that they employed the intercession of angels? and how is it that they did not adore Jesus Christ, seeing they accounted themselves unworthy to go immediately to him? Finally, how is it that they owned the angels for the supreme heads of their religion, seeing that they made use of their intervention only to come to God? This very thing was the motive of their erroneous practice. And one of the before-named ancients* adds expressly, that the service which they did to angels was praying to them; and also this abuse reigned a long time in Phrygia and Pisidia; and that even in his days there were oratories found dedicated to St. Michael:—a relation which has so stung one of the great cardinals of Rome,† that, all in choler against this author, (who lived almost twelve hundred years ago, and was besides one of the greatest and most learned spirits of antiquity,) he says that with his leave he has had ill luck in this particular. Whence you may see the respect that these gentlemen bear the ancient fathers, whom they have perpetually in their mouth. When they favour them, they are oracles. If they speak otherwise, their antiquity does not save them from being treated as ignorant and unlearned. But they allege that the apostle says of those of whom he speaks, that they held not the Head (that is, Christ Jesus). I grant it: but I affirm that this does not infer that they made profession of acknowledging him not. As from his saying that they were puffed up by their fleshly mind, and intruded into things which they had not seen, it follows

* Theodoret.

† Baronius.

not that they acknowledged either the one or the other of these things. So far were they from it that they made profession of humility, and it was under this very pretext that they worshipped angels, and boasted, as without doubt they did, of knowing well the things which they divulged. But the apostle speaks here of that which follows truly and legitimately from their doctrine, and not of what they avowed. For doubtless they made profession of Jesus Christ and of his gospel, and Paul clearly presupposes it through his whole discourse. But by the addition of their errors they denied in effect what they confessed with their mouth; and by this worshipping of angels took away from Christ the quality of being Head of the church, which in word they gave him. It is this with which the apostle here charges them, and on this he evidently founds this maxim, that whosoever takes the angels, or any other creatures, for his mediators and intercessors with God, he, in effect, renounces the mediation of Jesus Christ, and takes from him the glory of being Head of the church; this dignity no more admitting an associate than that of his regality, and being such as cannot be possessed by any one but himself.

But why do I stand considering what the opinions of these false teachers in other respects were? Let them have believed whatever else you please, sure it is that they worshipped angels, and that Paul accuses them of it, and reprehends them for it, and warns the faithful of following them in this particular. He does not say that they were sorcerers or atheists, that they did not serve or invocate God, and his Son Jesus Christ. He says that they worshipped angels, and severely reproves them for it. You do the same. Judge, then, whether the apostle's thunder does not fall upon you. But you will say, I do adore God and Jesus Christ. Indeed! do you not mock the world by defending yourself in that manner—as if you were accused of not acknowledging the Divinity of the father, or of the Son, and not of worshipping angels? But it is always the custom of these masters to substitute one or other of the ancients in their place, when they are accused of transgressing the ordinances of God and his apostles. The Lord forbids the bowing down ourselves before images. They avow they do it; but for all that pretend that the law thunders against the heathen of former times, and not against them. Paul condemns, with strong expressions, those who enjoin abstinence from meats. They confess it is their practice; but add, that it is the old Encratites, and Montanists, and Manichees whom the apostle means, and not they. In like manner here, being accused of worshipping angels, they frankly confess it, yea, boast of worshipping them, and excommunicate us for not doing so likewise. And thus while Paul protests so clearly that we must not serve them, they pay us off with this brave excuse, that it is not of them he speaks, but of I know not what old race of Jewish heretics; as if it were not manifest that he speaks in general of all those who at any time, and in any place whatever, take upon themselves to serve angels, forbidding us, under a heavy penalty, to let them master it over us upon any pretext whatever.

As for us, dear brethren, who know that the laws of God are universal and eternal, and that no age nor climate can dispense with them, or exempt the violaters of them from that righteous curse which they threaten; let us faithfully obey this holy and sacred direction which the apostle has given. Let us not heed the vain glosses and frivolous distinctions by which human subtilty endeavours to elude it, and colour over its own abuses. Let us observe sincerely what this great minister of Jesus Christ enjoins us. He forbids us to worship angels in point of religion. There is no reason that either the eloquence or subtilty, the splendour or the power of men, much less their pleasure and usurped dominion, should have more efficacy upon us than this heavenly authority. And praised be God for that he has given us the courage to obey his apostle in this particular, and to put away the worshipping of angels and men from among us, notwithstanding the strong contradiction of flesh and blood. Let us abide firm in this resolution. Let us adore none but God, since there is none adorable but he. It is just that he alone should be served among us, since it is he alone who has created and redeemed us.

But, beloved, remember I remind you, that rightly to render him his due glory it is not sufficient to have renounced the error of those ancient Phrygians whom the apostle here opposes, and of our adversaries of Rome, namely, the adoration of angels and departed saints; there must also be a banishing of all strange service, all idolizing of anything whatever. For if God cannot suffer those who serve angels and deceased saints, that is, the most excellent natures which exist, and such as have the image of the Deity most clearly resplendent in them, how much less will he endure those that adore gold and silver, the productions of the earth—or their own belly, the most shameful and infamous of all idols—or the flesh, which is but a vain and perishing figure—or the grandeurs of the world, which are but exhalations? And we who have renounced the first of these false services, how can we be excusable if we retain and exercise the second? Now would to God we were as free from the one as we are from the other.

But it must be confessed, to our shame, these latter kind of idols have still a great many devotees and servitors among us. That avarice which Paul calls an idolatry is but too much exercised among us; the flesh and vanity are here publicly served. Wretched men, where is your judgment? You do not serve the angels of heaven, yet you serve the metals of the earth. You do not adore spirits made perfect, yet you adore profane flesh. Neither the light of the sun, nor the brightness of the moon, has been able to seduce your hearts; and yet you have suffered yourselves to be seduced by the glittering of gold and silver, the false *Sol* and *Luna* of the chemists. You who have disdained to put your confidence in saints, have put your hope in gold, and said unto fine gold, Thou art my confidence. The belly, with shame and horror do I utter it, the belly is your God; yours, who have made this glorious promise, to have none but the Eternal only for your God. How can you hope that the Lord will suffer you to give him such monsters for companions—he, who is so jealous of his glory that he cannot suffer the angels themselves to be associated with him? Dear brethren, let us deceive ourselves no longer. Let us once for all put completely away all these false services; and exterminating every idol from among us, adore and serve none but God alone. Let him have the entire possession of our whole hearts; let him reign and exercise an absolute dominion in them, governing all the sentiments and motions of them at his will; that after having constantly adored him in spirit and in truth, we may hereafter receive from his holy, faithful hand the crown of glory, and eternity, which he has purchased for us by the merit of his only Son our Lord Jesus Christ; to whom, with him and the Holy Spirit, the true and only God, blessed for ever, be honour and praise unto ages of ages. Amen.

SERMON XXIX.

VERSES 18, 19.

Let no man beguile you of your reward in a voluntary humility and worshipping of angels, intruding into those things which he hath not seen, vainly puffed up by his fleshly mind, and not holding the Head, from which all the body by joints and bands having nourishment ministered, and knit together, increaseth with the increase of God.

DEAR brethren, the same pride which destroyed the first man at the beginning is the cause of the ruin of such of his posterity as perish. For if you consider it well, you will perceive that that is the thing which makes them despise or wrongly embrace the Christ of God, in whom alone stands our salvation. It was pride that kept the Jews from embracing this singular gift of Heaven, because, saith John, they loved the praise of men; even as our Lord reproached them, saying, "How can ye believe, which receive honour one of another?" And Paul expressly informs us, that the proud fancy they had to establish their own righteousness was the reason of their not submitting to the righteousness of God, Rom. x. 3. It was likewise pride that blinded the minds of the Gentiles, so that they saw not the wonderful things of the gospel of Jesus Christ. The haughty opinion they had of their own vain wisdom induced them to disdain the wisdom of God; and to account the cross of his Son foolishness, though it is an inexhaustible treasury of wisdom. Again, it is pride that has disseminated among christians themselves all the heresies which have grown up into any repute, from the nativity of the church to this hour. Ignorance animated with presumption has brought them all forth, and bred them up. For if the unhappy workers who divulged them had kept to the doctrine of God, and not launched out beyond that which he has revealed in his word; if the vain fierceness of their spirit had not imboldened them to attempt things above the reach of men; they would never have thought of corrupting religion with their falsely subtile inventions. It would have remained pure throughout, and sincere to this day, and the same as when the ministers of our Lord and Saviour delivered it at first to their disciples by word and writing. But their pride misleading them, induced them to attempt things above their capacity, and to adore and spread abroad their presumptuous imaginations as true secrets of God.

The apostle informs us, in this text, that this was the origin, in particular, of those errors and false services which certain seducers went about to introduce at that time among christians. We heard, in the last discourse upon this subject, what their error was, namely, that under colour of a false humility they taught the service or religious worship of angels. We are now to consider, by the assistance of God, that which the shortness of time hindered us from then explaining, namely, the marks of these false teachers, and the pernicious consequence of their error. For though the apostle's intimation of the thing itself is sufficient; his authority in the church is such, that it is not lawful for any man, whoever he may be, to teach or believe anything in the christian religion contrary to the sentiment of this great servant of God: yet, not content with enjoining the Colossians that they should not let these pretended doctors, who would cause them to serve angels, to beguile them of their reward, in order to add more weight to his exhortation, he explains to them the true motives of those seducers, and the cause of their error, and demonstrates also the dismal issue in which it involved them. For, as you have heard, he notices, first, their audaciousness and ignorance, when he says that they intrude into things which they have not seen. Next, he shows the source of these evils, namely, their foolish presumption, when he adds that they are vainly puffed up by their fleshly mind. And lastly, he represents to us the pernicious consequence of their doctrine, the fruit and result in which all their striving terminated, which was, that by their glorious services they in effect seduced and separated men from Jesus Christ, the true and only Head of believers, and so deprived them of that life, light, and salvation which this divine Head infuses into the members of his mystical body. For this is, in substance, the sense of the latter part of the text, in which the apostle says that these people did not hold "the Head, from which the whole body by joints and bands having nourishment administered, and knit together, increaseth with the increase of God." In these three heads the whole meaning of this text seems to me to consist. Wherefore, if it please God, we will examine them distinctly one after another; and, in the apostle's order, treat, first, of the boldness of these seducers; secondly, of their presumption; and lastly, of the consequence of their doctrine, which tends to separate men from Jesus Christ, the Head of the whole body of the church.

I. In the first place, this temerity, to intrude into things one has not seen, is ordinary enough with all sorts of men, ever since the venom of pride poisoned their hearts, but especially with all heretics: but it is peculiarly remarkable in those who teach the worshipping of angels; it being manifest that these blessed spirits, whose worship they establish, are of a nature much superior to ours, the order and operations of which are open to none of our senses. But when the apostle says they have not seen the things into which they intrude, his meaning is not simply, that the eyes either of their body or of their natural reason never received the species of these objects, nor apprehended or conceived the consequences and conduct of their being; but also that they neither had, nor could have, by the word or revelation of God, any certainty of the things they affirmed. For though the greater part of the matters of religion is above our senses; yet when God has revealed them to us, and as it were rendered them visible in his word, it becomes easy for us to know them by this means; and the Scripture too calls this knowledge a sight of them. Ezekiel means this when he reproaches the false prophets with following their own spirit when they had seen nothing, Ezek. xiii. 3; that is, they predicted and assured things for truth which the foolish imagination of their own spirit suggested to them, though, in fact, God had showed them no such matter in the light of his revelation. It was just so with those seducers whom the apostle censures in this place. They dogmatized and affirmed it as a clear case, that angels were to be served and invocated; and to persuade men of this, they delivered many things concerning their nature, and their intervention between God and us. Yet the truth is, that of all this they neither had, nor could have had, any certainty; they being things which they had never seen, either in the school of nature or the revelation of God.

All our knowledge and assurance necessarily comes from one of these three sources: namely, either from sense, and such is the knowledge we have of the things we see, hear, smell, touch, and taste; or from reason, such as human science, which is acquired or formed by discourse and natural reasoning; or, lastly, from the revelation of God, who reveals to us by the light of his word various objects and truths, which neither our sense nor our reason could perceive in nature. Now though reason causes men, by the consideration of things which exist, or are done in the world, to discern some principles and truths of religion; yet the whole of this is so small a matter, and withal so confused and imperfect, in consequence of the corruption of our understandings, that the word of God ought to be held for the sole assured foundation of religion; according to that which the apostle signifies to us in the Epistle to the Romans, chap. x. 17, that "faith cometh by hearing, and hearing by the word of God." When therefore he says here that the seducers intrude into things which they have not seen, he respects in general all those sources of our knowledge, and absolutely denies that these men had by them any of the things which they taught; but he also particularly refers to the third, that is, the revelation of God. And his meaning is, that the Lord had not showed them, nor caused them to see by his word, any of the things which they preached and desired to set up in the religion of christians. And though indeed they neither had, nor could have had, any certain knowledge of them; nevertheless they discoursed about them blindfold, and published their fancies, the visions of their brain, and dreams of their own spirit, for indubitable, necessary, and wholesome truths.

This conduct the apostle excellently sets forth by that word which we have translated "intruding;" a word that properly signifies entering into, setting foot on, and marching forth in some quarter, as on ground we have a title to. Whereby he points out the vanity of these false teachers, who did not merely busy themselves in a research of things above their capacity, (which is in itself a vain and ridiculous labour,) but also dared to speak of them, and make peremptory decisions about them: so, going above ground, and walking as it were in the vacuum of their own imaginations; mounting their thoughts to a region far above them; like that poor phrenetick of whom the poets speak, who having presumed to enter upon a strange element, and fly there, soon found his rashness punished with his ruin. The prophet makes use of a similar phrase, when, to represent his modesty, he says that he had not exercised himself in great matters, or in things too high for him, Psal. cxxxi. 1.

Dear brethren, we have no occasion to go so far back as the apostle's time for examples of this vanity. Our adversaries of the communion of Rome afford us a sufficient store; who retain the error of those whom the apostle here reproves, serving angels, as they also inherited their temerity, intruding into things which they have not seen. They magisterially pronounce, that men must serve and invoke angels and departed saints. They boldly define the religious worship that is to be given, and divide it into its kinds; naming one of them *dulia*, and the other *hyperdulia;* all with as much confidence as if they spake of things most obvious to sense. I urge not, for the present, that Scripture blasts this whole error, everywhere intimating that we ought to serve no one in religion but God alone, and with a loud voice anathematizing the worship of any creature. I pass by what it says particularly against the adoration and worshipping of angels; and also that which Paul expressly prohibits in the text. I keep singly to the rule he here gives me, that no belief be afforded those who intrude into things which they have not seen; and demand of these hardy doctors, in what region, in what part of divine revelation, have they seen these services, these *dulias*, and these *hyperdulias*, of which they so positively speak? Where is it that the Holy Ghost has showed them these bold doctrines? To what prophet has he revealed them? To what apostle has he signified them? Of what evangelist have they learnt them? Surely they must here of necessity be silenced. They have not seen one of these pretended mysteries in the book of God. They cannot show us any track of them anywhere, except it be in the fancies of Plato, and of the heathen philosophers, the disciples of demons, and not of God; men taught in the school of error, and not in that of truth. They proceed further yet, and give us discourses about the orders of angels, and distribute to them their business, and appoint them their ministrations; they rank the saints, and give to them each his charge and employment. And if you ask them how these spirits, being in heaven, hear our prayers and requests, and by what means they see the secret motions of our hearts; some of them answer, that the mirror of the Trinity, upon which they incessantly have their eyes, presents to them all the ideas of these things; others say that God reveals them to them some other way. But whence do they know this? It is neither sense nor natural reason that has showed it to them. If therefore they have seen it anywhere, it must be in the revelation of God. Yet it is clear, and they cannot deny it, that neither this pretended mirror, nor any one of their other conjectures, appears there at all. And one of their most famed authors sufficiently declares it: We do not know, says he, by any certain reason, whether the saints perceive our prayers or not, although we piously believe it: * as if it were piety, and not pitiful credulity, to believe things of which we have no assurance. But let him make what account of it he pleases. This is evident, that since he confesses they have no assurance of these things, it must of necessity be confessed also that it is extremely imprudent to intrude into them, except he will reject the authority of the apostle in condemning here most expressly those who intrude into things which they have not seen.

This vanity further shows itself in the things which they publish concerning the state of souls in their fabulous purgatory, the situation, the structure, and partitions of which they represent, together with the fire and torments of the spirits which are there imprisoned, with as much confidence as if they were just now come from thence after many years' stay in the place. Nevertheless, the truth is, that neither they nor their ancestors ever saw one particle of it, either in the Scriptures of God or in the nature of things; there being not a word anywhere of any one of these imaginations. That which they say of their transubstantiation, with its conditions and circumstances, and of the manner in which the body of Christ is present in every crumb of their host, and in every drop of their chalice; their positions, likewise, concerning their pretended sacrifice of the mass, and concerning the relative or analogical adoration of images, and concerning the characters which some of their sacraments imprint upon the souls of men; and, in one word, all the points of doctrine which we contest with them, are of the same nature. All of them are things which they have have not seen; they intrude into them, walk in them, and strut vainly; commanding the belief or practice of them under pain of damnation, however doubtful and uncertain they may be, and furiously anathematizing all those who make the least scruple to receive them.

As for us, dear brethren, who, through the grace of God, have learned to prefer his voice to the imaginations of men, and to fear the thunderings of heaven more than the fulminations of Rome, let us leave them in this vain humour; or rather let us pray to God to bring them out of it, and to give them to distinguish their own dreams from his declarations.

---

* Cajetan. in 22. q. 88. a. 5.

And, for our further safety, let us religiously keep to the apostle's direction. Let us never intrude into things which we have not seen. Neither let us be so simple as to follow those who do, or suffer ourselves to be beguiled by them. Let us rest in the things which God has clearly revealed to us in his word; which he has so set forth before our eyes in that divine treasury of his truth, that very children may there behold them. This portion is sufficient for us; if we cultivate it well, we shall find in it abundantly wherewith to inform our understandings, to calm our consciences, to sanctify our hearts, and to perfect all the faculties of our souls. Let no man presume "above that which is written," 1 Cor. iv. 6. Take heed of being wise above what is meet; but be wise to sobriety, Rom. xii. 3. Let the word of God be the rule of our science, and his book the bound of all our curiosity. All knowledge is obtained without knowing anything beyond it. This consideration alone is enough to preserve us from all the errors of Rome; for since the intruding into things which we have not seen is a temerity condemned here by the apostle, and in matters of religion we can have seen none but such as God has revealed in his word, it evidently follows, that we are obliged not only to refrain from believing, but also to proceed to the rejection of all the doctrines about which we are in contest with Rome, no one of which appears in the word of God. And it is manifestly sin to reduce them to practice, since, according to the apostle, "whatsoever is not of faith is sin." Rom. xiv. 23; it being certain that there cannot be any true faith of things which are not found in the word of God, seeing that the same apostle shows us that that hearing which produces faith in us is of the word of God, as we have before intimated.

II. But I come to the second point, where Paul condemns the arrogance and presumption of the false teachers. It is this properly that leads, or rather misleads, them into that Utopia of things they never saw. They are, says the apostle, vainly puffed up by their fleshly minds. By this understanding, or mind of their flesh, he means all the vivacity, ability, and acuteness with which nature has endowed us, to whatever degree of vigour and light reason of itself attains. For under the word flesh Scripture comprehends the whole nature of man; that is to say, not his body only, to which this name properly belongs, but also his soul, yea, even his understanding, his will, and his reason, which is the most excellent part of it. As sin, since it infected our nature, has in such a manner condensated, and corrupted, and altered all the faculties of our soul, that it has turned them, in a manner, into flesh and blood; not that it has, properly speaking, destroyed the nature of them, which, as you know, is still spiritual and immortal, but in consequence of its deadening the vigour, and vitiating and depraving the dispositions of them, having fastened us to the earth and to ourselves, and filled our affections and wills with so perverse and violent a love of the flesh, that all the light of our understandings is obscured and blackened by the contagion of this poison: and their conceptions are totally tainted with it, all our discourses and reasonings, in this miserable state, being nothing but flesh and blood, until the Spirit of God comes and reforms us, and of carnal and natural understandings, as were ours, makes them spiritual, by the infusion of his holy light into them. Thus it is that our Lord and Saviour said to Peter, "Flesh and blood hath not revealed this secret to thee, but my Father which is in heaven," Matt. xvi. 17. And Paul protests that "the natural man receiveth not the things of the Spirit of God," 1 Cor. ii. 14. It is therefore properly this reason or intelligence of the natural man, that is, of a man not illuminated from on high, which the apostle here calls the "fleshly mind."

But the good opinion which those seducers have of it he terms, with much elegance, a puffing up. For, to say the truth, it is but wind with which they are inflated, filled they are not. Now, not satisfied with having thus exposed their vanity, he further adds that they are puffed up vainly, that is to say, in vain, and without cause. For indeed, whatever may be the pretended acuteness of our mind, it is, in reality, so insignificant, it is a faculty so feeble, so limited, and of such narrow dimensions, that if it give us any vanity, it is without cause. They who best know themselves, and possess this part in a higher degree, well perceive it, and frankly confess that all the light of our understanding is but a vapour; its science, ignorance, and its ability, presumption. For who is there that does not daily find, upon trial, that the point of this so much esteemed understanding turns at the least difficulties, that its sight is dazzled at the meanest lights, and that its reason is confounded in the plainest meditations? And when we consider, not barely what each single person knows, but all the science that all mankind have acquired during the many ages that its greatest and most accomplished wits have been busied about it, we find that it is so little in comparison with that of which we are ignorant, that a drop of water has more proportion to the whole ocean. It is, therefore, without doubt, a vanity extremely foolish to make ostentation of it, and to presume much upon a man's self for so small an advantage. But it is a much worse extravagance still to take this understanding of the flesh for our guide in matters of religion which are all of them divine and celestial; while it is incapable of conducting us in the very things of nature, and of the earth, as experience enables us daily to see; so that we must conclude that all those who, laying aside the word of God, would instruct us in religion by the light of their own understandings, are imbued with as high a degree of senselessness as ever existed; and that, besides vanity, there is frenzy in what they do, and some such extravagance as those mad people showed who formerly attempted to raise the fabric of their tower up to heaven. This is just the malady of all the heretics and seducers that ever rose up in the world. Accordingly, you see that the apostle, in the Epistle to the Galatians, enrols heresy among the works of the flesh, because it is a production of its understanding, which, incited and heated by its presumption, brings forth this wretched brood. And it is remarkable that these same seducers, whose puffing up and pride the apostle here exposes, notwithstanding made profession of humility of spirit, as he himself testifies, to show us that we should not rely upon appearances; and that oftentimes under the habits, and looks, and outward actions of humility there are hidden hearts puffed up with vanity and swoln with pride. And such is, in reality, the genius of all those who would have their inventions to be valid in religion. Their having the audacity to exceed the institutions of God proves an insufferable arrogance, inasmuch as, instead of being content with his directions, and submitting to them with a humble and teachable spirit, they undertake to cut out new ways to heaven. I leave now to each one the care of applying this observation to those new rules, which the spirit of superstition has multiplied, for various ages, almost to an infinity. They all set the cross over their gates; the services they perform to angels and men, the habits they shape for their zealots, their countenances, and their very looks, and eyes ever fixed on the ground, promise a profound humility. But God knows what the reality is. Leaving, therefore, the dijudication of it to him, I only warn you not to suffer such fair outsides to deceive you; remembering how the apostle has here taught us that a profession of humility of spirit sometimes covers a soul vainly puffed up with the sense of its fleshly lusts, and also that not seldom this very humility and pretended mortification is the matter which feeds its pride, and maintains its flatulency.

III. But it is time to come to the third point, which contains the worst and most pernicious effect of this worshipping of angels, here condemned by the apostle; namely, that they who promote it, or adhere to and practise it, do not hold "the Head, from which all the body by joints and bands having nourishment administered, and knit together, increaseth with the increase of God." You know that this Head of which he speaks is our Lord Jesus Christ, eternal and true God made man, who died and rose again for the salvation of the world; and that the body of this Head is the church, the whole multitude of true believers. This comparison is so frequent in

Scripture, and the reasons upon which it is founded are so clear and so well known, that there is no necessity for me here to repeat them. We have to observe only the operation of this divine Head upon the body, and the benefits which it communicates thereto, both which the apostle touches upon. He says, first, that this Head nourishes the body of his church. Then, in the second place, that he knits the same together by joints and bands. And, lastly, that by this means he causes it to increase with the increase of God. All this is taken from the resemblances of natural bodies, from which this comparison is drawn. For you see that in nature the head first distributes to all the parts of the body such strength as is necessary for exercising their motions and sensations; it being, as it were, the common source from which the animal spirits, as they are called, the principles of motion and sensation, are by the nerves, as by so many channels, shed forth into all the parts of the whole frame, as well higher as lower, the most remote as well as the nearest; and when this influence and communication of the head happens to cease, you see the members which are deprived of it presently become paralytic and insensible. Then, further, the head does the body this office: it binds and keeps properly fastened to each other, by means of the same nerves, all the parts of which it is made up, both the harder ones, as the bones and cartilages, and the softer, as the muscles, and other substances. Finally, the head, by means of this continual influence, gives its body the ability to grow, and extend itself, and rise up by degrees to the measure of its due magnitude. The apostle therefore makes use of this natural image, to represent to us those spiritual benefits which we receive from the communion of the Lord Jesus, our mystical Head, and says,

First, that he furnishes his body, that is, gives it abundantly spiritual sense and motion, and, in a word, all the graces necessary for the exercise of a heavenly life; diffusing them into all his mystical members, that is, into all his believers, by means not of their animal nature, but of his divine and eternal Spirit. This Spirit, which he distributes to all and to each of his members, replenishes our eyes and senses with that light and vigour which is requisite for seeing, feeling, and tasting divine things. It sheds abroad peace and joy into our hearts, and curing our benumbed limbs, and opening our hands which vice had locked up, gives us the operations and motions of the life of God; and, in short, forms in us all the conceptions and virtues of the new man.

But he says, secondly, continuing this excellent metaphor, that this divine Head fitly knits together his body by joints and bands; expressing, by these words, that spiritual union which binds and joins all true believers to their Head and to each other. For as every member of the body has its particular temperature and qualities, very different from the rest, one being hard, another soft; one cold, another hot; one dry, another moist; and yet, being linked by those secret and imperceptible bands which, descending from the head, fasten them all together, make up but one only and the same body: so is it with the church. The faithful, of whom it is composed, are both in nature and grace infinitely different from each other. In nature: for some are of one nation, of one age, of one sex, of one condition, and others of another; one rich, and another poor; one learned, another ignorant; one noble, another of low extraction. In grace likewise: for who can utter all the differences of their gifts in this respect? But Jesus Christ, their mystical Head, notwithstanding this diversity, reduces them all into one and the same body; as Paul says elsewhere, "We being many are one body in Christ." He sets us together, and fitly unites us one with another, by these mystical joints and bands, of which the apostle here speaks; that is, the gifts and graces of his Spirit: and first of all charity, the universal bond of all the faithful, which ties them inseparably together, by the sentiments of a sincere and ardent love, and by all the motions, offices, services, and assistances which depend upon it. It is this spirit of charity that mixes all their souls into one; that renders them sensible of each other's weal and woe; that inspires into them the same prayers and wishes; and so governs their actions, that, though different, they yet all aim at the same mark, the glory of their Head, and the common edification of his members. Among these joints and ligaments of the Lord's body I also place the various graces with which he invests them, giving to this man one talent, and to that man another; to one zeal, to another knowledge; to one utterance, to another judgment. To the same, too, must be referred the different offices which he has instituted in his church, pastors, teachers, elders, and deacons; this various distribution approximating them to one another; the need they have of their brethren, and the succour they may afford them, admirably knitting and keeping up the commerce of their common charity, as Paul expressly observes in the Epistle to the Ephesians, chap. iv. 12; where, speaking of the different ministries which the Lord Jesus formed and erected among his people, he says that he made them for the perfecting or setting together of the saints, for the edification of his body.

But he adds a third benefit derived from this Head, which is as the sequel and fruit of the two former; that his body, thus furnished and compacted by its Head, increases with the increase of God, that is, with a divine and spiritual increase, arising from the efficacy of God, and tending to his glory; inasmuch as the church, thus united to its Head, and filled with the influences of his grace, is established, strengthened, and completed by degrees, in faith, in hope, in charity, in light, and in sanctity, until it attain unto the measure of its perfect stature in Christ. Such is the communion of the church with its Head Jesus Christ here described by the apostle.

And hence it appears how grievous is the error of those who worship angels, there being nothing in these words but what evinces it. First, then, the apostle says they hold not the Head. It is true that they do not profess to let it go. For they affirm themselves to be christians, and own Jesus Christ for the Prince and Author of their religion. But in reality and in effect they break the union which they should have with him in the character of Head, since they address themselves to angels as their mediators and intercessors with God. For it is giving them the office of head, which pertains to one alone; it being clear that this mediation, which is the source of our life, is the office of our Head. Again, their impudence plainly appears, in that Jesus Christ our Head furnishes his body with all necessary graces. For why should we seek in angels or saints what we have abundantly in Jesus Christ? Is there any grace, any light, any blessing, which we may not have from him? Nay, says the apostle, it is he that furnishes the whole body. He is the fulness of grace, an inexhaustible abyss of good. Surely, then, it is extreme vanity to address ourselves to any other, and to seek the waters of life and of salvation in petty by-streams, rather than in that full, fresh, abundant and only source which the Father has given us in this divine Head. If the worship of angels and saints were permitted, (which it is not,) it is evident it would be unprofitable, since we most assuredly have, in Jesus Christ alone, all the succour and assistance which we can possibly pretend to obtain from those creatures.

But that which the apostle adds, in the second place, namely, that this divine Head compacts and knits together his whole body, further powerfully opposes this error, which divides the church, and brings a manifest strange variety into its services; inasmuch as it multiplies the objects of its devotion, causing some to serve one angel, or one saint, and others another; some have a partiality for one and call themselves after him, and others adhere to another; as you plainly see by the example of those of Rome, who are divided into various bands and fraternities, according to the angels, the male and female saints, to whom they offer their devotion; not to mention that each of them has a particular service for his guardian angel, differing from the service of all others on account of its object, inasmuch as, according to their account, every one has his particular angel, different from those of others. Whereas the true body of Christ is all knit together in a perfect union, having but one only Head Jesus Christ, and one only religious service, one and the same faith, and one and the same worship.

Lastly, the apostle again strikes at the authors of this error, when he says that the body of the church being united, guided, and governed by its Head Jesus Christ, increases with the increase of God. For these people are accustomed to boast of perfecting and increasing the religion of christians by the addition of such services as they invent. But Paul informs us that this is not the increase which the church receives, which must be an increase of God, an augmentation and advancement in things which he has commanded and instituted; whereas these people grow only in the traditions of men, and inventions of the flesh, which add nothing to the true and legitimate magnitude of the body; it becomes by them more puffed up, not fuller; more deformed, not greater. They are like warts, and imposthumes, which disfigure and incommode the body, but are far from enriching or perfecting it.

Dear brethren, let us lay by all these strange doctrines. Let us hold fast to this holy and blessed Head, Jesus the Son of God, who has vouchsafed to take us for his body. Let us enjoy, with most profound respect, the great honour he has therein conferred upon us. Let us not be so ungrateful, or so imprudent, as to give that glory to another which belongs to him alone. Let vain men submit to other heads; let them profane this divine quality of head of the church, attributing it either to angels, or (which is yet worse) to a mortal man. For our parts, O Lord Jesus, we neither have, nor ever will have, any other head than thee. As it is thou alone that hast redeemed us, formed and associated us in the communion of thy body; so never will we address our devotions, our religion, our services, and invocations to any but to thee. It is on thee alone that we will live, and from thy springs alone we will draw. Likewise with thee are the words of eternal life. To which of the saints shall we turn? Without thee we can do nothing, and in thee alone we can do all things. Beloved brethren, this is the vow which I now present to the Lord Jesus in the behalf of us all, and I assure myself that there is not one of you who does not heartily say Amen thereto. It remains that we faithfully perform this great vow, rendering up ourselves to be guided and governed by the Lord Jesus Christ, since he is our Head; having no motion or sentiment but what descends from him, and receiving into our nerves and arteries his celestial and divine Spirit; sincerely renouncing the spirit of the flesh and of the earth, which animates the world. Remember that you are the body of Christ, and live in such a purity as may be worthy of so great a name. Above all, let us have those sacred bonds between us which fitly knit all the members of our Lord together; that is to say, the sentiments of a vigorous charity, communicating readily and cheerfully to each other the graces with which our common Head has furnished us, for our mutual edification: the rich, their alms to those that are poor; the wise, their instructions to the ignorant; the strong, their succour to the weak; those that are in prosperity, their consolations to the afflicted: increasing all of us continually with the increase of God, in faith and sanctification, and advancing daily some paces towards the mark and prize of our high calling. This is the discipline of the Lord Jesus. This is what he has commanded us, his apostles preached, and left in their writings, to us; not the worshipping of angels, and other such inventions of superstition, of which those holy men say not one word, except it be to refute and condemn them. Let us rest in their doctrine, and we shall have part in their bliss, through the grace of Jesus Christ, their Head and ours; to whom, with the Father and the Holy Spirit, the only true God, blessed for ever, be honour, praise, and glory to ages of ages. Amen.

SERMON XXX.

VERSES 20–22.

Wherefore if ye be dead with Christ from the rudiments of the world, why, as though living in the world, are ye subject to ordinances, (Touch not; taste not; handle not; which all are to perish with the using,) after the commandments and doctrines of men?

DEAR brethren, seeing that the apostle plainly shows in various places that the use of meats is a thing indifferent; and that if we eat we have not thereby the more, or the less if we eat not, 1 Cor. viii. 8; and even enjoins us to accommodate ourselves to the infirmity of our brethren, declaring that "it is good neither to eat flesh, nor to drink wine, nor to do anything whereby our brother stumbleth, or is offended, or is made weak," Rom. xiv. 21; it may seem strange to some, that in this Epistle, and in the First to Timothy, and elsewhere, he so earnestly insists upon this point, and employs so many words and reasons against those who prohibited certain sorts of meats to christians. But if you thoroughly consider the whole procedure of this holy man, and the motives for his giving such direction, you will find it in all its parts to be full of reason and profound discretion. For, first, there is a great difference between those with whom he bears, and those whom he rejects. The one were infirm, and the other insolent. The former, through want of knowledge, could hardly consider those things permitted which were prohibited by the school of Moses. The latter, in their rashness, attempted to bring christians under the yoke again. The error of those reached no further than their own persons. These would dogmatize, and give the church new laws. Wherefore the apostle is lenient towards the one, and severe against the others, according to the difference of their faults. And as to the thing itself, though it is no more a crime to abstain from any of the meats which God has created for our use than it is to eat them, yet to make this abstinence pass for a matter of necessity is a pernicious attempt. First, it is an overthrow or a diminution of our liberty, which having been purchased by the blood of Christ, ought to be very precious to us; for it is not just that the fancy or the tyrannical humour of men should bereave us of that which has cost him so dear. Moreover, such injunctions cause that to be thought necessary which is indifferent, and that to pass for a part of the service of God which is not so; an opinion which has dangerous consequences; for men, once possessed with this imagination, lose, in such exercises, a great portion of that time which should be wholly spent in the study and practice of the true commandments of our Lord Jesus. But, what is still worse, they easily imagine that they get by such abstinence from things permitted a licence to commit without danger things prohibited, and the privilege of having their obedience to God dispensed with on account of that which they render unto men; a conception which, as you perceive, undermines the foundations of that true and real sanctification, without which no man shall see God.

The apostle, well knowing therefore the venom of these doctrines, and seeing, on the other hand, the strong inclination that men have towards them, being likewise not ignorant (as experience has but too much verified) that there would always be people found to propagate them among christians, considered it necessary for the security of our faith to give us, in various parts of his divine Epistles, strong preservatives against the contagion of this pernicious error. You have heard already how he said concerning it, "Let no man judge you in meat or in drink;" completely repressing, by those few words, the temerity of all those who, for such things, bring the faithful to the bar, and condemn to the fire of hell for having but tasted of meats which they prohibit. He now resumes the same discourse; and having, in the two preceding verses, refuted the worshipping of angels, which the seducers taught in religion, he comes to their other ordinances, which concerned certain abstinences and devotions, which they imposed on christians as salutiferous, and necessary for humbling the spirit and mortifying the flesh; and, first, he refutes them by three excellent reasons which he urges against them; next, he rejects the vain and specious pretexts under colour of which they were recommended. The first of those three reasons which he advances against these pretended devotions, is taken from the liberty which Jesus Christ has purchased for us by his death, freeing us from all carnal and ceremonial services: "Wherefore if ye be dead with Christ, why, as though living in the world, are ye subject to ordinances," such as, "Touch not; taste not; handle not?" The second is drawn from the nature of those things themselves from which an abstinence was ordered: "which all are to perish with the using." And the third from the origin of such ordinances: instituted, not by the authority of God, but "after the commandments and doctrines of men." These are the three points of which we purpose to treat in this discourse, by the assistance of God; beseeching him to grant that we may meditate upon them to our common edification and consolation.

I. The apostle's last words were concerning the communion of the church with Jesus Christ its Head, who nourishes his whole body, and fitly knits it together by joints and bands, causing it to increase with the increase of God. Here he takes occasion to set before us again that enfranchisement from the yoke of ceremonies which we have by this holy and mystical communion with our Lord. This is his meaning in these words, we are "dead with Christ from the rudiments of the world." For, as we have showed before, the apostle calls the ceremonial ordinances of Moses's law the elements or rudiments of the world, because they were the first and lowest lessons of God's people; all of them consisting in material and worldly things, and in the use of, or in an abstinence from, either elements, or plants, and animals, and other fruits and productions of the world. But he seems in this place to signify by these words generally all services of this nature, whether those that Moses formerly instituted for the exercise of the childhood and minority of Israel, or those that other men afterwards introduced, of which sort were the devotions and ceremonies which the elders of the Jews and the Pharisees added to the law, and passed for traditions of antiquity, as we understand by the gospel, where in various places our Saviour notices them, and very sharply reproves them. Such again were the systems and devotions of those seducers whom the apostle here opposes, and all others similar to them, which, though instituted by different authors, and at different times, yet jointly consist in one and the same kind of earthly and material things, and tend to one and the same end, namely, the purifying and sanctifying of men, and the rendering the

Deity propitious and favourable to them by such exercises. This whole service is carnal, confined to certain corporeal things and actions in which it consists, as in meat and drink, in watchings and clothing; in men's washing and disciplining themselves, going in procession, or on pilgrimage, repeating certain words and forms of prayer: it also depends upon times, having its years, its months, its days, its festivals, and its very hours all regulated. This was the very form of the carnal or ceremonial service of the Jews, which was directly opposed to that other service which Jesus Christ gave us in his gospel, and which, instead of confining us to these childish scruples of times, of places, and of things, wholly consists in a pure and genuine worship of God, in loving and fearing him, in tenderly regarding our neighbour, in honesty and justice, and in a true and lively holiness. Accordingly, you know, that as the former service is termed carnal, the latter is styled spiritual. The one is a serving in shadow, the other in truth; the one in flesh, the other in spirit. It is then, in my opinion, all that first species of carnal services, from whatever source they flow, either the institution of Moses, or the invention of any other man, that the apostle here calls "the rudiments of the world," declaring that we have been freed from it by our Lord Jesus Christ; remaining no longer subject to all this childish and infantile discipline, nor bound up to hours, or times, or elements, or other things of the world; but being raised above all these, so that we may make use of them with full liberty, according to the interests of piety and charity, and not be any more in bondage to them, or dependent upon them.

But because Jesus Christ has procured us this great benefit by his death, and puts us in possession of it by the communion we have with him, Paul sets forth this grace, of his freeing us from subjection to the rudiments of the world, in terms which refer to that death, saying, not simply that we are delivered from such kind of services by Jesus Christ, but that we are "dead with him from the rudiments of the world;" an expression exceedingly graceful and elegant. It signifies, first, that we are no longer subject to these rudiments of the world. For the dead are out of all servitude. The laws no more demand anything of them. Neither their lords nor their masters have power any longer to require aught of them. Death breaks all the bonds that tied them to any subjection whatever. The apostle says, therefore, that we are dead to the rudiments of the world, to signify that we are freed from them; that we are no more subject to them, as he tells us elsewhere in the same sense, that we are "dead to the law," Rom. vii. 4; and again in another place, "I am," says he, "dead to the law, that I might live unto God," Gal. ii. 19. And thus, too, it is that we must take his affirmation that we are "dead to sin," Rom. vi. 2; that is to say, delivered from its tyranny. And because death puts an end to and abolishes the power and authority of the master, as well as the servitude and subjection of the vassal, Paul says indifferently that sin and the commandment of the old law are dead to us, and that we are dead to them, signifying by this expression that we are their subjects no more.

But Paul's expression here, that we are "dead with Christ from the rudiments of the world," shows us, in the second place, both the cause of our liberty—Jesus Christ, and the means by which he acquired it for us, namely, his death. We are dead to all ceremonial services, because our Lord has dissolved and abolished them in dying for us. His death has completed all the designs for which these rudiments of the world were, for a time, appointed. It has procured that righteousness which they represented, and exhibited that salvation which they promised, and brought in the substance of which they were but shadows. It has opened the house of God to the Gentiles, whom they excluded; put an end to the old testament, to which they pertained; and founded the new, an eternal, and immutable one, which they prefigured. Wherefore the veil of the temple was rent from the top to the bottom at the time that Jesus suffered death, for a token that the ancient worship, of which this veil was a symbol, became thenceforth abrogated and annulled.

Lastly, these words of the apostle further exhibit an apt resemblance between the Lord's death on the cross, and our freedom from the yoke of ceremonies. For as Jesus in dying divested himself of the life he led here below, during the days of his flesh, in infirmity, and in subjection to the elements of Moses, to take up a new one by his resurrection, which was to be free, divine and celestial; so we, in like manner, by virtue of the communion we have with him, and particularly in his death, lay down that former manner of life, which consisted in the childish exercises of some carnal abstinences and devotions, to live henceforth in the liberty of the children of God; serving him no more in shadow and in figure, but in spirit and in truth, with a conscience pure, and a heart not confined to the places, things, and times of the old world, but continually elevated to that new, incorruptible, and eternal one above the heavens, where Jesus Christ, the Author and Prince of our religion and salvation, dwells. Such is this evangelical truth here laid down by Paul at the beginning of the text, that we are "dead with Christ from the rudiments of the world."

Therefore you may see, by the way, how erroneous were their conceptious who placed the perfection of the faithful in the practice of these carnal systems and devotions, accounting those perfect who use them. Paul, on the contrary, terms them here "the rudiments of the world;" so that the subjecting of christians to such discipline is so far from being a perfecting and completing them, as these men pretend, that, on the contrary, it is a putting them back to their alphabet, and a reducing them, from the highest classes of the school of God, down to the lowest, there to become children again, and to lead a childish life with the disciples of Moses, in an apprenticeship to his rudiments, and under the scourge of his discipline.

The apostle, from this principle thus asserted, concludes against the false teachers, that all their ordinances, touching abstinence from certain meats, were vain, unjust, and tyrannical. "If therefore," says he, "ye be dead with Christ from the rudiments of the world, why, as though living in the world, are ye subject to ordinances?" Afterwards he notices and expressly specifies some of those ordinances which men would impose upon the faithful, namely, "Touch not; taste not; handle not." The force and the coherence of his argument is evident. It is an injustice, says he, and a tyranny, still to burden those with worldly ordinances who are dead to the world. You are dead to his rudiments through Christ, who has by his death abolished all this kind of carnal disciplines and services, and nailed up and torn upon his cross the obligation to them. By his grace, you live no longer in the world, in the school of figures and worldly ceremonies. You live henceforth in heaven, in the light and liberty of the Spirit. For Paul sometimes applies the word *world* to the state of God's people within their land of Canaan, in the school of their Moses, and the performance of a worldly and carnal service. And therefore he elsewhere terms the Levitical sanctuary "a worldly sanctuary," Heb. ix. 1. The faithful, then, being without this Mosaic world, it is clear, that no man can justly impose upon them in matters of religion any laws or ordinances of this nature; that those who attempt it outrage Him that freed them, and oppress the liberty of his people; and that every one may justly reject the yoke and oppose their tyranny.

Neither must it be alleged, that the ordinances in question are not those of Moses, but others quite different. For whatever ordinances they are, it is evident they are a yoke; and every yoke, whatever may be its nature and form, deprives us of our liberty. Besides, it is very probable that the apostle, as we have already observed, by "the rudiments of the world," intends not particularly the Mosaical service alone, but generally all such service as is bodily, and of the same nature with that of Moses. And finally, though it should be taken simply for the Mosaic laws, yet would Paul's argument be good and conclusive from the greater to the less; as he would then say, If you be set free from the yoke of Moses, which was framed and put upon the necks of the ancient people by the express appointment of God, how much more shall ye be free from that of men! If Christ has delivered you from those ordinances of which it cannot be denied that God was the author, how intolerable is the presumption of those men who burden you with their laws! Indeed, who can believe that God would have freed us from his own commands, to put us under those of others? and that his Son would have delivered us from a yoke of God, to load us with one of mortal men? and that he would have exempted us from the rod of Moses, to yield us up to the scourges of these new Rehoboams?

As to these ordinances which the apostle here specifies, doubtless they were those of the seducers, and not his own, as was imagined, against all semblance of truth and reason, by the author of the Comment on Paul that goes under the name of St. Ambrose, one of the ancients. Paul's previous caution, "Let no man condemn you in meat or in drink," sufficiently shows that they were the magisterial ordinances of these pretended legislators, who very severely commanded their people not only to forbear the eating, but even the tasting and touching, of such meats as they prohibited. Our adversaries of Rome understand the first of those three words to refer to the prohibitions in the Mosaic law, of touching or handling a dead body, for instance, or such other things as the Jews might not touch without being counted unclean. In the same manner they refer what is said of tasting to the prohibition of eating swine's flesh, and the hare, and other meats, the use of which was not permitted in the law; as if the false teachers, at whom the apostle aims, would have introduced among christians no other ordinances than those of the Mosaic law.

But this whole exposition is impertinent, and contrary to the apostle's meaning. If he had referred to those Jewish prohibitions, it would have been sufficient to have said once, Touch not, without superadding a third word of the same signification, namely, handle not. Not to urge that this cannot agree with that which follows, where he says that these things were set up "after the commandments and doctrines of men;" it being evident that the prohibitions in the Mosaic law were made by the authority, not of men, but of God; so that if the seducers had pressed nothing else, it would have been harsh, not to say false, to accuse them of making ordinances after the doctrines of men; and they would without doubt have answered, that they were founded upon the commandment of God. Finally, the apostle's assertion, that the things, an abstinence from which the seducers ordered, were all such as perished with the using, subverts this exposition, and evidently shows that the things forbidden by those false teachers were only meat and drink, and not dead bodies, or other substances, the touching of which was prohibited by the law. For since the things of which he speaks are consumed, destroyed, and all perish with the using; and, on the other hand, it is most evident that the things which the Jews were forbidden to touch are not at all of that nature (that is, such as perish in the using); it must of necessity be concluded, that it is not of them Paul speaks, but of those only which serve for the food of man, and which are all consumed by the use that is made of them in eating or drinking. And, in the end, we must come back to the interpretation our Bibles exhibit, which have very rightly rendered this passage in these words, "Touch" or eat "not; taste not; handle not." For though the first of these three words frequently and commonly signifies to touch, yet those who understand the Greek know that it is sometimes taken for to eat; of which our expositors have produced instances from good and irrefragable authors.

Now in these three words thus arranged the apostle represents to us, by the way, both the order of the scrupulous devotions of superstition, and the progress of the tyranny of these legislators. At first they forbid the eating of certain meats; that is, the use of them at your ordinary meals. If they win this ground, they proceed further, and will debar you even from tasting them. At last they possess you with scruple to touch them, as if the mere contact of such things were apt to pollute you. There is no end to the scruples of superstition, nor any measure in its devotions and observances. It heaps them up daily one upon another, and is never satiated with this vain food. It never says, It is enough; it is always saying, Give, give, like the wise man's horse-leech in the Proverbs, chap. xxx. 15. If it regulate your eating to-day, to-morrow it will give you laws for your clothing, and afterwards for each of the parts of your life; not leaving so much as your looks or your breathing free. It is a labyrinth in which poor consciences go on intricating themselves without any issue; and a snare which first takes them, then binds them fast, and in the end strangles them.

II. But let us now consider the two other reasons of which the apostle makes use, to show the vanity of the pretended ordinances of superstition, respecting meats, and eating, and drinking. The second, then, is taken, as we have already intimated, from the nature of those things from which abstinence was commanded. They are all, says he, things which perish with the using; that is, such as are consumed in doing us service. The very eating and drinking, by which they are taken, destroy them; and they are so feeble and infirm a substance, that they cannot be of use to us without being corrupted; and to nourish us, they must first perish; an evident sign that all the benefit we receive from them respects only this wretched mortal life, it being neither possible nor imaginable, that what perishes, and is consumed in us, should have any force or virtue for the life of our soul, which is immortal and incorruptible. So you see the apostle here presupposes this maxim, that neither religion, nor the service of God, properly and immediately consists either in the use of, or an abstinence from, any of those things which serve to maintain our common life, and are consumed in serving it; as he says elsewhere expressly, that "the kingdom of God is not meat and drink; but righteousness and peace, and joy in the Holy Ghost," Rom. xiv. 17. He makes use of the same reason again in another place. "Meats," says he, are "for the belly, and the belly for meats: but God shall destroy both it and them," 1 Cor. vi. 13. His Master and ours had used it before upon the same argument, to the same purpose, against the vain scruples of the Pharisees, the patriarchs of all this kind of discipline. "Not that," says he, "which goeth into the mouth defileth a man;" because, as he adds immediately after, "whatsoever entereth in at the mouth goeth into the belly, and is cast out into the draught," Matt. xv. 11, 17; that is to say, it perishes and is consumed with the using. Consequently, the apostle pronounces again, in consequence of the same doctrine, that "meat (that is, any certain sort of meat) commendeth us not to God: for neither, if we eat, are we the better: neither, if we eat not, are we the worse," 1 Cor. viii. 8; because, as he says in another place, "every creature of God is good, and nothing to be refused, if it be received with thanksgiving," 1 Tim. iv. 4.

Surely, were it not for the extreme blindness of men, there would be no occasion for us to repeat and confirm so easy a lesson with such diligence and in so many places; the sole light of reason, and the nature of things itself, teaching it so clearly. For who is there that does not perceive this truth, if he heed it ever so little? and that does not discover of himself that one is not the better or the more holy for eating herbs or fish, nor the worse or more vicious for living on other things? All this serves but to sustain the feeble nature of this poor body, and terminates there, without penetrating to the soul, whose essence is wholly spiritual. The conception of the understanding, the disposition of the heart, the habits which refer to them, and the actions that proceed from them, these alone make men good or bad, and their morals laudable or blamable; so that it is a gross and a deplorable error, though I grant that it has ever been, and still is, a very common one, to make a part of piety and holiness to consist in eating of, or abstaining from, certain sorts of meats.

III. The apostle contents not himself with citing the conclusions of reason and the nature of the things themselves, against the vain and pernicious ordinances of these seducers; but in order to overthrow them without recovery, and to take away all pretext of defending them, he makes use, in the last place, of a strong and invincible argument, drawn from their being established after the commandments and doctrines of men. Thus it was that God formerly struck at the vain services of Israel: "Their fear towards me (said he) is taught by the precept of men," Isa. xxix. 13. And the Lord Jesus overturns all the authority of the Jewish traditions in a similar manner, telling the scribes and Pharisees that it was in vain they honoured God, "teaching for doctrines the commandments of men," Matt. xv. 9. And it appears to have been from this that Paul took both the conception and the expression which he uses in this place. This reasoning, my brethren, is deserving the deepest attention. The apostle rejects the ordinances of the seducers, because they are commandments and doctrines of men. There is no man who sees not that this discourse has no consequence, unless by presupposing that nothing ought to be received in religion under the quality of necessary belief or service, except it be either taught or commanded of God. It is the doctrine of the apostle Paul in this place; the doctrine of the prophet Isaiah in that to which we have just referred; and it is the doctrine of Jesus, the Master of apostles and prophets, in his dispute against the Pharisees. O holy and precious truth! from how many errors wouldst thou deliver the world, if, according to the authority of our Lord, and those of his two grand ministers, men would examine all things by thee as their rule; and consider, when some article in religion is preached to them, not whether it be specious and have some appearance of reason, or whether it has been held by the sages of antiquity, or is now believed by the greater number of princes and people; but whether it is indeed taught of God in his word, or is merely commanded by men!

Dear brethren, by this short and simple method you may easily settle your thoughts about all the differences which rend christendom at this day. Take the book of God, and admit nothing into your belief but what you shall find either asserted or commanded there; refusing whatever the word of the Lord has not authorized. Sure I am that the sacrifice of the mass, and purgatory, and transubstantiation, and the monarchy of the pope, and the invocation of saints, and, in a word, all that divides us from Rome, will remain among those commandments and doctrines of men which Paul here casts away from our faith; and that nothing will be found among the commandments and doctrines of God, but those services and beliefs which are received and confessed by our churches. In the name of God, make trial of it, if you have not already done it; and you will see, that if our adversaries have doctrines of men for them, we have the doctrines of God, of his prophets and apostles, for us. I pass by other doctrines of Rome for the present. Only how can they defend their ordinances for the not eating of flesh during more than a third part of the year; commanding the faithful to live all that time upon nothing but herbs and fish, under pain of damnation; pressing this ridiculous law with so much rigour, that they do not acknowledge those for christians who transgress it; and punish them not with spiritual pains only, but, in the countries where the inquisition reigns, even with temporal, unto death itself? Is not this doing with a high hand that which the apostle here forbids, "Let no man judge you in meat or in drink;" and, "Why are ye subject to ordinances," namely, "Touch not, taste not, handle not?"

The assertion of our adversaries, that the apostle speaks only of the Mosaic prohibitions of touching the dead, and tasting the flesh of the hog and hare, we have already refuted. He speaks, in general, of ordinances which forbid the tasting of any sort of meat upon a religious account. And it is no way credible that he should grant the pope, or any other man, that which he denies to Moses, or should respect their laws more than his. Besides, all the circumstances and reasons which he notices or urges against the laws of the false teachers, are evidently of force against those of our adversaries. Those teachers ordained that there should be no eating nor tasting of certain meats. These men do the same. They recommended their abstinences upon pretence that they humbled the body, and did not spare it. This is exactly what our adversaries affirm of theirs. The apostle alleges against them that they stitched up again the veil of Moses, which had been rent in twain by Jesus Christ; and reduced that carnal and worldly worship into the church which had been abrogated and abolished by the cross of our Lord. Is it not a service of the same kind as that which is taught by those of Rome—a service which consists in things purely external and corporeal, namely, eating and meats? Paul adds, that the things from which the seducers required christians to abstain were all such as perished in the using. Those about which our adversaries make laws, are they not consumed in the very same manner—the flesh, which they forbid—the fish and herbs, which they command? Finally, Paul rejects the ordinances of the seducers, because they were doctrines and commandments of men. Those of Rome, to which the same quality adheres, ought not then to be any more tolerated than they. For however bold they may be, they durst not say that God appointed them. They only say that they are conformable to Scripture. But how can this be while they so rudely clash with the apostle's doctrine in this place?

As to their allegation, that the Hebrew children would not eat of the meats of the king of Babylon's table, the Scripture tells us they did it for fear of being defiled, Dan. i. 8, because the greater part of the meats of pagans was offered to idols. Besides, they doubted whether there might not be some of those things which were forbidden by the law of Moses, under which they lived; causes, as every one knows, that take place no longer, and are in effect very far off from the reasons of the abstinences of Rome. They produce also Daniel's three weeks, during which neither flesh nor wine entered into his mouth, Dan. x. 2, 3. They should add, what the Scripture expressly declares, that he "ate no pleasant bread" nor anointed himself all that while, because, as he says himself, he was mourning. It therefore follows, indeed, that those who mourn and are in affliction of spirit may, if they think proper, banish all the pleasures of their mode of living, even to those which are innocent, permitted, and ordinary, as Daniel did at that time upon his own judgment, and not from any public commandment. But it cannot be concluded from this that either there was then, or that there ought to be now, a law for perpetuity in the christian church, which forbids the use of meats for certain times of the year, which is precisely the thing that our adversaries pretend. I pass by Timothy's abstinence, who drank no wine; for there is little probability that it was through a religious scruple he abstained from it. Beside, he was a particular person, and did so at his own discretion, not by the order of any public law. And yet too Paul recommends to him to do the contrary, 1 Tim. v. 23; and, in fine, the question is now of meats, not of wine, which those of Rome prohibit to none at all. I also pass by the fasts of the Israelites on various occasions; as those of Anna, of David, of Esther, of John Baptist and his disciples: these have no communion with the abstinences in question. We do not refuse fasts, far be it from us. We do not simply and absolutely forbid even abstinence. For it is equally in a Christian's liberty to eat, or not to eat, any sort of meat whatever; neither the one nor the other is a sin, provided it be done in faith and charity. All that the apostle condemns, and we with him, and after him, is the tyranny that prohibits what God permits, and which makes that necessary which he has left free, and also the superstition that places the true service of God in things purely indifferent. It remains then for us to conclude, that this law of our adversaries is a doctrine and a commandment of men, since it has no foundation in the word of God.

But, which is more, it is evidently contrary to it. For the apostle writing to the faithful at Corinth, who lived in the midst of a heathen people, in whose markets and at whose tables all sorts of meats were indifferently sold and served up, he gives them this rule: "Whatsoever is sold in the shambles, that eat, asking no question for conscience sake." And, "If any of them that believe not bid you to a feast, and ye be disposed to go, whatsoever is set before you, eat, asking no question for conscience sake," 1 Cor. x. 25, 27. How does this accord with the Roman laws, which forbid so many sorts of meat for conscience sake? But this holy man has proceeded much further yet. He has not only refuted this error, he has also predicted it, and given us timely information of it; ranking abstinence from meats expressly among the articles of the false doctrine of those seducers, of whose coming he prophesied; describing them by dreadful marks, that we might have a just abhorrence of them, 1 Tim. iv. 1—3. Neither may it be answered, that he speaks of those who hold the nature of meats to be impure and polluted in itself. He attributes no such thing to those whom he condemns, and says simply that they would command to abstain from meats. If our adversaries do not so command, we do wrong to apply this text to them. But since they eminently command the thing, and so highly esteem the command, that they deny him the name of a christian who violates it, it is clear that of them also the apostle speaks. He says, it is true, that every creature of God is good, and was created to be used by the faithful with thanksgiving. He affirms this, I say, to refute this error; as we also make use of it to refute that of Rome. But he does not at all impute to them whom he opposes, that they formerly denied this truth; and hereafter we shall hear that those whom he in this place refutes ordained their abstinences, for the humbling of the spirit, and the mortifying of the flesh, altogether in the same manner as our adversaries do at this day, and not out of any opinion they entertained that the meats they prohibited were unclean or polluted in their nature. Accordingly, we read that the ancient christians, who lived about the end of the second century and the beginning of the third, did not forbear to condemn the Montanists' laws of abstinence, and to apply to them that passage of the First Epistle to Timothy, which we have just quoted; though those heretics protested, as they of Rome do at this day, that it was not intended against them, who believed, with Catholics, both the divinity of the Creator, and the goodness and purity of the creatures, but against the Marcionites and the Encratites, who denied the one or the other, or both of them together, as we learn by a certain book of Tertullian, in which he expressly pleads the cause of Montanus against the orthodox, whom in derision he calls *Physici*.*

* Tertul. lib. de Jejuniis. c. 15.

Having thus refuted the error of those of the Roman communion, I now proceed to answer their revilings. For upon the pretext of our disapproving the tyrannical law of their abstinences they accuse us of being Epicureans, and our religion altogether a religion of flesh and blood, and favouring gluttony and drunkenness; as if it were neither possible to commit excess with fish, nor to exercise sobriety with any other food. It is not in the present days only that this error, being unable to defend itself with reason, has had recourse to railing: the Jews at the beginning, seeing our Saviour live simply, without the pomp of their fasts and abstinences, called him a glutton and a wine-bibber, Matt. xi. 19; the Montanists afterwards cried out against the Catholics of those days, as they of Rome do against us at present, that the belly was their god, the buttery their altar, the kitchen their temple, a cook their priest, the steam of meats their Holy Spirit, and sauces their gifts of grace.* Let it not shame us to be treated as the Son of God was, with his first and best disciples. I might here say many things of our morals, and the morals of our adversaries, and perhaps it would be found that our carnival is no less sober than their Lent, and their abstinence many times as intemperate as our pretended dissoluteness. But it is better to refute their slanders by the honesty of our lives, than with the acrimony of our words.

Show then, dearly beloved brethren, by your sobriety, purity, and temperance, that it is not the love of the flesh, as calumny proclaims, but respect to truth, which makes you embrace the party you do. Defend your liberty in such a manner, as that you take it not for an occasion to live after the flesh, Gal. v. 13. It is this flesh which Jesus Christ has forbidden us. That of animals does not defile those who eat of it soberly, and with thanksgiving; but this flesh renders all those truly unclean who suffer themselves to be tempted with its pleasures. Abstain from all its lusts, 1 Pet. ii. 11. Have in abhorrence all its sweets. Eat not at any time of its fruits, and count it a grievous crime to taste of its dainties. It is of this flesh that we may without rigour lay the injunction upon you, Touch it not, and taste not of it. Let the acts of injustice and the pollutions and the vanities to which it carries men of the world be an abomination to you, and your meat as that of the Lord Jesus was, to do the will of God, and finish his work, John iv. 34. In particular, keep yourselves from the excesses of the season that is at hand. Abhor the disorders of the world, even more than you pity its superstition, and partake far less in its debauches than in its abstinences. Prepare yourselves also for that divine repast to which we are about to invite you, by all kind of good works of piety and charity; and above all re-

* Tertul. lib. de Jejuniis. c. 15.

member that the doctrine of the Lord Jesus is, to renounce ungodliness and worldly lusts, and to live soberly, religiously, and godly; and that his true discipline consists only in two points: the one, that we abstain, not from what is in its nature indifferent, but from what he has forbidden us, as contrary to piety towards him, or charity towards our neighbour, or honesty with respect to ourselves; the other, that we patiently and cheerfully suffer the pains and mortifications, not which a voluntary superstition assigns us, but which his holy and paternal hand dispenses unto us. This, dear brethren, is our Advent, this our Lent, and the true law of our abstinences. The Lord Jesus, who has given it to us, vouchsafe us his grace, that we may duly fulfil it to his glory, the edification of our neighbours, and our own salvation. Amen.

SERMON XXXI.

VERSE 23.

Which things have indeed a show of wisdom in will worship, and humility, and neglecting of the body; not in any honour to the satisfying of the flesh.

DEAR brethren, it is a truth acknowledged by the sages, both of the church and of the world, that man sets his affections only on things which seem to him to be good; whether they are so in reality, or through error of mind, he so considers them, when in truth they are not. Examine the motions of your own souls, and the designs and desires of your neighbours, as far as you can penetrate them. You will find without doubt, and discover without difficulty, that neither yourselves nor they love or pursue anything but what you account to be good, that is, tending to your benefit, and capable either of yielding you some pleasure, of affording you some profit, or of acquiring you some honour. Hence the philosophers defined good by its reference to our affections, and by the power it has to move and attract our desires, saying, Good is that which all desire. And hence impostors, who make a trade of seducing men, have always taken a great deal of care to give their errors and vain institutions some show of goodness; being aware that without this they would not be able to gain any man's affections, much less to have a train of followers in the world. This is to be seen particularly in religion, into which neither heresy nor superstition was ever introduced, except under the favour of this imposture; though spirits of different capacities, having meddled in the affair, there has been, accordingly, a great difference between their deceptions. For as those who would make a false stone pass for a diamond, or an emerald, or a ruby, endeavour, as far as cunning is able to counterfeit the truth, to give it the colour, the shape, the lustre, the sparkling, and other qualities of it, that by such a feigned resemblance they may deceive simple and inexperienced persons: so they who have endeavoured to corrupt religion, that they might cause the opinions and services which they introduced to be received for sound doctrines and systems, have, above all things, been solicitous to gild over their merchandise, and to colour it with some fair and specious pretexts, calculated to dazzle the eyes of men, to hide the defects of their doctrine, and to give it the appearance of that which in substance it is not.

It is this that the apostle Paul here observes in the doctrines and commandments of those seducers whom he encounters in this chapter. For having solidly and admirably refuted that superstitious discipline which they had introduced, and which consisted in a religious worshipping of angels, and in a scrupulous abstinence from certain meats, and in the observation of certain festival days, he concludes by exposing, in this last verse, the false colours, with which they in vain daubed it over. He acknowledges that it had, it is true, some show of wisdom, but denies that this was sufficient to cover its defects, or to oblige the faithful to receive it. Their ordinances, said he before, are "commandments and doctrines of men;" which indeed, he now adds, "have a show of wisdom in will worship, and humility, and neglecting of the body; not in any honour to the satisfying of the flesh." It is evident that he speaks of those human doctrines which he mentioned in the verse immediately preceding; and he says, first, that they have a show of wisdom; next, he represents particularly three things which give them this false show, voluntary service, humility of spirit, and rough treatment of the body, which they did not at all spare. These are, as it were, the three colours which, being mingled together by the artifice of the seducers, composed that paint which rendered their doctrine plausible, and gave it this false show of wisdom, which deceived the eyes of the simple. In compliance with this distinction, we shall treat of three points in this discourse: voluntary service, humility of spirit, and little care for the body; and then consider how error and superstition have always used them, and still, to this day, make use of them, to gloss their inventions. God grant us to be duly aware of them, and be pleased, for this end, so to guide and assist us by his Spirit, in discoursing upon them, that we may all bear away some edification and consolation.

The name of wisdom is great and honourable in the opinion of all people in the world. For other sciences have respect only to natural or human things, but wisdom relates to divine. Other branches of knowledge, too, are, for the most part, unprofitable to him who professes them; that of wisdom is salutiferous; signifying the skill of conducting one's way aright for the attainment of happiness, by the light of some choice and excellent truth. Consequently, this title of wisdom properly belongs only to the knowledge of God, which he has given us by his Son in the gospel, the only light that is capable of conducting us to supreme felicity. Accordingly, you know, it is the name that Paul ordinarily gives to it; as when he desires that the word of God may dwell richly in us in all wisdom; and when he says, in another place, that he speaks wisdom among them that are perfect, calling it, shortly afterwards, the wisdom of God in a mystery, the hidden wisdom; and the same he repeats in various places. Now, though the doctrine of those who corrupt the gospel, as did these seducers whom Paul opposes in this chapter, is most falsely called wisdom, yet so it is that its authors gave it the name, and would have it pass in the belief of men for a rare and a beneficial knowledge, more worthy of heaven than earth, and capable, indeed, of rendering those who follow it perfect and happy. The apostle acknowledges that the doctrine of the seducers of his time had this show of wisdom, but by his very granting them the show he denies them the truth of it; and his meaning is, that their doctrine had nothing but a false and a deceitful colour of wisdom, not the substance and reality of it.

I. Will worship, or voluntary service, is the first particular that gave these doctrines of the seducers this false show. They have, says the apostle, some "show of wisdom in will worship," that is, on account or because of the voluntary service which they introduced and taught; the observances and instructions which these men enjoined, as abstinence from certain meats, the worshipping of angels, and the like, being nothing else but voluntary services. A service may be called voluntary two ways: first, when he that performs it unto God, does it with affection and good will, without dislike or constraint; the love he bears this great and sovereign Lord sweetly bringing his soul under his yoke, and disposing him to account whatever he has commanded to be good and delectable. In this sense that free and sincere obedience which true believers render unto God, according to the gospel, may be styled voluntary, because it proceeds not from a spirit of bondage, as does theirs, who serve only because they are afraid; but from a spirit of love and of adoption, crying in their hearts, Abba, Father. Wherefore the prophet terms the new people, who rendered this frank and filial service unto God, under the gospel of the Messiah, a voluntary or willing people. "Thy people," says he, speaking to him, "shall be willing in the day of thy power," Psalm cx. 3. It is not in this sense that the apostle understands the voluntary service of which he speaks: for, first, though the terms voluntary service, which are taken up in the French to express what Paul has set down, may be so understood; yet true it is the Greek word he used in the original text is never so taken, as the intelligent know; for this kind of worship or service consists in things which God has expressly commanded, but the worship here meant by the apostle is not so.

We are to know, then, that the will worship of which he speaks is worship which God by his word never commanded men to render; but they present it to him merely of their own will, subjecting themselves and others to it because it is their pleasure, without any necessity imposed on God's part, who demanded no such thing of them. It is voluntary, not with regard to the manner in which it is performed; for in this sense, as we have said, the service of true children of God may be also termed voluntary: but with regard to its institution; the principle which introduces it, and presses the performance of it, being not the law or the authority of God, but simply the will of men, who of their forwardness undertake to do things to the honour of God, and for his service, which he for his part never ordered. The word therefore, in the language of the Greeks, is ordinarily taken in an ill sense, as importing superstition, because it is the property of this vice to invent various services at his own pleasure, and to pretend to satisfy the Deity with them.

But as the apostle points at that which gave the seducers' doctrine its show and lustre, it cannot be doubted that he means their service or worship was voluntary, not superstitious, though indeed it was so likewise. For superstition being generally decried, and known to be a vice, it is clear that in that character it is incapable of recommending any one's doctrine; nor were there ever found seducers so foolish as to profess that their worship was superstition; much less to boast of it, and to strive to render it acceptable on that account. But voluntary service charms men, and pleases their carnal sense. And false teachers generally glory in it, and propose it as a mark of the sublime wisdom of their doctrine. There are two sorts of it: the one wicked and shameful to the highest degree, which would make that pass for the service of God which he not only has not commanded, but has even expressly prohibited; as when the idolaters in the wilderness counted the festival which they kept before their golden calf, and the honours which they gave it,—things which God had expressly interdicted,—for worship performed to the Lord their God. Such also in effect was that religious serving of angels which the apostle censured before, though it cannot be doubted that the seducers who introduced it endeavoured, by various subtilties, to elude those passages of Scripture in which we are forbidden to do religious service unto any creature whatever. The other sort of voluntary service has a little more bashfulness and modesty than the former; when a man ordains and, if we may so speak, erects into the title of a divine service the observance of certain things which God has neither commanded nor forbidden, such as abstinence from certain meats, and the observation of certain days. It is properly to this rank we must assign that voluntary service which the apostle intends in the text. For they who institute such services as the former do not acknowledge that they are commanded of God, they only pretend that God has not forbidden what they command; glossing those passages in which he forbids it, and so artificially changing the true and genuine sense of them, that they cause it to be believed that the objects of their service are not comprehended in it.

Now that this gives their inventions a show of wisdom, as the apostle here says, and a lustre fair and plausible in the eyes of carnal men, is very clear. For, first, it seems magnanimous and heroic to be discontented with what God has commanded for his service, and to have the resolution to exceed it. That which he has commanded being evidently due, and of indubitable equity, it seems a small matter to do no more than this, because it is simply nothing else than the discharge of what a man owes; which appears not to be a virtue so exceedingly praiseworthy; for who ever heard of panegyrics made in a man's praise because he duly paid his debts? Accordingly, you see that presumptuous young man who is mentioned in the gospel made no great merit of all this. For when our Saviour told him simply what God commands us in his law, he answers disdainfully, that he had kept all those things from his youth, Matt. xix. 20; as if he had said that was his ordinary, his daily practice, and that he expected quite a different answer from so great a teacher. But when a man does that which he is not bound to do, he is admired; as we esteem him more highly who gives what he does not owe, than him who simply makes punctual payment of what he does owe. Besides, it seems an act of a great and extraordinary love to God, to subject that very thing to him which he has left free to us. The fear of the lash often compels a slave to do all that his master has commanded him; but it seems that nothing but love can induce him to do more. Again, this very boldness of daring to establish a certain sort of worship in the service of God has a kind of I know not what grandeur in it; because common sense, dictating to us that to ordain service for him is properly the act of a divine authority, we immediately take them for divine men who undertake such a work. The character of the human mind also, which appears in these voluntary services, may likewise cause them to be the more esteemed by men; every one naturally loving his own productions, and favouring his own works.

Whether it is for these reasons or for others, certain it is, that voluntary services are ordinarily esteemed and admired by men. And you see it clearly by what is done in the communion of Rome. For though, considering things thoroughly, no man can doubt that innocence, charity, and justice are much more excellent than those voluntary observances which are practised among them; yet it is evident that the latter are much more esteemed than the former. For the one they call simply good works; but the others exceed it. They are works of supererogation. They were obliged to forge this new word, our common languages having none lofty enough to express the extraordinary altitude of their merit. Hence the monks, if you believe them, are angels and demi-gods. They are looked upon as so many heavenly jewels, so many stars and luminaries: as the only ornaments of the earth and of their church. But they esteem thus highly none of those who without a frock, or little band, or particular rule, lead an honest and irreprehensible life in a secular habit. The reason of this difference is, that the former exercise themselves in such voluntary services as Francis, and Dominick, and Bruno, and Loyola have prescribed them, whereas the latter addict themselves to that which God has commanded them; though indeed no man can deny that to oblige men, to vindicate the oppressed, to succour the needy, and to assist the widow and the fatherless,—the things which God has commanded,—are incomparably better, and more excellent, than to put on a capouche, or to go with bare feet and shaven crown, or scourge oneself twice or thrice a week, which are things that men ordain. You see, also, that in that communion none are usually canonized (which is the highest honour they confer on piety) but such as have regularly fasted and disciplined themselves, and lived in celibacy, and, as they say, done miracles; things which God has not at all commanded in his word. As for those who content themselves with the religion and piety which God has ordained, and do not affect voluntary services; they must not pretend to be ranked among the saints of Rome. But I think there is yet another secret reason, which has as much or more efficacy than all the rest, in causing voluntary services to be so well received by men, namely, that great aversion which they naturally have against those things which are commanded of God; from the obligation of which they hope to redeem themselves, either in whole, or, at least in part, by means of human services. For however they may pretend that they find it very easy to render obedience to God's commands, yet in reality there is nothing to which they submit so unwillingly, and with greater pain; so that all the austerity of voluntary service is pleasant in comparison with it. Entertaining then this false prejudice, that by abstaining from what God permits, or by submitting to that which he does not command, they shall in reason oblige him to dispense with that which he does command, upon the hope of this exchange, they gladly embrace voluntary service, which indeed, as you are aware, they hold to be satisfactions; that is, a kind of ransom, at the price of which they are delivered from the punishment which they have incurred for not having served God as he has commanded. Thus you see, dear brethren, that voluntary service gives a lustre and a vain show of wisdom to human doctrines and traditions.

II. The second thing which contributes to this effect, and which renders these doctrines highly commendable, is humility of spirit. The apostle has already noticed the affectation and show of this pretended humility in one of the doctrines of these seducers particularly, namely, their teaching the worship of angels; which they did under the pretence that, by putting the faithful in subjection to those blessed spirits, they would thereby be humbled. Here he speaks of it more generally. For not only is the outside of false teachers commonly painted over with the colours of a great and deep humility, their discourse and all their procedure being full of submissions, and of a high profession of renouncing the advantages of vain-glory; but their institutions and discipline also promise humility, and seem to be so many exercises of it. And this is the thing, in my opinion, which the apostle particularly considers in this place. Look back, I pray, on the instructions of those seducers whom he opposes; I mean on those abstinences from certain meats, and the observations of certain days; does it not seem that this was exercising men in humility, since it abridged their liberty, and degraded them from the power which they possessed of disposing of these three things at their pleasure? To this we may add, that, in general, whoever subjects a man to his own law, humbles and abases him, putting a new yoke upon his neck, whatever may be the thing which he commands. The same mark of humility appears in the greatest part of the voluntary devotions which are in vogue, whether among pagans, Turks, or christians themselves. For they all, in a manner, reduce the habit and diet of their devotees to a low and abject state, and such as is of small esteem among men, and oblige them to things which seem to vilify and, in some degree, disgrace our nature. For the most part, they gave them filth for trimming, as the most ancient of the heathen poets says expressly of certain very devout priests, called Selli, or Sellians, that they always had foul feet and slept on the bare ground.* They cast down their countenances, and make them of a sad look; as our Saviour says expressly of the hypocrites of his time, that they disfigured their faces, Matt. vi. 16. And as for habits, who can recount all the diversities of them? It may suffice to observe in general respecting their materials, and form, and fashion, that these zealots have always adopted those which are not only coarse, and little esteemed, but such also as have something unusual and ridiculous in them. Their food wears the same livery; and you know there is at this day an infinite number who, to descend to the lowest degree of meanness, bind themselves by an express vow to mendicity or beggary, though God by express order forbade his people so to do; these men desiring rather to violate his command than to deprive themselves of so rare a humility. It is sufficient for their design that this strikes the eye. For there being nothing more natural to man than the desire of honour, and the passion for glory and distinction, and of showing every way, in person, in clothing, and in diet, the marks of some superiority and advantage over others; one can hardly look without admiration upon people who seem to renounce all this; especially when they are persons born and bred in such conditions as afforded them the means of possessing all these advantages at their desire. This without doubt creates a great prejudice for their doctrine, and causes it to be favourably received; it appearing impossible either that persons who so voluntarily divest themselves of that which others most earnestly seek, should not be influenced by a good spirit, or that doctrines which tend to humble our haughty and proud nature should be otherwise than holy and salutary.

III. There remains for us to notice the last and strongest of those three colours which compose the paint of human doctrines, and which gives them the greatest gloss, namely, neglecting the body. The apostle says that they "have a show of wisdom in neglecting of the body; not in any honour to the satisfying of the flesh." It is clear, and confessed on all hands, that he speaks of the austerity and rigour which these seducers assumed, both in their lives and doctrine, beating down their bodies, and giving them hard usage, without having any great care to satisfy their desires. All agree that this, in substance, is the apostle's scope and sense, as indeed his words necessarily and clearly signify. But when we consider the arrangement of these words, and the meaning of each of them in particular, there appears some difficulty, which has caused a

* Homer, Iliad. II. v. 235.

diversity of opinions among expositors. The difficulty precisely respects the latter clause alone, "not in any honour to the satisfying of the flesh;" which is word for word the meaning of the original. Some good and eminent servants of God, however, sever the word *honour* from the rest, interpreting the apostle thus, "They do not at all spare the body in that which is for the satisfying of the flesh." The honour of the body, in the apostle's language, is its purity and honesty, as he plainly teaches elsewhere, saying, The will of God, even our sanctification, is, "that every one should know how to possess his vessel in sanctification and honour," 1 Thess. iv. 3, 4. And to this honour he opposes, in another place, Rom. i. 26, all the filth and impurities of luxury, which he calls passions of dishonour, or "vile affections," as our Bible has translated it. Consequently, he styles marriage, which was instituted of God for the conservation of this honour of our bodies, "honourable in all," Heb. xiii. 4. The apostle, then, according to the sentiment of these interpreters, opposes this honour to the seducers' pretended mortifications. To preserve this honour, it is true we ought to spare our bodies, but religiously abstain from all that is contrary to it, denying our flesh all the pleasures of impurity. It is for this end alone that we are permitted to mortify our bodies; whereas the abstinences of these seducers were of another nature. For the rigour they used towards their bodies was to abstain, not from pleasures incompatible with sobriety, temperance, and chastity, but from certain sorts of meat, the use of which in no way defiles the body, nor violates, in any manner, the holiness in which it ought to be kept. This exposition, you see, is good and scriptural, and suits well with the apostle's terms.

The French Bible has followed another interpretation, no less pertinent, in taking the Greek word, which properly signifies honour or respect, for "having regard,"—they do not at all spare the body, and have not any respect, or any regard, for satisfying of the flesh. For a man regards what he honours; consequently *to honour* is often put in Scripture for *having a care of;* as when Paul commands Timothy to have a care of widows, he says to him, "Honour widows that are widows indeed," 1 Tim. v. 3; and this frequently occurs in other places. In the same manner therefore he says in this place, that these teachers did not at all spare the body, and took no care of it, not valuing at all the things which are requisite for feeding and satisfying the flesh. I think we may retain this exposition, as the simplest and easiest; and indeed it is the most common, and has been most generally followed. These false teachers then made this their contempt of the body, and the small care they took to nourish it according to its appetites, to be proclaimed aloud; referring thereto those abstinences which they enjoined from some kind of meats, declaring that this was to mortify their flesh, and to keep it in a wholesome discipline. What could be said more plausible? For as nothing is more unworthy the high designs of piety than adhering to the things of the carcass and the kitchen; so it seems that there is nothing more worthy of the things of heaven than contempt of this base and wretched nature. And the more passionate ordinary men are for their flesh, even to the making it their god; so much the more do they admire those who beat it down, instead of adoring it, as do they themselves. Accordingly, it is evident that most seducers have abused this colour to paint over their inventions and impostures. We read how the old idol priests "cut themselves with knives and lancets," 1 Kings xviii. 28, and other pagans rend their children and nobles with stripes before the altar of their feigned deity; nor can one think, without horror, upon the cruelties and barbarities which most of their priests and votaries exercised, and still to this day exercise, on their own persons in places where paganism bears sway. Their abstinences also were extreme; and there were sects, yea, whole nations, which scrupled to eat of anything that had had sense. The fastings and austerities of the Encratites, the Montanists, and Eustathians, ancient heretics of the christian profession, are famous in the writings of antiquity. Even the Mahometans, the most sensual and carnal of all infidels, make a show of not sparing their bodies. I pass by the prodigious and incredible austerities of their votaries, of whom some go almost naked, and so little spare their flesh, that they wound and gash it, both with incisions and burnings; others eat and drink but very seldom. Even all Mahometans in general most devoutly observe every year a kind of Lent, which they call Ramadan, fasting daily a whole month from morning till night without taking anything till the stars appear. Every one knows also how scrupulously they all abstain from wine, one of the most pleasing and esteemed refreshments of the body.

But it is no wonder, beloved brethren, that these people, who are without any knowledge of the apostle's authority, should suffer themselves to be seduced by such vain shows. Our amazement and grief is on account of our adversaries of the Roman communion, that this false lustre, so loudly decried here by an apostle whom they profess to acknowledge and reverence, should be sufficient to recommend to them doctrines purely human, and cause them to receive them for divine. For I may truly say that almost all their errors have been introduced under the three false colours which the apostle here so unceremoniously rejects, namely, voluntary service, humility, and mortifying the body. And they are not ashamed to recommend them still by these very things; alleging for the defence of their doctrines those shows with which pagans, heretics, and infidels have formerly painted over their impieties and superstitions, and the abuse of which the apostle expressly noticed and condemned. It is by this that they defend the worship of images, the invocation of saints, the abject submission in which they live to the prelates, and particularly to the bishop of Rome, the celebration of so many festivals, and a multitude of other abuses. Not being able to found them on the Scriptures of God, they plead that they are voluntary services, which are performed with a good intention, and tend to humble the spirit. Their fastings and abstinences, their watchings and pilgrimages, their whippings and discipline, and all the odd exercises of their monks, are not in the least commanded of God. But what of that? The more voluntary they are, say they, the more meritorious; and then, on the other hand, they mortify the body, which they spare not at all, having no regard to the satisfying of its desires. There is nothing which they might not pass as good and scriptural with this specious pigment. I might justly plead against these vain pretexts, that God's will ought to be the rule of ours, and that it is dangerous to trust our intentions in matters of religion, since it often happens that God holds that in abomination which most pleases our thoughts; and also that it is a proud and extravagant humility to give men a power over our consciences, which it is the prerogative of God alone to have; and that if the neglecting of or not sparing the body serves to mortify it, it follows not that we must place divine service therein. I might allege these, and many other things, and establish them by Scripture, to demonstrate the vanity of their pretexts; but at present I content myself with the apostle's example and authority. He acknowledges that the doctrines of those seducers whom he opposes had these three very colours, and that the same gave them a show of wisdom. And yet for all this he does not hesitate to reject them; paying so little regard to this their show, that he vouchsafes not to spend one word upon its refutation. However specious may be their doctrines, it is enough for their rejection that they were instituted and taught by men, and not by the Lord; clearly presupposing by this procedure that all christians should hold it for an undoubted maxim that religious service must be measured by the will of God, and not by ours; by his order, and not our fancy; and that the foundation of our humility is the respect we owe him, not to submit our consciences to any besides him. Let, then, the traditions of Rome, in other respects, be of what quality you please; let them have all the colours of wisdom; let them be voluntary and humble, and meet to mortify the flesh. You will do much by setting all this pompous show in view. You will gain much by displaying it before my eyes, and declaiming upon the advantages of those things. I cannot receive them except you show me that God has instituted them, and not man. The apostle has taught me to pay so little regard to these reasons, that I should not even vouchsafe to amuse myself with considering them. After having heard you, it is sufficient for me to tell you, as he says here to the seducers of his time, that if your doctrines have this show of wisdom which you attribute to them, they are, in conclusion, but human things, since God has not at all commanded them in his word.

Yet, upon thorough examination, it will be found, my brethren, that the most of their inventions want not the reality alone, but the colour and the very show of wisdom. For, I beseech you, what shadow of wisdom is there in this Lent, for instance, which they began the other day after the ordinary preface of their carnival? What reason or common sense is there, if it be free, that can affirm that it is wisdom, after licence taken for all kind of debauches and fooleries, to imagine that a handful of ashes will efface it all—that it is wisdom to believe that the eating of fish is fasting—that it is wisdom to think that the eating of herbs, or salmon, or green-fish is a sanctifying oneself—and that to taste but a bit of beef or mutton, during these forty days, is to defile one's soul with a deadly sin, meriting eternal fire? As if the whole nature of things were changed in a moment, and the living creatures of the earth, from being good and wholesome, as they were but four days since, became contagious and deadly. Is it wisdom to confine christianity to an observance, which has in it so little reason, and to say, as they do, that those who eat any flesh within this time are not christians? There is no understanding, however ordinary, that may not easily perceive that all this has no show of wisdom in it, to say no worse. And it is to no purpose to tell us that it is not the nature of the things themselves, but the commandment of their church, which causes them to be of this opinion. For if these things are not true in themselves, their church does wrong to authorize them; and besides contravening the rules of wisdom, it evidently violates those of charity, as it straitens the way to heaven, augments the difficulty of entering there, and damns men for things which, without its commandment, would be free and indifferent.

Let us lay aside then, I beseech you, my brethren, all these human commandments, which are so far from being just and necessary, that they have not, for the greater part, so much as that vain show of wisdom which the apostle granted that the doctrines of the seducers had in his time. Let us hold to the sacred and saving institutions of our Lord Jesus, which are all just, all reasonable, full of deep and truly divine wisdom. Let us believe, as he has taught us, that it is "not that which goeth into the mouth defileth a man, but that which cometh forth from the heart," Matt. xv. 11, 18; and that "the kingdom of God is not meat and drink; but righteousness, and peace, and joy in the Holy Ghost," Rom. xiv. 17. Let us serve him according to his own rule, and not according to the imaginations of men. Let our will be bound up in his; let it count itself happy in following his directions, and not presume to guide itself. Let it learn of him what it owes him, not be so arrogant as to define it according to its own fancy. The task he has given us is great enough for the employment of all our time and strength, without diverting it to any other object. It is in this that true humility consists, even in submitting absolutely to Jesus Christ, in refusing no service which he commands, in attempting nothing beyond his orders. He, it is clear, directs us to love God with all our heart, and our neighbour as ourselves; and that, denying ungodliness and worldly lusts, we should live soberly, righteously, and godly in the present world, looking for his glorious appearance. This, beloved brethren, is the rule of the Israel of God, which was delivered by Jesus Christ, preached by his apostles, confirmed by their miracles, and by the conversion of the world. Peace and mercy be to all that shall follow it. Amen.

SERMON XXXII.

CHAPTER III.

VERSES 1, 2.

If ye then be risen with Christ, seek those things which are above, where Christ sitteth on the right hand of God. Set your affection on things above, not on things on the earth.

DEAR brethren, if the study and practice of true holiness, which consists in the love of God and of our neighbour, had filled, as it ought, the hearts and lives of christians, they would never have amused themselves with those inferior devotions and carnal ceremonies, wherewith superstition has always fed, and to this day feeds, the world. This second sort of services was invented and introduced into religion to supply the absence of the other: for man well knowing that the majesty and beneficence of God oblige us to serve him, and that the charms and temptations of earth turn away his heart from the legitimate service of true and real sanctity, which we owe him, that he may not appear empty in the presence of this sovereign Deity, presents, instead of that which he requires of us, certain corporeal, childish, and spurious devotions, which, as they are our own invention, naturally please us. Accordingly, they are commonly called satisfactions, because they are performed to satisfy God for the omission of what was due to him; an evident sign that if men had fulfilled their duty, there would have been no need to employ themselves in these other exercises. Hence arose at the beginning those abstinences from certain meats, and those distinctions of days, and that worshipping of angels, which some seducers would have established among christians in the very days of the apostles. Afterward from the same source also issued the stations, the xerophagies, and other extravagancies of the Montanists, and of various heretics who disturbed the ancient church. In fine, from this very original have sprung the observances and voluntary services of Rome; those orders and rules of the many monks who now fill the world; quadragesimal rites, fasts and vigils, auricular confessions, pilgrimages, whippings, festivals, jubilees, chaplets, and fraternities, with a multitude of similar devotions which have obscured the christian religion. We may confidently say, there would never have been recourse to such things if mortification of the old man, if true piety towards God, and true charity towards their neighbour, had exercised and continually absorbed the affections and lives of christians. Their greatest zealots confess that their rules and discipline have no place in heaven, where holiness is perfected; and never had less on earth, than among christians of the first age, who were the best and most holy; all these human devotions having evidently sprung from the lax piety of christians, and the corruption of their manners.

Therefore the apostle Paul, having refuted in the preceding chapter, as you have heard, the pretended services and mortifications of the false teachers of his time, that the faithful to whom he writes might utterly be disgusted with and turned away from them, now lays before them the just duties and legitimate exercises of christian piety; the body of holiness, instead of shadows; the solid doctrine of the Lord Jesus instead of the vain and childish lessons of superstition; the true mortifying of the flesh, instead of the seducers' unprofitable macerations; and an abstinence from sin and the lusts thereof, instead of abstinence from certain meats; in fine, heaven, instead of earth. As a prudent gardener, who, after he has plucked up the weeds or unprofitable herbs of his garden, and well cleansed the ground, casts in good seeds, which are worthy to occupy the earth, and capable of yielding fruits useful for the food of men. By this means the apostle prevents an objection that superstition usually makes. For, being not able to maintain its petty services as holy and necessary in themselves, it has been wont to allege, that, whatever they are, it is better for christians to use them than to be idle. The apostle takes from it this vain pretence, showing the faithful that they have another task, which is much more worthy, and much more noble, namely, the study and practice of true holiness; so that superstition is guilty not only of a superfluous diligence, but of a pernicious temerity, in diverting christians from their legitimate and necessary work by those voluntary exercises wherewith it pretends to charge them. Let us then, dearly beloved brethren, keep off from the vain institutions of superstitions, whether ancient or modern, and keep to the discipline of Paul. Let us meditate, study, and practise what he enjoins us, and assure ourselves that, in observing and following his rule exactly, we shall have neither time, nor will, nor need to follow the rules of men. He employs all the remainder of this Epistle in these divine documents; and in the beginning of this chapter, after he has raised our hearts to heaven, he represents to us the general duties of sanctification which are necessary for all christians; thence passing to particulars, he instructs married persons, children, fathers, and masters in what they owe to one another, as you shall hear, if God please, in the sequel of these discourses. For the present, to explain the exhortation which he placed at the head of this excellent chapter which we have read to you, we will consider, by the grace and assistance of the Holy Ghost, first, the precept it contains, that we seek the things which are above. Secondly, the two reasons upon which he founds it; one taken from our being risen with Christ, and the other from Jesus Christ's sitting on high at the right hand of God. We shall observe upon each particular as briefly as possible the instructions they afford us, either for our edification and consolation in general, or particularly for our preparation for that holy and mystical repast unto which the Lord Jesus invites us against the next Lord's day.

I. The ancient Greeks ascribed to their most esteemed philosopher the glory of having brought down wisdom from heaven to earth, because he was the first that fixed the minds of his scholars on the investigation of their own nature, and what we owe either to ourselves or to other men; whereas the sages who lived before him employed themselves only in the contemplation of the heavens, and their motions, and the things dependent on them. But the Lord Jesus, the true Prince of wisdom and verity, instructs us in a better manner than he, who verily was but a blind leader of the blind. For all the philosophy of Jesus Christ is to loosen us from the earth and lift us up to heaven, and so to fix our minds and affections there, that we may dwell, and converse, and have our souls incessantly there, even now, however distant our bodies are from that happy habitation. It is very true, as that poor pagan judged, that contemplating the sun, and the planets, and the stars, and searching out their motions, and admiring their beauty, their light, their greatness, and other qualities, (which was all the employment of the first heathen philosophers,) does not much conduce to the perfection of our manners and the felicity of our lives. But it is not that on which Jesus Christ fixes us. He has discovered to us things on high within that nobler part of the world, which are infinitely more excellent and more necessary; and such as, if that pagan had seen, he would have made no difficulty to confess that true wisdom consists not in staying oneself here below on the earth, but in ascending up to heaven, and in viewing, loving, and admiring them continually.

For, first, he has revealed to us there a holy and glorious city, seated above nature and all its elements; a city, not mutable, and subject to perish, as inferior things, but settled, permanent, and eternal; the sanctuary of life and immortality, which God has built, and in which he has displayed all the wonders of his power and wisdom; the dwelling-place which he has prepared for such among men as, embracing his promises by faith, shall live here in his fear, and obey his commandments; and where he has already gathered and consecrated in his rest the spirits of such of the faithful as he has fetched out of the present world. Christ has made us see that there those blessed ones dwell with the armies of holy angels, and that thither he went himself when he had finished the work of our redemption upon earth. In this mystical paradise the true tree of life grows. There the rivers of pleasure run. There shines the true Sun that never sets. There are kept those divine flowers which can neither soil nor fade, with which the piety and patience of saints shall be one day crowned. There God manifests himself to his servants, and shows them the beauties of his countenance unveiled; and feeds them, and fills them with joy, and transforms them by this vision, into so many living images of his eternal and blessed nature. There are true glory and real pleasure, honour, felicity, and magnificence, the idea of which never entered either into our senses or into the very thoughts of our heart; in comparison of which all the pomp of the earth, and the glory of this heaven, in which we see the sun and the stars go their rounds, is but a shadow and a vapour. Again, as the creatures there possess true glory, so they exercise true sanctity. All that is seen of it here below, is but a little spark of the perfection of those blessed inhabitants of that celestial city. The love they bear to the Lord is there perfect, as well as the knowledge they have of him. Charity towards our neighbour, concord, union, truth, there reign absolute. Their souls have neither affections nor desires but which are conformed to the will of God. The light of his face governs all their motions; and shedding itself abroad continually upon them, maintains them in an eternal holiness, peace, and blessedness. The Lord Jesus has discovered to us all these wonders above the heavens, having brought life and immortality to light by the gospel. But further, he has certified us that these are things which concern us, and pertain to us; and that he has opened by his cross and resurrection the way that will most assuredly bring us to them. If we have the courage to follow him, of whatever condition or quality we may be, he will congregate us to this holy company of his servants; receiving our souls into his bosom upon their departure from this earth, and raising up our poor bodies themselves one day reinvested with his immortality and glory.

These are, dear brethren, the things which are above, which the apostle exhorts us to seek in the same sense that our Saviour commands us in the gospel to "seek the kingdom of God, and his righteousness," Matt. vi. 33; signifying by that term, first, that we propose heaven and eternity to ourselves for the chief end of our life, and place our supreme happiness in this rich possession; that we make it our grand and only design. And, secondly, that we employ in this noble pursuit all the might we have; seriously using all the means which the word of God prescribes, faith, prayer, piety, holiness; and flee, as a mortal pest, everything that keeps us off or turns us aside from this mark. The slothful, who does nothing all day but desire, and sets not his hand to the work, has no part in those heavenly things. His desire kills him, saith the wise man, Prov. xxi. 25; as one that feeds on nothing but wind. There must be knocking; there must be seeking; there must be working out our salvation with fear and trembling. This treasure is not for cold and languid wills, that evaporate altogether in vain wishings. It shall be that man's prize who shall take it with an ardent and a generous courage, and, impelled with a violent affection, spare neither pain, nor watching, nor labour to obtain it.

That which the apostle commands us in the following verse, namely, to mind the things which are above, amounts to nearly the same sense. For the word he uses comprehends the two actions of our souls towards objects we love; the one considering and thinking on them, the other desiring and embracing them in our affections. So you see he obliges us, first, to lift up our hearts to heaven, where the Lord Jesus is, and to have that blessed kingdom continually before our eyes, which God has there prepared for us, together with all those great eternal good things in which it consists. He requires that this thought fill our souls day and night; that it be the thought that has superiority in them, that governs all their motions; the thought that regulates our resolutions, and decides all our doubts; that in all things which present themselves we reflect, to see how they refer to it, and whether they are compatible with it. Such was the practice of the father of the faithful. He looked, says the apostle, for a city that hath foundations. And Moses, the grand legislator of the Jews, had respect, says the same apostle, unto the recompense; that is, as he explains himself in the text, they minded the things which are above. And this thought (as you see) is also necessarily joined with affection, with an ardent desire of possessing such amiable and excellent things, and with a steadfast hope of enjoying them at length.

This is then, my brethren, the first of those two duties which the apostle requires of us, namely, that we seek the things which are above. Now to it he annexes a prohibition, which follows necessarily from it, namely, that we seek not the things which are upon the earth; heaven and earth being so opposite, that it is not possible but that they who seek the things of the one must renounce the things of the other. The things of the earth are, as you know, the goods of the world, riches, gold, silver, honours, pleasures, and the like; all that which earthly men, the children of this generation, esteem and passionately love. He does not mean that we should have no care at all about the necessaries of the present life; for those good things being gifts of God, without which we cannot live, we may both acquire and enjoy with thanksgiving, yet not cleave to them; and use them, yet not abuse them. The apostle, you know, elsewhere commands us to care for our families, and to attend every one to his own business, and to labour with our hands, that we may walk honestly towards them that are without, and that we may have lack of nothing. But he forbids us to seek the things of the earth in the same sense that he commands us to seek those of heaven; that is, to place our chief good in them, and to desire them with choicest affection, and to prefer them before any other consideration. Thus those men sought the things of the earth, of whom the apostle declares their belly was their god, and that they gloried in their shame, Phil. iii. 19; and those in the gospel parable, Luke xiv., who preferred the care of their fields, and of their oxen, and the love of their wives, before the call of heaven. Such a one, in the Old Testament, was Esau, who chose a little pottage of lentils rather than his birthright. Such, in the New, were those sordid Gadarenes, who would have the Son of God depart, because he had occasioned the loss of their swine; and those who love their fathers, or mothers, or brethren, or other alliances, or worldly possessions, more than the Lord Jesus, or that prefer the praise of men before the praise of God. Such a one also was that foolish rich man, who thought himself happy enough because he had goods laid up for many years, and dreamt of nothing but enjoying them.

II. Now, though the bare dignity of heavenly things, and the mere meanness and unprofitableness of earthly things, should be sufficient to recommend the former, and to disgust us with the latter; yet the apostle, to urge us to duties so just as these, sets before us two excellent reasons. The first is drawn from our resurrection with our Saviour. He had touched it already in the 12th verse of the preceding chapter; and from thence he resumes it, and reminds us of it here, saying, "If ye then be risen with Christ;" that is to say, Since you are risen with the Lord, as I have showed before. For the particle "if" is used here, as it often is elsewhere, for illation and conclusion, not to express doubting; and imports as much as if the apostle had said, Since that, or seeing that. For the rest, you plainly see that the resurrection of which he speaks is not that of our bodies, which shall not be till the last day; but another mystical and spiritual one, already accomplished in us, by virtue of our Lord's resurrection, and the efficacy of his Spirit. He speaks of it also in Ephesians, chap. ii. 5, 6, that God "hath quickened us together with Christ, and raised us up together, and made us sit together in heavenly places in him." He explains to us the mystery of it elsewhere in these words, "We are buried with him by baptism into death; that like as Christ was raised from the dead by the glory of the Father, so we also should walk in newness of life," Rom. vi. 4. Every resurrection presupposes a death preceding. For to rise again is nothing else but for one to be restored to life who before was dead. Now the state of men under the dominion of sin the Scripture calls death, because they have no more sense or motion towards piety and holiness than the dead who rest in the grave have for the actions of this life. Ye were "dead in trespasses and sins," says the apostle to the Ephesians, chap. ii. 1, speaking of the time of their ignorance. Whence arises that which our Saviour says in the gospel, "Let the dead bury their dead;" and that which Paul says, The widow "that liveth in pleasure is dead while she liveth," 1 Tim. v. 6. When therefore, by the efficacy of the vocation of the Spirit and gospel of the Lord, a man passes out of this miserable condition into the state of grace; receiving the light of faith into his understanding, and love and sanctification into his heart; the Scripture, to express this wonderful change, says he is risen again. This is precisely the resurrection that Paul intends in this place.

He says that we are risen with Christ, first, because this blessed change which is accomplished in us by his grace is like that change which took place in him when he arose from the grave, where he lay for the space of three days. He was raised to life by power from on high. For as he then received the faculties of motion and sensation, of which he was deprived in the sepulchre; so we, in our regeneration, receive a spirit and a principle of life which we had not before. Again, as the Lord was restored to life by the glory of the Father, as the apostle speaks, that is, by virtue of the exceeding great and glorious power of God; in like manner are we renewed, and put into the state of grace, by the efficacy of the might of God, and not by the arm of man, or the operation of flesh and blood. Indeed, as the Lord, upon his rising again, recovered not simply that life which he laid down in his dying, but a much more excellent, glorious, spiritual, celestial, and immortal life; so we resume in our regeneration, not the life of the first Adam before sin, from which we were fallen, and which, however excellent, was nevertheless animal and mortal, that is, capable of being lost, as appeared by the issue; but another much more exquisite and perfect, a life eternal, immutable, and like that which the blessed angels live. Thus you see the resurrection of the Lord Christ is the idea and pattern of ours. But I add, in the second place, that we are said to be risen with Christ, because it is in him, and from him, that we have this grace; it being evident that faith, which is the first faculty of the new life, ingrafts and incorporates us into Jesus Christ; and as the vine branch does not live but in its stock, so man cannot live that divine life but in his Saviour.

I may add, we are risen again with Christ, because his resurrection is the cause of ours; as, if he had not risen from the dead, we should have remained in the darkness of our spiritual death. Christ coming forth out of his grave has opened and enlightened ours, and administered, out of his own store, all things necessary to deliver us from our miserable state of death, and to put us in possession of the life of heaven. His resurrection has confirmed our faith, showing us clearly that he is the Son of God, and that his gospel is true. His resurrection has assured our souls, giving us full proof that his death fully satisfied the Judge of the world. It has strengthened our hopes, making us see, by the example of our Head, that death, the most terrible of our enemies, cannot impede our happiness. Hence it has kindled love to God, and the desire of such great glory in our hearts; and, finally, produced in them the principles, habits, and dispositions of the new nature, which are necessary for our attaining to blissful immortality. Since, therefore, Jesus Christ in rising again thereby raised up our life, which had been ingulfed in hell and the curse, and brought to light the causes of faith, hope, and charity, the principal faculties of that new life we now possess, it is evident that we are risen in him and with him. From whence that which the apostle infers no less clearly follows, that we ought to mind henceforth the things which are on high, and seek them with all our affection. For the life to which we are raised up with our Lord is heavenly, and not earthly; divine, and not natural; eternal, and not corruptible. Since, therefore, every creature employs all its sense and affection about things suitable to its life, who sees not that the faithful are obliged, by the dignity they possess in being risen with the Lord, neither to breathe after nor embrace other things, but those that are on high, in which their new life properly consists? And such is the example he has given us. For being risen, he abode but a very little time here below, only as long as the work of our salvation required, and then ascended to heaven, to draw up our thoughts and affections thither, until our bodies also follow one day, being raised up thither, as his was, unto highest glory.

And this is the second consideration which the apostle here lays before us to persuade us to so just a duty; "Seek those things which are above, where Christ sitteth at the right hand of God." For if, as our Lord said, "where your treasure is, there will be your heart also," where should our souls be but in heaven, since in that blessed dwelling-place their treasure resides—Jesus, their good, their life, and their joy, in whom is hid all our felicity? Under the Mosaic law, the faithful always turned their eyes and thoughts towards the temple at Jerusalem, because it was the resting-place of the pledges of God's covenant with them, and of the most precious symbols of his presence and glory. Judge what our affection and earnestness should be for heaven, which contains the true ark of God, where all the fulness of the Godhead dwells, not in shadow and figure, but really and bodily? Yea, more; Jesus Christ is our Head, and we his members. How can we preserve this honour, but in keeping close to him, and following him faithfully, without ever separating from him, or withdrawing from that sanctuary where he dwells? And indeed he expressly assures us in the gospel that he willeth we should be where he is; and that where the dead body is, there also the eagles gather together; so if we are truly of the number of his eagles, it is not possible but we should take our flight to heaven, since this divine body of our Lord and Saviour is there.

And hereby you see, dear brethren, how distant the doctrine of Paul is from that of Rome. For whereas the apostle elevates our hearts from earth to heaven, Rome brings them down, as much as she can, from heaven to earth; fastening the hearts of her zealots on her material altars and *ciboria*, in which she pretends the Lord is enclosed, against the suffrage of the whole church, who have constantly applied these words of the apostle particularly to the sacrament of the eucharist, exhorting the faithful, when they celebrate it, to have their hearts above. Surely if Jesus Christ is here below, as Rome would have it, the apostle does wrong to command us to mind the things which are above; and worse again in urging, for a reason of it, that Jesus Christ resides above. If the Lord is in heaven, we ought, according to the apostle's instruction, not to seek anything on earth; how much less, I beseech you, ought we to seek the Lord himself there! I do not inform you that this is to be understood of the presence of the human nature of Jesus Christ, for you know that he is everywhere as to the essence and providence of his divinity. And as to the grace of his Spirit, and the efficacy of his will and institutions, we readily confess that it is not confined to the heavens; but extends and shows itself wherever he pleases, according to his promise to be in the midst of us, when we are assembled in his name.

But the apostle does not merely say that Jesus is in heaven. He adds, that he sitteth at the right hand of God. Many learned men have laboured much to explain these words; and some have strangely disguised them, as if they signified that our Lord's human nature had been invested with all the properties of the Divinity, which implies that it was transformed into a divine nature; a fancy which all true christians abhor, confessing that the two natures remain each of them in its integrity, having been united in Jesus Christ, but not blended together nor confused. The apostle, if we please to hear him, will tell us in two words what it is to sit at the right hand of God. For in 1 Cor. xv., speaking of the state to which Jesus Christ has been exalted in the heavens, and in which he shall remain to the end, instead of saying as the prophet in Psal. cx., from whom the expression was taken, that the Lord should sit at the right hand of the Father; he says simply, that he shall reign till he has put all his enemies under his feet; an evident sign that this sitting at the right hand of the Father is nothing but that supreme dominion which has been given him over all things, and which he does and shall exercise to the end of all ages, inasmuch as God has made him "both Lord and Christ," as Peter speaks, Acts ii. 36. And this consideration again mightily strengthens the holy apostle's exhortation. For since heaven is the throne on which the Prince of the universe sits, and from which he dispenses and governs all things at his will; there is great reason we should turn our eyes thither, and have this royal court of our Sovereign in mind night and day, to comfort ourselves under the trouble, which either the iniquity of men and devils, or the intemperance of other creatures, gives us, and to form our manners, and all the parts of our life, after the will and by the example of so great and so holy a Monarch.

Behold the lesson, beloved brethren, which the apostle gives us at this time, that we seek not low, but high things; not those of the earth, but the things of heaven; since we are risen up with Jesus Christ, who is set down on high in heaven at the right hand of God. Who in all the world would be more happy than we, if we maintained a good and firm resolution to obey him, and practise the thing which he enjoins us? These fears, and these desires, and so many other vain passions which trouble our whole life, would have no more place in us. Elevated far above that which men unprofitably covet, or possess, or apprehend, we should, with angels, enjoy a divine contentment. From that glorious heaven, where we should reside, we should despise the vanities and variations of the earth, and see its seasons revolve, and its elements rage, and its idols perish, and its pleasures fleet away, without any perturbation, being secure that none of its storms can ever reach that high and inaccessible region where our hearts and lives are. We should look upon death without terror, knowing that it could not take any of those things from us which we possess on high. We should suffer all the accidents of this life without emotion, because they can change no part of the things we have in heaven. The charms also and illusions of the world would affect us as little as its menaces and raging, because the fruition of a greater good would render us insensible to lesser ones, as the presence of the sun extinguishes the shining of the stars. Being content with heaven and its eternity, we should covet nothing more; and satisfied with so rich a portion, we could not envy any of the creatures the perfections and happiness they enjoy. Our whole life would be a perpetual festival, in which, free from the travail and turmoil of worldlings, contemplating in spirit the glory of the palace of our Lord, meditating on his promises, breathing after his benefits, and enjoying them for the present by faith and hope, we should in repose wait for the blessed day of our glorious triumph.

But, alas! how far are we from such a felicity! This wretched and perishing earth is the sole object of our minds. Our souls are no less fastened to it than our bodies. It swallows up all our thoughts; it possesses our affections; it engages our cares and labours, and has the use of all our time. We have no desires and love, but for the false goods which it shows us; nor fear and horror, but for the evils with which it threatens us. As for heaven, and the things it comprehends, we are so far from seeking them, that we do not so much as think of them, except it be dreamingly, or as an amusement, when we are told of them in this place; looking on the stately representations which Jesus Christ has drawn of them as an empty picture, beautiful indeed, and pleasing, but good for nought, save to feed our eyes with a short and profitless pleasure; not attracting nor engaging our desires. This is the cause why our whole life is miserable, full of griefs and fears, of weaknesses, regrets, and infelicities. The lightest strokes overturn us; the least losses and slightest afflictions bear us down; because not being fastened to heaven, the only firm and sure place of the world, we fluctuate, exposed to the mercy of all that comes against us. And as children cannot be appeased when their dolls are taken from them, because they have set all their affection on them; so trouble seizes us when we lose some of these toys of earth. There is no way to comfort us, because we have fastened our hearts to them. And, to say the truth, our condition is worse than that of other men; they are subject only to the evils which either the infirmity of nature, or (as they call it) the inconstancy of fortune, brings with it; whereas, besides these, the bad christian, who is a christian but in name, is exposed to the persecution of the world; so that, to speak plainly, no man is more foolish or wretched than he who has part in the temporal sufferings and hardships of true believers, and none in their consolation or blessedness, inasmuch as his profession exposes him to the hatred of the world, and his vice excludes him from the kingdom of God.

Awake, then, ye that are worldly, and come at once out of so dangerous an error. Let not the trumpet of heaven, the voice of our great apostle, have sounded now in your ears in vain. Add not this contempt to your other crimes. He has informed you of your duty. He has declared the reasons which oblige you to perform it. Take heed, lest if you shut your ears against Jesus Christ, who speaks by his mouth, you perish with this earth, and the things you seek on it. Do you not perceive that you shall never find there the happiness you seek? Has not the experience of so many millions of persons, who daily spend themselves in this vain labour, taught you that the things of earth are all of them but vanities and illusions, transient images, which promise pleasure, honour, and contentment, but afford none—which cure the maladies neither of the body nor the soul—which infinitely weary those that seek them, and never fill the hearts of those that possess them; multiplying their desires and their fears, inflaming and envenoming their passions instead of extinguishing them—which are subject to infinite mutations—of which men and elements may bereave you every moment—and which, considering the short and uncertain duration of the life we lead below, you can enjoy but a very little time, supposing that nothing deprives you of them before death? At that time, what will it profit a man to have gained the whole world, and lost his own soul? Matt. xvi. 26. Surely it is an incredible blindness, not only that a christian who has hopes of the world to come, but that even any reasonable man, should adhere with such ardent and obstinate eagerness to such wretched and fruitless things. We perceive it, and confess it, and make the most excellent discourses in the world upon it; and after all, the false lustre which we behold in these things has such a faculty to bewitch our senses, that there is not a person who does not suffer himself to be caught thereby. But the worst is, that besides error and vanity, it tends to eternal damnation. For men must not flatter themselves. None can serve two masters, nor look on heaven and earth together. He that seeks the one must of necessity renounce the other; it being no more possible to seek than it is to find, at once the things beneath and those which are above.

Faithful brethren, choose you, and take the better part. Leaving worldly men to labour in vain after the things of earth, and to seek in them what they shall never find; turn you your hearts and eyes towards heaven, as the apostle exhorts you. There, christian, is the felicity you desire. There dwell rest, and joy, and immortality, and the perfection of both soul and body. These are the only things truly worthy of your prayers and your pains. Seek them, and mind them night and day. Give yourselves no rest till you have found them, and feel the first-fruits and beginnings of them in your hearts. Let these thoughts sweeten your sufferings, and console you under your losses: In vain ye threaten me, ye people of the world. Ye cannot deprive me of what I possess, nor hinder me from finding what I seek; since upon the things of heaven ye have no power. Of whatever ye bereave me, the best part of my treasure, and the only part which deserves that appellation, will still remain entire to me. Let the same thought arm us against all temptations. Thou, tempter, promisest me the things of the earth; but I seek those of heaven, of which thou canst not dispose. Though I should lose all I have here below, even to this flesh itself, yet shall I find it again with a thousandfold increase in heaven. Let this thought again keep us continually employed in the good and honourable actions of piety, charity, and honesty. Let our manners resemble those of the inhabitants of that divine city which we seek. Let the light of their knowledge, the ardour of their love, the purity of their affections, shine forth now in our lives. To that heavenly life the new nature which Jesus Christ has given us, in raising us again with himself, obliges us. The thoughts and works of heaven are necessary productions of the principles and faculties of that life to which we have been raised up. You can neither be christians, without having part in the resurrection of our Lord; nor have part in his resurrection, except you walk with him, and wear that lightsome robe of sanctity with which he clothes all the associates of his resurrection. He himself calls us hereto from that lofty throne, whereon he sits at the right hand of God: Faithful soul, says he to each of us, look unto me, and I will give thee light. Fear not; for I govern the heavens and the earth. Only fix thine eyes, thy thoughts, and thy heart on me, and I will guide thee by my counsel, and receive thee one day into my glory. Dear brethren, this he promises us, and of this he will give us earnest next Lord's day, at his holy table. Let us do what he demands of us, or, to say better, let us pray him to perform it in us, and he will assuredly accomplish what he promises. Unto him, unto the Father, and unto the Holy Spirit, the true and only God, blessed for ever, be honour, praise, and glory, to ages of ages. Amen.

SERMON XXXIII.

VERSES 3, 4.

For ye are dead, and your life is hid with Christ in God. When Christ, who is our life, shall appear, then shall ye also appear with him in glory.

DEAR brethren, the Lord Jesus being not only the author and cause, but also the pattern and example, of that great salvation which God of his infinite mercy offers to mankind in the gospel, we cannot have part in it, or assuredly enter into this rich possession, without manifesting a resemblance to this sovereign Lord, and being so many copies of this divine original, where all his features and lineaments may appear, though in a form and measure much less perfect and eminent than his. Of this the apostle expressly informs us in his Epistle to the Romans, saying that those whom God "did foreknow," that is, love, and discriminate from the rest of men, according to his good pleasure, to communicate true faith and eternal salvation to them, "he also did predestinate to be conformed to the image of his Son," chap. viii. 28. For this cause he does us the honour to call us sometimes his "children," and sometimes his "brethren," Heb. ii. 12, 13, because of the resemblance we bear to him; the nature, condition, quality, and, as it is commonly termed, the fortune of children, following the fathers; and of brethren, being like their elder brothers. Whence the apostle concludes in the Epistle to the Hebrews, chap. ii. 11, that "He who sanctifieth," that is, the Lord Jesus, "and they who are sanctified," that is, the faithful, "are all of one," that is, of one and the same mass, of one and the same form and nature. And to make it plain to us, the Scripture compares him, sometimes to a vine, John xv., at others to an olive tree, Rom. xi., of each of which we are branches; both of them being things between which there is by nature a strict communion, both having the same constitution and qualities. And hence again it is that Paul calls him our first-fruits. When speaking of our death, and the resurrection which is to succeed it, he says that Christ was made "the first-fruits of them that sleep," 1 Cor. xv. 20; the first-fruits, as you know, being of the same condition and nature with the rest of those things out of the mass of which they are taken.

Now although this conformity of the faithful to the Lord Jesus is of great extent, yet it principally appears in two heads, in which the Scripture particularly considers it; namely, in his death, and in his resurrection; the happy remembrance of which we have celebrated this morning. For the death of Jesus Christ has produced a death like it in all true believers; reducing them, by its efficacy and virtue, to a state conformable to his, when he was stretched on the cross and lay in the sepulchre. In like manner, his resurrection transmits into them a life like that which he resumed when, having overcome death, he issued out of his grave. His death is not only the cause, but also the pattern, of ours; and likewise his life is both the principle and example of ours. Of this death and life, dearly beloved brethren, which are the effect and image of the death and resurrection of the Lord, we intend to treat in this sermon. For after having celebrated the memory of the death and resurrection of this great Saviour, and participated of both, by the virtue of his Spirit and our faith, upon what can we more pertinently meditate, than the precious fruit which each of them produces in us, and the images of these mysteries, which this divine dead and again risen person draws and forms in us; inasmuch as he changes us after a manner into himself, by an impression of his omnipotent influence; so that if we have truly received him, we are become dead, and have risen with him? Paul teaches us this excellent and saving truth, in the series of our ordinary texts, by the words which we have read for the subject of this exercise. In those which preceded, and which we expounded eight days since, this great apostle drew us from the earth, that he might elevate us to heaven, where Jesus sitteth at the right hand of the Father: "Set your affection," says he, "on things above, not on things on the earth." But because he knew how difficult such a transportation would be for persons who are still so many ways fastened to the earth, in order to work so high a design thoroughly into us, besides the reasons already represented, which were taken from our resurrection with the Lord, and from his presence and glorious sovereignty in the place to which he would elevate us, he further proposes two more for that end, in this passage: the one taken from our death; "For ye are dead;" and the other from that new life which we have received; a life hidden, it is true, for the present, in God, but such as will be plainly and fully discovered one day, at the manifestation of the Lord Jesus: "your life is hid with Christ in God." These are the two principal points we shall expound in this sermon, the grace of our Lord assisting; and him we invoke, praying that his word may effectually work in us, and his power to salvation thoroughly change us into the similitude, both of his salutary death, and of his glorious life; that being dead to ourselves, we may live henceforth only in him, to his honour, and the edification of our brethren.

I. Be not alarmed, christians, at the apostle's telling you, in the entrance, that "ye are dead." This death which he attributes to you is gain, and not loss; a donative from God's grace, and not an effect of his wrath, or an execution of his justice. I grant, that every death is the privation of some life which was possessed. But since there are miserable and execrable lives, it must be confessed that every death is not a calamity. For to be rid of a thing that harms us is not a calamity but a comfort. It is an advantage, and not a damage, to be deprived of a poison and freed from an accursed state. The death of which the apostle speaks is not the destruction of that happy life which the Creator gave us at the beginning, when man enjoyed within Paradise a continual exercise of the original rectitude of his nature, and the sweet and innocent fruition of the goods of the first world. The first Adam, and not the second, deprived us of this life; and as we received it in his person, so we have lost it by his crime, being heirs of his misery as well as of his sin. The life which is extinguished in us by the death here intended by the apostle, is that corrupted and sin-infected life which we have received from our first parents by carnal generation; a life contrary to the will of God, meriting his wrath, and obnoxious to his curse; the operation of a poisoned nature, and the acting of a blind understanding, a perverse will, and an irregular affection, the continual flux of an abominable pest, which, in the course of nature, could end in nothing but eternal death. It is that which Scripture calls the life of the old man, that is, of this altogether depraved and corrupt nature which we derive from Adam; and which, through error in its false wisdom, placing its felicity in the enjoyment of earthly things, adheres to them with inordinate desire, and neither acts nor labours but to acquire them; pursuing them with such a violent ardour, that everything holy, just, and honest it violates to attain its end. This is the life that the Lord Jesus destroys in all his true members, and to which his holy apostle says and means here that we are dead. The death of which he speaks is nothing but the privation of this pernicious and accursed life; the abolition of its principles, and the destruction of the habits on which it depends. We are dead, because, entering into the communion of Jesus Christ, we have put off this first life, which was natural, carnal, and earthly, and consisted in a perverse and vicious search and fruition of the perishing things of this old world, which advances to perdition. This he teaches us again in many other places, as when he says, that "old things are passed away;" that Christ having "died for all, then were all dead;" that they "should not henceforth live unto themselves," 2 Cor. v. 14, 15, 17: that we are "dead with Christ," "buried with him by baptism into his death;" made one and the same plant with him, by "the likeness of his death;" that "our old man was crucified with him, that the body of sin might be destroyed," Rom. vi.: that "they that are

Christ's have crucified the flesh with the affections and lusts," Gal. v. 24. And it is the same which he called "the circumcision of Christ," and the "putting off the body of the sins of the flesh," Col. ii. 11: the same which he represents in his own person, that he is "crucified with Christ;" and that it is no more himself that liveth, but Christ who liveth in him; and that the world is crucified unto him, and he unto the world, Gal. ii. 20; vi. 14. And it is the same also that Peter understands, when he says we have suffered with Christ in the flesh, that we should not live the rest of our time in the flesh, after the lusts of men, 1 Pet. iv. 1, 2.

Behold that penitent woman, whose history you have in the gospel. Before she had seen the Lord, she was a harlot, who lived in nothing but uncleanness, and had neither action nor thought but for the lusts of the flesh. But after she had heard the word of Jesus, and felt the efficacy of his Spirit, she soon cast away all her former life. She has now no longer that wanton and wicked heart, those unchaste looks, those impure desires. In vain you seek in her that debauched person who lived in infamy before. That person is no more there, but is dead. The sharpened arrows of the King of glory have penetrated her heart, and slain her, Psal. xlv. 5. Behold Paul before his conversion. He was a furious wild boar, inflamed to threatenings and slaughter; breathing out nothing but blood and destruction, Acts ix. 1; a murderer animated by pride and cruelty. Jesus spake to him on the way to Damascus. His word, like a two edged sword, pierced this fierce and unruly persecutor. He struck him dead, or, to say better, destroyed and consumed him in a moment. Seek not Saul in him any longer, that fierce and cruel man; he is no more there. He is dead, and so thoroughly dead, that you shall not find in him any semblance of what he was before. Again, take a view of those pagans of Colosse, of Ephesus, of Athens, and of other places, who were converted by his ministry. Before they were idolaters, committing all kinds of vices; their life was nothing but a continual practice of superstition and impiety, of avarice and ambition, of envy, cruelty, and injustice. Now, when they have passed through the victorious hand of the Lord Jesus, you see no more any such thing in them. He has extinguished in them all this kind of life. Those idolaters and ungodly wretches, those epicures and robbers, who lived in their persons before, are all dead. They are new men of another quality, in whom none of that which they were before remains any longer. There is not one of the truly faithful and living members of Jesus Christ but has undergone this death; the flesh has been slain in him, and the old man pierced, nailed, and crucified upon the cross of the Son of God.

I acknowledge, that as long as they are on earth, they resist the efforts and attempts of this old man, and hence that combat of the flesh lusting against the spirit, of which the apostle elsewhere speaks, Gal. v. 17. Yet I affirm, that true believers may be said even for the present to be dead with respect to the flesh, and the flesh dead in them. First, because sentence against it is given in the judgment of God, who has in his eternal counsel determined to extinguish and abolish, in all the members of his Son, that first life which they inherited from old Adam. Secondly, because the execution of this decree of God is begun and advanced in them for the present. The mortal blow the flesh receives in this life, from the hand of Jesus Christ, and cannot possibly recover again. Then, in the third place, because this execution already begun in them will not be long completing; natural death, which, considering the few days we spend here below, is not far from either of them, divesting first their souls of all earthly and carnal relics, and then the resurrection finally refining their bodies also at the last day, when earthly life shall be entirely destroyed and utterly dissolved. For these three reasons the apostle says here and elsewhere that the faithful are dead, with respect to the life of sin and of the flesh; not because they have not in themselves some remains of them, but because this death is ordained by the decree of God, and already begun in them, and will soon be infallibly finished. Even as we reckon among the dead a malefactor whom a supreme court has condemned to die, and a sick person whom a prudent and able physician has pronounced incurable; we do not hesitate to say, he is dead, because his death is inevitable, and all the life that remains for him is as nothing: so when a man has been mortally wounded, we immediately rank him with the dead, because a vital part is struck, and all the motions and perceptions he still has are but his last gaspings, and the final struggle which his life makes before it expires. It is the same with true believers. The flesh in them is wounded to death; and if it stirs, if it struggles, if it gives them any blow, at most it is a small matter in comparison with that life it formerly exercised in them. At that time it reigned in them. Now, if it fight, yet it no longer rules. It finds a spirit in them which resists it, which makes head against it; and in this, to it, fatal conflict, it loses by little and little all the blood and life it has yet left. Wherefore the Lord Jesus, whose death, as we have said, is both the cause and the pattern of ours, did not die in an instant, but by a lingering death, having continued five or six hours in an agony before he gave up the ghost. It is thus that the old man dies in the faithful. He is already pierced with the nails of our Saviour, fastened to his cross in a dying state, and without hope of recovery. Nevertheless he struggles still, and will be some time in this state, losing blood, and strength, and motion, and life, not all at once, but by little and little.

This is the condition of true believers. Whence appears the pernicious error of those men who, having the old man, not bound, nor pierced, nor wounded to death in them, but living and reigning at full liberty, and with his whole vigour, yet imagine that they belong to Jesus Christ, and are of the number of his true members. It is a fatal mistake. Jesus owns none for his but such as are dead with him; whose flesh is either already laid down and destroyed in the grave, as theirs who live in heaven; or at least nailed to his cross, as theirs who yet fight on earth. I confess the presumption of those who boast that they sin no more, and feel no longer in themselves any motion or opposition of the flesh, is extremely vain. But your error, worldling, is not a whit less, who, having sin reigning, and the flesh living in you, forbear not to persuade yourself that you are a true christian. If the flesh still breathes in a true christian, if it has still some motion and feeling in him, yet it has dominion in him no longer. It lives in him no more, it languishes in him, and is so weak, that it plainly appears to be in the pangs of death. Put it into this state, if you will be truly a christian. Fasten it to the cross of Jesus. Pierce it through with his nails and with his thorns. Make it drink of his vinegar. Take from it its pleasures; draw out its blood and strength.

Since this is our condition, since we by the beneficence of our Saviour are dead, in such a manner as we have now explained; you clearly see, christian, that the conclusion of the apostle evidently and necessarily flows from it, namely, that we should not seek any more the things which are on earth. For since we have in Jesus Christ put off that carnal and vicious life, for the maintaining and welfare of which earthly things are subordinate, who does not comprehend that it would be an insufferable folly for us to amuse ourselves still with them? It would be an error as ridiculous as if one went hunting after game, or buying precious stones and garments, for a person either already dead, or at least in the agony of death. Such a person has no more need of those things, they being good only to feed or decorate that life which he no longer possesses. Just so, christian, do you act, who labour so ardently in seeking after and acquiring riches and honours, and other goods of the present world. All this is the equipage of a life which you no longer have. The flesh, for whose delight and adornment those goods serve, is dead, or at least death-struck in you. It is crucified with the Lord; and a crucified one has nothing to do with meat, or jewels, or other things of the earth. "Thou fool," said our Saviour to the rich worldling in the gospel parable, "this night thy soul shall be required of thee: then whose shall those things be which thou hast provided?" Luke xii. 20. As if he had said, being dead, he could no more enjoy them. Christian, how is it that you do not consider, not only your dying before long, but that you are, to speak correctly, dead already—that there is no carnal life for you any longer—so as to conclude that you have therefore no need of all this earthly pelf, which with so much pain you scrape together? I confess that while we are on earth we cannot altogether be without it. But neither can you deny, that for living as a christian here we need but little of it, and for a little time, because we have little left us of that life for which it is necessary. Let us proportionably have little affection and adherence to it. Let us use it, but for necessity, and not for delight. Let us look upon the world with the eyes of pilgrims, taking only so much of it as is requisite for our passing on. Let us set before us the example of the life which our Lord led on earth, during the days of his flesh; for indeed it is the pattern of that life we should live here below after our regeneration. He sought neither the glory, nor the pleasures, nor the riches, of the world. He adhered not to any one of those things, but used what was necessary for his food and raiment with great sobriety and frugality; not tasting the fruition of it, and so little fearing to be deprived of it, that instead of the glory of the world, he voluntarily suffered extreme ignominy; poverty and nakedness, instead of riches; torments and the cross, instead of pleasures. And so you see, my brethren, how the consideration of our being dead in Christ Jesus should turn us aside from coveting and seeking earthly things.

II. But the life we also have in him should no less set us at a distance from them; and this the apostle sets before us, in the second place: "Ye are dead, and your life is hid with Christ in God. When Christ, who is our life, shall appear, then shall ye also appear with him in glory." It seems that the first words tend to prevent an objection, which might be made to the apostle, upon his saying that we are dead. For how does this consist with that which he asserted before, namely, that we are risen with Christ? If we are risen, we live; and if we live, it is not true that we are dead. But this difficulty is easily resolved. For, first, the life to which we are dead is the life of sin and of the flesh, as we have explained it; whereas the life to which we are risen in Jesus Christ is the life of Christ and of his Spirit. The one is the life of the old Adam, and the other of the new. Now it is not incompatible that one and the same person is deprived of the former, and possessed of the latter. Nay, on the contrary, it is not possible that such as live in the former manner should also live in the latter; and as in nature the generation of one thing naturally presupposes the corruption of another, so in grace the life of the second Adam necessarily infers the death of the first: so that from our being risen with Christ, it is so far from following we are not dead to the flesh, that, on the contrary, it thence necessarily follows we are dead to the flesh; it not being possible to affirm the former without supposing the latter, nor to place the life of Christ in us otherwise than by the death of Adam in us. An inevitable necessity requires the one to die that the other may live in us.

As for that life which we acquire by our resurrection with Jesus Christ, the apostle grants that it belongs to us, and that in this sense it may be said of us that we live, as he says frequently both of other believers in general, and of himself in particular. Yet, notwithstanding, he shows us again that this life of Christ is not manifested and completed in us; that it is for the present hidden in God with Jesus Christ: so that in this respect it might be said of us, while we are on earth, that we live not; and that we have not yet the life to which Christ has raised us; after the same manner as he shrinks not to say elsewhere, that our being saved is in hope, and we yet wait for the adoption, Rom. viii. 23, 24; as if we had not hitherto received the salvation and adoption of God. For the right understanding of this mystery, we must consider briefly what the apostle here says of it; and, first, what that life is which he calls ours; secondly, how it is hid in God with Jesus Christ; and then, lastly, what shall be that manifestation of this life which he promises to us at the appearing of Christ.

The life of the faithful is that which Jesus Christ gives them when he receives them into his communion, instead of the life he takes from them. That which he takes away was impure and vicious; this is pure and holy. That was natural and earthly; this is spiritual and heavenly. The principle of the former was a carnal mind, and an irregular concupiscence; the principle of the latter is a divine faith, and a just and reasonable love. The one consisted in a vicious enjoyment of the flesh and of the earth; the other is a sweet and a legitimate possession of the Spirit and of heaven. And as the former was mortal and perishing, no less than the flesh and the earth, from which it drew its nutriment; so the other is incorruptible and eternal, according to the nature of the Spirit who quickens it, and of heaven that maintains it. The fruits of the former were sin, shame, and damnation. The fruits of the latter are righteousness, honour, joy, and immortality. That first life, therefore, was rather death than life, being such as after a short and feverish agitation could not terminate but in eternal sufferings. And this, on the contrary, is alone truly worthy of the name of life, which name also the Scripture ofttimes purely and absolutely gives it; as when it says, "He that hath the Son hath life; and he that hath not the Son of God hath not life," 1 John v. 12; and that he that believeth in the Son is passed from death unto life.

But then, you will say, since we do believe, how is it that the apostle says our "life is hid with Christ in God," as if it were not in ourselves? Dear brethren, I answer, it is very certain that the Lord Jesus even at present gives all his true members the seeds and principles of this blessed life, which he casts into their hearts by his gospel; and preserves, augments, and fortifies them there gradually by the power of his Spirit, and the use of his word, his sacraments, and his discipline, to make them bring forth the excellent fruits of love and holiness. By reason of these beginnings, and of the sure title they give them to the plenitude and perfection of that life, they are said in Scripture to live, and to have eternal life at present; as we attribute to a plant the name and life of its species when it has taken root, and put forth some bud and verdure, though it has not yet attained its full growth and perfection. Yet it must be acknowledged, that the complete form of this life, which consists in perfect holiness, robed with glorious immortality, resembling that which Jesus Christ, our elder Brother, brought up out of his sepulchre at his resurrection, and carried with him into heaven forty days after, will not be communicated to us but in the world to come. For here, as you know, both our knowledge is imperfect, and our sanctity weak; as the apostle says, "Now we see through a glass, darkly," 1 Cor. xiii. 12. We have not yet apprehended, nor are already perfect, Phil. iii. 12. By reason of this he compares our condition here to childhood, during which there is imperfection in our thoughts, words, and judgments; whereas in that other blessed world we shall see face to face, and know as we are known, 1 Cor. xiii. 12; and all that is in part being done away, we shall be at the highest pitch of perfection, and in the full vigour of a truly mature age. Besides, this body, which makes up a part of our being, is yet subject to the laws of natural life, nor can it be sustained but by the use of earthly and corruptible elements, and by the low functions of eating, drinking, and sleeping: whereas that divine life which we have in Jesus Christ is freed from all these infirmities, requiring a celestial, and in some degree a spiritual body; which is preserved by the sole virtue of the quickening Spirit, without needing the assistance of any earthly and perishing things. Whence it appears that, to speak properly and exactly, we shall not have this blessed life till after the last resurrection. We now have but a title to it, and the first buddings, rudiments, and initials of it; which the apostle excellently signifies, when speaking of himself and of all the faithful, he says we "have the first-fruits of the Spirit," Rom. viii. 22; that is, to use Peter's words, as it were the first lineaments of this divine and spiritual nature, of which the Lord has made us partakers, 2 Pet. i. 4.

Wherefore Paul here at once very truly and admirably says that "our life," that is, the life we have by Jesus Christ, "is," for the present, "hid with Christ in God;" because the Father yet keeps it in his hand, reserving the full display of it in us until the time he has foreordained in his counsel. Until then it does not appear, but abides hid in God, as a sure and certain effect in its true and immutable cause. The world sees it not in us; and its first-fruits which we now have are so unknown to it, that, far from believing we have any life more excellent than its own, it accounts us, on the contrary, the most miserable and despicable creatures on earth, and thinks our life to be foolishness, and mere frenzy, and judges that its end will be without honour, as the author of the Book of Wisdom well expresses it, chap. v. 3. Indeed, God most frequently puts this heavenly treasure into earthen vessels, and chooses for this blessed life persons weak and contemptible, and such as are of no consideration among the men of the world; as Paul expressly observes, 1 Cor. i. 26—28: neither is there in them, more than was formerly in their Head, either form, comeliness, or anything that should induce those who see them to desire them, Isa. liii. 2. To which may be added the afflictions which extremely disfigure them, and darken the little lustre which they have. Amidst such inferiority and infirmities, it is hard to discern a single ray of that glory to which they are destined. In times of great temptation they themselves entertain doubts of it. And notwithstanding the Spirit who quickens them, most clearly, and with the strongest evidences, reveals for their consolation the perfections and wonders of their future life; yet they see and taste so small a portion of it, in comparison of what they shall have in the end, that it might well be said their life is hid in reference to themselves. And thus John informs us: "Beloved, now are we the sons of God, and it doth not yet appear what we shall be," 1 John iii. 2.

But we must not forget what the apostle here adds, namely, that our "life is hid with Christ in God;" whereby he signifies two things: first, that Christ is yet to a certain degree and in some sense hidden, with respect to the glory of his person. For though his salvation and dominion have been discovered by his gospel to every creature, both Jews and Gentiles; yet having withdrawn his raised and glorified human nature into the heavenly sanctuary, and from thence governing his kingdom by the secret operations of his Spirit, his person remains concealed from the eyes of the world. The great veil of the heavens, which environs the sanctuary into which he is entered, hinders us from seeing his glory, how sparkling and radiant soever it be. Secondly, the apostle signifies by these words that our life is properly and directly in Christ; that he is its source and its cause; and that in a twofold sense: the one, because he merited it for us by his sufferings; the other, because he produced and formed it in us by his Spirit; by reason of which he is called the Author and "the Prince of life," Acts iii. 15; and John says that life is in him, John i. 4. Then, again, our life is in Christ, as in its original pattern, wherein at present exists the true and perfect form of that sanctity, glory, perfection, and immortality, in which the life wherewith we shall be invested consists. Wherefore he is termed our elder brother, our principle or beginning, and our first-fruits, as we have said at the commencement of this discourse. Whence a great and a firm consolation is provided for us against all the tempests of the present world, when we consider that, however sad and frightful at times our desolation is, yet we live in God, and in his Christ. Christ is the sacred and inviolable stock that bears us, in which the sap of our life is perfectly safe, above the rigours of winter and heat of summer, and all other perils which threaten us. God is faithful, and Christ is living; and it is not possible that either the one should deny himself, or the other die. Since then the Father is the depositary, and the Son the stock of our life, let us assure ourselves, that though we feel it but feebly and faintly in ourselves, yet we possess it, and shall eternally have it, so as nothing shall be ever able to extinguish it. Let this sweet hope sustain us, and cause us to wait patiently for the term of that full and entire manifestation which the apostle in the sequel promises us: "When Christ, who is our life, shall appear, then shall ye also appear with him in glory."

His calling Christ our life is a noble expression, full of force and emphasis; similar to that which Jeremiah uses, when, speaking of the Lord's Anointed, he calls him "the breath of our nostrils," Lam. iv. 20, to signify that it is upon him our whole life depends, and that (if we may so say) it is by his sacred mouth we draw our breath. Thus the apostle's assertion, that Christ is our life, does not simply signify that he is the cause and author of our life, but that it fully and wholly depends upon him; that without him, and separate from him, we have not a drop nor spark of life; and that it is in him alone we have all the being, all the motion, and all the feeling which indicates the life of heaven. In very deed, it is he who has merited it for us by his death. It is he who has brought it to light by his gospel. It is he who has showed us a most accomplished pattern of it in his person, at his issuing out of his sepulchre. It is he who has given us the first-fruits of it by his word and Spirit, and preserves and increases them in us by his benediction. It is he who keeps the fulness of it for us in his treasury on high, as being the true Father of eternity. And, lastly, it is he who, taking this glorious life out of his heavenly cabinet one day, will put it on us with his own hand. Besides, we possess neither the beginning nor the perfection of it but in him, and by the benefit of our communion with him, because we are his members and branches, which cannot live but as united to their head, and incorporated in their vine.

The apostle therefore says, that when this sovereign and only author of our life shall appear, "then shall we also appear in glory." He has appeared once already, but in the flesh, as the apostle says, "God was manifested in the flesh." He shall appear again a second time, but in glory. This second appearing he means when the Lord Jesus descending from heaven with the host of his angels, and seating himself on a judicial throne, shall openly show to all the creatures of the world his glory and Godhead, which the heavens that contain his flesh on high, and the weaknesses that cover his mystical body here below, now hide from the earth. "Then," says the apostle, "shall ye also appear with him in glory." When this sweet and happy season arrives, you, as plants in the spring, shall receive your life, which, from that sacred stock in which it is now preserved, shall be diffused into you, and into all other branches of this vine of God, and crown you in an instant with its eternal verdure. The glory of which he speaks signifies the light, the perfections, the wonders, and the pomp of beatific life; perfect knowledge of God, love, sanctity, and joy; the immortality of our bodies, their beauty, their brightness, their strength, and impassibility; and indeed all the portions of that infinite good, the grandeur and excellency of which we shall never distinctly comprehend till we possess it. We shall then appear in this glory, first, because, in addition to the first-fruits of it, which we have, Jesus Christ shall give us the fulness of it, which we have not. Undoubtedly the greatest and most illustrious part of his glory, which now remains hidden in him, he then shall shed abroad upon us. Secondly, because the world, which now despises and treads us under foot, shall then see us in this glorious state. As Christ, our Head, shall be seen with astonishment by those who pierced him; so they who now outrage his members shall then see them in their glory, and be constrained to change their opinion, and to acknowledge those for children of God and his saints whom, in the present world, they deride and ridicule.

Thus you see, beloved brethren, what kind of life it is which Jesus Christ promises and communicates to his faithful ones, namely, the fruit of our faith, and of that divine food which we have taken this morning; the life of angels; the crown of saints; a pre-eminent and eternal felicity in conjunction with a pre-eminent and immortal glory. This is the rich treasury, the living and inexhaustible spring, of our consolation and sanctification. Judge, I beseech you, what manner of persons they should be who have so high and divine a hope, and whether it is not reasonable we should withdraw our thoughts and our affections from earth, to elevate them to heaven, since there our life is, and thence we expect our chief happiness. Christian, you that have a title for heaven, are you not ashamed to long for earth—you that are destined to a life which perishes not, to labour for the meat that perisheth—you that in Jesus Christ have the substance of true and solid happiness, to run after shadows? How much more generous and constant are the children of this generation in their vanity! Those among them who are of noble extraction, and especially such as are brought up in hope of a crown, would not labour in trade, or degrade themselves by mean conduct; and there are nations who totally refrain from commerce with other men, and account themselves defiled and profaned by having but touched a plebeian. And you who are the offspring of heaven, a child of the Most High, a brother of his angels, and an heir of his kingdom; you, that are nourished with divine manna in the hope of a heavenly life and an immortal crown; how have you the heart to grope in the mud and heap up dung—to intermix with the most miserable bondmen of the earth, and the profanest workers of iniquity? A king's son once refused to contend in the public games because he saw no kings do it. Christian, remember the dignity of your name; separate yourself from the exercises and diversions of the people of the world. Leave them the earth, out of which they came, and to which they shall return. Enter not into so ignoble and sordid a race, the race of mammon, in which you see none run but children of the earth, and the brood of vipers and serpents. Purify your minds and your bodies; never defile them with base and earthly thoughts or actions. Say not, "What shall we eat? what shall we drink? wherewithal shall we be clothed?" These are the thoughts and cares of bondmen. These are the discourses of pagans. This is all they seek. You, who are christians, and whose life is hid in Jesus Christ, seek his kingdom and his righteousness. Let this be your ambition, and all the desire of your souls. Let this divine life, and the glory with which it will one day crown you in the sight of heaven and earth, be night and day the object of your thoughts. Possess yourselves of it now with a holy impatience. Begin betimes to live as you shall live eternally. Let the contemplation of God, let the love of his beauties, let the meditation of his mysteries, let considering of and conversing with his Christ, be your employment and refreshment in the present world. Sanctify this earth during the time you tarry on it, and change it as much as possible into heaven, adorning it with an angelic life and conversation. This is the way to make sure your crown; for it will not be given in heaven but to those who have desired and sought it in the time of their abode on earth. None shall reap eternal life but they who have sowed to the Spirit. No man shall have fruition above but he who has hoped below; and no man hopes here below but he that cleanses himself from the filth of vice. He that hath this hope in Jesus Christ purifieth himself, says John. Represent incessantly to yourselves this glorious coming of the Son of God. Consider that he will not long delay. "Yet a little while, and he that shall come will come." Consider that he will come suddenly, as lightning, which in an instant shines out from the clouds; and as the thief, who comes at the moment he was least expected. How great will our confusion be, if he should surprise us in the disorder of our worldly affections and occupations! But God forbid that this should befall us. He has waited sufficiently for us. Let us employ that little time which is left us with so much the more care, the less care we have shown for that which is past. Let us watch, let us pray let us be doing. Let us work out our salvation with fear and trembling. Let us lead lives worthy of the name of christians, which we bear; worthy of the Master whom we serve, of the food he has given us, of the love he has borne us, and of the glory he reserves for us; cleansing ourselves from all filthiness of flesh and spirit, and waiting with a holy joy and settled patience for the revelation of this great God and Saviour, to his glory and our salvation. Amen.

SERMON XXXIV.

VERSE 5.

Mortify therefore your members which are upon the earth; fornication, uncleanness, inordinate affection, evil concupiscence, and covetousness, which is idolatry.

DEAR brethren, in all the designs of our lives, the end is the principle which moves us to act, and the rule of our actions. The fair aspect it presents inflames our hearts, and kindles in them the desire of possessing it; which thereby awakens the powers of our souls, and causes each of them to employ its ability and industry in the pursuit; the understanding gives its light to discover and make a due choice of means fit to conduct us to it; the will, and affections, and other faculties of our nature which depend upon them, use their operations to gain these means and set them in motion. All this is done, as you know and experience daily, only to attain the end we have proposed to ourselves. The ends at which men aim are infinitely different, and often contrary to each other, and consequently their courses also are very dissimilar; as if some went east and others west; or some took their way southward, and others their march northward. Yet notwithstanding such various intentions and endeavours, they are all incited and led on in the same manner; not one of them but the desire of some end which he loves has seized and swayed to action, and at length induced to take the course he steers, according to his zeal for its attainment, and the judgment which his understanding makes of means proper to bring him to it. The end therefore being the first spring that sets us going, the principle of our motions, and, as it were, the north star of our course, the guide and measure of our actions; you see, my brethren, that it infinitely concerns us to take it right; and having once taken it, to have it continually before our eyes, in order to refer and address all our labours to the same. Wherefore our Lord condemns those as unadvised and injudicious persons who enterprise a design without having first duly considered it; without having sat down, and taken their counters in hand, and exactly calculated the cost; that is, without having maturely and composedly examined what the thing is which they desire, and what abilities they have to attain it; as that ridiculous builder who laid the foundation of a tower, and was then constrained to relinquish it, not having wherewith to finish it. For this reason also the professors of moral philosophy, that they might rightly instruct their scholars, have been wont to set before their eyes the felicity of man, that is, his end, to enkindle a love and desire for it in their hearts; and then they proposed to them the means to be used to obtain it.

Such is the method which the holy apostle has followed in this part of his divine discourse which we are expounding. He showed us at the entrance heaven, and Jesus Christ, who reigns there, sitting at the right hand of his Father; together with that life, and immortality, and glory which he keeps for and promises to his faithful ones. This is the end to which we should tend. "Set your affections on things above," said he; and I persuade myself there is not a man so stupid and barbarous, upon whom an object so good and desirable does not make impression, and possess with love and a secret desire to obtain it. Now, though the splendour of so noble and so sublime a happiness should, as soon as it appears, extinguish all that fallacious appearance of earthly things in which the children of this world vainly seek their good, and which they foolishly take for the end of their lives; yet the apostle, to preserve us from this error, and fully inform us of our true end, has further expressly advised us not to place it in things here below. Mind not the things, says he, which are upon the earth. Having therefore each of you settled this divine end of your lives in his heart, according to the apostle's doctrine, look at it continually. Let it be night and day before your eyes. This thought alone is sufficient to direct all your steps; to govern all your actions; to purify your souls; to render you invincible against all your enemies; to preserve the peace and joy of God, and maintain his consolations in you amid the greatest storms. Yet this does not satisfy our apostle. Not content with having marked out our aim to us, and showed in general what we ought to decline, he details minutely the means we are to use for arriving one day at that blessed heaven whither he had elevated our hearts. He discovers and declares to us, one by one, the rocks and dangerous passages of our course, and, finally, goes over the most part of our duties in conducting this grand design. He begins with vices of the flesh and of the earth, the two most pernicious pests, and most contrary to the design on which, by the grace of God, we have entered. The apostle therefore commands us to commence an exterminative war, to fight, to weaken, to kill, and to destroy without pity, all that we perceive in ourselves to bear any affection or inclination to them: "Mortify therefore your members which are upon the earth." The Lord be pleased to bless now the voice of his apostle, and sink these words, which himself formerly inspired, so deep into our souls, that they may be at this time effectual to our sanctification; eradicating those accursed passions out of our hearts, which cannot live nor fructify there without dishonouring the gospel, and depriving us of that heavenly life to which we aspire.

The exhortation, you perceive, contains two parts: the first of which commands us, in general, to "mortify our members which are upon the earth." The other represents to us, in particular, some of these members of our old man which we are to mortify; namely, "fornication, uncleanness, inordinate affection, evil concupiscence, and covetousness, which is idolatry." These are the two heads which, the grace of God assisting, we will consider in this discourse: first, the apostle's general exhortation; and then, in the second place, the vices which by name and expressly he commands us to mortify.

I. As to the general exhortation, it is expressed in these words, "Mortify therefore your members which are upon the earth;" and to comprehend it aright, we must consider its meaning and coherence. An understanding of its meaning depends on that clause, "your members which are upon the earth." For every one sees that the term members cannot signify here, as it ordinarily does, the parts of which our body is composed, the hands, the arms, the feet, and the like; and as Paul uses it elsewhere, when he says, "Neither yield ye your members as instruments of unrighteousness unto sin," Rom. vi. 13. If this had been his intention here, there would have been no need to add, as he does, that these members are upon the earth, every one plainly seeing it. Besides, what he says in the sequel necessarily excludes this sense. For he puts uncleanness and covetousness in the rank of those members which he commands us to mortify; things which are not parts of our bodies, neither the being nor name in any way comports with them; but, indeed, vices of our souls, in which they properly reside, and whence they spread themselves over our whole nature, defiling and dishonouring it various ways. This addition leaves us no doubt but that these vices, and others like them, together with all filthy and shameful habits, from whence bad actions proceed, which he elsewhere calls the deeds of the body, and works of the flesh, are directly and precisely those members to mortify which he commands us.

But, you will say, how and why does he call them our members, seeing they are not the parts of our nature, which are all good and created of God, but rather the maladies, leprosies, and pests of our nature; supervening from without by the venomous breath of the old serpent, and his contagious intercourse—things that deprave, blast, eat out, and consume our being, so far are they from accommodating it, or adorning it, or affording it either the benefit or the beauty which the body derives from the diversity of members with which it is so admirably furnished? I answer, that this is very true, and that vices being the poison and ruin of our true being, cannot be properly called members of it; it being evident that a disease is nothing less than one of the members of the body which it afflicts. Yet, granting that, the apostle might, upon some other account, use this similitude, and compare the vices of human nature, in its present state, to the various members which constitute our body. Rightly to understand it, you will please to remember that it is a form of speaking very common in all languages, to compare those things to a body which are made up of an accumulation or collection of many parts, different indeed, but nevertheless united in order, some having a sequel and dependence upon the rest; hence we are accustomed to say, the body of an estate, of an army, of a town, of a family. A whole in which there is no distinction of parts, is called a mass; one in which some distinction is to be observed is termed a body. Hence it arises that the apostle compares that heap of vices and evil inclinations which exist in all men from their birth, and grows and gathers strength with age, he compares it, I say, to and gives it the name of a body. You may remember, in the former chapter he says that by our regeneration in Jesus Christ we have put off the body of the sins of the flesh. This same body of our vices is also often compared to an entire person, and called, as you know, the old man, or the old Adam. For, first, it is not one vice alone; it is a vast multitude of them; a mass of horrors; a hydra of evils; a mixture of many poisons; a heap of an infinity of orders; a complication of many maladies, which all at once make spoil of one and the same creature, and leave nothing sound or whole in it, from the sole of the foot to the crown of the head, to speak as the prophet, but cover it all over with wounds and bruises, with putrefied and inveterate sores. Then again, these maladies, though all pernicious and mortal, are different among themselves; there are infidelity, superstition, distrust, hatred, or contempt both of God and our neighbour, love of the flesh and the earth, pride, cruelty, sloth, luxury, intemperance, avarice, and a thousand such others. For who can so much as name them all? And though the confusion which always necessarily accompanies error and vice is truly very great among them, nevertheless there is some kind of order and sequence to be observed in them. For as knowledge should move and guide our nature, here ignorance governs this troop of monsters. Blindness is their guide, and error their director. And as in the right constitution of man the will follows the light of the understanding; here the will follows its darkness, and embraces those phantoms which the frenzy of its leader takes for solid realities. And as in the various diseases of the body a certain order and regularity is seen in their beginnings, their progress, and increase, nothing happening in them without cause; so in the sicknesses of the soul, they have their accesses, their inflammations, their returns, and their periods; that though there is nothing but a perpetual disorder, which displaces everything, and overturns all, yet all has its certain causes. Therefore, with much reason and elegance, the apostle compares this strange convention of numerous evils, which, though various, work with union and dependence, to a body; and each of those vices of which it is composed, as covetousness, fornication, and the like, to the members of a body.

He calls them our members, because the old man, which is made up of them, is wholly ours, and invests all the principles of our life from their root; it envelopes them, and mingles so deeply with them, that, so to speak, it is nothing but corruption and malady. This venom infects all the actions and impulses of our nature, its understanding, its affections and passions, together with the thoughts, words, and actions which flow from them; so that as our animal and natural life consists in the exercise of our members, and in their actions, in the same manner our moral life is nothing but a continual exercise of these vices, and of the sins they produce. This is clearly seen, if you consider the lives of profane and unregenerate persons; they are nothing but a continual exercise of vices, of ambition, of vanity, of covetousness, of luxury, and of sensuality, as they are addicted more or less to the one or the other of these sins; the perpetual flowing of a foul and muddy stream, which a corrupted spring daily sends forth, so that you cannot observe so much as one of its swellings or rollings exempt from its filthiness. And this may suffice for comprehending the reason why the apostle calls these parts of the old man our members. I do not agree with that interpretation which some propose, namely, that the members of our bodies, having been created of God, are ours only in respect of use, and not in respect of their original; whereas the members of the old man are ours, all manner of ways, having been made and formed in us by our own fault and naughtiness, and not by the hand of God, who created man upright and pure; man distorting and depraving himself. This idea seems to me more subtle than solid. For though the substance of it is true, yet it is so wide from the apostle's design in this place, that there is little likelihood he thought of it, when he here called the vices of our corrupt nature our members. Without doubt he does so only because it is in the exercising and acting of these vices that the carnal life of men consists.

For the remainder, if you remember what we said upon the preceding verses of the death of the old man in us, you will not think it strange that the apostle, after having said that we are dead, does not forbear to exhort us to mortify the members of this same life, which we have put off in Jesus Christ. For our being dead in this respect does not imply that the life of the flesh is entirely and absolutely extinct in us; (this will not be effected until we shall quit it at our leaving of the earth, and put on celestial bodies at the day of the resurrection;) but the Scripture thus speaks, first, because Jesus Christ has by his death, resurrection, and ascension into heaven destroyed and abolished all the causes that gave nutriment and sustenance to the life of the old man; and, secondly, because the old man has received his death-wound in each of us by the faith that ingrafted and incorporated us into Jesus Christ; so that if we persevere, it is not possible that he should recover. But this death of his, as we said, is not immediate. It is executed by little and little; and the exercise of a believer, during his stay here below, is to employ himself incessantly about it, daily to weaken and wound that flesh of his, which is already nailed to the cross of his Lord; to extinguish by little and little all the remains of its life; that is, to mortify his members, as the apostle here speaks. In this sense, you see, these two ideas are so far from having anything contrary or incompatible in them, that, on the contrary, the one evidently and necessarily follows from the other. For since we are dead in Jesus Christ, since the arrest for the death of our old man is past, since Jesus Christ has done on his part all that was necessary to execute it, since this flesh condemned is already fastened to his cross, it is evident that it ought to live no longer; and that, consequently, each of us should incessantly bestir ourselves to put it to death, by mortifying its members, beating down and weakening their vigour, driving deep into them our Saviour's nails and thorns, until they are effectually reduced to that state of death to which they were condemned, having no more motion or sentiment, or force, or life at all in us. Behold, my brethren, the thing the apostle means by these words, "mortify your members." To utter it in a word, he would have us weaken and extinguish the vices of our old man, and put them in such a state of death, that they shall have no more strength, nor vigour, nor motion.

But as this holy man's whole language is full of profound wisdom, I am of opinion he thus speaks to give a further blow to those seducers whose error he refuted in the foregoing chapter. These men, to recommend their discipline, declared that they did not spare the body; that they had no regard to the satiating of the flesh; that they opposed its pleasures, and humbled and mortified it. And you know that, at this very day, this is the language of those votaries who make christianity to consist in such exercises. They speak of nothing but their mortifications. Paul therefore here corrects the vain conceits of this error, and shows us what true mortification is, and that it is worthy of the study and exercise of the faithful. The members of the old man he instructs us to mortify, and not those of the body. Its vices, its fornication, and covetousness, and pride, we must quell and kill with blows, not our body. And as one of the prophets said to the superstitious of his age, who fasted, and afflicted themselves, and rent their clothes, "Rend your heart, and not your garments," Joel ii. 13; in the same manner, the apostle here opposes the internal mortification of sins, as only necessary and truly worthy of a christian, to the external mortification of the body, to which error did and still does confine itself. For, indeed, to what purpose is it to beat a man's breast, and rend his back, while sin in the mean time reigns in his heart? To what purpose is it to afflict the members of the body, while the members of the old man are left sound and whole—to stretch out the one upon the ground, and lie in ashes, while the others are in pleasure? It is not by a haircloth or a whip that vices are subdued. These things inconvenience the body, but surely do not improve the soul. They humble the outside; they hurt not within, but leave the old man there at full liberty, with his thoughts and lusts. And it is not without reason the apostle informs us elsewhere, that "bodily exercise profiteth little," 1 Tim. iv. 8. Experience has justified his words; the lives of those who addict themselves to such exercises being no better, yea, sometimes worse, than the lives of others. And it is not long ago since truth drew this confession from the pen of one of our greatest adversaries,* that such exercises many times injure men's spiritual advancement, because of a secret opinionativeness and pride which they beget and feed in some spirits, who become arrogant and haughty, and take occasion from them to despise those who lead a more moderate life. The apostle therefore would have us, instead of these childish and profitless exercises, to lay out our labour upon the mortifying of the members of the old man, that is, our vices.

To the same intent I refer what he adds, that these members "are upon the earth;" which is worthy of observation, whatever way you consider it. For, first, these vices are all upon the earth, if you respect either their rise, or their business, or, lastly, their end and desires. It is clear they all spring out of the earth, from admiration and connection with earthly things; they all creep on the earth, in its excrements or in its fruits, and rise no higher than its fumes and vapours; wretchedly cleaving to these sordid vanities, which they feel to fleet away and perish in their hands while they grasp them and are enjoying them. Where is covetousness? Where is luxury? Where is gluttony and ambition? For what do they seek? What do they desire? For what do they toil themselves? Surely you plainly see that the earth is their only element; that the metal which the one desires, and the flesh which the other longs for, and the messes which the third breathes after, and the vanities which are the passion of the latter; I say, you plainly see that all these are but earth, or fruits and productions of the earth. These members then of the old man fasten us to the earth, and not the members of this body; it is sin, and not simply this flesh. For as to our body, it needs but little for its preservation during the little time we pass here below, whereas the desires of vice are infinite. Whence it follows, according to the apostle's conception, that it is vice we are to mortify, and not the body; the members of the old man, and not those of the body.

* The Jesuit Petavius, l. 5. c. 3, De la Penit. Publique.

Then again, if you consider the places destined to be the abode of both natures, you will further see that the members of the old man, that is, its vices, are only upon the earth. There they make their spoil and exercise all their tyranny; there they live, there they die, there they rot, unprofitably consuming themselves in their own wretched filthiness. They have no place in heaven, where enters nothing but what is pure, where perfect sanctity lives and reigns eternally, crowned with immortal glory. But the members of our bodies, which superstition seizes and ridiculously afflicts, though they are for the present on the earth, and have need of its elements, yet they shall not remain there always. They shall be one day lifted up into the heavens, and enter into the sanctuary of God, and live on his manna, and partake of the fruits of the celestial tree of life.

Knowing now the meaning of this exhortation of the apostle, you may easily, without my saying any thing respecting it, comprehend the connection it has with the preceding words, which state that we are dead, and that our life is hid with Christ in God, and that we shall one day appear with him in glory. For since we are dead to the world, and called to the hope and the fruition of a heavenly life, which is hidden on high in Jesus Christ, and shall be one day manifested and given to each of us; who sees not that all this most strictly obliges us to draw off all our affections from the earth, and to cut all the ties that fasten us to it? that is, to mortify our members which are on the earth, all the vices that engage us and insnare us in the things of the earth.

It remains that we consider the vices or members, of the old man, which the apostle particularly names and expressly enjoins us to mortify: he mentions five in all; "fornication, uncleanness, inordinate affection, evil concupiscence, and covetousness." I conceive that the first four are related to one and the same head, and are but divers branches of one and the same stock, namely, luxury, or sensuality. Fornication is the principal species of them, the disorders of which are so evident and so well known, that no one can be ignorant of its nature. Uncleanness comprehends all the filth and pollutions which are contrary to the chastity and purity of our bodies, as incests, violations, and those other abominable furies of carnal passions, which transgress even the laws of nature, corrupt as it is. The word which we have translated "inordinate affection," signifies, literally, perturbation, or passion, in the original. But it is frequently used to express the passion of lubricity, and the filthy disposition of a voluptuous and effeminate heart, which easily receives the impression of all lascivious objects, and abandons itself to this kind of pleasures, and runs after and pours forth itself in a manner entirely to them. Evil concupiscence, which the apostle adds in the fourth place, is the source or the root of all this sort of vices. For though concupiscence is often taken in general for all irregular appetites and desires, whatever the objects are to which they are unduly carried; yet it sometimes signifies those in particular which respect the pleasures of the flesh, and we often use the word concupiscence in this sense in common language. Nevertheless I grant that in this place it may be taken in a larger extent, as importing inordinate coveting either of pleasures, or of profits and riches; because the apostle speaks here of covetousness also, and not of sensuality alone. He calls this evil concupiscence to distinguish it from that which, keeping within its just bounds, desires things lawful in a due manner and measure.

The last of the vices here touched by the apostle is covetousness, a vice no less known than the foregoing. Only the description he gives it is remarkable, in saying, "covetousness, which is idolatry." This title surprises us, every one well knowing that idolatry and covetousness are, to speak properly, two different sins: the first directly respecting religion and the service of the Deity, when men adore a thing which is not the true God, and render it those religious honours which belong to none but God; whereas covetousness is a moral sin, which consists in an excessive and immoderate adhesion to the goods of this world, makes men get them and possess them amiss, and contrary to the laws of justice and reason. These two things therefore being so different, why saith Paul that covetousness is idolatry? Dear brethren, I answer that he was in no wise ignorant of this, nor did he intend in this place to confound these two sins, which in many other places he most expressly discriminates and distinguishes; as particularly there, where making a list of the principal sinners who shall not inherit the kingdom of God, he sets down the idolater and the covetous severally, and each of them in his rank. But aiming here, in passing, to brand and blast this vice, and to give us a just horror of it, that we might not account it, as the greater part of men do, a light matter, and a lowness and weakness of spirit rather than a crime; he qualifies it with the name of idolatry, improperly, I grant, and figuratively, but very fitly for discovering its venom to us. And it is not here alone that he has done it. He brands this vice after the same manner in the Epistle to the Ephesians, chap. v. 5, where speaking of the covetous, he adds the very same thing, "who is an idolater." "Ye know, that no whoremonger, nor unclean person, nor covetous man who is an idolater, hath any inheritance in the kingdom of Christ and of God." Now this proposition, that covetousness is idolatry, may be pertinently explained two ways: first, by taking it as signifying simply that it is an abominable thing. For as there was nothing in all the horrors of paganism that was more severely prohibited of God, or more hated or abhorred among the Jews, than idolatry; hence they gave this name to everything which they detested, and I perceive that even to this day this form of expression is common among them; when they would signify that a thing is abominable, they frequently say it is an idol, or it is idolatry; so that we need not wonder if Paul, who follows the idioms and terms of the Jews' language, has said here, in a like sense, that covetousness is idolatry, to signify that it is a horrible and detestable vice. We meet with a similar expression, or rather indeed the same, 1 Sam. xv. 23, when the prophet, to show Saul how great the iniquity of the fault he had committed was, in not executing punctually that which God had commanded him, tells him that "rebellion is as the sin of witchcraft, and stubbornness is as iniquity and idolatry." There you see, by the names of the most abominable sins, witchcraft and idolatry, he signifies the heinousness of disobeying the voice of God, altogether as the apostle in our text expresses the atrociousness of avarice. I add in the second place, that though covetousness be not properly and formally idolatry, yet it has so much resemblance to it, that there is scarcely any other sin to which this name better agrees. The idolater looks on his idols with profound veneration; so does the covetous on his goods and coin. The one shuts up his idols; so the other does his. The one serves an image, and the other gold and silver; and when the idol is of either of these two metals, (as they frequently are,) they both serve the same thing, with this difference only, that the idolater serves it under one form and one way figured, the covetous under another; the one offers incense and sacrifices to his idol, the other immolates his heart and affections to his. Add hereto, that the covetous bears more love to the objects of his passion, and renders them more service, than he does to God; he puts his hope in gold, and saith to fine gold, "Thou art my confidence." And if you thoroughly examine his life, you will find that he serves none but mammon. Mammon is then his god; after the same manner as the apostle says elsewhere, that the belly is the god of voluptuous men: hence it follows that it cannot be denied but that he also is an idolater.

In fine, there are two things here to be observed. The first is, that under the names of these five vices, fornication, uncleanness, inordinate affection, evil concupiscence, and covetousness, the apostle signifies not merely the acts of these sins, which are also commonly called by the same names, but properly and precisely the internal habits of them, as seated in the soul. For they properly are the members of the old man; the acts are but his effects and operations. His meaning, therefore, is, that we cut them up to the very root; that we not only abstain from those vile actions to which they sway such as they possess, but that we mortify and extinguish them, to the end that these accursed sources of evil being once dried up, our life may remain pure and clean from all their filth. The other thing is, that we must not fancy the apostle meant to make here an exact enumeration of all the vices of the old man. He gives us but a small scantling of them, intending we should likewise mortify all the rest, as gluttony, drunkenness, and the like. For it would be no benefit to us to have cut off one of his members, if we let him live in respect of others. His life is our death, and while he preserves it whole in any of his parts we cannot be in safety. Let us labour, therefore, to extinguish it all. Eradicate all its lusts; repress all its stirrings; and smother all its sentiments. Let us make a deadly and irreconcilable war upon this whole brood of monsters. Spare we not any one of them. Let us exterminate them all as an anathema. Treating them as the ancient Israelites sometimes did the accursed nations of Canaan, and as the psalmist would have the little children of Babylon treated, desiring they might be dashed against the stones, Psal. cxxxvii. 9. It is in this case only that cruelty is laudable, and that a man may lay aside pity without blame. He that hath pity on the members of his old man is cruel to himself; to spare them is to destroy oneself, and to preserve them is to betray our own salvation.

This, then, my brethren, is the mortification which the apostle requires of us. Neither he nor any other of the ministers of Jesus Christ anywhere enjoins us to wear haircloth, or to disfigure our countenances with a multitude of fasts and watchings, or to go barefoot, or to put on a cowl, or renounce the use of any of the meats which God has created for our service; much less to cover ourselves with filth, or to gore ourselves all over with flagellations. God will one day say to those that amuse themselves in such mortifications, "Who hath required this at your hands?" Isa. i. 12; and, why have ye suffered so much in vain? Gal. iii. 4. The only mortification he demands of us is that of the old man; that we beat down our vices, and not that we rend our bodies; that we deface our passions and not our countenances; that we renounce our lusts, and not his gifts; that we give the discipline to our manners, and not to our shoulders. As for ourselves, my brethren, I acknowledge that we have renounced the mortification of the superstitious; the misery is, we do not practise that which was our Saviour's, though without it no man can have part in him or his kingdom; as the apostle intimates plainly enough here, where he does not own any person for a member of Christ risen, who is not dead; and elsewhere he affirms in express terms, that "they that are Christ's have crucified the flesh with the affections and lusts," Gal. v. 24. We amuse not ourselves in bodily exercise. No; but do we more heed that of the Spirit? We spare our hearts no less than our bodies, and do not treat the vices of the one any whit more roughly than the skin of the other. Men see sufficiently by the actions of our lives that the members of this old man, whom the cross of Christ has condemned to death, remaining very far from dead, are scarce wounded in us; that they are not so much as scratched; that they live in us in their full strength and vigour, and no more feel our Saviour's nails and thorns than if he had not died, or we had not believed in him at all. Our adversaries seek how to charge it home upon us, and it is the only one of their arguments that puts us to confusion. We easily answer all their other reproaches. There are none but this wherein our consciences force us to separate the cause of Jesus Christ and of his gospel from our own. For if his truth were to be judged of by the quality of our deportment, who could defend it, seeing the horrible disorder that generally appears in our lives? Let us consider only the two articles here touched by the apostle, unchastity and avarice. In conscience, is the one and the other of these two passions dead among us? Have they not as great a vogue as among the men of the world? Are the modesty of youth, the honesty of marriage, chastity and temperance, better practised here than elsewhere? Do the sordidness and eagerness of avarice less appear? Verily, (I am extremely ashamed to say it,) all is alike, except that those without confess, and chastise themselves, and macerate their flesh with some kind of fasts, and say their chaplet; whereby, at least, they show some sense of their guilt, though they apply ineffectual and ridiculous remedies to it. Whereas we, after committing the same faults, and dabbling in the same filth, come to present ourselves impudently here, without fearing God or having shame of men. And if the voice of the Lord, that resounds in this place, draw some sigh from us at our going hence, we return every one to our vices as pleasant and as obstinate as ever.

God is so good that he has hitherto waited for our repenting. But let us beware lest our obdurateness change his patience into fury, and constrain him in the end to punish such a refractory contempt of his word and his favours, and avenge the affront we show his gospel, by living so ill in such clear and divine light. Let us all descend into ourselves. Let us examine our carriage and our consciences. Let each one interrogate himself: Come, my soul, after so many months and years that Jesus Christ has so carefully instructed thee, what pains hast thou taken to conform thyself to him, and to imprint the image of his death and of his life upon thy behaviour? Hast thou nailed thine old man to his cross? Hast thou mortified his members? Hast thou deprived them of that wretched vigour which they display with so much efficacy in the children of disobedience? Do they leave thee at rest? or, when they begin to trouble thee, hast thou the courage to resist them? Does not avarice stretch out thine hand upon the goods of others? or does it not restrain thee from imparting of thine own to the poor? Hast thou not felt its vain solicitudes and fruitless melancholies—its insatiable cupidity and unbridled eagerness—and that impudence it has to despise and violate honesty, laws, and decency, for the satisfying its inordinate desires? But if avarice has not importuned thee, tell me, my soul, has not the lust of the eyes and the vanity of the flesh at one time or other insnared thee? Has not this traitorous Delilah lulled thee asleep? Hast thou guarded the glory of a Nazarene to which God has consecrated thee from her ambushments? Brethren, let us catechize our souls daily, and about our other duties as well as these. Let us not pardon them anything. Let us judge them righteously, and with inexorable severity; chastise them for all their faults; and, bringing them down at the feet of God, make them weep and groan in his presence. Let us reproach them with their ingratitude, and set before their eyes the benefits of God, and the offences with which they have recompensed him. Let us denounce also his judgments on them, and the horror of his dreadful vengeance; and not give them over until they have taken a full and firm resolution to return no more to their ingratitude. Above all, dear brethren, let us make them hate and detest those two pests which the apostle has today so solemnly condemned to die, namely, luxury and covetousness. Let us execute his just sentence upon these two passions, and cause them to suffer that death which they so many ways deserve. For, as to the first, it impudently profanes a body which belongs to Jesus Christ, was redeemed by his blood, washed with his heavenly water, fed with his flesh, and consecrated by his Spirit:—rends it from the communion of that divine body, of which it is become a member, to change it into one of the members of Satan:—bereaves it of its glory, and despoils it of its greatest honour; and drawing it out of heaven, whither God had called it, drags it into hell. I know well that men of the world flatter themselves, and extenuate this sin. And I am not ignorant that there are persons among ourselves who suffer themselves to be corrupted by these shameless sayings of the world. But why do we call ourselves christians, if we prefer the sentiments of the world, or of our own flesh, before the judgment of God? Paul, besides what he says of it here, protests aloud elsewhere, having spoken of adultery, fornication, and uncleanness, that "they who commit such things shall not inherit the kingdom of God," Gal. v.

21; and again, more formally, elsewhere, "Be not deceived; neither fornicators, nor adulterers, nor the effeminate, shall inherit the kingdom of God," 1 Cor. vi. 9, 10. Renounce either Paul, or this error of the world. If you persist in it, the apostle declares to you that you deceive yourselves; that is to say, instead of heaven, which you in vain hope for while you continue in this evil way, you shall in the end have hell for your portion, in the communion of devils, whose uncleanness you love more than the purity of Jesus Christ and of his saints. Neither may you plead to us the furiousness of this passion. God has provided for it, giving you an honest and a lawful remedy of it, namely, marriage. Why do ye not use it? But the love of libertinism, and the fear of an imaginary yoke, and an ambitious humour, withhold most men from adopting it; who would willingly say, what the doctors of Rome have not been ashamed to write concerning their priests, that marriage is a greater sin for them than fornication; whereby they sufficiently declare what opinion they have of this filth, since they prefer it before a thing which they rank among the sacraments. But the Epicureans among pagans, and monks among christians, have cried down marriage as much as they could, through a marvellous artifice of the enemy of our salvation, who rightly judged that by this pernicious doctrine he should involve a multitude of people in the villanies of luxury, and consequently in damnation. But if this vice be pernicious, the other, which Paul condemns here, is no less so. And his not being able to name it without giving it the title of idolatry evidently shows you what indeed it is. Ye covetous, let this thunderbolt break the charms of your illusion. Judge what a vice yours is, since the apostle calls it idolatry; and thereupon conceiving a just horror at it, renounce it for ever, and all those low thoughts in which it occupies you, to become henceforth liberal, charitable, beneficent, communicative, rich in good works. Instead of these perishing goods, which are exposed to the hands of men and the injuries of nature, labour to treasure up a foundation for the time to come, and to get together on high in the heavens those true and immortal riches which Jesus Christ, the Father of eternity, there keeps for us, and will one day give us, to enjoy the same for ever in supreme glory with himself and all his saints. So be it.

SERMON XXXV.

VERSES 6, 7.

For which things' sake the wrath of God cometh on the children of disobedience: in the which ye also walked some time, when ye lived in them.

DEAR brethren, if men had as great a measure of understanding and generosity as virtue has of beauty and attractiveness, nothing more would be required to induce them to love it and embrace it than exhibiting to them its image. This admirable object would quickly ravish their hearts, and in an instant kindle in them a sweet and everlasting flame of love, which would govern all the motives and sentiments of their lives; and consuming in a short time the vices and the foolish or unjust passions of their nature, fill their deportment with piety, honesty, and charity. One of those ancient sages of the world, whom they call philosophers, rightly acknowledged this truth, notwithstanding the darkness of his paganism, and said that if we could see virtue naked, that is, as it is in itself, it would inflame our souls with a marvellous love to it. For, indeed, what is there fairer and more amiable than virtue? the true and lively image of God, the supreme beauty of all beauties, the resemblance of angels, the fairest of all creatures, the only jewel of reasonable nature, the light of our souls, the ornament of our bodies, the advantage of our being above that of animals, the end and utmost perfection of the world, its just and legitimate governess, this vast universe having not been made and formed, but that she might happily possess it, governing and keeping it under her holy and divine laws! She sets all our affections in their true position, bowing them under the Creator, and raising them above the creature. She reduces all the faculties of our nature to their just symmetry, subjecting our passions to the will, and our will to reason. Resting content with the love of God, and the hope of his glory, she covers no unjust thing, and wrongs no person, no, not in desire and thought; but loves and obliges all men as much as she can, and sheds abroad continually upon them the sweet and innocent rays of her excellent light; remaining always holy, just, and honest without, always calm, peaceable, and happy within.

Who could look upon a thing so beautiful without loving it? Accordingly you may observe, that where there appears at any height, for instance, upon the throne of a nation, some image of it, though not fully to the life, nor complete, and everyway entire, but only rudely drawn, and in many respects imperfect, yet it fails not immediately to attract the eyes and hearts of the world. It proves the love and joy of the present generation, and the admiration of all posterity. Men bless it; heaven and earth delight in it; and the age that produced it is glorious by it; one single example of this nature being sufficient to adorn a whole country, and render the time in which it flourished for ever illustrious. What then would our delight be, if we beheld its true and accomplished image in all its lively colours, without defect, and without imperfection? It is true, God has portrayed it indeed to the life in the tables of his Scriptures; but the eyes of our souls are so dim, that we comprehend it only very imperfectly; and again, our sordidness and wretchedness are so extreme, that commonly we do not love things according to their inherent beauty and honesty, but according to the profit they afford us; and hate things not so much for their deformity and natural odiousness, as for the injury they may inflict upon us. This ignorance and mercenary humour, common to all men, is a cause why our Saviour contents not himself with proposing to us the beauty of holiness, and the deformity and disorder of sin, which is the proper mode of dealing with reasonable creatures; but accommodating himself to our infirmity, he incessantly sets before our eyes the good and evil which will redound to us from holiness and from sin, as we shall addict ourselves to the one or the other. He represents to us, on one hand, the happiness to which the saints are advanced who obey his will; and, on the other hand, the dreadful torments into which vice assuredly precipitates the wicked. And though his Spirit in part cures this ignorance and sordid disposition in as many as he regenerates, yet while we are on earth some relics of them remain in us. Hence he forbears not to use this method even with the faithful themselves.

You have a remarkable instance of it in the lesson of the apostle upon which we are now commenting. Having exhorted us to mortify our members which are upon the earth, that is, to renounce the defilements of luxury and avarice, to incline us to so just a duty, he represents to us in the text the judgments of God upon the obstinate slaves of these vices; they are things, says he, "for which the wrath of God cometh on the children of disobedience." He comprises in these few words the fearful and inevitable, but just, judgment of Heaven upon all those who, despising its goodness, abandon themselves to the one or the other of these vices. And then, in the following verse, he sets before our eyes, for the same purpose, the misery of our past life, which, as the life of children of rebellion, was sunk in the turpitude of these sins, and what infinite kindness God has shown us in drawing us from them; in which things, says he, "ye also walked some time, when ye lived in them." He does this to the end, that being seized with a just horror at our former state, and ravished with the sense of our present happiness, we might heartily renounce the service of our former masters, and live henceforth in that purity, honesty, and charity to which this new Lord calls us, who has vouchsafed to take us to himself, and to shed into us a new life and nature, as distant from our former one as heaven is from the earth. Now, as these are the two reasons which Paul urges for withdrawing us from those two principal vices of the profane; so shall they be, by the will of God, the two parts of this sermon. In the first, we will consider the judgments of God upon obstinate adulterers and covetous persons; and in the second, the misery of our former condition, when we lived in these vices, and could expect nothing in the sequel but the same effects of the wrath of God upon us. The Lord Jesus be pleased so to accompany our words with the virtue of his blessing, that those whom the loathsomeness, injustice, and horror of these vices have not been able to alarm, may now at least be plucked from them by the fear and terror of those dreadful judgments of Heaven, which are unavoidably prepared for all the children of rebellion.

I. The first part is expressed in these words, that "for these things the wrath of God cometh on the children of disobedience." I will not stay to inform you that, to speak accurately, wrath has no place in the divine nature. For who among you does not know that God is a Spirit most pure, most simple, and most blessed, enjoying an infinite calm and tranquillity; whose knowledge can never be surprised nor felicity disturbed, as we learn from Scripture, and even from reason? Now wrath, and such passions, consist in the agitation and emotion of the blood and spirits which stir them; being variously caused in us by our imagination, as the objects which it conceives are troublesome or satisfactory, present or future; the one producing in us sorrow, the other joy; some fear, and others hope; those of one sort wrath, those of another contentment or complacency. None of this, you perceive, can happen but where there is some mixture of humours and spirits, which, as they do not exist in God whose essence is most simple, it is impossible that any of these passions should agitate him, and least of all wrath, which is one of the most troubling and boiling of them all. But the Scripture, which addresses us in the dialect of children, often attributes these passions to God figuratively, to represent thus grossly the mysteries of his nature by the images of those things which are familiar with us, because they belong properly to our nature. Thus we must understand that which it calls the wrath of God. For it signifies by this term, not the perturbation of an agitated spirit, which cannot be in God, because of the sovereign perfection of his nature, but a just and reasonable will to punish the person that deserves it. This it terms wrath, by reason of some resemblance that appears between these two things. For a man who is in wrath eagerly desires to avenge himself upon the person who troubles him; and if it be in his power, he does it by causing him displeasure and afflicting him. So God treats those who violate his laws; he makes them suffer evil, and punishes or chastises them according to their deserts. But he does it without any perturbation, with a calm and composed will; whereas a man in wrath does it with emotion. And because we seldom act otherwise, there being few that avenge themselves without some trouble and rising of anger, it seems to us that it is the same with the Lord. Wherefore we say he is angry when he avenges his laws and punishes the crimes of his creatures, though, in reality, there is nothing in his action but the purpose and effect of an avengement, and not the disturbance of any passion. Hence it happens that the Scripture also speaks in a similar manner, frequently attributing wrath in this sense to God. And if you closely regard it, you will find that it gives this name either to the will which God has to punish men, the arrest and order which he passes for it; or to the effects themselves that follow his will, that is, the punishments he makes culpable persons suffer by his order. It is in this second sense the apostle intends it here, when he says that "the wrath of God cometh on the children of disobedience;" the wrath, that is, the judgments, evils, and executions of God, with which he punishes their rebellion according to the decrees of his avenging justice. He speaks in the same manner elsewhere, when he says that "the wrath of God is revealed from heaven against all ungodliness and unrighteousness of men, who hold the truth in unrighteousness," Rom. i. 18.

The expression, "the wrath of God *cometh*," some refer to the judgments which he frequently executes upon the voluptuous and covetous in this world; as if he had said that for these vices God has been accustomed to inflict his avenging strokes upon men. Others understand it of the punishment he will award them at the last day; and, indeed, the Scripture frequently so speaks of that great judgment, and the things which shall be done in it, saying that it cometh; elegantly signifying by that word the certainty and infallible coming of a thing which, it is true, as yet is not, but will not fail to be; as if it were a person who travelled, and was already on the way to the place where he would arrive. But I conceive the apostle encloses within this word the execution of both those kinds of judgments, signifying by it those great and dreadful torments into which God will plunge the wicked on the day of his anger, which will be the last effect of his wrath against sin, and also all the chastenings wherewith he scourges them in this life, which are, as it were, the first-fruits of his wrath, and so many samples and forerunners of his final vengeance. Paul comprises all this in his saying that "the wrath of God cometh." But this form of speech, that the wrath of God cometh upon men, is graceful and eximious, importing that the evils which arrive on earth do not happen at adventure, nor spring out of the earth itself, and their inferior causes simply, but issue from another source, namely, from heaven, which pours them down here below, as a storm or deluge, for inevitably enveloping and overwhelming those for whom they are appointed. They set forth from heaven, they travel towards us, and fall in the end upon the heads of evil-doers, by the order of the Most High, who marks out the whole course they are to take, and dispenses them with the same judgment that he does thunders, and tempests, and rains, which come upon us from on high by the guidance of his providence. And as you see, for the most part, in the works of nature, that these meteors do not come on a sudden, but after some signs which precede and presage their approach; in like manner it is ordinarily with the judgments of God. The thunder of his wrath, as well as that of nature, roars before it falls. God threatens the guilty before he strikes them, and almost always sends men some warnings, which are as couriers and harbingers of his wrath, to prepare them, that they may either divert it, by preventing it through their repentance, or receive it to remain with them. Thus, in Matthew, chap. xxiv., our Lord and Saviour predicts that the last judgment should be preceded by many great and terrible signs, for daunting the ferocity of sinners, and reducing them, if possible, to repentance; and in the same place he describes the prognostics of that dreadful vengeance which God was soon after to pour upon Jerusalem, and the whole nation of the Jews; and which failed not shortly to arrive punctually as he had foretold. He observes the same order still in his chastising families and nations; scarcely ever involving them in any calamity but he warns them of its coming before he executes it; which may be remarked, among others, in those horrible scourges which have made havoc in Christendom for these eight and twenty or thirty years.

But the apostle adds who they are upon whom the wrath of God comes, "upon the children of disobedience." It is a Hebrew form of speech, familiar in the Scriptures of both Testaments, to call that man the child of a thing who is addicted to it, and has in him the impression and tincture of it; as they call antichrist the son of perdition; that is to say, a lost man, one devoted and abandoned to perdition, who destroys himself in destroying others. And the Grecians, whose language is extremely polished and perfectly well formed, have not, however, disdained this form of expression, using often, the children of the Grecians, to signify Greeks themselves, and, the children of physicians, for physicians. In like manner here, these children of rebellion, of whom the apostle speaks, are the rebellious; such as disobey the will of God and his warnings, fiercely despise his counsel; those who, as Peter says, stumble at the word; who, whatever care God takes to declare his holy will to them, and to call them to repentance, will not hearken, but obstinately settle and harden themselves in their sins; by which they render themselves guilty of two heinous faults, unbelief and disobedience. For they reject the testimony of God, and esteem it a fable; sometimes even openly mocking it, which is a horrible outrage against the truth of God. Then next they disobey his voice, confirming themselves in doing what he forbids them, and in neglecting what he commands them. Such were those profane persons before the flood, who stubbornly despising the preaching of Noah, the herald of righteousness, continued impudently in the track of their corrupt ways; taking no heed to the admonitions of God and his servant. And Peter, by reason of this insolent contempt, terms them "disobedient," or unbelieving, 1 Pet. iii. 20. They did eat, saith our Saviour, they drank, they married, and gave in marriage, and perceived not the flood, until it came and bore them all away. Afterward the people of Sodom and Gomorrah did as much; who treated the holy and humble remonstrance of God's servant Lot to think on themselves, and the notice he gave them of the destruction of their cities, as raillery or frenzy, Gen. xix. 14. They remained obstinate in this profane security, until a deluge of fire and brimstone, pouring in a moment out of heaven upon them, and upon their abominable country, forced those dreams of their incredulity out of their heads, and taught them that there is nothing more true than the word of God, nor more false than an imagination of the security of sinners. Indeed, it is the crime of all those upon whom the wrath of God falls. They are children of rebellion, to whom may be applied (though to some more, to others less) what a prophet said to the Jews, They would not understand, but have pulled away the shoulder, and made their ears heavy, that they might not hear, and have hardened their hearts as an adamant, that they might not hearken to the law, and the words which the Lord of hosts sent by his Spirit, Zech. vii. 11, 12.

I acknowledge that this is properly the crime, first, of those who reject the gospel of the Son of God, the true word brought in by the Holy Spirit; and, secondly, of them that, living under the Mosaic covenant, rebelled against the word of God preached to them by Moses and the prophets. But I affirm, that even they are not exempt from it, who have sinned, or do sin, in the darkness of paganism. For though these people do not reject the word either of the gospel or the law, neither of which is addressed to them; yet they cannot be excused of contemning that other voice of God, which makes itself heard from heaven throughout all the earth, and sounds secretly in every man's heart, and privily calls them to repentance for their sins, to piety, honesty, justice, and rectitude. They profanely reject this sacred declaration of the Deity, without which God never left a man among the nations, no, not the most forlorn, or most desperately plunged in idolatry and viciousness, as the apostle teaches us in the Acts. They despise those admirable directions he gives them in the governing of the world, to seek him, feel him, and find him, Acts xiv. 17; xvii. 26, 27. They make light of the evidences he offers them in his administration of the universe of his eternal power and Godhead; and finally, abuse the riches of his mercy, of his patience, and of his long-suffering, by which his goodness invites and solicits all men to repentance, Rom. i. 20; ii. 4. Hence how astonishing, not only the justice, but even the gentleness and benignity, of God, who having right to punish men upon the first sin of which they are found guilty, yet does it not; but calls and invites them to repentance, and waits for them, and causes not his wrath to fall upon them, till, to the crime of their sin, they have added that of rebellion against that second way of salvation, which he in his loving-kindness offers them; namely, the way of repentance. For that which the apostle says here of fornicators, and the avaricious in particular, is true of all vices in general; the wrath of heaven cometh not upon them who are guilty, but when by their unbelief and obduracy they have made themselves children of rebellion; and there is not a sinner in the world, how great and enormous soever his crimes may be, but this good and all-merciful Majesty receives most readily to mercy, provided only he repent; according to the prophet's saying, that God willeth not the death of a sinner, but that he be converted and live, Ezek. xxxiii. 11; so that henceforth it is not simply sin that condemns men, but impenitence and unbelief. And the goodness of God so much the more gloriously appears in this his procedure towards them, for, that he might have the liberty of treating thus with them, he bought it (if I may so speak) at the price of the blood of his only Son, whom he (such is his goodness to us) delivered up to the death of the cross, to preserve the interests of his justice, which opposed this way of mercy which he determined to open unto men after their falling into sin. But this very thing shows us, on the other hand, how great the corruption of men is, and how untractable the furiousness of the passion they have for vice, in that, not content to be debauched from the service of their Sovereign, (which is of itself a horrible crime, and worthy of a thousand penalties,) they are so desperately in love with sin, that, to continue in it, they despise, and even reject, with an enraged insolence, all this holy and sacred mystery of the kindness of God, and are so enchanted and bestialized by the poisons of sin, that they prefer its short, vain, and wretched pleasures before divine grace and salvation, and less dread the wrath of their Sovereign, the society of devils, and the torments of hell, than the loss of that unworthy and shameful delight which the practice of sin, and the fulfilling of its lusts, gives them for a few days.

But we may further observe here the apostle's holy art, who, aiming to divert the Colossians from avarice, and the pollution of carnal pleasures, does not tell them that God will punish them heavily, if they do not avoid them: this language might have offended them, as implying that they had some inclination or disposition to such a fault. On the contrary, presupposing that this would not befall them, to give them dread of these crimes, he shows them their just punishments in the person of the unbelieving and rebellious; like a tender and a prudent father, who, to imprint a hatred of vice and drunkenness in the heart of his child, chastises the slaves in his presence, that the example of those vile and wretched persons may teach him what punishments he will deserve, if he, who is the son of his house, the heir of his freedom and estate, fall into any such disorder. For we must not fancy that because we have the honour to be allied to God, we may therefore commit with impunity those sins which the Lord punishes so severely in those that are without. Far from us be so sottish and so pernicious a conceit. God hates vice, and not persons; and whoever hardens himself therein, live he in any profession, pagan or christian, reformed or otherwise, he is a child of rebellion; and the advantage and excellency of the profession he makes is so far from exempting him from punishment, that it will aggravate it; it being most just, as our Saviour teaches us, that he who knew the will of his Master, and did it not, should receive more stripes than he who offends ignorantly, Luke xii. 47. And when a true believer falls through infirmity into some one of these disorders, (as, alas! happens but too often,) God plainly shows how much it displeases him, never failing to chasten it, except a prompt repentance prevent his rebukes. Judgment, says Peter, begins at the house of God, 1 Pet. iv. 17. And, He judges us, says Paul, and teaches us, "that we may not be condemned with the world," 1 Cor. xi. 32, as we shall assuredly be, if we persevere in sin without repentance and amendment. Hence the apostle, fearing lest some such imagination should abuse the Ephesians, gives them the same intimation, with express advice that they suffer not themselves to be beguiled with a false hope of impunity: "Let no man deceive you with vain words: for because of these things cometh the wrath of God upon the children of disobedience," Eph. v. 6.

But further, his specially threatening fornication, uncleanness, inordinate affection, evil concupiscence, and covetousness, in saying that "for these things the wrath of God cometh upon the children of disobedience," is not to signify that other excesses of such rebellious ones, as their cruelties, murders, ambitions, and similar enormities, should remain unpunished; on the contrary, he elsewhere expressly declares, that "the wrath of God is revealed from heaven against all ungodliness and unrighteousness," Rom. i. 18; and again, that there shall be "tribulation and anguish upon every soul of man that doeth evil," Rom. ii. 9. But he has denounced this wrath of God upon the luxurious and avaricious by name; because, among all vices, these especially provoke the vengeance of God, by reason of their vileness and enormity, and also for the disturbance they occasion in human society, the interest and preservation of which often forces the Lord to speed the execution of his judgments upon such sinners, and to punish them exemplarily in this world; that so by his severity he may cool the fury of those who, giving up themselves to the passions of these two accursed pests, would overthrow all order among mankind, if their rage were not repressed by some remarkable chastisement.

As for the truth of this sentence, "the wrath of God cometh for these sins upon the children of disobedience," since the apostle, who is the mouth of heaven, the oracle of Jesus Christ, pronounces it, no christian may doubt it. First, though they should go on altogether unpunished in this world, yet in the next it is certain that this burning wrath of the Almighty, which shall there manifest itself once for all, at the great and terrible day of the Lord, shall separate them for ever from the society of the blessed, and strike them down to hell, there to suffer eternally with devils the just punishments of their rebellion. For besides this clear text, the apostle in three other passages expressly enrols idolaters, fornicators, and adulterers among those who shall have no part in the kingdom of heaven, 1 Cor. vi. 9, 10; Gal. v. 21; Eph. v. 5. And elsewhere he says particularly of whoremongers and adulterers, that God will judge them, Heb. xiii. 4; and again, that God will destroy those who, by such pollutions, shall have destroyed or violated his temple, that is, their bodies, 1 Cor. iii. 17. In like manner, John assigns them "their part in the lake that burneth with fire and brimstone, which is the second death," Rev. xxi. 8. And as for the covetous, it is of them in particular Paul says that "the unrighteous shall not inherit the kingdom of God," 1 Cor. vi. 9; and elsewhere, that covetous desires "drown men in perdition," 1 Tim. vi. 9.

But besides this great and dreadful punishment which these vices will infallibly draw down at the last day upon the children of rebellion, they at present involve them in such various evils, that if the world's stupidity and passion did not blind it, it might easily perceive the truth of what the apostle affirms. For, first, that brutishness, and that horrible eclipsing of good sense and right reason, and that bestial addictedness to the vilest passions and actions, into which almost all the slaves of these vices are seen to fall, are an eminent and plain mark of the wrath of God upon them. The life of the debauched is nothing but a continual wandering out of the way. Consider Solomon, the wisest prince that ever lived, in whom shone so glorious and splendid a light of knowledge and wisdom, that he ravished his whole age, and attracted a great queen from the ends of the earth to come and behold his glory. After he yielded up himself to this infamous passion, he so lost all that force of spirit and judgment, that he became extravagant to such a degree, as to give up himself to idolatry, the utmost of all brutalities, in complacency to his concubines. The heathen poets, in their fables, to represent what is the ordinary sequel of this vice, make one of their heroes assume the habit and equipage of a woman, after he had once fallen into the snares of this wretched passion. It is an image of what still befalls those who suffer themselves to be taken in those snares: putting off by little and little all virtue and shame, they become effeminate, and so utterly lose their senses, that at length there is nothing so disgraceful, nothing so contrary to order, honour, and decency, but they readily do and suffer. The same is signified again by another fable of the same author, concerning some whom the potion of a sorceress transformed into swine and other beasts. The fable is pregnant with truth, and under feigned names and persons contains the history of the greater number of those miserable men whom fornication and adultery have bewitched. They lose heart, and judgment, and common sense, and commit so many follies and extravagances, that it is very easy to perceive it is no longer the soul of a man, but of a mere animal, that guides them. Hence comes so strange a metamorphosis, even in a Solomon, and in persons who otherwise seemed so cautious and prudent. Dear brethren, doubt not but that it comes from a secret judgment of God, who deprives them of that spirit and discernment of which they made such ill use, and who, so to say, degrading them from the rank of men, of which this vice has rendered them unworthy, drives them out among animals, delivering them up to a mind unfurnished with judgment, as the apostle elsewhere describes this dreadful vengeance of God, Rom. i. 21—23.

But besides mind and reason, who sees not that it also

usually takes away their strength, beauty, vigour, and health of body, bringing on them diseases which gnaw their very bones, diseases which rot and consume them before the time, and which, creating sharpest pains in all the parts of their miserable flesh, make it pay dear for the dishonest pleasures they have given it? Loss of goods is also one of the punishments which God commonly inflicts for this sin, permitting its very self to consume, by the irregularity of its foolish expenses, the means which are necessary for the support of the life of man and reduce those who serve it to a vexatious and shameful poverty. To which we may yet add numerous examples of tragical miseries, of which the lives of men are full, which God visibly inflicts on sins of this sort. It was for them that he sent the first deluge of water on the earth; and afterwards, a second of fire and brimstone upon the coasts of Sodom and Gomorrah. The debauches of Israel with Moab were the causes of the death of four and twenty thousand men, whom God consumed in his fury. And the tribe of Benjamin, though great and flourishing, was reduced to six hundred men, for the uncleanness of one of their cities. Who knows not that sometimes one man's adultery has caused long wars and ruined great estates? And among the instances of it, that is particularly lamentable of the Goths' empire; which having flourished in Spain a long time, was destroyed and utterly overthrown for a fault of this kind committed by one of their kings. This occasion brought in the Saracens, who, besides liberty and goods, took also the christian religion away from the most part of the people; introducing and maintaining Mahometism in those countries during many ages. It is not to be doubted but that the violent deaths and ruin of so many great ones, whom the world has seen, and still sees, perish with astonishment, are for the most part from the same source, even the debauches to which they have been carried. The accidents of particular families and persons infected with this leprosy are less marked; yet are they nevertheless very remarkable. And he that shall look narrowly into them, shall find in them admirable examples of the justice of God upon these kind of sins; and this in particular, that he commonly takes away his covenant from families where such disorders reign. I might easily show you similar footsteps of the wrath of God upon the covetous, whose unrighteousness he often punishes with loss of reason, of health, of honour, and of that very wealth which they love much better than their bodies, and even their souls; not to speak of the infamy which God sometimes pours upon them, and the horrible miseries into which he suffers them to fall, in their persons and in their posterity.

II. But I must pass to the other part of this text, and speak a few words upon it, and conclude. For the apostle, after this wrath of God, which he has represented as falling from heaven upon the children of rebellion, because of their pollutions and avarice, reminds the Colossians, that they themselves had formerly been in the same condition; "In the which ye also walked some time, when ye lived in them." To live in these sins is to have the principles of our life infected with their venom. To walk in them is to produce the actions of them. The one is the power and faculty of life, the other is the exercise and function of it. Having in oneself the principles and faculties of life, the apostle terms living, and by walking he understands a putting forth the actions of the same; as appears plainly by his saying elsewhere, "If we live in the Spirit, let us also walk in the Spirit," Gal. v. 25. A man that, for instance, is asleep, nevertheless lives, and has life, though he performs not the actions of it. As therefore to live in the Spirit is nothing else but to have the faculties and powers of our nature renewed, and as it were new-cast, and regenerated by the virtue of the Spirit of Jesus Christ; so, on the contrary, to live in sin is, in like manner, to have our understanding, and will, and the other powers of our nature, putrefied, and corrupted, and as it were, poisoned with Adam's sin, by the contagion of his flesh. And again, as those walk in the Spirit who exercise piety and holiness, and conduct all the actions and motions of their lives according to the will of the Spirit; so they, on the contrary, walk in sin who follow and fulfil its lusts, and employ themselves in no other exercise but serving it, and doing those evil works which naturally flow from its habits. But we have spoken largely before, if you remember, of this first life of old Adam, which the grace of the Lord Jesus has destroyed and mortified in us. We have only to observe in our way, that since the exercise of man in his state of nature before grace is to walk in vices and in grossest pollutions, it must be a great error to imagine that he should be able, in such a state, to produce works either meritorious, as some say, or preparatory to grace, as others pretend. All he does at this time, if you believe the apostle in the case, is not good, but to prepare for hell and merit the wrath of God; and to have any other opinion of it will be a diminution of the greatness of the grace of God towards us. Let us think then, beloved brethren, on that shameful and miserable state in which we naturally were, and should have continued for ever with the children of disobedience, living and walking in sins, the wages and fruit of which could be no other than eternal death, if the Lord, through his abundant grace, had not delivered us from such a condemnation. And remembering, as we ought, the greatness of the benefit he has conferred upon us, let us incessantly bless his mercy and goodness:—Thanks be ever rendered unto thee, O holy and merciful Lord, that us who were servants of sin, thou hast made free by thy Son, and given by thy Spirit to obey that express form of doctrine which has been delivered us by thy servants! Rom. vi. 17.

But as heretofore the vices in which we lived continually produced all kind of pollutions and sins; and henceforth, since the cross and grace of our Lord have dried up this source of impurity; let there no more appear any track of them in our manners. Let the holiness of that new man, of whose name and blood we boast, shine forth in all the actions of our lives. Above all, let us banish those two chief and accursed pests of luxury and avarice, for which you have heard before all the mouths of heaven opened to fulminate, against the rebellious who serve them, the curses of this world and of that which is to come. And if the ignorance of such as lived in error withheld not the wrath of God then from coming on them for these two kinds of sins, what must those expect now who commit the same crimes in the light of Jesus Christ? Sure, as much as the disobedience of the one is more grievous and enormous than that of others, so much more terrible will be the wrath that shall pour from heaven upon them, than all the judgments of God the world has seen in time past. Your ingratitude, christian, who so ill bear your name, and your disobedience, surpass in enormity all the unbelief, both of the first world and of ancient Israel; they rejected but the preaching of Noah and the ministry of Moses, whereas you outrage the gospel of the Son of God, and, as much as in you is, make him a liar. Yet you know how they were punished; you know the deluge which the crime of some brought upon all the earth: you know the abyss opened its mouth to swallow up others alive; heaven, and earth, and the elements were armed against them. If their punishment makes you tremble, why do you imitate their faults? yea, why commit you such as are more heinous and blacker than theirs? God is good and merciful, I acknowledge, but to *repenting* sinners. To those who mock at his instruction, and make a jest of his menaces, he is severe and inexorable. And if they amend not, they shall know sooner or later to their cost that it is a fearful thing to fall into his hands. May the Lord Jesus, whom we invocate, please to give us better things; so reforming this church by the power of his Spirit and of his word, that henceforth these crying sins be no more seen among us. Not the filth of luxury, nor the villanies of avarice which are the infamy of his people, the reproach of our profession, the scandal of such as are without, the shame of those that are within, and the ruin and eternal misery of those who obstinately continue in these vices; but rather let honesty, chastity, purity of body and spirit, charity, and liberality, and all other christian virtues, be seen to flourish and fructify in the midst of us, to the glory of God, to the edification of all within and without, and to our own salvation. Amen.

SERMON XXXVI.

VERSE 8.

But now ye also put off all these; anger, wrath, malice, blasphemy, filthy communication out of your mouth.

DEAR brethren, the philosophers have well and accurately observed, as each of us may perceive by his own experience, that besides understanding and will, there are in the souls of men two other inferior powers; one of which desires those pleasing things which sense presents to it, and the other flees from and avoids those that look troublesome. In the barbarous language of the schools, the former is called the concupiscible, and the latter the irascible. Both were given us by the Creator for our benefit, to act as two goads; one to urge us to seek and acquire what is profitable, the other to repel what is inimical. And in the primitive and legitimate constitution of our being, each of these two powers, exactly obeying reason, had nothing in their motions but what was good and just. Afterwards, by our fall, sin supervening, put them into great disorder; reason, which had lost its dominion, leaving them both without guidance, and most commonly favouring their errors instead of correcting them. For now desire embraces any gustful thing which is presented, and anger is stirred up against everything that seems displeasing, without heeding or following the judgment of right reason; whence proceed the greatest part of the sins and miseries of the life of man. Accordingly the principal task of those who would reform our manners, is to labour above all things to rectify these two powers of our souls, and gently to reduce them to the yoke of reason, that neither of them may ever move itself but as it commands or permits. Our apostle, therefore, having undertaken to give the Colossians, and other believers, who read this Epistle, the form of that sanctity to which the doctrine of our Lord Jesus Christ obliges, took care at the entrance to correct the movements of both these powers. He began with concupiscence and avarice, enjoining us to mortify all that is vicious in them, and religiously abstain from such excesses, which are the basest of carnal pleasures. To this end he reminds us of those inevitable punishments which these disorders always draw down from heaven upon the children of rebellion; that if the justness of the thing itself cannot persuade us, at least the fear of punishment may retain us in our duty. Having thus cleansed our concupiscence, he comes next to wrath; and, in the verse we have read, faithfully advises us to mortify likewise its passions, and all the evils they produce; that our lives may be not only pure and honest, but also innocent, calm, peaceful, and truly worthy of that Jesus Christ of whom we make profession, who is the supreme pattern of sweetness and benignity. "But now ye also put off all these; anger, wrath, malice, blasphemy, filthy communication out of your mouth."

Of the five things which he commands us to put off, "anger, wrath, malice, blasphemy, and filthy communication," the first four are either kinds or effects of that one and the same passion which we call *wrath.* The last refers to somewhat else; nevertheless he ranks it here with the other for a reason which you shall hear presently. This is the subject of which, by the will of God, we will treat in this sermon. Only before our coming to it, considering that there is nothing superfluous or useless in this holy apostle's language, we must discover, in short, the meaning and reason of those words with which he begins his exhortation, "But now ye also put off all these things." They depend upon the former verse, to which they most evidently refer. Paul there put the Colossians in mind of their ancient condition under the darkness of paganism, before the gospel shone on them. At that time, said he to them, you wallowed in the filth of avarice and luxury, as well as other children of the generation; ye walked and lived in these things. When, therefore, he adds here, "But now put ye off all these things," it is clear that he opposes to the time of their past ignorance the time of their present knowledge; their faith to their error; their christianity to their paganism; the day to the night, and the light to darkness; and by this means presents one reason to induce them to their duty, drawn from their present estate. For everything, as the wise man shows, has its time, and every season its business. The actions of the day are of one sort, and those of the night another; and a thing that becomes childhood is not sufferable in riper years. While you were in the darkness of paganism, that gross ignorance in which you lived rendered your vices less strange and more excusable, says the apostle. Now that you live in the light of Jesus Christ, with what excuse can you cover your faults any longer? The laws and customs of this divine kingdom, into which he has called you, are quite different from those of paganism, which you have renounced. Be content to have escaped out of them, and let it suffice you to have wretchedly lost so many years in the vices of ignorance, and to have so long fulfilled the will of the Gentiles. Now that God has graciously brought you to quit their errors, relinquish also their vices, and henceforth regulate your manners by the light which shines about you. Have no more intercourse with their works, since Jesus Christ has brought you out of their darkness. The apostle, in another place, explains this reason more at length, which he here only touches: "The night is far spent, the day is at hand: let us therefore cast off the works of darkness, and put on the armour (that is the garments) of light," Rom. xiii. 12. "Ye are all children of light, and of the day: we are not of the night, nor of darkness," 1 Thess. v. 6. "Old things are passed away; behold, all things are become new," 2 Cor. v. 17. Beloved brethren, would to God we had this consideration always before our eyes! It would be sufficient to divert us from the vices of the world, to which we suffer ourselves to be so easily carried. For if they rendered us guilty of death when we practised them in the darkness of ignorance, of what hells and maledictions shall we not be worthy if we commit them now? Now that we live in the light of the gospel, in the communion of saints and angels, who sees not, that if we live in sin, all these great advantages will turn to our misery, and that the honour of our knowing God and his Christ will serve no end but aggravating the guilt and augmenting the punishment of our sins? Let us then, christians, beware of abusing the gifts of God. Let us lead a life worthy of the condition to which he has called us, and of the age to which he has advanced us, and following the counsel of his apostle, now that we are under grace, in the kingdom of holiness, let us put off all these base lusts, which belong only to that state of error and ignorance out of which we are come.

The word which we have translated "put off" signifies simply lay by, or cast behind you; as when a man throws down a burden with which he was laden; and so our Bibles have rendered it, Rom. xiii. 12, where the apostle has used it; "Let us cast off the works of darkness. And it seems it would not have been amiss so to translate it in the passage before us, because it immediately follows, and "filthy communication out of your mouth," with respect to which the phrase "put off" is inappropriate, as you perceive. But this concerns the words only. The sense remains the same, that we rid ourselves of all the passions of vice, and cleanse our souls, our senses, and our mouths of them, and, as the apostle speaks elsewhere, using again the same word, cast off all this heavy and killing load of the sins of the world. We must not forget the word *also;* "ye also put off all these things." Some refer it to other believers, who strive after true sanctification; as if the apostle's meaning were that the Colossians should act like them. But nothing appearing in the text on which such an interpretation may be founded, I account it better to refer it either to the present state of the Colossians, which required, that as they formerly walked in vice, so they should now renounce it; or (which seems to me more appropriate) to the passions of which he had spoken. Besides fornication and covetousness, put off also all these things, namely, wrath and blasphemy, of which he now speaks. For indeed, friend, if you would be truly a christian, it is not enough that you rid yourself of one vice, you must also break with all the rest. As for restoring you to health, it is not sufficient to cure you of one malady, you must be healed of all; it being clear that while any one remains upon you, though you may be less sick than you were when you had many others with it, yet you will not be in health. Accordingly, to be a true christian, a disciple of the Spirit, and one of God's household, there is need of being delivered not only from some vices, but from all. If you have mortified the passions of luxury and avarice, I acknowledge it is much. But yet it is not all. Quit also those of wrath and blasphemy, since they alone are sufficient to destroy you, though you have no other. This is the instruction the apostle, after having ordered us to mortify the former of these vices, adds; "Put off also all these things; anger, wrath, malice, blasphemy, filthy communication out of your mouth."

The first two of these five words refer to one and the same passion, which we too well know, and indifferently call either wrath or anger. But in the language the apostle uses there is this difference, that the second of these words (which we have rendered wrath) properly imports a firm and fixed desire of revenge. The other which we have translated anger, or indignation, is the first trouble which arises in us when we enter into choler, that fire which on a sudden kindles in our spirits, and heating and agitating our blood, makes it boil about our hearts. One is the beginning, and the other the form and consistency of the passion. One is the first gust of the storm, the other the continuation of it. The one enkindles, the other burns, our hearts. The one puts fire to them, the other keeps it in. I confess this first boiling up of indignation is a less evil than formed wrath; but, notwithstanding, it is an evil. Wherefore the apostle would have us clear ourselves of them both. That malice which he adds, in the third place, is also, in my opinion, a certain kind of anger. I know well the word is of great extent, and signifies in general that venom and evil of sin which is diffused through any one of our passions, whichever it be. But here, as frequently elsewhere, I suppose it is taken for the malignity of anger; when a mischievous and vindictive stomach inwardly broods on its passion, and feeds its fire under the ashes, hatching some ill turn for the person it aims at, and waiting for opportunity to break out. Such a man works under ground, as miners do, and appears not till the ruin he prepares for his enemy is fully ready. His passion is like a stinted fire, that does not burn up till its season. Of all kinds of anger, there is none more black and malignant in itself, or more noxious and pernicious in its effects. Wherefore the apostle calls it malice, naughtiness, or malignity particularly; and it seems to be the same thing he elsewhere calls bitterness, when treating of the same subject, he says, "Let all bitterness, and wrath, and anger, and clamour, and evil-speaking be put away from you, with all malice," Eph. iv. 31.

But the apostle's indication of our duty is not obscure, and it would be loss of time to spend any more about its explanation. The sum of all is, that each of us in good earnest labour to practise it. For the evil that this holy man would take away from us is so common, that scarcely a person can be found exempt from it. I confess it is a great and almost incredible calamity, that man, who was created for humanity, and whose nature seems to be formed only for sweetness, courtesy, and gentleness, should be so corrupted, that there is no animal in the world more ferocious and malignant. The poison of serpents, the paws of lions, and the tusks of wild boars, are not more to be dreaded than most men's anger. I confess also, it is yet a much greater shame that christians, whom the discipline, spirit, and example of their Master should have transformed into sheep and lambs, that is, into creatures without gall and void of asperity; that they, I say, should be as much or more subject to the furies of this passion, than men of the world, brought up and fashioned in the school of vanity and error. But however shameful this fault is, we are constrained, by the very evidence of things, to acknowledge that it is too common among us. There are households where this demon of anger governs all at its pleasure, incessantly troubling the concord of husband and wife, the union of parents and children, and the peace of masters and servants. There is nothing done, nothing said, but in anger. You would say of these houses, that they are the fabled cavern of Æolus, where the winds shut up in it are heard night and day, roaring and blustering. There is no climate, no sea, no coast in all the earth, where storms are greater or more frequent. For whereas natural tempests happen but at some seasons of the year, in these miserable houses no calm is ever seen; and there needs but one petty action, one word, yea, one look, to raise storms of many days' continuance: as it is said of certain lakes in the mountains of Berne, that if one cast but a stone into them, the surrounding air becomes turbid, and is immediately filled with winds and clouds, which soon issue lightning, thunders, and excessive rain. Yea, there are some whose passion is so violent, that it cannot be kept within the enclosure of their houses. It issues out of doors, and without respect to the faces of those who pass by, without apprehension of scandal, audaciously shows itself in public, and acts its tragedies in the presence of all the world. Our anger will sometimes have even these sacred places for witnesses, in which it is not ashamed to make itself seen, and to utter the greatest indignities and provocations it can form before the eyes of this holy company, in the sight of God and his angels. And though this passion has always had too free course among us, I must needs say, my brethren, that quarrels, injuries, blows, fightings, even to the shedding of blood, were never seen so frequent as of late. O God! how can it be that the gospel of Jesus Christ, which is so assiduously and faithfully preached to you, should have so little influence upon you—should not only fail to plant in your souls that celestial and angelic sanctity, which it was sent to produce, but be unable even to restrain your deportment within the bounds of shame-facedness and decency? We are christians, and do things which honest men of the world, which disciples of heathen philosophy, would not have done. If they have not more holiness than we, it is certain they have more discretion.

But I forbear complaints, dear brethren, though, in truth, if there be any subject wherein grief, emotion, and even anger may be permitted, without doubt it might in this. Come we to the thing itself, and each condemning himself for his own particular faults, into which anger has heretofore transported him, amend for the future, and studiously endeavour to cure his soul of this passion. Let us give our hearts no rest until we have purged them of their gall, and tempered and seasoned them with the sweetness and gentleness of our Lord and Saviour. When we perceive in ourselves, or in our children, some inactivity of the liver likely to occasion diseases, or even some ill habit, such as stooping, or any other ungraceful posture of the body, we do our utmost to correct it, and readily submit to anything to attain our end. Would to God we were as careful to cure inclinations and passions contrary to a heavenly life! I durst say that we should not spend three months in such endeavours without wholly mortifying, at least very much mitigating and taming, this fierce and cruel anger, which causes so many mischiefs in the church and in the world. Though there were nothing but the apostle's prohibition, which so expressly orders us to quit and put off all kinds of wrath, this alone might suffice to give us an abhorrence of it. But the deformity and venom of the thing itself, if we consider it ever so superficially, will clearly justify this holy man's injunction, and force us to confess, that if he had said nothing of it, our own interest would induce us to do of our own accord what he enjoins us. For behold, I pray, what spoil this passion makes in the souls, in the bodies, and in the whole nature of those poor men upon whom it seizes. First, at the entrance it perturbs their judgment, and extinguishes the light of their understanding; and spreading its poisonous vapours through all the faculties of their mind, leaves them no clear sight of anything. In this agitation they conceive nothing but with perturbation, and see nothing but under strange colours; they no longer discern a friend from an enemy; they forget respect; they lose modesty and shame. It is no longer reason that guides them; but rage and impetuosity thrust them on, and carry them headlong. They are no longer men. Anger has transformed them into beasts or devils. The very heathen well observed it, saying, as we still read in their books, that this passion is a short madness, that it differs from madness in nothing but in its being of shorter duration. And the Holy Ghost makes the same judgment of it, when he pronounces, in Ecclesiastes, that "anger resteth in the bosom of fools," chap. vii. 9; and elsewhere he puts among the marks of a prudent, discreet man, that he restrains his wrath, and, as he expresses it, "covereth his shame," Prov. xii. 16; justly calling the follies and extravagancies which this passion causes us to commit, our shame.

For it stops not at that disorder which it creates within us. It soon breaks out and discovers its hideousness. For that blood which it has heated and made to boil about our hearts, rushing forth to the external parts, gives a new tincture to the countenance, and defacing its natural and ordinary form, and covering it, as we may say, with a strange and hideous mask, causes it to appear quite different from what it was before. The man has no longer his ordinary eyes. He has others of fire and of flame; a look wild and furious; a visage of a hundred colours, sometimes red, blue, or violet, sometimes pale and wan, according to the various motions of his fury. His veins swell, the storm within driving into them with violence a vast quantity of blood and spirits. His voice becomes rough, and loses its natural tone. His speech is confused and inarticulate, rushing forth all at once, without order and without distinction. He bites his lips, he grinds his teeth, and does a thousand other actions, so resembling the actions of demoniacs, that it is easy to see that the passion which torments him is a very demon. If you had seen yourselves in this state, I do not doubt that you would have been frightened at yourselves, and have hated the cause which so vilely disfigured you. But what need is there for any other glass in which to see the image of your anger than that with which your neighbours' passion daily presents you? That trouble, that fury, and that frantic demeanour, which you cannot without trembling behold in them, is a faithful portrait of your anger. When it seizes you, you are in no degree wiser, less frightful, nor insufferable than they.

But as in nature, when the wind and the thunder have roared for a time, there follow hail and fire, breaking forth from the clouds, and making dreadful havoc here below; so is it generally with the tempest of anger. After the noise and thunder of a thousand reproaches, and indiscreet, insolent, ridiculous speeches, in the end it usually comes to blows, which are dealt this way and that, without judgment or discretion. And when there happens to be resistance, when one angry man encounters another possessed with the same rage, as it frequently happens, how sad and shameful is the combat of two such furies, who, instigated by the demon that guides them, commit and suffer the vilest and deepest injuries! Who can utter the other evils which this execrable passion causes in mankind? It troubles the peace of families and states, stirring up in them sedition and wars. It is this that has invented duels, and, to authorize its rage, makes it pass for a point of honour; so blinding men, that they will have their honour to consist in offending God, and damning themselves, by shedding another's blood, and hazarding their own, which is undoubtedly not only the most false, but also the most foolish and senseless, error that ever was committed. It is anger that plots and executes most of the treasons, murders, and assassinations which are committed in the world. It is this that raises clamour. Quarrels and processes are its workmanship. It breaks the most sacred bonds of civil and domestic society, and teaches men shamelessly to tread under foot all laws, both human and divine. It instructs them to despise their own welfare and repose, in order to have only the satisfaction of disturbing that of other men. There is no vice that carries men so far, or that is apt to render them more unnatural. Judge what is its poison, and how cruel it is, since David, who otherwise was a kind and generous man, by only tasting a little of it, became so changed, that he marched forward his men with a resolution to pillage and massacre a whole poor innocent family, for the fault of only one man. And you know the inhumanity which this same passion induced Simeon and Levi to commit, causing them to put a whole city to fire and sword for one young man's indiscretion and folly. Consequently Jacob their father, even on his death-bed, calls them "instruments of cruelty," and curses the fierceness of their anger and the excess of their fury, Gen. xlix. 5, 7. But as anger easily thrusts on men, and precipitates them into all sorts of sins; so, on the other hand, it is infinitely contrary to piety and holiness. It drives the Holy Ghost, the author of all honesty and virtue, out of our souls. For he dwells not in noise and violence; and, as the Scripture says, in the history of Elijah's vision, he is not in those great impetuous winds that cleave the mountains, and rend the rocks, and shake the earth, 1 Kings xix. 11, that is, in wrathful souls. This Spirit loves peace and gentleness. Accordingly, he appeared to John Baptist under the form of a dove. By consequence, there is nothing that drives him sooner from us than the tumult of this blustering and tempestuous passion. And, indeed, instead of glorifying God, which is the first point of piety, wrath influences men to despise and blaspheme him. It disturbs and overturns all his service; it being impossible that a soul can pray to him and invocate him as it ought while it is in this agitation. And James tells us expressly that "wrath worketh not the righteousness of God," chap. i. 20. It is an enemy to charity; which desires the good and safety of its neighbour, whereas wrath wishes and procures his injury and ruin. It extinguishes modesty; it is incompatible with patience and humility; it expels consolation and joy. For what contentment or joy can there be amidst the tempests of this wretched passion, which disquiets all things, and keeps our spirits in a continual agitation? It makes us troublesome and tedious to every one; and instead of that sweetness and gentleness which should adorn our manners, it plants them with anxiety and ill humour, roughness, rashness, and sourness, as with so many briers, or nettles, which make all the world to shun our company, according to the wise man's counsel, "Make no friendship with an angry man, and with a furious man thou shalt not go," Prov. xxii. 24. We ought therefore to be obliging and accessible, and to attract strangers to us by our suavity, courtesy, and affability, for their edification; anger, on the contrary, drives away from us our very friends. For where is he who by choice, and without being by some necessity obliged, would live or converse with a person subject to this passion? Accordingly, you see, that whereas in other families every one rejoices at the master's arrival, in the house of an angry man, on the contrary, nothing is so much dreaded as his presence, because he always carries with him disturbance and tumult wherever he goes.

But if anger is troublesome to others, it no less incommodes its possessor, keeping his spirit in a continual state of perturbation, hindering all the sweet and delightful reflections of his mind, and breeding others which are black, cruel, and tragical. It disturbs his repose, robs him of his pleasures, and eats out his heart like a viper. And it is impossible that with all this it should fail to ruin, or at least to impair, the health of the body also, which, consisting in a certain equality and temperature of humours, and in the regular action and well-ordered motion of the blood and spirits, what can be imagined more contrary to it than this passion, which confounds and overturns all this inward economy of our bodies, turning and tossing our spirits, stirring and driving our blood hither and thither with extreme violence and rapidity?

Beloved brethren, these are the characters and principal effects of this passion. If reason, with which heaven has adorned your nature, be dear to you; if the presence of the Spirit of God and his holy image be valued by you as it ought; if you have any affection for the order, welfare, and happiness of your neighbours; if you take pleasure in their society; if you love the exercise of piety and other virtues; if you desire to preserve your souls in repose, and your bodies in health; obey the apostle's command, root out and put away anger from your hearts. Suffer not so dangerous a guest to lodge within you, the parent of quarrels and debates, the enemy of peace, the cause of hostilities and murders, the pest of families and estates, the storm of the soul, the poison of the understanding, the blinding of reason, the abhorrence of God and men, the ruin and hell of those whom it possesses. Never tell me that you cannot resist the tyranny of your irascible temper or that you did not begin first to be angry; but it was an injury from your neighbour which kindled your wrath, and you should pass for a man of no spirit if you suffered an affront without emotion and resentment. These are but pretexts and vain excuses, which cannot hide the shame of your fault. For as for nature, it forces no man to wrath: on the contrary, it loves harmony and tranquillity; and it would be a strange thing if we could not be men without having the impetuosity and fury of irrational animals. If the Creator has given you anger, he has also given you understanding to temper it, and reason to govern it, and the word and Spirit of his Son to mortify it. And as for offences received from your neighbour, the producing of them is no justification of your passion; it is a telling us the story and occasion of it. What, then, do you imagine that the Lord never forbids you to be angry but when nobody gives you cause? If your neighbour does well to be angry with you, why are you troubled at it? And if he does ill, why do you imitate him? His having begun is so far from justifying you, that I doubt whether this very thing will not aggravate your crime. For he who casts himself into an evil into which he saw another fall seems less excusable than he. His example, in which you might have seen the hideousness of this passion, should have kept you from it. And as to the judgment of men, if they be wise they will never impute it to you for faintheartedness that you have overcome your own animosity, since it is properly in this that the highest point of magnanimity consists; it being clear that the weakest persons of all, as children, and such as resemble them, are also ordinarily the most turbulent and choleric, and that true generosity is less subject to be moved and perturbed. But if the opinion of the vicious or ignorant affrights you, surely you have not yet profited much in the school of Christ, where the first lesson is to despise the fancies and maxims of the world, that we may rest in the laws and will of God.

Lay aside then all these nullities of excuse, and sedulously form yourselves to that sweetness and benignity which God requires. Shun all occasions of anger, and repel them when they occur. And to win this ground upon yourself, and to be always master of your own spirits, descend into yourselves, and consider well the meanness of your nature, and its little worth, that this body, which makes so much noise, is, in fact, nothing but dust and ashes; that this breath which animates it is a spirit, it is true, but full of ignorance and vanity; and, which is worse, covered with crimes worthy of hell, if God should judge you in rigour. Rid yourselves of that vain opinion of your nobility, of your riches, of your power, of your abilities, which puffs you up so much. For, to say the truth, all this is but a dream and a nonentity. Such a consideration would be excellent to keep down the stirring and boiling of your anger, which arises mostly from nothing but our presumption. For esteeming ourselves too highly, we consider it high treason for any man to offend us; and that to dare to attack us is a kind of impiety. But, on the other hand, let us also judge of our neighbours with more equity and reason; and think that, in the sight of God, they are as much, or, it may be, more than we; they are the workmanship of his hand, the portraits of his image, the redeemed of his Christ, and the denizens of his paradise, as well as we. If we looked upon them and ourselves in this manner, we should not be so easily or so vehemently troubled at their offences against us. Then, again, we should lift up our eyes higher, and meditate upon the providence of God, and take all the outrages which are committed against us as chastisements or trials which befall us by his order. It was this consideration that restrained David's anger on that just occasion for it which Shimei's insolence afforded: "So let him curse," said he, "because the Lord hath said unto him, Curse David," 2 Sam. xvi. 10. A noble speech! a holy declaration! If we act conformably with it, all the occasions of perturbation which men give us will be so many exercises of patience and humility. If they revile us, we shall bless them. If they outrage us, we shall bear with them. If they contemn and abase us, we shall put ourselves yet lower; and when they call us worthless people, we shall add, Yea, we are but dross and filth. If they reproach us with poverty or ignorance, we shall say in addition that we are but worms, conceived and born in sin.

This would be profiting by their outrages, and making the fury of other men the subject of our virtue and matter of our praise. It would be also of use, for forming us to meekness and patience, to have still before our eyes the patience and meekness of a Moses, of a David, of a Jeremiah, of a Stephen, and, above all, of our Lord and Saviour; "who, when he was reviled, reviled not again; when he suffered, he threatened not," 1 Pet. ii. 23; leaving us this glorious pattern, that we might follow his steps. We should also propose to ourselves the example of God himself, who is infinite goodness and love; who bears the blasphemies of his creatures, and instead of crushing them, causes his sun to shine on them, and waters their lands with his rain, inviting them so graciously to repentance. Which would you rather be, the disciples of this supreme Lord, and of his Son, and of his saints; or of those miserable vassals of sin whom the evil spirit possesses? And this again should sweeten our resentments towards those who offend us, even the remembrance that it is Satan who inspires into them all the evil which they say of us or do to us. They are but his instruments; while we attack them as if they were authors of the outrage; acting in this particular like dogs, which bite the stone that struck them; and touch not the person who threw it. The man is worthy of our pity. The devil, who instigated him, properly deserves our hatred. It is with this murderer that we should be angry. There anger would be just. But if by all these remedies we cannot prevent being sometimes incensed against our neighbours, at least let us stop when our perturbation boils up. Let us not add sin to our emotion, neither let the sun, as the apostle says, go down upon our wrath, Eph. iv. 26; but hold this for a certainty, that the shortest angers are the best.

Now if we can once divest ourselves of this wretched passion, we shall by the same means eradicate with it the other of blasphemy, or evil speaking, which Paul here annexes. For wrath is commonly the root from which this springs, or at least that which the apostle means, who uses a word that signifies a man's reviling his neighbour, a thing scarcely ever done but in anger. But all evil-speaking, whatever is its origin, is an accursed and deadly plant, the production and workmanship of the devil, the father of evil-speakers. For his trade, you know, is to calumniate, to detract, and to speak evil. They who do these things are his disciples, and it is from his suggestion and infusion that they derive the poison of their tongue. And as they have now part in his employment, so shall they one day participate in his torments; according to that which the apostle teaches us, that revilers shall not inherit the kingdom of God, 1 Cor. vi. 10. Indeed, since heaven is the inheritance of charity and holiness, what portion in it can detraction pretend to, which is so contrary to those two virtues, and gives them at once three deadly wounds; wounding and outraging by the same blow, not only the person of whom it speaks evil, but also the individuals to whom and by whom it is spoken? It wounds the reputation of the person of whom it speaks evil; and, as much as in it lies, deprives him of his honour, the most valuable of our external goods, and such as no riches can equal. It pollutes the ear of him who hears it, and makes such a poison glide through it into his heart as is apt to extinguish neighbourly charity: and fill him with suspicion, aversion, and hatred against his neighbour, even to the raising sometimes of scandalous and violent enmities and quarrels between them. Again, the detractor does not spare himself; but profanes his own tongue, and abuses it to the wounding and scandalizing of his neighbour; whereas it was given him by his Creator to be an instrument of benediction and edification. And this seems to be properly the consideration which the apostle here had in view. Having cleansed our hearts from the pollutions of wrath and malignity, he also purifies our mouths, taking out of them what is contrary to their sanctification. "Put away," says he, "anger, wrath, malice, blasphemy, filthy communication out of your mouth." And this is the reason why to blasphemy, or detraction, he adds filthy communication, because it defiles our mouths, and corrupts our speech, one of the most precious presents that divine bounty has made us; and that too that our mind might use it for the communication of its good and holy conceptions to others, for their consolation and edification. Whereas, on the contrary, he who indulges in filthy communication fills the ears of others with pollution, fouls the purity of their hearts, and shows the infection of his own; out of the abundance of which, as our Saviour says, his mouth speaks. For as offensive breath betokens some inward indisposition and corruption; so filthy and dishonest conversation discovers the impurity and unchastity that are in the soul of him who uses it. Hence the apostle in another place expressly puts this among other parts of christian sanctity, that our conversation be pure, chaste and honest; "Fornication, and all uncleanness, or covetousness, let it not be once named among you, as becometh saints; neither filthiness, nor foolish talking, nor jesting, which are not convenient," Eph. v. 3, 4. And again in another place, "Let no corrupt communication proceed out of your mouth, but that which is good to the use of edifying, that it may minister grace unto the hearers," Eph. iv. 29. Behold, beloved brethren, the divine doctrine of this great apostle. Let us conform our whole life to this; serving God in body and spirit; and sanctifying our hearts and mouths to his glory, and the edification of our neighbours; eradicating first out of our souls all asperity and bitterness, anger, wrath, and malice, and planting them with kindness, sweetness, and patience towards all men; then purging our tongues also from the poison of detraction, and from the filth of all dishonest communication, consecrating them as precious vessels to the praise of God, and the spiritual utility of men; to the end that there be nothing in our conduct but what is worthy of the discipline of our Lord Jesus Christ; and that after we shall have so walked in his fear, in all piety and honesty, he may hereafter receive us into his kingdom of glory, where, without holiness, none shall enter. Unto him, with the Father and the Holy Spirit, be all honour and praise, to ages of ages. Amen.

SERMON XXXVII.

VERSES 8, 9.

But now ye also put off all these; anger, wrath, malice, blasphemy, filthy communication out of your mouth. Lie not one to another.

AMONG the advantages which raise our nature above that of irrational animals, speech undoubtedly holds one of the first ranks; being the interpreter of the mind, the image of thought, the instrument of communication, the bond of society, the instructor of ignorance, the consolation of grief, the parent and nurse of friendship, and the sweetener of life. If you consider it in itself, what can be imagined more marvellous than this faculty, which represents, by a certain number of sounds, not very different from each other, the infinite variety of all those things which come into our minds; and bringing them out of that inaccessible and impenetrable recess, where our soul conceives and forms them within itself, makes them appear abroad; rendering that in some measure visible which was altogether invisible, and that corporeal which was purely spiritual? I well know that animals discover the passions and movings of their souls, joy, grief, fear, desire, by certain cries, which they utter as often as they are affected with them. But there is nothing in this that approaches to speech. For the voices of animals proceed from nature itself; whereas words of speech are an effect and an institution of reason. Those are confused and inarticulate; these distinct, and formed with excellent art. Those express nothing but the passions of a sensitive faculty; these represent the conceptions of the understanding. But speech is not less useful than wonderful. Without it, assemblies of men would be but so many herds of cattle, and their reason would do them little more service than if they had none at all. Whereas speech brings it forth, and renders it useful to us, communicating to many, and almost infinitely multiplying that which was at first in one soul only. For as a seal imprints its form upon all the drops of wax to which it is applied, so speech, gliding through the ear into the hearts of all that hear it, engraves on them that image of the mind and will of the speaker which it carries with it. It guides and keeps up the negociations, the treaties, the alliances, the arts, the sciences, and the instructions of men; and is the soul of their commerce and of their conversation, and, in a word, of all their humanity. It is by this that superiors cause themselves to be obeyed, and inferiors obtain the assistance they need; since it is this that makes both the will of the one, and the necessities of the other, to be understood. It is this that unites the souls of equals, and discovers what each has of reason and wisdom in himself, or of sympathy and aversion for others. It transfuses the soul of the one into the others, pouring into them their sentiments, their reasonings, their inventions, and their affections.

But as the abuse of the most excellent things is much more dangerous than that of things mean and common, so it is plain that the efficacy of speech is not less pernicious, when applied to evil, than useful and beneficial, when employed for good. It is as powerful to destroy as to edify; to infect, as to cure; and is equally capable of communicating to men health and sickness, life and death, according to the springs and intentions from which it is dispensed. Speech being of so great importance in the life of men, it is with great propriety that the apostle has taken care, in the rule he here gives us for our deportment, to cleanse it of the vices with which sin has polluted it. You may remember that, in the preceding text, he purged it of the poison of detraction, and of pollutions contrary to honesty, commanding us to put away blasphemy and filthy communication out of our mouth. Now, to the end that it may be thoroughly pure and legitimate, and truly worthy of a christian mouth, he takes out of it lying also, the most shameful of its defilements, and that which is most directly contrary to its natural constitution. "Lie not," says he, "one to another." And because, in the preceding sermon, shortness of time permitted us not to say all that we desired upon the two former vices of speech, we will resume that discourse now, with your permission; and treat, if the Lord please, of all those three sins of the tongue which the holy apostle has here forbidden; first, evil-speaking; then, in the second place, filthiness, contrary to honesty; and, thirdly, lying. May it please God to guide us in this discourse, and so purify our lips with the divine fire of that heavenly coal, with which he formerly touched those of his prophet, that henceforth our mouths may be so many living sources of benediction and edification, from which shall issue none but good and innocent, pure and honest, sincere and veritable speeches, to his glory, our neighbour's benefit, and our own salvation. Amen.

The apostle, in the original, makes use of the word "blasphemy," to signify evil speaking. For though the former term, in our tongue, imports words spoken to the offence of God, when things unworthy of his greatness, and holiness, and truth are attributed to him, or those which belong to him are denied him; or when that which is proper to his divinity is communicated to creatures; yet in the Greek, that is, in the language the apostle speaks, the word blasphemy generally signifies any offensive, injurious speech, whomever it concerns, whether God, or angels, or men. The truth is, this word, if we respect its origin or etymology, simply denotes injuring the reputation, or offending some one's honour; as the Greek grammarians have observed. Consequently, Paul uses it not only here, but also in other places to signify such revilings and detractions as are directed properly to men, and not to God; as when he says, in the first Epistle to the Corinthians, chap. iv. 13, "Being defamed, we entreat," it is in the original, being blasphemed; and when he enjoins Titus, chap. iii. 2, to admonish the faithful that they "speak evil of no man," it is in the Greek, blaspheme no man. That evil-speaking which he in this place so severely banishes from all christians' mouths is a vice so common, that no one can be ignorant of it. The world is full of it, and the church itself beholds but too many examples of it in those who make profession of her communion. But that no man may deceive himself, it will not be impertinent to represent the principal kinds of it. For as in a pestilence great diversity is found in the poisons which it comprehends, and in the manner in which they seize on human bodies; so is it with evil-speaking. It is a poison that has under it many different species, a mischief that puts forth various branches from one and the same root of bitterness. If you regard the form of it, one smites uncovered, another deals its blows in secret: the former reviles openly, and wounds the honour of a neighbour in his presence; the latter manages itself subtlely, and blackens his reputation in private, with so much greater effect, because it is in a place where no person appears to ward off its blows. If you consider the cause and occasions of it, some are incited to it by anger, others by hatred; some by a close envy, the most by a secret malignity of nature. Again, if you respect their design, some do it to avenge themselves of offences, which they believe they have received; others to satisfy their ill humour; and a third sort, merely to pass away the time. It may be, that the apostle here particularly aimed at open evil-speaking, which being pressed by the violence of anger, breaks out into revilings, since it is of this passion expressly that he speaks in the preceding words. Yet we must not imagine that he permits us to indulge in any species of this evil. For whatever difference there may be in other respects, this is common to them all, that they offend our neighbour, and deprive him, either in whole or in part, of the most precious of his goods, that is, his reputation. If it is a heinous sin to rob a man of his money, or his goods, or his lands; how much more grievous is his crime who attempts to bereave him of his honour, which is more to be esteemed than life itself! To which must be added, that goods may be recovered, and are actually very often recovered; but it is extremely difficult, and ordinarily impossible, for persons whose reputation evil-speaking has violated to repair the loss. And though the wound which an evil-speaker has given may be cured, yet it is scarcely ever so well and perfectly done, as to leave no scar remaining.

But besides reputation, which evil-speaking properly attacks, it most commonly takes away some of those other goods which depend upon it; yea, sometimes life itself. For both the affection of our friends, and the edification we afford our neighbours, being consequences of the esteem they have for us; who sees not, that the blows of a slanderous tongue deprive us of both these good things, in ruining that good opinion which was entertained of us? And if the person who takes in the poisons of evil-speaking be potent, and in high authority, how unspeakable are the miseries, and mournful the effects, which it produces! It was this accursed evil that formerly ruined David with king Saul, and drew upon him a long and a cruel persecution. It is this that in the courts of princes, and in the families of private men, daily causes thousands of disorders; that dissolves the best friendships; that sows distrusts; that enkindles hatreds; that embroils quarrels; that oppresses the innocent; that renders the fairest virtues hideous, and the greatest abilities suspected, often depriving church and state of the exquisite fruits that might be reaped from their being employed. And the psalmist, to represent this pernicious efficacy of evil-speaking, tells us that its detractions are "sharp arrows" shot by a strong man, and "coals of juniper," Psal. cxx; and Solomon his son, in a similar manner, compares the calumniator to a hammer, to a sword, and a sharp arrow; both of these expressions meaning that there is in nature neither metal, nor fire, nor weapon more dangerous than the tongue of a slanderer. It is of this we must properly understand what the apostle James says of the tongue in general, namely, that it is "a fire," yea, "a world of iniquity," which "defileth the whole body, and setteth on fire the course of nature and is set on fire of hell;" that "it is an unruly evil, full of deadly poison," James iii. 6, 8.

But setting aside the horrible effects which evil-speaking produces in all societies of men, its malignity and unrighteousness appear of themselves. For while the Lord desires us to consider the good qualities and perfections with which he has endowed his creatures, to the end that we might praise and esteem them, and imitate them, to his glory and our own edification, the evil-speaker looks upon nothing but their defects and vices. And as vultures fly over fair meadows, and flowery and sweet-smelling fields, and alight only on dunghills, and places full of carrion and infection; and as flies, without touching the sound parts of the body, fasten only upon sores and ulcers; so the evil-speaker, without so much as noticing what is graceful and happy in the lives of men, falls upon that which is weak and sickly in them. If they have chanced to stumble, as is very ordinary in this infirmity of our nature, it is upon this that he fixes; in this he takes pleasure, this he gladly exposes and publishes, amplifying and exaggerating it with his infernal rhetoric. It is by this he knows persons, it is by this he marks them out and describes them; as bad painters who represent nothing so exactly as the moles and scars of the faces which they draw, the deformity of the nose, the protuberance of the lips, and other such marks which they have from the birth, or receive by some accident. Charity covers sins, and forgets them; the evil-speaker divulges them, and remembers them perpetually, and takes out of the grave that which had been buried in oblivion, and brings it to light again. He loves pollution, and feeds on nothing but poisons and filth. And for this end he has always a sufficient store of such provision by him. His memory is a magazine, or rather a sink, where he heaps up the villanies, the sins, and the scandals, not of his own neighbourhoood, or his own quarter only, but of the whole city; yea, if he possibly can, of the whole state. It is from this diabolical treasury that he derives the subject of his sweetest thoughts and most pleasing entertainments. These things are his perfumes and his dainties. But he is not content only to rake together and lay open the imperfections which he finds in his neighbours; he is so malignant that he feigns more, and fancies some where there are none. He spreads it abroad for truth; and that he may persuade others of it, he artificially colours his fictions, giving out shows for truths, and shadows for substances. He so bitterly hates all good, that where he sees any he bespatters, blackens, and disguises it, and causes it to pass for evil. And as the snail sullies the lustre of the fairest flowers with its sordid slime; just so this bad man, by the poison of his malignity, defames the most grateful virtues, and turns them into vices. He takes valour for temerity, and patience for stupidity; justice for cruelty, and prudence for craftiness. Him that is liberal he calls prodigal, and the frugal person covetous. If you be religious, he will not fail to accuse you of superstition; and if you be free and generous, and far from superstition, he will accuse you of being profane. In fact, there is no virtue nor perfection for which this wicked man has not found an infamous name, taken from the vice that borders next upon it. To this iniquity he usually adds a base and black piece of treachery, when, to cause his poisons to be the more easily swallowed, he mischievously sugars them, beginning his detractions with a preface of praise, and with an affected commendation of the persons whom he intends to revile; protesting, at his entrance, that he loves and respects them, for the purpose of creating a belief that it is nothing but the mere force and evidence of truth that constrains him to speak evil of them. He kisses his man at meeting, and then murders him, as Joab formerly did: he crowns his victims before he kills them: a fraud which, notwithstanding its ordinary occurrence, is the blackest and most malignant that can be committed.

After these things, we need not wonder that God and his saints have abhorred evil-speaking, and universally treated it as one of the most detestable vices in the world. As for our Lord, he forbade it expressly to Israel of old, in those words, "Thou shalt not go up and down as a tale-bearer among thy people," Lev. xix. 16. "Thou shalt not raise a false report," Exod. xxiii. 1. And as for saints, David protests he will cut off the man that slandereth his neighbour privily, Psa. ci. 5; and among the qualities he gives the persons who shall dwell in God's holy hill, he says particularly, "he that backbiteth not with his tongue, nor taketh up a reproach against his neighbour," Psal. xv. 3. He curses this kind of people, and makes such vehement imprecations against them, in the 109th Psalm, as we do not find that he ever used against any other sort of sinners; and that truly with much justice, for there is no vice more malignant, or upon which the devil's marks are more express. Profit seduces the thief; pleasure precipitates the fornicator and adulterer; the honour of the world causes the murderer to commit his sin. The evil-speaker can allege no such motive; it being evident that he reaps from his vice no fruit at all. There redounds thence to him neither honour, nor profit, nor pleasure. "What shall be given unto thee," says the psalmist to him, "or what shall be done unto thee, thou false tongue?" Psal. cxx. 3; as if he had said that he could draw no advantage from it, and that by wounding and wronging others he got nothing for himself. It is a mere sin, a thing that has no allurement or temptation to excuse it; affording him that commits it nothing but the pleasure of the devil, who loves evil for its own sake, and seeks no other satisfaction in sin than the mere commission of it. Accordingly, you see that detraction and calumny is the proper exercise of the devil. At the beginning he slandered God to man, inducing him falsely to believe that God envied his perfection. He slanders men to God, mischievously accusing in his presence the service they render to him, of hypocrisy and impiety, as you see in the history of Job. It is for this he goeth to and fro in the earth, and walketh up and down in it. He takes all this pains only to find food for his evil-speaking, and matter for calumniation. And it is in this character John describes him in the Apocalypse, as "the accuser of our brethren, which accused them before our God day and night," Rev. xii. 10. There are then no sinners who more resemble this unclean and accursed spirit than evil-speakers. Their vice, and the pleasure they take in it, is the true and genuine image of Satan. Certainly the apostle accounted this sin so horrible, and so contrary to the legitimate and natural constitution of men, that he expressly puts detraction and evil-speaking among the fruits of that reprobate mind to which the Gentiles were delivered up because of their impiety, Rom. i. 29, 30. And elsewhere he instructs us to hold evil-speakers for anathematized and excommunicated persons, with whom we should have no commerce; but drive them even from our tables, as infamous harpies that would pollute our repasts. "I have written unto you," says he, "not to keep company, if any man that is called a brother be a fornicator, or evil-speaker; with such an one no not to eat," 1 Cor. v. 11. And as he banishes them from our communion in this world, so he expressly enrols them among those who "shall have no part in the kingdom of God," in the world to come, 1 Cor. vi. 10.

Flee then, beloved brethren, this mortal pest. Let not the bad examples and vain opinions of the world, which esteems and caresses it, deceive you. It is not by the examples nor maxims of this generation that a christian ought to shape his conversation. Whatever disguise may be put upon it, the intrinsic nature of this vice cannot be changed. The good companies in which it is found, the audience that is given it, the colours with which it is decked, do not hinder this evil-speaking from being blasted and accursed by our Lord, detested and interdicted by his holy ministers; the image and character of Satan; the daughter of envy, hatred, anger, and malignity; the mother of scandals; the incentive of discords; the scourge of all human societies, and at last an infallible inheretrix of hell. Flatter not yourselves, ye evil-speakers. Acknowledge the heinousness of your vice, and renounce it betimes; and know that otherwise you can have no part either in the grace or glory of Christ Jesus. Do not tell me that you say nothing but what is true. I doubt it much; it being difficult for an evil-speaker to tell any story of his neighbours, and not add something of his own. Yet suppose it to be so, and that the persons you censure are in truth guilty of all the turpitude you impute to them; you greatly deceive yourselves, if you think to be exempted from evil-speaking thereby. Doeg reported to Saul that he saw David with Ahimelech the priest, 1 Sam. xxii. And the Jews testified that the Lord Jesus had said he would raise the temple again in three days, Mark xiv. 58. Both were true; and yet the scripture condemns both Doeg and those Jews as very calumniators and false witnesses; and that justly, because their design in saying such things was to offend the reputation of those of whom they spake, and to hurt them. And, in general, whoever says evil of his neighbour is guilty of evil-speaking, though what he says of him is true, if he say it without necessity, in places, at times, and unto persons where there is no occasion to say it. To have discovered a fault is an evil, seeing that fear of scandal obliges us to hide it; and to wound by so doing the reputation of the faulty, is yet a further evil; it being evident that, except his salvation or public edification compel us, we ought not to awaken up nor stir such things. Neither excuse yourselves again, by saying that it is not a design to harm your neighbour, nor any hatred you bear him, that prompts you to speak amiss of him; but what you say is only to pass the time for want of better discourse. Wretched man, how would you deal with him if you hated him, since, having not, as you say, any ill will against him, you hesitate not to wound him in this manner? Your soul must needs be infinitely malign, since it makes a pastime of offending a person whom you hate not. As if a man, and he too a christian, had not matter enough to employ his tongue in celebrating the wonders of God, and perfections of his creatures, and as if it were not a much greater pleasure to speak of good than of evil. Renounce then, henceforth, this unworthy and infamous exercise, and leave it to devils, to whom it belongs, and to those baser and more impure spirits which resemble them. Put away all evil-speaking out of your mouth, and consecrate your tongues to the blessing of God and the edifying of men. Remember that excellent rule which the Lord has given us, "All things whatsoever ye would that men should do to you, do ye even so to them," Matt. vii. 12. There is not one of you that does not consider it a grievous offence to be slandered and ill spoken of; take heed, then, of treating others in that manner: cover their defects, if they have any; hide their faults, if they have happened to commit any; considering that you also are not exempted, and have need of the charity you exercise towards them. Employ yourselves in curing your own evils, rather than in discovering those of other men; and be more solicitous to correct your own defects, than curious to learn or publish theirs. Seek your contentment in your own good deeds, and not in the evils of others. And as it is not sufficient for a man that he does not steal, but he must also not conceal another's theft; so it is not sufficient, my brethren, that we refrain from evil-speaking ourselves, we must not so much as entertain the evil-speakings of others. Let us keep our ears as well as our mouths pure and free from this poison. Let us defend the absent, when they are ill-spoken of in our presence; favour their honour; and if we cannot otherwise do it, at least let us declare by our looks and countenance how troublesome detractive discourses are to us. This is often sufficient to silence them; for the vice is so weak and so shameful in itself, that, to beat it down, we need only to put it back. And this is the wise man's meaning, when he says, that as "the north wind driveth away rain, so doth an angry countenance a backbiting tongue," Prov. xxv. 23.

But having spoken of detraction, it is time to come to the other vice, of which the apostle here would purge our mouths. "Put away," says he, "filthy communication out of your mouths." This is so shameful a practice, that it has no place in the manners of the people of the world, who have ever so little honesty and gravity. And I cannot enough wonder at the extravagance of the ancient Stoic philosophers, who, maintaining virtue and honesty as to other things, still permitted their wise man to utter the most unseemly matters, shamelessly and without any cover whatever. It is certain that this licentiousness of the tongue cannot come but from the uncleanness of the heart; a soul chaste and truly holy, having all images of filthiness in abhorrence. And as this impurity of speech arises from corruption, so it evidently tends to it, infecting the minds and affections of those who hear it. And to this that Greek proverb, which the apostle elsewhere mentions, must be particularly referred, that "evil communications corrupt good manners," 1 Cor. xv. 33. For such discourses bring into our spirit filthy and abominable images, which, being received, make impression, and growing familiar with us by degrees take away the shame and horror we ought to have at dishonest things. I say as much of the unclean and perverse artifice of those who hide the impurity of their thoughts under covered speeches, and of a double meaning. For it is these sayings that sink deepest into the imagination, and do so much the more harm, as they are closer and more witty. And here I cannot forbear complaining of their abuse also who have administered auricular confession, as they call it, among christians, since it has been in use. For these men, under pretext of informing themselves of the state of the souls of those whom they confess, often put strange questions to them, and such as ill accord with modesty; whereby they commit two faults: the one is, that, contrary to the apostle's express prohibition, both here and elsewhere, they license themselves to say and hear dishonest things, changing the tongue of ministers of Jesus Christ, which should be nothing but sanctity and honesty, into a vessel of uncleanness, and their ear into a public sink of all the filth of a parish. The other is, that by such demands they open people's hearts to vice, and most dangerously put them in mind of evils of which they perhaps would never have thought. They are come so far in this matter, that, not content with corners, and the secret of their confessionals, they have also published great books upon this subject, which the most shameless would be hardly able to read without blushing. Such, among others, is that of a Spanish Jesuit,* in which he has heaped together so much filth, yea, some until now unheard of in the world, that other doctors of the Roman communion have been forced to make public declaration of the indignation and horror which this infamous volume has produced in them; though otherwise both the writing and the author are infinitely esteemed by those of his own order. As for us, my brethren, who are not in truth the companions, (as these gentlemen qualify themselves,) but the servants and disciples, of the Lord Jesus, let us form our mouths after his most holy example, and by the rules of his apostles. Let there be nothing in our language but what is honest, serious, and seasoned with the salt of grace, worthy of the ear, not only of the chastest virgins, but of angels themselves. For it is for this use that the Lord has given us a tongue, not to pollute the ears of our neighbours, not to teach them evils they know not, nor to induce them to discover to us what they know; but indeed, to edify them, to glorify the name of God, to show forth his wonders, and speak that language in this world which we shall eternally speak in that holy and glorious Jerusalem on high, into which no impurity nor filthiness shall enter.

There remains the third vice, of which the apostle would purge our speech, that is, lying—a vice that has greatest extent of all the rest, and such as men slip into with most facility; "Lie not," says he, "one to another." Truth is properly a correspondence and conformity of our conceptions with their object, when the image we form of it in our minds is such as the thing itself to which it has relation, as when we believe that a thing is or is not, which accordingly is or is not indeed. But truth of speech, to which lying is opposed, is measured by our conception, and not by the thing which is

* P. Aurelius.

the object of it; that is, our speaking is true when it accords, not with the thing itself immediately, but with the conception we have of it. It therefore frequently happens that a man speaks a thing which is false, yet does not lie; and, on the contrary, sometimes lies, though what he utters is in itself true: as when Jacob said that his son Joseph was dead, he lied not, because his tongue, in what he uttered, accorded with his heart, though the thing spoken was not true; and, on the contrary, if he had said, against the belief of his soul, that Joseph had been alive, he had lied, since he had spoken contrary to his own thought, though what he had said in that case would have been in itself true. Man, being a reasonable creature, is bound to endeavour not to possess any opinion or sentiment in anything but what is true and conformable to the reality of the thing, heedfully keeping himself from being surprised, and from falling into any error; yet this is not properly the duty which the apostle requires of us here. As indeed we must acknowledge, that through the weakness of our apprehensions and understandings, and amid that infinity of false appearances with which things or men continually present us, it would be very difficult, not to say impossible, to preserve ourselves from all error, and never be deceived in common life. The apostle demands of us a very easy and just thing, even that we never speak anything but what we believe to be true; and that in the commerce which we have with men our language be sincere and faithful, without fraud and without fallacy; naturally representing without what we conceive within; and that we never say one thing and think the contrary. The Scripture teaches us, in a multitude of places, that God hates lying more than any other vice; and the wise man says expressly, that lying lips are an abomination to him. Prov. xii. 22. The psalmist also, among other marks which he gives to the inhabitants of the hill of God, puts this for the very first, that they walk uprightly, and work righteousness, and speak the truth in, or as it is in, their heart, Psal. xv. 2; and elsewhere he says peremptorily, that God will "destroy them that speak leasing," Psal. v. 6. In sum, John proclaims in his Revelation, chap. xxi. 8, that the portion of "all liars" shall be in "the lake which burneth with fire and brimstone." Whence you see that the question here is not respecting a matter of decency, but a necessary duty, in which we may not fail without incurring perdition. The justice of it is so evident, that the sages of the pagans themselves have acknowledged it; leaving us in their books a thousand notable intimations of that roundness, and simplicity, and truth, which a man of honour and probity should inviolably observe in his whole life. For speech having been given to us by nature, or rather by the God of nature, to the end that we might signify and declare to our neighbours what we have in our hearts, it is clear that an abuse of it, to signify that which we do not think, is a violation of the law and institution of nature. And all true and generous minds have this sentiment so imprinted on them, that they cannot endure double persons; consequently, the prince of heathen poets makes his hero say, He hates no less than the gates of hell the man that says one thing, and hides in his heart another. Lying is a slavish vice, that proceeds either from baseness of spirit, from badness of conscience, or from vanity. Accordingly, you see, that it is extremely odious among all noble and civilized nations, and particularly in ours, where you know there is no outrage that is accounted more grievous, and more to be resented than to charge a man with lying. He who suffers it without justifying himself is held to be a man lost in honour, not among gentlemen only, but even among people of meaner birth; this generous and true sentiment having been handed down to us by our ancestors, that lying is an infamous thing, and the mark of a soul either wicked or witless; and that he who is not ashamed of it will make conscience of nothing; as, on the contrary, truth is the foundation of all virtue and honesty. But the Scripture shows us in two clauses what we should think of it, when, on the one hand, it names the devil the father of lies; and, on the other, calls the Lord the God of truth, and his eternal Son the truth itself; a consideration that renders the temerity of those so much the more insufferable, who, styling themselves the companions of Jesus, have not blushed to favour lying, by that doctrine of equivocations and mental reservations, as they call them, which they have published and practised in these last times. "But ye have not so learned Christ, if so be that ye have heard him, and have been taught by him, as the truth is in Jesus," Eph. iv. 20. He hates all lying and obliquity, in whatever manner they are disguised; and would not have his truth dishonoured by begging from its enemies' hand the help which it needs; that is, he would by no means have fraud and fallacy employed on his behalf; his providence is potent enough to defend it without such infamous succour. It is a maxim of his apostles, that we must not do evil that good may come. Lying is an evil contrary to the law of God and the ordinances of nature: there cannot therefore be any reason which gives us a dispensation to commit it.

Thus you see, beloved brethren, that which we had to explain concerning these three vices, which the apostle here banishes from the mouths of christians, evil-speaking, impurity, and lying. Let us obey his holy doctrine, and remembering that, according to James, "He that offendeth not in word, the same is a perfect man," let us diligently purge ours from all these impurities; and so govern our tongue, that it may not speak but of wisdom, nor pronounce but of judgment, and that all our discourses may be full of goodness, honesty, and truth; so that our Lord and Saviour, who is charity, purity, and sovereign truth, may own us for his, and after the conflicts and trials of this life give us part in the peace and triumphs of the next; receiving us into the society of those pure and holy spirits who live on high in the heavens with him, to bless him for ever: as unto him, with the Father and the Holy Spirit, the only true God, belong all honour and glory. Amen.

SERMON XXXVIII.

VERSES 9—11.

Seeing that ye have put off the old man with his deeds; and have put on the new man, which is renewed in knowledge after the image of him that created him: where there is neither Greek nor Jew, circumcision nor uncircumcision, Barbarian, Scythian, bond nor free: but Christ is all, and in all.

DEAR brethren, I know, and freely confess, that being called this day, through the goodness of God, to celebrate the memory of the death and passion of our Lord Jesus Christ, it is my duty, in order that you may be prepared for so important a service, to occupy your attention with things that relate to this great and divine mystery. But as I acknowledge that this is properly the service in which I should employ this hour; so I conceive that these words of the apostle Paul, which you have heard, and which occur in the chain of our ordinary text, are very suitable to that principal subject of our exhortation. For this putting off the old man, and this putting on the new, of which they tell us, are both of them the true effects of this death of our Lord, the remembrance of which we solemnize. If Jesus had not died, we should never have put off the old man, nor put on the new; since that without his death we could not have had the pardon of our sins, nor the grace of the Holy Spirit, nor the hope of immortality; all which are things absolutely necessary for divesting us of the old man, and reinvesting us with the new. But Jesus Christ having died on the cross, has there pierced through and fastened up our old man; and by the virtue of his sufferings created and formed in us another new man, as different from the old as heaven from the earth, and life from death. Therefore the apostle elsewhere concludes, from the death of Jesus Christ, the death of the old man in us, and the life of the new. "If one died for all," says he, "then were all dead: and he died for all that they which live should not henceforth live unto themselves, but unto him which died for them, and rose again. If any man be in Christ, he is a new creature," 2 Cor. v. 14, 15, 17. And in another place he says expressly, that our old man was crucified with Christ, that the body of sin might be destroyed, and that we, being dead to sin, might live to God through him, Rom. vi. 6, 11. Thus the death of Christ is at once the destruction of the old man and the production of the new; the one was abolished by it, and the other created. This flesh of the mystical Lamb, which God to-day presents to us, has slain our flesh and enlivened our spirit; and from his divine blood, in which the old man is drowned, has issued forth the new, created in righteousness and holiness; like as formerly the Israelite was seen to come out alive and glorious from that very gulf of the Red Sea in which the Egyptian lay sunk and overwhelmed.

But, O new wonder! as our Lord's flesh and blood is the principle that gives being to our new man, so is it also his nutriment. And as in nature, things are sustained by the same means which produced them; so in grace, the new man is preserved, increased, and strengthened by the same blood of Jesus Christ out of which he was formed. And that heavenly meat and divine drink, which you shall presently receive from the hand of God, are not given you but for feeding and perfecting your new man. I go yet further, and venture to say, that this new man, with whom the apostle would at this time invest you, is none other, rightly considered, than the same Jesus Christ whom we have put on at baptism, and whom we receive in the supper, propagated (if I may so speak) and portrayed in us by his own power; who transforms us into the likeness of his death and resurrection, because that entering into and dwelling in us, he forms in us a man like himself; who, as he did, dieth unto the flesh; and with him, leaves in his sepulchre all his old life, as an infirm and useless offal; and being enlivened with him, and adorned with his light, and endowed with a heavenly nature, leads thenceforth a spiritual and glorious life. Thus you see that the body of Christ was crucified and his blood shed; and that both are given us in the supper, to divest us of the old man, and invest us with the new. This is the end and fruit of all that mystery, to the participation of which you are this day called. Consider, then, that the best preparation you can bring to it is a serious meditation upon what the apostle here informs us. He exhorted the Colossians before to mortify the vices of their flesh, and all the infamous passions of that pagan life which they had previously led in the darkness of their ignorance; as fornication, covetousness, anger, evil-speaking, impurity of language, and lying. Now, to root up these and other such vices, and to comprise all the parts of sanctification in a few words, he commands us to put off the old man with his deeds, &c.

There are others who take these words for a reason of his preceding exhortation, drawn from that state into which Jesus Christ had put them by baptism; as if his meaning were, that they are obliged to renounce the vices he had been forbidding them; since in their baptism they put off the old man, on which these vices depend, and of which they make up a part; and put on the new, which is contrary to and incompatible with them. Whether you understand it thus, or take the text simply for a prosecution of the preceding command, showing us that, for the due execution of it, we must perform what is here added, all amounts to nearly the same sense. And for rightly comprehending it, we will treat, if God permit, of the three points which offer themselves in the apostle's words: first, of the old man, which we must put off; secondly, of the new, which we must put on, and the form in which it consists, namely, a renewing in knowledge, after the image of him who created it; and lastly, of that indifference of nations, and ceremonies, and conditions, which the apostle affirms in this matter, requiring nothing in reference to it but Christ, who is the all of it, and in all. May it please God so to enlighten our understandings rightly to discern this saving truth, and touch our hearts to love and practise it; effectually sanctifying us by the virtue of his word and precious sacrament, that we may all go out hence new men, conformed in purity, and charity, and every virtue, to that Lord Jesus, in whose name and communion we by his grace do glory.

I. The Scripture sets before us the person of Adam, and of Jesus Christ, as two different stocks of mankind, or as it were two opposite heads, or principles of this nature, which we call human. They have this in common, that both have a great number of children, which are issued from them, and depend upon them; and that each of them communicates to his own his being, his form, his life, and his condition, imprinting his image on them, which every one of them bears according to the quality of his extraction. They differ, or rather are opposite, in that one is earthy, the other heavenly; one has a carnal, vicious, infirm nature, full of ignorance and error, and subject to death and the curse; the other has a spiritual, holy nature, full of light and wisdom, acceptable unto God, immortal, and inheriting eternity. The one propagates in his children sin and death; the other communicates to them his righteousness, holiness, and life. The one transmits his nature by a carnal generation; the other imparts his to his descendants by a spiritual generation, and such a one as has nothing in common with flesh and blood. The nature of the one is depraved by the impoisoned breath of the old serpent, which creeps on the ground, and lives on the dust thereof; that of the other has been formed and preserved by the eternal and celestial Spirit. It is for these reasons that the Scripture calls each of these two persons simply man, because of their advantage, and their holding the first and principal rank, each of them in his kind. For the same reason again, it gives each of these two persons the name Adam; because they are each of them the Adam, that is to say, the father and author of his order; the one of sin and death, the other of righteousness and life. But, to distinguish them, it calls the one the first man, and the first Adam; the other the second man, and the last Adam, 1 Cor. xv. 45, 47. The former, having corrupted himself by his disobedience, has also infected us, leaving us vice and the curse for an inheritance. The latter, having repaired our fault by his obedience, has given us righteousness, holiness, and immortality. Adam is styled the first man, and Jesus Christ the second; because the one's corrupting preceded the other's repairing and reforming. Adam first defiled and poisoned his nature by sin; and then Jesus Christ manifested his, full of grace and truth. It is upon the same consideration that Adam is called the old man, and Jesus Christ the new. Taking in withal, that the first Adam shall be destroyed; whereas the second remains for ever. For it is the custom of Scripture to call that old which is ready to be done away, and that new which is firm and lasting. But because each of these two men communicates to those who are his the form and condition of his nature, according to that Scripture principle, that that which is born of the flesh is flesh, and that which is born of the Spirit is spirit, John iii. 6; Paul, therefore, giving the effect the name of its cause, by a figure ordinary in all languages, calls that form and condition of nature which each of us receives from the first Adam, by carnal birth, the old man; and, likewise, that form and condition which the faithful receive from Jesus Christ, by spiritual regeneration, the new man. This is what he means here, when he speaks of putting off the old man, and putting on the new; and elsewhere, in a passage similar to this, The truth, says he, which ye have learnt in Jesus, is, "that ye put off concerning the former conversation the old man, which is corrupt according to the deceitful lusts; and that ye put on the new man, which after God is created in righteousness and true holiness," Eph. iv. 22, 24.

Now as to that form of nature which we all receive from the first Adam by our carnal birth, every one well knows what it is, and in what it consists. For the Scripture declares, and all men's experience also teaches, that the nature of the children of Adam is extremely corrupt and vicious; smitten in the understanding with a horrible ignorance and blindness, and full of errors and false and pernicious maxims; infected in the will with violent and enraged love of a man's self, of the flesh, and of the earth, with brutish affections and passions. This nature is nothing but pride, ambition, injustice, avarice, luxury, envy, hatred, malignity, imprudence, fury, cruelty, and inhumanity. Such are all Adam's progeny while without the communion of Jesus Christ. There are no others born upon the earth; and whatever difference there is between men, with regard to climate, colour, and external appearance of life, the blood from which they come imprints this wretched form upon them all in common; which, seizing them at their birth, grows up and is augmented with age and exercise, rooting itself in them, and thrusting forth the habits of various sins, which in the end render them insufferable to God and their neighbours. And if the providence of heaven, for the preservation of mankind, did not repress the cursed fecundity of this evil, the disorder and havoc which it makes would be much greater than it is, and would proceed to infinity. It is then this mass of corruption, this hydra of vices, which the apostle calls "the old man," because it is the production of Adam, our old and first stock, in every one of us.

II. Hence it is easy to understand, on the other hand, what the new man is; that is to say, the form which Jesus Christ, the principle of the second creation, puts upon each of them that are his. For it is directly contrary to that of the first Adam, and comprehends in it all graces and virtues in opposition to the other's vices, as faith, wisdom, piety, charity, justice, meekness, honesty, temperance; and, in one word, a holiness like that of Jesus Christ, the image of which it is also called. It is this that Paul here styles "the new man," because it is the work, and likewise the portrait, of the Lord Jesus, our new Adam. And he describes it thus himself in this place. For as to the old man, he only names it, without saying any more of it. But he occasionally explains to us the nature of the new, saying that it "is renewed in knowledge, after the image of him that created it." In which few words he teaches us, first, that it is created in us, that is, produced by the operation of a divine power; in consequence of which we are called the workmanship and the creatures of God; and the apostle says elsewhere, that we were "created in Christ Jesus," Eph. ii. 10; whereas the production of the old man in us is not a creation, but a natural operation. For as it is indeed in our power to kill a man, but there is none, save God alone, that can raise him up again; so it was easy for Adam to destroy himself, and all of us with him, but to recover and re-establish us belongs to God alone. Adam could corrupt and deform our nature; but neither he, nor any of his, was able to repair or reform it into a new man. This appertains to none but the Creator. It is the work of a divine power.

Then again, the apostle shows us here who it is that creates this new man in us, saying that it is the same person after whose image it is created. For it is clear that the new man is after the image of Jesus Christ. It is, then, Jesus Christ that creates it in us. Vain man, give not the glory to your pretended free-will. It appertains wholly to the Lord. And we may truly say of this second generation, what the psalmist sings of the first, that it is the Lord, the eternal Word of the Father, "who hath made us, and not we ourselves," Psal. c. 3.

But the apostle in saying that this new man is renewed, teaches us another very important lesson, namely, that this piece of our regeneration, or the production of the new man, is polished and perfected by degrees in us; the Spirit of Christ working upon it during the whole course of our life upon earth, and adorning this his own creature by various reiterated operations with the graces and spiritual beauties it ought to possess, until it attain to the utmost and highest point of its perfection in the heavens, when there shall be seen a complete and angelical holiness shining forth in it with glory and blessed immortality.

Again, the apostle briefly touches upon the manner after which, and also the pattern by which, this renovation is wrought in us. Respecting the manner of it, he says that this new man is renewed in knowledge; thereby showing that Jesus Christ, for the communication to us of this new nature, which is in him as in its source, gives us the knowledge of his truth, and day by day augments it in us: for as ignorance and error are the principal deformities of the old man, and the cause of all the rest; so, on the contrary, wisdom and knowledge are the principal lineaments of the new man, by which are formed in us all the other virtues in which it consists, as love of God, charity towards men, and all the other holy habits which depend upon them; it being manifest that we love none but the things we know, and that proportionably to the knowledge which we have of them. Wherefore the Lord begins the admirable work of his grace by giving us knowledge. And we have an excellent illustration of this his method in the first creation of the world, where Moses expressly observes, that the first thing God created by his word was light, which is the symbol of knowledge, as darkness is of ignorance. At this the apostle plainly points elsewhere; "God, who commanded the light to shine out of darkness, hath shined in our hearts," 2 Cor. iv. 6. This light of knowledge, once lighted up in our souls by the Spirit of the Lord, quickly expels vice from them; and showing us the holy and glorious face of God in Jesus Christ, transforms us into his likeness, as saith the same apostle; "We all, with open face beholding as in a glass the glory of the Lord, are changed into the same image, from glory to glory, even as by the Spirit of the Lord," 2 Cor. iii. 18. It is this he means in the text, when he says of the new man that it is renewed after the image of him who created it, that is, of Jesus Christ our Lord. For he properly is the pattern by which that new nature of which we are made partakers is formed. He is both the author and pattern of it; and it is for this that it is called by his name, that is, the new man. Therefore the apostle elsewhere, to express the end and effect of his ministry toward the Galatians, says that he travaileth in birth until Christ be formed in them, Gal. iv. 19. He had no other design but to reinvest them with the new man. Certainly then the new man is nothing else but Jesus Christ formed in us; that is, nothing else but the form of this holy and blessed Lord, engraven and imprinted on us by the seal of his word and Spirit, which is precisely the thing he here calls his image. If you know Jesus Christ, you cannot be ignorant what this his form and image is. Jesus Christ is the Saint of saints, a man full of all purity, righteousness, charity, patience, constancy, and truth; and indeed of all the lights of holiness. Surely then his form and image can be no other than a genuine representation of these divine qualities, a soul in which appears a goodness, a humility, an honesty, I say not equal, (for it is not possible to arrive at so high a perfection,) but at least resembling his, and proportionate to it. And this is that which Paul elsewhere comprises expressly in two words, saying that "the new man is created after God, in righteousness and true holiness," Eph. iv. 24.

Thus, you see, brethren, what that old man and what this new man is of which the apostle speaks in this place. The one is the image of the first Adam, and the other of the second. He commands us to put off the old man with his deeds, and put on the new; a mode of speaking no less elegant than familiar in Scripture, which is accustomed to say of all the things that are found in any subject, that it is clothed with them. As when the prophets say that God is clothed with strength, with glory, and with magnificence; that he is clothed with justice; that he will clothe his priests with salvation, and their enemies with shame; that he will clothe the heavens with darkness: and so in a multitude of other places, where it is evident that the term clothing is taken figuratively, to express simply the putting off a thing in any particular subject, whether it be internally or externally. Whence it follows that to put off, on the contrary, is simply to quit a thing which one had, and rid himself of it. Thus, to put off the old man, is nothing else but to rid ourselves of his vices, and of his corruptions; to pluck up, for instance, out of our hearts his covetousness, and his ambition, and the habits of his other sins. But the apostle expressly adds, that we put him off with his deeds; that is to say, that we not only pluck up out of our hearts the habits of vices, which are, as it were, the roots and stocks of it, but that also we cut off from our lives all the actions, whether interior, as desires and lustings, or exterior, as other sins which proceed from it, and are so many fruits of this accursed plant. For, to speak properly, the old man is one thing, and the act of sin that issues from it another. The one is the corruption itself of our nature, the other is the effect which it produces; the one is as the plant, and the other as its fruit. For example, cruelty and covetousness are some of the very members of the old man; murder and stealing are acts of it. The apostle directs us to put off both, that neither vice nor its acts might have any place in us. In like manner, to put on the new man, is, on the other hand, to deck and adorn our understanding, our will, our affections, and all the parts of our life, with those excellent virtues in which the new man consists, as we have said before; to labour at it studiously, and take no rest till we have them formed in us, and our whole nature is covered and enriched with them.

But though these two words, to put off, and to put on, are in this passage figuratively taken, yet they show us, contrary to the gross and senseless error of some, that both the old man and the new signify the form and disposition, not the substance and very essence of our nature: for when a thing is utterly destroyed, we do not say it puts off what it had, but that it is perished; and when the substance of a thing is altogether newly produced, we say not that it is clothed, but created: so the apostle here commands us to put off the old man, and to put on the new. It is evident that in this renovation of our nature we do not lose the very substance of it, nor acquire another new one; but only quit that unworthy and wretched form which sin gave it, and assume another, which resembles that of Jesus Christ. I acknowledge that that old form which we put off had seized on, blasted, and disfigured all the parts of our nature, both internal and external; as also that the new one, which we receive in Jesus Christ, extends itself likewise to them all; in which respect both of them differ from a garment, which covers but the outside, and reaches not further in; yet they both are, notwithstanding, things differing from the subject itself, which is unclothed or clothed with them, as a habit is a different kind of thing to the body it covers. The one is as it were the rust, the poison, the malady, the loathsomeness, and the deformity of our nature; the other is the beauty, the health, the perfection, the ornament, and honour of it, and, as it were, the jewel that gives it all it has of worth and value. Neither let the terms of old and new man trouble you, for they are often made use of in all languages to signify the qualities, and not the very essentials, of our nature, as when we say of a person who was once vicious and debauched, but is now become honest and virtuous, that he is another man, a new man; though, to speak properly, he has the same substance, the same soul and the same body, he had before, and has quitted nothing of his former nature but the bad habits with which it was vested, not the substance of his being. Thus it is with regard to the old and new man; the substance of the subject remains the same under both; there is nothing changed but its form and quality. And it is thus also that we are to understand what, after the prophets, Peter has said, namely, that at the last manifestation of the Son of God there shall be "new heavens and a new earth," 2 Pet. iii. 13; for these creatures which now subsist shall not be annihilated. On the contrary, Paul says that they shall have part in the deliverance of the sons of God, Rom. viii. 21; but because they shall be purged from all vanity, and put into a state much more excellent than that in which they now sigh and languish, therefore they are called new heavens and a new earth.

As for what remains, the apostle enjoins us expressly, both here and elsewhere, to put off the old man and to put on the new, because in truth these are two different things, even as to depart from evil and to do good. It is very true that in the state men are in, no one puts off the old man without putting on the new; and so on the contrary. And again it is also true that the same Spirit of Jesus Christ which effects the one also effects the other, even as the sun by one and the same action dispels the darkness of our air and diffuses into it light; yet this does not prevent considering, simply and absolutely in itself, the putting off of the old man to be one thing, and the putting on of the new another. For the corruption of the old man is not a mere absence and privation of the sanctity of the new, neither is virtue a mere privation of vice, as darkness is nothing at all but a simple privation of light; otherwise it might be said that the new man is everywhere where the old man is not; and so, on the contrary, as where there is no light darkness of necessity takes place, and where there is no darkness there must be light. But though these two actions of putting off the old man and putting on the new are different in themselves, yet are they inseparably joined with each other; and in the state we now are in, it is impossible that any person can divest himself of sin, and of the misery of his old man, without investing himself with the new, because there is no other way of salvation but the communion of Christ, into which no one ever enters without putting on the new man. It is in this that all our salvation consists.

III. But because those false teachers which troubled the church at that time pretended, to the prejudice of this doctrine, that circumcision and various other external things were necessary in religion; as if they were sufficient to save us without the new man, or at least the new man were not sufficient to save us without them; the apostle rejects this error here which he refuted before, and to this purpose, in speaking of the new man, adds, "Where there is neither Greek nor Jew, circumcision nor uncircumcision, barbarian, Scythian, bond nor free; but Christ is all, and in all." His meaning is not that, among those whom Jesus Christ converts to new men by virtue of his gospel, there are none that are by extraction Jews or Greeks, barbarians or Scythians, and for condition bond or free, circumcised or uncircumcised; nor likewise that these differences are in themselves nothing, or ought not to be considered at all, either in nature or in the state and politic order. On the contrary he himself hereafter establishes the difference of bondmen and free, and commands us to observe it in civil life. But what he says must be restrained and appropriated precisely to his intention and design, without extending it any further. He speaks of the new man, and says that none of these differences take place in him. He means, therefore, simply, that in this respect (that is, in what concerns the nature of the new man) all these different qualities and conditions are no way important; that, with respect to it, they have no force nor virtue; that neither the superiority of the Jew, nor the advantage of circumcision, nor the liberty of the free, serves at all to bring us near the new man, and communicate him to us; that the knowledge of the Greek, the rudeness of the barbarian, the uncircumcision of the Gentile, and the meanness of the slave, do not remove us further from him; that a man can participate in him with the first of these qualities, and can with the last. It is the same thing that he says elsewhere, even that "in Christ Jesus neither circumcision availeth anything, nor uncircumcision, but a new creature," Gal. vi. 15; and again, that in Christ "there is neither Jew nor Greek, there is neither bond nor free, there is neither male nor female; for ye are all one in Christ Jesus," Gal. iii. 28.

He hereby excludes, first, the pretended advantage of the Jew above the Greek; for the Jews so foolishly presumed upon their birth, that they imagined it sufficient to render them acceptable to God, and they haughtily disdained the Greeks, as accursed and abominable, by the sole infelicity of their extraction. The men of Rome are at this day no wiser, for they only define christianity by an adherence to the see of their city. The apostle here condemns the vanity of both; proclaiming that neither the Jew nor the Greek, and consequently not the Roman or Italian, are of any consideration in godliness, so as to confer upon us or deprive us of the new man. And John Baptist had before cautioned the Jews against it: "Think not to say within yourselves, We have Abraham to our father," Matt. iii. 9. And it is this our Saviour meant, when he told Nicodemus that to enter into the kingdom of heaven he must be born again, John iii. 3; signifying that all that dignity of this carnal birth, which so mightily puffed up the hearts of the Pharisees and Jews, was but a thing of nought, and contributed not at all to the bringing them into his communion. And elsewhere, the Jews crying out that Abraham was their father, he answers them, that if they were the children of Abraham, they would do his works, John viii. 39; an evident sign that the children of the saints are they who do their works, as said one of the ancients,* and not they who take up their place; and that, as Peter said, "In every nation he that feareth God, and worketh righteousness, is accepted with him," Acts x. 35.

That which the apostle afterwards adds, of barbarians and Scythians, tends also to take away all difference of people in matter of godliness, against the vanity of the Greeks, who despised all other nations, and called them barbarians; esteeming none but their own, because of the great politeness of their language, the civility of their manners, and the study of philosophy and eloquence which flourished among them. Paul informs them that this vain excellency is of no value in christianity, and that the illiterature and political defects of barbarians do not alienate them from God, provided that, putting off the old man, they put on the new. The Scythians are those whom we call Tartars, and he makes particular mention of them, either because of their barbarity and extreme rudeness, inasmuch as they were accounted the most uncultivated and least polite of all barbarians, or, as some think, because of their probity, justice, and moral innocency.

After nations, he speaks also of the difference of ceremonies and conditions. To the former refers his expression, that in christianity there is neither circumcision nor uncircumcision, comprising under this one species all other similar observances of things external in religion, and not commanded of God; signifying that men are neither advanced towards the kingdom of heaven by being circumcised, nor set further from it by being without circumcision; and likewise, that, as he saith elsewhere, "if we eat, we are not the better; and if we eat not,

---

* Hierom.

we are not the worse." We see therefore how ill-founded is the ridiculous opinion of those who put a far higher estimate upon themselves, in point of holiness, than upon others, on account of these external and voluntary devotions; as, for instance, because they wear a cowl, or a certain particular habit, because they abstain from flesh, either continually, or during certain days, and do other such things, in which they are not ashamed even to place christianity. What the apostle adds, in the last place, concerning the bond and the free, also comprehends nobility and peasantry, riches and poverty, dignity and inferiority; and, in short, all that diversity of condition which divides men in the present world. Though these qualities put a difference between them on earth, they put none between them in heaven, nor in the mystical body of our Lord and Saviour, into which God receives us all indifferently, if he see the new man in us, and equally excludes those in whom he finds it not. The pomp of riches and honours, and the glory of great birth, recommend no one to him; meanness of extraction or of condition, and the misery of poverty, do not induce him to reject any. He strips all men of that habit that makes up no part of them, and judges of them only by that form of the old or new man which they bear within them.

Now having excluded all these things from the true constitution of piety, he informs us, in conclusion, in what its whole force and virtue consist. In this renovation of man "there is," says he, "neither Greek nor Jew, circumcision nor uncircumcision, barbarian, Scythian, bond nor free: but Christ is all, and in all." That which the Jews in vain promise themselves from their birth, and they that judaize from their circumcision, and the Greeks from their philosophy, and great ones from their dignity, Jesus Christ alone gives abundantly to all that are in him. He is all to them. For in him the Gentile finds Judaism and the nobility of Israel; all they that are of faith being children of Abraham, Gal. iii. 7. In him the uncircumcised have the true circumcision, which is not made with hands; barbarians, divine philosophy and the citizenship of heaven; bond-men, freedom of spirit; poor men, the treasures of eternity; abject persons, the glory of God, and the excellency of his kingdom. And as he has in him an abundance of all sacred and salutiferous things, so he has them for all: shutting not up the bosom of his grace against any, whoever he may be, and universally conferring on all those of his communion righteousness, wisdom, sanctification, and redemption; and, in a word, all graces requisite for conducting them to and putting them into the eternal possession of supreme felicity.

Dear brethren, it is this same blessed Lord, the fountain and the fulness of all good, that God presents to you at this time in his word and in his sacrament. Come ye all to him, seeing he is so bountifully offered unto you. Let no one imagine either that he may do well enough without him, or that he may not enjoy him. He is both necessary for the greatest, and accessible to the least. The dignity of masters, the abundance of riches, the extraction of the noble, the observances of the devout, and such other advantages, will be of no use at all in saving those who have them; so that Jesus Christ is no less necessary for them than if they had them not. The low estate of servants, the distress of the poor, and other similar disadvantages, hinder no one from approaching and receiving him. And as the brazen serpent, which prefigured him in the desert, was communicated indifferently unto all, great and small, poor and rich, noble and ignoble, and equally cured all those who looked on it; and again, as there was no remedy to be had against the bite of the fiery serpents but that alone; neither riches, nor nobility, nor science, nor any other quality being able to cure any of them: so is it with our Lord Jesus, he is equally both necessary and approachable for all. He offers himself to the great, he disdains not the least. He gives himself to both, and saves them all indifferently. Come ye then all unto him, whatever in other respects your condition or extraction may be. Lift up your eyes to him, and behold him stretched out for you upon the pole of Moses, crucified for your sins, and wounded for your iniquities; his flesh pierced with nails, his blood spilt on the ground; presenting to you in this scandalous, but healthful infirmity, the treasure of life and happiness. Bring unto him souls full of faith, reverence, and love, and prepare for the reception of him, not your bodily mouth or stomach, places, whatever superstition may say, unworthy to lodge him, but your hearts, your minds, your understandings and affections; that is, the nobler part of your being. There it is that he takes pleasure, there it is that he would dwell. Accordingly, it is there that he should operate and display his virtue unto the extinguishing of the old man, and the engraving of his own image. As the body is not the object of this his operation, so neither is it the seat of his presence, nor the throne of his majesty.

But you plainly see, my brethren, that this incomparable favour which he confers on you, in being willing to come and dwell in your hearts, obliges you to put off his enemy the old man, and to clear yourselves of all his pollutions, to eradicate the habits of all his vices, to smother all his desires, and to cleanse your whole life from all his deeds. This old man is the disgrace of your nature, the poison of your soul, the death of your life, the cause of your unhappiness. It is he that destroyed you, that banished you out of Paradise, that bereaved you of your true delights, that made you subject to vanity, to the wrath of God, the hatred of his angels, and the tyranny of devils. Divest yourselves of this corrupt and accursed habit. Give yourselves no rest till you be rid of it. Tell me not that this old man holds too fast; that you feel him cleaving to your inward parts. Where eternal salvation is concerned, there no excuse is to be taken. If you cannot rid yourselves of him in any other way, it would be better to pluck out your very bowels than to spare them and perish. But the truth is, we flatter ourselves; and that to keep this pleasing enemy with us, we make ourselves believe that he is part of us; as if we could not be men without polluting ourselves in the filth of his vices. Be not afraid of injuring or outraging yourselves by driving him from you. It is but the pest and poison of your nature, as we said before. Your life will not be, as you imagine, incommoded by it, but made more free and happy than it was. Besides, after the victory over him, which Christ has won upon the cross, it ill becomes us to complain of the strength of this enemy. All his strength consists only in our cowardice, our feebleness and effeminacy. Jesus Christ has taken from him all the true strength which he had. He has crucified him, and overthrown all the foundations of his tyranny and of his life, exhibiting to us the deformity thereof, and opening to us the way to liberty and the gate of the house of God. Instead of this wretched, sordid, and shameful form of life, let us put on that new man, who now presents and gives himself to us. Let us have him night and day before our eyes, as the only pattern of our true nature. Let us copy him completely, and faithfully engrave upon our souls all the features of his divine and glorious form. Let the image of this new Adam shine forth in our souls, and in our whole conduct.

Dear brethren, it must be acknowledged that hitherto we have greatly failed in this duty. For what is more unlike each other than we and Jesus Christ, to whose image we should be conformed? He is humble, meek, and patient as a lamb; we are fierce, proud, and irascible as lions. He did good to his enemies; and we hardly spare our friends. He loved the greatest strangers, and we hate our nearest neighbours. He was most pure and holy, and we are polluted with the filth of intemperance. He sought only his Father's glory and the salvation of men; we muse upon nothing but earth, and consider only our own interests. With this dissimilitude, or rather contrariety, how can we pretend to have put on the new man, which is created after the image of Jesus Christ? And how can it be otherwise than imagined that we rather bear the image of his enemy? Yet you are not ignorant what depends upon it; and well know that is impossible to have part on high in the glory of the new man, except we put him on here below. In the name of God, beloved brethren, and as your own salvation is dear to you, pursue this great and necessary design. Repair the negligences of the time past; and discharging, for the future, with good fidelity, what the apostle's word and the sacrament of this mystical table equally require of you, put off the old man, who has destroyed you; put on the new man, who has saved you, renewing you in the knowledge and likeness of this sweet and merciful Lord, who died and is risen again for you; that after you have borne on earth the image of his holiness and charity, you may bear it eternally in the heavens, together with that of his glory and immortality. Amen.

SERMON XXXIX.

VERSES 12, 13.

Put on therefore, as the elect of God, holy and beloved, bowels of mercies, kindness, humbleness of mind, meekness, long-suffering; forbearing one another, and forgiving one another, if any man have a quarrel against any: even as Christ forgave you, so also do ye.

DEAR brethren, that which the sacrament of the Lord's holy supper requires of us, and which, when we duly receive it, effects and produces in us, is the very thing which the apostle commands us in this text, and to which he forms us by these words. He directs us to be merciful, kind, humble, meek, patient, and ready to pardon one another. And the end and effect of the sacrament is to make us so: for it communicates the Lord Jesus Christ unto us; not that the substance of his body enters into ours, nor that his flesh is touched by our mouths and stomachs, (a thing both preposterous and impossible, and which is moreover unprofitable and superfluous,) but indeed transforms us into his image, and renders us like him, that is, humble, meek, patient, kind, and merciful, as he is, forming these divine virtues in us by the efficacy of his death, which is celebrated in this mystery. By which you see a remarkable difference between the heavenly food which we receive in this sacrament, and the earthly meat we daily take; for whereas the latter is, for the nourishing of our bodies, changed into their nature; the former, on the contrary, for the enlivening of our souls, transforms them into its own. Thus, since we have participated this morning of this precious sacrament, we cannot better employ the present hour than in meditating upon these words of the apostle, which contain and represent one of its principal effects. Consider them therefore, my brethren, attentively. And that we may discern whether or no we have truly communicated of the bread of heaven, let us examine whether it has produced and formed in our hearts that humility and kindness, and all those other virtues, which the apostle enjoins us in this place; and let us be assured that, without this, neither the Lord's favour in inviting us unto his table, nor the heavenly food there presented to us, will benefit us at all; and that so far from contributing to our salvation, it will aggravate our condemnation, according to the apostle's saying in another place, that "he that eateth and drinketh unworthily eateth and drinketh damnation to himself."

Paul, if you remember, having in general exhorted the Colossians to mortify the members of the old man, particularly nominated and specified some of his principal vices, as covetousness, fornication, malignity, wrath, and others, expressly enjoining them to put them away. But because it is not enough to refrain from evil, but there must be also a doing of good; so it is not sufficient that we abstain from vice, if we do not exercise the actions of virtue. This great apostle having forbidden the lusts and sins of the old man, commands us first, in general, to put on the new, as you heard a week since; and then, in the progress of his discourse, he points to some of the principal parts of this new man by name. It is precisely at the verses we have read that he begins to point out these qualities: "Put on then," says he, "as the elect of God, holy and beloved, bowels of mercy," &c. This exhortation he infers from the preceding verses, and proposes, at the entrance, a reason that obliges us to this pursuit, taken from the honour God has done us to choose us for his saints and his beloved. Next, he commends to us compassion, benignity, humility, meekness, patience, five virtues which refer, as you see, to the manner in which we are to behave towards our neighbours, and particularly towards those who suffer evil, or do us any. Afterwards he points out two acts of patience and benignity; the one is a bearing with, and the other the pardoning of, one another; and to incite us to them, he adds the example which our Lord and Saviour has given us. So we shall have three points of which to treat in this discourse, if the Lord will. First, the quality of the elect of God, "holy and beloved," which the apostle gives us at the entrance, to sway us to our duty. Secondly, the five virtues which he recommends to us, and the exercise of them in the matter of that forbearance and mutual forgiveness which we owe one to another. And finally, the example of Jesus Christ, which he sets before our eyes as an accomplished pattern, and a most effectual argument of our sanctification. Dear brethren, hear, meditate, and duly put in practice that divine lesson which the Lord Jesus gave you this morning in the mystery of his table, and now repeats by the mouth of his apostle.

I. The apostle deduces from what he had generally asserted in the preceding verses, that we "have put on the new man, which is renewed in knowledge after the image of him who created him." Thence he now concludes, "Put on then bowels of mercy, kindness, humbleness, meekness, long-suffering." The consequence is evident. For since we put on the new man in Jesus Christ, it is clear that these virtues being members and parts of this new man, it is our duty to put them on; and that without them, this new nature, which makes us christians, would remain imperfect in us. Brethren, mark well this reasoning, and learn by it how greatly they deceive themselves, who pretend, without these virtues, to the name and inheritance of christians; imagining that they are not necessary for all, but only meet for such as will be more perfect and more excellent than the generality of the faithful. It is a principle laid down in various places by the apostle, and acknowledged by the whole church, that no man is in Christ except he be a new creature. And he himself teaches us here, that whoever is a new creature must put on compassion, and those other virtues he names in order; surely it follows, then, that whoever has not put them on is not a new creature, and consequently is not a christian. If therefore you will be christians; if you will aspire to salvation, which God gives to none but to those who are christians, renounce that pernicious error, and embrace the pursuit of all these virtues with vigorous resolution, labouring incessantly in it until you have invested your souls with their habits, sentiments and affections, and filled your whole life with their actions.

It is the thing to which you are also evidently obliged, by the dignity of being the elect, the holy, and the beloved of God, of which the apostle in this place reminds you. Put on, says he, compassion, kindness, as elected of God, holy and beloved. The Hebrew grammarians have remarked that the word *as* is used in that language two ways: sometimes to signify the analogy and resemblance of one thing to another, and this they call the *as* of likeness; for instance, when our Saviour says, "Be wise as serpents, and harmless as doves;" and sometimes to signify, that the subject of which we speak has not the resemblance, but the reality, of that particular which we attribute to it, and this they term the *as* of verity. As when John says of our Lord Jesus Christ, "We beheld his glory, the glory as of the only begotten of the Father," John i. 14. His meaning is, not that Jesus Christ was like the only Son of God, but that he was so indeed and in truth and that the glory which he and his companions beheld in him was just such as the glory of God's true Son should be. An *as* of the first kind compares one thing with another; an *as* of the second compares a thing with itself. The first is a comparative particle, as the grammarians term it; and the second a rational one. The *as* here used by the apostle is of the second kind, not of the first; for he does not mean that we should addict ourselves to those virtues which he enjoins, as do certain other persons elected of God; but that we addict ourselves to them, because we have the honour to be elected of God ourselves. This *as* does not compare us with others, but with ourselves, and imports as much as if Paul had said, Seeing that, or since you are elected of God; containing in it this reasoning: Such as have the honour to be elected of God, his saints, and his beloved, ought to be clothed with humility, benignity, and meekness; since then you have in Jesus Christ the honour to be the elect, the saints, and the beloved of God, judge if you are not bound to put on all these virtues. We use the word *as* in the same sense often in common conversation; as, for example, when we say of a good man that he lived and died religiously, as a christian, that is, so as was meet for that quality of christian which he possessed; and when we advise a young man of good rank to be honest in all his conversation, as born of a good house, and issued from a noble and a virtuous father.

Of these three qualities which the apostle here gives the faithful, the first is, that they are elected of God. The election of God is the choice which he makes, according to his good pleasure, of certain persons, to call them to the knowledge of himself, and to the glory of his salvation. And this term election, signifies sometimes the resolution he has taken in his eternal counsel to choose and call them, which the Scripture elsewhere calls the determinate purpose of God, Eph. i. 11; sometimes the execution of this eternal determination, when God in time touches the men of his good pleasure by the efficacy of his word and Spirit, converting them to the faith of his gospel, and separating them by this means from the rest of men, who continue in the miserable state of their nature, through their impenitence and unbelief. The apostle, in my opinion, comprehends both these significations, when he says here that we are elected of God; that is, such as he has chosen and effectually separated from the world, according to his determinate purpose, calling us to himself, to serve him according to the discipline of his gospel. Now that this quality obliges us to put on all the virtues which he recommends to us in the words following is evident. For this very thing is the aim and end of his election, as the apostle elsewhere informs us, when he says that God hath chosen us in Christ, "that we should be holy and without blame before him in love," Eph. i. 4. And it is this that Moses formerly represented to ancient Israel, the type of the new: "The Lord," says he, "has avouched thee this day (that is, hath raised thee above other nations by his election) to be his peculiar people, and that thou shouldest keep all his commandments," Deut. xxvi. 18. Whence it appears how false is their calumny who accuse the doctrine of election of favouring vice and impenitence. If it were so, what could have less of reason in it than the apostle's discourse, who alleges our election to incite us to the studious pursuit of holiness? But it is quite contrary to what these men pretend. As God's election is the source of sanctification and good works, so the asserting and teaching it is an establishing and a founding of them. And they who make their boast of being elected of God, but in the mean time lead a licentious and profane life, mock God and men; and shall, if they amend not, infallibly perish in this false and vain error. For since God's election is never executed without converting and sanctifying a man; and it is impossible, on the other hand, that any one should know that he is elected, except by feeling the real execution of his election; it is evidently rashness and a palpable error to imagine that one is elected, except he is truly converted to God and endued with piety and charity.

Another quality which the apostle here gives us is, that we are holy, or saints; for he is not of the opinion of Rome, who calls none saints but those whom she has canonized. Paul acknowledges none for believers who are not saints. Accordingly, you know, that in the Creed, the church which is the body of all true christians, and not of the canonized only, is called holy, and the communion of saints. Indeed, since there is not a christian who has not been baptized into Jesus Christ, and received the Holy Ghost, according to the apostle's saying that "if any man have not the Spirit of Christ, he is none of his," Rom. viii. 9; how can he be a christian who is not a saint, seeing both baptism and the Spirit of Christ sanctify all those to whom they are truly communicated? Now that this quality of saints or holy ones, also obliges us to all the virtues that the apostle gives us in charge, in the following verses, is as clear as the sun at noon-day; for what else is holiness itself, but a piety and an exquisite charity, complete in all its parts, and adorned with every virtue? Besides, by sanctification we are dedicated and consecrated unto God, so that henceforth we ought not to dispose of ourselves but for his service and according to his will; which is nothing else than to live in all purity, honesty and virtue. And this is what the Lord signifies, when he so often charges his people to be holy;

"Ye shall be holy unto me," says he, "for I am holy; and have separated you from other people, that ye should be mine," Lev. xi. 44; xx. 26.

The third quality which the apostle here gives us is, that we are the beloved of God; that is to say, those of all men whom he most loves and highly esteems in his Son Jesus Christ. Since then the love with which God honours us obliges us to love him, and that we cannot fail in this reciprocal love without horrible ingratitude; it is evident that our being the beloved of God necessarily requires of us to put on all these virtues which the apostle is about to give us in charge. First, because it is a necessary and infallible effect of the love we bear to God to do what he commands us, and he commands us nothing else but the exercise of every virtue. "If ye love me," says he, "keep my commandments," John xiv. 15. Secondly, because true love transforms him who loves into the image of the thing loved; so that God being charity, justice, and holiness itself, it is impossible, if we love him truly, to do otherwise than put on all these divine virtues. Thus you see, believers, that the honour we have to be elected of God, holy and beloved, most strictly obliges us to do what the apostle commands us; this is, to embrace all the virtues he is about to represent to us; which he expresses in one word, bidding us to put them on, that is, that we seat them in our hearts, and show them in our lives; that we deck our souls with their habits, and adorn our manners with their acts. For it is this that is signified by the word put on, here figuratively used, according to the usual style of Scripture; as we informed you in expounding the preceding text, where the apostle exhorted us to put off the old man, and to put on the new.

II. The foremost of these virtues which he recommends to us are those five which he expressly nominates in the present text, mercy, kindness, humility, meekness, and patience. Mercy is a goodness and tenderness of spirit, which causes us to commiserate the miseries of others, to have compassion on them, and to take part in them, as if we suffered them ourselves. And the apostle, to show us how quick and deep this sentiment should be in us, commands us to put on, not mercy simply, but bowels of mercy, which is a mode of expression taken from the Hebrew language, in which the word bowels is often used to signify the emotions of pity and the tenderness of compassion; and this not without reason, it being clear that compassion affects and greatly moves the heart, the principal of our internal parts. It is not enough that we lodge pity in our looks, externally showing the movings and appearances of it. The miseries of our neighbours must descend into our hearts, and reach the depth of our bowels; they must affect them with a real grief, that may move them, and stir up all that is in our power to afford them succour. For the gospel of Jesus Christ does not at all approve of the rigidity of the Stoic philosophy, which plucked up mercy as well as other passions out of the bowels of its wise men; as if to compassionate trouble or grief were a thing unworthy of a virtuous person. Let him remedy the miseries of others, said they, but let him not feel them. Let him succour the men, but let him not be touched with their passion. First, that which they presuppose is false; namely, that to suffer oneself to be touched with sentiments of grief is a defilement or pollution of virtue. There is nothing unworthy of true virtue but vice: now grief is not a vice; it is a simple sentiment of nature: and in order to be wise, it is not necessary that a man should renounce the sentiments of nature: it is sufficient to govern them, and keep them within their bounds, and use them with reason. Again, this insensibility, which is a chimera and a fiction of their own, cannot take place in the soul of man, which God has formed unto affection and tenderness more than any other creature; as is evident by tears, of which none but man is capable. Lastly, whereas they would have the wise man succour the miserable without feeling their misery, this is both difficult and dangerous. For it takes away one of the sharpest incitements that spurs us on to assist them; it being clear that nothing more powerfully moves us to do this than compassion. We must not, as those people said, remedy other men's miseries without feeling them, which is both difficult in our nature, and would be unprofitable if it were easy; but, on the contrary, we must feel them that we may remedy them. So likewise there is nothing more cold and helpless than these insensible persons. For eradicating compassion out of our hearts, they put in them obduracy and inhumanity, which are infinitely more contrary to true virtue than grief and emotion.

Renounce we then, beloved brethren, this rough and inhuman philosophy. Let it be no shame to us to be tender and sensible of our neighbours' miseries. Let us hold compassion, not for an infirmity, but for a virtue, unto which God calls us by his commands, and by the examples, both of his saints, and of his Son himself, Jesus Christ our Lord: "Be ye merciful," saith he, Luke vi. 36. And one of his apostles exhorts us to be full of mutual "compassion, pitiful, courteous," 1 Pet. iii. 8. And our Paul goes so far as to command us to "weep with them that weep," Rom. xii. 15; and the truth is, our tears and our sympathies, if we can do nothing else, afford some ease to the afflicted. The saints of whom we are told in Scripture have all this character of sweetness and humanity. They were tender and full of compassion towards all afflicted persons: and, to produce no other examples, you know the miseries of men touched and pierced the heart of our Lord and Saviour, who wept when he saw the grave of Lazarus, and of whom it is said, that he "can have compassion on the ignorant, and on them that are out of the way," Heb. v. 2; and again, that he is "touched with the feeling of our infirmities," Heb. iv. 15. But besides the law of God, nature itself demands of us these sympathies; for men being our neighbours, that is, of one and the same nature with us, who does not see that it is reasonable that we should be touched with their miseries—and this the rather, as it may be our lot to be similarly afflicted ourselves, and one day to need that compassion and succour which they now crave of us?

After the movings of compassion, the apostle demands of us the succour and offices of benignity, which is a goodness of nature that takes pleasure in, and makes it its study to serve and oblige every one, and injure or disoblige nobody; that readily stretches out its helping hand to the afflicted, and freely communicates its goods to the necessitous: a thing which God commands us everywhere in his word, desiring us there to be communicative, to break our bread to the hungry, and impart our substance to those who are in need. The charge of stewards, or dispensers, which he has given us, obliges us thereto; for he has put into our hands all the wealth we possess, to the end that we should prudently and charitably dispense it to our neighbours. And as he promises great benedictions and recompenses, as well in this life as also in the next, to those who acquit themselves faithfully of this duty, and are kind and beneficent; so he menaces all those who shall fail to do it with grievous and eternal punishments, and treats them at very turn as persons not only cruel and inhuman, but also inequitable and unjust.

Unto mercy and kindness the apostle commands us to add humility, the basis and foundation of all christian virtues, the ornament of a believing soul, the mother of patience, the nurse of charity. There is no disposition of soul more pleasing to God or more profitable to men. I confess the exercise of it is difficult to man, naturally proud and wilful. But the light of the gospel of Christ, and the power of his grace, render that easy to us which is hard of itself. The pride of man surely springs only from his ignorance. If he knew himself as he ought, he would be humble, and instead of glorying in, would be ashamed of himself. Why then do not we, who know the vanity of our being, the feebleness of our bodies, the malignity of our hearts, the ignorance and folly of our minds, the perverseness of our affections, the uncertainty and misery of our life, the demerit of our sins, and the eternal woe of which they are worthy, completely clothe ourselves with a sincere and profound humility? After these considerations, how can we have any puff of pride? If you tell me, it is true, you were such by nature, but that the grace of Jesus Christ has made you otherwise; I answer, that in this you have cause indeed to acknowledge and glorify his bounty, but none to lift up yourselves. For you have nothing that is good but what you received from God; and if you have received it, why do you boast of it? The more he has given you, the more ought you to humble yourselves; as those branches bow most and bend lowest which are most laden with fruit. Thus you see that, being nothing in yourselves and having received of God all that you can have, it is just that you should be humble; not to mention here either the command for it, which God gives us in a thousand places, the graces he promises to humility, the pattern of it, which he sets before us in his Son Jesus Christ, or the ruin with which he menaceth the haughty.

After humility, the apostle lodges in our souls two of its daughters, namely, meekness and long-suffering, or patience. Meekness is properly that which we call gentleness; the greatest grace of our behaviour, and the most amiable ornament of our life. It receives every one with an open heart and a pleasing countenance. It is not easily provoked, and, as far as it can, takes all things in good part. It is affable, and judges not with rigour. It restrains the stirrings of anger, and notwithstanding the occasions offered for it, keeps and maintains itself in a sweet calm, without becoming angry, easily receiving, as far as reason permits, the excuses of those who have offended it, and being much more readily appeased than irritated. As this virtue is very grateful to others, so is it exceedingly profitable and beneficial to ourselves. For living with men, that is to say, with weak and wretched creatures, without gentleness, which sweetens all things, we must needs be in a continual irritation, and never have joy nor repose. Patience is the sister of gentleness; they both bear vexatious things without exasperation; only with this difference, that gentleness is exercised with reference to the sullenness, the ignorance, and the impertinence of those with whom we converse; patience undergoes greater evils, such as outrages and affronts, and those very afflictions which are sent us of God, as sicknesses, losses, and the like.

But for the better clearing of the nature of these two virtues, the apostle particularly recommends to us two eminent acts of them, extremely necessary for christians, and of singular use in our whole life, when he adds, "forbearing one another, and forgiving one another, if any man have a quarrel against any." The first of these acts pertains as well to meekness as to patience. For, first, if there be any defect either in the humour, or in the person, or even in the faith and piety of our brethren, provided it is not a capital crime, which tends to the overthrow of religion and salvation, we ought not for this to break with them, nor reject nor sadden them, but bear with them with all kindness, remembering both the need we have that the same equity and condescension should be used towards us in many things in which we are no more perfect than our brethren; and the example of our Lord and Saviour, who, according to the prophet's prediction, Matt. xii. 20, did not break the bruised reed, nor quench the smoking flax. Then, in the second place, if our neighbours have offended us, either by word or deed, we must not forthwith have recourse to revenge, as men of the world do; but endeavour to overcome them by gentleness, bearing their wrongs with a christian and generous resolution. The other act which the apostle commands us, and which likewise respects those two virtues, is our pardoning one another, if one has a quarrel against the other. This is more than that bearing with one another which he first required of us; for there are people found who bear with the sullenness or the infirmities of their neighbour, yea, with his offences, whether it be that they have not the means to avenge themselves, or that they deem it not expedient to do so for the present, who in the mean time keep and brood upon their resentments in the secret of their hearts, waiting for an opportunity to show them with advantage. Wherefore the apostle is not content with telling us that we should bear with one another; he further directs us to pardon one another; that is, efface out of our souls all resentment of an offence received, and eradicate all desire of revenge, heartily remitting to our neighbours the faults they have committed against us, as our Lord enjoins us, when he says that his Father will irremissibly punish us, if we do not from our hearts forgive every one his brother, Matt. xviii. 35. This duty reaches universally to all the faithful, and takes place in all kinds of subjects, as the apostle signifies when he adds indefinitely, "if any man have a quarrel against any," whatever the occasion of the quarrel be, whether injurious speeches given or actions done, either against ourselves or any one of ours.

III. But because Paul was not ignorant how difficult this piece of christian piety is, our flesh having no passion stronger and more difficult to be subdued than the resentment of offences and the desire of revenge, to reduce us to this forgiveness and divine patience, and to beat down the fierceness of our hearts, he proposes to us the example of the Lord Jesus, the Prince of our discipline and Pattern of our life; "As Christ," says he, "forgave you, so also do ye." He does the same also in the Epistle to the Ephesians, chap. iv. 32, where he sets before us the example of God forgiving us all our sins for his Son's sake. And what stronger reason than this could the apostle urge? For Jesus Christ being our Head and our elder Brother, unto whose image we ought to be conformed, according to the predestination of God; how shall we be his members, his disciples, and his living portraits, if we have nothing in us of that great and divine goodness which he has showed us? If he had only exercised it towards others, we should be bound to imitate him. But it is ourselves whom he has pardoned, and not others only; so that his example much more strictly binds us: for the inhumanity of that wretched servant in the parable, who, when he himself had been gratified by his master, would forgive his fellow nothing, is much more detestable than if his master had showed such kindness only to some other man. Nor does the Lord omit to mention to him that circumstance expressly: "Thou wicked servant," says he to him, "I forgave thee all that debt: shouldest not thou also have had compassion on thy fellow servant, even as I had pity on thee? Matt. xviii. 32, 33. Judge then what a hell our obduracy will deserve, if we, having experienced in our own persons the wonderful goodness of our Lord and Saviour mercifully forgiving us our faults, have hearts so refractory and so cruel as to refuse to forgive our brethren. He is our Master and our God, and we are but his servants and his vassals; or rather, we were his enemies, his fugitives, and his rebels. And notwithstanding all this, he forbore not to receive us to grace. Our faults were infinite in number, and extremely heinous and criminal, being committed against God, and consequently deserving eternal punishment; yet this hindered him not from pardoning them all. Think, then, if our pride is not altogether intolerable, who, being neither gods, nor kings, nor rulers, but poor worms of the earth, and brands plucked out of hell by the sole clemency of our God, have yet the stoutness to deny, not to our vassals, or our servants, but our neighbours, our brethren, the domestics and children of our common Master, the pardon, not of many faults, but of one or two only; not of such as are grievous, but of slight ones; not of capital ones, but such as are remissible; yea, sometimes rather pretended than real. Add to this, that, as for the Lord Jesus, no one prayed him to forgive us; there was nothing but his own goodness alone that induced him to do us this grace: whereas he, and his Father, and his Spirit exhort us and command us to forgive our brethren; and this too with promise to render us for ever happy if we do it, and threatening to condemn us to eternal fire if we fail of it. Thus you see how proper is this example of our Lord for the apostle's purpose and design.

But observe yet, in passing, that the comparison he makes between our duty in this behalf, and the grace of Jesus Christ towards us, evidently infers that the pardon of our sins which the Lord gives us is pure and simple, and without reservation of those temporal punishments and satisfactions which they of Rome pretend he exacts of them after he has remitted their faults. For as to us, it is clear that as often as our brother repents of having offended us we ought to forgive him, according to the command of Christ; and he would be a mocker and impious who would not remit him his fault, but on condition that he should be for some time punished for it in a fire. Since then the apostle directs us to forgive our brethren, as Jesus Christ forgives us, who does not see that this unheard-of rigour has much less place in the grace which we receive from our Lord, than in that which we do our brethren, by forgiving them when they have offended us?

This, my beloved brethren, is what we had to deliver for the exposition of this exhortation of the apostle. Would to God the practice of it were as common among us as the understanding of it is easy, and the justice of it evident! But we know well what he requires of us, and are not ignorant that it is our Master's will, neither can we deny that it is most reasonable; and yet we do it not. He commands us mercy and kindness, and nothing is more rare among us. They are as little to be seen here as in the societies of the world. We have for the most part little or no compassion for the miseries of our neighbours; for if we were touched with a true compassion for them, we should visit them in their sickness, we should succour them in their necessities, we should assuage their griefs; at least our tears would declare the part we take in their troubles; whereas nearly all of us do the contrary. We shun meeting the afflicted, as if misery were a contagious malady; and to colour our hard-heartedness, we feign that they are wicked and have verily deserved the evil which they suffer. So far are we from alleviating their unhappiness, that we insult it; and instead of oil and balm, we pour vinegar into their wounds; not considering that by adding calumny to rigour we do not justify, but redouble our cruelty. For if it were so, that the afflicted had been worse than you represent him, does it follow that you ought not to have pity on him? Do you owe compassion to none but the innocent? Good Lord! what would become of us, if God and men should so deal with us? For who of us is not culpable? You that reproach the poor afflicted unseasonably with their faults, really are you pure and without reproach before God? If you look narrowly into it, you will see that if you are not miserable, it is not because you have not deserved it as well as any other, but because God spares you, or reserves you perhaps for some sorer chastisement. But it is uncertain also whether the person whom you treat so ill is afflicted for the faults of which you accuse him or not; for, seeing the impenetrable depth of the judgments of God, no man can know of a truth how the case is; and in the uncertainty in which we are it is best to behave ourselves wisely towards the man, and to judge moderately of his affliction. After all, the

Lord has not made you inquisitor or judge of your brethren, that you should pity none but those whose innocence you should justify. He reserves the judgment of them to himself, and the authority to make it. For your part, who are infirm men as others are, he gives you order only to consider whether your neighbours, and especially your brethren, are afflicted, and if they are, to have pity on them, to feel their evils as sensibly as they do themselves; and after this first dressing by compassion, to follow the curing of their miseries with a gentle hand; liberally imparting to them your alms, if they be necessitous; your instructions, if they be ignorant; your credit and assistance, if they be oppressed; and your succour, if they need it.

But as we have little or no concern for the affairs of others, so have we too much for our own: our private interest swallows up all our thoughts and affections. We are solicitous for none but ourselves; and those hearts of ours, which see our brethren pine away, and languish, and die, without shedding so much as one tear, cannot endure the least puncture in our own skin without perturbation and being pierced through with grief. This delicacy makes us unable to bear anything. The heaviness, the simplicity, the least defect we see in our people about us, or in our friends, offends us. And though we have more occasion than any for the equity and indulgence of others, yet we can bear nothing from them; but imitating in this part of our lives the furious and extravagant rigours of Rome in her councils, excommunicate and anathematize indifferently all who cross us. And as for the offences which are committed against us, we make them so heinous, that if we were believed, they would all be taken for treasons, which cannot be pardoned without injustice, and considerable prejudice to all human society. Hence arise those hatreds and quarrels with which all among us are full, and which are kept on foot and perpetuated, to the reproach of the gospel and scandal of the world, between great and small, yea, between neighbours and nearest alliances, not so much as brethren and sisters exempted; neither the communion of grace nor of nature being sufficient to reduce our refractory and untractable stoutness to reason. Now, though this is deplorable, yet it is not to be wondered at; for the cause of it is very evident, even pride, which has taken up the place of that humility which the apostle commands us. It is this arrogance, and that haughty opinion, which every one has of himself, that renders us so cruel and unnatural, insensible to the miseries of the afflicted, and implacable towards those who have offended us. This is the poison that kills all sweetness and gentleness, all tenderness and humanity in us, and draws out of our bowels all the sentiments of the charity of Jesus Christ. Restore humility, and you will soon recover all those divine virtues.

But, dear brethren, enough of complaints; especially on so good a day, in which we have communicated at the Lord's own table. I would now much rather praise your virtues and graces, than reprehend your faults and vices. I shall therefore leave the charge of examining them to each one of yourselves, to be performed by you apart, under the eyes of God, and in the secret of your own consciences; and will, for a conclusion, content myself with exhorting and conjuring you to obey henceforth this command of the apostle, and to put on, as he enjoins, "bowels of mercy, kindness, humbleness of mind, meekness, long-suffering; forbearing one another, and forgiving one another, if any man have a quarrel against any, even as Christ forgave you." This is required of you by that sacred bread and wine which you all have taken together this morning at the table of Jesus Christ, and are the symbol of your union, and the badge of your concord. Has not that mystical cup indeed sweetened your hearts? Has it not mitigated your gall and bitterness, and mollified your stoutness, and expelled out of your minds all thoughts contrary to charity? This, again, that holy and glorious Lord, who has to-day been communicated to you, demands of you. Christian, saith he, I have showed thee mercy, that thou mightest do so to others; I have had pity upon thee, that thou mightest have compassion upon them; I have given thee my flesh and blood, that thou mightest impart thy good things to my poor members who need them; I have died for thee, that thou mightest live for them; and have satisfied thee with the bread of heaven, that thou mightest distribute unto them that of the earth; I have pardoned thy crimes, and drowned them all in my blood, that thou mightest cheerfully forgive the offences which they have committed against thee. Thus, my brethren, the Lord addresses us.

The name of christians, which we bear, and the quality of elect of God, holy and beloved, which is inseparably annexed thereto, also oblige us to the same service. For with what face can we say that we are elect of God, if we still abide in the commerce of the world, and its vices—or his saints, if we have no mark of his sanctity—or his beloved, if we despise his commandments? Finally, the interest of our own welfare and salvation likewise demands of us the same thing: for what is there more miserable than cruel, haughty, hard-hearted, and implacable souls; whom their own vices torment, night and day, in the present life, and the fire of hell will torment eternally in the world to come? And, on the contrary, what is more graceful or more happy than a church, in which reign pity and benignity, humility, meekness, and patience, those holy virtues which bind all the faithful together? It is there that the Lord has commanded life, and the blessing for ever, as the psalmist sings, Psal. cxxxiii. 3; it is there he pours forth the graces and consolations of his Spirit in this world, and will in the next distribute the crowns of his glory and of his immortality. Amen.

SERMON XL.

VERSES 14, 15.

And above all these things put on charity, which is the bond of perfectness. And let the peace of God rule in your hearts, to the which also ye are called in one body; and be ye thankful.

DEAR brethren, hypocrisy, that piece of wickedness which God most abhors, prevails to a great extent in human life. It not only counterfeits piety, performing external actions of religion, and hiding a profane and impious heart under this handsome veil; but also frequently puts on a false show of justice and goodness towards men, that, by this external appearance, it may deceive them, and through their credulity accomplish its dishonest and vicious designs. By this, first, it commits an iniquity of the blackest character; it being, as a wise heathen formerly said, one of the most unjust actions in the world to make a wicked wretch pass for an honest man. And, secondly, it unworthily profanes the acts of virtue, which are most holy and sacred; making them serve the passions and interests of vice, than which a more unclean and baser object cannot be imagined. For a hypocrite does good, not out of any affection which he has for virtue, but to get reputation, to win people's hearts, or to advance his own affairs. Ambition, or avarice, or pleasure, is the idol to which he sacrifices the noblest and most splendid actions. For instance, when he gives alms to the poor, it is not because he cares for them, as the scripture speaks of Judas, but he does it only to win credit. He gives, properly, to his own vanity, and not to the necessities of men. Again, when he acts the part of a merciful man, and forgives the offences of those who have injured him, it is not any sentiment of goodness, but merely the interest of his glory, that sways him so to do. There are a multitude of people who thus abuse beneficence and gentleness. Like expert tyrants, they make them the instruments of their lust; and when they perform any virtuous actions, it is not at the command of those virtues themselves, but in subserviency to their own vices; retaining a disposition to be cruel and inhuman, if their interest requires it. Such as are only virtuous in this manner are not so in reality. They are subtle and dexterous, but not good men. And though the external lustre of their good works is apt to deceive men, yet it will not be able to satisfy their own conscience, if they have any; and much less to commend them in the eyes of God, who judges of things by their inside and their reality, not by their appearance. For, in order that any act of beneficence, of clemency, of meekness and humanity, may be holy and acceptable unto God, it is requisite that it should proceed from a sincere love towards our neighbours. If it come from any other principle, it is of no value in reality, however plausible and pompous it may be in appearance. It is a false and spurious production; a fruit fair without, but worm-eaten and corrupt within. Besides that the thing speaks for itself, Paul also proclaims it in the 13th chapter of the first Epistle to the Corinthians; "Though I bestow all my goods to feed the poor, and have not charity, it profiteth me nothing."

Therefore, brethren, the same apostle, having before charged us to bear with one another, to forgive one another, and to perform all other acts of kindness, mercy, meekness, and patience, to purge our hearts and works from all the venom of hypocrisy, now adds, very pertinently, that, together with these virtues to which he has exhorted us, we are, above all, to put on charity, as that which is the soul of every true virtue, and without which the fairest and most esteemed actions are but, as an ancient doctor well said, glittering sins. And, besides all this, says the apostle, "put on charity, which is the bond of perfectness. And let the peace of God rule in your hearts, to the which ye are called in one body; and be ye thankful." You plainly see that he recommends to us three christian virtues, charity, the peace of God, and thankfulness. Now, as for the last of these, he only names it, without saying anything else of it; whereas, with reference to the other two, he briefly sets before us some considerations, to urge us to take up the studious pursuit of them. For he says of charity, that it is the bond of perfection; and of the peace of God, that we are thereunto called in one body. In compliance then with the order of our text, we will treat of three heads in this discourse, if God please: first, of charity; secondly, of the peace of God; and then, for a conclusion, make a few brief remarks upon gratitude, or thankfulness, about which the apostle speaks but a word.

I. There is no person in the church who does not know that charity is that pure, sincere, and virtuous love which each of us owes to other men, our neighbours, upon the account of that communion of nature we have with them, and principally because of the image of God, after which they all are created, according to the express command which he has given us to love them as ourselves. I grant that it has various degrees, and embraces men with some inequality, these more strictly, and those less, according to the differences of their merit and worth, as also of the union we have with them, either in a state of nature or of grace. Nevertheless, it extends itself to all, and does not account any one a stranger; but obliges and serves them freely, as far as its ability permits, and when occasion is offered. For our Lord and Saviour teaches us, in the parable of that poor man whom the Samaritan assisted, finding him in that pitiful state in which the thieves had left him, on the way from Jerusalem to Jericho, that every man that needs our help is our neighbour, Luke x. 36; so that God and right reason obliging us to love every one that is our neighbour, there is, doubtless, no man whom we ought not to love. But as charity has a much greater extent than the friendship of the world, so is its flame much more pure and holy. For, to say the truth, men of the world love none but themselves; it being evident that, if they affect any, it is not so much to do them good, as to draw profit or pleasure from them. But charity sincerely affects its neighbour, desiring to him and procuring for him that good which is necessary to make him happy. And the difference of these two affections comes from their causes. For charity issues from the love of God; whereas worldly friendship proceeds from that vicious and inordinate love which every one bears to himself: so that charity, loving our neighbour for God's sake, seeks nothing but God's glory, and the welfare of the person it loves; whereas, a man of the world, loving only for his own sake, accordingly seeks nothing but his own interests. And though this plainly appears in the whole conduct of each kind of love, yet it may be particularly observed in this one event, namely, that that affliction and misery which extinguishes worldly amity, makes the affections of charity to flame more than ever; an evident sign that the one is neither bred nor fed but by the fruit it gathers from the thing it loves; whereas the other, on the contrary, being kindled by that ray of the divine image which it sees engraven on the nature of its neighbour, is kept always burning, and the more it sees him need its compassions and good offices, the more it increases and redoubles its endeavours. It is this holy and christian charity which the apostle commands us to put on: "And above all these things, put on charity."

These words, as they lie in the original, may be taken two ways, both of them apt and good, and such as have their authors. Some interpret them, "and above or over all these things." Others, a little different, "and for all these things." Both agree that "all those things" which the apostle intends are the same he had spoken of immediately before; namely, those bowels of mercy, that kindness, that humility, meekness, and patience, which, in the preceding verses, he commands us to put on. Now, then, after the sense of the former of those interpreters, he means, that to this rich garment we should add charity; putting it uppermost, as a precious and useful robe, to cover and keep all the rest. Not that we must put on charity last, in regard of time, after all those other virtues; on the contrary, it ought to be first formed in us, as the parent by whom the greater part of the rest are to be brought forth. But the apostle makes use of this comparison upon the account of other resemblances which these things have with one another; and the authors of this exposition notice three of that kind: one, that as the robe we put over our clothes is greater and larger than our other clothing, so charity has a much greater extent than any of the before-mentioned virtues. For mercy succours only the miserable; kindness helps them only who have need of us; sweetness only caresses those with whom we converse; and patience only bears with those who offend us: but charity embraces them all together, and is affectionate towards our neighbours generally, both those that are in adversity, and such as are in prosperity; persons in affluence, as well as those who are necessitous; friends and foes; the perfect and the infirm; those who oblige us, and those who offend us; and those likewise who look upon us as indifferent. Secondly, as that last piece of our clothing, which also covers all the rest, and is most in sight, is commonly fairest and the richest; so likewise is charity, without doubt, more excellent than all the other virtues which make up a christian's clothing. Lastly, as the one marks out and distinguishes men, being usually the character of their rank and of their quality, in the town or in the state; so the other is the christian's livery, and a mark of the honour they have to be the children of God, and disciples of his Son; as our Saviour said, "By this shall all men know that ye are my disciples, if ye have love one to another," John xiii. 35.

These considerations are pretty and pleasing; but I doubt whether they are not over-fine, and somewhat too far-fetched. I should rather say that the apostle, by those words, "And above all these things put on charity," purely and plainly means, that above all, that is, principally, we should be owners of charity; signifying to us thereby, as he elsewhere teaches us at large, that it is the most excellent of christian virtues; so much so, that all the rest remain useless without it, being but so many vain and fallacious pictures, which have nothing of firmness or solidity in them. For instance, mercy without charity is but a weakness of nature. Without it kindness or benignity is but indiscreet profusion; courtesy, but deceitful tattle; humility, low-spiritedness; and patience, stupidity. It is the divine fire of charity that animates all these virtues, makes them perfect, and gives them all the nobility and acceptableness to God which they possess. It is with great propriety, therefore, that after the apostle had recommended them to us, he adds, that above all we have charity, as that which is of all the richest and most excellent. Not to speak here of the advantage he elsewhere gives it above all other parts of christianity, 1 Cor. xiii., even to preferring it, not only before the gift of tongues and miracles, before the grace of prophecy, and all the other wonders with which Jesus Christ adorned the beginnings of his church, but even before faith and hope; as that which will endure for ever, and flourish in the very sanctuary of immortality, whereas all those other gifts of God, which have their exercise only here below, shall cease; whence he concludes that charity is greater than all those other graces.

The other exposition, which interprets these words of Paul, "And for all these things put on charity," is also very pertinent, and what we have been saying sufficiently explains its sense. For since charity is the soul and the perfection of all the before-named virtues, which gives them all the value and worth they possess, the acts of them being vain without charity, as the apostle says, it is clear that for the possession of them charity must be had. Besides, it is this that excites them and puts them into operation, and also with a kind of necessity produces and forms them in our souls. For it is impossible that the man who truly loves his neigbour can be insensible to his distresses, if he is afflicted; or can forbear to gratify him with his beneficence, if he needs it; or stoop to his necessities, and humble himself about him; or bear with his defects, if he discover any; or treat him kindly; condescend to his infirmities, and seek to gain him, if he withdraw from his friendship; and patiently take his offences, if he so far forget himself as to do him any; according to the apostle's saying, that charity is patient, and kind, not envious, "is not puffed up;" that it "endureth all things, believeth all things, beareth all things," 1 Cor. xiii. 4, 5, 7. Wherefore he affirms elsewhere, Rom. xiii. 8—10, that "he that loveth others hath fulfilled the law," and that this command, "Thou shalt love thy neighbour as thyself," comprehends in it and summarily recapitulates all the duties enjoined in the rest of the commandments, and concludes that charity is the fulness of the law, that is, the thing that fills up all the articles of it. Hence John, the beloved disciple of the Lord Jesus, as we read in the church history, in his extreme old age, having no longer the strength, as formerly, to make long sermons in the assemblies of the faithful, contented himself with saying these few words, "Little children, love one another;" judging, and that rightly, that he had comprised in this short sentence all the true duties of christians. Since, then, the nature, fecundity, and efficacy of charity are such, you see what good reason the apostle had to recommend us to put it on, for our having and exercising that mercy, benignity, humility, meekness, and patience he told us of before.

His expression, that "charity is the bond of perfectness," has the same tendency. But here it becomes a question what that perfection is of which charity is the bond; and expositors labour to explain it to us. Some understand it of the perfection of all virtues, which this one binds and puts together, comprehending and embracing them all as we said just now; and the Romanists thence draw an argument to confirm their doctrine of justification by works. For, say they, those who perfectly fulfil the law are justified by the works of the law. Now since charity is, in this sense, the bond of perfection, it is evident that those who have true charity perfectly fulfil the law; consequently, they are justified by the works of the law. But letting pass for the present that which they presuppose, namely, that charity is here called the bond of perfection, because it binds together and comprehends in it the observance of all the commandments of the law, it is clear, however, that that which they pretend will not follow. First, because it is not sufficient for a man's justification by the works of the law that he fulfil it only after some certain time to his life's end. It is necessary that he should have fulfilled it from the beginning, and been exempt from sin, not only from his childhood and youth, as the young man pretended to be in the gospel, but even from his nativity. Supposing, then, but not granting, that he who has charity perfectly fulfils the law, without failing so much as in one point, this, as you see, would be done only from the time he had put on the habit of charity, and could not alter the fact of his having transgressed in various ways before. Since, then, the law justifies none but those that never violated it at any time, it is manifest that even if a christian should never violate the law after he has charity, yet he could not be justified by his works, nor would he be exempted from needing the grace of God for the remission of the sins which he committed before he had charity. But where grace is, there justification by works cannot have place, according to Paul's declaration in the Epistle to the Romans, chap. xi. 6: "If it be by grace, then is it no more of works: otherwise grace is no more grace. But if it be of works, then is it no more grace: otherwise work is no more work."

But I add, in the second place, that what they suppose, namely, that he who has charity perfectly fulfils the law, so as never to fail so much as in one point, is evidently false, and contrary to experience and Scripture. To experience; for who does not daily perceive how often, and in how many ways, those very men among the faithful offend, who have the greatest degrees of charity? To Scripture; for it plainly tells us in various places, that " if we say (they are the words of an apostle) we have no sin, we deceive ourselves, and the truth is not in us," 1 John i. 8. True it is, that charity does not cause us to offend; nay, such offending is, on the contrary, a deviation and a departure from charity. However, I affirm, it is no impossibility for a man who has true charity sometimes to falter in it, as you see it often happens in all habits; he who is endowed with them commits some actions not very consonant with them. A good archer, for instance, does not always hit the mark, and a good advocate does not always plead exactly well. It happens that the best writers, the most exquisite painters, and the most accomplished politicians, commit errors now and then in the matters of their profession. And it was said long since of the most excellent and admired piece of heathen poetry, that there are passages in it at which the author slept; whence others have derived the privilege of forgetting themselves in a prolix work. The same event attends the habits of moral virtues; for these do not so absolutely fill up the souls of men, that actions contrary to them do not sometimes escape those who have obtained them to an eminent degree, as experience shows, and philosophers have expressly noticed. Therefore neither are faults incompatible with the habit of charity, as we possess it here below. Only it withholds such as are truly endowed with it from committing them often; and when they are overtaken, it quickly touches them with regret, and moves them to repent of what they have committed. Since, then, that to be justified by works a man must present such works to God as have no need of pardon, it is still evident that charity, however perfect we may have it here below, is not capable of justifying us before God. If our adversaries will be obstinate, and maintain that charity is exempted from all sin, I will grant it of that charity which reigns on high in the heavens, being kindled and kept up by the vision of the glorious face of God; but I will say with St. Augustine,* that no man has such a charity upon earth; ours here is but begun and imperfectly formed. Yet the law requires of us a charity full and entire, and perfect in every particular. Surely, then, that which we at present have is not able to satisfy the law, and consequently cannot justify us.

But others conceive that, by this perfection of which charity is the bond, the integrity and unity of the church is to be

* Aug. Ep. 29. ad Hieron.

understood, because the perfection of bodies properly consists in the collection and colligation of the parts of which they are composed, those that want any one of them being not in a condition to be called perfect. These authors, therefore, consider that charity is here styled the bond of perfection, because it is this that joins and binds all the faithful together, by means of the mutual love which they bear each other. For my part, dear brethren, I think we must join together these two expositions, and reduce them to one; and understand the apostle's words, the bond of perfection, as simply importing that charity is a perfect bond, by a Hebraism very frequent through the whole Scripture; as when it speaks of a man of sin, or a man of peace, to signify a sinful man, or one who is peaceable or pacific; affections of infamy, for "vile affections," Rom. i. 26; and so in a multitude of other places. Here then, in like manner, the apostle says a bond of perfection, instead of a perfect bond; an exquisite bond, capable of binding up in perfection both all christian virtues in every faithful soul, and all the faithful in the church with each other. For as concerning virtues, charity binds them together, both by that common principle from which it causes them to spring, namely, love of our neighbour, and by that common end to which it directs them, namely, his benefit and edification. It gathers up and puts all of them together in its bosom, not leaving one out of its enclosure, because they are all necessary for it; mercy to comfort those whom it loves, benignity to succour them, humility to win them, gentleness to please them, patience to preserve them, and, in short, all the rest, to acquit itself of those duties it would perform towards them. And as for the faithful, who does not know that charity is the perfect bond of their union? The considerations of blood, of state, of interest, and of pleasure, sometimes bind other men together, but it is with a great deal of imperfection, these uncertain bonds being daily broken, and so badly compacting the persons they enclose, that they are soon separated, and sometimes even fall out with and injure each other. But charity is in very deed a perfect bond, that unites those whom it ties together so closely, and with such firmness, as neither the accidents of fortune, (as they call them,) nor the mutations of the earth, nor death itself, which dissolves all other unions and conjunctions in the world, can loosen them, or separate them from each other. It was this sacred bond that formerly made all the believers at Jerusalem to be "of one heart and of one soul," Acts iv. 32. It is a bond that all the force of men and elements can neither break nor untie; a bond stronger than death and the grave, as the mystical spouse sings in that excellent Song. It does not only join the souls of the faithful; it mingles and unites them, changes them into one body and one spirit, gives them the same will and the same affections.

II. Now, further, it is to form and preserve this holy union among us, that the apostle recommends to us the peace of God in the second part of this text: "Let the peace of God," says he, "rule in your hearts, to the which also ye are called in one body." For this peace of God is not that which we have with God by faith in Jesus Christ his Son; being appeased by the satisfaction of his cross, he looks upon us in him with a propitious and favourable eye, as a Father, and not as a Judge, not imputing our sins to us, which may be termed peace of conscience. But it is the peace which we ought to have with each other, all of us living amicably together, as children of one and the same Father, and heirs of one and the same grace and glory. It is the daughter of charity, and a fruit of that holy and christian love which binds us perfectly together. The apostle calls it the peace of God; first, because he loves it above all things, and upon this account he is often styled in the Scriptures the God of peace, hating nothing in the world more than trouble and discord, contentions and wars. Secondly, because he commands it everywhere in his word. And lastly, because he is the author of it, who gives it and inspires it by his Spirit into all those who are truly his children. And the apostle has expressly given it this title in this place, for the more effectually recommending it to us, and that he might induce us to receive it with the greater respect, as a thing of God, holy, sacred, and divine, which we cannot violate without offending grievously that sovereign Majesty to whom in so many ways it belongs.

He directs that this peace of God may rule in our hearts. The term which he uses in the original is admirably expressive and elegant; for it properly signifies, to have the superintendence of a thing, to be the judge and arbiter of it, to govern and regulate it, and give it law. That is, the apostle means that this divine peace should be the queen of our hearts, the mistress and governess of all our motions; which keeps them in due respect, and withholds them from ever attempting anything that tends to violate or disturb it; and if the resenting an offence, for instance, or an opinion of our own worth, or any other such consideration, begin to kindle wrath, or hatred, or animosity against our brethren, or to excite some other passion of a similar nature in our hearts, that this peace should forthwith advance, and stay the commotion and agitation of our minds, calming the storm, and speedily repelling all these sentiments of the flesh, as so many incendiaries, or evil spirits, without giving them entrance or audience; that it should enjoin and inspire into us humility and patience when we have been offended, regret and the making of satisfaction when we have offended any other; and cause us to seek carefully after all that it shall judge necessary to maintain amity and good fellowship among us, as kind words and obliging deeds; banishing both from our mouths and from our manners all that is apt to cause or keep up a division from our neighbours.

The intelligence which he communicates, that this is the peace of God, is enough to persuade us to give it such a place in our hearts. But that the apostle might overcome all possible obstinacy, he here further represents to us two other considerations which should constrain us to give it this superintendence over our souls. The one is, that we are thereunto called; and the other, that we are one body. As to the first, you know that our Lord and Master Jesus Christ everywhere calls us to this peace of God, and that he has given us precepts for it in his gospel, and examples of it in his life. For what was there ever in the world more meek and peaceable than this divine Lamb? He contended not, nor cried, and his voice was not heard in the streets, Matt. xii. 19, as the prophets foretold of him. He was gentle and lowly in heart. He never repulsed any; and received sinners with open arms, however bad and abominable they had been. He invited his greatest enemies to his salvation, and offered his grace to the most obstinate, and bore their contradictions without answering again, and their reproaches with silence, and their rage without exasperation; and wept bitterly for Jerusalem, because that rebellious city would not know the things of her peace. Such is the pattern he gave us; commanding us likewise expressly to be gentle, and harmless as doves, without gall and without bitterness, and to be in peace among ourselves, Mark ix. 50. And his apostles repeat this lesson to us in various places: "If it be possible," says Paul, "as much as lieth in you, live peaceably with all men," Rom. xii. 18. And it is for this that Jesus Christ came into the world, even to pacify heaven and earth, Jews and Gentiles; to extinguish enmities and wars, and change swords into ploughshares, and spears into pruning-hooks; to take away the poison of asps, and the cruelty of wolves, and the fierceness of lions, and transform bears and the most savage beasts into lambs, and make them all live and dwell peaceably and amicably together, Isa. ii. 4; xi. 6—8: finally, to make peace overflow as a river, Isa. lxvi. 12, as the ancient oracles had magnifically foretold; in consequence of which he is also expressly styled "The Prince of peace," Isa. ix. 6. And you know it was the legacy he bequeathed us, when he was preparing to die for us: "Peace I leave with you," said he, "my peace I give unto you," John xiv. 27; not to speak of the blessing and the dignity he promises those who shall love peace: "Blessed are the peace-makers: for they shall be called the children of God," Matt. v. 9. After all this, who can doubt that he calls all his people unto peace, as the apostle here affirms, since he forms them to it by his voice, by his life, by his promises, and by the whole design of his mediatorial office?

But besides the command and order he has given, the very state and condition in which by his vocation he has placed us manifestly requires it; and this the apostle represents to us, in the second place, when, having told us that we are called to peace, he adds, "in one body," or, to express the full and whole force of the Greek words, in one only body. It is a doctrine universally received, and most expressly asserted in various places of Scripture, that the whole church makes up but one only mystical body, of which Jesus Christ is the Head, and the faithful are the members, being animated under him with one and the same Spirit, and knit together by one and the same faith, hope, and charity. No one has part in the kingdom of heaven who lives not in the communion of this body. Surely then it should be one of our chief concerns to maintain peace among ourselves; and to put it, as the apostle directs, in the highest place of our hearts, that it may govern with supremacy all our thoughts, motions, and sentiments. For there are no natural bodies whose members do not agree and live with each other in a perpetual and inviolable peace. The societies of states and families, which are bodies, but of another kind, namely, political and economical, are governed in the same manner; their primary and most sacred law is, that all the orders and persons of which they are composed have peace with each other. Now if this has place both in nature and in the societies of mankind, how much more ought it to be observed in the church, which is a divine, celestial, and supernatural body! Our own interest naturally requires it; for as war weakens and ruins the states into which it thrusts itself, and whose members it divides; so, on the contrary, peace establishes, fortifies, and preserves them, according to that saying of our Saviour, "Every kingdom divided against itself is brought to desolation; and every city or house divided against itself shall not stand," Matt. xii. 25.

III. The apostle adds, in the close, "and be ye thankful;" which some refer to the same scope which the rest of the text has; as if he intended that those thanks we owe to God for the free favour he has showed us, in receiving us unto peace with him, also evidently requires us to maintain peace with our brethren. And I acknowledge that the argument is good and pertinent. Yet it is better to take this clause for an exhortation, which he gives us in general, to be thankful towards God and towards men. For as ingratitude is one of the blackest and most detestable vices, expressly enrolled by the apostle among the marks of those wretched times, whose extreme corruption he foretells in the second Epistle to Timothy, chap. iii. 2; so is it certain that gratitude or thankfulness, is a most necessary virtue: and, in my opinion, he went not very wide from the truth, who called it the mother of all other virtues.* It enkindles piety in our hearts, raises up the love of God and of his Christ, and urges us to serve and obey him, and, by consequence, to exercise all honesty and virtue. It is certain that upon this account no man sins without ingratitude. Add to this, that thankfulness is the source of all the services and duties which we perform to our princes, to our country, to our parents, to our superiors, and all who have obliged us; offices, as you know, which have a great extent in human life; so that it is with much propriety that the apostle, after charity and peace, gives us charge also touching thankfulness.

Dear brethren, these are the three virtues of which he tells us in this text. Let us not neglect any one of them; but embrace them all three, and deck our lives internally and externally with them. In the first place, above all, let us put on charity; as the soul of christianity, the perfect bond of our union, the mark of God's children, the abridgement of all our duties, and the mother of all virtues. Having it, you have all and without it, you have nothing. Without it, all the profession you make of the gospel, your prayers, your religion, and your services, are but an empty noise, "a sounding brass," as the apostle says, and "a tinkling cymbal," 1 Cor. xiii. 1. Because the Israelites wanted this, God held all their devotions and sacrifices in abomination. How much more will he reject yours, if you have the impudence to present him any without charity, now that his Son Jesus has so clearly shown you the necessity and excellency of it! For what can you allege any longer to excuse yourselves from this duty? Truly nature itself sufficiently obliged you before to love your neighbours, since they are your brethren, even after the flesh, issued from the same Adam, and the same Noah, animated by the same spirit, clothed with the same body, born and bred upon the same earth; and if you divest yourself of all the difference which vanity and opinion have created, you will see that in truth there is none at all between you and them. You are subject to the same accidents as they, and the death which at last brings them down will no more spare you than it does them. Having so intimate a connection with them, you ought to look upon them as your other selves, and love them as your near relations, and not account anything that concerns them foreign or indifferent. The heathen, who knew no more, had the understanding to draw this conclusion from it. But the cross of our Lord and Saviour has afforded us other reasons for

* Cicero.

charity, which are much more excellent and pressing. For he so loved men, that he died to save them. Christian, how can you hate or despise persons whom your Master has so much loved and esteemed, upon whom you see his blood, by which they have been washed and purified together with yourselves—his Spirit, with which they have been sealed as well as you—the first-fruits and earnests of that heavenly inheritance unto which they and you are called to live eternally together? It is by this that they are to be considered, and not by what they are upon this earth, which, with the whole heap of all its pomps, and riches, and nobility, and honours and other pieces of vanity, is but a figure which passes away and perishes. If your neighbour has nothing on the earth, if he is despised and accounted the filth and off-scouring of the world, as the apostle speaks, remember that he has his share in heaven, that he is an heir of this eternal kingdom, the child of God, and brother of Jesus Christ. Let this his dignity, which is so high and so precious in the sight of God and his angels, induce you to love him, to regard him, and to befriend him; let it mitigate your resentments, if he has offended you; let it stretch forth your hands to a ready communication of the succour of your alms, of your consolations, and of your good offices, if his necessity calls for them. For such is the nature of true charity; it loves not in words and with the tongue, but in deed and in truth. Let ours then abound in alms and in beneficence to the poor, in consolations and in good offices to the afflicted. Let it be firm and constant. Let not our brethren's ill successes, no, nor their offences, (if they happen to commit any,) be ever able to break this sacred bond of perfection, which spiritually joins us and them together in our Lord.

Let us also heedfully keep, as committed to our trust, that peace which Jesus Christ has left us at his death, and unto which he calls us in one body, by all his religious mysteries. This, says the apostle, is the peace of God; and he that keeps it may be sure to have God with him, according to the promise which the same apostle elsewhere makes: "Live in peace; and the God of love and peace shall be with you," 2 Cor. xiii. 11. Object not those petty reasons which flesh and blood inspire. Nothing must be heard against the peace of God. The apostle requires that it should rule in our hearts, that it should be the governess and superintendent of them. Account then every thought that would disturb it as rebellious, drive it out of your hearts and crush it as an infernal thought, which cannot come from any but the enemy, since it is contrary to the peace of Christ. Now here, dear brethren, I might make large complaints upon that rebellion, of which most of us are guilty, against this peace of God which the apostle sets up to rule in our hearts. We have shaken off its yoke. Flesh and blood, and their interests have driven it out from among us. It is so far from possessing the first place here, that it has scarcely any at all; and it seems that, offended with our contempt, it has quitted the church as well as the world, and is altogether retired into heaven. For all among us are full of divisions and discord, of suits, of quarrels, of little wars, which we make upon one another, with a scandalous eagerness and obstinacy. In the name of God, let us recall, beloved brethren, into our communion, this holy and blessed peace of God, unto which Jesus Christ and his gospel with so much importunity invite us, and henceforth give it that place in our hearts which the apostle assigns it. This is the best thanks we can render this great Saviour for the kindness he has showed us. And if we deny him that peace he demands of us for our brethren, I know not how we can ask his peace for ourselves, or clear ourselves of the foulest ingratitude. But I hope better things, and do beseech the Lord that he himself would shed abroad his peace into our hearts, and absolutely settle it in them: that we may see all his blessings abound in the midst of us, both those of the present life, and those of the life to come. Amen.

SERMON XLI.

VERSE 16.

Let the word of Christ dwell in you richly in all wisdom; teaching and admonishing one another in psalms and hymns and spiritual songs, singing with grace in your hearts to the Lord.

DEAR brethren, experience shows us that most things are sustained by the use of the same means which gave them being. Thus in nature we see that nothing more confirms, nor better preserves, the arts and sciences, than those very actions and exercises which formed them, and that nothing better maintains estates than the same prudence and valour which raised them. Also, as frequent converse with virtuous persons commonly enkindles in our hearts a love of an aim at probity, so does it advance our constant perseverance in it. Accordingly, in religion, the word of God, which produces faith and holiness in our souls, is the very thing which preserves and perpetuates it there. This word is the power of God, both to form the piety of his elect at first, and to keep it in them for ever after its formation. It is the parent, the nurse, and the guardian of the new man. It administers both the seed of our regeneration, and the milk of our spiritual nutrition. It is this that gives us spiritual life; it is this also that preserves it. It is upon this that both the beginnings and the progressions, the production and the perseverance thereof depend. Wherefore the holy apostle, having before exhorted the Colossians to christian sanctification, and pointed out the principal fruits of it, as mercy, benignity, patience, charity, and peace; now, to abridge this discourse, and comprise all in a few words, recommends to them the word of God, as the only means, not only to maintain and preserve, but even to perfect and complete, all the parts of their piety, as a living and plentiful spring from which they might draw both those virtues which he had named, and all others that were necessary for the perfection of their christianity. There is no need, says he, that I should take the pains to point out particularly to you all the graces which ought to beam forth in your actions, nor recommend singly those perfections which the name and profession of Jesus Christ requires of you. You have a good master near you that will teach them and excellently form them in you; I mean the word of Christ, which I deem it sufficient merely to recommend to you. Hear it, and practise it, and let it be familiar with you. To direct you to it, is to say all. You will want nothing if you hear, and study, and believe its intimations with that attention and respect which you owe it. "Let it dwell richly in you in all wisdom," &c.

This is the advice, beloved brethren, which the apostle before gave the Colossians; advice so much the more necessary for us now, because, besides the negligence and disgust of our nature, there are people found in this unhappy age who decry the word of God and do all they can to make christians suspect it, and to wrest out of their hands this precious treasure of faithful souls; an attempt unheard of in all the first ages of the church, and not to be believed, did not our eyes and senses testify it. Therefore, christians, if you have any zeal for your Master's glory, upon whose wisdom all the blame that is laid upon his word evidently reflects, if you have any love for the edification of your neighbours, and if you have any affection for your own salvation, hear with attention the apostle's instruction. Take home to you and keep with you this heavenly word, which he would lodge and have to dwell there. Defend these divine springs of life, of which all our fathers drank, against the attempts of these new doctors, who would by all means stop and fill them up; doing the house of Jesus Christ such wrong as the Philistines formerly did the family of Isaac, whose wells, as the sacred historian tells us, they closed up and filled with earth, to render them useless. Gen. xxvi. 15. Now, to guide you in this meditation, I will (if it please

God) consider in order, the two points that offer themselves in the apostle's text: First, that in which he recommends to us the study of the word of God, in these terms, "Let the word of Christ dwell in you richly in all wisdom." Secondly, that in which he represents to us some of the principal uses we ought to make of it: "Teaching and admonishing one another in psalms and hymns and spiritual songs, singing with grace in your hearts to the Lord."

I. All the terms which he uses in the first part are worthy of much consideration. First, his calling the word of God, which was delivered by the prophets and apostles, and is contained in the Scriptures of the Old and New Testament, "the word of Christ." It is the word of Christ, both because he is the subject and the end of it, and also the author of it, who inspired it by his Spirit into his servants; in the same manner as the apostle elsewhere terms all the afflictions of the new and of the ancient church even to those which Moses and the Israelites suffered in Egypt, the affliction and reproaches of Christ, Heb. xi. 25, 26, because Christ is both the cause for which the faithful are afflicted, and also the director of their affliction who sends and governs them by his providence. Whence it clearly follows that he is God, since all Scripture is by inspiration of God, and that he subsisted in the time of the patriarchs, and of all the ancient church, contrary to the impious doctrines of those heretics who deny the divinity of our Lord, and pretend that he had no subsistence in nature until he was born of the blessed virgin.

In the next place, we are to consider in what manner the apostle recommends to us the study of this word. He says not, Let it be among you, let it be read, let it be known of you; but using a term of much more force and efficacy than all that amounts to, he directs that this word of Christ may dwell in us. Dwelling, you know, is properly affirmed of men, and implies their taking up their abode, or living in this or that place, and being ordinarily and almost always there. Hence, as the most learned of the Jewish doctors has well observed,* the Scripture uses this word figuratively to signify the constant and settled abiding of one thing in another; though the thing which is said to dwell in the other may not be animate, and the other, in which it is said to dwell, may not properly be a place or a space that contains it. As when Job, execrating the day of his birth, wishes, among other things, that clouds may dwell upon it; meaning that that day may be continually covered with clouds, that it may never be without that sable and sad veil, and, as he explains himself, that darkness and the shadow of death may for ever pollute

* R. Moses Ben. Maim. in More Nevochim. l. l. c. 25.

it; though, to speak properly, it cannot be said that clouds, which are inanimate things, dwell anywhere, and much less dwell in a day or upon a day, which is not a place or comprehensive space, but a part of time. And it is also in this figurative way that we must take all those passages of Scripture in which God's dwelling is spoken of; as when he protests in Exodus, and frequently elsewhere, that he will dwell in the midst of the children of Israel, Exod. xxix. 45; Lev. xxvi. 12: a particular which the apostle applies also to the church of the New Testament, 1 Cor. vi. 16: the meaning is, that his majesty and his providence should always be with the faithful, and never forsake them, though, to speak properly, the Lord, who is an infinite essence, and fills heaven and earth without being enclosed by them, dwells nowhere. It is in this figurative sense that the apostle here uses the world dwell, and truly with much grace and emphasis, when he says, "Let the word of Christ dwell in you." His intention is, that it be constantly in you, and settled there, that it be an inmate of your hearts and lips, that it never leave them; and as our souls dwell in our bodies, to quicken them, and to govern all their motions, in the same manner, that this divine word be the soul of your hearts, abiding day and nigth there to conduct and regulate all your actions, that it be as well known and as familiar to you as the persons who dwell in your house, and pass their whole time with you.

But the apostle, not content with so vivid an expression, adds another term, to signify more fully how studiously we ought to fill all the faculties of our souls with this word of the Lord; "Let it dwell in you," says he, "richly;" that is, abundantly, and, as the French Bibles have it, plenteously, in such a manner as that there may be no part of its mysteries which is not found in you; that its promises, its commands, its assertions, its prophecies, its instructions, may be all entertained, and not one of them excluded; and that there may be no part of yourselves in which this divine guest is not admitted to lodge and to abide; your understanding, memory, will, affections, deportment; that it appear in your whole life, and shine forth there in such a manner as every one may perceive it. It is also to this that the last words which he adds, "in all wisdom," refer; in which he shows us the end and the immediate effect of this dwelling of the word of God in us; namely, the rendering us wise unto salvation, and the giving us all the wisdom that is necessary to glorify God, and obtain eternal happiness. He would have it dwell so abundantly in us, that we might derive from it all the knowledge it imparts, both of the things we should believe, and of the things which we should do to be saved. For it is this that he usually means by that wisdom which he recommends to us. And because this knowledge has many parts, some of which are useless without the rest, he says not simply, "Let the word of Christ dwell in you richly in wisdom," but "in all wisdom," to show us that it is not enough to study some part of this heavenly knowledge. This probably might have been sufficient for men under the Old Testament, who were but in their minority; a christian, being come to mature and full age, ought to know all the will of God, all his counsel, and all that admirable wisdom which he has revealed to us by his Son and unfolded in his Scriptures.

Thus you see, dear brethren, what is the meaning of this precept of the apostle. In it now we have a great many things to observe. And, first, his procedure, in that having commenced his discourse upon our sanctification, and not being inclined to enlarge upon it further for the present, he refers the faithful for the rest, not to the voice of the church, but to the word of Christ; an evident sign that it is not the church, as those of Rome pretend, but divine Scripture, which is the supreme directress of the faithful. It is true, that pastors are serviceable for their instruction, but it is as ministers only, and not as masters; nor do they minister of their own, but out of the stock of this divine word; beside which they ought to teach nothing of themselves; and if they do, they are not to be heard. Secondly, the express order which the apostle gives us, that the word of Christ should dwell richly in us, shows that it is the duty of pastors sedulously to exhort their flocks to the study, reading, and meditation of the divine Scriptures, and that it is incumbent on their flocks to addict themselves assiduously to it. Whence it follows, in the third place, that this word of Christ ought to resound continually everywhere; in the church in its public assemblies, in private families, and the very closets of its members: otherwise how would it dwell plenteously in us? Moreover, since the apostle speaks here to all the faithful in general, as well people as ministers, this Epistle being directed by him to all "the faithful brethren in Christ which are at Colosse," it is evident his intention is, that not only should all christians hear this word in the church, but that they should also read it each one in private if they can; and that such reading is not only permitted, but commanded, as profitable and necessary. Again, the apostle's requiring that it should dwell in them, yea, dwell richly in them, necessarily implies that it is not enough to know some general points of this heavenly doctrine; but that men ought to be fully and distinctly instructed in it, and in such a manner as that there may be no part of this divine treasure of which we are not possessed. The same appears further from the effect which the apostle would have us draw from it, namely, our abounding by means of this word, "in all wisdom;" a thing which has no place in those who have but a superficial, and, as they say, an implicit, that is, a confused, involved, and entangled, knowledge of it. Whence it clearly follows that the word of Christ contains all things necessary to salvation; it being evident that he who is ignorant of any part of them is not owner of wisdom, and much less of all wisdom; which yet the apostle intimates that we shall have, if the word of the Lord dwells richly in us.

Compare now the law and the discipline of Rome with this doctrine of Paul, and you will find such a difference, or rather, so palpable a contrariety, between them, as that the night and darkness are not more contrary to the day and its light. First, the apostle refers his scholars to the word of Christ, to learn there all the duties of christianity. Rome directs hers to the pope and his officers, to be instructed about their salvation. The apostle declares that the word of Christ is capable of giving us all heavenly wisdom, if it dwell in us. Rome asserts, that it is not sufficient for this end, and that it contains but some parts of saving wisdom, for the completion of which unwritten tradition must be added. The apostle would have this divine word dwell in us. Rome would not that it should; and introduces in its place I know not what kind of fabulous legends, with which she fills the world, giving them to her votaries for instructing and feeding their souls. The apostle directs that this word be read, both in public and in private, among the faithful; Rome ordains that neither the one nor the other shall be done. As for the public, if she show her assemblies any pieces of it, she shows them hidden, and wrapt up in a language not understood; that is, she reads them, and reads them not; it being evident that proclaiming the laws and ordinances of a sovereign to a people in a language which they do not understand, is the same in effect as if they were not proclaimed. It is holding out a candle, but a candle hid under a bushel; that is, a holding it not out. It is presenting the face of Christ to his people; but presenting it veiled and disguised, under such a form as they discern nothing of it. And as to private, you know with what indignity Rome treats christians, and how she forbids them to read their Father's Testament, and judges it a crime that they should handle books which were made for them, or see those letters which are expressly directed to them. And that the permission of this reading, which they give some tradesmen of this city, and that the boldness of some doctors, who deny even the clearest things, may not deceive you, I think it pertinent to represent to you here the doctrine of Rome touching this matter. Know then that in the Treatise and Index of prohibited Books, drawn up by the authority of the council of Trent, approved and published by the authority of Pope Pius IV., and of all his successors, one of their first rules runs expressly in these words: "Since it is manifest by experience, that if the holy Bible be commonly and indifferently permitted in the vulgar tongue, there is derived from it more damage than profit, in consequence of the temerity of men; the judgment of the bishop or the inquisitor must be abided by in this case; so that they by the counsel of the parish priest, or of the confessor, may grant the reading of the Bible in a translation made by some Catholic author unto such as they shall find capable of drawing from such reading, not damage or prejudice, but increase of faith and piety; and this license they must have in writing. As for those who shall presume to read it without such license, they must not receive absolution of their sins without having first rendered up their Bible into the ordinary's hands."* Thus far the papal law.

Was there ever ordinance more injurious to the word of God, and to his apostle's authority? First, their position at the entrance, namely, that the common reading of the Bible does more hurt than good, and causes more damage than profit, is horrible, and directly contrary both to the wisdom and goodness of God, and also to Paul's declaration. For who can believe that God would give such books to his church as are more apt to hurt them than to help? And how does his apostle recommend them to all christians indifferently, directing that this word dwell plenteously in them, if this is dangerous for them, and rather pernicious than profitable? And why does he promise us from it the fruit of wisdom, yea, of all wisdom, if the reading be so perilous? Is wisdom an evil and pernicious thing? But it is easy to comprehend the thoughts of Rome; she means assuredly that reading the Bible is prejudicial to her; that it discovers her impostures, and, giving wisdom to the simple, arms and fortifies them against her corruptions and pretended traditions. This is in truth the damage and loss she fears, and which makes her so careful to extinguish or set aside all glimpses of this heavenly light, to the end that she may reign at her ease by the favour of darkness. And if she would have sincerely represented her motives in this ordinance of hers, there would not have been the preface which we have just read, but such a one as this,—'It being evident by experience that the reading of the Bible is very prejudicial to the church of Rome, giving men the hardiness to reject the authority and doctrine of her pope, who not only is not found anywhere in this word of God, but even opposes it in various instances; for these reasons it has seemed good to her to shut up and restrain the knowledge of it as much as she can, since the abolition of it altogether is both impossible and scandalous.' This is their true meaning, this their true motive. And indeed you see how in conclusion they straiten this reading as much as

* Index Libr. Prohibitor. Reg. 4.

they possibly can. First, they will not allow men to read any version of the Scripture, though never so good and faithful, and exactly translated from the original texts, except it has (as they say) some Catholic for its author; that is, one or other of those people who, being passionate for the Roman cause, would weaken the words of the Scripture as much as possible, and sometimes even audaciously corrupt them for their own advantage; as you may plainly perceive by the example of him who, passing the bounds of the modesty of all others, has not long since put the express term *mass*, a stranger to all Scripture, into the book of the Acts of the Apostles; and written at the third chapter, that the prophets and teachers which were in the church of Antioch did say mass, against the warrant of the original, and of all ancient versions, the Syriac, the Arabic, and the Latin, which is itself canonized by the Council of Trent, every one of which says agreeably with the original, that those persons served or ministered to the Lord; contrary to the example of the vulgar versions of the Roman communion, as that of the doctors of Louvain, of Benedict, of Frison, and others; and, in fact, against the evidence of the thing itself, this latter version falsely supposing that there could be no divine service but its pretended mass. Judge by this sample what the versions of the Bible, made by these good catholics, are likely to be. But however altered and disguised these versions are in their own favour, they still fear them; well knowing that it is not easy so to sophisticate this heavenly word, as that it will not always have virtue enough left to confound their errors. Therefore they add another restriction, that for the reading of such Bibles there must be had a license, and in writing, not from the parish priest, (this is not sufficient,) but from the bishop of the diocess, or from the inquisitor (an office in the modern church, which is no more found in holy writ than the office of their mass). And yet they do not leave them an absolute disposal of the matter; but oblige them to assure themselves first, by conference and deliberation with the curates of the petitioners, that they are persons to whom the word of God will do no hurt; that is, will not give them a distaste for the Roman religion, which is in reality all the danger they apprehend.

Christians, do you not tremble to hear that these masters forbid what the apostle gives you orders to do—a thing that Jesus Christ himself commands you, when he says, "Search the Scriptures!" and that their dispensation must be had to do that which Jesus Christ, and his apostle enjoin you? The apostle says, "Let the word of Christ dwell in you;" and these gentlemen cry on the other side, No, meddle not with it. Cast not your eyes on it. Have not so much as the book in your houses, (which is far indeed from getting it to dwell in your hearts,) except one of our bishops or inquisitors give you permission for it. Oh, new and unheard-of theology! that a christian must have a dispensation from Rome, or one of her ministers, to obey Jesus Christ; and cannot do what Paul commands him, except the pope's officers give him a permission in writing. Can men more openly debase the authority of Christ and his apostle? Surely, what is commanded is a duty and that which is permitted (especially that for which one is obliged to have a permission in writing) is a thing contrary to our duty, as every one knows, and as you may see by the practice of Rome itself, where permission to eat flesh in Lent is indeed demanded, but not to eat fish in the carnival; because, according to their laws, the first is contrary to a christian's duty, and not the second. If, then, a christian must have a permission to read the Bible, it is evident that the reading of it is a matter of some contrariety to a christian's duty, that of itself it is unlawful and prohibited. Again, if such reading be duly commanded, it must of necessity be said that every one is obligated to read it, (at least every faithful man or woman that can read,) and that they no more need any one's permission to read the Bible, than to give an alms, or to comfort an afflicted person, or to obey their father or their prince. Paul's command, as you see, is express, "Let the word of Christ dwell in you." It is then our duty to read it and meditate upon it. It is then a manifest invasion of the apostle's authority to restrain us from reading it without any man's permission, whoever he might be. It is a changing what Paul has ordained. It is a taking it out of the rank of duties where he had set it, and placing it among transgressions. It is a making that to pass for prohibited which the holy apostle has commanded; there being no place for a permission, but in things which the laws of God or of men have forbidden.

Can a stranger thing be ordained? Yet they stop not here. For, fearing lest such a permission, though difficult and strait, and depending upon the will of their officers, should yet prejudice their religion, if any use were made of it, they withdraw nearly altogether the power to grant it, which they before gave the bishop and the inquisitor. For, in the observation which they add upon this fourth rule, they declare expressly, that "the meaning is not that there is by it any new power attributed to bishops or inquisitors, or to the superiors of regular societies, to give leave to any to read, or buy, or keep the Bible, or any piece either of the Old or of the New Testament, or so much as summaries or historical abridgments of the books of holy Scripture, in any vulgar tongue whatever; because (say they) they have hitherto been deprived of the power of giving such permissions by the Roman holy general Inquisition, and it must be inviolably observed."* See, I beseech you, a most manifest illusion! They forbid all christians to read the Bible without the bishop's or the inquisitor's permission; but they presently declare that no bishop or inquisitor has power to give any. Thus there shall no person be permitted to read it. Is not this an evident mockery of the world? But these men so greatly dread the Scripture, that they had rather become guilty of thus shamefully and openly deluding Christendom, than suffer any one to possess or to read so dangerous a book. They would rather favour their interest than their honour. And, indeed, such is the practice in Spain and Italy, and in the territories of the Inquisition, where this permission to read the Bible is not given to any man, whoever he may be; and where it is held for a capital crime, and a sure mark of heresy, to have in the house but a volume of the Old or New Testament in the vulgar tongue. So that of necessity those who, in these parts, permit this reading to some, are either guilty of violating the general ordinances of that church of which they profess to be members, or have some particular and extraordinary power from the pope to do as they do, which, however does not appear to be the case.

This crime would be less strange if it clashed only with this passage of the apostle. But it also overturns various other most express instructions which occur in the holy Scriptures. For God commands the king of Israel, who was a layman, not a clergyman, to write a copy of his law, and to have it by him, and read it diligently, Deut. xvii. 18, 19; and generally all his people to lay up all his words in their hearts and in their minds; to bind them for signs upon their hands, and for frontlets between their eyes, that is, to have them as familiar as their own hands and eyes; to teach them to their children, and discourse of them at home and abroad, lying down and rising up; and write them on the posts of their houses, and on their gates, Deut. xi. 18—20; vi. 7—9; which is just the same thing as Paul here briefly calls having the word of God to dwell in them. In fact, Luke praises the Ethiopian eunuch, because he read the Scriptures; and the men of Berea, because they consulted them daily, to know if the things which Paul and Silas preached to them, were so, Acts viii. 28; xvii. 11. Yet we nowhere read that they had leave of any papal bishops or inquisitors. And David pronounces that man blessed who meditateth day and night in the law of God, Psal. i. 1, 2. Again, the word of God being written, "that we might believe that Jesus is the Christ, and that believing we might have life through his name," as says John,

---

* Index Libr. Prohibit. observ. circa Regul. 4.

chap. xx. 31; and "for our learning," as says Paul, "that we through patience and comfort might have hope," Rom. xv. 4; it must of necessity be concluded, that, to forbid christians to read the Scriptures is evidently either to frustrate the intention of the Lord, or to accuse him of having been unable to give us Scriptures proper for his aim and our aid. I say as much, and that more positively, of the apostolical Epistles; which, being directed to the faithful clergy and laity, indifferently, there is no reason to restrain any of them from reading that which the first ministers of God wrote to them all.

The fault of our adversaries is so much the more inexcusable, as the ancient doctors, whom they so highly extol, are directly contrary to them in this particular. As Origen for one, who would have christians not only hear the word of God in the church, but exercise themselves in reading it at home, and in meditating on it night and day.* St. Hierom for another, who would have women and maids themselves to learn the Scriptures by heart.† St. Augustine for a third, who most earnestly recommends the reading of the word of God to the very catechumeni, that is, christians of the lowest form, such as had not yet received holy baptism.‡ St. Gregory the Great, that famous bishop of Rome, for a fourth, who gravely reproves a physician of the court because he took not the pains to read the words of our Redeemer every day. "For what is holy Scripture," says he, "but a letter from God to his creature? If you were in a far country, and there received letters from the emperor your master, you would not be at rest nor sleep at your ease till you had read them, and perceived what your earthly prince should have vouchsafed to write you. The Monarch of heaven, the Lord of men and angels, has sent and conveyed to your hands his letters about the concerns of your life. And yet, my son, you deign not to read them. Apply to them, I beseech you, and meditate daily upon your Creator's sayings."§ Thus wrote Gregory, more than a thousand years ago. Judge how far the language of later popes is from his spirit, and from his principles. I pass by other doctors of antiquity, who are no less contrary to this modern abuse, and will only mention further John of Antioch, bishop of Constantinople, to whom the church has given the name of Chrysostom, that is, golden-mouth, because of the richness and sweetness of his incomparable eloquence; he alone would furnish a man with enough to make a small volume, if any would put together all the passages of his works, in which he exhorts all the faithful, and especially those of the people, to an assiduous reading of the holy Scripture; and particularly in the

* Homil. 9. on Levitic. † Hierom, Ep. 14. et 30.
‡ August. lib. de. Catech. rud. c. 6, 8.
§ Gregor. in his Epistles, lib. 4. Ep. 40.

sermon which he wrote upon this very text of the apostle which we are expounding. "Hear," says he, "you that live in the world, and have wife and children, hear how he orders you, yea, you principally, to read the scriptures, not slightly, and heedlessly, but with great care and diligence." He would have them heed no other master: "You have," says he to them, "the oracles of God, and no one can teach you so well as these divine books." And a little after, "Have," says he, "the books of the Bible, the true medicines of the soul. Get, at least, the New Testament, the Acts of the Apostles, the Gospels. Let these be your perpetual masters and teachers. If any affliction befall you, loss of goods, of children, or of friends; if death itself present itself to you; make search forthwith in this book, as in the storehouse of celestial medicines, and fetch out of it the remedies that are necessary for the mitigation of your miseries: or rather, that you may not be put to the trouble of such search, lay them all up in your soul, and have them ready upon all occasions. Ignorance of the Scriptures is the cause of all our evils."* Thus far, Chrysostom. And truly, as you see, he was not of the opinion of the latter popes of Rome, who accuse, as you heard before, the reading of the word of God of doing more harm than good.

If the reading of them must be interdicted upon the pretence, that some unstable spirits wrest them to their destruction, it should be, in the first place, prohibited to bishops, priests, and monks; it being clear, if my memory does not deceive me, that those who have forged heresies by a misunderstanding of the Scripture were all of one of those three orders, and not of the common people. But it is a very wild expedient, and a remedy altogether extravagant, to condemn the use of things because of the abuse of them by some certain persons. By this account the best and most innocent things, and things most necessary for the life of men, should be taken from them; the light of the sun, the savour of meats, the excellency of wines, and fruits, iron, silver, gold, and other metals, the accomplishments of learning, and the wonders of eloquence. For which of these gifts of God does not the intemperance or the malice of men abuse? And, as the prince of pagan philosophers has rightly observed, there is nothing they so perniciously abuse as that which is of itself best and most profitable.† To conclude: since the same God, who knows the nature and the efficacy of his own Scriptures better than any, commands us all to read them, it is an insufferable temerity for a man to intrude with his advice, and change what the Lord has appointed, as if he were wiser than the Most High.

* Chrysost. Homil. 9. in Ep. ad Coloss.

† Aristot. Rhet.

II. But the apostle clearly refutes this calumny of Rome against Scripture in the other part of this text, where he sets before us the fruits and uses we ought to draw from it: "Teaching," says he, "and admonishing one another in psalms and hymns and spiritual songs, singing with grace in your hearts to the Lord." Elsewhere he informs us that "all Scripture is profitable for doctrine, for reproof, for correction, for instruction in righteousness," 2 Tim. iii. 16. Here, in like manner, he sets down, for the first fruit we are to gather from this rich knowledge of the word of God, that mutual teaching we owe to each other; for the second, admonition; for a third, consolation by the singing of psalms and spiritual hymns. As to the first, I grant the charge of teaching in the church principally pertains to pastors appointed for this purpose; yet there is not the most private believer who does not also in some measure participate in this function, when he has the gift and the opportunity, to edify men in the knowledge of true religion. Particularly fathers and mothers owe this duty to their children, husbands to their wives, masters to their households, the elder to the younger, and, in short, each one to his neighbour, when he has the convenience. Whence it appears again how far distant the apostle's sentiment is from Rome's. Paul would have the faithful entertain and instruct one another in the things of the word of God. Rome will not let any but the clergy have power to speak of them.

The second use we ought to make of the word of God is to admonish each other. Teaching properly respects faith; admonition has reference to manners. The Scripture furnishes us with that which is necessary to discharge both these duties; informing us plainly and plentifully, as well of things which are to be believed as those which are to be done. And it is incumbent on the believer to acquit himself in the matter according to the knowledge he has, instructing the ignorant and reproving the faulty, with a spirit of sweetness and discretion, as the apostle elsewhere prescribes. For every man ought to look upon his neighbour as his brother; to reclaim him, if he stray; to raise him up, if he fall; to clear things to him, if he doubt; and to have as much care of his welfare as of his own. Far be from us the cruelty of those proud spirits, who would not be solicitous in the least for their brethren's concerns; and who, if God should demand an account of them at their hands, would be ready to say, as Cain formerly answered, "Am I my brother's keeper," or schoolmaster? Now as we are to be charitable and prudent for the performance of this service to our brethren; so ought we again, in our turn, to receive it from them with patience and meekness; remembering how the psalmist says, "Let the righteous smite me; it shall be a kindness: and let him reprove me; it shall be an excellent oil," Psal. cxli. 5.

The third and last use the apostle directs us to make of the word of Christ is in psalms and hymns and spiritual songs, to sing from our hearts with grace unto the Lord. The so doing respects partly the glory of God, which we ought to celebrate by our singing, and partly our own consolation and spiritual rejoicing. For the Lord is so good, that he has provided even for the recreation of his children; and knowing that song is one of his most natural means, extremely proper both to dilate the contentment of our hearts, and render it full blown, as also to alleviate and mitigate their sorrows, he has not only permitted, but even commanded, us to sing to him spiritual songs. And to assist us in so holy and profitable an exercise, he has given us in his word a great number of these divine canticles, as the Psalms of David, and the hymns of various other faithful and religious persons, dispersed in various parts of the books of the Old and New Testament.

The apostle names three sorts of them, psalms, hymns or praises, and odes or songs. Now though there is no occasion to take much pains in exactly distinguishing these three sorts of sonnets; nevertheless I think their opinion very probable, who put this difference between them; that a psalm is in general any spiritual poem, whatever may be its subject; that a hymn particularly signifies sonnets composed to the praise of God; and that an ode, or song, is a kind of hymn of more art and variety of composition than others. You have various examples of them all in the Book of Psalms. First, all the compositions there are called psalms in general. But it is very evident they are not all of a sort. There are some in which are celebrated the goodness, the wisdom, and the power of the Lord, either towards David or towards the church, or with reference to all creatures. These are properly hymns, and such is the 18th Psalm, the 104th, the 145th, and many others. There are others in which are mystically and elegantly represented, with excellent skill, either the wonders of Christ, as the 45th, the 72nd, the 110th, and the like; or the histories of the ancient people, as the 78th, the 105th, and 106th. To these properly the name of odes, or songs belongs. It is with these sacred lyres, of which the word of Christ affords us both the matter and the form, that the apostle would have us solace ourselves. James gives us orders for it: "Is any among you merry? let him sing psalms," chap. v. 13.

The apostle calls all these sonnets spiritual, both on account of their author, who is the Holy Spirit, and also of their matter, which concerns only divine and heavenly things, the glory of God, and our salvation, not the vanities, passions, and follies of men, as carnal poems. He adds, "with grace;" signifying by that expression the sweet and saving effect of these spiritual songs, which profit and refresh at the same time. He would have us, in the third place, to sing from the heart; that is, not barely with the mouth, as hypocrites, but with the attention and affection of the heart. In conclusion, he directs us to sing to the Lord, that is, to the praise and glory of Christ, who is ordinarily signified by that term, the Lord, when it is couched singly, as it is here.

This is the rule he gives us for this holy and spiritual melody; a rule which Rome has as little spared as the other, which we have seen him prescribe, about our being studious of the word of God in general. For, first, she has banished from the church the singing of faithful people, and that so far, that those who are of her communion openly declare that to sing the Psalms of David, as we do, is great scandal to christians. Strange christianity! which is scandalized by singing that which the apostle commands; singing what celebrates the glory of God; singing what was indited by his Spirit, composed by his prophets, and tends only to the edification and consolation of faithful souls. Certainly, besides the authority of the book of God, it appears also by the writings of men, that formerly, in the ancient church, the christian people bore a part in the singing of psalms, and did it both in public and in private. Again, as to that which our adversaries make their clergy sing, with what conscience can they say that they sing it with the heart, since they who hear it, and the greater part of those who sing it understand it not? all their anthems being in Latin, a tongue long since dead and unknown to the people. Consider, too, whether the pomp, and the nicety, and the curiosity of their singing, and such a multiplicity of instruments as they mingle with it, and all the other artifices of their music, be not more proper for the pleasing of the ear than the edification of the spirit.

But, dear brethren, let us lay aside the defaults of others, and mind ourselves. First let us bless our good God that he has set up the word of his Christ again among us, in its light, and in its genuine use; and, acknowledging this grace from the bottom of our hearts, improve his favour. Let this word be the only governess of our hearts and lives. Let us hear its voice in public, consult it in private. Let us have these divine books, to which the Holy Spirit has consigned his instructions. Read them without scruple, and without fear of finding anything that is dangerous or venomous in them. They are the paradise of Jesus Christ, in which the tree of life grows, and whence flow the streams of holiness, joy and immortality, but a paradise where the old serpent never entered, where his breath and poison are unknown. Fathers and mothers, instruct your children in this wholesome study. Young ones, addict yourselves to it betimes. Fill your memories out of this treasury of wisdom. Men and women, old and young, rich and poor, learned and unlearned, receive ye all this divine guest whom the apostle has now lodged at your house. Let it dwell there (as he has ordered) richly and abundantly in all wisdom. If you receive and treat it with the respect it merits, it will cure your souls of all their maladies; it will inform your understandings of all heavenly truth, and purge them of all earthly errors and superstition. It will fill your hearts with love to God, and charity towards your neighbour, and by the efficacy of its truth extinguish all those petty passions that tie you to the world. It will comfort you in your troubles; it will fortify you in your weaknesses; it will sustain you in your conflicts; it will arm you against all sorts of enemies, and guide you in all your ways. It will sweeten your adversities, and govern your prosperity; and, to comprise all in a few words, it will conduct you to the haven of eternal salvation, notwithstanding all the storms of this wretched life. Employ likewise this word of the Lord to those uses which the apostle recommends to you, even to those mutual teachings and admonishings which you owe each other, giving and receiving them, as there is occasion, with a sincere and truly christian charity.

Finally, possess the liberty he gives you, of singing from the heart with grace unto the Lord psalms, and hymns, and spiritual songs. This Book of Psalms alone, if you learn it aright, is able to make you for ever happy. O God! of what a source of blessing and joy do they deprive themselves who reject or neglect it! It is a public magazine of heavenly wisdom, in which every one may find that which is meet for him; the ignorant, instruction; the learned, materials for study; the afflicted, comfort; and the contented, recreation. There are repentant tears for the guilty, and songs of thanksgiving for the faithful; preservatives against vice, attractives and excitements to piety, and lessons for all kinds of virtues. And the wonder is, that these high, useful, and necessary things are all presented to us there in the delicious sonnets of a graceful and a pleasing poetry, as in so many vases of pearl, and diamonds, and emeralds, to induce us to receive them the more readily. O wise invention of our great Master! in which we have together pleasure and profit, refreshment and instruction of soul, at once singing and learning what is most necessary for us. May it please him to bless this divine artifice, by which he invites and allures us to himself, and so touch our hearts by the efficacy of his Spirit, that as he draws us to him with these holy cords of his sweetness and love, we also may freely and cheerfully run after him, to the end, that having faithfully followed him in this world, he may in the next lodge us with himself, in the sanctuary of his glory, where, bearing our part with the angels, we shall bless and glorify him eternally. Amen.

SERMON XLII.

VERSE 17.

And whatsoever ye do in word or deed, do all in the name of the Lord Jesus, giving thanks to God and the Father by him.

DEAR brethren, the love which the Lord Jesus has towards us is so great, and the benefits which he has conferred upon us are so various and precious, that we are evidently constrained to give ourselves entirely to him, and we cannot withhold from him, without ingratitude, any part of what we are or have. He has laid down his life for us. It is just, therefore, that we again consecrate ours unto him. He has redeemed us at the price of his blood, and by this admirable ransom delivered from death and hell, not only our souls, but also our bodies and our whole nature. We are therefore wholly his, and have no more any other master but him; neither is there any justice in the world that will not adjudge him the propriety and possession of what costs him so dear. But though of right we are his vassals, yet it has pleased his love that we should belong to him under another and much more glorious title. For he has made us his brethren, having obtained of his Father that he should adopt us for his children, and accumulated this grace with all the highest favours to which creatures can be exalted. I mean, he has made us partakers of his inheritance, and communicated to us his nature and his Spirit, and crowned us with his immortality and with his glory. If he had not shed his blood for us as he did, who does not see that this his great and divine liberality would have purchased him all the life, and being, and motion we can have—and that to divert any part of it from his service, would be robbing him, and bereaving him with abominable sacrilege of a thing so legitimately, and for so many just and weighty reasons, belonging to him? If we are not the most unjust and ungrateful persons in the world, we ought all to have such sentiments, and consequently to look upon our nature and our life as things no longer ours, but Jesus Christ's; and dispose of them, not after our own fancy, and for our own interest, but at his pleasure and for his glory. And as you see that the servants of a prince (above all, those whom he has particularly obliged and favoured) set up his arms through all their houses, and adorn their halls and chambers with his picture, and have his praises always in their mouth, and fill up their whole life with his name and glory; so should we do to Jesus Christ, and with so much the more zeal, as he is a Lord infinitely more rich, more clement, more liberal, and more beneficent, than any monarch of the earth. Let our souls and bodies therefore bear his badges; let his glory appear exalted in all our actions; let the words of our mouths be dedicated to him, and our whole lives full of his name, breathing throughout nothing but his honour and service, without ever swerving from his will or from his interests. This, beloved brethren, is the lesson which the apostle Paul now gives us, in the words that you have heard. "And whatsoever ye do, whether in word or deed, do all in the name of the Lord Jesus, giving thanks to God and the Father by him."

By these words he concludes that excellent exhortation which he makes to all christians in general, of whatever sex, age, or condition. He began it at the 1st verse of this chapter, and continues it on to our text, pointing out briefly, but divinely, as you have heard in the preceding exercises, our principal duties; on one hand, the mortifying of the flesh with its lusts, as fornication, covetousness, wrath, and the like; on the other hand, the study and exercise of all christian virtues, as humility, kindness, patience, gentleness, charity, and peace. To all these he adds our knowledge of and continual meditation upon the word of God, with psalms and spiritual hymns. Upon this we dwelt in our last discourse. Now that he might not stay to treat severally of all the other duties of christians, which would be prolix, and even infinite, and a discourse of too great extent for an epistle, before he passes to that particular exhortation, which he addresses in the following verses to certain ranks of believers, as to married persons, to fathers, children, servants, and masters, he closes his first matter with the precept which he here gives us; a precept truly excellent, and well worthy to crown his exhortation, since it comprehends in a few words all the duties of a christian, both those which the apostle has expressly pointed out, and those which his design of brevity caused him to pass over in silence, without speaking of them by name. To the end that we may give you an exposition of it, we will endeavour, by the grace of our Lord, to explain, in order, the two parts which offer themselves in it; First, that whatever we do, either in word or deed, we do it all in the name of the Lord Jesus. Secondly, that we give thanks by him to God and the Father.

1. When the apostle pronounces, that all we do, in word or deed, be done in the name of the Lord Jesus, he clearly gives him our whole life. For these two things which he subjects to him, words and works, comprehend all the other parts of our life; it being evident that nothing issues from us, but what may be referred to the one or other of them; they are either

words or works. Words are the fruits of our mouths; works are the effects or actions of our other parts and faculties. I acknowledge, that, besides this, our spirit also acts within us when it knows or considers things, and desires or rejects them. But besides that these internal actions might be put into the rank of our works, by extending the word a little beyond its ordinary signification (as in effect some interpreters do give it such meaning here); besides this, I say, it is evident that most of the conceptions, and affections, and resolutions of the soul refer to words and external works, as being the principles and motives of them. For it is impossible that our words and works should be in the name of our Lord and Saviour, except our understandings and wills so address them; and it is properly this action of the soul which the apostle signifies, when he orders that we do all in the name of Christ. The tongue indeed pronounces the words, and the hands and other parts of our bodies execute those actions which are called works; but it is the spirit that moves them all, and directs and guides their functions to the end or design which it has proposed to itself, and draws them from such motives as it has conceived and formed within itself. And it is properly upon this that the difference of men's actions depends. It is this character that gives them the name and title they have in christian morality. Works that are the same as to the external action sometimes prove nevertheless very different, and even contrary; one good, another bad; because the spirit that produces them is not the same. As, for instance, the alms of an ambitious man and of a true believer have no external difference; the act of one in this respect is the same as the other; yet if you consider the inward springs of them both, you will find that the one is a piece of vanity, and the other a fruit of charity. Consequently, notwithstanding all their external resemblance, they are in reality works of quite a different nature; the one evil and condemned of God, the other good and acceptable to the Lord. The one, with all its outside paint and colour, is an act of vice, the other of virtue. The same is to be said of those two kinds of preaching which the apostle mentions in the Epistle to the Philippians, chap. i. 15—17: the one, of those that preached Christ through envy and of contention; the other, of such as preached him of good will and of love. The language of them both was the same; but the diversity of their designs render their actions so different, that those of the one, to say the truth, were a sacrilege and an abomination; those of the other, one of the best and most excellent works of christian piety and charity. Thus you see the rule which Paul gives us to order all the external actions of our lives, our words, and works; even that we "do all in the name of the Lord Jesus."

The rule is short and easy, but of vast and almost infinite use. As a little square serves an artificer to design and mark out a multitude of lines, and to discover and correct all those which are amiss; so by this little rule which the apostle puts in our hands, there is no human action respecting which we may not certainly ascertain, whether it is right or wrong, good or evil, and conformable to the will of God or otherwise; neither is there any part of our lives which this rule, if we take care to adjust them by it, is not capable of guiding and forming to perfection. Now as the name of God in Scripture signifies sometimes that Hebrew word of four letters which the Lord takes for his name and memorial, distinguishing himself by that appellation from all those gods to whom the error of nations wrongfully gave that quality, and the honours due to it; so likewise the name of Jesus is sometimes taken for this very word Jesus, which (as you know) is the name that was given to him by the express command of God. And so those of the communion of Rome seem to understand it, in that passage of Paul, where it is said, "That at the name of Jesus every knee should bow, of things in heaven, and things in earth, and things under the earth," Phil. ii. 20; uncovering as oft as they hear the word Jesus pronounced; as if the apostle's meaning were, that all creatures, celestial, terrestrial, and infernal, should do reverence when those two syllables Jesus are uttered. In which truly they are much mistaken; the import of that passage being quite the contrary. It is not thus either that Paul takes the name of Jesus in our text; as if he simply intended that in our actions and discourses we should not fail to intermix always the word Jesus, having it incessantly in our mouths, and never doing nor saying anything without pronouncing it first. Far be it from us to imagine that such a thought should fix upon the apostle's mind. It is not the word, nor the letters or syllables, of this name that he recommends to us. I grant, we cannot have it too much in our mouths, provided it flow into them from the heart, and that it be a religious and respectful consideration which makes us mention it, and not a vain and childish superstition, as if there were some secret virtue annexed to words.

We are to note then, in the second place, that as the name of God is very often taken in Scripture for the power, the authority, the will, respect, and consideration of God; so in like manner is the name of Jesus. Thus Moses, foretelling the coming of the Messiah, says, "And it shall come to pass, that whosoever will not hearken unto my words, which he shall speak in my name, I will require it of him," Deut. xviii. 19. "Which he shall speak in my name," that is, by my order and authority, and in acquitting himself of the charge which I have committed to him; and it is thus we frequently read that the prophets spake in the name of God; that is, by his express command, they being sent and dispatched from him. And it is said of Elisha, that he cursed the children that reviled him "in the name of the Lord," that is, by his authority, 2 Kings ii. 24. And this form of speech was so common among the Jews, that the priests and elders demanded of the apostles, in whose name they had done that miracle, Acts iv. 7; meaning upon whose authority and by whose order they had undertaken it. The same exposition is to be given of that which the psalmist sings, "We will remember" or boast in "the name of the Lord our God," Psal. xx. 7: that is, in his help and power; and speaking of God's faithful people, "They shall rejoice," says he, "in thy name," that is, in the confidence they have in thy power and goodness; of the same import is that which he adds, that the horn of his anointed shall be exalted in his name, Psal. lxxxix. 16, 24; that is, by his might, and by the virtue and order of his providence. So David, entering into combat with the Philistine, "Thou comest to me," says he, "with a sword, and with a spear, and with a shield; but I come to thee in the name of the Lord of hosts, the God of the armies of Israel, whom thou hast defied," 1 Sam. xvii. 45. "In the name of the Lord;" that is, for his glory, which thou hast reproached, and in assurance of his protection and succour; in the same sense that king Asa meant it on a like occasion: "Help us," says he, "O Lord our God; for we rest on thee, and in thy name we go against this multitude," 2 Chron. xiv. 11; that is, in thy quarrel, and with confidence in thee.

It is therefore in the same manner we are to take this phrase, in the name of Christ, which often occurs in the books of the New Testament, as in Matthew, prophesying and casting out devils in the name of the Lord, that is, by his authority and in his might; and when men are said to come in his name, Matt. vii. 22; xxiv. 5; that is to declare themselves his, and to affirm themselves sent by his order: to speak and teach in the name of Jesus Christ, Acts v. 28; and likewise to be assembled in his name, Matt. xviii. 20; that is, for his cause, and unto his honour, and with confidence in him. It is in this sense the apostle takes these words in our text: "Do all things in the name of the Lord Jesus." He means, first, that we refer all we do to his glory, and take his honour for the end of all our actions; and secondly, that we act according to his will and order; and lastly, with an entire confidence in him: not presuming anything of ourselves, as if we were able to do anything by our own strength; nor expecting any success, but only from his favour and benediction. Such is the rule which the apostle here gives us.

By this you see, first, that he banishes from our lives all the unfruitful works of darkness, that is, all vicious actions, actions contrary to justice, to charity, and to other christian virtues; it being evident, that if we do nothing but in the name of the Lord Jesus, we shall do none of these things; since they are all opposed to his will, his commands, and his glory. Secondly, by the same means he perfects and enlivens all those of our works, which of themselves and in their nature are good and commanded of God; ingrafting them by this rule upon the true motive from which they ought to proceed, and directing them to the true end to which they ought to tend, which is without doubt the name of Christ, and cleansing them from all that impurity and vice with which vanity or self-love might taint them. Good will be truly good, if we do it in the name of Jesus Christ; that is, for his sake, upon consideration of him alone, without seeking the approbation and acceptance, or the interest and service, of any other. Lastly, by the same rule, the apostle sanctifies those of our words and actions which are in their own nature indifferent, purifying them by the name of the Lord from the filth and abuse with which the vices of men pollute them, and elevating them to a degree of moral goodness which they had not of themselves, in that he consecrates them to the name of the Lord, and makes them to serve grace, whereas of themselves they were instituted only for the uses of nature. For instance, if you observe this rule of the apostle in your eating and drinking, which, as every one knows, are actions indifferent in their own nature; first, this sacred name of the Lord Jesus will purge the exercise of them of the excesses of intemperance and drunkenness on the one hand, and of the vain and foolish scruples of superstition on the other. Secondly, being referred to the honour of God, and accompanied with invocation of his grace, and thankful acknowledgment of his bounty, from indifferent, as they were in themselves, they become good, and holy, and acceptable unto God.

I willingly grant, however, that we must not so take the apostle's precept, as if we were obliged in every act, even to the least word we utter, to raise our thoughts actually to the name of Jesus Christ, and expressly implore his assistance by a particular prayer, and formally eye his glory. It is sufficient that we frequently and ordinarily make this application of mind to the name, to the command, to the help, and to the glory of our Lord. But it is necessary that we have the habit of this holy disposition so formed and radicated in our hearts, that even when time, or place, or some other necessity surprises us, and gives us not the leisure to think actually on the name of the Lord, our souls may still lean that way, as of themselves being so habituated to it, as, without other discourse or consideration, they may as to the substance discharge this duty; and never do nor say anything that tends not to the glory of our Saviour, and is not conformable to his will, and consistent with the resolution we all ought to have, of relying on Jesus Christ alone, and referring none of our actions to any other end than to his honour.

II. But I come to the other part of our text, which the apostle adds, that we give thanks by Jesus Christ unto God and the Father. These words may be taken two ways; either for another precept apart added to the former, or for some part and dependence of it. In the first relation, it is a new order the apostle gives us, to thank God for the benefits he has vouchsafed to us in his Son. He gives the same order to the faithful at Ephesus, in nearly the same words: "Giving thanks always for all things unto God and the Father in the name of our Lord Jesus Christ," Eph. v. 20. Under the second consideration, the words are a reason of what he recommended before, and the title, under which we ought to do all things in the name of the Lord Jesus; namely, for rendering unto God the Father by his Son the thanks we owe him: so that our whole life may be only homage, and a perpetual act of gratitude to God by Jesus Christ his Son our Lord. For it is not to be doubted that the best and most proper means of thanking God the Father for those infinite benefits he has conferred upon us, by the communion of his Son, is so to frame our lives, that we neither do nor say anything but in the name of his Son; that is, as we have explained it, according to his will, and for his glory. Now though it is not of much consequence which of these two expositions we follow, since in reality the thing is still the same; yet it seems to me the latter is more pertinent, because it better and more clearly connects the apostle's words.

Thanksgiving is one of the most necessary and universal offices of a christian. For if it is ingratitude to receive a kindness from any one with indifference, and without giving him thanks for it, what moment of our lives is there in which we ought not to perform this duty to God? First of all, this being of ours, this life, this body, this soul, and all the faculties of our nature, are his largesses, which, notwithstanding they are common to us with other men, are not to be despised, but ought to be considered as effects of an infinite goodness. Then, again, to what thankfulness does not the sending of his Son into the world, and the death he suffered for us by the will of his Father, constrain us? What shall I say of those infinite blessings he has obtained for us, the remission of our sins, our adoption to the number of his children, the glory and immortality for which we hope? Add to this, his continual providence, both over his church in general, and over each of us in particular; his favourable bearing with us, however great are not only our infirmities and imperfections, but even infidelities and ingratitudes; the admirable constancy of his divine grace, which our indignities can neither overcome nor put off; and though often refused, or ill received, yet ceases not to follow us; but he comes again towards us every morning, and despatches daily some new herald to solicit us to repentance: this sun that shines about us; this air with which he refreshes us; so many various fruits of the earth, with which he feeds us; the word of his gospel, by which he instructs us; his sacraments, at which he feasts us; the voice of his Spirit, either to comfort us, or awaken us in our evils; the strokes of his paternal discipline, which he so aptly administers, tempering them in such a manner that it is easy to see he scourges us for our amendment, to win us, not to destroy us. And if we love our neighbours as we ought, what ample matter of thanksgiving does God's dealing with them afford us! His forbearance to some, waiting for and inviting them to repentance; the grace which he exercises towards others, either in bringing them to or preserving them in his Son: the admirable gifts, so richly and so wisely diversified, which he imparts to one; and the prosperous success with which he favours the employment of others; there being not a person in the church however ignorant and inconsiderable in our eyes, to whom this good Master has not given one or other of his talents. If we had the tongues and voices of all the angels of heaven, yet could we not worthily acknowledge, or repay with sufficient thanks, a goodness so inestimable, and in every way so infinite.

But observe, that it is to God and the Father the apostle orders us to make our thanksgivings; and reasonable it is that the glory of it should be given to him, since he is the first and head spring of all. Not but that we may rightly address our praises as well as our petitions to the Son also, and the Holy Spirit, according to the examples of it which the apostles themselves have left us in various places of Scripture. But both in the creation, and also in the restoration of the world, the Father is still represented to us as the first principle of the action, the Son and the Holy Spirit acting next; as persons who subsist in such order, that the Father is the first, the Son the second, and the Holy Ghost the third; though, setting aside this order, and the distinction of their persons, their nature is in all things and every way the same, with respect both to essence and properties or attributes, and to all essential operations.

The apostle prescribes yet further, that it be by Jesus Christ we render thanks to God the Father. First, for that he is as it were the first and the chiefest channel by which all this goodness of God is poured forth upon upon us. For it is he alone who has acquired all the graces which mankind possess: in consequence of which he is called the Sun of righteousness, the Light and the Saviour of the world, the Prince and the Author of life, in whom dwelleth all the fulness of the Godhead bodily. And secondly, because our thanks themselves cannot be grateful to the Father, nor come into his presence before the throne of his grace, except they are addressed and presented by Jesus Christ, who alone is able to perfume both our persons and our poor performances with that odour which is necessary for all that would appear without confusion before this Supreme Majesty. Thus, beloved brethren, we have endeavoured to deliver to you an exposition of these words of Paul.

There remains now the chiefest point of all, even that you engrave them deeply on your hearts, and take them for the rule of your whole lives, applying them to each one of your actions, and making those wholesome uses of them for which this great apostle gave them. I will point out some of them at present, beseeching God to bless them to your edification, and leave the rest to your own pious meditation. Observe then, first, for the confirmation of your faith, that excellent proof the apostle gives us here of the divinity of the Lord Jesus. For as the Epistle to the Hebrews concludes it, from the Father's calling him his Son, and treating him differently from what he does the angels, the highest of all creatures, Heb. i. 5, 6; so may we reason, in like manner, from this passage of Paul, and say as that Epistle says of the angels: of which of the prophets or the martyrs, or the apostles, or of the angels of heaven, was it ever said to the faithful, Do all things in his name? Surely the faithful, both in the Old Testament and in the New, neither believe, nor hope, nor rejoice, nor speak, nor act, but in the name of God; and there is not one to be found in the divine records whose piety, and the exercises which depend upon it, are addressed to a mere creature. Here, as you see, the apostle requires, that not only some part of our faith, but that our whole life, and all our sanctification, should be referred to the name of the Lord Jesus. It must be therefore necessarily concluded, that he is not a mere creature, but very God, of an infinite goodness, power, and wisdom, eternally blessed with the Father. It is impossible that an inferior nature should be the support, the foundation, the last and highest end of all the works and words of all the faithful. Either all the Scriptures of God are to be effaced, and new ones made after the fancies of heretics, or it must be confessed that this Jesus is God, to whom they give a name capable of being both the beginning and the end of all parts of the lives of all the faithful that are or ever shall be in the world, conformably with their own assertion elsewhere, that he is the Father of eternity, the Prince of peace, our great God and Saviour.

Judge again, my brethren, if it is not an outrage to him, and an investing of creatures with some part of his glory, to require, (as those of the communion of Rome do,) that part of the piety, the good works, and the very faith of christians, be in the name of saints of both sexes; who, however sublime and excellent the dignity you give them, cannot, after all, be set above the rank of creatures. We daily hear them repeat their orisons, count their beads, ask and give alms, one of the choicest sacrifices of christian religion, make their pilgrimages for devotion, build their temples, consecrate their images, and their holy places, and their most precious possessions, and indeed their own persons, to the name of the blessed Virgin, of St. Peter, of St. Denis, and a multitude of other creatures ancient and modern. Adversaries! where find you the institution of these devotions? In what prophet or in what apostle have you read a command for them? In what Gospel, or in what Acts, and in what divine histories have you observed examples of them? What would Paul say, if he were in the world, to see his discipline so strangely forgotten among men who make profession to hold him for one of their principal apostles? He recommends to us not one of these names to which you devote yourselves. He speaks of none but that of the Lord Jesus; it is in that name alone he commands us to do all, whether in word or deed; because indeed "there is none other name under heaven given among men, whereby we must be saved," as said Peter, Acts iv. 12, the same Peter whom you pretend to be the head and the foundation of your popes. Paul surely gave and preserved this glory to his Lord's name alone with so much zeal and jealousy, that understanding how some in the church of Corinth joined in some measure the names of his servants with it, calling themselves, some of Paul, others of Apollos, others of Cephas, and others of Christ, 1 Cor. i. 12; as you see among our adversaries at this day, some call themselves of Augustine, others of Francis, and others of Jesus; this holy man exclaims against it as a sacrilege, and an utter overthrow of religion. "Is Christ divided?" says he, "was Paul crucified for you? or were ye baptized in the name of Paul?" 1 Cor. i. 13; prescribing by these words, or rather by this flash of lightning, that the faithful ought not either to call or distinguish themselves, or to glory in, or to speak, or do anything in religion in any other name than that of this holy and merciful Lord, who was crucified for them, and in whose name alone they were baptized. Yea, he thanks God that he had administered baptism but to few of them, lest any one should thence take occasion to believe or to say that he had baptized in his own name. Then, shortly afterwards, resuming the discourse, so much took he the thing to heart, he says, "Are ye not carnal, while one of you says, I am of Paul; and another, I am of Apollos? Who then is Paul, and who is Apollos, but ministers by whom ye believed, even as the Lord gave to every man? Ye are God's husbandry, ye are God's building," 1 Cor. iii. 4, 5, 9. Is not this telling us plainly that we ought neither to bear the name of any other than God, nor act in matters of piety in any name but that of Jesus Christ, in which likewise he here commands us to do and say all that we shall act in word or deed.

But having considered what the apostle affords us here against error for the instruction of our faith, let us now observe what he teaches us for the correction of our manners, which is his principal intention. He teaches us, my brethren, that if we will be truly faithful persons and christians, as we profess to be, we must have Jesus Christ continually before our eyes; must examine, address, and suit our actions, our speeches and purposes, unto the name of Christ; take it for the north star in our course, and, in one word, for the rule of our whole life. That we never do anything, little or great, otherwise than in his name. That his name be the only motive inducing us to speak and act, and the only mark to which our words and actions tend. Think now, first, how great our confusion ought to be. The apostle directs that whatever we do in word or deed, we should do it all in the name of the Lord Jesus; and most of us, on the contrary, do almost nothing in his name. Heaven and earth are witnesses that the name of Jesus has no part in our works or words. They are all consecrated to his enemies; they are inspired by their spirit, and aim at nothing but their interests. Tell me, ye covetous, is it in the name of Jesus Christ that ye toil night and day to heap up dross? Is it he who taught you those black arts and inhuman dexterities, to spoil the orphan and the widow to enrich yourselves? Have you had the confidence to call upon the name of Jesus, that he might teach you and guide your hands to work deceit and bless your violence? Is it to advance his glory and give his name a good odour, that you make yourselves famous among the vassals of mammon; not disdaining any part of his drudgery, however distasteful to God and man? And you that are ambitious, can you indeed persuade yourselves that those vanities which absorb your attention are so important to Jesus Christ—or that it is in his name you lose your time about them? You also whom the flesh and its pleasures drown in their filth, I ask, is it in the name of Jesus Christ you are employed? Is it for his glory, or according to his will? I say as much of the revengeful, and the drunken, and of all those that serve any one of the other vices, which Jesus Christ has expressly condemned and forbidden. Not one of all these acts in his name. Dear brethren, let us renounce these things if we will be christians. Let us never make any enterprise, never commence any action, without first considering whether it may be done in the name of the Lord Jesus; that is, whether it is such as we may with a good conscience implore his help to finish, and judging whether it is proper to advance his glory, and is conformable, or, at least, not contrary, to his will and interests. Hereby we are constrained to banish out of our lives, first, all vicious actions, of which none can be done in the name of Jesus Christ, since they are all displeasing to him. And they who, in designs of such nature, have the impudence to ask assistance of him (as some there are, into whom superstition has inspired this foolish conceit, that they may do evil for a good end); these, I say, offend Jesus Christ excessively, rendering him guilty of their crimes as much as in them lies, and inviting him to take part in their vices. But this rule of the apostle not only obliges us to eschew evil and abstain from sin, it requires, also, that what good we do must be done for Christ's sake, and in his name; that in our alms, and in our devotions, and in all the acts of our piety and charity, we should seek nothing but his glory, the fulfilment of his will, and the advancement of his kingdom, and not the praise of men, or the interest of our own affairs. It is taking his name in vain to do otherwise. It is profaning the actions of virtue by employing them in the service of flesh and blood; which actions of their own nature, and by God's intention, are to be done only for his glory, and for the name's sake of his Son.

Again, this maxim of the apostle's embracing generally all the actions of a christian, both in word and deed, it is evident that it ought to regulate those also which are in their own nature indifferent, and to restrain us from doing any such acts, except when they may be done in the name of Christ. For though the nature of them is indifferent, the use of them is not so, but must be governed by the good and the evil that may thence redound either to or against the glory of God and the edification of men, as the apostle says elsewhere; "All things are lawful for me, but all things are not expedient: all things are lawful for me, but all things edify not," 1 Cor. x. 23. Whence you see, how vain is the pretext of those who excuse the excess of their dress, of their tables, and of their houses, by the liberty which they pretend the Lord has given them to clothe, and feed, and lodge themselves as they think proper, alleging that he has not forbidden them velvet, or silks, or gold, or silver, or precious stones, or tapestry, or any sort of furniture, nor excluded from their tables any kind of meats or services, they being received with thanksgiving. I grant the use of these things, generally speaking, is free, they all being created of God for man; yet each of you ought to observe certain rules about them, and this one particularly, namely, that you consider whether the thing is such as you may do it in the name of Jesus Christ; whether the money you waste in it might not be better employed in the service of his poor, or of his sanctuary; whether your making men believe that you are vain-glorious, or intemperate, or voluptuous, by clothing, or lodging, or treating yourselves more richly and more magnificently than becomes your condition; whether this opinion of yourselves, I say, which you give your neighbours does not scandalize them, and is not prejudicial to the name and interests of our Saviour.

Hence, again, appears how inexcusable are they who marry with persons of a contrary religion. I confess that marriage is honourable, and that it is not prohibited to any; but this action, as well as all others of a christian, must be done "in the name of the Lord Jesus;" and so much the rather, as it is more important, and continues as long as our lives. Wherefore the apostle expressly modifies the liberty he gives to the believing widow by this exception; She is at liberty, says he, to marry again; "only in the Lord," 1 Cor. vii. 39. Now judge if it be a marrying in the Lord, when you make alliance with a person alienated from your communion; who will be a snare to pervert you from it, will pluck the name of Christ out of your house, and consecrate your offspring to error; and be so far from helping you in the exercises of your piety, that the person will disturb them.

Finally, this saying of the apostle shows us also what we are to think of dances and balls, and such other vain pomps of the world. If you can truly say that it is in the name of Christ you mask and dance, I will acknowledge that you fail not of your duty in it. But if it is clear, and manifestly known, as it is, that the Lord Jesus has no part in these follies; that in them his name is blasphemed rather than glorified; that his Spirit breathes not in them, but indeed the spirit of Satan and the world; that scandal is given in them, but no edification received; confess it a thing contrary to your duty. Add not impudence to guilt; acknowledge, if you are a christian, that it is a violation of the apostle's command to participate in such things, which neither are nor can be done in the name of our Lord Jesus Christ. I warn you particularly of it, because we are entering on the season in which the world is wont to give itself the greatest license for such indulgences. Dear brethren, let not its ill example seduce you. Let not the custom of the age, nor the pleasing of men, induce you to forget the respect which you owe to the apostle's voice, and the church's consolation. Seek your joys in the service of your Lord and Saviour, and in the meditation and imitation of his life; and having always before your eyes the love he bears for you, the death he suffered for you, and the heaven to which he calls you, love him with all your heart; and whatever you do, whether in word or deed, do it all in the name of this sweet and merciful Saviour, rendering thanks to God and the Father by him, unto his glory, and the edification of your neighbours, and your own salvation. Amen.

SERMON XLIII.

VERSES 18, 19.

Wives, submit yourselves unto your own husbands, as it is fit in the Lord. Husbands, love your wives, and be not bitter against them.

DEAR brethren, as man is subject to a twofold consideration; first, with regard to his nature simply, as he is a reasonable creature; secondly, with reference to his condition, or the rank he holds in human society; that is, as either a master or a servant, a magistrate or a subject, or the like: so there devolve upon him, according to these two respects, two different duties; those of the first description are general and common universally to all men; the others, of the second, relate only to some certain order of persons. I place in the first rank piety towards God, honesty, temperance, justice, and charity, and such other virtues, from which neither sex, age, nor condition is exempt, because every man, whatever he is otherwise, being a reasonable creature, is bound upon that account to practise all those virtues, as a perfection and ornament meet for such a nature. I include among the duties of the second order, the service that bondmen owe their masters, the obedience of children to their fathers, the dependence of wives in relation to their husbands, and the like; which pertain, as you see, only to persons in such conditions, and not to all men generally. This difference has produced in the schools of heathen sages the distinguishing of active philosophy into various parts: the first, which they call moral philosophy, or ethics, explains that first description of common and general duties; the others treat of the second, namely, the economics, which regulate and form the several different conditions which constitute a family, namely, husband and wife, parents and children, master and servants; and the politics, whose task is to expound the duties of all the various orders which compose an estate, as the prince and the subject, the magistrate and the citizen, men of the long robe, and of the sword and the like.

The apostles of our Lord, in those writings which they

have left us, where they have unfolded to us the divine philosophy of their Master, have also followed the same order, though their difference is otherwise very great. For they set before us, in the same manner, some general duties, which oblige all christians of whatever quality, and in whatever degree of society they are placed, whether civil, domestic, or religious. And though this part, being once well comprehended, has in it a great and almost sufficient light to direct and govern all the rest; yet they forbear not to descend to the particular duties of each of those states and conditions which the faithful occupy in human society. Thus the apostle Paul has done in this Epistle; for after having exhorted us all, in general, to piety, holiness, and charity, which belong to all christians equally, as you have heard in the preceding exercises, he now addresses himself in particular to each of those three orders of which a household is composed; the first of which is the husband and the wife; the second, the father and the children; the third, master and servants; giving each of them a good lesson for their conduct in the condition to which God has called them. Elsewhere he regulates the duties of subjects with reference to the civil powers under which they live; of the faithful with reference to their pastors, and reciprocally of pastors with reference to their flocks; not omitting deacons, the other part of ecclesiastic ministry; and this not in one place only, but many. In consideration hereof, before we proceed any further, permit me, I beseech you, to make here, at the entrance, one general reflection upon the holy apostle's manner of treating his subject.

Whence comes it that, having been so careful to instruct and to direct in particular each of those different ranks of persons which then were, and still are, in the church, they never dropped one word respecting the duties of three kinds of conditions, in which, in the present day, Rome makes the chief, and, in a manner, the all, of the christian commonweal to consist, I mean the pope, sacrificers or priests, and monks. The apostles instruct the lowest masters how they ought to treat their attendants, and the simplest presbyters, or bishops, that is, pastors, how they ought to feed their flocks. They never tell the pope in what manner he ought to deport himself in that great government of all christendom which, as it is said, has been given him of God. The apostles inform the most abject slaves of the servitude they owe their masters, and every flock of the deference and respect it owes its pastors. They never speak a word, either to single believers or their guides, of that infinite subjection which they are obliged to profess to the pope, or of kissing his feet, or of submitting the conscience, or any other such thing. The apostles exactly inform bishops or pastors of the duties of their charge; of preaching, exhorting, instructing, of watching, of correcting, of censuring, and of excluding the scandalous from communion. They never order any sacrificers to offer a propitiatory host unto God for the sins of quick and dead, nor tell them of the preparations, ceremonies, and observances necessary for this purpose; nor of purifying, by means of an auricular confession, the consciences of such as are to participate in such a sacrifice; nor of the precautions and subtilties which are necessary for the right administration of it. The apostles vouchsafe to take the pains to enter into families, and there regulate the demeanour of husbands and wives, of virgins and widows, of fathers and children, of masters and servants. Why say they nothing to monks, or to the solitary, as hermits and anchorites, or to those who live associated in separated dwellings? Why do they not somewhere instruct the guardians, the abbots, the superiors, and generals of these orders? Why do they not exhort their inferiors to yield them a blind obedience? Why say they nothing of their three vows, and of the means of well observing them? And why give they no instructions to religious women, who, imitating the zeal of men, shut themselves up in convents? But what do I say, that they nowhere regulate the conduct and particular duties of these three sorts of conditions? I say more than this, they make no mention of them at all, neither expressly nor implicitly. And if you read the books of the New Testament, you will find that there is no more mention made in them of the pope, and the sacrificers, and the monks of Rome, than of the brahmins of India, or the bonzes of Japan, or the mufti of the mussulmans. Whence comes so strange a silence, so universal an oblivion? Is it that the thing was not worthy of the apostle's care and pen? But how can that be imagined, since, if you believe those of Rome, it is upon these three orders that christianity depends? For as to the pope, he is the head of the church, and exercises so necessary an imperial power, that out of his communion there is no salvation. And as for priests, or sacrificers, it is they alone that purify the souls of men, both by the absolution they give to those whom they confess, and by that deity which they deliver to such as they communicate. Lastly, as for monks, their order is the state of perfection, they are the angels of the earth, the glory and the rampart of the church, the sole patterns of evangelical piety and holiness; wherefore they call their fraternities religions, and disdaining their old name of monks, each sect of them styles itself religious; as if the piety of other christians did not deserve to be called religious, in comparison with theirs. Whence comes it, then, that the apostles have so forgotten these three sorts of people, which are as highly or more necessary in the church than the four elements in the world? Dear brethren, you plainly see the reason; and if passion did not blind our adversaries, they might see it too as well as we. The apostles have said nothing to these three sorts of people, because there were none such among christians in their time. Had there been then a pope and sacrificers in the church, the apostles without doubt would have told them their duty, as well as bishops and elders, that is, pastors. And if there had been monks and devotees, they would undoubtedly have spoken to them, as well as to men and women who live in wedlock. Since they did it not, we may be certainly assured that neither of these three plants was sown or set by Jesus Christ or his apostles; but they have all sprung up since their days, partly from the imprudence, partly from the superstition and corruption, of men, who also affording them cultivation, have raised them by degrees to that prodigious greatness which now for several ages they have possessed. And this we say at the commencement, on account of the care which the apostles had in general to form and regulate the duties of the various conditions of persons which are found in the church.

As for Paul's precept in this place, he speaks, first, to husbands and wives; next, to fathers and children; and last of all, to masters and servants; following in this the natural order of the things themselves. For if you consider the dignity of them, the union of husband and wife is the most excellent, and that upon which the others depend; or if you regard their rise, man was a husband before a father or a master; God gave Adam a wife before he gave him children or servants. Now though in this prime union the husband possesses the first place, yet the apostle begins with the wife, and does the same in the two following orders, instructing children before fathers, and servants before masters; either because the subjection in which wives, and children, and servants are placed is more difficult and displeasing to our nature, than the love and government of husbands, and fathers, and masters; or because the subjection of the one is the foundation upon which the other's good government depends. We will handle at the present no more than the lesson which he gives to wives and husbands, contained in the text which you have heard, reserving that which concerns children and fathers, servants and masters, for another opportunity.

I. The wife's lesson is for words short, but for sense of considerable weight and extent. "Wives," says the apostle to them, "submit yourselves to your own husbands, as it is fit in the Lord." In which words, first, he commands married women that subjection which they owe to their own husbands; and, next, shows them the manner of that subjection, "as it is fit in the Lord." As for subjection, it is an order that God has established generally in all things which constitute any kind of body, whether in nature, or in either angelic or human society, that some should depend on others. Thus you see in plants the other parts depend upon the root, and in animals upon the heart, and they all upon the soul that causes them to live. Among men, there is no state without a superior that governs, and inferiors that are governed. In the composition of the world itself, as it is one total, you know that earthly things depend upon the heavens, these govern all the rest; neither is there any union, any body, or natural compacted frame in the whole universe, the whole of whose parts are entirely equal. God, whose wisdom is infinite, has so ordered it for the benefit of things themselves; those that are feeble and imperfect finding their perfection in the conduct of such as are more perfect, and the more perfect reaping advantage and dignity from the subjection of those that are less. This induced the apostle to say in another place, that God is not a God of confusion, or of disorder, but of peace. It follows therefore that to resist subjection when persons are called to it, is to thwart his will and disturb his order; a mark also, not of fortitude and courage, but of folly and malignity, to oppose it; agreeable to that which experience taught the heathen themselves to observe, even that good men are easy to be governed, and that those who most unwillingly endure a superior are always such as have least worth. It having therefore pleased God, according to this general disposition of his wisdom, that in marriage man should be the head, it is with propriety that the apostle exhorts married women to be subject.

That word comprises all the duty of the condition to which God calls them; and therefore the Holy Spirit uses it almost always on this subject; as in the Epistle to the Ephesians, chap. v. 22, where these very same terms occur; and in the Epistle to Titus, chap. ii. 5, That, says he, they be "discreet, chaste, keepers at home, good, obedient to their own husbands;" and in the First Epistle of Peter, chap. iii. 1, "Ye wives, be in subjection to your own husbands." I know well that the expression displeases our nature, which, in the corruption that sin has brought upon it, hates all, even the most lawful, subjection. And perhaps it is upon this account that the apostles have so often recommended it to christian women, that they might instruct them to combat this sentiment of our depraved nature, and submit themselves to God's arrangement. But certainly, setting aside the word, and the disorders which our sin sows in every condition, there is no harshness in this conjugal subjection; there is nothing in it but what is pleasant, beneficial, and advantageous, both to the wife herself, and also to the whole family. For it is an error to think that all subjection is hard and vexatious. That which the body owes to the soul, and the members to the head, that which the air and the earth render to the heavens, has nothing of constraint, nothing shameful in it; on the contrary there is in it that in which the glory of the body, and the members, and the elements consists. Among the angels themselves, whose being is full of perfection and glory, there is a kind of subjection, the inferior angels having dependence upon their chiefs. And in the terrestrial paradise, if sin had not banished us thence, amid the delights and perfections of a happy state, the wife would not have been exempt from being subject to her husband; an evident sign that this subjection is not incompatible either with her felicity or with her glory; and that all the bitterness now found in it arises not from the thing itself, but from sin, which has altered it, as it has all the other parts of our life and nature. For, in reality, what does this subjection signify, but a just and rational, a sweet and amiable, dependence of the wife upon the husband, like that of the body upon its head, or upon its soul?

Of this subjection, the first part, which is as the root and stock of all the rest, is a sentiment and disposition of heart; when the wife acknowledges in her soul that the husband God has given her is her head, and, as the wise man says, her guide; who, in the due order of their life, ought to have the first place; and that she is inferior to him, since she is his wife, whatever advantage she may otherwise have above him, whether in wealth or in nobility, yea, even in prudence and abilities. If she has once settled this holy and respectful persuasion in her heart, she will no more find anything of harshness or difficulty in all that subjection which she owes her husband. This sentiment alone is sufficient to form her to it, and to bow, without any constraint, all the actions of her life that way. And it is this, in my opinion, that the apostle means, when he says elsewhere that the wife should "reverence her husband," Eph. v. 33. Such was the sentiment of Sarah, whom Peter proposes to christian women for a pattern of their demeanour. She called Abraham her lord, as that apostle expressly states, 1 Pet. iii. 6, declaring by such respectful language in what esteem she held her husband, and that she regarded him as her superior, and the guide and governor of her life.

In addition to this reverence, the wife's subjection comprehends also the complacency she ought to have for her husband, fashioning herself to his mind, and divesting her own disposition of all that she sees offensive to him, to put on his affections and manners in everything as far as piety and honesty will permit; bending and accommodating her inclinations and humours in such manner to her husband's, that she may be as a faithful mirror to him, in which he may see his own image. This, you will say, is difficult. Certainly it is so; but only to those who bear their husbands little respect and love, and it is still more difficult to those who do not love them. She that loves her husband ardently, that looks upon him as the head which God has given her, as her weal, and her honour, and her glory, will easily discharge this duty, yea, take pleasure in it, it being the nature of true love to transform sweetly, and without constraint, the person loving into the beloved.

Lastly, this subjection comprehends the care a wife ought to have of her husband's person and family; all which the Scripture comprises in two words, when it terms her a help which God has given him, like unto him, that is, another self. That she love him constantly; be a consolation to him in adversity, and an augmentation of joy in prosperity; and, as the wise man has it, "do him good all the days of her life," Prov. xxxi. 12. That she train up his children, the sweet pledges of their amity and union, in all probity; and form them betimes to render him happy. That she keep his house, as Paul expressly orders, Tit. ii. 4, 5, govern his family, and hold all in it in good order; and, in the end, to consider that this is the business to which God calls her, even to employ all her cares, all her labour and vigilance, to the contentment, welfare, and honour of her husband; and that it is in this her own glory and felicity consist. Such is that conjugal subjection which the wife owes to her husband.

But the apostle, to establish and regulate this subjection, after giving it in charge to christian women, adds, "as it is fit in the Lord." I say in these words he first establishes that duty of subjection which the wife owes to her husband. For saying that this is "fit in the Lord," he shows us that the will of God is that this should be performed, and that it is his order and institution that the wife should be subject to her husband. This receives evidence first from the particular which we learn from Moses, even the Lord's saying expressly to Eve, and in her to all women, "Thy desire shall be to thy husband, and he shall rule over thee," Gen. iii. 16. The order also which he followed in the creation manifestly proves that this was his intention. For he created Adam first, and then afterwards Eve; an evident sign that Eve was made for Adam, and not he for her. And it is for the same end, likewise, that he formed Eve of one of the ribs of Adam, to show that the woman belongs to the man; that she is his own, as being made and formed of matter that was his; and that he has title to her and a right over her. Paul has prudently noticed it: "Adam was first formed, then Eve," 1 Tim. ii. 13. And elsewhere, "The man is not of the woman; but the woman of the man. Neither was the man created for the woman; but the woman for the man,"

1 Cor. xi. 8, 9. The nature of both sexes teaches us the same truth, as well as the order and manner of their creation; for though both in substance are the same being, alike rational and capable of immortality, yet it is evident that the constitution of woman is more weak, less active, and not so proper for government. It is this Peter means when he terms her "the weaker" or fragile "vessel," 1 Pet. iii. 7. And to this refers what the master of heathen philosophers has written,* that the woman reasons, consults, and deliberates more feebly and less resolutely than the man. Whence he concludes that her virtue or perfection is to serve, and not to rule; that is, to follow rather than to guide, and to obey rather than to command. Which is nevertheless to be understood of the generality, and the ordinary, natural, and legitimate constitution of each sex; it being otherwise very manifest that some women are found, not only as much, but a great deal more, reasonable, vivid, and active than some men. Upon these reasons all nations have rightly judged, as the Scripture expressly teaches us, that in marriage the woman ought to be subject, not one of those which have adopted the institution of marriage being found but what has so regulated it. Paul adds yet another reason, drawn from the fault which the woman committed in giving ear to the serpent, and upon this inducing her husband to disobedience. "Adam," says he, "was not seduced, but the woman being deceived was in the transgression," 1 Tim. ii. 14. For since they both fared so ill upon the husband's obeying the wife, it is very reasonable that the wife should resume the first order, and without putting off the yoke any more, as she did then, obey and be subject to him, whom she so unhappily undertook to govern, to the extreme misery of both.

But though all this is true and evident, yet I think the apostle intends here something more. For when he directs wives to be subject to their husbands, "as it is fit in the Lord," by the term "Lord" he understands, according to the ordinary style of the New Testament, not God simply, but Jesus Christ; and represents to them the honour they have of being in the communion of this sovereign Lord, to urge them on to a faithful discharge of this duty. For though it is a thing of bad grace, and contrary to the laws of God, that the wife should either assume superiority over her husband, or, however that be, refuse him this just subjection; yet there is no state nor religion, in which it is more unseemly, and less permitted, than in the discipline of Christ; first, because he has discovered and established the dignity, sanctity, and indissoluble union of the married state, to which this subjection appertains, much more clearly and excellently than ever did any lawgiver, not Moses

* Aristot. in his Polit. l. 1. c. 8.

himself excepted. Secondly, because as he has far better, and much more perfectly than any other, formed all his disciples in general to peace, and meekness, and humility; and women in particular to that decency, and modesty, and reserve which is proper for their sex; it is evident that christian wives are much more bound to submit to the subjection of which we speak, which is a thing depending on those virtues than any other persons of their sex. Moreover, the interest of their religion requires this performance at their hands, if law and reason had not imposed subjection on them; to the end that it might appear by their obedience that Jesus Christ does not disturb the just order of human societies; but, on the contrary, forms both men and women to all kinds of righteousness and honesty much more exactly and affectionately than do other religions. Lastly, the gospel of Jesus Christ having in various places taken marriage for a symbol of the union which is between him and his church, he has by that practice authorized and confirmed the duties of the two married parties, and particularly the subjection of the wife, since she is the image of the church, which ought to be subject to Christ; a matter which the apostle has elsewhere excellently made use of in this subject: "The husband," says he, "is the head of the wife, even as Christ is the head of the church. Therefore as the church is subject unto Christ, so let the wives be to their own husbands in everything," Eph. v. 23, 24. Thus you see with how much truth and wisdom the apostle here says to christian women that "it is fit in the Lord," (that is, in Jesus Christ,) that they should be subject to their husbands; it being clear from all that we have been saying, that all the considerations of the discipline of this same Lord, and of the communion they have with him, so strictly bind them to this duty, that if they fail of performance, besides the fault and the disorder which they commit against the law and institution of God and nature, they also particularly offend the Lord Jesus, outrage the mysteries of his gospel and scandalize his people.

But I have said that the apostle also by these words regulates and limits that subjection which the wife owes to her husband. For adding to the rest, "in the Lord," or, according to the Lord, he evidently shows that it reaches no further than to such things as do not offend Jesus Christ. She is subject to her husband I acknowledge, but only in things in which she is not rebellious against God. She ought to please him, but on condition that she displease not their common Lord. She owes him her obedience, and her assistance, and her service in adversity, and in all the troubles of household affairs, but not in sin. The will of Jesus Christ is the true boundary of her subjection and complacency. She ought to proceed so far; but further she may not pass without perishing. Whatever tie we have to any creature, it still leaves the rights of God entire, because our obligation to him is the first and most ancient, the strictest and most necessary of all. And if the husband pretend to oblige his wife, or the father his child, or the prince his subject, to the violation of any of the commands of God; that is, either to do what he forbids, or not to do what he enjoins; in this case the faithful soul is to remember that "we ought to obey God rather than men," Acts v. 29; and that if we love father or mother, husband or wife, children, or brethren, or sisters, or even our own lives more than Christ, we are not worthy of him, nor can we be his disciples, Luke xiv. 26; Matt. x. 37.

II. But having thus heard the lesson which the apostle gives the wife, let us now hearken to that which he gives the husband: "Husbands, love your wives, and be not bitter against them." He commands them to love them, and forbids them to be bitter against them; and in these few words he comprises all their duty. This duty is not less just, but indeed more agreeable and pleasing than that which he prescribed the wives. And observe, I pray, the apostle's prudence. For when he had allotted the woman subjection for her share, consequence seemed to require that he should give the man command and government for his. But he does it not. He established the man's authority sufficiently by putting the woman in subjection to him; and, in general, his strength and the other advantages of his sex cause him to assume too much. Wherefore, instead of saying, Husbands, govern your wives, or command them, or of using some such word, importing authority, he says to them, "Love your wives;" to sweeten on the one hand, the subjection of the wife, and to temper, on the other, the authority of the husband. Wife, let not your subjection fright you; the apostle subjects you not but to a person who loves you. Husband, let not your authority make you insolent. If the apostle subject your wife to you, it is only to the end that you love her. Derive no vanity either of you from the advantages he gives you. If the love which the husband owes his wife make her haughty, let her remember that withal she is subject to him who loves her. And if the authority which God gives the husband flatter him, let him not forget that the wife only submitted to him to oblige him to love her the more.

Further, this love which the apostle would have husbands cherish for their wives, is a sacred and sincere affection; produced in their hearts, not simply by that pleasing form and that grace and sweetness which naturally make men love and solicit this sex, and which, however perfect and charming, is at most, but a flower of a very short and uncertain duration; but principally by the will of God, who has joined them with them, who has given them to them for companions in their good and bad fortunes, for helps in all the parts of their life, for a perpetuation of their name and lineage, for diminishing their troubles and augmenting their joys. This perpetual and indivisible union which binds them together, and which of two persons has changed them into one flesh; which has mingled together all their interests, and in their dear children, inseparably combined and confounded their blood and very nature; all this, I say, must kindle in the soul of husbands a pure and an inviolable love to their wives. Then again, this love must flow forth from the heart into the external actions, discovering and evidencing itself by such continual effects as may be truly worthy of it. For love is not a dead picture, nor a vain fancy, nor an idol without life and action. It is the most lively and active of all our sentiments. It is a will that affects and sets all the power one has into operation to procure some good to the person whom it loves. The first effect of this love is to be pleased in the presence of that which a man loves, and not be able to suffer the absence of it long without disquietude; the second, to communicate to it all a man possesses that is good; and the third, to guard and preserve it from all injury and molestation.

It is thus the apostle would have husbands love their wives, even, first, that they live ordinarily with them, as far as the necessity of their affairs permits; not finding sweeter diversion nor more pleasing company anywhere else. Then, next, that they carefully make them partakers of the graces God has given them, and principally in all that concerns the salvation of their souls, which is the greatest good of all; faithfully directing them about it both by good and holy conversation, and also by pure and virtuous deportment. It is in this they ought to exercise that advantage which nature and the apostle give them, showing themselves to be truly the heads and guides of their wives, in the matters of God's service, and of holiness of life; for this end making provision of all necessary knowledge, that if they at any time consult them in their doubts, as Paul commands, 1 Cor. xiv. 35, they may be able to instruct them; lest, in defect of it, it might be said of them, as a prophet formerly said of idols, that they are teachers of nothing but lies, Hab. ii. 18. But to these cares for the soul the husband ought to add those also which respect the present life; labouring in his vocation, and imparting to his wife a share of all the substance he possesses or acquires proportionably to her need of it, either for her own necessary food and raiment, or for the maintenance of her children and family, as is suitable to her condition. It is this the apostle means when he commands husbands to love their wives.

But he forbids them, in the following words, to be "bitter against them;" that is, to be froward to them; requiring that all their conversation with them be full of sweetness and amity. The pagans themselves have observed the justness of this duty, as what we read of one piece of their devotions bears witness. For, when they sacrificed to that idol whom they called Nuptial Juno, because they gave her the superintendence of marriage, they were accustomed to take the gall out of the victim, and to cast it behind the altar, signifying by this, as say the interpreters of their ceremonies, that there ought to be no gall nor bitterness in marriage. The apostle's meaning, then, is that the husband first purge his heart of all this sourness and bitterness; that he never suffer hatred, malevolence, anger, provocation, fretting, nor disgust to enter there against a person whom he ought to love as himself. Next he would have the husband cleanse all his words and actions from the same poison. For if he who is angry with his neighbour without cause, and gives him the least reviling word, deserves torment, as our Saviour declares; of what hells is not he worthy who outrages his own flesh—her, whom he ought to cherish and tenderly love as Christ does his church? But, if the apostle commands a christian to use no offensive or opprobrious speech against his wife, he as little permits him to show bitterness of spirit by an angry, sad, and obstinate silence; which is not less provocative and sharp, to say the truth, than the most outrageous reproaches. In conclusion, by this clause, the apostle further, and with greater force of reason, banishes from conjugal converse, the cruelty, rigour, and tyranny of those boisterous, barbarous husbands, who treat their wives as bondservants, denying them that share which the laws of God and man give them in the government and administration of the household. And the utmost degree of this inhumanity is, when to revilings and contempt they add blows and excesses of hand; an outrage which the authors of the Roman civil law thought so unworthy of the conjugal alliance, that they permitted the wife so treated, to separate from her husband, approving and authorizing her divorce, if she can prove he struck her.

Thus, dear brethren, you have heard what we had to deliver for the exposition of this text. It teaches us all in general, first, that all sorts of people may and ought to read Paul's Epistles, and consequently all the holy Scriptures; for why should this holy man address this language to wives and their husbands, to children, and their fathers, to servants and their masters, if he meant not that all these persons should be permitted to read this letter? Christians, fear not to read what the apostle has vouchsafed to write to you. It is in vain that some forbid you to read that which it is his desire you should practise; none can know better than he how those Epistles which he wrote must be used. Then again, he here shows us how unjust is the indiscretion of those who have so ill treated the worthiness of marriage, that by their manner of speaking of it, you would suppose that they held it to be incompatible with christian purity. Paul everywhere maintains the honour of this holy order, and never at all prohibits or disparages it. Also, as the precepts which he gives to masters, to pastors, and others, clearly authorize the right and the dignity of those conditions; so is marriage established by the lesson which he here writes, and often elsewhere, to married persons. But the devil knowing well that this holy institution of God is infinitely profitable to men, both to preserve them from temptations to incontinence, one of the broadest ways to hell, and also to sweeten the harshness of their natures, by the tenderness of conjugal and paternal affections, and for various other purposes, of great importance to civil life, and to piety itself; the enemy, I say, not ignorant of this, has subtlely made a hatred or contempt of marriage, to insinuate itself into the spirits of a sort of men, under various plausible pretexts; so as that, in conclusion, christians (who would think it?) have ventured to consider it a piece of sanctification to abstain from it, and in the sequel prohibited it to the ministers of religion. For our parts, beloved brethren, we constrain none to marry. If any have received this grace of God, that they can contain and live pure out of this state, let them forbear to do so, if it seem to them good. Only we say two things: first, that the making use of it is free to all; there being no dignity nor profession in the church excluded from this divine permission. Secondly, that to such as have not the gift of continency, marriage is not only permitted, but even necessary; and of whatever rank they may be, their marrying is so far from offending God, that they offend him much if they marry not.

In conclusion, we add a serious exhortation to all who are in this state, that they sedulously put in practice the lesson which Paul has now given them, even that wives be subject to their husbands, as it is fit in the Lord; that husbands love their wives and be not bitter against them. Many complain of finding thorns in this condition instead of the roses they hoped for. Men charge it upon the pride, the levity, the vanity, the gorgeousness, the frowardness, the obstinacy, and the tongues of their wives, and lay many other odious reproaches upon them. Women, on the contrary, impute all this mischief to the husbands, complaining, some of their contempt, and want of love; others of their niggardliness towards them, and profuseness in other ways. Some declaim against their idleness, and the little care they take of their affairs; others against their excesses and intemperance. There are some who are angry at their speaking, and others at their silence; and, in short, they forget not one ill treatment which they have received. I know well that, upon strict examination, some fault would be found on each side; and that if there should be an apparent cause to reprehend wives, there would be no less cause to censure husbands. But I had rather lay aside all this vexatious process; and conjure you, dear brethren and sisters, in the name of God, to do the same: sparing one another's honour, consider what you are, and what a union God has called you to; and each one for his part acknowledging your defects in the duty it requires, terminate all your complaints in a reciprocal pardon; and forgetting all that is past, endeavour to procure to one another, in the state you are, that peace and contentment which hitherto you have not possessed. Do what the apostle bids you, and you shall find as much sweetness as heretofore you have tasted bitterness. For as there is nothing more wretched than a marriage in which the wife has no respect for her husband, and the husband no love for his wife; so neither is there anything in the world more happy, than a marriage in which the wife by a humble and respectful submission, and the husband by a sincere and faithful love, have their hearts and wills united in a holy concord. As the first of these two conditions is a hell, so the second is a very paradise.

Finally, my brethren, since Jesus Christ is the spouse of all faithful souls, you see what service and submission we are bound to render him. May it please this divine spouse, from that nuptial palace where he dwells, to make us smell the odour of his mystical perfumes, and to form our souls to all the obedience, the fidelity, and service which we owe him, and govern us by his Spirit, as he has purchased us with his blood; that, after having here beneath sighed for him, we may hereafter eternally enjoy him, according to his promises and our hopes. Amen.

SERMON XLIV.

VERSES 20, 21.

Children, obey your parents in all things: for this is well pleasing unto the Lord. Fathers, provoke not your children to anger, lest they be discouraged.

DEAR brethren, among all the mutual offices by which the society of men is preserved, those incumbent on children towards their parents, and on parents towards their children, are without doubt of the first order and most necessary. It is upon them that all the rest in some measure depend, and they are in human society what the foundation is in an edifice; the foundation once demolished, all the building falls to the ground; so the subjection of children, and the superiority of parents, once removed or unfixed, the ruin of all other parts of society necessarily follows. For if a man neglect his children or misgovern them, how will he duly and humanely treat servants, or subjects, or any other persons? Again, if a child shake off the yoke of his father and mother, how will he bear that of a master or a prince? There is no likelihood that the one or the other having failed in offices so sweet and natural toward persons that are so nearly in connection with them, will ever rightly discharge any of those which they owe to persons more remote, and with whom they have much less union. Whence appears the admirable wisdom of the providence of God, who, for forming us to the duties of love, subjection, and obedience, which are necessary in the civil or ecclesiastical society in which we are to live, puts us at first into the bosom and under the conduct of our fathers and mothers, that there, as in a sweet and suitable school, we may timely learn the bending of our spirits to love and respect for men; and after this previous apprenticeship, find the yoke of those superiors under whom we are to live in church or state less irksome. For one that has been a good child in the house will without much trouble be a good subject in the state; and likewise he that is a good father will easily prove also a good master, a good magistrate, a good pastor, if God should call him to any of those charges. Wherefore Paul requires, among the other qualifications of a bishop or pastor that he "rule well his own house, having his children in subjection with all gravity; for if a man know not how to rule his own house, how shall he take care of the church of God?" 1 Tim. iii. 4, 5. These reciprocal duties therefore of parents and children being of so great importance in the whole life of men, it is with propriety that our apostle takes care to regulate them in the text which we have read, immediately after having in the preceding verse stated those of husband and wife. He speaks first to children, according to the general order of beginning with the inferiors, which he observes in all this part of his institution, for reasons which we pointed out in our last discourse. "Children, obey your parents in all things: for this is well pleasing to the Lord." Then he prescribes to fathers also what pertains to them, in these words, "Fathers, provoke not your children to anger, lest they be discouraged." These are the two heads of which we will treat in the present sermon, if God so please: first, the duty of children; and secondly, that of fathers.

I. As to the first of these, we are to consider the apostle's command, contained in those words, "Children, obey your parents in all things:" and then the reason of this command, which the apostle annexes, "For this is well pleasing to the Lord." He directs the command to children, and uses here, in the original, a term which signifies any person begotten of another, his fruit, his production; a term that consequently comprehends all children of both sexes, that is, both sons and daughters; and of whatever degree, that is grandsons with regard to their grandfathers, as well as sons with regard to their fathers; for the word "children," according to the sense and authority both of Scripture and of the learned in the laws, includes both. Let all those therefore to whom this title belongs, remember that to them is this injunction of the apostle's addressed. Let not daughters urge the weakness of their sex, nor sons the strength and excellency of theirs, as a reason why the obedience they owe should be dispensed with, since, notwithstanding the difference of their sexes, they are all equally children. Nay, the weakness of maids is so far from diminishing, that it strengthens their obligation, inasmuch as it renders the guidance of those who brought them into the world so much the more necessary for them, as they are of themselves more infirm; and the fitter the strength of young men makes them to serve their fathers and their mothers, so much the more do they owe them obedience. Tell me not that time or fortune, as they call it, has freed you from this subjection; to whatever years you have attained, and whatever degree or honour you possess, you remain unalterably your father's and your mother's children; so that since it is unto this name the apostle affixes the obligation you have to obey them, it is evident that there is neither age nor office that can or should give you a dispensation from it. The Scripture sets before us an eminent example of it in Joseph, who, though of ripe years, and the father of a family, and a great lord in Egypt, where he was the second person in the state; yet all this made him not forget that he was Jacob's son; and when he knew that he was come into the country, he went immediately to meet him, Gen. xlvi. 29; his dignity withheld him not from rendering this honour to his father. He bowed down his purple before him, and notwithstanding the extreme inequality of their conditions in the world, he respected him always as his father.

But let us see what that duty is which the apostle here commands children to perform. "Obey your parents in all things." The law of God uses the term honour, "Honour thy father and thy mother." But it amounts to the same thing. For sure it is, that under this honour which the legislator enjoins just obedience also is comprised; and in the same manner, under the obedience which Paul commands is that respect which is one of the principal sources of it, understood and presupposed. Only it may be noticed, that perhaps he chose the word obey, the more effectually to show us what that honour is which we owe our fathers and our mothers; that it is not a vain respect, which consists merely in countenances and in ceremonies; but a true and real reverence, accompanied with obedience, so as to execute readily and cheerfully what they order us to do, learn what they teach us, correct what they dislike, and forbear to do what they forbid us. And by this the apostle condemns the hypocrisy of those who give their parents respect and civilities enough, as to words and gestures; but take no pains to do any thing they desire of them. Like that mocker in the parable, who having promised his father to go and labour in his vineyard, yet went not, Matt. xxi. 30.

But the apostle, to anticipate the vain pretexts with which impiety inspires ill natures, orders children not simply to obey their parents, but to obey them in all things; extending their authority to an infinity; nor shutting up within any bounds that power which God and nature have given them to command the persons they have brought into the world. Why then, you will say, is it true indeed that fathers and mothers have so vast and immense an authority; and that their children, whom God has created reasonable, are obliged notwithstanding this advantage to obey all their commands, however harsh and contrary to the light of their judgment? Dear brethren, if you consider the thing in itself, according to its own nature, and the terms of its first institution, it is very true that the authority of parents is so great, that children are indeed obliged to obey them generally, and without exception, in all things they command them. Nor does this disagree with that advantage of reason with which God has honoured children. For if things had continued in their due order, fathers would command their children nothing that were contrary to right reason. Now I confess that sin has disturbed this order, and it oft happens that those who are fathers command their children unjust things; yet neither can it be denied, that in this case they decline from the quality of fathers, and become tyrants. For the name of father involving in it an unfeigned love of the child, a love desirous of his good, and most remote from all that is contrary to his welfare; it is evidently a renouncing of this quality, when a father would oblige a son to things that are evil, and incompatible with the duties of a reasonable creature. It is therefore this abuse and this corruption of our nature, brought in by sin, that has bounded the paternal power, which of itself continuing in its right use, would be absolute; it is this that has obliged both divine and human laws to annex to it certain just and reasonable exceptions; which the apostle in another place, where he treats of the same subject, has comprised all in one word: "Children, obey your parents in the Lord," Eph. vi. 1; that is, as far as you may without disobeying the sovereign Lord, both theirs and yours; as far as their commands thwart not God's orders. And the words which he adds in the text itself necessarily lead us to this: "Obey them in all things: for this is well pleasing to the Lord;" an addition that evidently restrains the obedience of children to that which is pleasing to God; so that if the father happen to command that which displeases God, the child is obliged by all kinds of rights to regard more the will of God than the will of man; this maxim remaining firm and immovable, that whatever we owe to an inferior and subordinate power, the rights of the superior and sovereign must still remain entire. For since it is God who gave the father himself all the authority he has, it is clear that he has none against God; but that, as the child ought to obey him, so he ought to obey God. When he does it not, but by an insufferable felony casts off the yoke of this heavenly Father, to whom both he and we owe infinitely more obedience than to all the men on earth, it is just to deny him that obedience which he gives not to God; it is just that, of two contrary commands, the one of God, the other of a man, we prefer the divine before that which is human. As if a father should command his son to be an idolater, or to kill or to hate his neighbour; or should forbid him to embrace the service of God, or to make profession of the gospel of his Christ; in these cases, and others similar, disobedience would be just, and obsequiousness criminal. And to this properly that saying of our Lord and Saviour refers, Luke xiv. 26, "If any man come to me, and hate not his father, and mother, and wife, and children, and brethren, and sisters, yea, and his own life also," (that is as another evangelist expounds it, Matt. x. 37, if he love these more than me,) he is not worthy of me; "he cannot be my disciple."

Saving this just and reasonable exception, children owe their fathers that obedience in all things which the apostle here enjoins. And first in those which are of themselves good and holy, and conformable to the divine will; besides that the law of God obliges us all to them, the command of a father moreover obliges anew his children; and if they fail in it, besides the crime they thereby commit against God, they commit another against paternal authority, which shall be charged on them, and punished apart, as a different sin, and worthy of its particular penalty. Secondly, the child again owes obedience in medial and indifferent things; that is, things which are morally neither good nor evil, the extent of which is very great. Though such things are free of their own nature, yet they are so no more to a child after the father's order. His command draws them forth from that indifference in which they lay, and renders them necessary with reference to him. And here must no self-flattery take place. I wish (and it is their duty, as we shall hear presently) that fathers would command nothing but what is humane and equitable: yet if they forget themselves, and pass these bounds, however harsh and troublesome may be their commands, obeyed they must be, if they contain in them nothing impious, or contrary to the divine law; according to the express order that Peter gives servants to be subject to their masters, "not only to the good and gentle, but also to the froward." The reason for children with reference to their fathers is the same in this respect as that for servants with reference to their masters. You see, then, beloved brethren, the just extent of all those things in which the apostle would have children obey their parents.

Whence it appears how unrighteous, and dangerous, and contrary to the word of God is the doctrine of those of Rome, who enfranchise all christian children from this paternal authority and power, daughters at twelve, and sons at fourteen; giving them liberty at an age so young to go from their parents' house, whether they are willing or not, and retire from under their obedience into the cloisters of their monasteries; where they have erected an assured sanctuary and an inviolable safeguard for the rebellion of children against their fathers and mothers. There, under the umbrage of a false devotion, they entertain children in idleness, and foment their impiety, tyrannically giving them a dispensation from that obedience, and those just succours, which by all the laws of God and men they owe to the sacred persons of those who gave them being in the world. The father demands of them the assistances and consolations which he promised himself from them. He shows them his gray hairs and his limbs trembling through age; he conjures them by the life he gave them, and by the cares he took to train them up. He summons them to render him the just rewards of his pains, and not to despise the tears and entreaties of a person to whom they are indebted for their life. The mother all in mourning presents them the paps that nursed them, and sets before their eyes the tenderness of her affection, and all the ties of nature. And they both together point them to the bar of God, that they may see themselves condemned at his dreadful tribunal, to pay the honour which they owe them. What say our adversaries upon this? They say that children ought to look upon their fathers and their mothers without emotion; that neither their words nor their weeping should make any impression upon them; that if they cannot enter into the monastery otherwise than by treading their bodies under foot, they ought to have no compunction at all at so unnatural an action; that it is piety to be cruel and insensible on such an occasion. They say that the monastic vow has broken all the bonds of filial subjection; and that the child who has made it no longer owes anything to father or mother; that he is dead to them, and they have no more power over him than if he were out of the world.

O unrighteous, and cruel, and unnatural doctrine! How could these men more plainly contradict the holy apostle? The apostle says, "Children, obey your parents in all things: for this is well pleasing to the Lord." And these masters say, Children, obey them not in all things: if they forbid you to be monks, scorn their order. If they command you to abide with them, begone against their will; for you would do a thing displeasing to the Lord if you did not disobey them. Neither let them tell us here that they are now grown up. If they cease to be children by attaining to twelve or fourteen years of age, I will acknowledge that they are no longer subject to their parents. But if they must confess that no age divests them of this quality, it must be acknowledged that neither does any give them a dispensation from obedience, since the apostle commands it to all such as are children. They excuse themselves upon the account of devotion. This would pass, if the father called his child to impiety, or commanded him to deny Jesus Christ, or to serve idols. But this father and this mother, who would keep their child at home, are christians as well as monks are; and their house makes a part of that of Jesus Christ as well as the cloister in which he is kept. The obedience they demand of him is a duty commanded by the law of God, and very far from being contrary to it. I urge not at present that the vows by which he is pretended to be bound are contrary to the word of God, as particularly that of mendicity; are rash, as that of celibacy; are injurious to the Lord, as that of the blind and absolute obedience which they promise to a mortal man. Let them go for permitted. Certainly, at least, they are not necessary; and they themselves, great admirers as they are of them, confess that one may serve God and obtain his kingdom without the precincts of a monastery; and that neither beggary, nor single life, nor the frock, are things absolutely necessary to salvation. There is neither a place where one may not serve Jesus Christ in spirit and in truth, nor a habit but what is compatible with piety. Now the child ought to obey his father in all that God has not prohibited. Since then he has not prohibited the living abroad out of the houses and habit of Benedict, of Francis, of Loyola, and such other institutors of monastic life; every child is necessarily bound not to enter into them when his father forbids it. But, you will say, what if he has made a vow to enter? If he has, he has acted against the duties of piety and charity; and if it is an error to make such vows, it is blindness and obduracy to keep them. The first and most inviolable of our vows is that which binds us to the obedience of God, and after him to the obedience of our parents. If we have chanced, through imprudence or otherwise, to tie up ourselves elsewhere, we must speedily break the bond, and make no scruple nor conscience to break it, but to observe it. Besides the evident reason we have for it, and the confession of all wise men, who hold that vows made against moral duty are not binding, the word of God expressly makes this decision: "If a woman vow a vow unto the Lord, and bind herself by a bond, being in her father's house in her youth; if her father disallow her in the day that he heareth; not any of her vows, or of her bonds wherewith she hath bound her soul, shall stand," Numb. xxx. 3, 5. Here you see that vows, though in other respects good and lawful, are not binding, if made by children of the family, without their father's consent. And this is yet more forcibly concluded from the lawgiver's adding, that the vows of a married wife, disallowed by her husband, are null and void, Numb. xxx. 6—8; it being evident that the authority of a father over his child is much greater and more strict than that of a husband over his wife.

And hither must that censure be referred which our Lord and Saviour passed upon the Pharisees, who, under colour of the religion of vows, also annulled the honouring of parents by their children, so expressly commanded in the law. "God," he says, "commanded, saying, Honour thy father and mother: and, He that curseth father or mother, let him die the death. But ye say, Whosoever shall say to his father or his mother, It is a gift, by whatsoever thou mightest be profited by me; and honour not his father or his mother, he shall be free. Thus have ye made the commandment of God of none effect by your tradition," Matt. xv. 4—6. For the right understanding of our Saviour's discourse, and of that tradition of the Pharisees which he opposes, we are to know that the Jewish rabbis, as we learn by their own books, attached very great importance to vows, holding the religion of them absolutely inviolable. Moreover, they enlisted into the rank of vows, not those only which were legitimate, and conceived in a solemn manner, with terms of a full extent, as when one said, I make a vow unto God not to taste wine, or strong drink, during the space of forty days, and the like; but also all other words, in whatever form conceived and uttered, whether upon deliberation, or in anger, or otherwise, by which one devoted anything whatever, either expressly or covertly; as, for instance, if a man in a fit of anger, or in the trouble of a quarrel with his neighbour, was led to say through indignation, Let me die if ever I do thee any service; the rabbis took this for a true vow, and accounted such a man bound in conscience never to do that person any service against whom he had uttered such words. Now because the *corban*, that is, the sacred gifts given to the temple, was a thing which they esteemed most inviolable, and the offerings there kept might not be employed to any profane use, nor any private person put his hand into the treasury for that purpose upon pain of death; it became customary to signify that the use of a thing was totally interdicted to any one, to say that it was to him *corban*, that is, he was no more permitted to make use of it than of the sacred gifts, which in their language were called by that name. When, therefore, it happened that a son, through dislike or anger at his father, once was induced to say, All that of which you might have profit by me is a gift, or *corban;* that is, you shall never be the better for me, or you shall never draw service or profit from me, no more than from the *corban;* the Pharisees, and other rabbis, held that such a man was obliged by this vow to do his father no service any more; and they judged him innocent and blameless, though he never did him any, however pressing the father's necessity might be, alleging that the religion of a vow was above the natural obligation of children towards their fathers and their mothers; which was indeed to annul the law of God by their tradition, as our Saviour charged them. Judge, if those of Rome do not the same thing, dispensing with the obedience of children due to parents, upon pretence of monastic vows, in the same manner; and if, consequently, we have not all the reasons in the world, to apply to them what our Lord said of the Pharisees, even that they make the commandment of God of none effect by their tradition.

Let us then lay aside, since the Lord so enjoins it, all human inventions; and simply and faithfully keep to the will of our sovereign Master, as he has declared it to us in his word. You see that in the text it is the only reason the apostle brings to enforce this duty upon children. He might have urged the justice of the thing itself; it being evident that we owe respect and honour to those who gave us both life and education, and if not all, at least the greatest part of whatever help and honour we possess and understand. He might have argued from nature, which has engraven this law in the heart of animals themselves; whom we see, especially while they are young, to be subject to those that brought them forth. He might have produced the custom of all nations, even the least civilized not excepted, who by their practice, and some of them by their laws, have authorized the veneration of parents, as of sacred persons; and have noticed (as it is indeed very remarkable) that the pagans, both Greeks and Romans, so highly esteemed this duty, as to give it the same name they gave to the fearing and worshipping of God, calling not only devout and religious persons pious, but those also who were industrious to honour and to serve their fathers and mothers; consequently, they held that excesses committed against parents were to be punished in the same manner as violations of the honour of the Deity.* The apostle might have produced all these things, and many others. But he does it not. He alleges nothing but the sole will of God, as the best, the strongest, and the most considerable of all reasons. Children, obey your fathers and your mothers in all things. Why? Because this, says he, "is well pleasing to the Lord." If you be a christian, this is sufficient to persuade you to render to your parents that obedience which the apostle commands. For how can you neglect what is pleasing to that Lord upon whom depends all your salvation, who has been so good to you as to redeem you from eternal perdition by the death of his only Son, and to give you, in him, his Spirit and his peace, and the assured hope of everlasting life?

That this dutifulness of children towards their parents is well pleasing unto him, besides that the apostle, whose authority is irrefragable, expressly asserts it here, the Lord himself evidences in various ways: first, by his commandment, engraven by his own hand at the head of the second table of the law, "Honour thy father and thy mother." Secondly, by the promise he annexes to it, "to prolong your days upon the earth," if you are diligent to discharge this duty. In the third place, by the punishments he threatens to children who disobey their father and mother, ordaining in the political laws of Israel, that they should be publicly stoned by all the people of the city where they dwelt, Deut. xxi. 18; and elsewhere, that they should irremissibly put to death him who cursed his father or his mother, Exod. xxi. 17; Lev. xx. 9. In another place he pronounces by the mouth of wise Solomon, that the lamp of such a man "shall be put out in obscure darkness;" and that the ravens of the valley shall pluck out, and the young eagles eat, the eye of him that mocketh his father, and despiseth the instruction of his mother, Prov. xx. 20; xxx. 17. Again, the Lord's calling himself our Father, and honouring us with the name of his children, that he might induce us to serve him, sufficiently shows of what kind, and how holy and inviolable, is that obedience which we owe to parents; "If I be a father," says he, "where is my honour?" Mal. i. 6. Even pagans have acknowledged that the performance of this duty is well pleasing to the Deity; witness some of their poets confidently promising a long and happy life to such as shall honour their fathers and their mothers, and pay those just attentions to their old age which are due to it.

---

* Val. Max.

But it is time to come to the other head of the text, in which the apostle, after having reduced children to their duty, turns himself to fathers, and advises them to use the power he has given them moderately, and in such a manner as that their conduct may tend to their children's benefit, and their own happiness: "Fathers," says he, "provoke not your children, lest they be discouraged." This provocation which he forbids is an ill effect which the abuse of paternal authority produces in the hearts of children, when fathers act with too much rigour, and treat them too roughly; which happens in a great many ways. First, when they deny them a just allowance, and what is necessary to maintain them suitably to their birth. The apostle has judged this so enormous a sin, that he hesitates not to say that he who commits it "hath denied the faith, and is worse than an infidel," 1 Tim. v. 8. Secondly, Fathers provoke their children when they give them unrighteous and inhuman commands, as when Saul would oblige Jonathan his son to hate and persecute David, a very virtuous and innocent person; upon which this generous son, most unworthy of so bad a father, was vexed and inflamed with anger, 1 Sam. xx. 34. If the daughter of Herodias had had any spark of this good nature, she would have been in the same manner offended at that cruel and barbarous command her mother gave her to ask of king Herod the head of John the Baptist in a charger, Matt. xiv. 8. It is also provoking a child when, without any necessity, he compels him to perform sordid and servile actions, and such as are beneath his birth. In this rank too I put those who, without cause, assail their children's ears with contumelious words, whether they are inspired by present passion, or an ill-favoured custom has habituated their tongues to such venomous conduct. For we see some who cannot speak to their children, nor reprove them, nor so much as call them to them, in any other dialect, but discharge at every turn a hail-shower of maledictions and opprobrious terms upon them; a kind of behaviour most abject and odious, extremely unworthy of any honest and ingenuous man, especially of a christian, whose mouth ought to be a source of blessing, and have nothing issue from it but what is grave, and holy, and proper to edify. But neither is there any person with whom a wise man should less deal in this manner than his child, whom such indiscretion dejects, and infinitely dismays, if he has ever so little spirit and sensibility. It was with this black and piquant salt that Saul seasoned the remonstrances which he made to Jonathan: "Thou son," says he, "of the perverse rebellious woman, do not I know that thou hast chosen the son of Jesse to thine own confusion, and to the confusion of thy mother's nakedness?" 1 Sam. xx. 30. Are these the words of a father, and not rather of an enemy, yea, of a barbarous enemy, who has neither honour nor civility? as indeed it was anger that spake, and not reason; and he suffered himself to be so transported by the fury of his passion, that after such a tempest of rude words, he failed not to throw his lightning, casting a javelin at him to smite him. And this is the height of those excesses which the apostle intends here by that provocation which he forbids, when fathers chastise their children either without cause or without measure, and beyond what they deserve. For if justice oblige us to keep our minds free and composed in punishing the greatest strangers and the most heinous malefactors, that we may exactly proportion the penalty to their faults, as the Lord expressly commanded the judges of his people, Deut. xxv. 2, 3; how much more should a father, whose name breathes nothing but benignity and sweetness, observe the same moderation when his business is to chasten his child? God gives us examples of it in his treatment of his children, chastising them indeed, but, as he himself says, "with the rod of men, and with the stripes of the children of men," 2 Sam. vii. 14; that is moderately, and with a human rod, a rod tempered with gentleness and benignity.

The apostle, to dissuade fathers from this fault, shows them the evil which it produces: "Provoke not your children," says he, "lest they be discouraged." For there is nothing that more dejects the heart of a child, especially if ingenuous, than this rigour and roughness of a father. First, it saddens him, when in the countenance and actions of that person, to whom of all men in the world he should in reason be dearest, he sees nothing but anger and aversion. This grief often casts him into languishings and fatal maladies, which make fathers regret and execrate, though vainly and too late, their unhappy and imprudent severity. Then, again, this conduct intimidates children, and deprives them of all courage for any good and honest undertaking, and smothers in them all the fire and vivacity they possessed. For, finding themselves so ill treated by their own fathers, what can they hope for from other hands? Some, which is yet worse, are by this means hardened, and, together with sensibility and nature, lose all shame and modesty, and fall at last, by degrees, into desperate impiety, no longer paying any regard to God or men, which is the utmost and most horrid degree of vice. Consider, if the fear of so great a mischief does not oblige all fathers who have any remains, I will not say of piety, but even of judgment and good sense, to take heed that they provoke not their children.

Brethren, I beseech you, improve now this instruction of the apostle's. Children, to whom first he addresses his discourse, render to your fathers and mothers in all things the obedience he commands you. Remember the life they gave you, the pains they have taken to preserve it to you, the cares they have had to adorn and enrich it both with necessary knowledge, and with conveniences requisite to render it happy; the fears and tears they have been and, at every turn, are still in for you; their patience in bearing with the weaknesses of your infancy, and the extravagancies of your youth; the tenderness and constancy of the love they bear you, a love so great, so ardent, that you are the principal object of their desires; that they prefer your happiness to their own, and toil only for you, and have you night and day in their hearts; the vows with which they follow you everywhere, craving nothing of God more instantly than your advancement and happiness; and looking on you as the principal subject of their hopes and their joy. Have not so unnatural a soul as not to feel all these strict obligations which you have to love, and serve, and honour them. Pay their love with your respects, and their pains with your obedience; and be not so wretched as to render them trouble and affliction for so many benefits as you have received of them, nor so ungrateful as to frustrate the just hopes they have conceived of you. Certainly you would owe them this obedience if no other consideration obliged you than what is founded in themselves. But there is more than this. The apostle assures you that, in performing your duty to men, you will please God, the Father of spirits, and Ruler of the world. This, saith he, is pleasing unto him. He will reckon it to you as a part of the piety you owe him, and charge himself with the services you shall render to those whom he has given you as authors of your being. It is the best and the most pleasing devotion you can offer him. Miserable superstition, that goest to seek in cloisters for exercises pleasing to God! There was no occasion to go out of the father's house for this. Thou hast enough at home with which to please the Lord. As for the particular exercises about which monks are busied in their cloisters, we know not whether they please God, who never commanded them. But for the services which our parents demand of us for their consolation, and the easing of their lives, we cannot doubt that they are most pleasing to him, since he commands them, and his apostle assures us here expressly of it. Consider, I pray, the imprudence of these people. They say they would please God, and that it is their whole aim to obtain his approbation. In the meantime, to attain to this, they renounce their obedience to their parents, which is pleasing to him, and subject themselves to the fancies and the rugged rules of certain men, of which they neither have, nor can have, any assurance that they please God. Is not this to quit a certainty for an uncertainty, and to do the wrong way what one pretends, to go further off from what one seeks, and to cast oneself upon what he would eschew? But you, brethren, better instructed by the word of the Lord, seek to please him in doing that which he orders you, and in employing that time and labour in serving and obeying your parents, which superstition loses in its painful, but vain and fruitless, exercises. This is the way to be pleasing unto God, and to secure to yourselves that crown of blessedness which he has promised to such children as faithfully discharge this duty.

As for you, believing parents, nature itself, and the interest of your own happiness, so forcibly impel you to love your children, and to treat them well, that if the apostle had forborne to give such an express direction against provoking them, I think there would not have been much need to say anything of it. We offend much more on the other hand; I mean, in excess of affection and softness of indulgence: forgetting that to treat them so laxly is, in truth, to hate, and not to love them; to destroy, and not to train them up. The apostle forbids you to provoke them, but does not hinder you from correcting, reproving, and chastening them if they deserve it. He directs only that your conduct be just and temperate; that it keep a mean between the two extremes, the roughness of severity, and the remissness of indulgence. The care you owe them is, to form them to true virtue, to the knowledge and the fear of God, to charity, justice, and honesty towards men; to give them examples of these in your lives, and inculcate the lessons of them with your lips. Whereas we ourselves ruin their manners, and early instil into them our vices, almost before they know them. Our greatest care is to keep their courage high, and instruct them in pride, and inure them to vanity, as if nature had not given them enough of it. And to this they who have the means fail not to add the ball, and dance, and comedy. And that they may the better learn these grand lessons, fathers and mothers give them examples of them. We need not wonder, if, under such education, we see our youth so badly conduct themselves; if they become insolent; if they have little sentiment of true piety; if they treat those so much amiss to whom they owe most respect. Brethren, if you have children, remember, that besides the interest you have in their virtue and their vices, you shall render an account for them unto God, who has given them to you to train them for his glory, and for the edification of his church, and not to please the world, or to serve vanity.

But, dear brethren, of whatever state or condition we are, let us further take out two lessons which the apostle here gives us. The one is, to render all of us to God an exact and humble obedience in all things, since we have the honour to be his children. It is this that the child owes to his father. We are not his if we obey him not. We falsely vaunt ourselves in that glorious title, if we neglect the duty to which it binds us. The other lesson is, that the will of God should be the only rule of our lives; so that we do nothing but what is pleasing unto him. This is the sovereign reason of our duties, not to attempt anything that displeases him, nor neglect anything that is agreeable to him. This rule is of vast and perpetual use in all the parts of life. And omitting other things for the present, I beseech you only to apply it to the pastimes, the balls, the banquetings, and comedies of the present season. Each of you consult your own conscience upon this, if it is informed by the word of God, and ask it if these exercises of the world are verily pleasing to God; and whether, in running after them with the multitude, you can assure yourself you do that which delights him. If it answer, that there is no reason to believe it, but very much to the contrary; in the name of God, my brethren, follow this resolution of your own conscience. Abstain from these works of darkness; spare the church; give it no scandal; expose not its name and its profession to the scorn of those without, by engaging them in the disorders of the present generation. Let your manners have no less purity in them than your faith; and let there be a difference between the very entertainments of children of God and of others. Give to the poor what is cast away usually in such follies, and you shall acquire a firm and solid consolation, which shall never be followed with repentance and regret, but go on still increasing, until it be changed into that eternal and incomprehensible joy which is kept for us in the heavens by our Lord Jesus Christ; to whom, as to the Father and the Holy Spirit, the true and only eternal God, be honour, praise, and glory, unto ages of ages. Amen.

SERMON XLV.

CHAPTER III. 22—25, TO CHAPTER IV. 1.

Servants, obey in all things your masters according to the flesh: not with eye-service, as men-pleasers; but in singleness of heart, fearing God; and whatsoever ye do, do it heartily, as to the Lord, and not unto men; knowing that of the Lord ye shall receive the reward of the inheritance: for ye serve the Lord Christ. But he that doeth wrong shall receive for the wrong which he hath done: and there is no respect of persons. Masters, give unto your servants that which is just and equal; knowing that ye also have a Master in heaven.

If mankind, after the devastation which sin has made, has anything left that is laudable, advantageous, and conducive to welfare, it is, without doubt, the order of those societies which compose it. For this correspondence, and this harmony of several persons, different in themselves, and yet knit together by the mutual offices they perform to each other, and by that common end to which they direct them, is an effect and production of a very perspicacious and exquisite reason, and bears such evident marks of it as no one can help perceiving, if he apply his mind ever so little to this consideration. The thing is such as made a heathen * formerly say, that that grand and supreme divinity which governs the world sees nothing on earth more agreeable to him than the bodies of families and republics established among men, and governed by good and equitable laws. For as there is nothing, not only more unsightly and deformed, but also more disadvantageous, than confusion; so, on the contrary, there is nothing that is at once both more beautiful and more beneficial than order. For order, setting everything in its place, and uniting all together by the coaptation and combining of particulars, cherishes and preserves the whole; and by their union frames up a body which, conjoining in one the forces and perfections of each of them, becomes, by this means, extremely fair and most important. This is the reason why the apostles of our Lord and Saviour

* Cicero.

carefully discriminated this order from those defects and imperfections which their Master came to correct in the world. And as their holy discipline batters, overthrows, and brings to nought all that the unrighteousness and pride of sin has reared up among us; so it also establishes and mightily confirms the civil and domestic societies which it found in mankind, as so many holy and necessary institutions of God our Creator.

You have heard with what affection Paul recommends to christians the sacred and inviolable duties of husbands and wives, of fathers and children, for preserving domestic society in its integrity among us. Now, that he might leave no disorder at all in it, he speaks to servants and masters; and in this text discreetly regulates the subjection of the former, and the domination of the latter: representing to each excellent considerations, taken from fundamentals of gospel doctrine, to sway them to their duty. This subjection of servants, and superiority of masters, shall be the two points of which we will treat, if God permit, in this discourse; observing briefly the particulars they may afford for our common edification and consolation.

I. He insists most upon the first point, which respects servants; because subjection is bitter, and a thing to which our nature is loth to submit, especially in the condition in which servants at that time were. For it was not with them as it is now with ours, who are persons in reality free; and being able to dispose of themselves, only let out their services for a time, and upon certain conditions, without divesting themselves of the liberty in which they were born. The servants of the ancients, in the apostle's time, and among the nations to whom he wrote, were slaves, which belonged to their masters, and were theirs by the same kind of property as were their cattle. They could not dispose of their own persons, nor of their children, but by the authority and will of their masters. The law of servitude was of the same nature among the Jews also, excepting only that such servants as were of the Hebrew race went out of that condition, and were set at liberty, when they came to the year of jubilee, as is evident from various passages in the books of Moses. The apostle, knowing how harsh this condition was to men, took a particular care to sweeten it, and to recommend the duties of it to such as divine Providence had ranked in it; lest disgust at so strict a subjection, and love of liberty, should induce them to shake off the yoke, and to disturb the order of public society by their rebellion. First, he orders them to obey; next, he prescribes them the manner of this obedience, "not with eye-service, as men-pleasers;" and, finally, in the last two verses of this chapter, he sets before them some considerations, taken from the benignity and justice of God to incite them to a faithful discharge of their duty.

1. The command of obedience is expressed in these words, "Servants, obey in all things your masters according to the flesh." The very names of which he makes use show the justice of the duty which he gives them in charge. For since they are servants, and those whom they serve are their masters, it is evident that they are obliged, by the reason and nature of the things themselves to render them exact and faithful obedience. But his saying of masters, that they are their masters "according to the flesh," mitigates the rigour and the meanness of servitude, limiting the power of masters and superiors, and extending it no further than to temporal and corporeal things, not to the soul and conscience. Man may be master of our flesh, God alone is Lord over our spirits. Whatever be the subjection of our bodies, we have still our souls free and dependent on none but God their Creator, who alone has the power as well as the right to do them good or evil; as our Lord and Saviour reminds us: "Fear not them," says he, "which kill the body, but are not able to kill the soul: but rather fear him which is able to destroy both soul and body in hell," Matt. x. 28. It is with this distinction that we are to take the obedience which the apostle recommends to servants "in all things:" his meaning is, in all things that lie within the master's power, and purely and singly refer to the flesh, not reflecting on or touching the interests of the spirit. For if our master according to the flesh command us things contrary to the will of our Master according to the spirit, that is, of God; in this case it is evident that we ought to obey God rather than man; and that if we owe much, and in some sense even all things, to men, yet we owe them nothing to the prejudice of God; and that there is nothing which we should not rather suffer than fail of that first and eternal servitude which we owe to our Creator and Redeemer.

This holy doctrine of the apostle shows us first, that the Lord Jesus Christ does not at all disturb the order of human societies. He leaves to every one in them the just rights of which they are possessed, to persons or things. He subjects us unto himself, and unto God his Father; but without doing wrong to Cæsar, or to any of the lawful powers that govern either estates or families. He intends that all his should render to them what they owe them; he destroys only the treacheries and tyrannies of sin and Satan. Herod, dread not his coming; he will neither pluck your sceptre out of your hand, nor diminish in anything the rights of your crown. His design is to give you heaven, not to bereave you of the earth; to enfranchise you from the slavery of vices, and not to deprive you of the service of your subjects. Whence it appears how unjust and scandalous is the presumption of those who, under the pretence of gospel liberty, would abolish all dominion and sovereignty among christians; accounting it incompatible with the state of grace: and theirs no less, who subject, even in respect of temporals, all who are christians, not the greatest monarchs excepted, to one mortal man; making their crowns to depend upon his will, and giving him authority to depose them, and to loose their subjects from the yoke of their obedience; teaching also by the same means, that a christian prince who falls into heresy loses the right he had over his people. Can anything be said more pernicious, or more contrary to the apostle, who would not that paganism itself, a matter worse than heresy, should make masters and superiors lose any of the lawful rights they have over their christian slaves? Secondly, the apostle's limiting the authority and power of masters over their slaves, in things of the flesh, naming them their "masters according to the flesh," shows us that there is none but God alone who is our Master according to the spirit. It follows, therefore, that those who under any pretext whatever peremptorily invade the lordly ruling of our souls grievously err, and usurp a dominion which belongs to none but God; an attempt of which those of Rome are evidently guilty, inasmuch as they put the consciences of all christians in subjection to their pope and council; whereas the holy apostles expressly declare, that they have no dominion over our faith, 2 Cor. i. 24; and command all the ministers of Christ to feed the flock committed to them, not as being lords over God's heritage, but so as that they may be a pattern to them, 1 Pet. v. 2, 3.

2. But I return to Paul, who having in general directed servants to render that obedience which they owe to their masters according to the flesh in all things, adds the manner in which he would have them to obey them; "not with eye-service, as men-pleasers; but in singleness of heart, fearing God." He first purges the conduct of christian servants of a vice very ordinary with persons of that quality; namely, "eye-service;" because they have no other design but to please men. They do not think themselves bound by reasons of conscience to do their masters any duty or service, but only by those of their own interest. And so they serve them no further than they judge necessary for exempting themselves from that chastisement which they should incur if they failed to obey, or for procuring some recompense by winning their favour. They respect nothing but this in all the obedience they render them. Consequently, when they see their master present, they play the good husbands, as we say, and labour at their work with most officious diligence and care. But if he turn his back, they return to their nature, caring for nothing less than for his service: like that evil servant in the parable, who seeing that his master delayed to come, commenced his debauches, and began to outrage his lord's household, and waste his goods.

All the servitude of these people is but a comedy. And as players put on their disguise, and act their parts, when there is an assembly of spectators; so these only do their duty when their master looks on. And if they thought they could deceive his eyes and knowledge, or avoid his correction, or save their salary, they would surely never take the pains to obey any of his commands. It is this fallacious and truly servile disposition of heart which the apostle here forbids to christian servants, when he says that they should not serve to the eye, as aiming only to please men.

But instead of this, he would have them serve in singleness of heart, fearing God; that is, sincerely, without fraud or feigning, and having more respect to God than men. To that eye-service which he had mentioned he opposes singleness of heart; and to the pleasing of men, the fearing of God. The Scripture is accustomed to attribute two hearts, or a double heart, to a feigning person; because he makes show of one intention, and yet has another quite different: so has he who serves to the eye. To see him, you would say that he loves his master, and desires his profit; yet under this deceitful mask he hides thoughts and affections quite opposite; heeding nothing less than the interests of him whom he serves. But the servant whom the apostle here describes has but one affection and one thought; and having learned in the school of Christ that it is just and reasonable that the servant should obey his master, he serves his, to fulfil this piece of righteousness, and acquit himself of his duty, in which he would consider himself deficient if he did otherwise: so that bearing about everywhere this sentiment with him engraven in his conscience, there is neither place nor time in which he does not faithfully serve his master, whether he be absent or present, seen or unseen.

To this the apostle further adds, that he must fear God. Others refer the condition of servants only to man; he would have a christian know, that God is the author of it; that it is he who has appointed it; and would have us approve our fidelity in it, when his providence has called us to it. Think not, saith he, that you have to do with none but men. It is God who has put you in this state. Do not imagine it sufficient to respect and please the eye of your master. You must reverence and satisfy the eye of God, whom you cannot deceive, nor please at any lower rate than by doing your duty exactly and sincerely. But the apostle would not have a christian simply to do all his master commands him. He would also have him do it cheerfully, and with the heart: "Whatever ye do," says he, "do it heartily;" that is, first, not by constraint and with murmuring, but voluntarily; and, secondly, with affection for those who command you.

Verily, you will say, a hard law. For if the master be froward; if he command, as it often happens, things that are difficult, and harsh, and inhuman; how is it possible a servant should work with any cheerfulness? I answer, that our flesh finds it difficult to relish such obedience, and cannot suffer so hard a bit without reluctance and resistance. But the fear of God inclines us to account those things sweet which are in their own nature very harsh. If you look upon man only, I acknowledge that you have some ground to think it hard, that one, who is in reality no more than a man as you are, should have you in such subjection to his will. But if you lift up your eyes higher, and consider that it is God who has instituted this order, that it is he who has called you to this condition, that the master whom you serve is his minister and officer, then the roughest of his commands will become supportable to you. And it is to this the apostle reduces you, when, to bend you to this sweet and willing obedience, he advises you to do all things as unto the Lord, and not as unto men. Consider, says he, that it is to Jesus Christ, and not to a mortal man, that you render your services. Respect this sovereign Lord in the person of your masters; and think that it is he who orders you to do all that they command you. For he it is likewise who has given them to you by his providence for masters. Withal, he declares expressly in his word that it is his will you should obey them. Admire now, christian, I pray, the virtue of the gospel, which, like the branch cut down by Moses, sweetens the bitterest things, and so changes their nature, that, of distasteful and forced, it makes them pleasing and voluntary. What is there harder or more abject than the servitude of a slave? The gospel changes it into a devotion, into a religious service; that is, into the noblest and most voluntary of all human actions. The believer directs that obedience unto Jesus Christ which an infidel gives only to his master. He does that for his God which the other does but for a man. Wherefore he does it cheerfully and heartily, while the other does it only by constraint, and with regret. Hence the apostle says elsewhere, that a servant "called in the Lord is the Lord's freeman," 1 Cor. vii. 22. Not that he ceases to do his former master the service he was accustomed; from this he is so far, that he now becomes much more faithful and profitable to him than he was before; as Onesimus, the servant of Philemon, who, after he once knew Jesus Christ, went voluntarily to put himself again under his old master's yoke, which during the darkness of his unbelief he had cast off, Philem. 10. All the difference is, that whereas in the time of his ignorance he had respect merely to his master's will and authority, now he has little regard thereto, considering principally those of his Lord and Saviour; so that, to say the truth, it is him he serves, and not a man. Christ hath freed him from man's yoke, and put him under his own; since henceforth his aim in all he does for man is chiefly to please, not man, but Jesus Christ.

3. To form the spirits of christian servants to this holy disposition, the apostle represents to them, in the last two verses of this chapter, that the Lord Jesus is indeed the true Master and Superintendent of their whole lives, who sets them their task, and looks on their labours, whatever condition they are in, and will not fail when his day is come to make up a true and faithful account with them, largely recompensing such of them as shall be found to have honestly discharged their duty, and severely punishing the negligent. Do all things "as to the Lord, and not unto men; knowing that of the Lord ye shall receive the reward of the inheritance: for ye serve the Lord Christ. But he that doeth wrong shall receive for the wrong which he hath done: and there is no respect of persons." First, he would have them be certain that their servitude shall not be in vain nor unfruitful, if they acquit themselves in it as he has prescribed; and if their masters according to the flesh have no regard to it, their sovereign Lord will not fail to give them their pay and recompense. Next, he shows them what this recompense is which they are to expect from the Lord: it is "the reward of the inheritance." There is no one in the school of Christ who does not well know that this inheritance of which the apostle speaks, is that blessed and glorious immortality which Jesus Christ has purchased for us by the merit of his death, and calls us all to the possession of by his gospel. Now see how prudently the holy apostle has balanced his expressions of it! He calls it a reward, or guerdon, that is, a retribution and a prize; to the end that he might raise our hearts to this sublime hope, and incite us thereby to labour cheerfully for the receiving of so rich a recompense. For as prizes are given only to those who have laboured and striven; so this life of God is prepared only for those who shall, in their vocation, have fought a good fight, and kept the faith, and duly finished their course. And as the prince promises a soldier honour, and the master a workman wages; and the one performs, if the others discharge their duty; so the Lord promises us his kingdom, and will, according to his faithfulness, assuredly give it to every one that believes and perseveres. On this account the holy apostle calls that blessed life for which we hope a reward, or guerdon.

But lest this term should cause us to presume upon some merit in our labours, he pertinently adds another name to cure us of that error, and calls it "the reward of the inheritance." For an inheritance, as all know, comes not by merit, but by a different title, even because one is a child of the family. Expect then, faithful souls, this divine retribution, not from the dignity or merit of your works, but from the bounty and munificence of God; who, having freely adopted you into the number of his children, will give you part in this eternal inheritance; to which neither you, nor any mortal man, had naturally any right. It is his grace, his faithfulness, and his promise, that confer upon you all the share in it which you have. And his goodness and word being immutable, you ought to expect it with as much assurance as if you merited it, though you acknowledge that you never can. But because it might seem strange that the apostle should promise christians the reward of the inheritance of the Lord for services done to men, he repeats what he had intimated before, namely, that, to speak properly, it is Jesus Christ they serve, and not men; "for," says he, "ye serve the Lord Christ." It is true, this sovereign Lord is in heaven, in perfect glory, and has no need of our services, much less of such as slaves and mercenaries perform towards their masters. But such is his goodness, that he allows that as done to his own person which we do to men according to his command and for his sake. Thus he assures us in the gospel, that it is to him we give all the alms, the visits, and assistances, with which we gratify the least of his servants in his name: You have done it unto me, says he, in that you have done it to one of the least of these, Matt. xxv. 40. All the duties of that obedience which he commands us are of the same nature in this respect. Doing them unto men, we do them unto Jesus Christ, who has commanded them; therefore it is also unto him that the least and lowest services pertain which men, for his sake, perform to the masters, unto whom the order of his providence has put them in subjection; so that he being infinitely good and liberal, they ought to attend assuredly to that precious recompense which he promises to those who serve him.

But if so high and glorious a hope is not sufficient to affect us, and sway us to that willing obedience which he requires, let us regard, at least, the penalty he denounces in case we fail of our duty. It is this the apostle here sets before the eyes of christian servants, when, after proposing the reward of the heavenly inheritance to those who discharge their duty, he adds, "But he that doeth wrong shall receive for the wrong which he hath done: and there is no respect of persons." It is a general sentence, reaching all men of every condition, servants or masters, men or women, poor or rich. Whoever does another wrong, either by positive outrage, or by not rendering that which he owes him according to the laws of the gospel, shall receive at the hand of the supreme Judge that which he has unjustly done; that is, be paid for his fault, and punished with a penalty exactly proportioned to his crime. Nor should any one persuade himself either that the misery of his condition will move the Judge to pity him, or that the splendour and grandeur of his quality will blind his eyes, and so conceive the possibility of an escape. In this divine judgment, no regard, says the apostle, is paid to the look or outside of men. God will weigh your cause alone, not consider your person. And as he will not take notice of the rich or the mighty, not of lords or monarchs, so as to spare them, if they have lived in the practice of unrighteousness and violence, neither will he regard the poverty or meanness of the lowest, so as to exempt them from the punishment which their injustice or infidelity deserves; but, as he formerly commanded the judges of Israel, Lev. xix. 15, he will judge justly, not honouring the countenance of the potent, nor respecting the person of the poor. Whence it follows, that servants who rob their masters, or serve them not as they ought, shall surely suffer for their injustice; since, granting that men let their wickedness pass unchastised, yet the supreme Judge of the world will not fail to call them to their trial one day, and bring to public light the infidelities, the thefts, and acts of disobedience which they think they have hid safely enough in the darkness of their deceits, and condemn them to the just torments which they have merited, by violating the sacred orders he has made for human society, and doing that to others which they would not any should do to them. Such is, brethren, the apostle's instruction to servants.

II. Let us now peruse what he prescribes to masters: "Masters," says he, "give unto your servants that which is just and equal; knowing that ye also have a Master in heaven." First, he gives them in charge their duty; secondly, sets before them an excellent reason to sway them to it.

1. Their duty is to render justice and equity to their servants. It must not be imagined that the power of masters over their servants is unlimited. A mutual justice there is between them, which obliges them to each other reciprocally; and either of them who trespasses against the rules thereof is faulty. And as it is just that servants should obey and be subject, so is it likewise just that masters should be of good conduct, and give proper remuneration. It is this which the apostle means by that justice which he charges them to render to their servants. It comprises work, maintenance, correction, and wages. So that masters are obliged, for the right discharge of this duty towards them, to act in these four points with all prudence and equity, giving them a reasonable task to do, sufficient food, moderate chastisement, and a proportionate salary. They that do otherwise, and transgress in these things, either by defect or excess, do not render to their servants what is right; as, for

instance, those who overburden them with toil or strokes; and they who, on the contrary, let them live idle and in intemperance; those who diet them ill, or too well; and lastly, they who defraud them of their wages, which is one of the most horrid and cruel acts of injustice that can be committed.

But besides right or justice, the apostle would have masters render also to their servants equity. The word he makes use of in the original properly signifies a certain equality and correspondence, that should appear between the offices of the one and the deportment of the other; so that as the servant obeys in singleness of heart, and in the fear of God, the master likewise should command holily and religiously; and that as the one serves with joy and respect, in like manner the other should govern with mildness and affection. In a word, right comprehends all that refers to justice, and equity all that pertains to christian charity and gentleness.

2. To reduce the faithful to this holy moderation, he orders them to remember that they also have a Master in heaven. His meaning is, that the dominion they have over their servants is not absolute, but dependent on God, and, by consequence, such as ought to be regulated by his word and will. If they have people beneath them, they have a Master and a Sovereign above them, who is the common Lord of them all, and unto whom they are to give an account of the treatment which their servants shall receive at their hands. He says particularly that this Lord is in heaven, to hold them the better to their duty by the consideration of so redoubtable a Majesty; who is not here beneath on earth, the place of misery and vanity, but on high in heaven, sitting on an eternal throne, and from that glorious habitation of light and immortality considers and governs all things at his pleasure; nothing coming to pass in his whole empire, but what he plainly perceives, and of which he most justly judges. This great Lord is above all; and there is neither master nor prince of such elevation among men who is not under his feet. He is superlatively holy, just, and good. He loves all his creatures, and concerns himself in the wrongs of the meanest and most contemptible of them; hating nothing more than injustice and insolence, outrage and cruelty; possessing, withal, an infinite wisdom and an almighty power which none is able to resist. Surely, then, consideration of the empire and sovereign dominion which he has over us is very proper to keep us within bounds, and to restrain us from abusing the power which he has given us over persons subject to us; nor could the apostle put those who have servants in mind of anything more pertinently that should oblige them to render them right and equity. Thus we have explained his instructions. It is now for you, beloved brethren, to make your profit of them, and to gather the fruits he offers you in them, for

the amendment of your lives and the consolation of your souls.

First, ye christians, whom the meanness of your birth, or, as they call it, of your fortune, has reduced to the condition of servants, rejoice at the honour done you by this great minister of Christ, who disdains not to address his holy voice to you. Set the care he has of you against the contempt that men cast upon you. Let his speaking to you comfort you, and raise your hopes of the inheritance of God. Think well upon the declaration he makes, that the persons to whom you are subject are your masters only in reference to the flesh. Your servitude will not be eternal. Nay, it will not be very long, nor extend further at most than to the end of that carnal life which you lead upon the earth. When this earthly tabernacle is once dissolved, you shall enter into the glorious liberty of the children of God; and then there will no more be any difference between you and your masters. For the present, your better part is already in possession of this liberty; namely, that spirit which God has formed in you after his own image, and which in spite of all the outrages of men, will ever remain master of itself, if you give it to Jesus Christ, the great emancipator of mankind, who faithfully and speedily enfranchises every one who receives and embraces his truth. Only take heed that you abuse not his grace; as if the spiritual liberty with which he has gratified you discharged you from doing faithful service to your masters after the flesh. The more he has illuminated you in the knowledge of himself, the more fidelity and love do you owe. For besides other reasons, the fear of God and the will of Jesus Christ now oblige you to obey them; so that the serving them makes up a part of your piety. According to the manner in which you acquit yourselves in this, whether well or ill, God will give you or deny you his inheritance. But besides your own interest, the glory also of the gospel is concerned in the case. For your faults defame our religion, and cause it to be taken for a licentious discipline; whereas your fidelity will produce us praise. Every one will be constrained to acknowledge the holiness of our doctrine, when they shall see it reform the deportment even of men and maid servants. And this the apostle expressly represents to you elsewhere. "Exhort servants," says he, "to be obedient unto their own masters and to please them well in all things; not answering again; not purloining, but showing all good fidelity; that they may adorn the doctrine of God our Saviour in all things," Tit. ii. 9, 10. Do not excuse yourselves on account of the ill humour and rigour of your masters. Remember the words of Peter, who obliges you to serve not only such as are good and gentle, but also the froward, 1 Pet. ii. 18. Take their ill treatment for an occasion by which God would exercise and refine your faith. Receive those strokes of the rod from his hand, and not from theirs, making them matter for your patience and a trial of your faith. Let the eye of Jesus Christ, who looketh on you; let his favour and benediction, which always accompany sufferings for conscience sake; let the hope of his inheritance for your salary, sweeten all the pains of your servitude. However ungrateful men may be to you, your patience shall not be left unrewarded, if ye persevere in it constantly for Christ's sake.

And you, masters, who so much desire to have faithful and obedient servants, render to them that justice and equity which the apostle commands you. Though your extraction or estates set you above them in human society, yet your nature is the same as theirs. You are subject to the same infirmities. One and the same death will consume you both; nor will there be any difference between your dust and theirs. You shall appear before the same Judge, and the tribunal at which you shall be examined will have no more complacency for you than for them. That Lord whom you see over you is their Creator and Redeemer as well as yours. He has put them under you only to govern them, not to tyrannize over them; to have care of them as his creatures and children, not to tread them under foot as worms. Remember, he will treat you as you shall have treated them. You are his servants as they are yours; or rather, they are your brethren, and you are not worthy to be so much as his vassals. You and they are one and the same flesh, that came out of the earth, and unto earth shall return; but neither they nor you have anything in common with God. He is in the heavens, and you crawl in the dirt. He is the King of glory, and you are but dust and ashes. Yet such is his goodness, that notwithstanding this infinite inequality, he has not disdained your nothingness. He has pardoned your sins; he has washed you in the blood of his Son; he has forgiven you all your debts; he has communicated to you his divine nature. Respect his graces, and have no less gentleness and goodness for your own flesh and blood than this sovereign Lord has had for you who were his enemies. With what face will you beg mercy of him if you are inexorable to your people? How can you hope for the grace of your master, if you have none for your servants? I beseech you both, have these holy thoughts night and day before your eyes, that you may faithfully discharge those mutual duties which the apostle enjoins: the one, subjection and obedience; the others, justice and equity; both of you living in such a holy correspondence, as that the loyalty, the respect, the humility, the submission, and the diligence of servants may go in conjunction with the gentleness, gravity, liberality, and benevolence of masters. If you so act, you will be happy; the families where you live together in this manner will become the wonder of the earth, and the honour of the church. The blessing of Heaven will fall continually on them; and besides the contentment and repose which this kind of life will give you abundantly for the present, it will also bring you hereafter into the possession of the heavenly inheritance.

But, dear brethren, it is not enough that those masters and servants only to whom Paul particularly speaks profit by his instructions. We all have in them something to learn, of whatever quality and condition we are. For since he would have servants render so exact and so frank an obedience to their masters according to the flesh, judge what kind of obedience we owe to that highest Lord whom we all have in heaven. The master according to the flesh gave not his servant the being he has; and if he redeemed him, he redeemed only his flesh, and that at the price of a sum of money only. Ours made us, and it is by his liberality alone that we hold all the being, life, and motion that we have. Nor has he only created us; he has also redeemed the whole of us, our soul and body, flesh and spirit; not with silver and gold, which are corruptible things, but with his own precious blood, having voluntarily sacrificed his life to preserve us from death and give us a happy immortality. No master ever had so much right to command his servants as he has to command us. Let us obey him then in all things without reservation, and consecrate our whole life to his service, the whole of which we have once and again received from his grace. Neither is it with this Lord as with masters according to the flesh; these oftentimes command things unjust, or dishonest, things contrary to our salvation, which we cannot do without destroying ourselves. He commands us nothing but what is just, honest, and reasonable, what is worthy both of himself and of us. Wherefore the most abject bond-servant owes his master but a limited obedience; whereas we owe ours such as is absolute and infinite. His yoke is easy and his burden light. He demands only that we love him, and our brethren for his sake; that we live honestly and holily, that is, be happy. O ungrateful and execrable creatures, if we deny a Master to whom we owe so much, so just, so reasonable, so beneficial, and so blessed an obedience!

Again, judge, ye faithful, if the bond-servant ought to obey his master in singleness of heart, cheerfully and with affection, as the apostle says, with what ardour, promptitude, and devotion should we serve ours, who is not only almighty and all-wise, but also goodness, love, clemency, and beneficence itself! Then, as for the bondman, though he ought to serve his master at all times, and in every place, yet his master sees him not always; whereas we are ever under the eye of ours. He has a full view of us, sees us within and without; nor can we hide ourselves in any place where he is not present. We cannot speak a word, nor form the least thought in the secret of our hearts, but he is a witness to it, knows the whole as soon as ourselves. Now surely there is no slave so senseless and shameless as that the master's eye will not keep him in order, and compel him to obedience. If such a one be idle, or exorbitant, he is not so but in the other's absence. Since then we have ours always present, what remains but that we never be idle, that we employ all our time in his service, bearing respect to his divine eye, that looks upon us, and is over us, both day and night?

Again, even when the serving of a man is in question, the apostle would not have the slave to serve merely to please the man; such great integrity and probity does he require in all our performances. Judge then how much more holy, and pure from all interest, that obedience should be which we render to the Lord Jesus, God blessed for ever. Undoubtedly they who serve him to please men, to gain their esteem, and acquire a reputation for sanctity among them, or to draw thence any other profit; they, I say, besides being ridiculous and vain, commit also a great and an inexcusable sacrilege; profaning the name of God and the sacred acts of religion, and most unrighteously abusing them for worldly ends. Such are those hypocrites, Matt. vi. 2, who fast, and pray, and hear the word of God, and celebrate his sacraments, and give alms, to be seen and had in honour; that, in short, serve God only to please men. They, says Christ, have their wages. They are paid; they have nothing more to look for at God's hands. For such vain and deceitful service they shall have no other reward than that vain and deceitful breath which they have coveted, and foolishly preferred to the glory of God.

Let us eschew at once these people's misconduct and their misery; and, according to the apostle's prudent and divine injunction, whatever we do, whether the action be addressed to God, or respect our neighbour, do it all as unto God, and not as unto man. Let us seek for no other spectator nor remunerator than him alone. Let us be content with his approbation, and with the testimony of our own consciences, whatever censure men may pass upon us; being assured, as Paul here adds, that if we serve the Lord, if it is he we obey, if it is to his will and glory that we consecrate and direct the course of our lives, we shall infallibly receive from his bountiful hand the reward of the inheritance; and, on the contrary, that they who act unjustly, and, despising his truth, are injurious either to his majesty or his creatures, shall receive what they have unjustly done without respect of persons. Looking for so great and dreadful a judgment, at which the least of our actions, whether they be good or evil, shall be examined in presence of the assembly of the whole universe, what manner of persons, I beseech you, ought we to be, in all holy conversation and godliness? 2 Pet. iii. 11. Let us search our hearts, and make inspection into all the parts of our life; let us cleanse our souls and bodies from all filthiness and impurity, and timely judge ourselves; wounding and cutting off, with the righteous sword of a lively and serious repentance, all the evil we find in ourselves; and living henceforth justly, soberly, and religiously, without scandal before men, and with all good conscience in the sight of God; that we may next week present ourselves at his holy table, to our edification and comfort, and appear at the last day before his sacred and dreadful tribunal without confusion, to the glory of Jesus Christ who has redeemed us, and to our own eternal salvation. Amen.

SERMON XLVI.

VERSES 2—4.

Continue in prayer, and watch in the same with thanksgiving; withal praying also for us, that God would open unto us a door of utterance, to speak the mystery of Christ, for which I am also in bonds: that I may make it manifest, as I ought to speak.

DEAR brethren, prayer is the christian's sacrifice, the holiest exercise of his devotion, his consolation in troubles, his stay in weaknesses, the principal weapon he uses in combats, his oracle in doubts and perplexities, his safety in perils, the sweetener of his bitterness, the balm of his wounds, his help in adversity, the support and ornament of his prosperity; and, in a word, the key of the treasury of God, which opens it to him, and puts into his hand all the good things which are necessary both for this life and for that which is to come. It is for this reason that the holy apostles give it to us in charge with so much affection and diligence in all their divine instructions which are come to our hands. Not to seek further off for instances of it, you see how Paul, being upon the point of concluding this excellent Epistle to the Colossians, after he had informed their faith, and regulated their manners, and explained their duty, both in general towards all men, and towards particular individuals, within the societies in which they live, sets an exhortation to prayer at the head of some other directions, which he adds before he concludes: "Continue in prayer," says he, "and watch in the same with thanksgiving." And, in truth, it is with much propriety that he reminds us of so important and so necessary a duty. For since God is the Father of lights, from whom cometh down every good and perfect gift, how can we, without his favour and benediction, either acquire or preserve the faculties and habits of this divine life, unto which the holy apostle would form us, together with the virtues that relate to it? Since then prayer has the promise of obtaining from his liberality whatsoever it shall ask of him in faith, it is upon good ground that the apostle directs the Colossians to address themselves continually to God by prayer, for the meet and faithful discharging of those duties which he prescribed them. After this, he adds two other directions: the one, of conversing wisely with those who are without; and the other, to season their speech, the principal instrument of conversation, with the salt of grace. Whereupon he concludes this Epistle with the praises of Tychicus and Onesimus, who were the bearers of it; and with salutations he makes them on the behalf of some then with him; adding his own to the Colossians themselves, and likewise to the faithful of Laodicea. This is the substance of this last chapter of his letter, as you shall hear more particularly, by the will of God, in the following sermons. At present we purpose, his grace assisting, to consider what he says of prayer in those three verses which we have read; and to do it in order, we will treat of the two points that offer themselves in the text, as they are there presented to us. First, of prayer in general; "Continue in prayer, and watch in the same with thanksgiving." Secondly, of their praying particularly, and expressly for him, which he requires of them: "Withal praying also for us," &c.

I. Man being in some measure secretly conscious of his own weakness, and knowing how little succour second causes can afford him for the preservation and the happiness of his life, is in a manner naturally inclined to call to his aid by prayer that veiled and invisible Deity, whose providence he scents in everything, though he perceives not its form. All religions in the world give clear and very express testimony to this truth, there never having been any known that had not its prayers and litanies addressed to God; and the greatest idolaters, and the most deplorably wicked men, are accustomed to cry out when a danger surprises them, O Lord, help me; O God, deliver me; lifting up their eyes at that time to heaven, as if nature itself in that case compelled them to do homage to that Majesty which they outrage or blaspheme through the rest of their lives. But what nature too imperfectly teaches us, we learn plainly and fully from the Scripture; where we have both express commands to call on God, and promises of favourable audience, and examples of all holy men under each of the covenants, whose supplications the Holy Spirit has taken care to preserve for us in these sacred registers of the church. Paul presupposing therefore here that the faithful to whom he wrote had this exercise of prayer familiar among them, according to that common principle of nature and of Scripture, only regulates the manner of performing it, advising them to persevere in it, to watch in it, and to accompany it with thanksgiving.

As for perseverance in prayer, it is not without reason that he expressly gives it to us in charge. For though the duty is not only very just, but even most necessary; yet we are of ourselves so cold and sluggish, and so indisposed to the performance of it, that we all need the heavenly voice of this minister of God to excite us to it. Presuming that we have the things we need in our own power, or shall find them in the sufficiency of nature, and not considering how they all depend upon the hands of God, we remit the assiduous invocation of him and make not use of prayer but on extraordinary occasions, when human succour fails us, as the manner is in tragedies, where the Deity is not brought in but at some difficulties, which no created power or prudence is able to clear. On the other hand, we are so proudly delicate and tender, that if we are not heard as soon as we have spoken, we fly off, and are ready to say, as that king of Israel once did, "Why should I wait for the Lord any longer?" 2 Kings vi. 33.

To cure ourselves of so pernicious a humour, and that we may persevere in prayer, according to the apostle's advice, let us consider, in the first place, the continual need we have of God's assistance: for since it is in him that we have being, life, and motion; since it is he who sends poverty, and makes rich; who sets up, and puts down; who dispenses health and sickness; who brings down to the grave, and brings up from thence; who governs the hearts of men, and the elements of nature: since it is he, again, who begins, who polishes, and perfects all the work of grace, and crowns it with glory; who effectually produces in us both to will and to do of his good pleasure: it is evident that without the help of his holy and most happy hand we can never possess any good, either in our own persons or in our families, either in the state or in the church; nor be preserved, and secured, or freed, and saved from any evil of any kind whatever. You cannot refuse belief of this great truth without imputing falsehood at once to the Scriptures of God, and the depositions of nature, both which everywhere harmoniously declare and aver it. Yet if you credit it, why do you not consider what it necessarily infers, namely, that having continual need of God's assistance, you are by your own interest bound to implore it continually —and that as you cannot pass a day without his favourable succour, so neither should you spend a day without calling on his name? Look, I beseech you, upon poor beggars, with what earnestness, with what indefatigable perseverance, they spend whole days, nay, their whole life, in petitioning us! It is a sense of their necessity that gives them this constancy and inspires this courage in them. Dear brethren, we have infinitely more need of the succours of God than these poor people have of ours. Why are not we at least as earnest, as constant, and as assiduous in beseeching him, as they are in asking alms of us? As for them, our flintiness is such, that generally they reap little or no fruit of their perseverance in asking of us; whereas the Lord, according to the riches of his infinite goodness and power, never sends away ashamed such as persevere in prayer to him. He has so promised, he daily so performs, and the experience of the church in all ages assures us of the truth of his word. I confess, he does not always immediately give us what we crave. But if we be constant, if, undismayed at his first denials, we press him with a vigorous and an ardent faith, there is nothing that perseverance will not in the end draw from his bounty. It was thus that Jacob obtained the blessing he desired. He wrestled stoutly with God all night, and had power over him; he wept, and begged favour, and constantly holding fast his Lord, "I will not let thee go," said he, "except thou bless me," Gen. xxxii. 24—26; Hos. xii. 4. The Canaanitish woman in the Gospel took the same course, and was heard in the same manner. She bore our Saviour's first denials without dismay, and those hard words, "It is not meet to cast the children's bread to dogs," astonished her not. She received this great blow with fortitude; it did not induce her to discontinue her supplications; and her holy importunity came off victorious, having drawn from our Lord's mouth that sweet and desirable answer, "O woman, great is thy faith: be it unto thee even as thou wilt," Matt. xv. 22—28. Imitate this violence. It offends not God. It appeases him. The Lord himself commands it expressly, and teaches us that we ought to pray always, and not faint, by the parable of that poor widow, whose importunity overcame the obduracy of the unjust judge, and drew that from him in the end to which neither the fear of God, nor the respect of men, could sway him. This judge was wicked and cruel, yet the perseverance of a woman conquered him. How much rather shall ours bear away what we desire of God, who is goodness and clemency itself! As for that judge, it was his nature, and the disposition of his heart, that rendered him cruel and inexorable; but if the Lord grant not our first requests, it is not that he means indeed to be sparing of his benefits towards us. In truth, he is more willing to give them than we are to receive them. This is but a mysterious act of his wisdom; and by such delays he would exercise our faith, inflame our desires, and try our constancy. He hides himself that we might seek him. He retires, that we might press after him; and holds back his blessing, that we might pluck it from him. His favours are no boons that should be faintly desired. We do not know the value of them, if we do not esteem them worthy to be asked with importunity. The favours we sue for at the courts and palaces of men are only terrestrial things, things of little value, and of a short and uncertain duration. Yet what do we not do to obtain them? We besiege their gates in the morning early; we abide there till late at night; we suffer their denials and disdains, and oftentimes even their reproaches, and the outrages of their domestics. They drive us from them; they call us troublesome people; they regard our importunity as impudence, or insolence. We swallow all these affronts; and, after all, forbear not to come on again, inventing, if possible, some new submission to soften them; so great and pressing is our desire of those things for which we petition them. Christians, do you not blush at having more passion for things of the earth than for things of heaven? Are you not ashamed to solicit the justice or the favour of men with more earnestness than the grace of God—to have more patience and perseverance in seeking to win the heart of a worm of the earth, than to overcome the King of kings? Your salvation is concerned. The grace you crave of him is the abolition of crimes that merit an eternal death; and that which you solicit from him is not a piece of ground, or a house, or a small sum of money, or some years of a temporal life, or liberty: it is heaven and eternity which you beg, the treasury and palace of his Christ, the peace and joy of his Spirit, an immortal liberty, an immortal life and glory. It is for this, beloved brethren, that we should be violent, eager, and obstinately importunate. It is for this we should spend days and nights in solicitation at the feet of God, and seize resolutely on him, and protest to him, with a firm and fixed determination, that we will not quit him till he grant our desire. No, Lord, thou shalt not escape me. Either thou must suffer day and night my importunities, or I obtain what I petition for. I will give thee no rest until thou hast fulfilled the desire of my heart. I will have it from thy hand, or die begging it. Such, christians, is the perseverance which the apostle commands us here, and again elsewhere, when he gives us orders to pray without ceasing.

I have only two remarks to add: the first is, that we must not understand these words as if he desired us to quit all other exercise, and lay aside the labour of the callings in which God has placed us, and do nothing but pour out prayers; as certain extravagant heretics, called the Euchites, that is the Prayers, formerly interpreted it. The apostle, who orders us here to pray without ceasing, commands us also to labour, and that with such necessity, as that he sentences that man not to eat who does not labour. These acts of our piety do not thwart each other. Prayer seasons and animates labour; it hinders it not. That perseverance in it which is our duty does not consist in unintermitted prayer, but in prayer frequently resumed, and assiduously reiterated, so that neither the trouble of waiting, nor despair of obtaining, nor any other consideration, makes us give over the diligent practice of it.

The other advice we have to give you in reference to this subject is against superstition, which regulates prayers, you know, by the clock, and scrupulously ties men up to the number and to the words of their petitions. A christian, who has his conversation in heaven, above time, and the motions that make it, measures his devotion by things themselves, and makes his prayers, not at the toll of a bell, but at the signal of his need: he lengthens or ends them, not according to the number of beads in a chaplet, but according to the movings of his heart.

Now after perseverance in prayer, the apostle requires of us also vigilance in it: "Continue in prayer," says he, "and watch in the same with thanksgiving." I freely yield that the faithful may steal away some hours from their repose, and employ them in prayer, provided it is done without superstition. Nor do I deny that the prophets, and the apostles, and the christians of the primitive church, often did so; rising at night, and spending either in private or in their churches, some hours in prayer and other exercises of piety. Yet it seems to me that it is not of these watchings the apostle here speaks. For there is another kind of watch, which we may call the watch of the soul; and it is only an attention of mind, when we keep all our faculties in a good state, lively and working, not asleep, nor drowned in idleness, or in love of the world, or in its errors and vanities; but awake, and elevated unto God, heeding him, and intent upon his work; looking unto Christ, and for his day, and expecting his salvation with earnestness and constancy. It is thus that the soul of that prophet watched, who waited more attentively for God than the morning watchmen for the break of day, Psal. cxxx. 6. And to this must be referred those numerous passages of the New Testament which command us to watch: "Watch and pray, that ye enter not into temptation," Matt. xxvi. 41. "Watch; for ye know not when the master of the house cometh," Mark xiii. 35. "Let us not sleep, as do others; but let us watch and be sober," 1 Thess. v. 6. "Watch ye, stand fast in the faith, quit you like men, be strong," 1 Cor. xvi. 13. "Be watchful," Rev. iii. 2. "Blessed is he that watcheth," Rev. xvi. 15. And the same often elsewhere. For as the apostle elegantly says of a widow who spends her time in the pleasures of sin, that she "is dead while she liveth;" so may we say in the same manner of a person who thinks not upon God, nor his service, nor minds the occasions of doing good and holy works, however active and busy he may be in the affairs of the world, that he sleeps while he is awake. This mystical sleeping is an insensibility of soul for the things of God. The waking, or watching, opposite to it, is the attention, the sensibility, and the action of the soul about the things of salvation. It is true, that this kind of watching is necessary for us in all the parts of our lives, and that no season, no occasion should ever find a christian asleep in this sense. But as prayer is the most excellent of all our services; so it particularly requires of us this watching, this attention. I consider, therefore, that it is precisely this which the apostle means, when he commands us to watch in prayer. He would have us bring to it a soul awakened, not overwhelmed in the cares and passions of the world; not laden and weighed down with thoughts of the flesh; not spiritless and languid, but stretched forth, and lifted up to God; not heedless of what it does, or heeding it by halves; but minding the things it asks of him, and that Christ in whose name it presents its requests to him.

By which you may judge in what manner we are to regard most men's prayers, which are pronounced by the mouth alone, without any attention of heart, from custom rather than from any solid devotion. Certainly, since prayer ought to be made with watching thereunto, it is evident that these people's supplications are, to say the truth, dreamings, and not prayers. They are vain words, like to those which a man sometimes utters in his sleep. Those of Rome are so far from removing christians from this abuse, that they precipitate them into it, by that strange and extravagant law for their services, which orders the performance of them in a language which the people understand not. Our hearts are so vain, that they can hardly keep close to the things and words we understand. I beseech you, what attention can they have for those which they understand not? And how do they watch in praying, who are so far from thinking upon what they say, as that they know not what is meant? Magpies and parrots are capable of prayer and of devotion, if the uttering a few words, without understanding them, is praying to God.

But the apostle would have us further add to prayer giving of thanks. And truly with great propriety. For how can we ask of God new favours, if we make not our acknowledgments to him for those which we have already received? This duty is so rational, that if no other consideration called for it, the thing itself would oblige us to perform it. The having received a benefit is cause enough for rendering of thanks. It is an odious ingratitude, to have and use the gifts of God without expressing to him our thanks for them. But besides ingratitude, it is impudence also, to present ourselves to God and ask new benefits of him, if we thank him not for the old. It is with this therefore that all our prayers should begin; and there is no kind of rhetoric so powerful to persuade him to give for the future as an acknowledgment of what is past. He loves to sow his mercies upon such ground as receives them with gratitude; and he readily hears the vows and prayers of those who have a deep and respectful sense of the favours which he has conferred upon them. Now tell me not that you have not yet received anything from his liberality. There is not a man, however wretched and forlorn, that this divine sun of grace and bounty has not visited, and to whom he has not imparted some of his benefits. How much more has he done it towards you, whom he has honoured with his covenant! and to whom he offers his gospel, and his Christ, and in him all the treasures of his grace and glory! For I omit this body and this soul, this breath and light, and that multitude of other good things, which he communicates unto all men in the course of nature. But how can you, without being dead, or at least utterly stupid, possess no gratitude for the grace which he has showed you, in calling you to his communion, and thereby to the hope of salvation and eternity? Yet though he has done you so many favours already, he forbids you not to crave more of him. His goodness is an inexhaustible deep. Beg and pray boldly. All that he requires of you is, that you do it with thanksgiving; that you tender him your thanks for his first favours, if you would have him grant the requests you make to him for further graces. This is it, dear brethren, which the apostle enjoins the Colossians, concerning prayer in general, even that they persevere in it, "and watch in the same with thanksgiving."

II. He next solicits them, in the second part of our text, to pray particularly for him: "Withal praying also for us, that God would open," &c. As to this, I will not stay to chastise the silly subtilty of the superstitious, who conclude, from the apostle's requiring the Colossians to pray for him, that therefore we may also pray the spirits of the departed saints, which are in heaven, to do us the same office. This is as rational as if I should infer from Paul's writing this Epistle to the Colossians, that therefore we have warrant to write letters to the dead. These Colossians, of whom Paul demands the assistance of their prayers, were persons living here beneath on earth, persons with whom he had mutual commerce in such offices of charity. He wrote to them, they answered him. He knew his words would reach them, and he looked again for theirs; whereas we have no such commerce with the deceased. And as for the reply which is made, that they know our desires and hear our prayers, it is a fancy asserted without proof and without reason, such as nothing but the passion of a bad cause has inspired error with, and which we must not believe, since the word of God, which is the rule and measure of our faith, says nothing of it. However this may be, since God, who everywhere commands us to pray, nowhere orders us to pray to men departed; since the apostle who presses the Colossians, and various other believers who were alive, to pray unto God for him, nowhere solicits them, either by his order or by his example, to do him the same office, by addressing prayers to deceased saints; we cannot be faulty in keeping religiously as we do to the commands of God, and the examples of Paul, and the other saints of the Old and New Testament, who have indeed prayed unto God, and verily required the aid of the prayers of living faithful people, but never invocated or solicited the dead to pray for them. All that can be duly concluded from this example of the apostle is, that while we war here below under the ensigns of Jesus Christ, the charity that unites us all into one body obliges us to pray for each other, and not only pastors for their flocks, but also flocks for their pastors. Who was then, or who has since been, greater than Paul? Yet you see how he disdains not the prayers of private christians. He disdains them not, said I? He demands them, and requires them expressly. Elsewhere he demands the same assistance of the Ephesians and the Thessalonians.

Hence we may conclude, that for any one to have the title given him of a mediator between God and us, it is not sufficient that he pray unto God for us. For by this account the Colossians, praying for Paul according to the directions which he gives them and the request he makes of them, might and should be styled his mediators with God, which is infinitely absurd, as every one would confess. Whence, first, is refuted the abuse of those who give this glorious quality to pastors, calling them mediators between God and the people; an abuse against which St. Augustine cried out long ago, saying, that "if any man boasted he was a mediator between God and his flock, good and faithful christians could not suffer him; but would look upon him as an antichrist, and not as an apostle of Jesus Christ:" and concluding, that "all christian men recommend each other unto God by their prayers; but that we have one only true Mediator, him that maketh request for us, and for whom none makes request, namely, our Lord Jesus Christ."* Hence, secondly, appears further, that supposing that departed saints pray to God for each of us in particular, (as those of Rome pretend,) yet this would not be sufficient to acquire the title of mediator, which they give them; seeing that flocks praying for their pastors are not therefore their mediators; it being evident that to merit this title there must be offered to God for us, besides prayer, a propitiation capable of supporting it, and of acquiring us the favour of the Father, a thing that pertains to none but the Lord Jesus; the prayers which we make for one another having no other efficacy than what our common Head gives them, unto whom they ascend in the heavens, and in whom is the propitiation for our sins, as St. Austin excellently saith.† It is the express doctrine of Paul, who, having said that "there is but one Mediator between God and men, even the man Jesus Christ," immediately adds, as a reason for this title, that he "gave himself a ransom for all," 1 Tim. ii. 5, 6.

But let us now see what prayers the apostle requires of the Colossians, and what particular he would have them crave of God for him. Being a prisoner at Rome, one would have thought that he would have desired above all things to be set at liberty. But behold, I beseech you, the generosity of this holy man, and how nobly he despises the interests of the flesh. He says nothing of this. He would have them entreat God to open to him the door, not of his prison, but of utterance, that he may publish the mystery of Christ. This is all his heart is set upon. He takes no thought for his ease or liberty. He has no sentiment nor desire but for the exercise of his ministry; that is, for the advancement of the glory of God and for the edification of men. He is content, provided he may successfully disseminate his Master's gospel. If his prison hinder him from doing this conveniently, and to such a latitude as he would if he were free; in this case only, and from no other design, would he have prayer made to God to release him from his bonds. If not, his chain is indifferent to him, provided it obstruct not the course of the gospel, and that notwithstanding his bonds the word of God be not bound, 2 Tim. ii. 9. This is all he craves of the Lord, and all that he desires others should crave for him, that he "open," says he, "a door of utterance;" that is, give him, in his providence, the opportunity and ability to preach it, removing from before him the aversion, and hatred, and fury of men against this holy doctrine, and those other scandals which the devil never fails to raise in its way, as so many thick and impenetrable gates, to hinder this divine sceptre of Christ from entering in among men, and

* Lib. 3. cont. ep. Parmen. c. 8. † Ibid. paulo post.

accomplishing the good pleasure of God upon them. He uses the same phrase in another place in the same sense, and the reason of it is evident. For speaking of the fair occasion he had to preach at Ephesus, he says that a great door and an effectual was opened to him by the Lord, 1 Cor. xvi. 9; and again, to signify the same thing with reference to the country about Troas, he affirms that, being come thither on the account of the gospel of Christ, he found the door opened to him by the Lord, 2 Cor. ii. 12.

In process, he adds the end for which he desires the Lord would grant him such an opening: "To speak the mystery of Christ, for which I am also in bonds." "The mystery," that is, the secret, "of Christ," or the gospel, the most sublime and admirable of all the revelations of God. It is called a mystery, both here and in other places, Rom. xvi. 25; Eph. vi. 19; Col. i. 26; ii. 2; because it is a wisdom hidden of itself to men and angels, such as no created understanding could have ever penetrated; this counsel which God had taken to save men by the cross of his only Son being above the conception of all creatures; and one may say of it in truth, with the apostle in another place, that it is things which "eye hath not seen, nor ear heard, neither have entered into the heart of man," 1 Cor. ii. 9. He gives us the sum of it in another text, where he clearly explains what this mystery of Christ is: "Without contradiction," says he, "great is the mystery of godliness: God was manifest in flesh, justified in the Spirit, seen of angels, preached unto the Gentiles, believed on in the world, received up into glory," 1 Tim. iii. 16. Now he calls this grand secret the mystery of Christ; first, because Jesus Christ is all the fulness thereof, that is, the sole subject that fills up the whole of it. Consequently, the apostle, who was an excellent and most consummate preacher of it, for rightly discharging his office, determines to know nothing among those to whom he preached but "Jesus Christ, and him crucified," 1 Cor. ii. 2. Secondly, because it is the Lord Jesus who first revealed it unto men; who brought it out of the abysses of the divine wisdom, and from under the figures and obscurities of the old law, where it lay hid during preceding generations, Rom. xvi. 25; Eph. iii. 9, and communicated it to the holy apostles in the light of that heavenly Spirit with which they were baptized on the day of Pentecost; and afterward set it, by their ministry, before the eyes of Jews and Gentiles.

It is not in vain that the apostle says here, by the way, he is a prisoner for this gospel of his Master. For what allegation could be more proper, or more potent, to affect the Colossians, and render them prompt and earnest to pray unto God for him, and for the progress of the gospel, than a remonstrance that it is for this holy and glorious cause he suffers—and that this mystery of Christ, which he so passionately desires to publish, is so divine, as that he hesitated not to seal its truth by a constant and courageous endurance of the captivity in which he was held? But after this opening the door of utterance, the apostle would have the faithful crave of God further, that he may manifest the gospel as he ought to speak; that is, preach it in such a manner as may be worthy of so sublime a subject, with proper liberty, diligence and fidelity. For it is not enough to have once received of God gifts necessary for the execution of this holy office, he must preserve them in us by a continual influx of his light, and give us the courage, the zeal, and spiritual prudence to use them in such a manner as is proper for the edification of men.

Thus you see, beloved brethren, what the apostle formerly demanded of the Colossians, both in general, and for himself in particular. And consider that this great minister of Christ now demands the same things of you by our mouths; in general, that you "continue in prayer, and watching in the same with thanksgiving;" and in particular, that you pray for us, who have the honour to preach the gospel to you. As for prayer, we have before sufficiently justified the necessity of it. It remains only that you make your profit of it; that this holy exercise be ordinary in your families; that this sacrifice be there daily offered unto God morning and evening; that you do not undertake nor begin anything before you have dedicated it unto God by prayer. Instruct your children and servants in the same devotion, that there may not be a person within your doors who does not understand this divine liturgy of all christians, and exercise himself in it. Then take heed to acquit yourselves in this duty as you ought; that is, to perform it with fervency, attention, vigilance, and perseverance; to wash your hands in innocency, to purify your souls and bodies, for the presenting them to this supreme and most holy Divinity, without offending his sight. You know what the prophets say of those whose hands are full of blood, that they are an abomination to the Lord; that he is weary to bear them; that he abhors their devotions, and disdains their vain oblations; that he hides his face from them when they dare stretch out their polluted hands unto him; and will not hear their prayers, though they should multiply them to the utmost. "Wash you," says he, "make you clean; put away the evil of your doings from before mine eyes; cease to do evil; learn to do well; seek judgment, relieve the oppressed, judge the fatherless, plead for the widow," Isa. i. 13—17. This, christians, is the incense with which the Lord would have you perfume your offerings of prayer, that they may be pleasing to him. Hearken to his voice, if you desire he should hear yours. Obey the word of his gospel, if you would have him receive the words of your supplications. We complain that we have long prayed in vain: but let us not disparage his veracity; rather confess that we have not prayed as we ought; that is, with such faith, such repentance, and amendment of life, as necessarily should have accompanied these sacrifices. Henceforth then, for it is yet time, turn ye unto him with all your heart, and lift up pure hands, without wrath and doubting; and vigorously persevere in this holy exercise, with assurance that he will hear you.

But, dear brethren, among other things which you should crave of God, pray to him also for us, that he would open unto us the door of utterance, to the end that we may declare the mystery of Christ, and manifest it to you as we ought. For, if Paul, a chosen vessel, made and formed immediately by the hand of heaven, consecrated by Christ's own voice, and filled with the treasures of his Spirit in all abundance, notwithstanding required the assistance of the Colossians' prayers in the administration of this charge; how much more is the succour of yours necessary for us: for us, I say, who in comparison with him are but children! We conjure you, therefore, both by the glory of our common Master, and by the interest you have in his work, that you never fail to remember us in your sacrifices of prayer; but always beseech this supreme Lord to perfect his strength in our weakness, to give us a mouth fit to declare his mysteries, and to purify our lips, as he formerly did his prophets, untie our tongue, as he did that of Moses, and fill our souls with that divine fire which once suddenly animated his apostles; clearing up our minds unto a distinct knowledge of his gospel wisdom; inflaming our hearts with the zeal of his house, and cleansing them from the filth of all human passions. Now, if the Lord, inclined by the ardour and constancy of your prayers, vouchsafe to confer upon us some small portion of his grace, look on it as a thing that pertains to you; a thing given in answer to your prayer, and for your edification. Use it, and make advantage of it. Let it not be said that this great mystery of Christ was declared unto you in vain; and that it being manifested to you as it ought, you received it not as you should. God keep you from such an unhappiness. For, however weak our preaching may be, it is notwithstanding sufficient, my brethren, to render every one inexcusable, who shall not have received it with faith; neither your ears nor consciences being able to deny that we declare unto you all the counsel of God in his Son Jesus Christ. Let us all in common beseech him to deal so graciously with each of us, that all may rightly discharge their duty; that we may speak unto you, that you may hearken unto us, as it is meet; and that being knit together by a firm and indissoluble love, we may prosperously advance his work in all holiness, innocence, patience, and constancy, to the glory of his name, the edification of those among whom we live, and our own salvation. Amen.

SERMON XLVII.

VERSES 5, 6.

Walk in wisdom toward them that are without, redeeming the time. Let your speech be alway with grace, seasoned with salt, that ye may know how ye ought to answer every man.

DEAR brethren, while the church of Christ is here on earth, it is its lot to sojourn, for the most part, amidst people of another profession. For though the merit of our Lord and Saviour is sufficient to bring all mankind into the communion of God, and though his salvation is tendered by his own will and order to all those who have his gospel preached to them; yet such is the obduracy and blindness of our nature, that most men abide out of the covenant of God, wickedly and foolishly rejecting the great honour which he offers them. There are various whole nations which, irritated with the same fury, have utterly shut the door against Jesus Christ, refusing to suffer any of his servants within their coasts. And even of those in which he has some reception, it is commonly but a small part that acknowledge him; the greatest and most considerable in the world persecuting him, or deriding his mysteries. Even in private families the gospel sometimes makes this partition. The same roof often covers persons of different religions. It is a division which Jesus Christ has raised in the world; not that he positively willed and designed it, or that such is the nature of his doctrine; this properly tends only to unite all things, and recombine earth with heaven in an eternal peace; but it grows from the wicked and the cruel disposition of men, who despise his counsel, and disdain their own salvation. The kingdom of Christ thus remains as it were inlocked with foreign states, and his faithful ones are mingled among persons of a contrary religion, with whom this common habitation of necessity obliges them to have much commerce.

This is the reason why the apostle, having regulated before most of the duties of our life, here in a few words points out in what manner we should converse with these aliens in faith, among whom we are dispersed. And this direction was at that time the more necessary, as christians in those beginnings, which were as the nativity of the church, saw themselves environed on all sides with Jews and pagans, the two religions which then occupied the whole universe. And this was peculiarly the case with the Colossians to whom he writes this Epistle, as they dwelt in a city and a province of which the people were much addicted to the most infamous of heathen superstitions. He commands them, first, in general, to walk wisely towards those that are without, and redeem the time. Next, he orders them in particular to be careful of their speech, one of the principal and most important pieces of the commerce which we have with men: "Let your speech," says he, "be alway with grace, seasoned with salt, that ye may know how to answer every man." This exhortation, my brethren, well suits ourselves, and is proper for the condition in which we are, living under powers and among countrymen of a religion different from ours. Let us consider it therefore, and practise it with care. To help you to a right understanding of it, we shall, if God will, treat in the presentation of the two parts it contains, first, our conversation with those who are without in general; secondly, the qualities in particular which our speech ought to have in that converse; noticing upon each of them what we shall judge proper for your edification and comfort.

I. The apostle's general exhortation consists of two heads: the first is, that we walk wisely towards those that are without; the second, that we redeem the time. As to the first, I presume you all know, without my informing you, that the apostle here signifies by the word walking, according to the ordinary style of Scripture, living and conversing; and again, that he means by those who are without, such as are not of our communion, but, in point of religion, follow other sentiments and services than what we profess to embrace in conformity with the gospel of Jesus Christ. He gives them the same denomination also in another Epistle, where, after ordering us to shun the company of some who are called brethren, that is, who make profession of our communion, while they lead a wicked and scandalous life, he adds, "For what have I to do to judge them that are without?" 1 Cor. v. 12. He directs then that we converse wisely with them; that is, that in all our negociations and conversations we exercise much prudence and circumspection. Not that he permits a foolish and indiscreet deportment towards the faithful that are of the same body with us. God forbid. A christian's whole life ought to be prudent and advised; and whoever he converses with, he ought to govern his actions with judgment, and do nothing without reason, remembering the rule his Master gave him for ordering all his conduct, "Be wise as serpents, and harmless as doves." But because they without are usually enemies to our religion, and detest, or at least are ignorant of, or despise, its mysteries, every one sees that it concerns us, in treating with them, to use much more restraint and consideration than when we treat with our brethren. As when a soldier is in an enemy's country, he stands much more upon his guard, and marches, as they say, with bridle in his hand. Besides, you know, if persons are only strangers, we treat them with more care, and, if I may say it, with more ceremony, than our acquaintances. A brother lives with us without design, a stranger is a spy. The one bears even with those actions in which a severe judge would find something to reprehend. The other does not pardon anything; nay, is offended sometimes at the most innocent actions. Being persuaded of the charity of the former, we live securely with him; nor does his person put us in pain, because he approves of all that accords with our rule. With a stranger it is not so. Besides the care we ought to have to act rightly in all transactions with him, we must also be further anxious to act so as to please him. It is, therefore, with much propriety that the apostle directs us to live and converse wisely with them who are without; that is, to exercise in all our deportment towards them more attention, prudence, and consideration than we do in the other ordinary transactions of our lives.

The first point of christian wisdom in this deportment towards them is, to observe the end to which it ought to be directed; the second, to discern the persons; and the third, to choose such means as are proper for our design. As to the end, whether an accidental encounter causes us to treat with those who are without, or whether some design lead us to it, we ought always to aim in it, either to edify them and win them to Christ, or, at least, to prevent their taking any offence or disgust at our religion. In the commerce which the subjects of a civil state have with foreigners, it is enough that they keep sound and entire the fidelity they owe their prince, and the love and respect they have for their laws and government of their own country. It is not necessary, nor will it be suffered, that they should attempt to withdraw a stranger from his subjection to that power under whose sceptre he was born, because it is a lawful subjection, and whoever would unfix it intrenches upon another's right, which cannot be done without injustice. But in the matters of religion it is not so. It is not enough that you preserve yourselves from theirs who are without, you must endeavour, if you can, to draw them from it, and bring them over unto yours. For in this you do no one wrong: you hurt nothing but error, nor diminish the right of any but of superstition and impiety, and of Satan, the common enemy of mankind, who inspires them. You do not acquire anything for Jesus Christ but what lawfully pertained unto him, since he of right is Lord of all men, both because he created them and has redeemed them. You do an act of justice in reducing bond-servants under the yoke of their true and lawful Master, whom error had enticed from it. Thus, as often as you treat with those who are without, you ought to propose to yourselves the edifying of them in reference to religion, and to have a will and a desire in your hearts, like Paul's wish for Agrippa, and for the rest that heard him; "I would to God, that not only thou, but also all that hear me this day, were both almost, and altogether such as I am, except these bonds," Acts xxvi. 29.

But it is not enough to have a good end, there must be an application of proper and fit means; and for this purpose the diversity of the persons with whom we have to do is to be carefully considered. For the same things do not suit all. Wisdom therefore being obliged to diversify its conduct, according to the difference of those with whom it treats, a christian must, together with that good intention he brings with him to such encounters, diligently discern the persons with whom he is engaged; not only with respect to their different conditions in the world, or their different capacities, but also principally with regard to their humour and their disposition with reference to religion. For they who are without have not all of them an equal aversion for ours. There are some who have a sweet, a humane, and tractable spirit, and who hate not our persons, though they approve not our sentiments. There are others who are furious, and look upon us as monsters, whom they could with all their hearts, as one may say, devour. For it is the property of error and of superstition to inspire their zealots oftentimes with these cruel and inhuman passions. You will again meet with spirits who, though perhaps they rise not to this excess of rage, yet are reckless and obstinate, and having smothered, or, as Paul speaks, seared up with a hot iron all sentiments of true conscience, reason, and honour, are wilfully become a prey to error, and have stopped up their ears, and all the entrances into their understandings, against the word and light of truth, with a determined resolution not to admit anything that is contrary to their opinions, and rather to renounce the quality of reasonable creatures, than the maxims of their false religion. That there must be very different demeanour towards these different sorts of persons must be manifest to every one. And our Saviour plainly tells us as much, when, notwithstanding the order he gives his apostles to publish his truth on the house-tops, he yet advises them expressly elsewhere not to cast their pearls before swine; and the reason he annexes is remarkable, "lest they trample them under their feet, and turn again and rend you," Matt. vii. 6: plainly signifying by these words, as experience sufficiently confirms, that the spirits of those of whom he speaks are irritated and inflamed by that very endeavour which is used to cure them; and that this, so far from amending them, renders them more fierce and cruel. But now this discrimination of persons is not made in order that we may have liberty to hate the one, and love the other: for a christian's religion permits him not to hate any man; it indispensably obliges him to love all, whatever may be their nature, their religion, or their disposition towards us; yea, it requires him even to bless those that curse him, and do good to them that persecute him, and to pray for and be kind to them that crucify him, Matt. v. 44. He considers these differences of men only for the regulation of his deportment; for diversifying, not the passions of his heart, but the actions of his life towards them. For though his conduct varies towards different individuals, yet his heart is the same towards all; and, to say the truth, it is the love that he has for them, rather than any other reason, that causes him to deal diversely with them.

To come then to the choice of such means as are necessary, and may be suitable for the end that we propose to ourselves in this kind of conduct, christian wisdom excludes from the number, first, all evil actions, all actions that are contrary to piety or justice. We owe this respect not only to God and our own consciences, but also to men, and especially to such as are without, that we at no time do that which is sinful before them. For unjust or impious actions, besides the venom they have in themselves, have also this bad property, that they are directly contrary to the end we ought to have in our deportment towards persons without; which is, as we have said, the winning them to Christ. Instead of attracting and bringing them on, such actions drive them off and disgust them, inducing them to judge ill of our religion by the bad fruits it produces in us, and to suspect that our belief is like our works, and our gospel as false as our lives are foul. It was this that Nathan noticed in king David's sin: "Thou hast given great occasion to the enemies of the Lord to blaspheme," 2 Sam. xii. 14. And Paul says respecting the evil lives of the Jews, "Thou that makest thy boast of the law, through breaking the law dishonourest thou God? For the name of God is blasphemed among the Gentiles through you," Rom. ii. 23, 24. The heathen formerly took the same offence at the misconduct of bad christians, and did not forbear to reproach them with it. The men boast, said they, that they are delivered from the tyranny of Satan, and are dead to the world; yet their affections and lusts no less overcome and master them than ours do us, whom they call slaves of Satan. For what avails this baptism, with which, as they pretend, they have been washed; and that Spirit, which, as they say, governs them; and that gospel, respecting which they make so great a noise; since their whole life is full of filth, and flesh, and disorder? Accordingly, you see how the apostle, among other reasons which he urges to divert the faithful from things contrary to justice and honesty, does not forget to press this for one, "that the name of God and his doctrine be not blasphemed," 1 Tim. vi. 1; and in another place, "that the ministry be not blamed," 2 Cor. vi. 3; and, "that they may adorn the doctrine of God our Saviour in all things," Tit. ii. 10. So the first thing we owe to those who are without is a pure and constant innocence in all our commerce with them. The beginning and the first point of prudent converse in this respect is, that we neither say nor do anything in all the communications we have with them, which they may justly accuse of wanting devotion towards God, or of covetousness, or cruelty, or any other unseemly or unjust passion towards themselves.

But after abstinence from evil, we owe them also the performance and practice of that which is good; first, by rendering to them readily and uprightly all that is their due by the laws of God and of nations; to princes, fidelity and obedience; to magistrates, respect; to kindred and countrymen, amity; each in their degree: and, as Paul says elsewhere, "tribute to whom tribute is due; custom to whom custom; fear to whom fear; honour to whom honour. Owe no man anything, but to love one another," Rom. xiii. 7, 8. Let sovereigns see us zealous for their service; private men, open, sincere, and trusty in all the affairs we have with them, religious observers of our contracts and our words, honest debtors, mild and humane creditors, courteous and helpful neighbours. Let them not find us faulty in reference to any of the offices of an honest and a civil life. For God forbid that we should ever admit into our hearts so impious, so barbarous, and inhuman a conceit as some harbour, namely, that it is lawful to break promise with such as are without, and to deceive or use a person ill when we can plead that he is not of our communion. On the contrary, it is to these that we must show most justice and integrity; these of all men, are the persons towards whom we must acquit ourselves of all that we owe them with the greatest exactness and scruple. And he who thinks to draw me into his opinions by an act of injustice, cruelty, or perfidy, is so far from succeeding, that he makes me believe with much reason that the religion which permits him such things, and excuses them under colour of a good intention, and pretends that they are serviceable for greater glory to God, is an impious and abominable superstition, and much worse in this particular than the sects and disciplines of pagans themselves, who, however ignorant they were, never held any of these horrible maxims. God will not be served at all with unrighteousness and treachery; and to declare or to suppose that he takes pleasure in such services, is one of the geatest outrages that can be committed against him. They are grateful to the devil, and to none but him. A christian looks not upon any man on earth as his enemy; he knows that they are all the creation of the Lord his God, and that his Master died for them, and shed his blood to save them. He respects this character in them, however disfigured by vice or error. And he renders them these dues not from fear of their power, or their ill will, as some would persuade us, who say that the primitive christians submitted to their heathen emperors and magistrates only from motives of prudence, or rather from a world-like craftiness, because they were the stronger, and themselves the weaker; and that, had they the means, they would have plucked the sceptre out of their hands, and without scruple trampled that diadem under foot which they appeared to honour with such humility. No, dear brethren, this is not the nature or the foundation of a christian's conduct towards those that are without. It is God, it is his conscience, and not simply some other consideration, that obliges him to live with them as he does; according to the apostle's doctrine in another place, where he says, we "must be subject, not only for wrath," that is, for fear of vengeance, and of the sword which the magistrate bears in his hand, "but also for conscience sake," Rom. xiii. 5; which in the same manner extends to all other duties; that is, we must pay our creditors, keep our word, perform our promises, honour our fellow subjects, live honestly with them, though they are not of our religion, not only to avoid the evils we should incur by doing it not, but also for conscience sake; so that whatever impunity, yea, whatever advantage, we might expect for neglecting such duties, we yet never neglect them, accounting ourselves bound to do them by a supreme and indispensable law, namely, the just and holy will of God.

But besides these things which we owe, christian prudence, in its conduct towards those without, makes use of others also, which in rigour of right we owe not. For it aims not simply to do that which is strictly just, but also to win those with whom we treat; so that if anything, to which otherwise justice obliges us not, may be serviceable to this its end, that reason is sufficient to make us do it. On which account it opens the bosom of our humanity, courtesy, and beneficence to those that are without, to give them all the assistance, favour, and succour that we can in their need, as often as they ask it, yea, when they ask it not. We should in this case imitate the goodness of our Lord, who maketh his sun to shine and his rain to fall even on them that blaspheme him. Make me not those frigid and frivolous excuses, that they are out of our communion; that they hate us; that they do us evil; that they are ungrateful. This is good discourse for a worldling, who measures his duties by nothing but his own interest. As for you, who are disciples of Jesus Christ, it is the least thing you should consider. You should principally respect the glory of God, the service of his Son, and the edification of men. Do good then to all, as your heavenly Father does; disdain no one whom he has made. Account any one your neighbour who has need of you, be he Samaritan or pagan. It signifies not, if he is but a man. There is nothing more effectual to persuade him that your religion is holy and divine, than this virtuous and generous deportment. At least you will by this take from him all pretext of calumniating your profession. You will remain justified in his thoughts, and oblige him, if he is ever called to give testimony of you, to speak in that glorious and honourable language which the probity and innocence of the primitive believers formerly drew from the mouths of pagans, "Such an one is a good man, and there is nothing to be blamed in him but that he is a christian."

Again, for our living prudently with those that are without, it is one principal duty incumbent on us to accommodate ourselves to them as far as piety will permit; not needlessly opposing them at any time; nay, willingly yielding them some part of our rights; bowing and conforming ourselves to their laws, their humours, and wills, in things indifferent; that they may see it is not capriciousness, nor hatred, but the force of our consciences alone, that constrains us to dissent from their religion; and that, setting this aside, and our consciences cleared, there is nothing that we would not both do and suffer to pleasure them. Such was the apostle's practice; and he has left us an excellent example of this holy prudence, which he proposes and represents at large in the 9th chapter of the first Epistle to the Corinthians, ver. 19—22. "I have made myself," says he, "servant unto all, that I might gain the more. Unto the Jews I became as a Jew, that I might gain the Jews; to them that are under the law, as under the law, that I might gain them that are under the law; to them that are without law, as without law, that I might gain them that are without law. To the weak became I as weak, that I might gain the weak: I am made all things to all men, that I might by all means save some." Let us imitate this holy example of the apostle; only take heed to limit, as he did, this complaisance to things which we have power to dispose of, that is, to such as are free and indifferent for us; not extending it to those that are evil, and prohibited in the school of Christ, as contrary to piety or sanctification; remembering the lesson which the same Paul elsewhere gives us, that there is no fellowship between righteousness and unrighteousness, nor communion between light and darkness, nor concord between Christ and Belial, 2 Cor. vi. 14, 15. Finally, this prudent demeanour towards those without, which he here prescribes, requires that we avoid, as much as possible, all actions and speeches that offend them; and that, saving those to which our religion necessarily and inevitably obliges us, there escape us not any that may displease them.

The clause, "redeeming the time," which the apostle adds, contains the utility and fruit of this wise and prudent demeanour which he has enjoined the Colossians towards those that are without; the meaning is, that by governing themselves in that manner they would gain time, and mitigate, by such an address, the rigour of that difficult and dangerous season in which they lived, being surrounded by the aversions and persecutions of the heathen. I well know that there are some who expound these words differently; saying that they signify that the Colossians were to repair their loss of the time past by well employing the present altogether in a good, a holy, and a prudent way of life. For this is what we commonly call redeeming of time. Others, with more propriety, say the apostle's intention is, that we should seek and purchase, even at the price of what is dearest to us, occasions to edify those that are without, and make no difficulty of losing somewhat in matters of estate, or ease, or even in point of honour or reputation, to obtain the means of obliging them. For it is true that the word the apostle uses here in the original often signifies an occasion and opportunity, rather than time simply. But though both of these conceptions as to the thing itself are true and christianlike, yet they appear to me to be a little beside the apostle's scope and intention here. Moreover, the interpretation I proposed at first is more conformable to the style of Scripture; for the phrase which Paul uses in this place is found verbatim in the Greek version of the prophet Daniel, at the 2nd chapter, ver. 8, where king Nebuchadnezzar tells the Chaldeans he knew well they would redeem the time; meaning, as our Bibles have aptly rendered it, that they would "gain time;" that is, would fain escape, and smoothly get out of that difficulty into which they perceived they had plunged. To the same sense the apostle here, though on a very different subject, bids us to redeem the time, by walking wisely towards them that are without; that is, that we should, by such prudent and dexterous conduct, sweeten their spirits, and skilfully divert the storm of their fury, as an ill influence, which might overwhelm us; gliding gently on, and gaining time, until things, governed and ordered by the providence of God, have changed their posture.

It is also to this that that reason evidently refers which the apostle annexes to this very command, in a passage of the Epistle to the Ephesians, conformable and parallel to our text: "Walk circumspectly," says he, "not as fools, but as wise, redeeming the time, because," he adds, "the days are evil," chap. v. 15, 16. He would have us to use much circumspection in ordering our lives, and to redeem the time, because it is evil; that is, troublesome, and difficult to pass, in consequence of the ill disposition towards us of those among whom we live, they being ready at every turn to destroy us, and to execute their malevolence upon the least occasion of exasperation that we give them. Therefore, as a wise mariner at sea, when the wind arises, and the waters threaten, and the presages of a tempest appear, hauls in his sails and prepares for the storm, then, accommodating himself to the violence of the waves, lets drive a little, not daring to bear up full against it, all to gain time, and redeem himself by such care and conduct out of so sad and angry a season; so the apostle would have us use the same industry to ward off the blows which are menaced by the unfavourable disposition towards us of those without: he would have us not take all our liberty with them, but manage our words and actions prudently, accommodating ourselves as much as we can to their temper, and avoiding all that is apt to provoke them, giving them no occasion to injure us; that if it be possible we may by such holy and advised conduct gain time, eschew an ill encounter, and redeem ourselves from the troubles and disorders with which it threatens us. It is a reason of the command he gave us to walk wisely towards them that are without. For besides the glory of God, and the edification of men, which calls for this endeavour at our hands, as has been said, our own good, our safety and preservation also, necessarily obliges us to it; it being evidently impossible for us to subsist in the state in which we generally are, if we do not with a great deal of care and prudence turn aside and assuage the ill affections of those among whom we live, and upon whom, in a human way, our lives and liberties depend.

II. But after this general exhortation, the apostle gives us another for the government of our speech in particular, which we must now explain with all possible brevity. "Let your speech," says he, "be alway with grace, seasoned with salt, that ye may know how ye ought to answer every man." I must needs say that this is requisite in all the discourses of the faithful, whoever they speak to, and that their mouth ought to be a treasury of benediction, out of which should issue not a word but that is holy, full of grace, and good, as the apostle says elsewhere, to the use of edifying; that is, proper to edify them that hear it. But as in the preceding verse, though wisdom is necessary in all the parts of our conduct, he gave it us in charge particularly in reference to our commerce with such as are without; in the same manner here, pursuing the same subject, he appropriates those characters, which ought to appear generally in all the words of our mouths, to that discourse and converse in particular which we have with persons without. Besides the continuation of his discourse, which there is little likelihood he would here suddenly break off without reason, his adding that of answering every one, &c., confirms me further in this opinion; those words evidently referring to the answers we are to make to those without, when they interrogate or question us about our religion; as appears by Peter's making use of nearly the same words on the same subject; "Be ready always," says he, "to give an answer to every man that asketh you a reason of the hope that is in you with meekness and fear," 1 Pet. iii. 15. Now truly the apostle had good reason to take the pains himself to regulate our speech on such occasions, namely, when we converse with those without about our sentiments in matters of religion. For certainly this is the most tender part of all our converse with men, and that which should be managed with the greatest exactness. It is a very slippery passage, and the events frequently are of great importance, and have long and considerable consequences, for good and for evil, according to men's different conduct in it. And if there is any case in which the tongue has any reason to boast of great matters, as James says, chap. iii. 5, without doubt it is in this; an answer here, as it is qualified, being capable of amending or impairing the condition of a whole christian people: a wise and moderate discourse having sometimes averted or stayed the persecution of the church, and appeased the rage of its enemies; whereas, on the other hand, a speech, though in substance true, yet being indiscreet and ill-placed, hath often inflamed the hatred of the mighty, troubled the peace of the church, and caused a thousand disorders and devastations. The apostle then would have us, on this occasion, that is, when we speak with those without, more than on any other, govern our lips with so much judgment, that there may not a word break out but what is seasoned as it ought to be: "Let your speech," says he, "be alway with grace, seasoned with salt."

He presupposes, in the first place, and before proceeding to other things, that it has its principal virtue, namely, truth, which is the soul of it, according to that general rule he elsewhere gives us, to speak truth every one with our neighbour, Eph. iv. 25. But in conjunction with this his intention is, that our speech should have these two further qualities: first, that it be with grace; and, secondly, that it be seasoned with salt.

The grace he requires in it is not that which is given to a discourse by the ornaments of rhetoric, which respects only the pleasing of the ear, and consists in a choice of elegant words, and in a sweet and grateful composition. The grace a christian ought to seek for and have in his speech is, so to utter truth as not to offend the hearer; that it express our minds without exulcerating his; that it have neither gall, nor venom, nor virulency; that it be simple, humble, and modest; without reviling, without scoffing, and other such stings as may inflame those with whom we speak. The other particular which he adds, namely, that it be well salted, that is, prepared, and, as it were, seasoned with an exquisite prudence, refers in substance to the same thing; for, as salt desiccates meats, and eats out the moisture and putrid humour of them, leaving a sharpness in them pleasing to the taste; so this christian prudence, with which he would have all our speech imbued, works out all that it might have in it superfluous and noxious, and tempers it in such a manner, that the force and vigour which it leaves pleases the spirit, and enters gratefully into it. The masters of common rhetoric, likewise, taught that there should be salt in their scholars' speeches. But it is not that which must season a christian's deliveries. By this salt which they esteem, they mean certain pleasantnesses that border upon raillery and jesting: expressions that are quick, but offend not; that touch the spirit, but do not gall it. We, for our part, pass by this artifice, and draw the salt with which our speeches are to be impregnated from quite another vein, even a holy christian prudence, which avoids all that may displease or scandalize our neighbour, and chooses what is proper to edify him; so seasoning discourse, that nothing unsavoury or insignificant be uttered, which might disgust him at our persons or our religion. This salt cleanses our conversation, first, from all expressions that are either noxious and dangerous, as those that lead to vice, or are vain and fruitless; and, secondly, of all that may offend those with whom we talk, and alienate them from our religion. For this end, that knowledge is necessary of which the apostle speaks in the following clause: "that ye may know," says he, "how ye ought to answer every man." It is clear that this grace of speech, seasoned with salt, does not teach us how we ought to answer every man; but, on the contrary, this science or knowledge, when we have it, seasons our speech with its necessary grace. The words, therefore, "that ye may know," must be understood of the event and success; as if the apostle had said, Let your speech be with grace, and seasoned with salt, so that it may appear that you know how to answer every one. Or the word *know*, which he uses in the original, must be taken for as knowing, and as judging and discerning, how we ought to answer every man.

First, his calling our discourses an answering, intimates that we should not commence such kind of conferences inconsiderately, nor enter upon them without judgment and deliberation; being called to it either by some one's demand, or by the voice of such a necessary occasion as obliges us to speak.

Then, again, he shows us that we ought to diversify our speech according to the difference of persons, and in this it is that that discerning of persons which we touched upon before must do us service. There are those to be met with, whom it would be best not to speak to at all. The dispositions of some may suffer a firm and free discourse. The temper of others requires a more soft and tender treatment. As you see that meats for several bodies must be variously prepared, according to their different constitution; so we should diversely season our speech, according to the diversity of spirits.

Such, dear brethren, is the holy and wholesome lesson which the apostle gives us in this place. Let us practise it diligently, and regulate by it our speech and deportment in all the commerce we have with those without. Let us not hide our sentiments in religion from them, but explain ourselves to them in such a manner as may be proper both for their edification and our own safety. First, let us never speak of them but in season; and when occasion offers itself for it, do it with that gravity and decency which are due to so high and so important a subject. Next, let us take out of our speech all the stings that might incense those who hear us. Let it not have in it anything reproachful or offensive, anything that scents of hatred or contempt. Let it be sweet, and full of affection and respect. Let it bear the image of a well-disposed and a truly charitable soul, and breathe nothing but the good and the edification of our neighbour. And as for truths themselves, let it discover, and with full liberty expose, such as are grateful to our adversaries, as, thanks be to God, there are many; in particular, I make bold to say, all those that are principal and essential in religion, about which they make no contest with us. As for others, which consist in a rejection of their errors, and consequently cannot but be odious to them, we must deliver ourselves about them with much discretion; meekly showing them the reasons of our sentiments, that they may see it is not out of wilfulness that we depart from their belief, but by the constraint of necessary reason. Let us forbear atrocious and opprobrious terms, and keep a just medium between flattery and unworthy complacency, which covers silence, or disguises the malady, on one hand, and indiscreet and furious zeal, which angers and envenoms it, instead of healing it, on the other. Error is a sore which must be neither neglected, nor roughly handled; it must be touched tenderly, and in such a manner as, if possible, not to put the patient to pain.

See how Paul took such a case in hand. He was at Athens, a city full of so much impiety and idolatry as cut him to the heart. And having discovered the offence, he reasoned against it; when they had brought him forth, and asked him what then his doctrine was, he does not tell them that they were idolatrous, and impious, and brutish to worship wood and stone, though all this was very true. But the prudent minister of God saw well that if he had proposed this truth so crudely to them, he would have lost himself, and not at all have edified them. What does he then do? He gives them at first some praise, acknowledging that they were extremely devout. He then tells them of that unknown God to whom they had consecrated an altar; and thence dexterously takes occasion to preach to them the true God; insinuating the truth so skilfully, that, to hear him speak, one would think he had not brought it from abroad, but found it there among them. This was truly speech seasoned with the salt of grace. Let us imitate, I beseech you, brethren, this rich example of prudence and modesty, rather than the eruptions and indiscretions of zeal without knowledge, which serve only to irritate those that are without, and draw the bad effects of their aversion and hatred upon those that are within. But let us have yet more care to order our ways than our words. We cannot usher in our discourses with a better or more persuasive preface than a good and holy life; if we walk wisely with them that are without, as the apostle charges us; if we eschew not only evil actions, but those also that have the appearance of evil, and are reputed of men to be such; if we show them nothing but piety, honesty, humility, charity, meekness, and sincerity; if we affectionately seek and embrace occasions to oblige them, and to do them service; if we patiently bear the offences they commit against us, and revenge not ourselves but by offices of beneficence. This conduct, if we follow it, will mitigate some of them, and entirely gain others. It will invite the king, our sovereign lord, and his ministers, to continue and more and more confirm to us that sweet and precious liberty of conscience, which having been given us in this great state by his father's clemency and wisdom, has been hitherto preserved to us by his grace. Finally, this conduct will render our doctrine honourable in all things, and make the name of the Lord Jesus whom we serve to be glorified: and being acceptable to him, will draw down his benediction upon us; and after the first-fruits of his bounty, which he will enable us to taste in this life, introduce us hereafter to the full and eternal possession of his immortal glory. Amen.

SERMON XLVIII.

VERSES 7—11.

All my state shall Tychicus declare unto you, who is a beloved brother, and a faithful minister and fellow-servant in the Lord: whom I have sent unto you for the same purpose, that he might know your estate, and comfort your hearts; with Onesimus, a faithful and beloved brother, who is one of you. They shall make known unto you all things which are done here. Aristarchus, my fellow-prisoner, saluteth you, and Marcus, sister's son to Barnabas, (touching whom, ye received commandments: if he come unto you, receive him;) and Jesus, which is called Justus, who are of the circumcision. These only are my fellow-workers unto the kingdom of God, which have been a comfort unto me.

Dear brethren, the infinite wisdom of God is very clearly manifested in his works, not only by the admirable disposition of the parts of which they are composed, and the exquisite order in which he has ranked them; but also in that there is nothing about them without its utility. View the world, this vast and first master-piece of his hand; consider the Scripture, his other work, the second and more excellent discovery of his will and nature; and you will not observe anything in either of them but what is of use, both for the completion of the whole, and for the benefit, edification, and consolation of men. I acknowledge that among the parts of these two works of God, there are some more useful and more necessary than others; some, in which his wisdom and goodness shine bright, and beam forth an abundant light; others, in which they are but dimly seen. However, there is not any, though little and dusky in appearance, but what has its usefulness. It concerns us, therefore, not to despise one of them, but heedfully to remark whatever of worth the Creator has put in them all, that we may both give him the glory of it, and by it benefit ourselves. The truth is, we should insist most upon those in which the wonders of this great Author's hand are most resplendent; yet so as that we neglect not the rest when by his providence we meet with them.

In conformity with this order, having hitherto considered the divine instructions, both concerning faith and manners, which this Epistle of the apostle to the Colossians contains, we now present you the latter part of it, in which this holy man recommends certain particular persons, and salutes others, both in his own name, and in the name of some of his friends and colleagues in the gospel of Jesus Christ. Disdain not, dear brethren, this conclusion of the apostle's divine letter, nor imagine that it can yield you no profit, because it is not so luminous, and quitting the rich and weighty subjects with which we have entertained you, speaks of particular persons only. If it had nothing at all in it but the names of some faithful men, yet would it merit consideration. For if we take pleasure in hearing and learning the names of the captains, the officers, and the ministers of our ancient kings, and even of strange princes, who have been anything great and illustrious in their times, as an Alexander, a Cæsar, or such others; how much more regard should we have for those who had their share in the fortune and achievements of Paul, and held some rank with him in the house and service of Christ, our supreme and eternal Monarch! For I affirm, and every reasonable person who shall seriously consider the subject will agree with me, that the exploits of Paul and his associates, under the name and ensign of Jesus Christ, are much greater, and more admirable, than all the lofty deeds of the most renowned conquerors. So that if the grandeur of a transaction gives us the curiosity to inform ourselves of the names and qualities of those who figured in it, this alone ought to be no little satisfaction to us; even that we find, in this passage of Paul's Epistle, the names of seven or eight of these the Lord's generous warriors, who, coming out of various quarters to rank themselves on each side of our great apostle, combated the enemy at Rome, that is, in his strongest hold, and there in spite of all his fury, planted the empire and the trophies of their Master.

But besides the just and lawful pleasure which such a knowledge may give us, this passage will also afford us various other very useful instructions; the Spirit who guided this sacred writer dictating not a word that is not full of wisdom. And this reverent opinion we ought to have of all things contained in the book of God. For as when in the shop of an intelligent and able herbalist you see dry and withered simples, which have neither smell, taste, nor colour, you believe however that they have some secret virtue, which lies hidden under that poor and unpromising appearance; presuming that they would not else have been ever laid up in such a place: so when in the holy Scriptures you meet with some passage or other, which at first seems little worthy of consideration; emitting, if I may so speak, no smell, showing no colour, to affect or excite our perceptive faculty; be assured that under this unattractive outside there is undoubtedly some spiritual utility contained; for that Jesus, the sovereign Physician of souls, has laid up nothing in this divine shop which is superfluous or without use. You will by experience find it true, if you take the pains to examine attentively, and, as our Saviour speaks, to sound this text of the apostle's which, containing only some recommendations and salutations, which are little remarkable in appearance, will nevertheless afford you various instructions very useful for the edification of your souls.

Now, to assist you in this meditation, we will employ the present hour, by the will of God, in pointing out to you some of the most remarkable among them. And that we may proceed in it with some order, we will handle the two parts of this text distinctly, as they are presented to us in the text. In the first, which comprehends the first three verses, the apostle recommends to the Colossians two considerable persons whom he sent to them, namely, Tychicus and Onesimus. In the second, which extends through all the rest of the text as far as the 12th verse of the chapter, he presents them the salutations of certain faithful servants of God, who then sojourned at Rome, and were near him.

I. Upon the first of these two general heads, there immediately offers itself to our observation the zeal and affection of this holy man for his Master's flock, and withal his wisdom and spiritual prudence. He was prisoner at Rome in the chains of Nero, uncertain of the issue of his captivity; persecuted by the Jews, hated of the heathen, and, for a surcharge of affliction, turmoiled by the malevolence and cruel designs of some who called themselves christians. One would think that in so great, so confused, and so terrible a combat he would have been mindful of himself only; and that in his condition he could only have received the succours of other faithful men, and not have afforded them any. There is not a man of us who, finding himself in a similar danger, would not have considered himself excused from taking to heart the necessities of others, and have believed that he had just cause to gather up and fix all his cares on his own need. But this holy minister of God, to whom a most ardent charity rendered the interests of his Master's sheep much dearer than his own, makes quite a different judgment in the case. Neither his irons, his prison, the fury of the Jews, the cruelty of the heathen, the inhumanity of false brethren, nor death, nor the sword, that hung continually over his head, was able to put one moment out of his heart that care of the churches which held him, as he very truly says elsewhere, incessantly besieged from day to day, 2 Cor. xi. 28. Knowing then the trouble the Colossians were in for him, and the attempts that false teachers made upon their faith, he contents not himself with writing this divine letter to them; that is, with sending them in this paper a living and abundant source of consolation and of succour against the horror of persecutions, and the imposture of seducers; he despatches also two messengers to them, to inform them exactly of all the particularities of his imprisonment, to tell them by word of mouth various things which could not be written, and to discourse upon and explain those upon which the brevity of a letter had not permitted him to enlarge. For that such was the cause of his sending them he himself expressly declares: "They shall make known to you," says he, "all things which are done here:" and speaking of Tychicus, one of them, He shall declare unto you, says he, all my estate. For, for this purpose have I sent him unto you. In the following words again he intimates another reason; "that he might know," says he, "your estate." True it is, that there are some manuscript Greek copies which read it a little differently, namely, that ye might know our state. And truly it is thus the apostle speaks of his sending the same Tychicus to the Ephesians. I have sent him to you expressly, says he, for this end, that ye might know our state. But it signifies little which of these two ways we read the apostle's words. For there is fair probability, that as the Colossians were in pain for him, so he was likewise in pain for them; both because of the persecutions which the faithful were then everywhere subject to, and also on account of the trouble, which he understood that church received from some false teachers; so that, to satisfy this common and reciprocal desire which the Colossians and he had to receive certain and exact news of each other, he sent Tychicus to them, who might inform them of his, and learn theirs, to impart the same to him.

He adds the last and principal purpose of sending Tychicus, that, says he, he might "comfort your hearts." For it was certainly the consolation of these faithful people that the apostle sought. But, you will say, what consolation could the report of Paul's affairs afford the Colossians, since Tychicus left him in prison at Rome, that is, in the mouth of the lion, as he himself says in another place? Dear brethren, it is true that the apostle then abode still in that sad state, and it is true that it was on this account that the Colossians were in pain. But yet these two messengers had many things to say to them that were proper to mitigate their trouble, and to ease their pain; first, that the apostle was still alive, safe and sound, as Daniel formerly was in the den of lions; nay, that he was not without hope of being set at liberty. Then again, and which is the principal, that his faith and piety were so far from being weakened by this rude temptation, that they were become more firm and lively than ever, shining in this trial as fine gold in the furnace; that, instead of being afflicted at it himself, he comforted others; the Spirit of God continually maintaining christian joy and peace in his heart amid this tribulation, and preserving the same fresh and full, as formerly he preserved the bush of Moses in the midst of the fire. And lastly, that if his body was bound, yet the gospel was not so, the apostle with a high and invincible courage frankly preaching in his irons, and changing by a divine miracle his prison into a school of Jesus Christ; opening too, by the efficacy of his example, the mouths of many brethren to preach the word boldly without fear; his whole affliction serving, by the providence of God, to effect a much greater advancement of the gospel, as he says elsewhere, Phil. i. 12. This relation, as you see, was very proper to console the hearts of the Colossians; not to speak of the knowledge and capacity of Tychicus in the things of the kingdom of heaven, which enabled him to do these faithful people this good office, in representing to them the doctrine and the promises of our Lord and Saviour, the necessity and utility of the cross, the life and the crowns to which it leads, the eternal weight of that excellent glory which this light and transient affliction works, 2 Cor. iv. 17, and similar intimations, of which the whole gospel is full. For you must not imagine that this Tychicus and this Onesimus whom he sent to them, were simple messengers, who had no other ability but to make a faithful report of what they had seen and heard of Paul's affairs. They were two excellent persons, endowed with great gifts, and well instructed in the knowledge of God; yea, as it is certain of the one, and very probable of the other, called to the holy ministry. And it further heightens the apostle's charitable affection towards the Colossians, that he should deprive himself for their consolation of the presence and assistance of two such persons, at a time when they were so valuable and so necessary to him.

But in this choice his prudence appears no less than his affection and goodness. First, more generally, in that he employed about this affair persons proper for the purpose for which he sent them. And secondly, in particular, that one of the two whom he chose, namely, Onesimus, besides other qualities which he possessed, was a Colossian, and therefore a person who should have the more credit with them, as their own countryman. It is true, that Epaphras, of whom he will afterwards speak, had the same quality. But it seems that a particular consideration withheld the apostle from employing him in this commission, even that he had already exercised the holy ministry among the Colossians, and preached that very evangelical doctrine to them which was now troubled by false teachers, as we understand by the first chapter of this Epistle. He then being interested, and as it were a party in the quarrel, the apostle very prudently employs other persons, namely, Tychicus and Onesimus, that their faith and doctrine appearing conformable to that of Epaphras, the Colossians might the more easily perceive that his was not particularly his own, but in truth the Lord Christ's and his apostles; and that, as the Scripture says, in the mouth of these two or three witnesses the word might be established.

But the apostle, to give them credit with the Colossians, and render their ministry fruitful, informs them of the good and commendable qualities of each. As for Tychicus, he calls him his beloved brother, and a faithful minister, and fellow-servant in the Lord: titles, as you see, very honourable. He qualifies him after the same manner in the Epistle to the Ephesians; to whom he despatched him upon the very same business as he does here to the Colossians. Whence it appears that this holy man was one of those extraordinary ministers, whom the scriptures of the New Testament particularly style evangelists. These were as aids to the apostles, assisted them, followed them, and were variously employed by them according to the necessities of the church, sometimes in one place, sometimes in another, without being fixed to any particular flock, as are ordinary pastors, and making no longer stay anywhere than the apostle's orders required. Such a one, for instance, was Titus, whom Paul left in Crete to finish the erection of the church, Tit. i. 5, and afterwards sent into Dalmatia to preach the gospel there. Such a one again was Timothy, and Crescens, 2 Tim. iv. 10, and many others. And truly the charge which the apostles had, being of such a vast extent as to embrace the whole universe, necessarily required that they should be assisted by such helpers and inferior ministers, who might be employed in such places as they themselves could not go to or tarry in.

Our adversaries, to give you this intimation by the way, commit an error in this matter, when they apply to bishops what they read in the New Testament of this sort of ministers. For it is true indeed that the evangelists were superior to the common and ordinary pastors of each church, and held the next place to the apostles, whose lieutenants in a manner they were. But it is false to assert that any such ministers were, or were intended to be, in the church after the apostles' decease. Their ministry was extraordinary, and subsisted no longer than the apostleship did, for which properly it was instituted. And hence it plainly appears that the bishops of the Roman communion can by no means pass for ministers of this order, since they have each of them their title or diocess, to which they are confined, and have no power to exercise their ministry elsewhere; whereas the evangelists had no flock that was properly and particularly assigned them, but were as general attendants, who by the apostle's order, and according to the necessities of churches, transported themselves sometimes to one, and sometimes to another; to countries and people very far asunder; as you see by the example of Titus, who, having been employed in ordering the churches of Crete, came back when that was done to Paul, who a long time afterwards sent him into Dalmatia, a country, as all know, very far distant from the isle of Candia. Tychicus then was a minister of this rank, abiding near to Paul's person, to receive and execute his orders, as you see, both by the passage before us, which shows us that he sent him to the Colossians to edify and comfort them; and by the second Epistle to Timothy, chap. iv. 12, and the Epistle to the Ephesians themselves, chap. vi. 22, where we read that he sent him to Ephesus upon a similar design; and by the Epistle to Titus, chap. iii. 12, whom he directs to despatch Tychicus. And it should seem he was consecrated particularly to this ministry, when he was named among those who were to accompany Paul in his voyage from Greece to Asia, Acts xx. 4, about the fifty-third year of our Lord, that is, three or four years before the date of the Epistle to the Colossians.

The praises which the apostle here gives him show us with what zeal, care, and courage he acquitted himself in this sacred ministration. For he calls him, first, his beloved brother; declaring thereby both his christianity, for the faithful, you know, all called each other brethren, and the particular affection he bore him, loving and esteeming him as an excellent person, and one endowed with very amiable qualities. He styles him, in the second place, a faithful minister. The latter word signifies his office. He was not simply a christian; he was a minister in the house of God, that is, an evangelist, as we have showed you. The other expresses his conduct, and good conscience in the discharge of his office. For however holy and divine it is, it cannot avoid sometimes falling into ill hands, and adorning profane or negligent men, who ill acquit themselves in it, and dishonour it by the foul blots of their life or their doctrine. The apostle bears witness for Tychicus that he is none of that unhappy number, terming him not only a minister, but a faithful minister; a commendation that comprises the whole perfection of a true minister, according to that which the same apostle teaches us elsewhere: "Let a man so account of us," says he, "as of the ministers of Christ, and stewards of the mysteries of God. Moreover it is required in stewards, that a man be found faithful," 1 Cor. iv. 1, 2. He that is faithful acquits himself in the ministry committed to him trustily, according to the will and order of Christ, of whom he received it; which, as you see, comprises all its parts and perfections.

But here, as we proceed, it will not be impertinent to repel, with the authority of this phrase of the apostle, as with a firm and excellent buckler, an accusation drawn up by those of Rome, who reproach us that we give pastors a new name, and such a one as is not used in the language of the church, while we commonly call them ministers, a name, as they pretend, pertaining only to deacons, who are ministers, as every one knows, of an order inferior to that of pastors. Dear brethren, would to God that in the disputes we have with those of Rome questions were only of words! It would be easy for us to accommodate ourselves to their language; nor would we make any scruple to call the pastors of the church, as they do, by the names of priests and bishops, which we confess all the ancients, and even the holy apostles have used in this sense. It is the abuse and corruption of things which has caused us to quit these words; and seeing that the common speech of people had appropriated them to new offices, and such as were unknown to the apostles, meaning by the word priest a sacrificer, and by that of bishop a pontiff, or superior of sacrificers, we have left these names to them, with the things they signify among them, as utterly contrary to the institution of God: and that our pastors might not be confounded with theirs, as if we held them for sacrificers and pontiffs, instead of the names of priest and bishop, which the abuse of public speech has corrupted, and swayed to this sense, we have called them ministers, a name, as every one sees, very modest, and most suitable to their office, which, as to the whole of it, is nothing but a ministry: and though I acknowledge that this word, in Greek the very word deacon, is often used to signify their order who have care of the poor of the churches; yet this passage of the apostle plainly shows us that it is not so peculiarly annexed to the office of deacon, as that it may not be employed to signify pastors themselves; for it is precisely the term he uses here, for expressing that quality of pastor, or evangelist, which Tychicus had, when he affirms him to be a faithful minister: not to allege at present that he uses the same word very frequently in other places, to signify not only the office of preachers, but the apostleship itself, the highest of all ecclesiastical charges: as when he says, "Who then is Paul, and who is Apollos, but ministers by whom ye believed?" 1 Cor. iii. 5; and elsewhere he styles them, "ministers of the new testament," and "ministers of Christ," 2 Cor. iii. 6; xi. 23.

But I return to Tychicus, of whom the apostle says, in the third place, that he is his "fellow-servant in the Lord." Not that he was also an apostle; but since Paul in his apostleship, and Tychicus in his ministry as an evangelist, served one and the same Lord, and were of the same Master's house, referring all the duties of their different offices to his glory, and the good of his household, as their common end, and labouring, though with unequal authority, in the same work, namely, preaching the gospel, and administering the sacraments, it is evident that in this respect Tychicus was fellow-servant with this great apostle. His acknowledging him here so to be was a direct means to gain him full credit with the Colossians; for if they honoured the apostle, how could they despise a person whom he owns for his beloved brother, for a faithful minister of the gospel, and his fellow-servant? Now by his thus honouring Tychicus, you may see how far from this apostolical meekness and modesty some are, who, boasting themselves to be their successors, tread other ministers of the church under their feet, and so little consider them their associates, or treat them according to that quality, that they look on them as their vassals: giving out themselves to be their princes, their kings, and lords; and advancing themselves to an almost infinite height, not only above each of them apart, but even the whole assembly of them in a general council; nay, above the whole sacred body of Jesus Christ itself; that is, the entire church, which they affirm to be born their subject, and entitle themselves its monarchs, not forbearing to put even the greatest princes and emperors under the yoke of their domination, and to exact of them, as a mark of lowest servitude, the kissing of their feet.

But this holy and admirable humility of the apostle appears further still, in his speaking as he does of Onesimus, whom he sent with Tychicus to the Colossians: he is, says he, "a faithful brother," &c. For who, think you, was this Onesimus, whom he so honours as to call him his "faithful and beloved brother?" Dear brethren, it was a poor fugitive bond-servant, that is, a person of the meanest and most despicable condition of any at that time; as Paul himself gives us to understand, in the Epistle which he wrote in favour of this at length happy fugitive unto Philemon the Colossian, his master; where he plainly intimates, that this poor man, stealing from his master's house, had fled into Italy, and got to the city of Rome for safety. But oh the admirable providence of God, who knows how to carry on the salvation of his elect by ways which we cannot comprehend! the apostle happening to be prisoner there, and Onesimus, led by his curiosity, or some other such occasion, having heard him, was so affected at his preaching, as of a pagan, he became a christian; of a servant of Philemon, a freeman of Jesus Christ; and instead of that temporal impunity for the crime committed against his master which he sought at Rome, he there found the eternal remission of his sins, and the salvation of his soul. This is that which Paul elsewhere means, when he says that he begat him in his bonds, Phil. 10. Now, the apostle having showed him the fault he had committed in deserting his master, he resolves to return home to him, and voluntarily render up himself to his yoke again. And that Philemon might pardon his offence, he makes him the bearer of a letter, which he writes him on this subject; a letter so full of all the most express testimonies of a tender and ardent affection, as sufficiently proves that he in truth accounted him, as he here terms him, his beloved brother.

But some of the ancient writers of the church further intimate, that Onesimus profited so well in the knowledge of God and in piety, as notwithstanding the meanness of his condition after the flesh, he was advanced to the sacred ministry of the gospel, and executed it in the church of Ephesus. And truly the employment the apostle gives him here, with reference to this whole church, and the company of Tychicus, with whom he associates him, and the honourable title he gives him, styling him not only his beloved brother, which every christian might be termed, but likewise faithful, seems to show that he had some office; upon the account of which, for his conscionable acquitting himself in it, this testimonial of faithfulness is given him. And in this, I conceive, the apostle also makes a secret opposition between the good conscience with which he demeaned himself in this employment, and the unfaithfulness he had formerly showed to his master during the time of his ignorance; if he has been before unfaithful, says he, he is now faithful; after nearly the same manner as the apostle elsewhere, alluding to the word Onesimus, which was his name, and in Greek signifies profitable, says of him to Philemon his master, he "was in time past to thee unprofitable, but now profitable to thee and to me," Philem. 11. This, dear brethren, is that which the first part of the text contains.

II. We come now to the second. In it the apostle presents to the Colossians the salutations of three faithful persons, all the three jointly ministers of the gospel, and by nation Jews, who were then at Rome, to serve, and assist, and refresh him in his imprisonment: "Aristarchus," says he, "saluteth you," and so the rest in order. Whence we may observe, first, in general, what was the zeal and charity of those primitive christians; that the hatred and rage of the world was not able to keep them from rendering their duties and services to the confessors and martyrs of Jesus Christ even in prisons; nor from hastening to them from places very far off to succour and comfort them: it being evident that, of the eight persons mentioned here, and in the following text, some came from Greece, others from Asia, and some again from Syria and Palestine, that is, many hundred leagues, to visit and serve Paul. And by these salutations, which for their part they send to the Colossians, you see how these holy and charitable souls were affectionate to flocks as well as pastors, and to those who were absent as well as to them who were present. And again, the apostle's vouchsafing to act as their secretary on such an occasion, shows us that he approves these offices of civility, that is, salutations of such as are present, and by letter of such as are absent. In truth, a christian, whose charity and unfeigned cordial love of men is the principal virtue, and as it were the soul and one of the prime principles, of his life, ought to acquit himself sedulously in all due offices of humanity; and if there is in the deportments of other men anything humane and praiseworthy, he should practise it, and sanctify it to his Lord's use.

As for these three persons in particular, the apostle gives each of them his eulogium. The first is Aristarchus, a native of Thessalonica in Macedonia, a person noted in the history of the Acts, where you see him all along inseparably adhering to Paul, a companion in his travels and in his trials, running the danger of his life with him in the sedition at Ephesus, Acts xix. 29; at his departure then following him into Greece, into Macedonia, into Asia and Judea; and at last embarking with him when he was carried prisoner to Rome, Acts xxvii. 2. For this cause the holy apostle, in acknowledgment of so admirable a zeal, makes him a sharer with him in his crown, terming him a captive, or prisoner, with him; inasmuch as though those unjust judges had not condemned him, yet he took as great a part in the captivity of Paul as if sentence had been given against his own person.

The second is Mark, whom he signalizes by the honour he had to be the nephew of Barnabas, his cousin german, one of the most excellent disciples of our Lord, and that laboured in his work with the greatest zeal and fervour, as you see in the history of the Acts, and some of the ancients have even attributed to him the divine Epistle to the Hebrews. The glory of this holy man being very great in all the churches of God, the apostle conceived it a sufficient recommendation of Mark to say he was his sister's son. He adds only, "concerning whom ye have received commandment." I am much of their mind, who understand these words of some letter that Barnabas had written them in recommendation of him. And to this the apostle adds his own counsel to them, saying, "if he come unto you, receive him." Some conceive that he thus writes, because of that ill understanding that formerly happened between him and Barnabas, on the occasion of Mark, Acts xv. 39, to show now that there was no relic of it in his heart. However that may be, it is certain, as we read in the Acts, that Mark betrayed a little weakness at the beginning, quitting Paul and Barnabas in Pamphylia, without any reason, amidst their conquests, Acts xiii. 13. But afterwards the grace of God so mightily strengthened him, and so eminently employed him in converting nations, that besides the memory of it which remains in all the monuments of antiquity, he has also drawn from the pen of Paul two or three very honourable testimonies; this for one, and another like it in the Epistle to Philemon, ver. 24, where he mentions him among his fellow-workers; and the most advantageous of all in the Second to Timothy, chap. iv. 11, "Take Mark," says he, "and bring him with thee; for he is profitable to me for the ministry."

The third of those whom the apostle here mentions is "Jesus, called Justus." It is probable that his true name was Jesus, and that Justus was but the name which the Latins and Greeks gave him, calling him Justus instead of Jesus; it being usual with them to alter foreign names in that manner, when they pronounced them in their own dialects. We have of this servant of God no other memorial at all. For though some conceive that it is the same Justus of whom mention is made in the 18th chapter of the Acts, to whose house Paul retired at Corinth, when he saw the Jews resist his preaching; yet this seems not possible, because this man was by extraction a Gentile, and uncircumcised, though he had some knowledge and fear of God, as appears by Luke's terming him a religious man, or one that worshipped God; a character he ordinarily gives to persons of this condition; as to Cornelius the centurion, and various others; whereas Justus who is here in question was indeed a Jew, and circumcised, as Paul shows, adding immediately, of him and the two others just mentioned, "who are of the circumcision:" and he praises them all three in common, saying that they alone, that is, of their nation, were his fellow-workers unto the kingdom of God, and protests that they were a consolation to him; a great and an illustrious testimonial given them, that they laboured with him in preaching the gospel for the advancement of the kingdom of God, that is to say, for the edifying of the church, which the Scripture ordinarily calls the kingdom of heaven, and in the same sense the kingdom of God. Now this is what the apostle says of these three servants of the Lord.

It remains, for a conclusion, that we intimate to you briefly what edification you ought to draw from those particulars which we have noted in the apostle's present text. And, first, by the pain the Colossians were in for Paul, and by the care Paul takes for their consolation, you may see the ardent and cordial affection which the flocks and ministers of Christ should have one for another. Make you profit of it, you who are the Lord's sheep, and tenderly compassionate the labours and the sufferings of your pastors. Ye pastors, do likewise, and prefer, before all interests of your own, the edification and consolation of those sheep whom the great Shepherd has redeemed with his blood. Then again, the love which these five faithful men here mentioned bore to Paul, they keeping ever near him, and cheerfully and constantly obeying his orders, shows us with what fervour we should serve those who suffer for the gospel; and with what zeal we should inseparably adhere to the apostles of Jesus Christ, the teachers and founders of the church. For though their persons are no longer here below, yet their doctrine is and will remain here to the end; and in this respect they are still in their sacred writings sitting as it were on twelve thrones, judging all the Israel of God.

Moreover, the apostle so liberally praising all the persons of whom he here speaks, may inform us with what candour we should acknowledge the graces which God has imparted to our brethren, diffusing the sweet savour of their good name through the church, and honouring their zeal and their fidelity with our testimonials, to their comfort and the edification of their neighbours. Far from us be envy, and malignity, and pride, passions of a base alloy, and unworthy of a truly noble christian disposition. Let not the graces and dignity of Paul induce him to despise Onesimus; I mean, let not the advantages of such as are greatest cause them to disdain the least.

But let us consider particularly the examples of each of those five faithful men, and imitate them. For it is to this end that the holy apostle has proposed them, and thought meet to consecrate the memory of them in his divine and immortal Epistles; not that he might induce us to dedicate festivals to them, or render them religious worship, or invocate them as our mediators; away with such a thought, for all this appertains to God only. The true honour we owe them is to serve God after their example, and conform our lives to theirs, and draw the portrait of their high and holy virtues on our dispositions and our actions. Let us imitate the fidelity of Tychicus, the repentance and faith of Onesimus, the courage and the patience of Aristarchus, the assiduity of Marcus and of Justus in the matters of the kingdom of God. Let not meanness of birth or of condition, let not the greatness of sins, discourage any. Jesus Christ rejects neither the poor nor the guilty that come to him with faith; witness Onesimus, who, though a bondman and fugitive, yet so effaced all this ignominy, that he has praise from the mouth of the apostle, and his name engraven here in the temple of God, among the names of the most illustrious of his servants. If you have followed the Lord constantly and uniformly, as did Tychicus and Aristarchus, thank him for the grace which he has showed you, and go on from good to better. If it has befallen you, as it did Mark, to slacken at any time in the work of your heavenly calling, resume likewise, as he did, your former vigour, and return again to that condition, that it may be said of you, that you are useful for the Lord's service.

In general, beloved brethren, let us all be as these holy and happy persons were, fellow workers with the great apostle unto the kingdom of God, burning with him in a holy zeal to glorify Jesus Christ; living with him in all pureness and holiness; employing with him our tongues, our hands, and our pens, for the conversion of men, and edification of the church; and finally courageously suffering with him, when the Lord calls us thereto. It is this way, christians, that we shall get to that heavenly kingdom in which Paul is lodged after his combats, and there receive with him, from the merciful hand of our Father, the glorious crown of immortality, which he on his great day will give to us, and to all those who shall have loved the appearing of his Son; unto whom, with him, and the Holy Spirit, the only true God, blessed for ever, be honour, praise, and glory, to ages of ages. Amen.

SERMON XLIX.

VERSES 12—18.

Epaphras, who is one of you, a servant of Christ, saluteth you, always labouring fervently for you in prayers, that ye may stand perfect and complete in all the will of God. For I bear him record, that he hath a great zeal for you, and them that are in Laodicea, and them in Hierapolis. Luke, the beloved physician, and Demas, greet you. Salute the brethren which are in Laodicea, and Nymphas, and the church which is in his house. And when this epistle is read among you, cause that it be read also in the church of the Laodiceans; and that ye likewise read the epistle from Laodicea. And say to Archippus, Take heed to the ministry which thou hast received in the Lord, that thou fulfil it. The salutation by the hand of me Paul. Remember my bonds. Grace be with you. Amen.

DEAR brethren, the Lord Jesus being upon the point to quit the earth, and making as it were a declaration of his last will, charges his disciples above all things to love one another with a sincere and ardent affection, like that which he bore towards them. This mutual love he appoints to be the badge of our profession: "By this," says he, "shall all men know that ye are my disciples, if ye love one another," John xiii. 35. Accordingly, you know, that his Spirit failed not to imprint this divine mark upon those first christians whom he formed in the city of Jerusalem by the apostles' preaching, animated with the virtue of his heavenly fire. "The whole multitude of them," says the sacred history, "were of one heart and of one soul; neither said any of them that aught of the things which he possessed was his own; but they had all things common," Acts iv. 32. This union and admirable correspondence continued a long time among the faithful, and was observed by the pagans with wonder; witness he who, about two hundred years after the birth of our Lord, reproaches christians, that they know one another by certain secret signs, and love almost before they are acquainted, and all of them call one another indifferently brethren and sisters. Now, as error and passion abuse the best things, this poor ignorant person takes their holy and divine concord for some execrable conspiracy, and refers the mystery of their amity to infamous commerces; whereas all their union grew from heaven, and was founded upon piety, breathed nothing but honesty and holiness, and tended only to the glory of God, and the supreme happiness of men. Besides the apostle's writings, which, being exposed to public view, plainly showed to the dispassionate how pure, and honest, and holy were the laws of their charity, the manners, the lives, and actions of those primitive christians also evidently justified them; there are left us, God be thanked, various excellent accounts in the books of the first antiquity, by which the wonders of the charity and mutual love of those holy men plainly appear. And not to speak of others, you have fair and illustrious marks of it in this conclusion of Paul's Epistle to the Colossians, who shows us that his prison neither hindered various faithful men from joining themselves unto him in this affliction, nor him nor them again from minding absent christians, and charitably embracing the churches of Colosse, Laodicea, and Hierapolis. You here see the love of pastors to their flocks, the dear affection of flocks to their pastors, and the divine communication of churches one with another. If therefore it be a good and pleasant thing, as the psalmist sings, Psal. cxxxiii. 1, to see brethren maintaining a due intercourse with each other, grudge not this hour, my beloved, which we yet invite you to spend in the consideration of this text, having not been able to finish it entirely in our last sermon. Let this admirable amity of the first christians rejoice you, and give you an ardent desire to imitate it. Have one for another sentiments and movings of heart like to theirs.

You have already heard how Paul, having informed the faithful at Colosse that he sent Tychicus and Onesimus unto them, to declare to them his state, gives them the recommendations of Aristarchus, and Mark, and Jesus. He now adds those of Epaphras, and Luke, and Demas; and then his own to the church of Laodicea, and to a faithful man named Nymphas, with an order to impart this his Epistle to them, and to inform Archippus of his duty; whereupon he ends with his ordinary salutation, conjuring them to remember his bonds, and recommending them to the grace of God. For deducing these four points, by the assistance of God, in the same order as they are couched in the text, we must first consider who these three persons were whose salutations the apostle presents to the Colossians.

I. The first of the three is Epaphras; of whom he spake before in very honourable terms at the beginning of this Epistle, chap. i. 7, 8, where he styles him his "dear fellow-servant," and "a faithful minister of Christ;" and gives him the glory of having instructed the Colossians in the knowledge of the gospel, and of having taken the care to let him know the charity they had for him. Here he qualifies him in the same manner, "a servant of Christ;" that is, his minister, and an officer of his house in the work of the gospel. Moreover, he informs us that this holy man was a Colossian; that is, was born in their city, or at least made his ordinary abode there: "Epaphras," says he, "who is one of you, a servant of Christ, saluteth you." Some learned men* are of opinion, that it is this same pastor whom the apostle calls Epaphroditus, and of whom he speaks so well, in the Epistle to the Philippians, chap. ii. 25. But I do not see that this conjecture is either founded or followed by any of the ancients. I confess that the name Epaphras is a contraction of Epaphroditus; and such a diminution is ordinary in the Greek and in the Latin tongue in the proper names of men. But if it were one and the same person, there is no reason why the apostle should name him differently in these two Epistles: in the one contractedly, and with diminution; in the other the name at length and entire; considering withal, that no part of what is said in those two places concerning him induces us to believe it was the same man, but rather infers the contrary. For it seems that Epaphroditus was pastor of the church of Philippi in Macedonia, whereas Epaphras was pastor of Colosse in Phrygia; two cities and provinces very different, and separated from each other by much land and sea: the second situate in Asia, and the former in Europe.

The apostle contents not himself with telling the Colossians that Epaphras saluteth them. To this testimony of his affection for them he adds various others, that he may gain him their hearts, and strengthen the tie of amity and good correspondence more and more between this pastor and his flock. He says, first, that he always strives in prayer for them, "that," says he, "ye may stand perfect and complete in all the will of God." Prayer is the best office that we can perform towards those we love. But pastors particularly owe it to their flocks, not only in their assemblies, where they serve for the mouth of the company to present their requests, their vows, and their thanksgivings unto God, but also in private, and even when they are absent, upon some occasion of importance for the good of the church, as doubtless that was which at that time held Epaphras at Rome by Paul's order. Though he

* Grotius.

was far from their abode, he had them incessantly in mind; and distance hindering him from rendering them his other services, he assisted them with his prayers. The apostle signifies both the assiduity of them, when he says he prayed alway; and the fervency and earnestness of them, when he says he laboured for them. This word is admirable, and excellently represents the efficacy of his prayer. Think not, christian, that he who prays for you contributes nothing to your welfare, and that his prayers are but words and voices cast into the air. It is the best part of your battles; you have no succour more active than the repose of a man of God, who prays for you with faith and perseverance. It is he who, as Moses formerly, standing on the mountain and rapt up in spirit into the heavenly sanctuary, defeats Amalek, your spiritual enemies; and by the uplifting of his hands draws down the blessing of heaven upon your arms. He oftentimes even takes those rods out of the hand of God which he is about to lay upon you; and courageously wrestling with him, after Jacob's example, quits him not until he has obtained his demand. Such is the combat that Epaphras fought in the behalf of his Colossians, being night and day in prayer for them.

But what is it that he demanded of God for them? The apostle shows it expressly, when he says he strove for them in prayer, that they might "stand perfect and complete in all the will of God." He desired not for them the riches, honours, and pleasures of the world, the usual passion of men, slight and perishing goods; unprofitable, and oftentimes even pernicious, to those who possess them. He prayed God to give them the best blessings; perseverance in his love, in his fear, and in obeying his will. For it is this that the apostle's words signify. He demanded, first, that they might be "perfect and complete in all the will of God;" and secondly, that they might abide firm in this perfection. By "the will of God" he means those things which God wills, and loves, and which he commands in the gospel of his Son; in the same manner as he elsewhere says, our hope, for the things we hope to obtain; and, the promise of God, for the things he has promised us. He thus explains himself, when he says expressly in the first Epistle to the Thessalonians, chap. iv. 3, that the will of God is our sanctification, that is, that we be holy; which, as you see, is no other than the thing which God wills. It is that will of God which elsewhere he calls good, and acceptable, and perfect; which comprehends in it all the particulars of our duty; that is, in few words, faith and piety towards God, and charity towards our neighbour. For this is that which God wills, which he ordains and commands all men in the gospel of his Christ; even that we believe in him, embracing with a pure and thorough faith the truths which he has vouchsafed to reveal to us, and chiefly the promise of our salvation by the cross of our Lord Jesus; and that in the sequel we serve him religiously, renouncing all impiety; and love our neighbours, living with them in all justice, temperance, and benignity. This, brethren, is that will of God which the apostle intends; and observe, he says not simply, in the will, but in *all* the will of God. For there are people who would be content to do some part of what God wills, provided they might be excused the rest; as for example, to believe the truth which God has revealed, but not to do the good works which he has commanded; or to exercise some of them, but utterly fail in others: as they who live fair with men, but remain in impiety, and in the profession of error; or those, on the contrary, who make profession of error; or those, again, who make open profession of the pure service of God, but spare not either the goods or honour of their neighbours; or who, abstaining from one vice, license themselves to others; who are chaste, but covetous; or liberal and beneficial to the poor, but corrupt and incontinent. This partition is unjust, injurious to God, impossible in truth, and incompatible with the nature of the things themselves. And it is to inform us of this that the apostle says here expressly, "in all the will of God," to the end that no man might imagine it sufficient to embrace a part only of what God wills. Epaphras desired therefore that his Colossians might be perfect and complete in all this will of God; that is, as we have now explained it, in all the things which God wills, which he requires of us, which he commands men to do; that they might be perfect in faith, perfect in piety, perfect in charity, and in all virtue and holiness.

The two words by which he expresses himself, namely, perfect and complete, signify nearly one and the same thing; and the Scripture uses them indifferently, to set forth a being entire, one in whom none of the parts of piety and sanctification are wanting. Now this perfection, or integrity, in all the will of God, comprehends two things: the one is, that we know it, that we understand exactly all that God wills, all that he requires of us as he has revealed it in his word. The other is, that we pursue and effectually practise this will which we know. The first of these two points the apostle recommends to us elsewhere: "Be ye not unwise," says he, "but understanding what the will of the Lord is," Eph. v. 17; and in another place he commands us to prove it, Rom. xii. 2. The necessity of the other point our Lord Jesus Christ shows us, when he says in the gospel according to Matthew, chap. vii. 21, "Not every one that saith unto me, Lord, Lord, shall enter into the kingdom of heaven; but he that doeth the will of my Father which is in heaven." I acknowledge that, while the believer is here below, there want many degrees, both in his knowledge of the will of God, and in the obedience he renders to him, of that ultimate and supreme perfection unto which he shall one day attain in heaven, according to the apostle's assertion in the first Epistle to the Corinthians, chap. xiii. 12, that now we see through a glass darkly, and know but in part; but then we shall see face to face, and know as we are known. Yet, setting this comparison aside, this does not hinder that measure of faith and holiness to which the faithful at present attain from being properly termed a perfection and completeness; because it is without hypocrisy, reaching to internals and externals, and includes all the parts of true piety and chastity, not one left out. And it is in this sense that the truly faithful are often in Scripture called perfect and complete; that is, with reference to the state and measure of the present life, for distinguishing them, not only from profane and wicked men, who embrace no part of the will of God at all; but also from hypocrites and carnal christians, who consider only a part thereof, halting between two opinions, and are thoroughly and absolutely neither in Christ nor of the world. Epaphras had reason to desire this perfection for his Colossians, since that no one without it can inherit everlasting life. And they who teach, that it is not universally necessary for obtaining salvation, and that it is a matter of counsel, as they call it, not of command; they, I say, are grievously mistaken, and by this pernicious error open a door of license to wicked men, and furnish them with pillows upon which to sleep in mortal security.

For our parts, dear brethren, let us follow the prayer of Epaphras, and take good heed that we never count that superfluous or unnecessary which he so instantly begged of God for his flock and sheep. And knowing that they shall have no part in heaven whose righteousness does not exceed the righteousness of the scribes and Pharisees, and that Jesus Christ will receive in thither none but those who have done the will of God his Father, let us apply ourselves with all our might to know it and fulfil it. Let us give ourselves no rest, until, by prayers and tears, and by continual labour and exercise in the gospel, we have attained to perfection and completion in all the will of God. Yet it is not enough to attain to this, we must abide and stand firm in it, as the apostle here says, persevere constantly to our last breath in this noble and blessed undertaking; neither the menaces nor the caresses of the world, neither the sophisms of seducers, nor the scandals of false brethren, nor the weaknesses of our own flesh, ever prevailing over us to make us vary. For you know that the crown of salvation is for them alone who persevere. It is thus that Epaphras strove to obtain of God, by his ardent and assiduous prayers, that the Colossians might abide perfect, and complete in all the will of God.

But because the apostle knew how much it concerned this people to be firmly persuaded of the affection of their pastor, that he might assure them fully of it, he gives them the authority of his own testimony. "For," says he, "I bear him witness, that he hath a great zeal (that is, a very ardent affection) for you, and them of Laodicea, and of Hierapolis." These were two cities of Phrygia near to Colosse, where the Lord Jesus had churches that served him in the faith of his gospel. And that of Laodicea is one of the seven to whom he caused to be written by John those excellent epistles which are read in the first chapters of his Apocalypse. You see what care the apostle takes to set Epaphras right in the spirit of his flock. Whence you may judge how execrable is the rage or envy of those who, contrary to the example of this holy man, endeavour, by their detractions and ill offices, to alienate or slacken the inclination of churches towards their pastors, and in so doing render their ministry unprofitable to them. But, to proceed.

After the salutation of Epaphras, the apostle presents them that of Luke and Demas: "Luke, the beloved physician, and Demas, greet you." It is the constant opinion from all antiquity, that the first of these two is the same Luke, who wrote the third of our Gospels, and the book of the Acts of the Apostles, two of the most excellent pieces that we have in the divine writings of the New Testament. And indeed, besides the name of Luke, his own history, as it appears to me, leads us to this opinion. For he himself relates that he embarked with Paul, when he was carried prisoner into Italy; and that he came with him to Rome, as you may see in the last two chapters of the Acts, where he describes this voyage. Therefore, being there with the apostle, there is all the probability in the world that he is the person of whom Paul speaks in this place; it being not found that mention is made in Scripture of any other faithful man of that name. He calls him physician, because of his former profession; as you see that Matthew is sometimes termed a publican, because he was so before his conversion. But that same heavenly call that had changed Matthew from a publican into an apostle; and in ancient time, of a keeper of sheep, made David a pastor of nations; wrought a similar miracle in Luke, and, of a physician to the body, made him a physician of souls. His two books show us how able he was in this divine art; and as often as you read them at home, or hear them publicly here, where because of their excellency, they are both of them explained to you, be assured that they are a quantity of wholesome medicines presented to you, to be applied to your souls as you have need. I well know that there are some modern expositors who refer what the apostle here says to another Luke; but they produce no valuable reason. They allege, indeed, that the apostle would have adorned this person with some more illustrious eulogy, if he had spoken of Luke the evangelist; but this is extremely feeble. Is it not a very glorious qualification to call him his well-beloved? It is a great honour to have the love of so holy an apostle, and an assured testimony of piety and virtue. Withal, it is not always necessary to accompany the names of illustrious persons with all the eulogies they merit. The apostle, in the Epistle to the Hebrews, naming Timothy, whose praise and great advantages in the work of the ministry, and in all virtue, every one sufficiently knows, calls him simply his brother Timothy.

The other, on whose behalf he salutes the Colossians, is Demas. In the Epistle to Philemon, written at the same time with this, and in which he makes mention of most of the persons here named, he places Demas, with Mark, and Aristarchus, and Luke, among his fellow-labourers; whence it appears that he was a minister of the word of God, of the order of those who served for helpers to the apostles, and are styled evangelists. But after he had for a space ran well, after he had appeared with praise among the lights of the church, alas! he lost in the end this fair crown of glory. Paul, who vouchsafed to give his name such an honourable rank in two places of his epistles, in a third tells this lamentable story: "Demas," says he, "hath forsaken me, having loved this present world, and is departed unto Thessalonica," 2 Tim. iv. 10. From this doleful example, let us all learn, dear brethren, and particularly such of us as God has called to the holy ministry, to stand on our guard, and to mortify in ourselves worldly lusts, as avarice, the love of life, pleasures, ambition, and similar passions, which ruined Demas. And if the dragon cast down some of the stars that shined in the heaven of our churches; if the flesh and the earth, the food and the fulness of Egypt, and the false grandeurs of Chaldea, cause them unworthily to quit the design and the hopes of mystical Canaan, let us not be astonished at it. We are not better than the apostles. If all the light of their wisdom and miracles could not keep Demas from becoming bankrupt of the truth, we ought not to think it strange, if there happen to be among us some whom carnal appetites and vanity precipitate into the same fault, notwithstanding the clearness and evidence of our holy doctrine.

II. But it is time to pass on to the second part of our text, in which the apostle orders the Colossians three things: first, to salute those of Laodicea on his behalf; secondly, to communicate this Epistle to them; and thirdly, to inform Archippus of his duty. "Salute," says he, "the brethren," that is, the christians, "which are in Laodicea, and Nymphas, and the church which is in his house." This Nymphas dwelt either in the city of Laodicea itself, or in the country near it, as some, in my opinion, without necessity suppose. The apostle names him in particular, because doubtless he was one of the most considerable persons of the flock at Laodicea, and Paul's affirming that he had a church in his house sufficiently testifies the zeal of his piety. This church was not a place in his house where the assemblies for religious exercises were held, (for the Scripture never uses the word church in this sense, which is now common among christians,) but it is his household, and the persons of which it consisted, who all made profession of christianity with him, and were confirmed and edified therein by his instructions and good examples. Whence appears the vanity of the pretension of those at Rome, who only acknowledge that for a church which figures in the world, and carries with it the pomp of multitude and prosperity. The church of Jesus Christ is found wherever he is known, served, and adored according to his gospel; within the enclosure of the walls of a house, or in the very caverns of mountains, and coverts of the wilderness, whither the Holy Spirit expressly foretells us that the spouse of the Lamb shall be sometimes constrained to retire.

The second order which the apostle gives the Colossians is worthy of consideration. "When this Epistle," says he, "is read among you, cause that it be also read in the church of the Laodiceans; and that ye likewise read the Epistle from Laodicea." First, his directing that this Epistle should be publicly read in the assemblies of these two churches, shows us that the Scriptures of God were given to us, to the end that all the people of Christ, clergymen and laymen, small and great, should hear and read them, and not that they should be put into the hands of one certain class of persons only, as if this treasure belonged to none but them. And hence appears the abuse of those who only read the Scriptures to their people in a language which they do not understand, which is as bad, yea, in my opinion worse, than if they read them not at all. For not to read them is simply to bereave the people of the profit they might make of them; whereas to read them in an unknown tongue, is not only to deprive them of their edification, but also to mock them, and not less to offend God, by perverting his word in such a manner from its due use and end. What shall I say of their outrage, who accuse these divine books of ambiguity, of obscurity, of seeming contradictions and errors—who say that the reading of them is dangerous, and more apt to corrupt and embroil the faithful than to instruct or edify them? O holy apostle, why didst thou put so dangerous a book into our hands—a book full of thorns, and void of fruit? Why didst thou order them to read it in their assembly; to impart it unto neighbouring churches, and enjoin them to read it also? Why didst thou not fear lest thou shouldst infect the spirits of thine innocent disciples, and insnare them in some heresy by the darkness of thy riddles; or shouldst sow some disorder in their hearts by the ambiguity of thine expressions? Dear brethren, the apostle answers that his gospel is clear; that it is covered only to unstable spirits, and such as are engaged in some evil passion; that this Epistle is not any seed of error, but a remedy against seduction; a vessel full, not of poisons, but of preservatives and antidotes. But I perceive what is the matter. The Scriptures seem to these gentlemen dangerous; because, saying nothing of their pope, of their mass, of the worship of their saints and images, nor of their purgatory, and such other points; nay, saying many things which are evidently contrary to them; they easily induce those who read them with attention to believe that these doctrines have been invented by men, and were never taught by Jesus Christ and his apostles. This book troubles them, because they find not their reckoning in it. It is obscure, because what they love does not there appear. It is ambiguous, because it pronounces nothing clearly or expressly in favour of the opinions which they are resolved never to forsake.

Again, this imparting of Paul's Epistle to the Laodiceans, which the Colossians were to do by his order, shows us that there ought to be a holy and charitable commerce between the churches of Jesus Christ with reference to spiritual things; that a church which has received any grace from God which tends to edification should not grudge it to others, but affectionately communicate to them all that may serve for their instruction. And this communion ought to take place particularly between neighbouring churches, such as those of Colosse and of Laodicea. And it is upon this example, and upon the reason on which it depends, that the uniting of the churches of the same provinces in synods is founded; a thing instituted and observed from the beginning of christianity down to our days, and still very profitably practised and kept up among us, by the goodness of God.

This mutual communication of neighbouring churches appears yet further, in the apostle's ordering the Colossians, in the third place, to read also the letter from Laodicea after imparting to them his. "When this Epistle," says he, "is read among you, cause that it be read also in the church of the Laodiceans; and that ye likewise read the Epistle [which came, or was written] from Laodicea." It is demanded what this second Epistle is of which he speaks. Many theologians of the communion of Rome answer, that it was a letter which Paul wrote to the faithful of Laodicea, at the same time he wrote this to the Colossians; whence they conclude, that this piece being lost, as well as various other writings of prophets and apostles, it cannot be pretended that the canon of holy writ is perfect, and contains all things necessary to our salvation. Others, again, from thence infer that it is the church which gives the Scriptures the authority they have among christians; since, of the Epistles of Paul, it has left this in particular out of the canon of divine books, and retained only those fourteen which are in our hands. But there is nothing sound or solid in their argument; which concludes badly, and presupposes what is false. For suppose the apostle had written an Epistle to the Laodiceans, and that it was lost, (as I would not affirm that Paul and his fellow-brethren the apostles never wrote anything to any particular person or to any church but what has been handed down to us,) suppose it, I say; who told them that this loss makes the canon of our Scriptures defective? Who told them that there was in that letter some article of faith necessary to our salvation, which is not found in the other parts of the Bible which we now have? Again, who taught them thence to conclude, that it is the church who authorizes the divine books? I grant she is the keeper and depositary of them, as the synagogue formerly was of the books of the Old Testament, according to the apostle's saying, that unto them were committed the oracles of God; and that it belongs to her charge to preserve them, and read them, and recommend them to every one. But that it is the authority of her voice and testimony which gives them the price and value they have, either in themselves, or with reference to faithful souls, cannot, in my opinion, be said without outraging the majesty of their author, by making the divinity of the instruments of his wisdom to depend upon the fancy of men; as the Romans formerly submitted the worship and divinity of their gods to the decrees of their senate. They were not gods except it so pleased men. If it were certain that the apostle had written an Epistle to the Laodiceans, and put it into the hands of the church, it should be concluded, not that she has the power to authorize what divine books she pleases, but rather that she has greatly failed in her duty in having so negligently kept a heavenly jewel. But the worst yet is, that all that they say about this pretended Epistle of Paul to the Laodiceans is a vain conceit, and has no other foundation than their imagination. I well know that in our fathers' days a learned man* published one under that name, having found it in three or four libraries. But the piece is so gross and so ridiculous,

* Faber. Scapulensis.

that it has been universally rejected, as the work of an impostor, who abusing his leisure, forged this trifle, and shamelessly fathered it upon Paul. Some of the ancients also make mention of a document bearing the same name, whether it were different from this or resembled it; but the ancients who speak of it all unanimously decry it as an apocryphal book, and one issued out of an heretical shop, and framed at pleasure after Paul's death. And, in truth, one of the first writers of the Latin church declares,* that a famous heresiarch, named Marcion, had changed the title of the Epistle of Paul to the Ephesians, and instead of this name, which it always bore in the church, impudently called it the Epistle to the Laodiceans; and indeed in the Epistle to the Ephesians, those words occur which Epiphanius reports to have been cited by Marcion out of the Epistle to the Laodiceans.† This has given a certain writer‡ occasion to fancy that Paul indeed sent and addressed the same Epistle to the Laodiceans which at the same time he wrote to the Ephesians, these two churches having had need of the same remedies; and that it is this Epistle the apostle means in this place, directing the Colossians to take a copy of it, and read it in their assembly. All this would pass, if it were at all grounded; but it is too much confidence or credulity to think to persuade us of it upon the credit of Marcion, the most impudent impostor that ever troubled the church, and one that in particular played with the books of the New Testament, contracting them, maiming them, and changing them at his pleasure with an infernal license. Besides, this supposition agrees not with Paul's words. For he does not say, as these persons pretend, that the Epistle in question was written to the Laodiceans. True it is, the Latin interpreter has rendered it, the Epistle of the Laodiceans, but this would signify, as every one sees, that the Laodiceans had written it, and not that they had received it, either from the apostle or from any other. Yet though the Latin would suffer this rude gloss, it is clear the original cannot be made to bear it without undertaking (as these new doctors do, truly with presumption enough) to change the words of it, which we find uniform in the Greek copies, and which the ancients observed there, above twelve hundred years ago. For they clearly import, as our Bibles have faithfully translated and represented, that this Epistle had been written or sent from Laodicea; so that we must necessarily understand them, with the ancient Greek fathers, of an Epistle written, not to the Laodiceans, but from their city.

Now the apostle telling us no more of it, either here or elsewhere, we need not wonder that those who have had the

* Tertul. 1. 5. c. 17. cont. Marcion. † Heres. 43. cont. Marcion. ‡ Grotius.

curiosity to inquire what this letter might be, have fallen upon different opinions, as in a matter both obscure, and besides of no great necessity. Some of the ancients say that it is the first Epistle of Paul to Timothy, written from Laodicea; as is expressly reported by an old tradition, which is read still to this day at the end of that Epistle. And the truth is, it cannot be denied that this Epistle contains various instructions fit to edify the Colossians about the business of those seducers whom Paul here opposes; they taught a discrimination of days and meats, and this is there expressly condemned. And whereas it is alleged against these authors, that the apostle had not been in the city of Laodicea; consequently, he could not have thence written any letters, either to Timothy or any other; they perhaps would answer with an ancient author, Theodoret by name, that the history of the Acts assuring us Paul had traversed Phrygia, it is not very improbable that he passed through Laodicea, the capital city of the province. As to his saying, in the 2nd chapter to the Colossians, that he had a great conflict for them, and for those at Laodicea, and for all such as had not seen his face in the flesh; this shows indeed that the apostle had care even of those of the faithful whom he had not seen, but not that they of Laodicea or of Colosse were of the number; and that the sense of these words is, he was in pain, not only for them whom he had seen and known, but even for the christians he never saw. Yet because this exposition may seem a little forced, it is better and more easy to adhere to the common opinion, followed by the greater number of expositors, both ancient and modern, even that the Epistle from Laodicea, here mentioned by the apostle, was a letter written by the church of Laodicea to Paul; which letter he desires the Colossians should read in their assembly, because it contained things which he judged helpful to their edification; perhaps concerning the persons, or the errors, or the procedures of those very seducers whom he combats in this Epistle. This, in my opinion, is that which may be said in the matter with greatest probability.

There remains the third and last order he gives them: "Say to Archippus, Take heed to the ministry which thou hast received in the Lord, that thou fulfil it." We learn from the Epistle to Philemon, that Archippus was a fellow-soldier of the apostle's, that is, a minister of the holy gospel. The meaning then is, that the church should direct him, on Paul's behalf, to mind both the quality of that excellent ministry, and the authority and divinity of the Lord, in whose name he had been called to it, that he might acquit himself worthily in it, and diligently fulfil all its functions, leaving no part of them unperformed. It is thought that some negligence or other defect of this pastor might have induced the apostle to cause this advice to be given him; but, for my part, I would not without a more pressing reason suspect such a thing of a person whom the apostle had so much honoured as to call him his fellow-soldier, in the Epistle he wrote at the same time to Philemon; and should rather believe that Archippus, having been newly received into this sacred charge, the apostle would encourage him by this direction to a good discharge of his duty. However this may be, you see he gives the body of the church a power to address some remonstrances sometimes to its own pastors; an evident sign that they are not the masters and lords of it, as those of Rome pretend, but ministers and officers only.

He adds in conclusion, "The salutation by the hand of me Paul." The rest of the Epistle had been dictated by the apostle, and written by another hand. He writes these and the following words himself, with his own hand; and it was his ordinary practice so to do, as he declares elsewhere, 2 Thess. iii. 17, to assure his letters by this mark against the fraud of falsifiers, who even then impudently dispersed forged letters under his name; as he himself in another place intimates to us, 2 Thess. ii. 2. Yet, before he concludes, he conjures them to remember his bonds, as an excellent seal of the truth of his gospel, and an irrefragable testimony of the affection he bore to them, and the rest of the Gentiles, for whose sake he suffered these things; which consequently obliged them to love him, and to pray the Lord ardently for him; and above all to imitate his constancy and his patience on similar occasions, if they should be called to suffer. After this he gives them his blessing in these words, "Grace be with you. Amen." He means the grace of God in Jesus Christ his Son our Lord; and it was not possible to crown this divine letter with a fairer and more appropriate conclusion.

Let us bless God, my beloved brethren, who has vouchsafed us the grace to read and to explain it throughout in these holy assemblies; and pray him that he would please to continue the same liberty and tranquillity still to us, causing his word to fructify among us. At present, let us particularly meditate upon the remarkable lessons which this conclusion contains, to the end that we may sedulously practise them, each of us according to our vocation. Let ministers mind the direction given to Archippus, and imitate the example of Epaphras, in loving cordially their flocks, in striving for them by prayer, by word, and by deed; fulfilling their ministry, and so demeaning themselves in it, as may be worthy both of the excellency of the charge, and of the respect and love they owe to the Son of God, who has honoured them with it. Let flocks have reverence and amity for their pastors, and live in good intelligence with their neighbours, as Colosse and Laodicea, mutually communicating all things which tend to their common edification. Let the Epistles of Paul, and the books of his fellow-brethren, the prophets and apostles of the Lord, resound eternally in our assemblies. Let their voice alone be there heard, and their doctrine alone received, and let every tradition which is not marked with their seal be banished thence. Let heads of families imitate the zeal of Nymphas, so conscientiously training their children and their people to piety; and so regularly establishing the exercises of it among them, that it may be truly said of them, they each have a church in their house. And let all of us together, of whatever order or condition, study to be perfect and complete in all the will of God, and persevere unto the end in this holy profession; remembering also the bonds of Paul, and the sufferings of the faithful, by which God has confirmed the truth of his gospel; and so walk in the steps of these blessed ones, enjoying the favours of God with thankfulness, and undergoing his chastisements and trials with patience, that his grace may be with us for ever both in this world and in the world to come. Amen.

GENERAL INDEX.

THE END.

These are books God has put His stamp of approval upon, by preserving them for generation after generation, century after century, that grace and truth may continue to abound in the ones He has chosen to love.

PURITAN COMMENTARIES

Cs19	MATTHEW HENRY'S COMMENTARY, 6 volumes in 3	$35.00
Cs3	EXPOSITION OF EPHESIANS 1 & 2, Thomas Goodwin	6.95
Cs4	EXPOSITION OF EPHESIANS 3 - 6, Paul Bayne	7.95
Cs5	EXPOSITION OF I JOHN, John Cotton	7.95
Cs9	EXPOSITION OF MINOR PROPHETS (Obad.-Zeph.), Hutcheson	6.95
Cs14	EXPOSITION OF TITUS, Thomas Taylor	8.95
Cs18	EXPOSITION OF PROVERBS, Charles Bridges	8.95
Cs19	EXPOSITION OF THE SONG OF SOLOMON, John Gill	5.95
Cs6	EXPOSITION OF HEBREWS, John Owen, 7 volumes in 4 (unabr.)	37.50
Cs20	EXPOSITION OF ROMANS, Robert Haldane (January, 1970)	5.95
Cs23	EXPOSITION OF JAMES, Thomas Manton (January, 1970)	5.95
Cs24	EXPOSITION OF JOHN, George Hutcheson	4.95
Cs25	EXPOSITION OF COLOSSIANS, John Daille (January, 1970)	7.95
Cs26	EXPOSITION OF EZEKIEL, Patrick Fairbairn	6.95
Cs27	A TREASURY OF JOB, Vol. I (of 3), Green, Joseph Caryl, Green	9.95
Cs21	EXPOSITION OF LEVITICUS, A. A. Bonar (January, 1970)	5.95
Cs22	EXPOSITION OF I PETER, John Brown, 3 volumes in 2	14.95

DOCTRINAL AND DEVOTIONAL CLASSICS

Dc2	CHRIST OUR PASSOVER, Stephen Charnock	3.95
Dc6	MAN'S GUILTINESS BEFORE GOD, Thomas Goodwin (Jan.,1970)	6.95
Dc7	THE MORAL LAW, Ernest Kevan (from Anthony Burgess)	3.95
Dc8	THE COMPLETE WORKS OF JOHN BUNYAN, 4 volumes in 3	19.95
Dc9	THE OBJECT & ACTS OF JUSTIFYING FAITH, Thos. Goodwin	7.95
Dc10	AN ALARM TO THE UNCONVERTED, Joseph Alleine	2.50
Dc11	CHRISTIAN LOVE AND ITS FRUITS, Jonathan Edwards	4.95
Dc12	THE EXISTENCE & ATTRIBUTES OF GOD, Stephen Charnock	9.95
Dc13	THE SAINTS' EVERLASTING REST, Richard Baxter (Dec., 1969)	4.50
Dc14	THE REFORMED PASTOR, Richard Baxter (Dec., 1969)	2.95
Dc15	KEEPING THE HEART, John Flavel (Dec., 1969)	2.50
Dc16	HEAVEN OPENED, Richard and Joseph Alleine (Dec., 1969)	3.95

PURITAN PAPERBACK CLASSICS

Pb2	AN ANTIDOTE TO ARMINIANISM, Christopher Ness	1.00
Pb3	AN ALARM TO THE UNCONVERTED, Joseph Alleine	1.00
Pb5	CALVINISM TODAY & FIVE POINTS OF CALVINISM, H. Bonar, John Calvin, John Gill, Thomas Goodwin, Jon. Edwards, Fuller	2.75
Dc4	THE FIVE POINTS OF CALVINISM, as above, only in cloth bind.	4.50
Pb6	HUMAN NATURE IN ITS FOURFOLD STATE, Thomas Boston	2.25
Pb8	THE RARE JEWEL OF CHRISTIAN CONTENTMENT, Burroughes	1.50
Pb10	THE VANITY OF THOUGHTS, Thomas Goodwin (Dec., 1969)	1.25
Pb11	THE DOCTRINE OF PARTICULAR REDEMPTION, John Gill	.50
Pb17	THE RESURRECTION OF THE BODY, John Bunyan	1.50
Pb24	ABSOLUTE PREDESTINATION, Jerome Zanchius	1.95
Pb36	JOB'S TRIUMPH OVER SATAN, William Henry Green	1.75
Pb34	A HISTORY OF REDEMPTION, Jonathan Edwards	2.95
Pb37	GOD'S SOVEREIGNTY, Elisha Coles	2.50

PUBLICATIONS BY MODERN AUTHORS

Tc2	MULTILINEAR TRANSLATION OF SYNOPTIC GOSPELS, Green	3.95
Pb38	BAPTISM: ITS MODE & SUBJECTS, Alexander Carson	2.95
Pb21	THE PHILADELPHIA CONFESSION OF FAITH (Baptist)	1.50
Pb30	BIBLICAL ARCHAEOLOGY, Allan A. MacRae	1.50
Pb31	THE LIVING SCRIPTURES, translation of N.T., by Jay Green	.95
En1	THE ENCYCLOPEDIA OF CHRISTIANITY, Volume I of 8	15.00
En2	THE ENCYCLOPEDIA OF CHRISTIANITY, Volume II of 8	12.50
Pb32	CALVINISM TODAY, YESTERDAY AND TOMORROW, Jay Green	.95
Pb33	GOD'S EVERLASTING LOVE FOR HIS CHOSEN PEOPLE, Jay Green	.75

www.ingramcontent.com/pod-product-compliance
Lightning Source LLC
Chambersburg PA
CBHW060447100426
42812CB00025B/2725

* 9 7 8 1 5 8 9 6 0 1 3 5 2 *